Routledge Handbook of Sport Governance

The *Routledge Handbook of Sport Governance* is a comprehensive and authoritative survey of the wide range of issues shaping sport governance. It considers the evolution of the sport industry from a largely amateur, volunteer-driven sector into the globalised business that it is today and examines how professionalisation has fundamentally shifted the governance landscape for sport organisations and all those working within sport.

Written by a team of leading sport management scholars from around the world, the book is organised around five key themes:

- Part I: Overview of sport governance
- Part II: Environmental context and policy perspectives
- Part III: Ownership structures and governance models: Implications for sport governance
- Part IV: Board roles in the governance process
- Part V: Future sport governance challenges

Each chapter reviews the most recent research available and, in some cases, presents new data to support previously published studies. As sport governance is a relatively young field, each chapter maps future research needs to provide direction for sport governance scholars. A special feature of the handbook is a series of nine shorter research chapters in Part IV examining board roles in the governance process, tying theory to the day-to-day practical aspects of running a sport organisation.

With broader and deeper coverage of the key issues in contemporary sport governance than any other book, this handbook is essential reading for students, researchers and practitioners working in sport business and management.

David Shilbury is Foundation Professor of Sport Management and Director of the Deakin Sport Network and the Centre for Sport Research at Deakin University, Australia. He is non-executive Director of Golf Victoria and a NASSM Research Fellow, as well as being a recipient of the Dr Earle F. Zeigler award in 2011. He was the Foundation President of the Sport Management Association of Australia & New Zealand (SMAANZ) from 1995 to 2001 and was the inaugural SMAANZ Distinguished Service award recipient in 2009. He is former Editor of the *Journal of Sport Management* and *Sport Management Review* and his research expertise is in sport governance and strategy.

Lesley Ferkins is Professor of Sport Leadership and Governance at Auckland University of Technology (AUT), New Zealand and Director of the AUT Sports Performance Research Institute New Zealand (SPRINZ). As an action researcher, Lesley has worked closely with boards of national and regional sport organisations in NZ and Australia to develop governance and leadership capability. Lesley is Associate Editor of *Sport Management Review* and sits on the editorial board of the *Journal of Sport Management*. She is also Independent Director for Tennis, New Zealand.

Routledge International Handbooks

Routledge Handbook of Language Acquisition
Edited by Jessica S. Horst and Janne von Koss Torkildsen

Routledge Handbook of Identity Studies, 2e
Edited by Anthony Elliott

Routledge International Handbook of Poverty
Edited by Bent Greve

Routledge International Handbook of New Digital Practices in Galleries, Libraries, Archives, Museums and Heritage Sites
Edited by Hannah Lewi, Wally Smith, Dirk vom Lehn and Steven Cooke

Routledge International Handbook of Human Trafficking
A Multi-Disciplinary and Applied Approach
Edited by Rochelle L. Dalla and Donna Sabella

The Routledge Handbook of Comparative Rural Policy
Edited by Matteo Vittuari, John Devlin, Marco Pagani and Thomas Johnson

Routledge International Handbook of Masculinity Studies
Edited by Lucas Gottzén, Ulf Mellström and Tamara Shefer

Routledge Handbook of European Welfare Systems, 2e
Edited by Sonja Blum, Johanna Kuhlmann and Klaus Schubert

Routledge International Handbook of Heterosexualities Studies
Edited by James Joseph Dean and Nancy L. Fischer

Routledge Handbook of Contemporary European Social Movements
Protest in Turbulent Times
Edited by Cristina Flesher Fominaya and Ramón A. Feenstra

The Routledge International Handbook of Military Psychology and Mental Health
Edited by Updesh Kumar

Routledge International Handbook of Green Criminology
Edited by Avi Brisman and Nigel South

Routledge Handbook of Sport Governance

Edited by David Shilbury and Lesley Ferkins

LONDON AND NEW YORK

First published 2020
by Routledge
2 Park Square, Milton Park, Abingdon, Oxon OX14 4RN

and by Routledge
605 Third Avenue, New York, NY 10017

First issued in paperback 2021

Routledge is an imprint of the Taylor & Francis Group, an informa business

Publisher's Note
The publisher has gone to great lengths to ensure the quality of this reprint but points out that some imperfections in the original copies may be apparent.

British Library Cataloguing-in-Publication Data
A catalogue record for this book is available from the British Library

Library of Congress Cataloging-in-Publication Data
A catalog record has been requested for this book

Typeset in Bembo
by Deanta Global Publishing Services, Chennai, India

ISBN 13: 978−1−03−223915−6 (pbk)
ISBN 13: 978−1−138−34123−4 (hbk)

Contents

Figures

Tables

Contributors

Christos Anagnostopoulos is Assistant Professor at University of Central Lancashire (Cyprus) and Associate Professor at Molde University College (Norway). His research interests lie in corporate social responsibility and governance in sport. Christos has recently co-edited the first ever Research Handbook on Sport Governance (Edward Elgar). He is also the author of the Code for Good Governance for the Cypriot National Sport Federations. He serves as the research coordinator of the EU Erasmus+ project 'Good Governance Enhancement through e-learning for Sport Volunteer Board Members' (GReFORM).

Emmanuel Bayle is Professor in Sport Management at the Institute of Sport Sciences of the University of Lausanne (ISSUL), Switzerland. His research interests lie in Sport Management (Global sport leaders, Governance in sport organisations, CSR and sport), CSR and in nonprofit management.

Gonzalo A. Bravo is Associate Professor in Sport Management at West Virginia University, USA. He holds a master's degree in sport administration from Penn State University, USA and a PhD in sport management from The Ohio State University, USA. In 2016, Bravo completed a sabbatical semester in Brazil and from 2014 to 2017 he was a visiting scholar at the University of Pittsburgh's Centre of Latin American Studies, USA.

Jean-Loup Chappelet is Emeritus Professor of public management at the Swiss Graduate School of Public Management (IDHEAP) at the University of Lausanne, Switzerland. He launched the first sport management course in Switzerland in 1995 and was the Director of the Executive Master in Sport Organisation Management (MEMOS), an Olympic Solidarity programme, for 12 years (1999–2011). His research is focused on sport governance and Olympic events management.

Josephine Clausen holds a PhD in Sports Science and Physical Education from the University of Lausanne, Switzerland. Her main research topics are related to international sport organisations, including studies on professionalisation, governance, gender equity and event legacies. Prior to her PhD, Josephine worked for the UCI, the international cycling federation.

Geoff Dickson is at La Trobe University, Australia. His research interests centre on governance, interorganisational relationships, risk, law, leadership and consumer behaviour.

Alison Doherty is Professor of Sport Management in the School of Kinesiology, Faculty of Health Sciences at Western University, Canada. Her research interests are in the area of nonprofit and voluntary sport organisation capacity, with a particular focus on governance and volunteerism.

Rochelle Eime is Professor of Behavioural Epidemiology who has over 15 years of research experience with the sport and recreation sectors relating to both public health and sport management. Rochelle is the Director of the Sport and Recreation Spatial program of research (www.sportandrecreationspatial.com.au) which focuses on investigating sport and recreation participation, facilities and health for evidence-based decision-making.

Hallgeir Gammelsæter is Professor of Social Change, Organisation and Management at Molde Specialised University in Logistics, Norway. He teaches courses in management and organisation theory, including on the sport management program. His research focuses on the organisation and governance of commercialised sport. He has served in different positions with the European Sport Management Association and is currently Associate Editor at the *European Sport Management Quarterly*.

Luiz Haas is a PhD student in the Faculty of Human Kinetics at the University of Lisbon, Portugal. He is a former president of the Brazilian Association for Sport Management (2015–2017). His research is focused on the management of sport organisations and sport governance.

Spencer Harris is Associate Professor of Sport Management at the University of Colorado, USA. He has worked in sport development since 1993 and has worked for the University of Hertfordshire, Sport England and Right to Play. He completed his PhD at Loughborough University in 2013 focusing on the governance of the London 2012 Olympic Legacy. His research interests centre on sport governance and specifically the sport, politics and power relationship.

Coral Ingley is Associate Professor of Management at Auckland University of Technology, New Zealand. She is Founder and Director of the Corporate Governance Centre in the University's Faculty of Business and Law and teaches corporate governance and responsibility in the MBA programme. Her research focuses on board behaviour, the role of governance in stakeholder engagement, board leadership in sustainability and corporate social responsibility, as well as governance in small firms and urban governance. She is also a professional member of the New Zealand Institute of Directors.

Paul Jonson is Governance Consultant for Oceania Rugby and a Judiciary Member of the New South Wales Touch Football Association. He is a former Associate Professor at the University of Technology Sydney, Australia and the inaugural President of the World Association for Sport Management.

Joon-ho Kang is Director of the Centre for Sport Industry and Professor of Sport Management at Seoul National University, South Korea. He launched the Global Sport Management graduate program at Seoul National University, the first sport management graduate degree program in Korea. He designed and has been running the Dream Together Master Program, which is the Korean government's national project for global sport development. His research interests are sport development, sport marketing and sport event legacy.

Adam Karg is Senior Research Fellow and Director of the Sport Innovation Research Group at Swinburne University of Technology in Melbourne, Australia. His research focusses on sport consumer behaviour, organisational design and innovation applied to sport. He is engaged in a wide range of research, consulting and advisory roles with governing bodies, agencies, sport technology start-ups and professional sport teams.

Lisa A. Kihl is Associate Professor of sport management in the School of Kinesiology at the University of Minnesota, USA. She is Director of the Global Institute for Responsible Sport Organisations and Affiliated Scholar with the Tucker Centre for Research on Girls and Women in Sport. Her research interests primarily focus on the intersection of sport ethics, policy and governance.

Dongfeng Liu is Professor of Sport Management and Co-Dean of the School of International Education at Shanghai University of Sport, China. Dr Liu is Vice-President of the International Association of Sports Economists.

Becca Leopkey is Assistant Professor in the Department of Kinesiology at the University of Georgia, USA. Her main areas of research interest include sport event organisation, event legacy and international sport organisations.

Josh McLeod is Research Fellow in the Sport Management Program and the Centre for Sport Research at Deakin University, Australia. His research interests are in the area of sport governance, ownership in sport and organisational change.

Trevor Meiklejohn is Senior Lecturer in Sport Marketing and Management at Unitec Institute of Technology in Auckland, New Zealand. Trevor's research interests reside primarily in sport governance with a particular focus on the governance of new and emerging sports.

Tracy Molloy is with the School of Sport and Recreation, Sport Leadership and Management Department at Auckland University of Technology, New Zealand. She has significant industry experience as a national and international sport board member and a long-term member of the Australian and New Zealand Sports Law Association. Her research interests are sport governance and integrity with her PhD studies focussing on the use of nomination committees in the director selection processes of New Zealand national sport organisations.

Michael L. Naraine is Lecturer in Sport Management at Deakin University in Melbourne, Australia. From 2020 Michael will be an Assistant Professor with Brock University. Michael's expertise is in digital sport management, examining both the content and analytics of technological engagement, as well as the strategic management of innovation and technology within sport organisations. He sits on the editorial boards of *Case Studies in Sport Management* and the *International Journal of Sport Communication*. Michael is also a research fellow of the North American Society for Sport Management.

Ian O'Boyle is Associate Professor in Management at the University of South Australia. His research expertise is in the area of sport governance and leadership with a focus on the nonprofit sporting context.

Norm O'Reilly is Professor and Assistant Dean of Executive Programs in the Gordon S. Lang School of Business & Economics at the University of Guelph, Canada, where he is also the founding Director of the International Institute for Sport Business & Leadership, a think tank devoted to improving the sport business globally. He was previously the Richard P. and Joan S. Fox Professor of Business and Chair of the Department of Sports Administration at Ohio University's College of Business, USA.

Barbara Osborne is Attorney and Professor with a joint appointment in Exercise and Sport Science and the School of Law at the University of North Carolina at Chapel Hill, USA. Prior to this she worked for 15 years as an athletics administrator in intercollegiate athletics. Her current research focuses on legal issues in intercollegiate athletics, Title IX and women's issues in sport.

Milena M. Parent is Professor in sport (event) management in the School of Human Kinetics at the University of Ottawa, USA. She is also Lecturer and Tutor in the Olympic Solidarity-funded Executive Masters in Sport Organisation Management (MEMOS) program. Her research focuses on sport event and sport system governance.

Adele Pavlidis was awarded her PhD in 2013 from Griffith University, Australia and was recently awarded an Australian Research Council Discovery Early Career Research Award (DECRA) to continue her research into women's participation in contact sports.

Pamm Phillips is Professor and Director of Sport Management Programs in the Deakin Business School at Deakin University, Melbourne, Australia. She conducts research that builds the capacity of sport organisations thereby enhancing the quality of life for those who work and participate in sport organisations and has conducted a range of industry funded research projects that have affected national sport policy. She is an editorial board member for leading sport management journals.

Jonathan Robertson is Lecturer in the Sport Management program at Deakin University, Australia. He teaches undergraduate and postgraduate courses in Sport in Society and Sport Organisation Theory, as well as the Sport Management Practicum program. His primary research interests are in the areas of social responsibility in sport organisations, social change and organisational theory.

Michael (Mike) Sam is Associate Professor at the University of Otago, New Zealand and co-director of the NZ Centre for Sport Policy and Politics. His research encompasses policy, politics and governance as they relate to the public administration/management of sport. Mike is President of the International Sociology of Sport Association (ISSA) and serves on the editorial board of the *International Journal of Sport Policy and Politics*.

Geoff Schoenberg is Senior Consultant at Sport Australia and previously a research fellow at Deakin University, Australia. His research has focused on behaviours, group dynamics and decision-making in sport governing bodies across Canada, Australia and India. In his current role, he works with national sport organisations on governance transformation projects and develops governance frameworks for the sport sector.

Oskar Solenes is Associate Professor in Sport Management at Molde University, Norway. He is a historian with a special interest in the socio-cultural dimensions of sport, as well as organisational questions in sport organisations such as volunteerism and governance. He has also been part of several EU-funded projects, as the National Sport Governance Observer.

Popi Sotiriadou is Associate Professor of Sport Management and the Director of the Bachelor of Business Innovation at the Griffith Business School, Griffith University, Australia. She is a Senior Fellow of the Higher Education Academy and has expertise in managing high performance sport, organisational capacity for athlete development, governance and gender and sport development processes.

David Thorpe is Sessional Lecturer in Sports Law in the School of Law at Sydney University, Australia and is on the Editorial Committee of the Australian New Zealand Sports Law Journal. He was a member of the Athlete Selection Appeals Panel (Australia) in the 2016 Olympics.

Frank van Eekeren is Senior Consultant and Researcher in the School of Governance at Utrecht University, the Netherlands. He is manager of the research focus area sport and society at Utrecht University and studies public value creation in and through sport organisations, including sport for development.

Geoff Walters is Reader in Management at Birkbeck, University of London, UK and Assistant Dean of the Management Department. He teaches on the MSc Sport Management programmes and also works with UEFA on the MESGO and MIP executive management programmes. His research focuses on two areas: organisational governance and the role of the board; and network governance, the nature of power dynamics and how networks evolve and are shaped over time.

Erianne A. Weight is Associate Professor of Sport Administration and Director of the Center for Research in Intercollegiate Athletics as The University of North Carolina at Chapel Hill, USA. Her research is directed by a vision to increase opportunities for athletic participation and education through understanding the financial, educational and administrative impacts and opportunities for growth within intercollegiate athletics. She is a Research Consultant for Collegiate Sports Associates within Division I US intercollegiate athletics with a focus on athletics and higher education organisational culture, climate and student well-being.

Hans Westerbeek is Professor of International Sport Business at Victoria University, Australia, where he also heads up the Sport Business Insights research group. He holds adjunct appointments at the Free University of Brussels, Belgium, the Central University of Finance and Economics Beijing, China and the Real Madrid Graduate School, Spain.

Masayuki Yoshida is Associate Professor of Sport Management at Hosei University, Japan. His research interests include sport marketing, sport consumer behaviour and sport sponsorship. He is a Research Fellow of the North American Society for Sport Management.

Géraldine Zeimers is Postdoctoral Researcher at UCLouvain, Belgium, based at Deakin University, Melbourne, Australia. Her PhD research examined the implementation of corporate social responsibility in nonprofit sport organisations. She studied the implementation of CSR by sport federations from an inter-organisational and an organisational learning perspective. Her current research focuses on organisational changes in nonprofit sport organisations and sport governance.

Part I
Overview of sport governance

An overview of sport governance scholarship

David Shilbury and Lesley Ferkins

Introduction

Sport governance scholarship has a short history. The first sport governance-related manuscript published in the *Journal of Sport Management* was in 1996, some nine years after the establishment of this journal in 1987. This article, by Kuga (see Table 1.4), focused on the governance of intercollegiate athletics and the perceptions of faculty as key stakeholders. Interestingly, this is the only sport governance article published in the three leading sport management journals concentrated on the sports system in the USA. *Sport Management Review* published its first sport governance paper in 2003, five years after its inception in 1998, and the *European Sport Management Quarterly* published its first sport governance manuscript in 2003, two years after its commencement in 2001. Hoye and Cuskelly co-authored both articles, with the first published in *Sport Management Review* examining professionalisation of governance systems, board–executive relations and the role of the board (see Table 1.1). The second article, published in *European Sport Management Quarterly*, investigated board dynamics and specifically board power and performance in voluntary sport organisations (see Table 1.2). These two articles provide an insight to the general trend of articles published in the three leading journals, most of which tackle governance in sport systems formerly grounded in amateur and voluntary delivery systems.

Of the 1642 articles published in the field's three leading journals, 49, or nearly three percent of these papers were sport governance research focused. The *Journal of Sport Management* published 21 (2.7%) sport governance articles from its inception in 1987 through the end of 2018. *Sport Management Review* published 15 (3.3%) papers and the *European Sport Management Quarterly* 13 (3.2%) manuscripts until the end of 2018. On any measure, the proportion of papers focused on sport governance research is small. As will be argued in this chapter, and implicitly through the commissioning of this research handbook of sport governance, sport governance is a more important area of theory and practice than the current scholarship devoted to it implies.

The purpose of this introductory chapter is to overview the scholarship dedicated to sport governance and to explain the motivation for this handbook. In total, 29 chapters compose this handbook, with all chapters dedicated to various aspects of sport governance research and practice. Forty-two authors from 14 countries have contributed to this handbook. Each chapter reviews specific elements of sport governance identifying relevant research themes and communicating what is currently known about sport governance as well as identifying future research directions. In summary, this is a research handbook designed to survey the field and its progress specifically in relation to sport governance scholarship. As already indicated, the volume of sport governance scholarship in the three leading sport management journals reveals that scholarship in this domain may not have assumed the prominence and importance it warrants. This view is predicated on the importance of leadership in the governance process and the role of boards and individual directors in setting the standards and direction for individual sport organisations and, therefore, sport collectively.

Sport governance forms part of the broader sport management landscape. By definition sport management covers a wide array of subject areas, ranging from management, human resource management, marketing, sport economics, sport sociology, sport history, finance, sport and the law, data analytics, information systems and, naturally, the study of the sport industry and its component parts through which the management of people and organisations is executed. The context is clear, and in general, it is a unique context (Chalip, 2006; Shilbury, 2012). Sport organisations throughout the world have been on a journey of professionalisation, moving from amateur volunteer-driven entities to increasingly commercialised organisations managed by paid staff and change processes that have involved experimenting with the most efficient means to govern, manage, organise and deliver sport (Auld, 1997; Enjolras, 2002; O'Brien & Slack, 2003; Siegfried, Schlesinger, Bayle & Giauque, 2015). During this period of professionalisation, the focus of this research has traditionally been on paid staff and their interactions with volunteers involved with the delivery of sport (Cuskelly, Boag & McIntyre, 1999; Koski & Heikkala, 1998; Thibault, Slack & Hinings, 1991).

Governance practices were largely an afterthought in these changing times until commercial pressures and the need for heightened accountability began to emerge as important for the ongoing survival and legitimacy of sport organisations. This is somewhat ironic, as the majority of directors of sport organisations worldwide are volunteers. High-profile sport organisations including the International Olympic Committee and Fédération Internationale de Football Association (FIFA) are just two examples of how change in governance practices have been demanded as a consequence of various governance challenges. *The Economist*, in 2015, writing in response to the demise of former FIFA President Sepp Blatter, captures the cultural background that has led to poor governance and the inevitable need for sport to "clean up its act":

> Last, the governance of too many sports is opaque, juicily monopolistic, badly monitored – and wholly unsuited to the big-money age. Some sports (such as professional tennis) and places (such as Finland and South Korea, which have cracked down on match-fixing in football) have caught up. Others have, like FIFA, proved ill-equipped to combat predation and too hospitable to unscrupulous officials. Football is not the only vulnerable game; scandal has struck pastimes as obscure as handball. Villainous politicians, such as some of the many involved in Indian cricket (a swamp of fixes and backhanders), are often in on the act.

As indicated, the bulk of directors or members of boards of sport organisations worldwide are volunteers, but their role and motivations for undertaking this important task has not attracted the research attention it warrants. Ultimately, the accountability for the performance of sport organisations and for sport generally resides with individual boards of the plethora of sport organisations worldwide. Pielke (2015), in an extract from the *Global Corruption Report*, identifies the obstacles to accountability in international sport governance. He stated:

> Through the contingencies of history and a desire by sports leaders to govern themselves autonomously, international sport organisations have developed in such a way that they

have less well-developed mechanisms of governance than many governments, businesses and civil society organisations. The rapidly increasing financial interests in sport and associated with sport create a fertile setting for corrupt practices to take hold. When they do, the often-insular bodies have shown little ability to adopt or enforce the standards of good governance that are increasingly expected around the world. (p. 29)

This brief evidence supports the need for sustained research to understand the theory, processes and practices of sport governance as well as the motivations for directors elected or appointed to sport boards. As sport management scholars, we have a role to play in contributing to understanding what good governance looks like in various sport organisations across all levels, including professional sport, national and regional governing bodies and community sport.

The term governance stems from the Latin language and means to steer. In its simplest forms it requires oversight of the organisation's performance and its compliance with relevant regulations and the law. Contemporary governance has evolved to become a much more complex and multi-faceted function performed by boards to ensure the legitimacy of sport governing bodies at both international and national levels. As Tricker (2012) has noted, the performance role includes oversight and approval of strategy formulation and policy, and, through compliance, monitoring, supervising and oversight of accountability. Assessing and managing risk and, increasingly, obligations to social responsibility add to the layers of complexity associated with the role of boards. Moreover, many of the world's governments who support sport through funding have demanded compliance with a range of principles of good governance. Australia, New Zealand and the United Kingdom are just three countries to recognise and codify the importance of sport governance to ensure the delivery of quality sport at all levels. These principles and the rationale for this action are explored in more detail in Chapters 4–6.

The term "sport governance" has come to mean the practice of governance applied to the sport context (Hoye & Cuskelly, 2007). In a more detailed definition of sport governance, Ferkins, Shilbury and McDonald (2009) stated that sport governance is "the responsibility for the functioning and overall direction of the organization and is a necessary and institutionalized component of all sport codes from club level to national bodies, government agencies, sport service organizations and professional teams around the world" (p. 245). The focus of this handbook on sport governance is, in essence, on the board and its role and functions in performing the governance process. A board of directors is a group of elected or appointed people entrusted with and accountable for the leadership and governance of companies, nonprofits and, in this case, sport organisations. This handbook focuses on what these people (referred to as directors in this handbook) do collectively as individual boards and their responsibilities and functions in leading and governing sport. How directors are elected and/or appointed and the various ownership models and governance structures that lead to their election is further considered in Chapter 7 and Chapters 9–12.

Two forms of governance pervade the literature and are central to this handbook: a) organisational governance – the work of the board of a single organisation (Cornforth, 2012), and b) systemic or network governance – interplay between organisations, often in the same sport or same network (i.e., tennis, golf, IOC, NOC) (Henry & Lee, 2004). The second, systemic or network governance, is particularly important given the number of countries in which federated governance structures exist. Federated governance structures include a hierarchy of sport organisations in the same sport in the same country including a national sport organisation, state, provincial or regional sport organisations, as well as local clubs. As Cornforth (2012) has argued generally, "most governance research has focused on the boards of unitary organisations and has neglected the governance of organisations that have more complex structures" (p. 3).

More specific details of the implications of this form of governance structure are outlined in Chapters 7 and 13; but in summary, this form of structure has given rise to a raft of volunteer, cultural, structural and adversarial encounters (Shilbury, Ferkins & Smythe, 2013) demanding further global investigation of this form of governance in a plethora of sport settings. Research investigating federal sport structures and associated governance processes emerged in the following analysis of published sport governance scholarship.

Sport governance scholarship and alignment with the sport governance charter

Governance charters are now commonplace in most organisations. The purpose of a governance charter is to help people involved in governance, namely directors and CEOs, and company secretaries in the corporate sector to develop their systems, policies and procedures. A good charter covers a wide range of issues including defining governance roles and the role of the board, board functions, risk and compliance and key board processes. Although these higher-level headings serve to provide some insight to the contents included in a governance charter, each section contains considerably more detail as it relates to board functioning and responsibilities, and often with multiple appendices operationalising various processes. In summary, the charter is a major policy document which establishes the parameters of board functioning.

Consistent with the importance of a governance charter in organisational life, this chapter has adapted the use of the governance charter model developed by Kiel and Nicholson (2003). In their work with multiple organisations, Kiel and Nicholson developed this model to help directors and boards define their work. In this chapter, we use an adapted version of this charter to help map the existing sport governance scholarship identified in the three main journals in the field of sport management. The summary outcomes from the amount of this scholarship were noted in the opening paragraph to this handbook. To refresh, in the three leading journals, 49 (3%) articles have been published specific to sport governance. Although not many, this chapter maps the main content of each article against the sport governance charter to ascertain which of the four areas of the charter has been the focus of previous research.

This mapping is only representative of the research published in the three identified journals, and, clearly, there is more sport governance work published in other sport management journals as well as mainstream management and governance journals. Later in this chapter, the work of Dowling, Leopkey and Smith (2018) is used to overview the sport governance scholarship more broadly across the field. The three-journal analysis is indicative, however, of the proportion and volume of scholarship to date – particularly given the prominence of the three journals reviewed. This analysis also shows the number of sport governance articles published by year, indicating how governance has, in recent years, slowly attracted more research interest by sport management scholars.

Figure 1.1 shows sport governance articles published by year since 1996, when the first sport governance manuscript was published in one of the three journals assessed. Apart from 2003, there was limited work published in relation to sport governance until 2009 (four papers) and 2010 (seven papers). Since 2010, there has been a steady flow of sport governance research with four papers published in 2016, 2017 and 2018. Although, in relative terms, a small proportion of work when compared to other areas of sport management, it nonetheless shows a slight increasing trend. In 2010, all of the published articles focused on sport systems grappling with the professionalisation and commercialisation of voluntary sport systems.

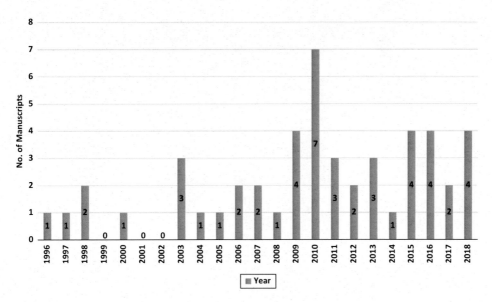

Figure 1.1 Sport governance manuscripts published by year.

Three of the articles in 2010 were published in the Australia/New Zealand context (McDonald & Sherry; Sibson; Ferkins & Shilbury) dealing with club member perspectives of sport board performance, gendering of sport organisation boards and developing board strategic capability in a federated network of sports. The remaining articles emanated from Canada (Hamm-Kerwin & Doherty), the United Kingdom and Europe (Ferrand, Henry & Ferrand; Gammelsaeter; Enjolras & Waldahl). Hamm-Kerwin and Doherty's work examined intragroup conflict in non-profit sport boards and both Ferrand et al. and Enjolras and Waldahl examined election to the board and democratic processes in voluntary sport organisations, while Gammelsaeter focused on commercialisation in the context of institutional logics. All seven papers reflect ongoing and consistent themes in sport governance research, all of which are illustrated in Figure 1.2, the sport governance charter.

The adapted governance charter shown in Figure 1.2 is composed of four quadrants: 1) Defining governance roles and motivations, 2) improving board processes, 3) continuing improvement and 4) key board functions. Within each quadrant, the key areas of responsibilities are shown. For the purposes of this analysis, the original charter has been adapted to "fit" the sport industry. Specifically, key areas added to the model include leisure and professionalisation, volunteer directors and motivations in quadrant 1, defining governance roles and motivations; board dynamics in quadrant 2, improving board processes; performance in quadrant 3, continuing improvement; and integrating regional entities and managing stakeholders in quadrant 4, key board functions. The addition of these six areas highlights some of the unique aspects of sport management that influence governance processes and the subsequent themes driving research.

Figure 1.2 shows that, of the 49 published sport governance articles, 14 aligned with quadrant 1 defining roles and motivations, nine with quadrant 2 improving board processes, three with quadrant 3 continuing improvement and 19 with quadrant 4 key board functions. Three of the remaining articles focus on ownership structures and do not neatly fit within the sport governance charter. The final article is a scoping review of sport governance research, which is

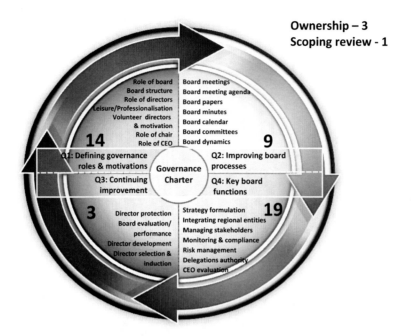

Figure 1.2 Sport governance charter. Adapted from Kiel & Nicholson, (2003). Boards that work.

considered later in this chapter to overview sport governance scholarship beyond the three main journals reviewed in this section. Each of the articles shown in Tables 1.1–1.5 include the codes that informed to which quadrant each article was allocated. The organisation of this scholarship using the sport governance charter quickly indicates where the major research foci have been between 1996 and 2018.

Quadrant 4 (Table 1.4), key board functions, generated the largest number of research articles. The various co-authored articles published by Shilbury, Ferkins and O'Boyle with nine of 19 publications dominate this quadrant. The work of Ferkins and Shilbury, in particular, illustrates the growing interest in the governance of federated sport structures with a focus on developing and understanding strategic capability of volunteer sport boards. Invariably, this work revolves around the challenges of working with regional sport boards to ensure alignment of purpose within a sport. Significantly, this stream of research brought together governance theory and processes with the strategy literature in the context of volunteer directors and the challenges they confront in moving from an operational to a strategic focus in the governance of sport organisations. More recently, Shilbury, with O'Boyle and Ferkins, extended their work to the investigation of collaborative governance as a mechanism to govern effectively across a network of sports. In addition to mapping a research agenda in collaborative governance, the remaining manuscripts examined the utility of collaborative governance by an NSO when using the strategic planning process to harness a collaborative national plan, the role of stakeholders and stakeowners in sport governance and the role of trust in collaborative governance.

Research in relation to stakeholders was the next most prominent theme. Kuga (1996) in intercollegiate athletics, Esteve, Di Lorenzo, Ingles and Puig (2011) in sport clubs and Garcia and Welford (2015) in relation to supporters and football governance all focused on varying areas of

Table 1.1 Quadrant 1 – Defining governance roles and responsibilities

No	Manuscripts	Themes
1	Parent, M. M., Naraine, M. L., & Hoye, R. (2018). New era for governance structures and processes in Canadian national sport organizations. *JSM, 32*(6), 555–566.	Design archetypes/ Government policy/ Professionalisation
2	Walters, G., & Tacon, R. (2018). The 'codification' of governance in the non-profit sport sector in the UK. *ESMQ, 18*(4), 482–500.	Codification of governance functions/Board roles
3	Adriaanse, J., & Schofield, T. (2014). The impact of gender quotas on gender equality in sport governance. *JSM, 28*(5), 485–497.	Board structure/Roles
4	Shilbury, D., & Ferkins, L. (2013). Sport governance encounters: Insights from lived experiences. *SMR, 16*(3), 349–363.	Leisure/Professionalisation/ Role of the board
5	Dimitropoulos, P. (2011). Corporate governance and earnings management in the European football industry. *ESMQ, 11*(5), 495–523.	Board structure
6	Enjolras, B., & Waldahl, R. H. (2010). Democratic governance and oligarchy in voluntary sport organizations: The case of the Norwegian Olympic Committee and confederation of sports. *ESMQ, 10*(2), 215–239.	Board structure/Roles
7	Yeh, C. M., Taylor, T., & Hoye, R. (2009). Board roles in organisations with a dual board system: Empirical evidence from Taiwanese non-profit sport organisations. *SMR, 12*(2), 91–100.	Role of the board
8	de Barros, C., Barros, C., & Correia, A. (2007). Governance in sports clubs: Evidence for the Island of Madeira. *ESMQ, 7*(2), 123–139.	Role of chair/CEO
9	Schulz, J., & Auld, C. (2006). Perceptions of role ambiguity by chairpersons and executive directors in Queensland sporting organisations. *SMR, 9*(2), 183–201.	Leisure/Professionalisation/ Role of chair
10	Hoye, R., & Cuskelly, G. (2003). Board–executive relationships within voluntary sport organisations. *SMR, 6*(2), 53–73.	Leisure/Professionalisation/ Role of the board
11	Kikulis, L. (2000). Continuity and change in governance and decision making in national sport organisations: Institutional explanations. *JSM, 14*(4), 293–320.	Leisure/Professionalisation/ Roles
12	Cuskelly, G., McIntyre, N., & Boag, A. (1998). A longitudinal study of the development of organizational commitment amongst volunteer sport administrators. *JSM, 12*(3), 181–202.	Leisure/Professionalisation/ Volunteer director motivation
13	Auld, C., & Godbey, G. (1998). Influence in Canadian national sport organisations: Perceptions of professionals and volunteers. *JSM, 12*(1), 20–38.	Leisure/Professionalisation/ Roles/ Volunteer director motivations
14	Inglis, S. (1997). Roles of the board in amateur sport organizations. *JSM, 1*(2), 160–176.	Leisure/Professionalisation/ Roles

stakeholder influence. A key theme in the stakeholder related publications was the governance of major events. Parent (2016) examined stakeholder perceptions of the democratic governance of major sport events; Naraine, Schenk and Parent (2016) examined stakeholder network governance; and finally, Parent, Rouillard and Naraine (2017) again concentrated on network governance and sport events. Strategy formulation and collaborative governance, and stakeholder's role in the governance process dominated articles in quadrant 4 with 15 of the 19 manuscripts.

Table 1.2 Quadrant 2 – Improving board processes

No	Manuscripts	Themes
1	Ferkins, L. Shilbury, D., & O'Boyle, I. (2018). Leadership in governance: Exploring collective board leadership in sport governance systems, *SMR, 21*(3), 221–231.	Board dynamics
2	Takos, N., Murray, D., & O'Boyle, I. (2018). Authentic leadership in non-profit sport organization boards. *JSM, 32*(2), 109–122.	Board dynamics
3	Adriaanse, J., & Schofield, T. (2013). Analysing gender dynamics in sport governance: A new regimes-based approach. *SMR, 6*(4), 498–513.	Board dynamics/Gender
4	Sibson, R. (2010). "I was banging my head against the wall": Exclusionary power and the gendering of sport organizations. *JSM, 24*(4), 379–399.	Board dynamics
5	Hamm-Kerwin, S., & Doherty, A. (2010). Intragroup conflict in non-profit sport boards. *JSM, 24*(3), 245–271.	Board dynamics
6	Hoye, R. (2007). Commitment, involvement and performance of voluntary sport organization board members. *ESMQ, 7*(1), 109–121.	Board dynamics
7	Doherty, A., Patterson, M., & Van Bussel, M. (2004). What do we expect? An examination of perceived committee norms in non-profit sport organisations. *SMR, 7*(2), 109–132.	Board dynamics
8	Doherty, A. J., & Carron, A.V. (2003). Cohesion in volunteer sport executive committees. *JSM, 17*(2), 116–141.	Board dynamics
9	Hoye, R., & Cuskelly, G. (2003). Board power and performance within voluntary sport organisations. *ESMQ, 3*(2), 103–119.	Board dynamics

Table 1.3 Quadrant 3 – Continuing improvement

No	Manuscripts	Themes
1	Hoye, R., & Doherty, A. (2011). Nonprofit sport board performance: A review and directions for future research. *JSM, 25*(3), 272–285.	Evaluation/Performance
2	McDonald, H., & Sherry, E. (2010). Evaluating sport club board performance: A customer perspective. *JSM, 24*(5), 524–543.	Evaluation/Performance
3	Ferrand, C., Henry, I., & Ferrand, A. (2010). Gendered identities in self-descriptions of electoral candidates in a French national sport federation. *ESMQ, 10*(5), 531–552.	Director selection

The remaining four papers all relate to monitoring and compliance through conflict of interest (Sherry & Shilbury, 2009), corruption (Lee, 2008; Mason, Thibault & Misener, 2006) and accountability as it relates to FIFA (Pielke, 2013).

Quadrant 1 (Table 1.1), defining governance roles and motivations, generated the second largest number of manuscripts. This quadrant was dominated by research examining the leisure focus of sport and the motivations of directors and the tensions inherent in the professionalisation of sport, design archetypes and governance generally. Role ambiguity, design archetypes and change were the key constructs underlying these papers, as scholars examined continuity,

Table 1.4 Quadrant 4 – Key board functions

No	Manuscripts	Themes
1	Parent, M., Rouillard, C., & Naraine, M. (2017). Network governance of a multi-level, multi-sectoral sport event: Differences in coordinating ties and actors. *SMR, 20*(5), 497–509.	Integrating network actors/Stakeholders
2	Naraine, M., Schenk, J., & Parent, M. (2016). Coordination in international and domestic events: Examining stakeholder network governance. *JSM, 30*(5), 521–537.	Integrating network actors/Stakeholders
3	O'Bolye, I., & Shilbury, D. (2016). Exploring issues of trust in collaborative sport governance. *JSM, 30*(1), 52–69.	Integrating regional entities
4	Shilbury, D., O'Boyle, I., & Ferkins, L. (2016). Towards a research agenda in collaborative sport governance. *SMR, 19*(5), 479–491.	Integrating regional entities
5	Parent, M. (2016). Stakeholder perceptions on the democratic governance of major sports events. *SMR, 19*(4), 402–416.	Managing stakeholders
6	Ferkins, L., & Shilbury, D. (2015). Board strategic balance: An emerging sport governance theory. *SMR, 18*(4), 489–500.	Strategy formulation
7	Garcia, B., & Welford, J. (2015). Supporters and football governance, from customers to stakeholders: A literature review and agenda for research. *SMR, 18*(4), 517–528.	Managing stakeholders
8	Ferkins, L., & Shilbury, D. (2015). The stakeholder dilemma in sport governance: Toward the notion of "stakeowner". *JSM, 29*(1), 93–108.	Managing stakeholders/ Integrating regional entities
9	Shilbury, D., & Ferkins, L. (2015). Exploring the utility of collaborative governance in a national sport organization. *JSM, 29*(4), 380–397.	Strategy formulation/ Integrating regional entities
10	Pielke, R. (2013). How can FIFA be held accountable? *SMR, 16*(3), 255–267.	Monitoring & compliance
11	Ferkins, L., & Shilbury, D. (2012). Good boards are strategic: What does that mean for sport governance? *JSM, 26*(1), 67–80.	Strategy formulation
12	Esteve, M., Di Lorenzo, F., Inglés, E., & Puig, N. (2011). Empirical evidence of stakeholder management in sports clubs: The impact of the board of directors. *ESMQ, 11*(4), 423–440.	Managing stakeholders
13	Ferkins, L., & Shilbury, D. (2010). Developing board strategic capability in sport organisations: The national–regional governing relationship. *SMR, 13*(3), 235–254.	Integrating regional entities
14	Ferkins, L., Shilbury, D., & McDonald, G. (2009). Board involvement in strategy: Advancing the governance of sport organizations. *JSM, 23*(3), 245–277.	Strategy formulation
15	Sherry, E., & Shilbury, D. (2009). Board directors and conflict of interest: A study of a sport league. *ESMQ, 9*(1), 47–62.	Monitoring & compliance
16	Lee, P-C. (2008). Managing a corrupted sporting system: The governance of professional baseball in Taiwan and the gambling scandal of 1997. *ESMQ, 8*(1), 45–66.	Monitoring & compliance
17	Mason, D., Thibault, L., & Misener, L. (2006). An agency theory perspective on corruption in sport: The case of the International Olympic Committee. *JSM, 20*(1), 52–73.	Monitoring & compliance
18	Ferkins, L., Shilbury, D., & McDonald, G. (2005). The role of the board in building strategic capability: Towards an integrated model of sport governance research. *SMR, 8*(3), 195–225.	Strategy formulation
19	Kuga, D. (1996). Governance of intercollegiate athletics: Perceptions of faculty members. *JSM, 10*(2), 149–168.	Managing stakeholders

Table 1.5 Ownership

No	Manuscripts	Themes
1	Dowling, M., Leopkey, B., & Smith, L. (2018). Governance in sport: A scoping review. *JSM, 32*(5), 438–451.	Scoping review
2	Buchholz, F., & Lopatta, K. (2017). Stakeholder salience of economic investors on professional football clubs in Europe, *ESMQ, 17*(4), 506–530.	Ownership
3	Gammelsæter, G. (2010). Institutional pluralism and governance in "commercialized" sport clubs. *ESMQ, 10*(5), 569–594.	Ownership
4	Smith, E. (2009). The sport of governance – a study comparing Swedish riding schools. *ESMQ, 9*(2), 163–186.	Ownership

change and design archetypes (Parent, Naraine & Hoye, 2018; Kikulis, 2000), organisational commitment of volunteers (Cuskelly, McIntyre & Boag, 1998), board paid staff relationships and decision-making (Auld & Godbey, 1998; Hoye & Cuskelly, 2003; Schulz & Auld, 2006) and the role of the board in amateur sport organisations (Inglis, 1997; Shilbury & Ferkins, 2013).

Other articles focusing on the role of the board, but with less emphasis on professionalisation, included codification of governance principles (Walters & Tacon, 2018), gender quotas and equality (Adriaanse & Schofield, 2014), dual board systems in Taiwan (Yeh, Taylor & Hoye, 2009), role of the chair (de Barros, Barros & Correia, 2007) and board structure and roles (Dimitropoulos, 2011; Enjolras & Waldahl, 2010). Clearly, the emphasis on professionalisation and its impact on volunteer directors and their motivations to become a director is evident in this quadrant. This also highlights one of the unique aspects of sport management, the tensions between a leisure-oriented product and the need to be more businesslike through professionalisation. In other words, "play" versus "business". Volunteer directors, given their leadership and governance responsibilities, find themselves at the heart of this tension.

Nine papers aligned to quadrant 2 (Table 1.2), improving board processes. Interestingly, all nine papers were board-dynamics motivated, with none dedicated to the procedural aspects of governance in terms of board meetings, papers, agendas, minutes, calendars and committees. Intragroup behaviour (Hamm-Kerwin & Doherty, 2010), cohesion and norms (Doherty & Carron, 2003; Doherty, Patterson & Van Bussel, 2004), power (Adriaanse & Schofield, 2013; Sibson, 2010; Hoye & Cuskelly, 2003) and commitment and involvement (Hoye, 2007) were the key group process themes to emerge. More recently, two papers allocated to this quadrant signify an emerging theme and perhaps a shift in thinking in the sport governance literature – the role of leadership in governance.

Authentic leadership in nonprofit organisations (Takos, Murray & O'Boyle, 2018) and the introduction of the concept of collective board leadership (Ferkins, Shilbury & O'Boyle, 2018) signifies this shift. This thinking contrasts with the existing research on sport governance, which has often concentrated on elements such as structure, process and policy. As Takos et al. (2018) observed, "Findings suggest that the nature of relationships between board members, particularly the chair and chief executive officer, is more positively influential on board functionality if characterised by authenticity and likely to lead to higher levels of trust, reduced disharmony, and limiting the formation of harmful subgroups" (p. 109). The role of leadership in board processes is highlighted through these findings. Similarly, Ferkins et al. (2018) examined the need for collective board leadership in managing inter-board dynamics in a federated structure, which firmly places board dynamics and unity as central to behaviours between boards.

Quadrant 3 (Table 1.3), continuing improvement, showed the least number of publications. Two of the three articles in this quadrant examined evaluation and performance (Hoye & Doherty, 2011; McDonald & Sherry, 2010) with the third investigating director selection (Ferrand, Henry & Ferrand, 2010). It is interesting to note that little work has studied director selection despite the debate surrounding the election of delegates to a national board in a federated model and the increasing reliance on the appointment of independent directors.

The final cohort of articles did not fit neatly into the sport governance charter. Three of the four papers examined ownership structures, which ultimately shapes the composition and approach to governance. Given the influence of ownership on governance, this is an area worthy of future research. Chapters 9–12 in this handbook examine current ownership structures in various regions of the world mapping potential future research directions. Finally, the last paper identified in this analysis also did not fit neatly into the sport governance charter. The work by Dowling, Leopkey and Smith (2018) did not focus on any one specific element of governance but was a timely scoping review of all the sport governance-related work published between 1980 and 2016. A summary of the findings is discussed in the next section.

Scoping review

The scoping review undertaken by Dowling et al. (2018) aimed to map the extent and range of research in sport governance. This process is similar to an audit, in which the body of work is identified and the key themes interrogated. Based on these results, it is possible to identify future research opportunities, given that one of the key ingredients of good scholarship is to undertake and publish research that informs and adds to the body of knowledge. In other words, the research process should advance and inform theory rather than simply communicate that which we already know. The search for peer-reviewed sport governance articles undertaken by the research team involved accessing four databases including SPORTDiscus, Scopus, Web of Science and Science Direct to ensure the widest coverage. Ultimately, after a series of refining processes, the search identified 243 sport governance-related articles. Dowling et al. (2018) reported the following descriptive statistics:

- The majority of articles (68%) were carried out in not-for-profit (n = 82) or spanned multiple sectors (n = 82).
- The most common study population was national sport organisations (n = 26), and leagues (n = 22).
- England (n = 30), Canada (n = 27) and Australia (n = 27) were the countries of most focus;
- Of the 243 articles published, 18 were published between 1982 and 2003, whereas 225 were published between 2004 and 2016.
- Approximately 27% of all sport governance articles were published in the three leading sport management journals (p. 3).

Dowling et al. (2018) used Henry and Lee's (2004) categorisation of governance types to guide the identification of published research. The three governance types include organisational (or corporate), systemic (or network) and political. Organisational governance is "concerned with normative, ethically informed standards of managerial behaviour" (Henry & Lee, 2004, p. 24). Systemic governance is "concerned with the competition, cooperation and mutual adjustment between organizations in business and/or policy systems" (Henry & Lee, p. 24) and political governance "is concerned with how governments or governing bodies in sport 'steer', rather than directly control, the behaviour of organizations" (Henry & Lee, p. 24). Consequently, the scope of articles included in this review was slightly wider than the previously reported published work in the three leading sport management journals. This signifies the complexity of defining sport governance and where governance starts and stops in relation to the role and functions of management as well as its role in society more generally.

The research team classified 74 articles as organisational governance, 49 as political governance and 120 as systemic governance providing insight into the range and scope of work published across all sources. In terms of study type, 144 were identified as empirical studies, 82 as review articles, 11 as theoretical in focus, five as case study and one as a research note (Dowling et al., 2018). The majority of work, therefore, was empirical, although the need to define, conceptualise and theorise is clearly present with 93 papers in the review and theory categories. These results highlight the important conceptual work required to clarify and define key interrelationships that lead to future empirical studies. This handbook is designed to survey the research undertaken in sport governance across a range of specified areas. As is indicated in the next section, this handbook has not only been written to capture research informing sport governance, but to also communicate future research directions based on what has not yet been studied and where there is the need to advance theoretical and practical understanding of sport governance.

Organisation of research handbook

The governance of sport has been an important component of sport management education and scholarship since the inception of sport management as an area of academic study in the 1960s in the USA. However, over the past 20 years, there has been a marked growth in interest by scholars in how sport is governed. As interest in the complexities, challenges and opportunities of good governance within a variety of sport contexts has become more prominent, there has been a growing awareness of the difficulty of determining the scope and boundaries of the activity. As previously indicated in this chapter, initial academic scholarship focussed on the work of the board, also known as organisational governance. A system-wide view has also begun to influence our understanding of the phenomenon (Shilbury, O'Boyle & Ferkins, 2016). However, sport governance is still a contested notion, meaning different things to different people in different parts of the world. After approximately 20 years of nascent growth in sport governance scholarship, it is timely to present a cohesive collection capturing progress and to help challenge and direct sport governance research into the next few decades. This research handbook is, therefore, an important contribution to the evolution of thinking in sport governance. Overall, the purpose of this handbook is to both map sport governance scholarship as well as provide a definitive account of the theory and practice of sport governance.

Specifically, this handbook aims to:

1. *Map out the territory of sport governance as a topic of research and practice.* What does sport governance encompass? What has been the focus of our scholarship efforts and what has this revealed? How has sport governance been explained in theoretical terms and what theories help explain the practice of sport governance?
2. *Offer an understanding of the global environmental context and varying government policy perspectives that have influenced the evolution of sport governance.* What have been the key environmental influencers in sport governance within and across nation states? What legal and regulatory influences shape governance practices? Why is governance so critical to sport codes? What is the role of governance within sport service and non-code sport organisations? How has the professionalisation of sport influenced the governance of sport and sport leagues?

3. *Explain evolving ownership models and the interrelationship of ownership and sport governance.* What is the range of different ownership approaches in sport and how is this evolving? How does ownership influence sport governance?

4. *Detail and analyse our present understanding of board roles and the sport governance process.* What is the role of the sport board and how is a board structured and comprised? What are the motivations behind board contribution? What is the significance of board dynamics and relationships? Why is strategy important for sport boards? How are sport boards held to account?

5. *Identify sport governance challenges and research opportunities.* Why might collective board leadership be of significance for the future of sport governance? How might a focus on diversity in the boardroom and in sport governance systems impact future research and practice? Why might social responsibility and integrity be important for sport governance into the future?

To achieve these outcomes the handbook is organised around five sections:

- Part I: Overview of sport governance
- Part II: Environmental context and policy perspectives
- Part III: Ownership structures and governance models: Implications for sport governance
- Part IV: Board roles in the governance process
- Part V: Future sport governance challenges

Part I of the handbook contains two chapters designed to set the scene for the remaining four sections of the text. Chapter 1, as is now clear, has provided an overview of the sport governance scholarship to date by examining published sport governance papers in the three leading journals in the field. Coupled with the work of Dowling et al. (2018), this introductory chapter has provided an overview of sport governance research to date. This chapter, together with Chapter 2, provides the foundation for the handbook by identifying published research, and in Chapter 2, working towards a theoretical understanding of sport governance.

Part II considers the environmental context in which sport governance exists. Comprised of six chapters, this section of the handbook examines the legal and regulatory environment and its influence on sport governance. In other words, what types of laws and regulations dictate how boards should function and act? This chapter is complex as corporate law pertaining to governance will vary from country to country. The intent, therefore, is to map out the underlying principles that typically shape legal statutes in the context of corporate law or other relevant statutes.

A suite of four chapters moves the environmental context to government policy and the shaping influences on sport governance. For example, many government departments of sport have developed a range of governance principles by which national governing bodies should comply. How these principles have been shaped and used to support government policy is an integral aspect of these chapters. The remaining two chapters in this section of the handbook examine the traditional sport governance structures that have shaped the sport system, from international sports federations to national sport organisations and their member associations. This structure has ultimately shaped governance practices to date. This analysis extends to examining non-sport code service agencies such as institutes of sport, Active Partnerships in the UK, sports commissions in the USA and lobby and advocacy organisations established to influence government policy and funding support.

Part III of the handbook dedicates four chapters to understanding ownership models of professional sport across various regions of the world. This is an important suite of chapters, as there has been limited work undertaken to understand how different ownership models shape governance practice and what changes in terms of governance practices when ownership changes. The remaining three chapters are dedicated to the governance of three specific areas, international sport federations, the governance of intercollegiate athletics given its special focus in the USA and the governance of hallmark events. The governance of hallmark events, in particular, highlights a range of challenges in bringing together diverse stakeholders for a finite period to oversee and monitor the delivery of these events.

Part IV of the handbook is unique, as it assesses the role of the board and directors and, although tackled from a research perspective, the nine chapters in this section could form the basis of readings for a course in sport governance. Certainly, with the other chapters in the handbook, it becomes an excellent resource to support the teaching of a class in sport governance. Part V of the handbook deals with future challenges in the intersection of leadership and governance, gender, gender quotas and diversity generally, social responsibility and integrity and how boards grapple with the complex issues associated with match-fixing, for example, and corruption, accountability and transparency. Finally, the handbook concludes with an overview of the research directions to emerge throughout each of the five sections of the handbook.

Summary

Chapter 1 is the first of two foundation chapters in this handbook examining sport governance research. It has provided an overview of the volume of published sport governance research in the three leading sport management journals. This analysis not only identified the volume of work, but it also categorised the work by theme and aligned it to the sport governance charter. This chapter, therefore, has provided clear direction on the emergent themes of sport governance research and how it relates to the work of boards and the practice of sport governance. Quadrant 4, key board functions, was shown to have produced the greatest number of articles, with most focused on the challenges of a federal model and the need to improve board strategic capability, integration with regional member associations and managing stakeholders.

This analysis of the three leading journals was complemented by the recently published work of Dowling et al. (2018). This work provided an overview of the number of sport governance-related manuscripts published within and beyond the field of sport management. Dowling et al. identified 243 sport governance research related articles spanning the globe. In both cases, data to emerge from these analyses show that sport governance research is a relatively recent phenomenon. Dowling et al. (2018), for example, showed that 225 of the 243 articles identified have been published since 2004.

Chapter 1 provided an overview of sport governance scholarship. It outlined the rationale for this handbook and described how it is organised. It also provided a sound platform from which to move from an understanding of existing sport governance scholarship to an examination of the theoretical basis of sport governance. Chapter 2 will review relevant theories applicable to sport governance and work towards a theoretical understanding of sport governance.

References

Auld, C. J. (1997). Professionalisation of Australian sport administration: The effects on organisational decision-making. *European Journal for Sport Management, 4*, 17–39.
Chalip, L. (2006). Toward a distinctive sport management discipline. *Journal of Sport Management, 20*, 1–21.
Cornforth, C. (2012). Nonprofit governance research: Limitations of the focus on boards and suggestions for new directions. *Nonprofit and Voluntary Sector Quarterly, 41*, 1116–1135.

Cuskelly, G., Boag, A., & McIntyre, N. (1999). Differences in organisational commitment between paid and volunteer administrators in sport. *European Journal for Sport Management, 6*, 39–61.

Dowling, M., Leopkey, B., & Smith, L. (2018). Governance in sport: A scoping review. *Journal of Sport Management, 32*, 438–451.

Enjolras, B. (2002). The commercialisation of voluntary sports organisations in Norway. *Nonprofit and Voluntary Sector Quarterly, 31*, 352–376.

Ferkins, L., Shilbury, D., & McDonald, G. (2009). Board involvement in strategy: Advancing the governance of sport organizations. *Journal of Sport Management, 23*, 245–277.

Henry, I., & Lee, P. C. (2004). Governance and ethics in sport. In J. Beech & S. Chadwick (Eds.), *The business of sport management* (pp. 25–41). Essex: Pearson Education.

Hoye, R., & Cuskelly, G. (2007). *Sport governance*. Sydney: Elsevier.

Kiel, G., & Nicholson, G. (2003). *Boards that work. A new guide for directors*. Sydney: McGraw Hill.

Koski, P., & Heikkala, J. (1998). Professionalization and organizations of mixed rationales: The case of Finnish national sport organizations. *European Journal of Sport Management, 5*, 7–29.

O'Brien, D., & Slack, T. (2003). An analysis of change in an organizational field: The professionalization of English rugby union. *Journal of Sport Management, 17*, 293–320.

Pielke, R. (2015). Obstacles to accountability in international sports governance. In G. Sweeney (Ed.), *Global Corruption Report: Sport* (pp. 29–38). Milton Park Abingdon, UK: Routledge.

Siegfried, N., Schlesinger, T., Bayle, E., & Giauque, D. (2015). Professionalisation of sport federations – a multi-level framework for analysing forms, causes and consequences. *European Sport Management Quarterly, 15*, 407–433.

Shilbury, D. (2012). Competition: The heart and soul of sport management. *Journal of Sport Management, 26*, 1–10.

Shilbury, D., Ferkins, L., & Smythe, L. (2013). Sport governance encounters: Insights from lived experiences. *Sport Management Review, 16*, 349–363.

Shilbury, D., O'Boyle, I., & Ferkins, L. (2016). A research agenda for collaborative sport governance. *Sport Management Review, 19*, 479–491.

The Economist. (2015). Bigger than Blatter. Retrieved 21 June 2018, from https://www.economist.com/leaders/2015/06/06/bigger-than-blatter

Thibault, L., Slack, T., & Hinings, B. (1991). Professionalism, structures and systems: The impact of professional staff on voluntary sport organizations. *International Review for the Sociology of Sport, 26*, 83–98.

Tricker, R. I. (2012). *Corporate governance: Principles, policies, and practices*. Oxford, UK: Oxford University Press.

2

Theoretical underpinnings of sport governance

Lesley Ferkins and David Shilbury

Introduction

The focus of this chapter on the theoretical underpinnings of sport governance is distinguished from Chapter 1, which more closely considers sport governance literature, topics and empirical studies. This chapter is one step removed from empirical endeavour in sport governance as it seeks to chart and analyse the theoretical landscape. The framework chosen for this chapter follows a multi-level view of governance encompassing the individual level, the board level, the organisation level and the broader system level of sport organisation interactions (see Figure 2.1). This augments the sport governance charter (Figure 1.2) used as the basis for Chapter 1, which is primarily board level focused.

The idea of a multi-level conceptual model to embody leadership and governance research in sport management is a notion recently offered by Welty Peachey, Damon, Zhou and Burton (2015) to map leadership scholarship. Jones, Wegner, Bunds, Edwards and Bocarro (2018) also used this thinking to explore shared leadership within a sport-for-development organisation setting. In governance, such multi-level thinking was adapted by Ferkins, Shilbury and O'Boyle (2018) to position major theories used within sport governance at various levels within a federated sport governance system. For the purposes of this chapter, it is considered helpful for mapping theoretical influences for sport governance scholarship and have further adapted the thinking of Ferkins et al. (2018) in presenting Figure 2.1.

All three articles noted above, point to work within our parent disciplines in leadership and governance – specifically, the work of Hitt, Beamish, Jackson and Mathieu (2007) in advocating for multiple level research in management and the need to build theoretical bridges across levels (i.e., individual, groups, subunits, organisations, interorganisational networks, environments). "The central theme of multi-level thinking is that organizational entities reside in nested arrangements" (Hitt et al., 2007, p. 1387). The authors also noted that much of the management research has been confined to a single level. As with using more than one theory to explore a phenomenon, potentially the added complexity and challenge of multiple levels of investigation has also created barriers for such scholarship. In sport governance, Dowling, Leopkey and Smith's (2018) scoping review identified that 121/243 (49.8%) were systemic governance studies. This contrasts 74 of the 243 articles (30.3%) that they classified

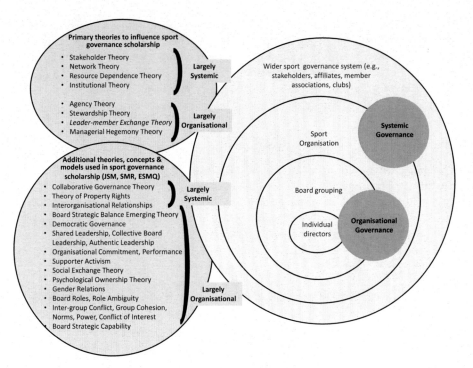

Figure 2.1 Theories influencing sport governance scholarship.

as organisational governance studies. These figures indicate a growing interest, nonetheless, in moving beyond single-level investigation.

In this chapter, a multi-level framework (Figure 2.1) is used to show the primary theories that influence sport governance scholarship and at what level of the sport system they have largely been deployed. Figure 2.1 also captures additional theories, concepts and models that have been used in the 49 articles published in our major journals (*Journal of Sport Management, Sport Management Review* and *European Sport Management Quarterly*) between 1987 and 2018, as presented in Chapter 1. As with the primary theories, Figure 2.1 also indicates at what level the additional theories, concepts and models have largely been deployed. This analysis highlights how a range of concepts, as distinct from established theories, have influenced sport governance scholarship. Like the established theories, these concepts are drawn from our parent disciplines, and it is interesting to note that there are few "indigenous" or "homegrown" theories of sport governance. This presents a major opportunity for sport governance scholarship going forward.

While acknowledging the three types of governance offered originally by Henry and Lee (2004) and later by Dowling et al. (2018) in their scoping review (i.e., organisational, systemic and political), this handbook concentrates on the first two forms. This is because they are considered central to our established definition of governance and are most prevalent within the sport governance literature (refer to Chapter 1). Further, it was also found that a number of the articles attributed to the political type of governance captured by Dowling et al. (2018) did not necessarily consider or focus on governance as a concept within the study (see for example, Parent, Rouillard & Leopkey, 2011). That said, as with Chapter 1, this chapter also leans on the work of Henry and Lee (2004) and Dowling et al. (2018) as a way to "ring fence" existing scholarship in sport governance about which this chapter spotlights the theoretical influences.

The chapter begins with a wide-angle discussion about the nature of theory in sport governance. It then presents a section on the primary theories to influence sport governance scholarship followed by a section on those theories, concepts and models beyond those originally offered by Ferkins et al. (2018) but found within the 49 articles published in our major journals. Each section references the associated levels of sport governance interactions (individual, board, organisation, system) as they relate to organisational or systemic sport governance.

The nature of theory in sport governance

Perhaps encouragingly for our discipline of sport management, sport governance scholars have approached their work through a range of different theoretical lenses (Dowling et al., 2018). Arguably, a trend in sport management scholarship has been to increasingly draw from multiple theories, usually from more established contexts or disciplines (i.e., business, economics, marketing, sociology, leadership etc.), in order to help explain sport management phenomena (Doherty, Fink & Cunningham, 2016). In addition to engaging with different theories for different sport governance topics, a number of researchers in sport governance have also acknowledged the value of applying a multi-theoretical approach to one particular sport governance phenomena (Dowling et al., 2018; O'Boyle, 2012; Ferkins & Shilbury, 2015). An example of this is our work in exploring board strategic capability within the nonprofit sport context (Ferkins & Shilbury, 2010; Ferkins, Shilbury & McDonald, 2005). Early in our journeying with this topic, we identified the need to draw from multiple theories to help explain the phenomena of board strategic capability (Ferkins, Shilbury & McDonald, 2005). Later we became more explicit in explaining how and why we drew from multiple theories: "To begin, agency and stewardship theory were at the forefront … but, as the stories emerged, a broader range of theory (especially collaborative governance theory) … was drawn upon" (Shilbury, Ferkins & Smythe, 2013, p. 351).

In considering the importance of theory in qualitative enquiry within sport management, Shaw (2016) also encourages us to consider our engagement with theory as being less about establishing *a* theoretical foundation, which might be rigid and singular, and more as something scholars can weave into the research as we progress through the study. She asks whether there is a need to establish a theoretical position before a project or whether it is possible to work with theory in a more flexible way. Certainly, our experience with sport governance above demonstrates a malleable relationship with theory. The value of this is that it is unlikely that any one theory can fully explain the complexity of what might be occurring within a board, organisation or sport system setting (Cornforth, 2012). Particularly in qualitative research, where an emergent and inductive approach is valued, the freedom to draw on multiple theories as the research unfolds potentially offers a way to yield rich insights (Shaw, 2016).

The trend to work with multiple theories has been argued, in governance work beyond sport, as a basis for which to move past agency theory as a singular lens through which governance might be viewed (Ansell & Torfing, 2016; Leblanc, 2004; Miller-Millesen, 2003). Until recent times, agency theory has tended to dominate the governance literature, which has influenced conclusions that the central role of the board is to control and monitor the CEO (Judge, 2009; Roberts, McNulty & Stiles, 2005). However, as Miller-Millesen (2003) found in her study of nonprofit boards, the integration of multiple theoretical explanations (in her case, agency theory, resource dependence theory and institutional theory) "… reveals a promising accumulation of wisdom regarding the roles and responsibilities of non-profit boards" (p. 541). In the corporate setting, Judge (2009) too is encouraging of the need to maintain our search beyond agency theory "for a more context-sensitive theoretical perspective on governance dynamics" (p. 123); albeit, such a quest still appears to be predicated on a more encompass-ing *single* theory of corporate governance, as his following statement implies. "The mission of CGIR [Corporate Governance: An International Review journal] is to identify and/or create a rigorous and relevant theory of corporate governance that applies equally well throughout the global economy" (p. 123).

Contrasting such a view is Shaw (2016) who noted that, in sport management (qualitative approaches), "We are not searching for *the* theory, rather one or many that may help us to under-stand a little bit more that we did" (Shaw, 2016, p. 22). Hoye and Doherty (2011) also advocated for an integrated approach to theorising in relation to sport board performance. In reviewing theoretical models on board performance from both the for-profit and nonprofit governance settings, they highlighted the few studies that had specifically integrated multiple theoretical perspectives. Despite the dearth of a pluralist approach, Hoye and Doherty (2011) present a strong argument for why they themselves established an integrated model of board perfor-mance. In this they emphasised the importance of multiple theoretical perspectives (i.e., agency theory, resource dependency, institutional theory, group decision-making processes, legal theory, managerial hegemony) in influencing the factors they chose as central building blocks for their model (i.e., environmental factors, individual factors, organisational factors, board factors). It is curious to note that, despite such endorsements, a multi-theoretical approach has tended to be the exception rather than the norm (Ferkins & Shilbury, 2015). Perhaps this is because it is dif-ficult enough to work with one theory, and that by incorporating more than one we add even greater complexity, challenge and confusion into our scholarship.

Nonetheless, Ansell and Torfing (2016) offer a competing argument for why it is important to strive for more expansive theoretical explanations, even at the risk of confusion, in our theo-rising of sport governance:

> There is no comprehensive and all-encompassing theory of governance, and the future development of such theory seems neither likely nor desirable. The competing theoreti-cal approaches and conceptualizations offer different analytical perspectives and tools that permit students of governance to mix and match them in their search for an appropriate theoretical framework for addressing a particular research problem or research question. Hence, a problem-driven study of contemporary forms of governance is better off choosing between a large array of sharp and distinctive special-purpose theories than relaying a blunt, unified all-purpose theory. (pp. 110–11)

In line with Shaw (2016), studies in sport governance might benefit from incorporating mul-tiple theories to study a particular phenomenon of interest. This might particularly be the case as scholars push beyond board and organisation level settings into network or systemic types of governance research contexts (Dowling et al., 2018).

What do we mean by theory in sport governance?

The above sentiments point towards the need to continue our efforts to clarify and evolve an articulation of what is meant by theory. The focus on sport governance clearly sits within our now well-established global discipline of sport management. As scholars in this field, what do we understand the purpose and value of theory to be? How do we understand the nature of theory, and how might we define our notion of theory? In a valuable resource for sport manage-ment scholars, Cunningham, Fink and Doherty (2016) sought to understand better how people engaged in theory-building processes for our discipline in producing the *Routledge Handbook of Theory in Sport Management*. Prior to this work, Cunningham (2013) noted in a special issue on theory development that, as a group of scholars committed to sport management, we have not necessarily critically examined theory and its place in our field. This certainly seems to be the case for the specific area of sport governance.

The handbook draws on Cunningham's (2013) definition of theory as "statements of constructs and their relationships to one another that explain how, when, why and under what conditions phenomena take place" (p. 1). This thinking is also evident in the way Zhang, Kim and Pifer (2016) chose to explain the importance of theory in quantitative enquiry within sport management. They drew on Sutton and Staw (1995) to emphasise that the purpose of theory is to explain the connections among phenomena; "it is the answer to queries of why, depicting the rationale behind certain actions, events, structures and thoughts" (Zhang et al., 2016, p. 9). Shaw (2016) (from a qualitative view) offered that, for her, the presence of theory marks the difference between a casual conversation in the pub and an academic discussion. Perhaps also, simply put, theory helps to explain *why*. Why do boards behave as they do? Uncovering the *why* potentially sets us up to guide future action or behaviour. The uncovering of why also necessitates close attention to context, acknowledged as a central element in the theorising process (Ansell & Torfing, 2016; Cunningham, et al., 2016; Judge, 2009).

From a governance standpoint in their theory-building process, Ferkins and Shilbury (2016) worked with the definition offered by Doherty (2013) that theory is a set of concepts that elucidates the relationships among these ideas. In also aligning with Cunningham (2013), Ferkins and Shilbury (2016), stated, "A good theory also explains what might happen and why under certain circumstances" (p. 126); thus, theory not only explains why but might also be instructive for future circumstances. Ansell and Torfing (2016) help shed light on the meaning of theory for governance scholars (albeit beyond sport). They offer that theories of governance can be described as analytical constructs which are developed by empirical endeavours and reasoning. They add that theories of governance encompass "a good deal of imagination and creativity" (p. 11). Thus, they are abstract, yet heavily influenced by context, and aim to define, explain and understand how organisations and societies are governed (Ansell & Torfing, 2016).

Finally, in seeking to explain the nature of theory in sport governance, we agree with the ideas of Cunningham et al. (2016) that theory has a broader utility for both advancing a scholarly domain (i.e., the discipline of sport management and sub area of sport governance) and is also significant for teaching. It allows "students to move beyond a descriptive awareness of phenomena to a deeper understanding of how, why and when activities occur and, as a result, they better understand action in which they can engage to influence those activities" (Cunningham et al., 2016, p. 4). This notion is akin to Shaw's (2016) position that theory is something that goes well beyond a casual conversation. From our own experience in sport governance, we firmly align with the idea that theory does indeed inform practice and vice versa. The deployment of action research to carry out many of our sport governance studies has shown us this (see Ferkins & Shilbury, 2016). Kurt Lewin, often recognised as the father of action research is famous for his statement, "There is nothing more practical than a good theory" (1952, p. 169). We wholeheartedly agree.

Primary theories to influence sport governance scholarship

This chapter now turns specifically to considering those primary theories that have been noted to influence sport governance scholarship (Hoye & Doherty, 2011; Naraine, Schenk & Parent, 2016; O'Boyle, 2012; Walters & Tacon, 2018). In this a comprehensive account of all theories is not used, instead this chapter aligns with Ferkins et al. (2018) in capturing the regularly deployed theories; those that particularly "speak" to our domain (the usual suspects). As noted earlier, sport governance scholarship has drawn from more established contexts (i.e., for-profit and nonprofit governance) and this choice of influencing theories reflects this (Clarke, 2005; Hoye & Doherty, 2011; Judge, 2009; Miller-Millesen, 2003).

Figure 2.1 captures eight such theories (top left, Primary theories to influence sport governance scholarship). These eight theories have been divided into those considered to have largely been used in systemic sport governance (n = 4) and those more connected to organisational governance (n = 4). It is also emphasised that these distinctions are by no means definitive. Some theories, for example institutional theory and, to a lesser extent, resource dependence theory, also feature in studies that might be more strongly associated with organisational governance (e.g., Ferkins & Shilbury, 2010; Gammelsæter, 2010). Further, Hitt et al. (2007) caution us in their discussion of multi-level research in management about the challenges of assigning levels for not only theory but in how the data was derived and the level of analysis. Figure 2.1 aligns theories and concepts used in sport governance scholarship with the predominant contextual level at which data collection and analysis was focused (i.e., individual directors, board grouping, individual organisation and a wider system involving multiple organisations).

The notion of organisational governance has come to be associated with studies that focus on individual directors, the board grouping as well as the individual sport organisation (Dowling et al., 2018; Ferkins et al., 2018; Henry & Lee, 2004). It therefore follows that agency theory, stewardship theory, leader-member exchange theory and managerial hegemony theory have been deployed primarily for these contexts. Moreover, in many instances, these theories have specifically been used to explain the interaction between the board and CEO. For example, Mason, Thibault and Misener (2006) used agency theory to explore corruption, with a specific focus on individual members/directors, and the functions of management within the International Olympic Committee. Dimitropoulos (2011) drew on agency theory to analyse the impact of particular corporate governance qualities on the earnings management behaviour of football clubs in Europe (i.e., board size, board independence, managerial ownership, institutional ownership, CEO duality).

Leader-member exchange theory was used by Hoye (2003, 2004, 2006) to analyse the dyadic relationship between board chairs and paid executives within Australian state sport organisations. Hoye (2004) credits Dansereau, Graen and Haga (1975) for their early work in developing this theory, noting that Kent and Chelladurai (2001) were the first to introduce it to sport management. Managerial hegemony is probably a theory more closely associated with corporate (organisational) governance as distinct from broader management studies (Dallas, 1996). As its name suggests, managerial hegemony theory sheds light on the conundrum that, while the board has legal power, the actual responsibility for the organisation is often assumed by management (Stiles, 2001). This idea proved particularly helpful for studies in sport governance that focused on board–CEO power dynamics (e.g., Ferkins, Shilbury & McDonald, 2009). For Ferkins et al. (2009, p. 268), managerial hegemony was described as the "tail wagging the dog" and was a basis for encouraging greater board involvement in strategy design to balance CEO influence. The practical use of this theory was made possible as part of an action research study involving a change process with a national sport organisation board group.

Which theories are most used?

Of the four theories largely associated with organisational sport governance in Figure 2.1, agency theory is arguably the most prevalent. It appears the most regularly (five times) in the 49 articles drawn from our three major journals, and it has also been widely cited as the dominant theory of corporate (organisational) governance beyond the sport domain (Van Ees, Gabrielsson & Huse, 2009). If not specifically used, it often makes an appearance in a review of literature that is associated with organisational sport governance (Hoye & Doherty, 2011; O'Boyle, 2012). Of the four theories largely associated with systemic sport governance, institutional theory appears to be the most widely used. It also appears most regularly in the 49 articles (five times), albeit that it appears to cross both organisational and systemic approaches. Like institutional theory, stakeholder theory and network theory are major theories well-used in sport management scholarship to explore relationships beyond a single organisation focus (Babiak, Thibault & Willem, 2018; Byers, Parent & Slack, 2012). It is therefore no surprise that they have also been deployed for the purposes of understanding systemic governance dynamics. In addition, seven of the eight primary theories captured in Figure 2.1 appear across the 49 articles drawn from our three major journals. The exception is leader–member exchange theory used by Hoye (in italics) (2003, 2004, 2006) but not published in our three journals (*JSM, SMR, ESMQ*).

The drive to view the study of governance as something beyond the confines of an individual organisation boundary or board group setting (i.e., organisational or corporate governance) has seemingly fuelled arguments to adapt a more expansive approach to governance theorising (i.e., to move beyond agency theory for example). Cornforth (2012) has been a strong advocate of the need to push beyond the organisational horizon and encompass multiple organisations in a governance system. While Cornforth's work is grounded in the nonprofit setting (and not within sport), his thinking has particularly aligned with those sport governance scholars who have focused on the challenges of governance in a federated sport network (O'Boyle & Shilbury, 2016; Ferkins & Shilbury, 2015).

This broader view of governance (systemic governance) has thus driven engagement with theories such as stakeholder and network theory, introduced more latterly to the sport governance domain (Ferkins & Shilbury, 2015). The work of Parent (2016) and Parent, Rouillard and Naraine (2017) are examples of how stakeholder and network lenses have been applied to understand governing relationships beyond single organisation entities (in their case, involving sport events). Again, in keeping with systems viewpoints and the many overlaps between categories, levels, theories and approaches, Figure 2.1 *indicates* these interactions, rather than definitively concludes that this is where they sit and, indeed, that all theoretical influences have been captured.

Additional theories, concepts and models used in sport governance scholarship

This section focuses on theories, concepts and models that are additional to those primary theories already noted to influence sport governance scholarship. The fourteen bullet points in the left-hand bottom corner of Figure 2.1 have been derived from consideration of the 49 articles published in the three identified journals (*JSM, SMR, ESMQ*). In this there are a further five theories that have featured in articles from the 49 that have not been regularly identified as theories of sport governance (Ferkins et al., 2018). These are collaborative governance theory, theory of property rights, board strategic balance (emerging theory), social exchange theory and psychological ownership theory. The remainder of those listed as additional are considered concepts and models.

Doherty (2013) offered an explanation for how to understand the distinctions between theory, concepts and models in sport management. She noted that while theorising is the act of forming or proposing a theory, conceptualising is the act of forming or developing a concept. She also explains that a concept is understood as an idea or notion. "Taken together, then, one theorizes by conceptualizing various ideas or notions and how and why they relate to each other" (p. 7). This is helpful in considering the 14 bullet points in Figure 2.1, of which only five were specifically identified by the authors in the sport governance articles to be theories. The remainder were referred to as concepts and models and thus referred to this way. Doherty (2013) also points out that a conceptual framework or model can be considered the structural representation of ideas and notions. Therefore, in following her previous logic, a theoretical framework or model "is the structural representation of the relationships among the concepts" (p. 7).

The five theories noted in Figure 2.1 in the additional theories and concepts circle all appear to meet this criterion in that they represent relationships among multiple concepts and ideas. Collaborative governance theory, for example, is a theory that has attracted increasing interest within the public and government sector for the purposes of investigating cross-sectorial governing relationships (Emerson, Nabatchi & Balogh, 2012). It speaks to how multiple organisations, across sectors, go about working together to achieve common goals and outcomes that may not be possible by working in isolation. The tenets of collaborative governance theory are also founded on a formalised consensus-orientated process that involves collective decision-making (Ansell & Gash, 2008).

Shilbury, Ferkins and Smythe (2013) introduced collaborative governance theory to sport governance (albeit a single sector) as a way to understand the tensions and dynamics associated with a sector in transition from an amateur ethos towards a more professional and commercial orientation. Embedded within the theory are concepts such as power and structure, leadership and motivation and decision-making (Ansell & Gash, 2008). These concepts and ideas were used in a theorising process by Shilbury, O'Boyle and Ferkins (2016) to explore how and why they relate to each other in the context of governance within a sport system such as a federated network. The purpose of that particular article was to explore the utility of collaborative governance theory to further enlighten future sport governance research of a systemic nature. Thus, Figure 2.1 associates collaborative governance theory with systemic governance.

Like institutional theory, the positioning of board strategic balance theory (Ferkins & Shilbury, 2015, 2016) potentially crosses both systemic and organisational governance. This is because one of the concepts of board strategic balance speaks to a system level of governance. Specifically, the idea of the board of a national governing body integrating its state or regional entities into the governing role is central to this theory. The other five concepts embedded within board strategic balance theory are more associated with board and organisation level governance. Additionally, board strategic balance appears to be the only indigenous theory for sport governance. In other words, all other theories (concepts and models) have been drawn from parent disciplines (commonly corporate governance, management, leadership etc.). Ferkins and Shilbury (2016) explain how they first borrowed concepts and theory from other disciplines to iteratively build their emerging theory as follows:

> Twelve years on from our first tentative steps in seeking to contribute to the way sport is organized, managed and led by focusing on those who govern, we moved beyond conceptual and empirical work to establishing a theory indigenous to the sport governance setting. The extensions and applications of our original topic of board strategic capability have occurred in a highly iterative manner. We began with existing theory, borrowed from other settings, which we used to add insight and explain the sport governance phenomenon. In using it as a tool of analysis, the amalgamation of existing theory with insights from the boardroom situation created new thinking and, ultimately, a new theory. (p. 123)

How concepts and models have been used in sport governance

The remainder of the 14 bullet points in Figure 2.1 are largely organisational sport governance ideas. The exception is inter-organisational relationships (Ferkins & Shilbury, 2010) which, as the name suggests, is firmly associated with multiple organisations and therefore highly relevant for systemic sport governance. Concepts of shared leadership (Hoye & Cuskelly, 2003), collective leadership (Ferkins et al., 2018) and authentic leadership (Takos, Murray & O'Boyle, 2018) are also associated with organisational sport governance because of how they have been used in the respective studies to explain board level interactions. This focus on the concept of leadership in governance is also an emerging area of investigation for sport governance which holds much promise for both organisational governance and systemic governance (Erakovic & Jackson, 2012).

Concepts of board roles (Yeh, Taylor & Hoye, 2009), role ambiguity (Schulz & Auld, 2006), inter-group conflict (Doherty, 2010), group cohesion (Doherty & Carron, 2003), norms (Doherty, Patterson & Van Bussel, 2004) and trust, power and control (Hoye & Cuskelly, 2003) are also more obviously associated with the board grouping in Figure 2.1. In these studies, the focus was often on a single organisation board and therefore related strongly to organisational sport governance. Also situated within organisational sport governance, is the work of Adriaanse and Schofield (2013, 2014) which deploys gender regimes to explore gender dynamics and the vexing question of gender quotas in sport governance. They founded their work on an established tradition of research relating to gendered organisations (Acker, 1990; Connell, 2009), as well as a stream of research in sport management on gender relations (Claringbould & Knoppers, 2012; Inglis, 1997; Sibson, 2010). Adriaanse and Schofield (2014) described gender regime as a theoretical concept, but also drew from Connell (2009) who established a theoretical model of gender regime. This theoretical model has been built on four concepts and ideas of gender relations (i.e., production relations, power relations, emotional relations and symbolic relations). Adriaanse and Schofield's (2013, 2014) work further exemplifies the nuanced distinction between *theory*, *concepts* and *models* while also offering powerful insights into the critical issue of board quotas in sport.

To conclude this section, two further theories, namely, psychological ownership theory and the theory of property rights, are considered. These theories sit alongside the concept of supporter activism and were used to investigate ownership – an emerging theme in sport governance noted in Chapter 1. The theoretical lens used by Smith (2009) was the theory of property rights in order to explore congruence between strategy and structure in different organisational forms as it relates to the act of governance within Swedish riding schools. The context within which Smith (2009) engages this theory appears to cross both organisational (organisation form) and systemic (multiple riding schools/organisations) types of governance, hence the placement in Figure 2.1.

In staying with the ownership theme, Garcia and Welford (2015) were interested in the notion of supporters in football governance, focusing a review of literature and research agenda on the role of supporters and, in particular, teasing out conceptualisations of supporter activism. They helpfully make the distinction between micro-level studies, which they refer to as individual clubs/supporter groups) and macro-level (government/policy). In this they asserted that:

> Academic attention thus far is broadly divided into two areas with little overlap between them: analysis of supporter engagement at the macro … level with a top-down focus, and sociological "bottom-up" case studies of supporter engagement and activism at the micro level … (p. 517).

This is an interesting observation, albeit specifically focused on supporters and football governance, but nonetheless has relevance for this particular chapter and the way this chapter has sought to associate theories, levels and types of governance investigation. Potentially, as our collective understanding of theories used in sport governance and therefore of sport governance practice evolve, it may be beneficial to actively seek ways to "overlap" organisational and systemic governance.

Summary

This chapter has explored the theoretical underpinnings of sport governance. Figure 2.1 charts theories, concepts and models used in the scholarship of sport governance and the level and type of governance with which they have largely been associated. The level and type of governance has primarily been determined by the empirical context of the study (i.e., individual, board, organisation or wider system) and/or whether the conceptual focus is within a single organisation (organisational governance) or involves multiple organisations (systemic governance). Figure 2.1 was supported by a discussion of the primary theories to influence sport governance scholarship, four of which were identified as being associated largely with systemic sport governance (stakeholder theory, network theory, resource dependence theory and institutional theory). A further four were identified as largely associated with organisational sport governance (agency theory, stewardship theory, leader-member exchange theory and managerial hegemony theory).

The primary theories appear to have found their way into sport governance scholarship because of their prevalence and utility within our parent disciplines. Some appear to have been specifically sourced from the study of corporate governance or governance in nonprofit (non-sport) settings (e.g., agency theory, stewardship theory, managerial hegemony theory). Others were key players within sport management prior to their deployment within sport governance (e.g., stakeholder theory, network theory, resource dependence theory, institutional theory) (Byers et al., 2012).

As noted in Chapter 1, sport governance scholarship has a relatively short history, with the first article in the three major journals published in 1996. A survey of articles from 20 years of nascent growth in sport governance scholarship has demonstrated a theoretical landscape previously established in non-sport settings and that, potentially, those primary theories have continued to serve the nuances of the sport management context. A good example of this is the rapid adoption of stewardship theory alongside agency theory as a way to explain the role and purpose of the board in a nonprofit sport setting (Shilbury, 2001). Stewardship theory contrasts agency theory by focussing on the broader responsibility by the board to act as guardians of the organisation and its future (Davis & Schoorman, 1997).

This positioning expands on the ideas of agency theory, which is largely restricted to notions of delegated authority assigned to the board (because of separation of ownership) to act on behalf of the shareholders for profit maximisation (Donaldson & Davis, 1991; Fama & Jensen, 1983). Both these theories have, in the early stages of sport governance scholarship been useful in driving an understanding of the purpose and role of the board in sport organisations. As Carver (2010) noted, "Because governance is a social construct rather than a natural phenomenon, theory must be driven by and anchored in the purpose of boards rather than derived from analyses of current practices" (p. 150). Drawing on stewardship theory to more fully explain the purpose of a nonprofit sport board (e.g., Shilbury, 2001) is in keeping with Carver's (2010) argument.

Figure 2.1 also supported a discussion of additional theories, concepts and models used in sport governance scholarship from 49 articles in the three major journals since 1996 (*JSM*, *SMR*, *ESMQ*). This discussion revealed that sport governance scholars have sought an ever expanding theoretical and conceptual basis to explain a range of themes and topics. These have largely been associated with organisational sport governance. Thus, interestingly, where authors have identified that they have engaged with theory (as distinct from a concept or model), this has largely been for the purposes of investigating systemic governance interactions. Conversely, where authors have positioned their work by drawing on concepts and models (and not naming a theory or theories), this has been for the purpose of exploring individual directors, board groupings and individual organisation dynamics. This may be explained by a maturation process whereby organisational sport governance has tended to be the "first cab off the rank" and the focus of early work (Hoye & Doherty, 2011). More latterly, systemic sport governance has gained momentum as a focus of sport governance scholarship (O'Boyle & Shilbury, 2016; Parent, 2016).

In addition to charting the theoretical underpinnings of sport governance, this chapter explored the nature of theory in sport governance, teasing out the distinctions between theories, concepts and models. One observation from this is that sport governance scholars have engaged a mix of theories, concepts and models, as well as the deployment of multiple theories to explore both a particular topic as well as a range of governance topics and themes. Figure 2.1 demonstrates the diversity in the deployment of theories, concepts and models, whereby the usual suspects appear (e.g., agency theory, institutional theory), but these are joined by an ever increasing collection of theories and conceptualisations. These ideas, perhaps not surprisingly, seem to be closely related to each other. For example, the ideas embedded within stakeholder theory and network theory offer similar and complementary thinking and have been used together to explore particular governance themes and contexts (e.g., Naraine et al., 2016). As previously noted, agency theory and stewardship theory also share overlapping yet complementary ideas. This observation extends to the additional theories, concepts and models where we have attempted to group similar ideas in the bullet point list in Figure 2.1.

Once such grouping is concepts and theories of leadership. Leader-member exchange theory has been used by Hoye (2003, 2004, 2006) as a primary theory to influence sport governance scholarship because of the early influence of this work within the scholarly community (Takos et al., 2018). This theory has also been associated with the concept of shared leadership, principally to explore board–CEO dynamics (Ferkins, et al., 2009) within organisational sport governance. More latterly, the concept of collective board leadership has been introduced as a way to examine both board level leadership and the systemic level of governance interactions between organisations (Ferkins et al., 2018). Takos et al. (2018) added authentic leadership to explore board member interactions in organisational sport governance. This small cluster of interrelated theories and concepts of leadership in governance also reveal that this particular terrain of sport governance is theoretically underdeveloped. As Takos et al. (2018) noted, "Despite the wealth of research in leadership it is somewhat paradoxical that the fields of leadership and governance rarely engage" (p. 109). The fact that scholars from more established disciplines of governance have not yet embraced this interrelationship presents an opportunity for sport governance to lead the way.

A final and major observation about the theoretical underpinning of sport governance scholarship is that, to date, there have been few indigenous theories developed specifically within and for the sport governance domain. The emerging theory of board strategic balance in Figure 2.1 appears as the only indigenous theory of sport governance. In their handbook on theory development in sport management, Cunningham et al. (2016) noted that many theories in use in sport management are adapted from parent theories or disciplines, which are informed by general management literature, yet, importantly, are grounded in the contextual factors and nuance that are potentially not evident within other sectors. In this way borrowed theories and concepts have been adapted and extended (e.g., see institutional theory in Babiak et al. 2018). This observation appears particularly salient for sport governance. As sport governance evolves, the opportunity exists, however, for indigenous theory development to augment our existing collection. As Cunningham et al. (2016) urge, where no relevant theory exists, or existing explanations do not fully capture the distinctive nuances and features of the sport setting, we need to drive towards developing our own theoretical basis.

While it could be argued that theory development grounded in the practical setting of sport governance, and therefore potentially case studies are important, Garcia and Welford (2015) offer another perspective in their conceptual article on the role of supporters in football governance. They argued that,

> There is a need to go beyond the single case study, using methodologies that include … different clubs, different divisions and even different countries, if possible, so that their experiences can be compared. That is to say, designing research methodologies that revolve around theory, concepts and variables, rather than cases. (p. 525)

Perhaps a combination of a grounding in practice and, to Carver's (2010) point, purpose (and therefore future practice), as well as a methodological design that encourages indigenous theory development (e.g., action research) are elements worthy of consideration in our theorising efforts. For sure, theory development should "continue to evolve as it is adapted, tested, refined and extended …" (Cunningham et al., 2016, p. 401) in order to advance practice of sport governance.

References

Acker, J. (1990). Hierarchies, jobs, bodies: A theory of gendered organisations. *Gender and Society*, *4*(2), 139–158.

Adriaanse, J., & Schofield, T. (2013). Analysing gender dynamics in sport governance: A new regimes-based approach. *Sport Management Review*, *6*, 498–513.

Adriaanse, J., & Schofield, T. (2014). The impact of gender quotas on gender equality in sport governance. *Journal of Sport Management*, *28*, 485–497.

Ansell, C., & Gash, A. (2008). Collaborative governance in theory and practice. *Journal of Public Administration Research and Theory*, *18*, 543–571.

Ansell, C., & Torfing, J. (2016). Introduction: Theories of governance. In C. Ansell & J. Torfing (Eds.), *Handbook on theories of governance* (pp. 1–17). Northampton, MA: Edward Elgar Publishing.

Babiak, K., Thibault, L., & Willem, A. (2018). Mapping research in interorganizational relationships in sport management: Current landscape and future research prospects. *Journal of Sport Management*, *32*, 272–294.

Byers, T., Parent, M., & Slack, T. (2012). *Key concepts in sport management*. Thousand Oaks, CA: Sage.

Carver, J. 2010. A case for global governance theory: Practitioners avoid it, academics narrow it, the world needs it. *Corporate Governance: An International Review*, *18*, 149–157.

Claringbould, I., & Knoppers, A. (2012). Paradoxical practices of gender in sport-related organizations. *Journal of Sport Management*, *26*, 404–416.

Clarke T. (2005). Introduction: Theories of governance – reconceptualising corporate governance after the Enron experience. In T. Clarke (Ed.), *Theories of corporate governance* (pp. 1–30). New York: Routledge.

Connell, R. (2009). *Gender*. Cambridge, UK: Polity.

Cornforth, C. (2012). Nonprofit governance research: Limitations of the focus on boards and suggestions for new directions. *Nonprofit and Voluntary Sector Quarterly*, *41*, 1116–1135.

Cunningham, G. (2013). Theory and theory development in sport management. *Sport Management Review*, *16*, 1–4.

Cunningham, G., Fink, J., & Doherty, A. (2016). Developing theory in sport management. In G. Cunningham, J. Fink & A. Doherty (Eds.), *Routledge handbook of theory in sport management* (pp. 3–20). New York: Routledge.

Dallas, L.L. (1996). The relational board: Three theories of corporate boards of directors. *Journal of Corporation Law, 22*(1), 1–25.

Dansereau, F., Grean, G., & Haga, B. A. (1975). A vertical-dyad linkage approach to leadership within formal organizations: A longitudinal investigation of the role making process. *Organizational Behavior and Human Performance, 13*, 46–78.

Davis, J. H., & Schoorman, D. F. (1997). Toward a stewardship theory of management. *Academy of Management Review, 22*(1), 20–48.

Dimitropoulos, P. (2011). Corporate governance and earnings management in the European football industry. *European Sport Management Quarterly, 11*, 495–523.

Doherty, A. J. (2010). Intragroup conflict in nonprofit sport boards. *Journal of Sport Management, 24*, 245–271.

Doherty, A. (2013). Investing in sport management: The value of good theory. *Sport Management Review, 16*, 5–11.

Doherty, A. J., & Carron, A. V. (2003). Cohesion in volunteer sport executive committees. *Journal of Sport Management, 17*, 116–141.

Doherty, A., Fink, J., & Cunningham, G. (2016). Themes and directions for theory in sport management. In G. Cunningham, J. Fink & A. Doherty (Eds.), *Routledge handbook of theory in sport management* (pp. 397–403). New York: Routledge.

Doherty, A. J., Patterson, M., & Van Bussel, M. (2004). What do we expect? An examination of perceived committee norms in non-profit sport organisations. *Sport Management Review, 7*, 109–132.

Donaldson, L., & Davis, J. H. (1991). Stewardship theory or agency theory: CEO governance and shareholder returns. *Australian Journal of Management, 16*(1), 49–64.

Dowling, M., Leopkey, B., & Smith, L. (2018). Governance in sport: A scoping review. *Journal of Sport Management, 32*, 438–451.

Emerson, K., Nabatchi, T., & Balogh, S. (2012). An integrative framework for collaborative governance. *Journal of Public Administration Research and Theory, 22*, 1–29.

Erakovic, L., & Jackson, B. (2012). Promoting leadership in governance and governance in leadership: Towards a supportive research agenda. In A. Davila, M. Elvira, J. Ramirez & L. Zapata-Cantu (Eds.), *Understanding organizations in complex, emergent and uncertain environments* (pp. 68–83). Basingstoke, UK: Palgrave Macmillan.

Fama, E. F., & Jensen, M. C. (1983). Separation of ownership and control. *Journal of Law and Economics, 26*, 307–325.

Ferkins, L., & Shilbury, D. (2010). Developing board strategic capability in sport organisations: The national–regional governing relationship. *Sport Management Review, 13*, 235–254.

Ferkins, L., & Shilbury, D. (2015). Board strategic balance: An emerging sport governance theory. *Sport Management Review, 18*, 489–500.

Ferkins, L., & Shilbury, D. (2016). Developing a theory of board strategic balance. In G. Cunningham, J. Fink & A. Doherty (Eds.), *Routledge handbook of theory in sport management* (pp. 114–131). New York: Routledge.

Ferkins, L., Shilbury, D., & McDonald, G. (2005). The role of the board in building strategic capability: Towards an integrated model of sport governance research. *Sport Management Review, 8*, 195–225.

Ferkins, L., Shilbury, D., & McDonald, G. (2009). Board involvement in strategy: Advancing the governance of sport organizations. *Journal of Sport Management, 23*, 245–277.

Ferkins, L., Shilbury, D., & O'Boyle, I. (2018). Leadership in governance: Exploring collective board leadership in sport governance systems. *Sport Management Review, 21*, 221–231.

Gammelsæter, G. (2010). Institutional pluralism and governance in "commercialized" sport clubs. *European Sport Management Quarterly, 10*, 569–594.

Garcia, B., & Welford, J. (2015). Supporters and football governance, from customers to stakeholders: A literature review and agenda for research. *Sport Management Review, 18*, 517–528.

Henry, I., & Lee, P. C. (2004). Governance and ethics in sport. In J. Beech & S. Chadwick (Eds.), *The business of sport management* (pp. 25–41). Essex: Pearson Education.

Hitt, M., Beamish, P., Jackson, S., & Mathieu, J. (2007). Building theoretical and empirical bridges across levels: Multilevel research in management. *Academy of Management Journal, 50*, 1385–1399.

Hoye, R. (2003). Who's leading, who's following? Leader-member exchange theory and voluntary sport boards. *Annals of Leisure Research, 6*, 103–113.

Hoye, R. (2004). Leader-member exchanges and board performance of voluntary sport organizations. *Nonprofit Management & Leadership, 15*, 55–70.

Hoye, R. (2006). Leadership within Australian voluntary sport organization boards. *Nonprofit Management & Leadership*, *16*, 297–313.

Hoye, R., & Cuskelly, G. (2003). Board power and performance within voluntary sport organisations. *European Sport Management Quarterly*, *3*, 103–119.

Hoye, R., & Doherty, A. (2011). Nonprofit sport board performance: A review and directions for future research. *Journal of Sport Management*, *25*, 272–285.

Inglis, S. (1997). Roles of the board in amateur sport organizations. *Journal of Sport Management*, *1*, 160–176.

Jones, G., Wegner, C., Bunds, K., Edwards, M., & Bocarro, J. (2018). Examining the environmental characteristics of shared leadership in a sport-for-development organization. *Journal of Sport Management*, *32*, 82–95.

Judge, W. (2009). Editorial: Towards a global theory of corporate governance. *Corporate Governance: An International Review*, *17*, iii–iv.

Kent, A., & Chelladurai, P. (2001). Perceived transformational leadership, organizational commitment, and citizenship behavior: A case study in intercollegiate athletics. *Journal of Sport Management*, *15*, 135–159.

Leblanc, R. (2004). What's wrong with corporate governance – A note? *Corporate Governance*, *12*, 436–441.

Lewin, K. (1952). *Field theory in social science: Selected theoretical papers by Kurt Lewin*. London: Tavistock.

Mason, D., Thibault, L., & Misener, L. (2006). An agency theory perspective on corruption in sport: The case of the International Olympic Committee. *Journal of Sport Management*, *20*, 52–73.

Miller-Millesen, J. L. (2003). Understanding the behaviour of nonprofit boards of directors: A theory-based approach. *Nonprofit and Voluntary Sector Quarterly*, *32*, 521–547.

Naraine, M., Schenk, J., & Parent, M. (2016). Coordination in international and domestic events: Examining stakeholder network governance, *Journal of Sport Management*, *30*, 521–537.

O'Boyle, I. (2012). Corporate governance applicability and theories within not-for-profit sport management. *Corporate Ownership & Control*, *9*, 335–342.

O'Boyle, I., & Shilbury, D. (2016). Exploring issues of trust in collaborative sport governance. *Journal of Sport Management*, *30*, 52–69.

Parent, M. (2016). Stakeholder perceptions on the democratic governance of major sports events. *Sport Management Review*, *19*, 402–416.

Parent, M., Rouillard, C., & Leopkey, B. (2011). Issues and strategies pertaining to the Canadian governments' coordination efforts in relation to the 2010 Olympic Games. *European Sport Management Quarterly*, *11*, 337–369.

Parent, M., Rouillard, C., & Naraine, M. (2017). Network governance of a multi-level, multi-sectoral sport event: Differences in coordinating ties and actors, *Sport Management Review*, *20*, 497–509.

Roberts, J., McNulty, T., & Stiles, P. (2005). Beyond agency conceptions of the work of the non-executive director: Creating accountability in the boardroom. *British Journal of Management*, *16*, S5–S26.

Schulz, J., & Auld, C. (2006). Perceptions of role ambiguity by chairpersons and executive directors in Queensland sporting organisations. *Sport Management Review*, *9*, 183–201.

Shaw, S. (2016). Importance of theory in qualitative enquiry. In G. Cunningham, J. Fink & A. Doherty (Eds.), *Routledge handbook of theory in sport management* (pp. 21–29). New York: Routledge.

Shilbury, D. (2001). Examining board member roles, functions and influence: A study of Victorian sporting organisations. *International Journal of Sport Management*, *2*, 253–281.

Shilbury, D., Ferkins, L., & Smythe, L. (2013). Sport governance encounters: Insights from lived experiences. *Sport Management Review*, *16*, 349–363.

Shilbury, D., O'Boyle, I., & Ferkins, L. (2016). A research agenda for collaborative sport governance. *Sport Management Review*, *19*, 479–491.

Sibson, R. (2010). "I was banging my head against the wall": Exclusionary power and the gendering of sport organizations. *Journal of Sport Management*, *24*, 379–399.

Smith, E. (2009). The sport of governance—a study comparing Swedish riding schools. *European Sport Management Quarterly*, *9*, 163–186.

Stiles, P. (2001). The impact of the board on strategy: An empirical examination. *Journal of Management Studies*, *38*, 627–651.

Sutton, R., & Staw, B. (1995). What theory is not. *Administrative Science Quarterly*, *40*, 371–384.

Takos, N., Murray, D., & O'Boyle, I. (2018). Authentic leadership in nonprofit sport organization boards. *Journal of Sport Management*, *32*, 109–122.

Van Ees, H., Gabrielsson, J., & Huse, W. (2009). Towards a behavioural theory of boards and corporate governance. *Corporate Governance: An International Review*, 307–319.

Walters, G., & Tacon, R. (2018). The 'codification' of governance in the non-profit sport sector in the UK. *European Sport Management Quarterly*, *18*, 482–500.

Welty Peachey, J., Damon, Z. J., Zhou, Y., & Burton, L. J. (2015). Forty years of leadership research in sport management: A review, synthesis, and conceptual framework. *Journal of Sport Management, 29,* 570–587.

Yeh, C. M., Taylor, T., & Hoye, R. (2009). Board roles in organisations with a dual board system: Empirical evidence from Taiwanese nonprofit sport organisations. *Sport Management Review, 12,* 91–100.

Zhang, J., Kim, M., & Pifer, N. D. (2016). Importance of theory in quantitative enquiry. In G. Cunningham, J. Fink & A. Doherty (Eds.), *Routledge handbook of theory in sport management* (pp. 9–20). New York: Routledge.

Part II
Environmental context and policy perspectives

3

Legal and regulatory aspects of sport governance

Paul T. Jonson and David Thorpe

The context of regulation of governance

Governance is defined in Chapter 1 of this handbook as "oversight of the organisation's performance and its *compliance with relevant regulations and law*" (emphasis added). This acknowledgement of the role of the law in regulating sport governance is often overlooked and under-researched (Forster, 2016). Indeed, in terms of research focus, what is evident from the sport management literature is the absence of consideration of the role of the law makers – the courts and the parliaments – in determining sport governance practices. To illustrate, Gammelsaeter and Senaux (2013) noted:

> …when many of the studies reviewed here suffer from not being situated in an explicit governance context, this does not mean they are flawed. Rather it reflects…a lack of engagement in studying football in more typical governance disciplines such as management and organisation studies. (p. 154)

Surprisingly, but typically, they ignore the discipline of law. Yet, it is our very firm view that law is the key element to sport governance. Having said that, there is no worldwide regulatory body for sport organisations. So, the question remains: In the absence of an overseeing agency, "how can the sports world regulate itself – that is, control and improve its governance" (Arcioni, 2016, p. 76)?

Governance itself can be categorised in three ways (Henry & Lee, 2004): Systemic, organisational, and political. **Systemic** governance is concerned with competition, cooperation and mutual adjustment between organisations and business and/or policy systems. **Organisational** governance (also described as corporate) is concerned with normative, ethically informed standards of managerial behaviour. **Political** governance is concerned with how governments or governing bodies "*steer*" rather than directly control the behaviour of organisations…through strategies such as regulation and inducement, rather than through direct action and control. This regulation is fundamentally a product of the broader social, political, cultural and economic environment in which sport takes place. The focus of this chapter is on the latter – political governance/steering – and, more particularly, how governments (through legislation) and courts (through precedent and apposite decisions) regulate sport governance.

The influence of law on sport governance reveals an attempt by courts and legislators to balance the organisation's desire for autonomy – to conduct its affairs in the best interests of the sport – against the need for the law to regulate the behaviour of entities within its jurisdiction. For example, salary caps and player drafts are prima facie restraints of trade but will nonetheless be enforced where the sport has a legitimate interest to protect and the restraint is reasonable in meeting that interest. Corporate law regulates a sport's constitution and the obligations of office bearers. Criminal law dictates broad standards of behaviour and punishes wrongdoers and, more recently, international agreements have led to laws regulating anti-doping measures and the recognition of arbitral bodies such as the Court of Arbitration for Sport. For decades the law established through courts – the "common law" – has guided how a sport deals with internal matters, for example, contractual obligations, restraint of athlete transfers and athlete discipline. Statute law, as will be explicated below, has a profound influence on sport policy at a board and organisational level.

From a management perspective there is much to be said for freedom of action unrestrained by the "niceties of the law". In a free society the rules adopted by a sporting organisation are almost entirely its own affair, developed autonomously to suit its perceived needs and its preferred governance structure. Clearly, there is a great advantage in rules being made by a governing body aware of what is needed for success, housed by experts nurturing and guiding the organisation and making expedited decisions undisturbed by outside forces unfamiliar with the requirements of the sport. This prized legal right should not be undervalued. And yet, as desirable as it may seem, complete autonomy is rarely beneficial. Experience teaches us that unrestrained autonomy leads to damaging excess. The law, accordingly, being generally reflective of societal standards, has nudged the decision-maker in the direction of sense and soundness. The law, in essence, serves to constrain the actions of governors and management, it discourages destructive excesses and controls unbridled power.

It was recognised in 2006 by the Independent European Sports Review (Arnaut, 2006) that the lack of external regulation has a negative impact on issues of transparency, accountability and standards of club governance, and, as a result, there have been calls for governing bodies and leagues to ensure that "appropriate regulatory controls are put into place to protect the principles of sound financial management and transparency in football clubs" (p. 26). In Europe at least, "there are an increased number of government regulations/codes to be adhered to and such stipulations apply to sports NGBs (NSOs) and affiliates…including, financial reporting standards, auditing, health and safety requirements, child welfare, ethics, disability, employment policies and the like" (Bourke, 2013, p. 120).

O'Boyle (2012) noted, a "complex relationship exists between the governance structure that operates within a sports organisation which is sufficient to satisfy its management, and the *legal* pressures that are placed upon an organisation from *external* forces" (p. 336, emphases added). It is these external forces – the courts and the legislatures – that are regulating or "steering" the former, that is, the governance structures and processes of sport associations. As Hoye and Cuskelly (2007) stated: "The statutory requirements, corporate and nonprofit governance codes and guides to principles and standards, including those specific to sports governance, stipulate how sports organisations should determine their governance structures, systems and processes and what sort of behavioural standards are expected of those in charge of fulfilling the governance role" (p. 178).

This chapter will focus on the law created by statute and by courts and not on the corporate and nonprofit governance codes and guides to principles and standards which are considered in other chapters. Moreover, this chapter will *not* be looking at intervention by international governing bodies such as the IOC or FIFA on national governing bodies, nor that of governmental authorities such as Sport Australia (formerly the Australian Sports Commission) or UK Sport, as these too are covered elsewhere in the book. It should be noted that while these latter "codes and guides" and "regulatory interventions" do impact on the governance of a sport organisation, they are not mandated "legal" controls, but rather seek to guide the national body through policy or "suggestion". As Lee (2004, cited in Gammelsaeter & Senaux, 2013) noted, only states and major political institutions (which includes courts) possess the necessary power to impede the pursuit of private commercial interest to undermine the broader interests of sport. Indeed, the advent of professionalism, commercialisation, globalisation, demands for equity (such as spurned by racial and gender discrimination), growing media and public surveillance of sport and its governing bodies, a growing litigious society and conspicuous failures of governance by sport organisations have all influenced the legislative changes and common law growth witnessed over the past 10 to 20 years.

The legal framework

As has been noted by Keohane (2006, quoted in Pielke, 2013), "Since there is no global government, global governance involves strategic interactions among entities that are not arranged in formal hierarchies" (p. 256). Whilst it may be thought the United Nations (UN) is *the* "global authority", in reality the UN has no law-making power as such. Under Public International Law, countries, often utilising UN procedures, enter treaties or make declarations to achieve particular objects of international concern. These do not become law until adopted by a sovereign government through their law-making processes. As we shall see below, the Treaty of Lisbon, which is pertinent to sport governance in Europe, is one such international agreement, while the World Anti-Doping Code (WADC), as promulgated through the World Anti-Doping Agency (WADA), has been adopted by both governments and international and national sport organisations (NSOs) to regulate governance and behaviour. Hence, the regulation of governance of sport at the international level is ultimately by agreement among national governments or by NSOs and umbrella bodies. Furthermore, the enforcement of the local laws fulfilling an international agreement rests with the courts and governments of the respective countries (as well as the sport associations). The special case of the European Union (EU) shall be examined. It is also worth noting that some countries widen their jurisdiction by applying domestic law beyond their territorial borders. For example, in 2015 the United States Department of Justice successfully prosecuted several FIFA officials with racketeering and money laundering despite several of these offences being committed offshore (see for example, *United States of America v. Bedoya,* 2015).

Currently, there is little international legislation that can be directly applied to sport. The exceptions to this rule (spectator violence, doping, match-fixing and corruption) are covered by four international treaties or conventions. However, "there is an increasing tendency for governments that have ratified these treaties to draw up or amend national laws in order to cover sport" (Chappelet, 2018, p. 730).

All International Sport Organisations (ISOs) – unless an unincorporated or unchartered association – have some form of legal status, even if confined to the jurisdiction of a "home" country, and are therefore legally accountable in that jurisdiction. As noted by Pielke (2013), "legal accountability refers to the requirement that international bodies and their employees must abide by the laws of relevant jurisdictions in which those laws are applicable" (p. 279). Thus, for example, both FIFA and the IOC are both subject to Swiss Law as that is where they are incorporated and chartered.

Indeed, most ISOs are based in Switzerland where they have benefitted from a quasi-unregulated system. The "Swiss Civil Code provides only very basic minimum requirements for associations that come under Swiss jurisdiction, while the overall Swiss legal framework allows for large degrees of both fiscal and organisational autonomy and limited prosecution of private corruption" (Geeraert, 2015, p. 27). Furthermore, while corruption in Swiss-based international sports organisations is a criminal offence under Swiss law, the laws are not as rigorous as might be expected.

This is not to say that FIFA and, all other ISOs legally based in Switzerland, can escape legal scrutiny in all other countries; rather, in terms of the regulation of their governance, the law of Switzerland is applicable. Indeed, as Pielke noted (2013), because FIFA, like the IOC, operates in countries around the world, with its members and sponsors subject to the laws of those participating nations, FIFA has a significant exposure to relevant national legislation…(but its) formal accountability is to Swiss law under its articles of incorporation" (p. 263). Hence, it is the Swiss government and courts that regulate and steer the governance of FIFA (Pielke, 2013) and indeed all other sport organisations which are legally constituted in Switzerland, including the IOC. This is to be contrasted with the legal actions taken by the US authorities against senior members of FIFA's governing body for "alleged large-scale corruption, tax evasion and money laundering among others" (Meier & Garcia, 2015, p. 890). Exceptionally, however, FIFA is able to dictate the behaviour of national governments towards its members. As Meier and Garcia (2015) point out, if in FIFA's eyes football's autonomy is not respected, the affected country may see their FIFA membership suspended by FIFA. This may be seen as FIFA being independent of legal regulation; however, it is not an absence of legal authority that allows this to happen but rather, as evidenced in Greece, Spain and Poland, a lack of will by the nation states due to the social and political backlash they might, or indeed will, endure (Meier & Garcia, 2015).

It has been argued that "the globalization of sport has shifted the legal regulation of the international sport system increasingly towards the private authority of international sport bodies such as the IOC, WADA, the Court of Arbitration of Sport (CAS) and ISOs" (Foster, 2003 cited in Findlay, 2016, p. 69). However, as was detailed above, the ultimate authority to ratify such international instruments rests with national governments. This authority of national governments and the workings of Public International Law to regulate sports governance of international and national sport organisations can be illustrated by the role of the national states in adopting and respecting European Union and court decisions.

The European Union

The European Union (EU) itself is established under treaties adopted by the 28 member states. The current principal legal document is the Treaty on the Functioning of the European Union (TFEU – The Lisbon Treaty) which amended the Treaty on European Union and the Treaty establishing the European Community (OJC306, 17.12.2007) and came into force on 1 December 2009. The Lisbon Treaty contains no article formally enshrining the supremacy of Union law over national legislation, but a declaration was attached to the Treaty to this effect (Declaration No 17). The Lisbon Treaty, however, for the first time clarifies the powers of the Union. It distinguishes three types of competences: exclusive competence, where the Union alone can legislate, and member states only implement; shared competence, where the member states can legislate and adopt legally binding measures if the Union has not done so; and supporting competence, where the EU adopts measures to support or complement member states' policies. Member states may only sign international agreements that are compatible with EU law (Facts Sheet of the European Union, 2018).

Under Article 6(e) of the Lisbon Treaty, the EU has competence to carry out actions to support or supplement the actions of the member states in the field of sport, while Article 165(1) sets out the details of a sports policy, stating that the Union "shall contribute to the promotion of European sporting issues while taking account of the specific nature of sport, its structures based on voluntary activity and its social and educational function" ("Sport" Facts Sheets on the European Union, 2018).

This is described as a "supporting competence" in that the EU in this instance can only coordinate or supplement the actions of the member states of the EU. From a legal point of view, the importance of the provision is essentially symbolic as it merely legitimises EU action already taken in the field of sport and, in addition, will not change the approach of the Court of Justice of the European Union (CJEU) in sport cases. Furthermore, given that the EU offers sports bodies a degree of "supervised autonomy", it is claimed that "EU institutions do not have a proactive role in directly regulating sports governance, but that they play a supervisory role to ensure sport organisations behave within the limits of EU law" (Geeraert, 2014, p. 303). However, it has been noted that if sport governing bodies are not respectful of principles of good governance, they can expect their relative autonomy to be curtailed (Interview European Commission Administrator July 2013, in Geeraert, 2014, p. 304). As Geeraert (2014) noted, "sport bodies seem to be willing to engage with the EU due to a latent fear of EU law" (p. 316). But, Garcia and Weatherill (2012) contend that "(t)here is no suggestion in the Treaty that the European Union is equipped to play a powerful role in regulating sports governance" (p. 251). Furthermore, Weatherill (2011) argued Article 165 does not allow the EU to usurp the proper place of sports organisations in selecting their preferred system of governance and emphatically does not elevate the EU to the position of general "sports regulator" in Europe.

Despite this negativity and circumspection, it is contended that the EU can control international sport organisations such as the IOC, FIFA and UEFA through the enforcement of EU law by the CJEU and the European Commission. As Geeraert and Drieskins (2015) stated, "that is because sports rules issued by ISOs often fall within the realm of the EU's internal market competence, most directly in relation to freedom of movement and competition law" (p. 1453). The CJEU itself has mainly built upon the principle of freedom of movement when dealing with sport cases. This was most graphically illustrated by the Bosman case (1995). In 1990 a professional footballer of Belgian nationality, Jean-Marc Bosman, was placed on a compulsory transfer list by his club, RC Liege, after he refused to sign a new contract that would have reduced his pay to a quarter of that earned previously. Following doubts about a transfer to a French club, RC Liege suspended Bosman, preventing him from playing for any other club that season. Bosman claimed that the transfer rules and the UEFA rules, which permitted European national associations to limit the number of foreign players, were unlawful. The matter was ultimately referred for opinion to the European Court of Justice, which determined that the transfer restrictions were an "obstacle to the freedom of movement of workers and were prohibited" under Article 48 of the EC Treaty.

By contrast, competition law has mainly had an impact on sport organisations because of the far-reaching powers of the European Commission (the executive arm of the EU) as public enforcer. In short, the EU does have power in limited circumstances to directly regulate ISOs based in Europe. The reason being that the EU's competences only cover a limited range of these ISO's activities. Moreover, as Geeraert and Drieskins (2015) also point out, sanctions by the EU "lack political support, since the EU member states have diverse views on the appropriateness of public interventions in sport and they traditionally respect the autonomy of the ISOs to regulate football" (p. 1456).

It should be noted that in addition to the EU "law route" to control the behaviour of Europe- based ISOs, there is also the EU sports policy route. The cornerstone of the European Commission sport policy is the promotion of open and fair sports governance, which it seeks to promote through the Social Dialogue principles, under EU social law contained in Article 154 TFEU (Serby, 2016). The role of policy in shaping sports governance – including in the European Union – is discussed in greater depth elsewhere in this book (see Geeraert & Drieskins, 2015).

To conclude on the EU and its role in steering sport governance, the EU – via the CJEU and the Commission – has the capacity to curtail the autonomy of ISOs. However, the Commission never truly operates autonomously of the member states (Geeraert & Drieskins, 2015). The reason for this is the EC sports policy, which appears to elevate the importance of social dialogue in sports governance (Serby, 2016). In short, "the EU has formally assumed a competence in sport through Article 165, and, arguably, the EC has staked a claim to be a de facto EU sports regulator" (Serby, 2016, p. 49). This means at the European Union level, a difficult balance has to be found between allowing total autonomy and establishing extensive government intervention in the governance of sport organisations legally based in Europe (Geeraert, Scheerder & Bruyninckx, 2013). A significant product of Public International Law is the World Anti-Doping Code (the Code) designed to steer sport bodies in their governance of doping by athletes to enhance performance.

The World Anti-Doping Code and Agency

The *World Anti-Doping Agency* (WADA) is a Swiss private law foundation with its formal legal base in Lausanne Switzerland, however its operational headquarters are in Montreal, Canada (WADA, 2018). WADA was founded in 1999 as an international independent agency composed and funded equally by the sport movement and governments of the world with the aim of bringing consistency to anti-doping policies and regulations within sport organisations and governments right across the world. Its key activities include scientific research, education and development of anti-doping capacities (Forster, 2013). Following the creation of the initial World Anti-Doping Code in 2004, WADA was tasked with overseeing acceptance, implementation and compliance of the Code, the core document that glues together anti-doping policies, rules and regulations worldwide (WADA, 2018). One commentator formed the view that "since its establishment WADA has been extremely successful in developing a coordinated approach to doping in sport by bringing together three sets of stakeholders: governments; ISOs; and event organisers" (Houlihan, 2014, p. 273).

One of the problems in the globalised environment for sport governance is "jurisdiction". That is, who has authority over an international sport and its stakeholders and participants. Governance involves "compliance with regulations and law" as defined at the outset of this chapter. Accordingly, due to Public International Law as outlined above, sport organisations must ensure they comply with the worldwide rules that have been adopted to prevent doping practices in sport, namely the World Anti-Doping Code (the Code). The Code has its legal basis and authority in the UNESCO (United Nations Education Science and Cultural Organisation) International Convention Against Doping in Sport, 2005. Houlihan (2014) described the Convention as "providing governments with a secure legal basis for acceptance of the Code" (p. 266). Indeed, the Convention represents the first time that governments around the world have agreed to apply the force of international law to doping. This is important because there are specific areas where only governments possess the means to take the fight against doping forward.

The Convention also helps to ensure the effectiveness of the World Anti-Doping Code. As the Code itself is a non-government document that applies only to members of sports organisations, the Convention provides the legal framework under which governments can address specific areas of the doping problem that are outside the domain of the sports movement. As such, the Convention helps to formalise global anti-doping rules, policies and guidelines in order to provide an honest and equitable playing environment for all athletes. There is a degree of flexibility as to how governments can give effect to the Convention, either by way of legislation, regulation, policies or administrative practices. Entered into force on 1 February 2007 – becoming the most successful convention in the history of UNESCO in terms of rhythm of ratification after adoption – the Convention is now the second most ratified of all UNESCO treaties.

The World Anti-Doping Code – first promulgated in 2004 with the most recent iteration in 2015 – is the core document that harmonises anti-doping policies, rules and regulations within sport organisations and among public authorities around the world. Ever since it entered into force, the Code has proven to be a powerful and effective tool in the harmonisation of anti-doping efforts worldwide. This has been demonstrated by the overwhelming support of governments and sports in accepting the Code, in addition to the growing body of jurisprudence from CAS in supporting the principles of the Code (Thorpe, Buti, Davies & Jonson, 2017). Importantly, all major international sport organisations that are affiliated with the IOC are required to adopt the Code. This is a contractual arrangement. The Code itself is monitored by the World Anti-Doping Agency (WADA).

The Court of Arbitration for Sport

Predating WADA and the WADA Code as an international sport governance regulatory authority is the Court of Arbitration for Sport (CAS). CAS was conceived in 1981 by the then President of the International Olympic Committee (IOC), HE Juan Antonio Samaranch and was established by the IOC in March 1983 after a wave of litigation placed the Olympic movement under severe pressure. The purpose was to set up an arbitration institution which would deal with disputes directly or indirectly linked with sport. More particularly, it was created to offer a specialised authority capable of settling international disputes and offering a flexible, quick and inexpensive procedure (the last point is somewhat problematical today) (Thorpe, Buti, Davies & Jonson, 2017).

Forster (2016) contended that "CAS's decisions have no legal standing in the legal system of any country" (p. 3). This is not correct. Chartered under Swiss law and governed by its own statutes and rules of procedure, the CAS was recognised as a true court of arbitration by a decision of the Swiss Federal Tribunal (*Gundel v. FEI/CAS*, 1993). It is correct to say, however, that enforcement and recognition of CAS awards are reliant on sovereign government legislative recognition or by contractual agreement between sport organisations and participants in their organisation.

The primary objective of the CAS is the settlement of sports-related disputes through the use of mediation or arbitration provided by panels composed of one or three arbitrators. In principle, two types of disputes may be submitted to the CAS: Those of a commercial nature and those of a disciplinary nature. In such disputes that may bear on questions of principle, or on pecuniary or other interests relating to sport and in providing for the resolution of such disputes, the CAS provides the infrastructure. Article R27 of the Code provides that the Code applies whenever the parties have agreed to refer a sports-related dispute to the CAS (Court of Arbitration for Sport, 2019). The dispute may arise out of a contract containing an arbitration clause or be part of a later arbitration agreement (Thorpe, Buti, Davies & Jonson, 2017).

Whether an appeal will be available to the domestic courts will depend on the nature of the challenge – for example, on the propriety of the rules and regulations of the sporting body.

However, in the context of amateur sports, this is unlikely, given that most membership agreements with national sporting bodies and affiliation agreements between NSOs and international federations generally contain clauses excluding the jurisdiction of the domestic courts and ensure that the CAS is the ultimate court of appeal (Thorpe, Buti, Davies & Jonson, 2017).

The Court of Arbitration for Sport becomes an element of sport governance regulation principally by contractual agreement. That is, many sport organisations stipulate that members of their association and participants in their events must submit to and abide by CAS determinations and that they forego any appeal to the courts in relation to the determination itself. Submission to CAS jurisdiction is obligatory for sports that wish to compete in the Olympic Games. Accordingly, CAS is accepted as something which must be included in the overall governance and management of the sport. The CAS is therefore a significant institution in the realm of sport governance at all levels (Thorpe, Buti, Davies & Jonson, 2017).

In summary, both CAS and WADA are legally domiciled in Switzerland and have to comply with Swiss laws which, as we have seen before, places the Swiss legal system in a special place in sport governance. However, it should be noted that because WADA is often dealing with drugs which are illegal drugs in many national criminal codes, few governments are willing to completely delegate sports anti-doping to WADA. The International Intergovernmental Consultative Group on Ant-Doping in Sport (IICGADS) is an outcome of this reluctance. It is a means by which governments can govern WADA. Around 200 national governments have ratified UNESCO's International Convention against Doping in Sport. This, coupled with IICGADS, gives WADA the governmental mandate it requires (Forster, 2013).

Hence, most international and national sport organisations must – by force of statutory law, common law and CAS determinations, and contractual agreement between the ISO and their national federation members – have, as part of their governance, compliance with the Code and cooperation with WADA. This is a requirement by all those national governments who have adopted the UNESCO International Convention Against Doping in Sport of sport organisations who are legally based within their jurisdiction.

Governance regulation by sovereign states

Legislative regulation of sport governance can occur at three levels: Local/regional, national and international (Public and Private International Law). Thus far this chapter has considered the regulation of sport governance at the international level. However, most of the "steering" occurs at the national level. The mantra of sport organisations in western liberal democracies may be characterised as "governance of sport is an internal matter, and external forces (namely governments) should stay out" (Mehta, 2016, p. 2). As is now illustrated, the level of governmental regulation throughout the world varies from providing various legal frameworks within which a sport organisation may govern to total governance of sport by the government. Again, it should be noted that this chapter is focused on legislated and case law requirements for sport governance as opposed to policies and charters that may, for example, set expectations for a sport organisation that wants to receive public funding.

It should also be noted that, in the jurisdictions that are member states of the European Union, "the law" also entails provisions and regulations of European law as was discussed above. Consistent case law of the European Court of Justice holds that sport is subject to European Union law in so far as it constitutes an economic activity (van Kleef, 2014). A number of nation states' regulations as found in the literature will now be reviewed to illustrate the range of regulatory "steering" by the state (through legislation and courts) of governance by sports associations.

United States of America

At the national level, "the United States has long eschewed any formal system of sport govern-ance, preferring instead to rely on market forces and institutions established outside govern-ment…(rendering) a sport governance system that avoids policy-driven solutions and when forced to develop policy, often undermines its legitimacy by failing to provide within the policy any mechanism for implementation or enforcement" (Green, Chalip & Bowers, 2013, p. 21). Only three policies govern sport or aspects therein: Title IX of the Education Amendments [1972 (PL92-318)] and the Americans with Disabilities Act [1990 (PL 101-336) amended 2008 (PL 110-325)] whose provisions prohibit discrimination in settings where sport may occur; and, The Amateur Sports Act [1978 (PL 95-606) amended 1996 (PL 105-227)] which directly addresses sport governance in the United States, but has proven ineffectual. It was formulated with the explicit purpose of keeping government out of sport governance. It vests the US Olympic Committee (USOC) and its National Governing Bodies with the power "to coor-dinate and develop amateur sport in the United States…". However, the only requirement provided to assist with enforcement is that the USOC must provide a report to Congress each year regarding its activities.

American courts have also chosen to keep sport free from government oversight. In *Flood v. Kuhn* (1972), the Supreme Court upheld the ruling that baseball was not the kind of commerce that American anti-trust laws were intended to regulate, so professional sport leagues in the United States are not subject to the same kinds of anti-trust oversight to which all other private businesses in the United States are subject. Green, Chalip, and Bowers (2013) noted that govern-ment has involved itself with sport provision at local and regional levels, which has necessitated some involvement in governance at those levels; however, since states largely choose not to do so, sport is left to local and county governments. As a result, entrepreneurs are free to run their teams and their leagues as they see fit within the confines mandated by American business law. Consequently, each professional league has its own rules and systems for governance.

Australia

Australia is governed with a mix of statutory and common law across the nation, plus distinc-tive and differing law from state to state. Most NSOs are incorporated under the Australian Corporations Act (2001) and mostly as Companies Limited by Guarantee at the behest of Sport Australia (the national government's commission to operationalise sport policy). This ensures that these NSOs must comply, in their governance, with the full requirements of Australian corporate law including the rules overseeing directors' duties. This is also true of most clubs in the Australian professional leagues where there is a mix of public companies limited by guaran-tee and private companies limited by shares (Phat, Birt, Turner & Fenech, 2016). While at the state (regional) and local level most sport organisations will incorporate under, and are therefore regulated by, the Association Incorporation Acts. The rules surrounding governance under these Acts are very similar to those under the national legislation. In terms of case law, the most cel-ebrated case was that of *Buckley v. Tutty* (1971) wherein it was ruled that attempts to constrain off contract professional athletes was a restraint of trade and not open to governing bodies.

Canada

NSOs in Canada are incorporated under the federal Canada Not-for-profit Corporations Act, SC 2009 c 23 (NFP Act) which governs the development and promotion of their respective sport across Canada. Despite the fact that they are private independent bodies, NSOs are responsible for carrying out the federal government's sport policy objectives. Similar to NSOs, provincial sport organisations (PSOs) govern individual sports within the provinces. PSOs are funded by each provincial government's department responsible for managing sport, fitness and recreation in the province.

The struggle for control over the resources of the national organisation is not simply a case of divisions with the PSOs (Provincial sport organisations) wrestling control away from the NSO. In Canada the PSOs, more often than not, own the NSO and thus can use authority rather than persuasion or politics to gain or assert power (Parent & Patterson, 2013). At the professional level, sports clubs from major Canadian cities participate in most North American professional leagues. Although there are various ownership models available to sports teams, some professional leagues restrict ownership to a particular model. For instance, National Hockey League (NHL) teams – from both the US and Canada – are organised either as partnerships or private corporations to avoid regulations and disclosure requirements associated with public ownership. The NHL ultimately prefers to work directly with identifiable major shareholders or entrepreneurs who own NHL clubs. The ownership model of professional teams may also vary depending on the market in which they operate. For example, two Canada Football League teams, the Saskatchewan Roughriders and the Edmonton Eskimos, have thrived under the community ownership model because this model particularly caters to their small but vibrant fan bases (McLaren, 2018).

In an effort to encourage good corporate governance, the federal government requires NSOs to comply with government policy to qualify for funding. Sport Canada encourages (as distinct from "requires") NSOs to have governance practices that enshrine the following principles: A commitment to mission and guidance by a strategic plan; clarity of roles and responsibilities; effective financial control; a focus on human resources; and transparency and accountability for outcomes and results (Sport Canada, 2011, p 3). Canadian law imposes a wide range of duties and liabilities on directors of NSOs. Many of these duties and liabilities are prescribed under the NFP Act, while others are established by other federal, provincial and territorial statutes (McLaren, 2018).

Russia

Smolianov (2013) reported that "sport governing organisations in this highly centralised, integrated and increasingly democratic system carry difficult responsibilities for fair spending of state money, ethical achievement of ambitious goals, enforcement of rules and control over doping and corruption" (p. 75). Professional sport had started to develop and is being developed now largely within the army, including commercial and relatively independent soccer, ice hockey and basketball as well as other Olympic sports. Whereas, "preparation of athletes for international competitions is led by the government and state sport authorities who put national goals above interests of particular organisations. Coaches run this sport system as they are employed by the state and rewarded according to achievements of participants" (pp. 75-6).

The Ministry for Sport, Tourism and Youth Policy of the Russian Federation issues new laws and revives old laws pertaining to sport across all socioeconomic spheres. Under direct presidential supervision, a Council for the Development of Physical Culture and High Performance Sport and for the Preparation of the 2012 Olympic and 2014 Paralympic Games was established. The Russian government also provides direct guidance for sport societies particularly those fostered within public service organisations. All sport-related organisations and activities are guided by the 2007 Federal Law on Physical Culture and Sport based on the following principles:

- Free access to sport
- Unified nationwide legislation…in compliance with international agreements
- State guarantees of sport-related rights to citizens (includes anti-discrimination)
- Interaction between federal and local governments in the field of sport, between sport authorities and federations, and development of all types and components of sport as a social and educational voluntary activity.

"The above-mentioned law serves as a guide for the Sport Ministry's governance of amateur and professional sport, which it exerts based on advice from medical, biological and pedagogical scientists it employs" (Smolianov, 2013, p. 80). Ljubownikow and Crotty (2014, cited in Kral & Cuskelly, 2017) provided evidence from Russia where a new law was passed to make NSOs more accountable and transparent.

South Africa

Sport governance within the South African environment can be seen as the structure and processes put in place by the government which allow national sport bodies to develop strategic goals and direction, monitor their performances against these goals and ensure that their respective boards act in the best interest of all South Africans. It is Sport and Recreation South Africa (SRSA) whose main task is to develop the policy framework within which the governance of sport in South Africa is managed. A key player in South African sport governance is the local authority. They are in direct contact with the sites of delivery and have the primary function to develop a policy framework for the governance of sport at a local level that takes both national and provincial policies into account. National federations are responsible for the implementation of government policy on sport and recreation at national, provincial, and local levels (Bester, 2013).

United Kingdom

In the UK much of the regulation has come from UK Sport and the Department of Culture Media and Sport, however, this is primarily policy-based regulation rather than statutory. The regulation of governance throughout the UK is similar to that in Australia and Canada. Many NSOs are first and foremost accountable to their key funding bodies – government (via funding from the Sports Councils) and, for a select few, commercial sponsors. Strategic decisions taken by Boards of NSOs are therefore affected by government policy (Walters & Tacon, 2013). Hence, the government has decreed it unacceptable that any organisation receiving public money should have governance standards that fall short of existing standards such as those contained in the UK Corporate Governance Code. In 2016, Sport England and UK Sport launched "A Code for Sports Governance" – a new set of gold standards of governance. The Code sets out levels of transparency, accountability and financial integrity and applies to any organisation seeking public funding regardless of size and sector, so it includes national governing bodies of sport, clubs, charities and local authorities. In relation to statutory compliance, the Code deals with the legal, regulatory and compliance policies, processes and procedures that a well governed sport organisation should have in place (Stephens, 2017).

The vast majority of professional sports organisations such as the football clubs are incorporated as public or private companies (Farquhar, Machold & Ahmed, 2005). Hence, they too must comply with the UK Corporate Governance Code. This is a significant improvement to past practices which were described as "(taking) advantage of a lack of guidelines in terms of disclosure, the appointment of directors, induction and training of directors and risk management practices" (Michie & Oughton, 2005 cited in Phat, Birt, Turner & Fenech, 2016, p. 71).

In England, the unincorporated association has traditionally been the most common structure used by the majority of sports clubs and governing bodies. An unincorporated association is comprised of a group of individuals who are consensually (rather than contractually) bound together by the constitution or rules of the club. As these entities are not recognised as having legal personality, the members may be personally liable for the debts of the club if these debts cannot be met from the assets of the club or under an insurance policy, or liability may attach personally to decision-making committee members who contract outside the organisation's purview. For this reason, many sports organisations prefer the structure of an incorporated association in the form of a company. The tradition of English company law has been to give members a considerable freedom regarding the internal organisation of the company.

China

The decisive governance power of Chinese sport is still in the government's hands. This power-centralised system leads to the government having a monopolistic position in dealing with the emerging public investment and is seen as an obstacle for China's sport reformation and commercialisation (Hong & Huang, 2013). In their view, it will be hard for China's market-oriented sport industry to develop unless government switches its role from steering to leveraging.

Brazil

In 1988, sport in Brazil achieved constitutional status. Article 217 established the autonomy of sport organisations; priorities of public funding; and a clear distinction for the governance between professional and non-professional sport organisations. This saw a shift in the way sport was organised and governed. The Zico Law in 1993 provided a new structure for governance and established the principles and guidelines for the functioning of sport organisations. In 2003, the Moralising Club Law (Law 16672/2003) imposed administrative responsibilities on professional football clubs and established penalties for club directors in cases of mismanagement (Bravo, 2013).

Bravo (2013) noted "sport clubs in Brazil represent the keystone of its entire sport system. Although most clubs are private organisations, their development has been highly dependent on sport policies enacted at the federal level" (p. 152). Recently, the Brazilian Olympic Committee (COB) was "steered" by the IOC, as well as the Brazilian Sports Ministry (after threats by the Ministry that the COB would not be certified and would cease to receive public funding to the COB and its affiliated entities) and relevant Brazilian legislation to adopt a new sports governance model (Barracco, 2018).

Middle East

Sport governance in the Middle East and North Africa is marked primarily by the lack, or at best the rudimentary beginnings, of understanding of what the concept entails in terms of procedure, transparency and accountability. Dorsey (2013) reported that "the ruling Al Sayed family retains its grip on sport. Major soccer clubs remain the playground of princes... (and that) governance in a swath of land stretching from the Atlantic coast of Africa to the Gulf meant little more than regime control and subjection to the regime's whims and political designs" (p. 160).

Scandinavia

Persson (2013) reported that in Scandinavia sport is entrusted with autonomy to run itself and its activities. Further, the financial tradition of supporting sport in Scandinavia should be understood as what Henry and Lee (2004) refer to as political governance. Mutual trust (between central government, local authorities and the sport movement) has resulted in sport organisations being entrusted with relatively large amounts of autonomy to organise sport with financial support from states and local authorities.

Greece

Under the Greek Constitution, Article 16(9) states: "athletics shall be under the protection and ultimate supervision of the State and that the State shall make grants to and control all types of athletic associations". Quick and Costa (2013) advised that the Standing Committee of Educational Affairs sets the legislative framework for sport and is responsible for supervising the implementation of policies and programs of the General Secretariat of Sport. Meanwhile, professional sport leagues in Greece are established under a ministerial decision from the Minister of Cultural Affairs upon receiving an application from the representative sports federation. However, while the leagues are established by the state and controlled according to Greek sports law, the clubs themselves are prohibited from becoming public companies which has consequences for both accountability and decision-making (Quick & Costa, 2013).

Cyprus

The Cyprus Sport Organisation (CSO) is a non-profit, semi-governmental organisation acting as the supreme authority in the Republic of Cyprus and responsible for the development of sport. Every athletic and developmental activity comes under the jurisdiction of the CSO. The CSO activities include the establishment of national federations, provision of grants to sport associations and promotion of international relationships (Charalambous-Papamiltiades, 2013)

Based on the research case study of governance in sport of Cyprus national sport governing bodies reported by Charalambous-Papamiltiades (2013), it is inferred that the majority of the NSOs are incorporated non-profit organisations. Many of the professional football clubs, it can also be inferred, are corporate for-profit organisations.

Germany

In Germany, the standard organisational structure is the registered association (*eingetragene Verein*) which is regulated in § 21–79 of the German *Bürgerliches Gesetzbuch* (*BGB*). As the German *BGB* only provides a minimal legal framework, the articles of association can deviate from most statutory provisions given that only few are of "imperative" law. The minimal legal requirements of the articles of association include the purpose, the name and the seat of the association and the indication that the association is to be registered. Furthermore, the law stipulates that the articles contain provisions regarding membership, the composition of the board and the general meeting (Franck, 2010; van Kleef, 2014).

Switzerland

In Switzerland too, the chosen legal form of most sports organisations is the association. An association is a group of natural or legal persons organised as a corporate body and is governed by Art. 52–79 of the Swiss Civil Code. The association is the most liberal of legal entities in Switzerland. It is subject to fewer legal requirements than other corporate structures in terms of both the internal and external organisation. Moreover, in Swiss law, the freedom to create and enforce rules is also limited by two provisions in the Civil Code that constitute the application of human rights between private persons. These provisions maintain the prohibition not to violate the rights of personality. With regard to professional sports, the company is gaining ground as an organisational structure for clubs. However, all national and international federations seated in Switzerland are organised as associations. Furthermore, under Swiss law (Article 69b of Switzerland's Civil Code) large ISOs based in Switzerland must undergo financial audits (Chappelet, 2018).

One of the fundamental principles of Swiss private law is the freedom of the parties in the design of their legal relationships. Consequently, the right to freely organise one's association does not only entail the composition of the articles, but rather the design of the entire regulatory system. Under Swiss law the freedom of association thus comprises the creation, application and enforcement of rules. This broad conception of *Vereinsautonomie* and its liberal application in Swiss association law is generally considered the main reason why most international sports federations have chosen this country as their seat. As a result, the practical importance of Swiss law on organised sports cannot be underestimated (van Kleef, 2014).

France

In France, the promotion and development of sport is recognised as a matter of public interest, which results in the French state taking a much more prominent role in the organisation of sports compared to the other countries. As in many other countries, the general organisational form of clubs and governing bodies is the association, governed by the French law of 1 July 1901 relating to the contract of association. However, when sports associations reach €1.2 million in annual revenues from the organisation of paying sports events or a total of €800 000 in annual remunerations, they have the legal obligation to manage these activities in a corporation subject to the *Code de commerce*. In France too, the articles of association are subject to both the freedom of contract and association and can be freely determined. In the organisational structure of sports in France, a pivotal role is played by the sports federations. As in most other jurisdictions, the federations are associations and serve to organise the practice of one or several sports disciplines. The French state recognises different levels of national federations: Certified federations and delegated federations. The normative power of certified and delegated federations is supervised by the minister of sports. Any modification of the articles of association, procedural rules, the disciplinary regulations or financial regulations must be reported. If the modifications are inconsistent with the certification granted to the federation, the minister will demand the necessary corrections. The law further requires the rules be fit for the application of regulations of the international federation as long as these are compatible with French law. Aside from the general principles of law, French sports federations must comply with the principles of equal access to sport and equal treatment (van Kleef, 2014).

Future

As noted by Dowling, Leopkey and Smith (2018), "Legal issues have profound implications for governance arrangements, especially the rules and regulations that dictate them" (p. 433).

As illustrated, legalities shape the nature of governance arrangements and the types of governance models adopted (e.g., China vs. European sport governance models), and power dynamics of actors within governance networks are often enforced through legal means (e.g., EU law, government funding).

Initiatives at the policy level by ISOs have their value, but they have not managed to involve the world's governments. All of the evidence shows that these global governance bodies do not govern themselves well, and little evidence suggests this will soon change (Forster, 2016). Sport has become a global phenomenon and transnational legal responses are necessary (Hendrickx, 2016). One area for future research is whether a more effective solution than voluntary "alliances" or "partnerships" would be to adopt an international convention linking national governments and sport organisations. Chappelet (2018) contends:

> Adequate sports governance cannot exist without greater government involvement in regulating international sport and, consequently, national sport. Only governments can provide a national legal framework and prepare the ground for drawing up a treaty or convention as the basis for international sports legislation. (p. 732)

On this last point, we are of the view the ground could also be prepared with the major ISOs. It would be necessary to conclude an international convention adopted by all countries involved in international sport (as was done for WADA and, in effect, with CAS) to ensure public authorities across the globe cooperate in steering the fight to eliminate misguided governance. However, there is room for greater consideration of the use of treaties and conventions to control ISOs and NSOs in their governance, including processes for financial management in particular. As Chappelet (2018) noted:

> Sport organisations and their governance are destined to combine elements of corporate governance with aspects of democratic governance. Only intergovernmental treaties can provide the international legal framework needed to oversee this new form of sport governance. *Benefits and drawbacks of such a convention should be further studied.* (p. 732, emphasis added)

Chappelet (2018) also proposed "the creation of a specialist body to help monitor and help improve the governance of all international sport organizations" (p. 727). Similarly, Arcioni (2016) recommended a World Sport Governance Agency (WSGA): A legally and financially independent organisation able to support all stakeholders in sport at the national and international levels in order to improve governance structures. It would be the recognised body for audit and certification of good governance. These assertions need to be more fully fleshed out and critiqued. A major gap in the research is the exploration of how the law and commerce (i.e., management and governance) intersect to help shape the governance of sport organisations. In particular, how have independent commissions which are elected/appointed on the basis of expertise and experience – often commercial – as opposed to boards, which are elected on the basis of being representative of the members, performed from a governance perspective? Future research on and theoretical consideration of the role of grassroots membership on the governance processes, including election of directors, and in decision-making is also warranted given the membership focus of many sport organisations. In summary and conclusion, this chapter ends where it started. Despite a clearly established link between structures of governance and overall organisational performance in sport, an acknowledgement exists that research and the body of literature relating to this area must be increased (O'Boyle, 2012).

References

Arcioni, S. (2016). The creation of an independent body for the control of governance in sport worldwide. In Y. V. Auweele, E. Cook & J. Parry (Eds.), *Ethics and governance in sport* (pp. 75–83). Abingdon: Routledge.

Arnaut, J. (2006). *Independent European Sports Review*. Retrieved 2 April 2019, from http://eose.org/ress ource/independant-european-sports-review/

Australian Corporations Act. (2001) (Cth).

Barracco, R de P. (2018). From corruption and scandal to reform: How the Brazilian Olympic Committee overhauled its governance model. *LawInSport*. Retrieved 22 February 2019, from https://www.law insport.com/topics/articles/item/from-corruption-scandal-to-reform-how-the-brazilian-olympic-co mmittee-overhauled-its-governance-model

Bester, P. (2013). South Africa. In I. O'Boyle & T. Bradbury (Eds.), *Sport governance, international case studies* (pp. 90–106). Abingdon: Routledge.

Bosman case. (1995). Union Royale Belge des Societes de Football Association ASBL vs Jean-Marc Bosman, Royal Club Liegeois SA vs jean-Marc Bosman and others and Union des Associations Europeennes de Football (UEFA) vs jean-Marc Bosman [1995] C-414/93 [ECJ].

Bourke, A. (2013). Sports governance in Ireland: Insights on theory and practice. In S. Soderman & H. Dolles (Eds.), *Handbook of research on sport and business* (pp. 112–125). Cheltenham: Edward Elgar.

Bravo, G. (2013). Brazil. In I. O'Boyle & T. Bradbury (Eds.), *Sport governance, international case studies* (pp. 142–155). Abingdon: Routledge.

Buckley v. Tutty. (1971). 125 CLR 353, 373.

Chappelet, J-L. (2018). Beyond governance: The need to improve the regulation of international sport. *Sport in Society*, *21*, 724–734.

Charalambous-Papamiltiades, M. (2013). Cyprus. In I. O'Boyle & T. Bradbury (Eds.), *Sport governance, international case studies* (pp. 212–228). Abingdon: Routledge.

Court of Arbitration for Sport. (2019). Retrieved 22 February 2019, from https://www.tas-cas.org/en/ index.html

Dorsey, J. M. (2013). The Middle East. In I. O'Boyle & T. Bradbury (Eds.), *Sport governance, international case studies* (pp. 156–166). Abingdon: Routledge.

Dowling, M., Leopkey, B. & Smith, L. (2018). Governance in sport: A scoping review. *Journal of Sport Management*, *32*, 438–451.

Facts Sheet of the European Union. (2018). Retrieved 22 February 2019, from http://www.europarl.europ a.eu/factsheets/en/sheet/5/the-treaty-of-lisbon

Farquhar, S., Machold, S., & Ahmed, P. K. (2005). Governance and football: An examination of the relevance of corporate governance regulations for the sports sector. *International Journal of Business Governance and Ethics*, *1*, 329–349.

Findlay, H. (2016). Accountability in the global regulation of sport: What does the future hold? In Y. V. Auweele, E. Cook & J. Parry (Eds.), *Ethics and governance in sport* (pp. 69–74). Abingdon: Routledge.

Flood v. Kuhn. (1972). United States Supreme Court (1972) No. 71-32.

Forster, J. (2013). Global sport organisations. In I. O'Boyle & T. Bradbury (Eds.), *Sport governance, international case studies* (pp. 260–276). Abingdon: Routledge.

Forster, J. (2016). Global sports governance and corruption. *Palgrave Communications*, *2*, 15048. doi:10.1057/ palcomms.2015.48

Foster, K. (2003). Is there a global sports law? *Entertainment and Sports Law Journal*, *2*(1), 1–18.

Franck, E. (2010). Private firm, public corporation or member's association governance structures in European football, *International Journal of Sport Finance*, *5*, 108–127.

Gammelsaeter, H., & Senaux, B. (2013). The governance of the game: A review of the research on football's governance. In S. Soderman & H. Dolles (Eds.) *Handbook of research on sport and business* (pp. 142–160). Cheltenham: Edward Elgar.

Garcia, B., & Weatherill, S. (2012). Engaging with the EU in order to minimize its impact: Sport and the negotiation of the Treaty of Lisbon. *Journal of European Public Policy*, *19*, 238–256.

Geeraert, A. (2014). New EU governance modes in professional sport: Enhancing throughput legitimacy. *Journal of Contemporary European Research*, *10*, 302–321.

Geeraert, A. (2015). *Sports governance observer 2015. The legitimacy crisis in international sports governance*. Copenhagen: Play the Game.

Geeraert, A., & Drieskens, E. (2015). The EU controls FIFA and UEFA: A principal-agent perspective. *Journal of European Public Policy*, *22*, 1448–1466.

Geeraert, A., Scheerder, J., & Bruyninckx, H. (2013). The governance network of European football: Introducing new governance approaches to steer football at the EU level. *International Journal of Sport Policy and Politics*, *5*(1), 113–132.

Green, B. C., Chalip, L., & Bowers, M. T. (2013). United States of America. In I. O'Boyle & T. Bradbury (Eds.), *Sport governance, international case studies* (pp. 7–19). Abingdon: Routledge.

Gundel v. FEI/CAS. (1993). 1 Civil Court, Swiss Fed Trib.

Hendrickx, F. (2016). What if sport and the law have become interlocked? In Y. V. Auweele, E. Cook & J. Parry (Eds.), *Ethics and governance in sport* (pp. 136–144). Abingdon: Routledge.

Henry, I., & Lee, P. C. (2004) Governance and ethics in sport. In J. Beech & S. Chadwick (Eds.), *The business of sport management* (pp. 25–41). Essex: Elsevier.

Hong, F., & Huang, F. (2013). China. In I. O'Boyle & T. Bradbury (Eds.), *Sport governance, international case studies* (pp. 124–141). Abingdon: Routledge.

Houlihan, B. (2014). Achieving compliance in international anti-doping compliance: Analysis of the 2009 World Anti-Doping Code. *Sport Management Review*, *17*, 265–276.

Hoye, R., & Cuskelly, G. (2007). *Sport governance*. Sydney: Elsevier.

Kral, P., & Cuskelly, G. (2017). A model of transparency: Determinants and implications of transparency for national sport organizations. *European Sport Management Quarterly*, *18*, 237–262.

McLaren, R. (2018). *The Sports Law Review*. Retrieved 22 February 2019, from https://thelawreviews.co.uk/edition/the-sports-law-review-edition-3/1151392/canada

Mehta, R. (2016). The future of sports governance: Will sport sustain its traditional model of autonomy? Retrieved 22 February 2016, from https://www.sportslawbulletin.org/future-sports-governance-will-sport-sustain-its-traditional-model-autonomy/

Meier, H. E., & Garcia, B. (2015). Protecting private transnational authority against public intervention: FIFA's power over National governments. *Public Administration*, *93*, 890–906.

Michie, J., & Oughton, C. (2005). The corporate governance of professional football clubs in England. *Corporate Governance*, *13*, 517–531.

O'Boyle, I. (2012). Corporate governance applicability and theories within not-for-profit sport management. *Corporate Ownership & Control*, *9*, 335–342.

Parent, M., & Patterson, D. (2013). Canada. In I. O'Boyle & T. Bradbury (Eds.), *Sport governance, international case studies* (pp. 54–73). Abingdon: Routledge.

Persson, H. T. (2013). Scandinavia. In I. O'Boyle & T. Bradbury (Eds.), *Sport governance, international case studies* (pp. 167–183). Abingdon: Routledge.

Phat, T. H., Birt, J., Turner, M., & Fenech, J-P. (2016). Sporting clubs and scandals – lessons in governance. *Sport Management Review*, *19*, 69–80.

Pielke, R., Jr. (2013). How can FIFA be held accountable? *Sport Management Review*, *16*, 255–267.

Quick, S., & Costa, G. (2013). Greece. In I. O'Boyle & T. Bradbury (Eds.), *Sport governance, international case studies* (pp. 184–198). Abingdon: Routledge.

Serby, T. (2016). The state of EU sports law: Lessons from UEFA's 'Financial Fair Play' regulations. *International Sports Law Journal*, *16*, 37–51.

Smolianov, P. (2013). Russia. In I. O'Boyle & T. Bradbury (Eds.), *Sport governance, international case studies* (pp. 74–89). Abingdon: Routledge.

"Sport". (2018). Facts Sheets on the European Union. Retrieved 22 February 2019, from http://www.europarl.europa.eu/factsheets/en/sheet/143/sport

Sport Canada. (2011). Pursuing effective governance in Canada's national sport community, Ottawa. Retrieved 22 February 2019, from www.sportlaw.ca/wp-content/uploads/2011/12/FINALGovernancePrinciplesEN.doc at 3

Stephens, E. (2017). A guide to the UK's new code for sports governance. *LawInSport*. Retrieved 19 March 2017, from https://www.lawinsport.com/topics/articles/item/a-guide-to-the-uk-s-new-code-for-sport-governance

Thorpe, D., Buti, A., Davies, C., & Jonson, P. (2017). *Sports Law* (3rd ed.). South Melbourne: Oxford University Press.

United Nations Education Science and Cultural Organisation International Convention Against Doping in Sport. (2005). Learning to live together, anti-doping. Retrieved 19 December 2018, from http://www.unesco.org/new/en/social-and-human-sciences/themes/anti-doping/international-convention-against-doping-in-sport/

United States of America v. Bedoya. (2015). US District Court, Eastern District of New York, 3 December 2015.

van Kleef, R. (2014). The legal status of disciplinary regulations in sport. *The International Sports Law Journal*, *14*, 24–25.

WADA. (2018). What we do. *World Anti-Doping Agency*. Retrieved 19 December 2018, from https://www. wada-ama.org/en/what-we-do

Walters, G., & Tacon, R. (2013). United Kingdom. In I. O'Boyle & T. Bradbury (Eds.), *Sport governance, international case studies* (pp. 107–123). Abingdon: Routledge.

Weatherill, S. (2011). EU sports law: The effect of the Lisbon treaty. Oxford Legal Studies Research Paper No. 3/2011. Retrieved 19 December 2018, from https://papers.ssrn.com/sol3/papers.cfm?abstract_id=1747916

4

Sport policy systems and good governance
Insights from Europe

Christos Anagnostopoulos, Frank van Eekeren and Oskar Solenes

Introduction

Sport is a fundamental pillar of European civil society. European governments have acknowledged the benefits that sport provides in terms of social cohesion, health and national pride, and also the economic benefits related, for example, to jobs and tax revenue (Jack, 2018). According to the European Commission's official statistics, sport accounts for three percent of Europe's Gross Domestic Product (http://ec.europa.eu). However, the European "sport movement" (that is, "the group of the leading sport organisations in each country" (Chaker, 2004, p. 6)) has faced several challenges during recent decades concerning the development and implementation of sport regulatory policy. Many factors have led to the "governing of sport" becoming very challenging. These include an uncertain legal framework, increased cross-border activity, the global approach that sports clubs and organisations have adopted, regulatory requirements of international federations and ever more complex laws, both from national governments and the European Union (EU) (Geeraert & Drieskens, 2017).

Historically, sports organisations in Europe have enjoyed considerable autonomy in running and regulating sport. However, this autonomy has faced interventions from commercial interests, courts, governments and regulators and the EU (Anagnostopoulos & Winand, 2019). A common denominator of such interventions is the notion of "good governance" and its application in the wider European sport environment. The attentiveness towards good governance is not surprising when state funding commitments (such as providing support for sport activities and participation in international competitions; making investments in hosting sport events, or bids to do so; or acquiring broadcasting rights for public broadcasters) require that the management of these resources meets certain objectives but does so via ethical processes (Frossard, 2018).

Since 2007, good governance has been at the heart of the EU's sports policy. Indeed, there has been an increase in the number of public reports that have centred on good governance in sport (Parliamentary Assembly of the Council of Europe, 2012). As an insight into the scale of policy (funded) research, a search for "good-governance-sport" on EU's Erasmus+ webpage (as of 6 February 2019) identified 76 completed and/or ongoing projects in the five preceding years (from 2014 to 2019). This indicates the growing realisation that good governance is fundamental to improving the performance of sport organisations, especially enhancing their resistance to corruption (Geeraert, 2019). For instance, the Council of Europe emphasised that "[t]he mainstreaming of good governance principles in the management of sports bodies is seen as an appropriate way to prevent and mitigate unethical behaviours including corruption" (Council of Europe, 2016, p. 1).

Against this background, this chapter reviews the role of sport policy systems in shaping sport governance practice in Europe. It does so by largely drawing on two studies commissioned and/or funded by the European Commission: The *VOCASPORT Report* (Camy, Clijsen, Madella, & Pilkington, 2004) and the *National Sports Governance Observer: Benchmarking Sports Governance Across National Boundaries* (*NSGO*) (Geeraert, 2018). The next section starts by offering the framework that maps out different types of national policies evident in the EU Member States, before outlining how the NSGO sought to inspire European national sports federations to enhance the quality of their governance by measuring governance and building capacity. The chapter then discusses the national policy of selected European countries (Cyprus, the Netherlands and Norway) that fall into one of the VOCASPORT categories and have varying NSGO indexes. The chapter concludes by offering some directions for future research as well as how the four NSGO dimensions can be conceptualised by the means of a metaphor.

Good governance and sport policy systems in Europe

The EU, along with European sport organisations, are fully engaged in promoting good governance in sport. In October 2013, the EU Expert Group on Good Governance adopted recommendations on the Principles for Good Governance of Sport, which serve as a guide for action for sport organisations. The principles were addressed to governments and to the sport movement at three different levels: Grassroots sport organisations, national sport governing bodies and European/international federations. These *principles*, with the appropriate application by the sport organisations, could satisfy the definition of good governance as set in the *recommendation* as follows:

> The framework and culture within which a sports body sets policy, delivers its strategic objectives, engages with stakeholders, monitors performance, evaluates and manages risk and reports to its constituents on its activities and progress including the delivery of effective, sustainable and proportionate sports policy and regulation. (Expert Group Good Governance, 2013)

The recently concluded EU Sport Ministers Resolution on the EU Work Plan for Sport (2014–2017) included measures to strengthen cooperation at EU level, including enhancing good governance, skills and qualifications in sport. During the same period, the European Commission started putting more emphasis on good governance in European Sport, with the view to revealing existing good governance initiatives and good practices and to monitor whether sport organisations voluntarily declare their commitment to the implementation of good governance principles within their organisation. The objective of the above actions has been to address the great diversity of sport governance among the Member States of the EU.

VOCASPORT

In order to address the scarcity of related sport policy reports on an EU level, the Sports Unit of the European Commission contracted Jean Camy and colleagues (2004) to develop a comparative report on the different types of national policies evident in the EU Member States (VOCASPORT Research Group, 2004). The *VOCASPORT Report* classified the various national sports policies based on four parameters:

a) What **role the public authorities**, particularly the State (represented by the relevant ministry), played in regulating the system. This can include defining the role that sport plays in the country, defining participants' responsibilities, determining funding conditions, the provision and maintenance of sport facilities and overseeing how the various processes are implemented.

b) The **extent to which the actors in the sports system are coordinated and engaged,** and **the form** of such coordination. The involved parties can be completely autonomous or totally coordinated (as in the case of market forces). Regarding the form of coordination, in certain countries a particular party will be dominant and set the limits of intervention; in others, formal documents clearly describe the coordination and the level to which each actor will be involved.

c) What **roles the involved actors** – particularly the voluntary, public and private sectors – play in delivering sport provision.

d) How **suitable the supply is to changes in demand**, including mechanisms for evaluating new demands and also approaches and responses to such demands.

Based on the above parameters, the national sports policy systems in Europe can have one of four main configurations. According to Camy et al. (2004, p. 53), these systems demonstrated the following characteristics:

a) The active role of public authorities in regulating the system that characterises its **bureaucratic configuration**. All systems will have legislative frameworks (that is, laws regarding sport) that are specific to the field. Such systems involve rules laid out by a public authority whose legitimacy (both political and democratic) means it does not have to negotiate greatly with other players. Voluntary sports movements act through "delegation". There is sometimes a lack of social partners and the impact of consumers/users and entrepreneurs on sports policy implementation is often low.

b) A characteristic of the **missionary configuration** is the strong presence of a voluntary sports movement that has influential decision-making autonomy. Such movements are given responsibility by state or regional authorities to orient sports policy, despite a contractual logic gradually developing. The presence of social partners is minimal and voluntary managers have more legitimacy than employees. It is rare for users to be able to adopt a consumer position and entrepreneurs have variable roles.

c) A characteristic of the **entrepreneurial configuration** is system regulation caused by the demand (social or economic) for sport. It is difficult to stop the market directly regulating supply and demand. Essentially, public authorities set a framework that enables the market logic to play out, and the voluntary sports movement needs to adapt to the tendencies of entrepreneurs and maintain its position within this context.

d) **Social configuration** involves the social partners' presence within a system that is subject to cohabitation/collaboration among public, commercial and voluntary actors rather than being dominated by a single player. Despite potential tensions, the primary concern of the representatives of employees and employers tasked with system governance is the common good that sport brings.

Christos Anagnostopoulos, Frank van Eekeren and Oskar Solenes

National Sports Governance Observer (NSGO)

Most recently, the NSGO report (Geeraert, 2018) investigated whether and to what degree the principles of good governance across Europe are established. Eight European partners assessed the governance of national federations responsible for administering football, handball, swimming, tennis and athletics (plus any other three from triathlon, field hockey, skating, rugby, basketball, skiing, gymnastics and a national umbrella federation). The aim has been a cross-country comparison of the governance of the same sports. Based on the NSGO tool, which divides good governance into four essential dimensions (transparency, democratic processes, internal accountability and control and social responsibility) and the methodology underpinning the NSGO's 46 principles of good governance and their 274 indicators (see www.nationalsportsgovernanceob server.org), the report demonstrated that the degree of good governance in European national sport federations varies considerably.

The following case descriptions of Cyprus, the Netherlands and Norway attempt to illustrate how European sport is equipped (or otherwise) to tackle good governance challenges. These countries were chosen based on three criteria: (1) The countries to be discussed should have been part of the NSGO project, (2) the selected countries should demonstrate different configurations of the sport policy system and (3) their overall NSGO index scores should differ. On this basis, the cases are Cyprus (as a bureaucratic configuration and with the weakest NSGO status), the Netherlands (as a social configuration and with an overall good NSGO status) and Norway (as a missionary configuration and with highest close to very good NSGO index score). Figure 4.1 offers an overview of the NSGO's (European) participating countries along with the assigned (VOCASPORT) configurations as per their sport policy system. The following sub-sections tease out three case descriptions that fall under three different configurations of national sports policy systems that, at the same time, demonstrate different levels of good governance practices.

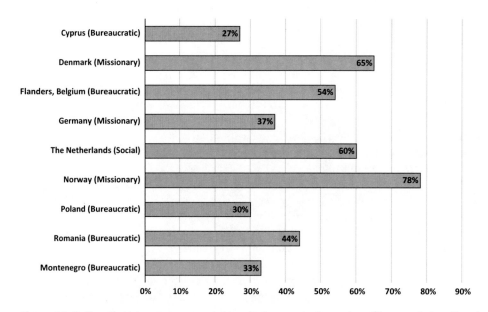

Figure 4.1 National sports governance observer index scores. Reproduced by permission. Play the Game. National Sports Governance Observer, Danish Institute for Sports Studies, p. 33.

Cyprus: An example of bureaucratic configuration

With a population of around one million people, Cyprus (officially, the Republic of Cyprus) is among the smallest Member States in the EU. The state heavily influences the operation of the entire sport sector, so Cyprus falls under the category of a "bureaucratic configuration". The first law to deal with sport issues in that country was Law 41/1969, which essentially established the Cyprus Sport Organisation (CSO) as the country's supreme sport authority. The CSO, which is a semi-governmental non-profit organisation, is supervised by the Ministry of Education and Culture and the President of Cyprus (through the Council of Ministers), which appoints nine volunteers to sit on its Board of Directors for a 30-month term. Although the board does not require government approval to make most of its decisions, it does require such approval for the annual budget, supplementary budgetary measures and to purchase and/or build sport facilities (Chaker, 2004).

In order to carry out public sports policies, the CSO has 267 employees in four departments (sports, technical, finance and human resources). The CSO's annual budget of roughly €25 million[1] comes from football pools, a tax on betting on horses, and the national lottery (Chaker, 2004). From this budget, the CSO provides (a) financial support (approximately 45 percent of the total annual budget), counselling and supervision to sports federations and clubs, (b) help in developing and maintaining sport facilities, (c) financial and technical support to develop and manage the national Sport for All programme, and (d) the "Athletes' Health Certificate" across the sport spectrum.

The CSO's Sports Academy promotes education and training for people involved in the administrative and governing bodies of sport organisations, particularly the administrative personnel and volunteer board members of the sport federations. The Academy aims to constantly upgrade the knowledge of sport stakeholders, and to cooperate with all stakeholders in order to educate and train them regarding the management and administration of sport organisations.

Although Cyprus' sport federations have organisational structures to facilitate good governance, the country has an average NSGO index 27 percent indicating "weak" scores on all four dimensions. This has made Cyprus the "negative outlier" across the countries examined in the NSGO project. A striking feature within the "internal accountability and control" dimension is that it does not include a multi-annual strategic plan – an essential aspect of organisational performance and among the most important duties of the elected volunteer board members (Ferkins & Shilbury, 2012). The federations do make sure that the general assembly provides basic supervision of the board and do have robust financial controls (particularly from the CSO itself). Despite this, given the federations' size and capacity, the board members perform many operational activities that blur (and in some cases erase) the separation of powers between the management/administration and the board. Therefore, a code of ethics and procedures to identify and manage conflicts of interest should be implemented and Cyprus should strive to achieve higher standards of governance.

With regard to the "democratic processes" dimension, basic democratic procedures are safeguarded by several concrete clauses in the statutes and internal regulations (clear election procedures for board members, a quorum for the board holding general assembly meetings at least annually, etc.). That said, the most contentious matter in Cyprus's sport environment is the need to establish term limits for board members. Also, a much wider integration of key stakeholders (especially the athletes, as it seems that only the coaches are currently involved) in strategic planning would help improve the democratic processes.

The low score in the "transparency" dimension (30 percent) is unfortunate, given the admission by representatives from the sampled federations that all of the relevant information could have been made available on their official website. In this case, it appears that the lack of capacity (personnel, technology) was the cause of the low score, rather than a lack of willingness to comply.

In terms of the "social responsibility" dimension, it does not appear that the Cypriot sport federations have taken much action at all (score of 5 percent). The few steps that were taken were almost exclusively the result of the "umbrella" organisation that was examined (the Cyprus National Olympic Committee), which follows the IOC's guidelines on some of the issues (such as doping) examined within this dimension.

Based on these somewhat concerning results, the CSO has, under the "bureaucratic configuration" started to reevaluate and enhance Law 41/1969 by including articles to support good governance, particularly within the national sport federations, and enable the CSO to take action when good governance breaches are reported. The CSO's first policy action was to introduce the first Code of Good Governance for the National Sport Federations in Cyprus. This document was heavily influenced by the NSGO project and comprises four dimensions, 15 focus areas and 55 articles.

Although the Code has been in effect since June 2018, federations had until the end of that year to start implementing its provisions. This six-month period enabled the national sport federations to make the necessary statutory changes to align with the Code's provisions. By 2019, every federation was expected to follow the Code's framework, and the CSO's management and control mechanisms would be extended by the end of that year by assessing how the federations had implemented the Code. The Code does not make concrete references to non-compliance penalties because it is designed to be a tool to support the federations. However, the extent to which the Code's provisions have been implemented will have significance when revising the CSO's subsidisation criteria for the federations.

The provisions in Cyprus's Code are largely similar to comparable policy-oriented documents in places like Flanders and the United Kingdom. However, there are certain points related to organisational conformance and performance. These are the need to introduce term limits for volunteer members of the board; the importance of designing multi-annual strategic plans for all federations, whatever their size; the need to have a "conflict of interests register"; and the value of educating and training volunteer board members, athletes, coaches and administrators by collaborating with educational providers, including academic institutions.

Holistically, adopting the Code is expected to directly impact all of the boards (including the approximately 400 volunteers who sit on them) and the 354 sports clubs that are affiliated with and funded by the federations. Implementing the Code is also expected to indirectly impact 56,000 registered athletes, 400 elite athletes, 133 sport club trainers, and 40 national coaches (Anagnostopoulos, 2018).

An example of social configuration: The Netherlands

The Netherlands is a founding member of the European Union and has roughly 17 million people. The country's sports system is a social configuration, which suggests that the development of sports policy is a collaborative process involving the government and civil society through the voluntary sports movement. The country's main sports policy actors are the Ministry of Public Health, Welfare and Sports, the municipalities and volunteers as represented by the national sport federations, local volunteer sports clubs and the national umbrella organisation, known as the National Olympic Committee and National Sports Federation (NOC*NSF).

The Ministry of Public Health, Welfare and Sports acts as the political mouthpiece of the NOC*NSF and has the primary role of coordinating and encouraging sport. The national government accounts for around ten percent of government spending related to elite sport, policy programs for the sports sector and for knowledge and innovation. About one percent of government spending is borne by the provincial government. The 380 municipalities are responsible for the largest share of government spending on sport. Approximately 90 percent of government spending, corresponding to 1.2 billion euros, comes from municipalities. This money is spent from the freely available resources in a municipality and is not linked to a statutory target for sport. Of this budget, 85 percent is spent on construction, design and operation of sports facilities (van den Dool, 2018). As municipalities are now increasingly viewing sport as an area in which public value can be created, social utilisation of sport has grown in importance within their sport policy agendas. The municipalities use public grants to encourage volunteer sports clubs to capitalise on their public value. Thus, volunteer sports clubs are now involved in implementing municipalities' policies rather than just being the places where sport is organised.

The Netherlands has 75 national sport federations, which incorporate the country's 24,000 local volunteer sports clubs. The main task of these federations — which are established by the sports clubs — is to represent the clubs. The federations unite within NOC*NSF, which represents the federations in relation to the government. The NOC*NSF is viewed as an independent entity that is responsible for all sport in the Netherlands, from grassroots to elite levels, including paralympic sport, and for distributing funds from the national lottery to the federations. The NOC*NSF is an independent body, but its decisions must be approved at a general meeting of the representatives from the federations; thus, the federations actually make the final decisions regarding policy and budget.

The code of good governance in sport, published in 2005, deals with the governance of the national sport federations and requires the federations to comply with its 13 recommendations or give a good reason for not doing so. The NOC*NSF encouraged the federations to align themselves and their processes with the code. Since January 2011, federations have had to comply with certain minimum quality requirements in terms of maintaining basic sport management principles and the generally accepted rules of the relevant sport. Failure to adhere to such requirements could lead to a federation no longer receiving lottery funding. In practice this did not occur until now. Checks on adherence to the minimum quality requirements are done through an annual self-assessment that the federations complete. Given the presence of such a framework, the eight Dutch federations had an unsurprisingly high average NSGO index score of 60 percent, indicating "good" status.

The national sport federations in the Netherlands are relatively transparent in terms of their members, multi-annual policies, agendas, statutes, internal regulations and minutes from their general assemblies. However, they are less transparent regarding the remuneration of their board members and the decisions they make. The fact that the long-term decisions of the general assembly are easy to follow (through annual reports), but the policies and decisions of the board are not, is noteworthy.

The federations had the lowest average score (54%) regarding the "democratic processes" dimension, largely because of the relatively low scores for principles related to stakeholder involvement. Sport federations generally have clear agreements about how athletes are involved in decision-making processes, but such agreements do not relate to referees, coaches or volunteers. In contrast to Cyprus, the Dutch national sport federations had the highest scores regarding term limits and retirement schedules for board members. On the other hand, they had a notably low score related to implementing gender equality policies.

Within the dimension of "internal accountability and control", the Dutch federations achieved the highest score in terms of having a distinct organisational structure that takes the principle of separation of powers into account. While the federations have provisions in place for effective financial supervision, both internal and external, such provisions are lacking for evaluating their own composition and operation as are procedures related to the premature resignation of board members.

The "social responsibility" dimension was incorporated to varying degrees in the studied sample of Dutch federations. All had policies promoting sport for all, which is unsurprising given the federations' traditional connection between elite and recreational sports. The federations generally give much more attention to issues like doping or sexual harassment in sport than to strategies promoting environmental sustainability or gender equality.

It would be of interest to observe what impact the latest national agreement on sport (the Sportakkoord) will have, particularly as it is the result of common efforts among sports organisations, local and national government, the provinces, the private sector and civil society organisations. As part of the Sportakkoord, the NOC★NSF currently is, in close collaboration with national sport federations, municipalities, sport associations and other stakeholders (such as sponsors), developing a new code of good governance in sport. The new code aims to create a national framework that can also be implemented in local sports clubs taking their specific context into account. The code will be accompanied by a support program focused on training, knowledge dissemination and practical assistance for sport organisations (van Eekeren & de Kwaasteniet, 2018).

An example of "missionary configuration": Norway

Norway is a member of the European Economic Area and has just over five million people. The umbrella confederation for all sports in Norway is the Norwegian Olympic and Paralympic Committee and Confederation of Sports (NIF). The NIF's General Assembly is held every four years and is the supreme governing body for organised sport in the country. It develops laws related to sports; such laws make no reference to the national constitution and do not require parliamentary approval. Delegates represent Norway's 54 national sport federations and 19 regional NIF confederations (branches of NIF that have bi-annual general assemblies of their own). These national and regional associations oversee more than 12,000 clubs and 360 sports councils at the municipal level.

The Norwegian model has been likened to a sports policy system, which *VOCASPORT Report* (Camy et al., 2004) referred to as the "missionary configuration". This model is decentralised from state policy making, but internally centralised with guidance from the NIF, whose constitution has effectively monopolised Norwegian sports. This arrangement is effective in terms of sport governance in that national sport organisations must comply with NIF standards; it is also efficient, in that these organisations use the NIF as a resource regarding areas for which small associations (in particular) may be unable to sustain a professional office.

All of the NIF's club and organisation members are volunteers and none of its members are incorporated. Companies do not have any voting power in Norwegian sports, all members have equal rights and individual members (aged 15 and over) can vote in their club's annual assembly and be selected to represent their club at regional or national levels. There is no individual membership in national sport associations or confederations; all membership is club-based (NIF). Professional athletes, including foreign ones, can only work or compete in domestic competitions if they become members of an association club.

As sports have become increasingly professionalised and commercialised, there has been an increase in the number of private stakeholders in Norwegian sports. The rule that only members can vote has blocked the access of these stakeholders to the NIF's decision-making bodies and members. Some sports involve a lot of private money, but clubs must still have an association structure that enables them to participate in competitions and in formal decision-making processes. However, such associations often collaborate with corporations that are established solely to finance a club. Such organisations are prevented from having an influence via the NIF system, but they can exert power through other means, including the financial assistance they provide.

Sport in Norway is rarely politically controversial. As a result, the autonomy of volunteer sports has widespread political support, and the NIF has been viewed as an efficient means of developing and implementing sport policies. This virtually apolitical approach is partly due to the fact that the national budget does not include any public financial support for sports, so sports issues are not debated in political forums. Because sports are financed by the national lottery, funding depends on how profitable the lottery is rather than on politics.

The Norwegian NSGO index is 78 percent, which is "good". The overall score would have been "very good" if the dimension of "democratic processes" had achieved a score of 80 percent or more (as was the case in all other three dimensions). In terms of transparency, a strong point of the Norwegian federations is their publication of policy documents, agendas and minutes from general assemblies, sports rules and administrative regulations. However, they can improve in terms of explaining the board's work and providing information about board members and the background to important rulings. It is important to improve this area to avoid claims of closed and undemocratic processes.

The dimension in which the Norwegian federations scored lowest was "democratic processes". This may appear surprising given Norway's reputation as a society that emphasises democratic values. The federations are generally good at ensuring democratic elections for board members and standing committees, and all organisations appear to have clear regulations regarding gender equality on the board. However, areas for improvement include setting term limits for board members, making the board's composition both differentiated and balanced (apart from gender), and including internal stakeholders such as referees, coaches and athletes (Solenes, Gammelsæter & Egilsson, 2018).

Norwegian sport federations achieved a score of "very good" regarding internal accountability. They have internal committees for financing and auditing, financial control systems and clear conflict-of-interest procedures regarding board members. However, they could improve in terms of establishing early retirement procedures, board supervision of management and a code of conduct for board members and management.

Regarding "social responsibility", the Norwegian federations have implemented policies to combat doping and match-fixing and consulted with their member organisations in terms of management and governance. Improvements could be made vis-à-vis promoting policies for environmental sustainability and athletes' careers outside the sport and in achieving fair treatment for athletes.

Against the above-mentioned NSGO scores on the four dimensions, it should be noted that the almost very good governance standards in the Norwegian sport environment have not been a result of a prescriptive policy of how national sport federations should govern themselves (for example, through a compulsory Code for Good Governance). Rather, the Norwegian government has produced a number of descriptive white papers almost every decade since the early 1990s (see: 1991/1992; 1999/2000; 2011/2012). These were all based on broad pillars such as sport for all, voluntary sports, elite sports growing out of grassroots sports, regulations on children sports, gender equality and a mixture of public and private funding that together formed the roadmap for a transparent, democratic, accountable and socially responsible sport landscape.

Concluding remarks and future research directions

This chapter has sought to offer insights on European policy systems and standards of good governance. However, it is beyond the scope of this chapter to suggest that there is a correlation (let alone causality) between certain configurations and good governance standards (that is, NSGO index scores). Beyond the more likely case that a national policy system may exhibit aspects of more than one configuration (Henry, 2009), the simple intention has been to illustrate three different sport policy systems *and* (rather than *in relation to*) good governance performance of their national sport federations.

The descriptions seem to confirm that specific configurations influence the way in which good governance is approached. It is striking that, in the bureaucratic configuration of Cyprus, legislation is seen as the instrument to promote good governance; in the social configuration of the Netherlands, the relevant stakeholders work together on a new code and support program; and that, in the missionary configuration of Norway, the government has formed a broad road-map for the entire sports landscape. Next to this, contextual factors, such as culture and history, will undoubtedly play an important role in the good governance approach, which implies that it will not be easy to apply a different, apparently more successful, approach to good governance in a different setting.

At the same time, however, the above observations suggest some potential future issues and areas worth of research. One question that deserves further investigation is why the average standards of good governance in Norwegian sport federations are higher than those of some of their Cypriot and Dutch counterparts (Geeraert, 2018). Such research must look at both structural and cultural factors. Regarding the former, strategies for achieving common high governance standards can be highlighted by comparing centralised good governance policies. Regarding the latter, the federations' implementation of good governance beyond formal requirements can be explained by certain factors, including the professionalisation of the sport sector (Shilbury & Ferkins, 2011; Siegfried, Schlesinger, Bayle & Giauque, 2015), spill-overs from other sectors and the broader presence within the countries' culture of shared governance-related norms. Therefore, also at the organisational level, further research could consider the resistance of individual federations to pressure, either cultural or structural, to implement good governance. Such resistance can either be endogenous (if it comes from inside the organisation) or exogenous (when federations face pressure from stakeholders that prevents them from implementing good governance) (Geeraert, 2018).

In conclusion, given that incidents of poor governance have not gone unnoticed by governments (irrespective of the degree of intervention), national sport federations must gain and/or retain their legitimacy. As a final takeaway message, it is suggested that the different policy configurations in conjunction with the four NSGO dimensions of good governance could be viewed by using an "umbrella" as a metaphor. Sport federations can safeguard democratic processes by ensuring transparency and guaranteeing accountability and control, thus protecting themselves against pressure and/or criticism from different stakeholder groups related to how these organisations operate – put differently, embracing the umbrella's protective and deflecting abilities. At the same time, turning the umbrella "upside down" one can also collect and incorporate goodwill, as happens with actions related to social responsibility, such as dual careers, collaboration with universities for research and training and environmentally related actions. The umbrella is an integration mechanism in which public demands, expectations and the confines of social acceptance and prestige can be detected, gathered, scanned and fulfilled – in other words, what the future of researching and practicing good governance in sport should all be about.

Acknowledgements

Material for this chapter has been extracted from the National Sports Governance Observer (NSGO) funded by the European Commission under the Erasmus+ programme. Special thanks to Play the Game: Danish Institute for Sports Studies.

Note

1 In 2018. Before Cyprus was hit heavily by the financial crisis (in around 2015), the CSO's annual budget exceeded €40 million.

References

Anagnostopoulos, C. (2018). NSGO country report: Cyprus. In A. Geeraert (Ed.), *National Sports governance observer. Final report* (pp. 49–66). Aarhus: Play the Game: Danish Institute for Sports Studies.

Anagnostopoulos, C., & Winand, M. (2019). Introduction to the research handbook on sport governance. In M. Winand & C. Anagnostopoulos (Eds.), *Research handbook on sport governance* (pp. 1–8). Cheltenham, UK: Edward Elgar Publishing.

Camy, J., Clijsen, L., Madella, A., & Pilkington, A. (2004). *Vocational education and training in the field of sport in the European Union: Situation, trends and outlook (VOCASPORT)*. Lyon: European Observatoire of Sport and Employment. Retrieved 23 March 2019, from http://eose.org/wpcontent/uploads/2014/03/voc asport-Final-Report-English-Version.pdf

Chaker, A. N. (2004). *Good governance in sport – A European survey*. Strasbourg: Council of Europe Publishing.

Council of Europe. (2016). *14th Council of Europe conference of ministers responsible for sport: Final resolutions*. Budapest: Council of Europe.

Expert Group 'Good Governance'. (2013). EU work plan for sport 2011–2014. Deliverable 2. Principles of good governance in sport. Retrieved 23 March 2019, from http://ec.europa.eu/assets/eac/sport/lib rary/policy_documents/xg-gg-201307-dlvrbl2-sept2013.pdf

Ferkins, L., & Shilbury, D. (2012). Good boards are strategic: What does that mean for sport governance? *Journal of Sport Management, 26*, 67–80.

Frossard, S. (2018). Foreword. In R. Jack (Ed.), *Good governance initiatives in sport at national level. Good practice handbook for the sports movement* (no. 9) (pp. 56). Directorate General of Democracy, Enlarged Partial Agreement on Sport (EPAS), Council of Europe, Brussels.

Geeraert, A. (Ed.). (2018). *National sports governance observer. Final report*. Aarhus: Play the Game: Danish Institute for Sports Studies. Retrieved from https://playthegame.org/knowledge-bank/publications/ national-sports-governance-observer-final-report/ee07c9d7-130d-4599-a9ba-a996008fb1a4

Geeraert, A. (2019). The limits and opportunities of self-regulation: Achieving international sport federations' compliance with good governance standards. *European Sport Management Quarterly*, Advance online publication. doi:10.1080/16184742.2018.1549577

Geeraert, G., & Drieskens, E. (2017). Normative market Europe: The EU as a force for good in international sports governance? *Journal of European Integration, 39*(1), 79–94.

Henry, I. (2009). European models of sport: Governance, organisational change and sports policy in the EU. *Hitotsubashi Journal of Arts and Sciences, 50*(1), 41–52

Jack, R. (2018). *Good governance initiatives in sport at national level. Good practice handbook for the sports movement* (No. 9). Directorate General of Democracy, Enlarged Partial Agreement on Sport (EPAS), Council of Europe, Brussels.

Parliamentary Assembly Resolution 1875. (2012). Good governance and ethics in sport. Final version. Retrieved 23 March 2019, from http://assembly.coe.int/nw/xml/XRef/Xref-XML2HTML-en.as p?fileid=18258

Shilbury, D., & Ferkins, L. (2011). Professionalisation, sport governance and strategic capability. *Managing Leisure, 16*, 108–127.

Siegfried, N., Schlesinger, T., Bayle, E., & Giauque, D. (2015). Professionalisation of sport federations – a multi-level framework for analysing forms, causes and consequences. *European Sport Management Quarterly, 15*, 407–433.

Solenes, O., Gammelsæter, H., & Egilsson, B. (2018). NSGO country report: Norway. In A. Geeraert (Ed.), *National sports governance observer. Final report* (pp. 160–176). Aarhus: Play the Game: Danish Institute for Sports Studies.

van den Dool, R. (2018). *Monitor uitgaven sportgemeenten: een overzicht van de uitgaven in 2017*. Utrecht: Mulier Instituut.

van Eekeren, F., & de Kwaasteniet, R. (2018). NSGO country report: The Netherlands. In A. Geeraert (Ed.), *National sports governance observer. Final report* (pp. 140–159). Aarhus: Play the Game: Danish Institute for Sports Studies.

5

Government policy and sport governance
Canada, New Zealand and Australia

Michael P. Sam and Geoff Schoenberg

Introduction

The subject of governance is growing in academic circles. Its popularity is evident in its recent general coverage in handbooks by various publishers (cf. Bevir, 2011; Levi-Faur, 2012; Winand & Anagnostopoulos, 2019) and in handbooks, like this one, examining governance as applied to a specific field or context of study. Organisational (or corporate) governance has received most of the attention in sport management and with good reason. It builds upon the long-standing concern for volunteer boards, strategy and principal-agent relations involving staff, sponsors and event organisers. Likewise, what is called "systemic governance" in this volume has demonstrated an equal prominence owing to the importance of understanding organisational networks, partnerships and the exercise of authority within the wider sector.

Governance, in many ways, is not particularly new to sport studies; though that is not to say that the concept cannot add new insight, particularly given that contemporary strands in governance thinking bring together perspectives from political studies, economics, sociology and management (Grix & Phillpots, 2011). This chapter specifically focuses on the relationships and overlaps between policies and governance within the sport sector in Canada, New Zealand and Australia. Policy in this chapter is understood in a very broad sense as any combination of rules/regulations, goals/commitments or programmes/practices initiated by government and its agents. The focus is thus on how the sport sector is steered via government policy and how this shapes subsequent governance practices. The chapter ultimately seeks to generate additional understanding of how sport is coproduced within a plural and fragmented sector.

Governance as "steering"

Governance, in very simple terms, is the process of governing. Governance is most often explained through a metaphor of "steering" and, in contrast to, "rowing" (Rhodes, 1997). The metaphor is useful for several reasons. First, "steering" suggests that governance is more closely linked with aspects of policy, planning and strategy than it is with day-to-day implementation and operations. Second, and most importantly, steering elicits the idea that the direction of policies and programmes is not clear-cut owing to the fact that service delivery is increasingly coproduced.

States rely heavily on non-state actors to achieve their aims; for example, a policy goal of creating "national identity" might rely on hosting major sporting events, which in turn requires the cooperation of private and public sector interests.

The focus of governance thus surrounds the process of steering networks of organisations that span different jurisdictions, levels of authority and institutional arenas. Governance in this sense, is concerned with coordinating horizontally (across areas of, say, health and education) as well as vertically (from local to national to international), hence the emergence of concepts such as joined-up governance, network governance, regulatory governance and democratic governance.

The explosion of interest in governance has come at a time in which governing has become increasingly complex. For those interested in corporate governance, it emanated from the variety of actors influencing the activities of firms such as shareholders, regulatory agencies, distributors, manufacturers and financial institutions. Simultaneously, governance theories emanated from researchers examining emerging forms of government who were unsatisfied with hierarchical/bureaucratic models of politics that could not adequately explain third-party service delivery and public-private partnerships. What these perspectives share is an acknowledgement of the *plural nature of "making things work"*.

Regardless of its foundations, the concept of governance has much to offer in understanding sport. In large part, this is because sport is organised across public, private and non-profit sectors. Indeed, its delivery and development are characterised by pluriformity (Bevir, 2011) and, as such, one of the primary concerns for all involved is how each other's activities are coordinated (or whether they should be). As described below, the increasing attempts of governmental actors to influence the governance of national sport organisations (NSOs) is indicative of the expanding network with which sport-governing bodies must grapple. While the federated model is still predominant, meaning that the relationships between provincial/state bodies and the national body are potentially the most important node, the network of influential actors is expanding.

Where coordination is a central principle of governance, it is important to understand the main organisational modes of governance: Hierarchies, markets and networks (Rhodes, 1997; Sam, Batty & Dean, 2005; Williamson, 1985). Each mode can be understood as an organisational means for coordination and steering. Each represents a pure type, but most sport systems display characteristics of each (Sam, 2017).

Hierarchies are perhaps the most intuitive form of coordination, typically understood within the command and control structures of governments or large firms (Williamson, 1985). In countries like Russia, China and South Korea, sport systems are organised hierarchically such that organisations are not autonomous, but rather directed from those above them. This type of unitary structure enables close control over subordinate organisations because there are clear lines of accountability for performance (or lack thereof). Steering is thus enforced through formal rules, procedures and policies.

Markets, in contrast, are a means of coordination characterised by competition and consumer choice. The activities of organisations within markets are coordinated and governed not by rules and directives but by signals, such as costs and prices. In its broadest sense, sport development is coordinated by a market, where sports with the most popularity garner the bulk of registered participants. Less popular sports vie for market share and effectively compete with one another for numbers. How is this a governance mechanism? Consider a sport wanting to organise a new weekly youth competition on a Saturday morning (a popular time slot for other sports). While it is free to position this new sport "product", it does so at its own risk. The new sport competition may go ahead, but organisers may have to adjust times (or seasons) based on whether it can generate enough customer interest. Thus, unlike a hierarchy, the coordination of the sector's activities is achieved without a higher authority or hierarchically located superior. Steering is effectively self-regulated.

Networks are a means of social coordination achieved not by rules or market signals, but by trust and negotiation among/between organisations. Organisations in a network are autonomous (and have their own goals), but agree to work together to pursue a common aim. In sport, the most common term to describe this governance mode is "partnerships". Regardless of the different nomenclatures (such as inter-organisational relationships), networks of autonomous organisations working together represent a *hybrid* mode of coordination and, importantly, this is the defining feature of contemporary governance. The emergence of networks has coincided with the recognition that organisations cannot go it alone to address "wicked problems" (like youth inactivity) that cut across sectors like health, education and sport (Sam, 2009). Likewise, for NSOs, working with/through networks at state/provincial and regional levels is fundamental to achieving elite and community sport outcomes (e.g., the federated model for Australian NSOs). Networks are also apparent between different programme deliverers like schools, sport clubs or city-owned facilities.

In sum, since governance is principally concerned with steering, its analytical focus is concerned with:

- The *architecture* of the sector including the organisational links, inter-dependencies, partnerships and authority structures therein;
- The *instruments* or *means* through which these networks are steered and coordinated (e.g., policies, programmes, regulatory regimes).

The case descriptions below examine the state of sport governance in three countries and attempt to answer questions across three broad areas in relation to each:

1. *Characteristics of the system*: What does the system look like? What are its structural characteristics (federal/state/local), club system, etc.? What are the patterns of authority between them? What are the goals of each partner/stakeholder and how are they complementary or different?
2. *Government policies and strategies*: Since government agencies in all three countries have a general mandate to oversee/steer sport, what instruments do they deploy to do so? To the extent that central agencies want to shape the sport environment, how do they go about it? Do they roll out "national programmes"? Do they create competition between NSOs? Do they create new "coordinating agencies"? Do they promote best practice via informational campaigns? Do they commission reports, taskforces and inquiries?
3. *Effects of policy on governance*: What are the outcomes of these governance forms? What is occurring in terms of modernisation/professionalisation, organisational changes and reforms? What can be anticipated in terms of democratic input, funding patterns or new forms of organisation?

Canada

Canada (pop. 37 million) is one of the world's largest and most geographically dispersed states, with a population density of just four people per square kilometre. Its system of government is based in federalism and principled on the division of responsibilities/powers between federal

67

and provincial levels. These divisions pose a recurring challenge for federal sport policy-makers. Long considered as a subset of education, sport is the responsibility of the ten provinces and three territories. As such, each province has a central agency responsible for sport promotion and development typically operating under a provincial ministry (e.g., Alberta Sport Connection, Sport Nova Scotia and Sports Québec). These agencies in turn, support their respective provincial sport organisations (PSOs). While cities and local municipalities remain the primary providers of sport facilities in the Canadian system, other organisations such as the YMCA maintain a significant presence in some urban centres. While the individual PSOs may operate hierarchically, the provincial sport system is best characterised as a network with lead agencies (like Sport Manitoba) continually seeking more coherence and uniformity across their network partners.

At the federal level, Sport Canada, a branch within the Department of Canadian Heritage, oversees sport. The main organisations under its purview are the NSOs. As with their provincial counterparts, NSOs are autonomous non-profit organisations that often rely on government funding for their survival. Sport Canada steers this part of the sport sector via its various funding programmes. Its Sport Funding Accountability Framework (SFAF) sets the conditions and criteria for funding NSOs. Among these conditions are requirements for bilingual (French/English) delivery, along with expectations for enhanced participation opportunities and improved performances at Olympic/Paralympic Games and world championships (Sport Canada, 2018).

Much of Sport Canada's activities are circumscribed by the Canadian Sport Policy (CSP) – a shared vision between federal, provincial and territorial governments. First tabled in 2002, and later revised in 2012, the CSP remains the blueprint for Sport Canada to deliver on four objectives, specifically to enhance: Participation (more people playing more), excellence (elite sport), capacity (a modernised development system) and interaction (a connected and coordinated system). The CSP is notable in its explicit concern for integrating the various levels and jurisdictions (federal, provincial/territorial, municipal) (Sport Canada, 2012).

One of Sport Canada's primary roles is therefore a facilitative one in maintaining a dialogue between federal and provincial partners (Sam, 2011). The relative autonomy of the provincial sport systems has demanded a commitment to work collaboratively through joint policy statements of federal-provincial/territorial ministers who are responsible for sport, physical activity and recreation. The Priorities for Collaborative Action (e.g., 2017–2022) is a significant steering mechanism designed to achieve alignment and integration horizontally (between the provinces) and vertically (between national/federal and provincial bodies). The joint plan currently has nine priorities, dealing with various dimensions of sport delivery such as ethics, alignment with the education sector, participation among under-represented groups, athlete support and good governance. The collaborative nature of the federal and provincial/territorial priority-setting marks an entrenched imperative to coordinate the disparate provincial sectors. Insofar as these plans are "complemented by the individual action plans of each (provincial) government", they foreshadow the likelihood of isomorphism among partners over time. While diplomatic exchange is a reflection of federal-provincial/territorial relations more generally, integration is rendered more complex by the fact that the governance of sport must extend beyond ministries and departments, to also include the web of non-profit organisations at national, provincial and regional levels.

The patterns of rule and authority in Canadian sport are thus extremely diffuse, with governance achieved through collaboration rather than by fiat (Sam, 2011). Even in relation to high performance sport, where systems are typically coordinated hierarchically (Bergsgard, Houlihan, Mangset, Nodland & Rommetvedt, 2007), Canada's High Performance Sport Centres and Institutes consist of coalitions comprising public (Sport Canada + provincial agency), non-profit (e.g., Canadian Olympic Committee, Own the Podium, Coaching Association of Canada) and corporate interests. Among these, Own the Podium (OTP) is most reflective of this complex public-private partnership approach. Sport Canada effectively outsources its elite sport strategy implementation to OTP via funding contributions ($62 million for "enhanced excellence"). In turn, OTP determines priorities and coordinates funding to NSOs in conjunction with the Canadian Olympic Committee, the Canadian Olympic Foundation, the Canadian Paralympic Committee, provincial and territorial governments as well as corporate partners.

In this diffuse network, one of the most unique governance features of federal-level sport thus surrounds the continual state support of quasi-advocacy groups (Sam, 2011). The *Sport Matters Group* for example, operates as a "think tank" and, while it is partially funded by Sport Canada, it lobbies the federal government on a number of issues (e.g., sport infrastructure, increased funding to the sector, etc.). More issue-specific steering bodies take the form of quasi-advocacy groups such as the *Aboriginal Sport Circle* (a national voice for aboriginals in sport), *Athletes Canada* (a collective voice of national team athletes), the *Coaching Association of Canada* (a collective supporting coaching interests) and Canadian *Sport for Life* (promoting the Long Term Athlete Development model) and the *Canadian Association for the Advancement of Women and Sport and Physical Activity* (advocating for the interests of girls and women). Importantly these organisations are all funded by Sport Canada and are aligned with key aspects of the central agency's policies and the CSP. Steering in this way is clearly *not* achieved hierarchically but rather via third-party network partners that work across jurisdictional boundaries.

In this way, Sport Canada's governance resembles a kind of "meta-governance", that is, the steering and coordination of self-organised or self-regulated networks (Jessop, 2011; Torfing, 2012). In this perspective, Dowling and Washington (2018) suggest that OTP and Canadian Sport for Life are governance mechanisms through which Sport Canada can achieve its wider objectives (and with less apparent contradiction). Meta-governance pursued in this way, they argue, is an extension of programme-based modernisation programmes such as quadrennial planning and the more recent SFAF (Havaris & Danylchuk, 2007; Sam & Macris, 2014; Whitson & Macintosh, 1989). The consequences of this governance approach (in relation to autonomy or isomorphism) on individual organisations are comparatively discussed later in this chapter.

New Zealand

New Zealand (pop. 4.5 million) is a small, unitary state, with some elements of decentralised authority to local authorities and regional bodies. Sport in New Zealand remains largely delivered through the system of linked clubs, regional associations and national federations. However, for youth (13–18), sport in secondary schools is becoming a growing feature of the sport system owing in part to the prestige it offers for schools aiming to maintain or grow enrolments. Territorial local authorities (i.e., local governments) remain a key source of support for sport facilities, particularly with respect to swimming facilities and other large multi-use complexes.

The governance of New Zealand's sport system is largely directed from the centre. Structurally, the central agency Sport NZ is a crown entity, an arm's length non-departmental body operating on behalf of the Ministry of Culture and Heritage. Sport NZ is governed by a board of directors consisting of eight to ten members appointed by the Minister of Sport and Recreation with responsibility for strategic direction and leadership. As board members are neither representatives of regions, nor of particular sports or levels of the sector (i.e., national/local), they are not accountable to partner organisations or clubs. Sport NZ's steering of the sector (including its strategy, programmes and activities) is therefore a reflection of the ruling government.

Alongside Sport NZ sits High Performance Sport NZ, a subsidiary organisation responsible for achieving elite sport objectives. It too has its own appointed board of directors, with operations largely devolved into the country's high-performance centres or sport-specific hubs. Sport NZ's community sport participation objectives are largely pursued through a network of 17 regionally based organisations called regional sports trusts. These are autonomous non-profit charities funded from a combination of local government sources, lottery grants and Sport NZ programme contracts. Since they are not formal arms of Sport NZ, the regional sports trusts are variable in the relative emphasis they place on sport, recreation and physical activity. They are also variable in the demographics they serve, their geographical size and mandates (Keat & Sam, 2013).

NSOs have historically been one of the main "partners" and contractors of Sport NZ programmes. Typically governed via a mix of regional representatives and independent board members, these organisations are also autonomous from state control. However, to say they are autonomous does not mean they are immune to pressures from the central agency. Both Sport NZ and High Performance Sport NZ exert a substantive influence in these organisations through their respective conditional and targeted funding schemes (Sam, 2012; Sam & Macris, 2014).

Sport NZ's most explicit governance mechanism in this regard is characterised by the creation and maintenance of competitive markets among/between NSOs (Sam & Macris, 2014). The use of markets as a governance mechanism has been a distinctive feature of New Zealand since 1985, after it became the first to adopt widespread new public management reforms in the public sector (Boston, Martin, Pallot & Walsh, 1996). New public management refers to the global movement from the 1980s in which management techniques and theories drawn from business management were applied to public organisations (Pollitt & Bouckaert, 2004). From the 1990s onwards, NZ's central sport agency began to change how it funded organisations, from eliciting "voluntaristic responses" to tying conditions with funding through contracts (Sam, 2009). Since 2002/2003, the central agency has targeted funding to a select number of "priority sports" to get the best return on investment.

Based in these principles, Sport NZ has been effectively treating NSOs as independent contractors. Where NSOs have to make a case for funding upwards to Sport NZ, the environment is characterised by contestability and competition. Because Sport NZ focuses its support on capable organisations, targeting those that "can effectively and efficiently deliver" and those best able to demonstrate outputs (Sport New Zealand, 2012, 2013b, p. 15), the system elicits little in the way of trust and cooperation (which characterises networks). Notably, sport at this central level lacks any network of organisations that can mobilise to either support or restrain the authority of Sport NZ.

The focus on targets and outputs is a reflection of Sport NZ's own treatment by the government. The agency reports on a number of different performance measures such as: 1) The number of sport participants, 2) the number of participant opportunities, 3) the number of joint community sport projects, 4) the number of coaching plans developed in NSOs and 5) the number of volunteers within the sector and so forth (Sport New Zealand, 2013a). In regards to elite sport, High Performance Sport NZ explicitly uses results to legitimise its strategy of performance-based budgeting. For example, it recently noted, "These (2013) results once again demonstrate that our strategy of targeting sports with the potential to win on the world stage is a successful formula" (High Performance Sport New Zealand, 2013, p. 1).

Similar to Sport Canada, NZ's central sport agency at times defers normative/political elements of its strategy to independent bodies. It creates partnerships with a range of community organisations to show congruence with public values (Sam & Ronglan, 2016). For example, in 2002, Sport and Recreation New Zealand (the predecessor to Sport New Zealand) established an advisory committee, *Te Rōpū Manaaki*, to bring its operations in line with principles of the Treaty of Waitangi (New Zealand's founding document). The committee was intended to operate as a source of strategic policy advice and an advocacy group, having as one of its objectives "to evaluate the benefits of utilising a 'by Māori, for Māori' approach" to sport delivery (Te Rōpū Manaaki, 2005, p. 1).[1] A more recent initiative focuses on gender equity in the governance of sport. In partnership with the New Zealand Olympic and Commonwealth Games Committee, Sport NZ aims to bring more women into the boardrooms of national organisations. Taken together, these initiatives can be interpreted as governance instruments aimed at coordinating NSOs.

Another way in which Sport NZ tries to coordinate sector activities is through its various benchmarking exercises and tools for organisational "self-assessment". The agency has a long history of publications (e.g., "Nine Steps to Effective Governance") and programmes (e.g., *SportsMark, Organisational Development Tool* and *Sport Compass)* – all of which aim to improve the governance capabilities of partner organisations. While at various times Sport NZ has introduced quality certifications such as the *Club Warrant of Fitness* and the more recent *Governance Quality Standard* (Sport NZ, 2017), it has not been overt in linking funding directly with evaluations of good governance.

Australia

Australia (pop. 25 million) is geographically large and divided into six states and two territories invoking comparisons with Canada due to similar forms of government and low population density (with concentrations along the East Coast of Australia similar to Canada's concentration of population centres near the USA border). Australian sport is, predominantly, organised in a federated system with different governing bodies at each geographic level (i.e., local clubs, state sport associations, national sport organisations). Thus, the majority of participation is at the club level with local municipal governments providing the bulk of sport facilities. At the federal level, the prime contribution is through support for NSOs and the Australian Institute for Sport. Rather than direct government intervention, Sport Australia[2] is a statutory agency of the federal government with its independent board of directors appointed by the Minister for Sport. Thus, Sport Australia is the primary pathway for government influence in sport and is the principal policy-maker at the national level.

In considering recent sport policy in Australia, there are two policies regarding the overarching direction of sport: *Australia's Winning Edge* in 2012 and the recent *Sport 2030* in 2018. Complementing these whole-of-sport views (of particular importance to this chapter) are governance-specific policies and documents released by Sport Australia. Together, the strategic direction documents and the governance documents carry influence within the broader sport sector. Consideration of these documents provides insight into how Sport Australia influences sport governance practices in Australia.

Australia's Winning Edge adopted an investment approach by targeting money to sports and athletes most likely to deliver success. Part of this approach involved pushing sport organisations towards recommended governance practices and shared services models (Sport Australia, 2012a). While not directly contrasting the Winning Edge platform, the new policy of Sport Australia, *Sport 2030*, does make substantive shifts in the direction for sport in Australia by putting more onus on the NSOs by reducing the aid available through Sport Australia and reducing the role of the Australian Institute for Sport (Sport Australia, 2018a). Furthermore, Sport Australia advocates for a "One Management" approach in sport governance where key elements of the sport (e.g., financial systems) are centralised and managed by the national body while the state governing bodies retain independence in their governance (Sport Australia, 2018a). While these national strategies provide a bird's-eye view of the vision Sport Australia has for governance, a better understanding is gleaned from examining the policy papers and documents specifically focused on governance.

In 2012, Sport Australia released *Sports Governance Principles* to articulate "a clearly stated position with respect to the governance of national sporting organisations to which the ASC provides taxpayer monies" (Sport Australia, 2012b, p. 1). This report included six principles, which NSOs were expected to integrate into the governance of their organisation. These principles were primarily focused on issues related to the board of directors (e.g., composition, processes, reporting). Later, a second policy was released which outlined a series of mandatory sport governance principles to which NSOs are expected to report against every year and could be tied to subsequent funding (Sport Australia, 2015). These mandatory principles saw Sport Australia adopt a broader view of governance to include organisational practices and structures in addition to board-specific recommendations. Notably, this document also advocated for a unitary governing model as opposed to the traditional federated model noting that where federated models persist, there should be an emphasis on practices associated with the terms of collaborative governance or collective leadership (Sport Australia, 2015).

In 2016, a further paper on governance reform was released. Perhaps in response to negative feedback regarding Sport Australia's strong preference for the unitary model in the *Mandatory Principles*, this report emphasised and encouraged a "unified approach" (i.e., collaborative governance or collective leadership) (Sport Australia, 2016). There was much less emphasis on organisational governance with more focus on systemic governance and the relationships between state and national governing bodies as well as between the states themselves. In another shift, this paper highlighted financial considerations related to good governance. While previous governance papers had highlighted the benefits of good governance for the good of the sport, this paper specifically acknowledged the financial reasons for good governance (Sport Australia, 2016). These included benefits to the organisation (e.g., better cost efficiencies when systems use shared structures) but also the need to be accountable for public funding. Sport Australia specifically mentioned the obligations for good governance associated with $AUD 120 million of taxpayer money. In 2018, the focus on systemic governance issues (e.g., voting structures and voting rights) and the federated/unitary model debate continued to be a focal element within a discussion paper released by Sport Australia (Sport Australia, 2018b).

While the predominant policy influence into sport governance occurs at the national level, state and local government sport policy can also influence governance. Given the number of states and the numerous local councils, a full review of all policies and associated influence is well beyond the scope of this chapter. Unlike the federal level – where there is a separate statutory agency with primary responsibilities for sport – sport policy falls directly within a government office or department at these more localised levels. Primarily this leads to funding being the primary carrot and stick used by state governments, whereas local governments with smaller budgets are more likely to use access to facilities to influence sport clubs. For example, the state of Victoria has pledged to no longer fund state sport organisations without a minimum of 40% female board members by 1 July 2019 (Sport and Recreation Victoria, 2015). As a final example, the City of Moreland instituted a policy requiring clubs wanting access to council facilities to have women's teams and women on the board of the organisation (Moreland City Council, 2016).

Discussion

Ultimately, it is worth noting a few trends regarding the intersection of government policy and sport governance in Canada, New Zealand and Australia. The first is that, in all cases, governments have taken an increasing interest in steering the sport sector as a whole. Gone are the days in which federal/national sport agencies are simply mandated to support and facilitate the activities of the sector. In addition, they now endeavour to lead their respective networks as a means of generating measurable policy outcomes. A crucial element of this sectoral leadership is the coordination of the numerous sport organisations that cut across public, private and non-profit sectors. Invariably, the fragmented architecture of sport has translated into persistent governmental efforts to integrate organisations, their goals, activities and modes of operations. While in Canada, this aim is explicitly termed "integration" and framed in relation to sectoral coordination, the same ideals resonate with the "whole-of-sport" policy paradigms in New Zealand and Australia.

One way in which this kind of sectoral steering can be achieved is through the advancement of shared principles and values. This explains the periodic use of government-led task forces, inquiries, reviews and the like seeking to create a sense of shared vision among diverse organisations. Government agencies have all deployed "soft" tools, such as discussion papers, or the commissioning of various consultant reports as a means of informing national strategies, plans and "roadmaps". The aim of having shared principles also explains the establishment of federal/national level initiatives (e.g., coach education programmes) that can normatively shape NSO development by underlining the importance of national leadership and best practice.

A second, closely related trend is that government agencies in all three countries are becoming increasingly concerned with the internal governance practices of the various sports. This is partly in recognition of the fact that their own effectiveness depends on well-functioning partner sport organisations. To this end, both central and provincial/state agencies continue to facilitate the development of effective governing boards through a myriad of programmes, training and consultancy services (see, for example, Hill, Kerr & Kobayashi, 2016). At the same time, an increasing emphasis on accountability has translated into more conditions placed on NSOs to receive funding. Sport Canada is probably the first documented case to use funding as a lever to induce managerial reforms within these organisations (Macintosh & Whitson, 1990). However, since then, investment funding has become an explicit policy driver in the three countries, with monies allocated to NSOs based on their perceived *capability* to achieve the broad goals of participation and excellence (cf., Sam, 2015; Sotiriadou, Gowthorp & de Bosscher, 2013).

Importantly from a governance perspective, an NSO's capability presumes control and coordination of the activities of sub-national level networks. Thus, underpinning governmental forays into the internal governance structures is the belief that NSOs ought to have coherent lines of accountability across all levels: National, state/provincial, regional and local/municipal. In governance terms, what is being advanced is a more hierarchical relationship between those levels as well as between the state and the NSOs. Yet, while national strategic planning exercises and whole-of-sport delivery models are clearly aimed at developing a hierarchy of goals and priorities among partners in these networks, they stop short of legislating new patterns of authority. The frustration with this kind of volunteristic response seems most evident in the Australian context in which Sport Australia has endorsed the benefits of a unitary model of sport governance as an alternative to the federated system.

This marks a significant trend in that government agencies have become increasingly bold in influencing the governance structures of individual organisations. Indeed, the trend is more pronounced in Australia and New Zealand than in Canada, perhaps due to the arm's length nature of Sport Australia and Sport NZ compared with Sport Canada's hierarchical location within a government ministry. In New Zealand, for example, Sport NZ has increasingly used market competition to effectively build its demands into the investment contracts NSOs are compelled to sign. Through these contracts, it has occasionally requested NSOs change the composition of their boards as a condition for funding and, in some instances, it has sought to have a say on the individual board appointments. Given Sport Australia's explicit mandatory list of governance principles, it is perhaps safe to say that this agency is likely to be the most assertive in terms of coercing governance reforms within NSOs. Taken together, the trend towards bolder government influence speaks to the observation that, irrespective of the emergence of partnerships and networks, these modes of governance continue to operate in the "shadow of hierarchies" (Héritier & Lehmkuhl, 2008).

A number of issues are apparent within these governance prescriptions. By tying access to funding to governance practices, Sport Australia and other Australian governmental organisations are seeking to influence how NSOs are governed. While earlier efforts focused on improving sport governance acknowledged differences between sports and their different governance practices, recent reports suggest an isomorphic vision for sport governance as well as a willingness to use resources to advance other government priorities. While government priorities have featured prominently for the past two decades, the view that organisations should be compelled towards a common unitary model suggests a growing preference for hierarchies over networks.

Perhaps the most pressing challenge for government agencies seeking to alter the governance structures lies with convincing provincial/state, regional and local affiliated partners that a unitary model will be any more effective than the federated model that currently exists. Governmental attempts to influence organisational governance does, in some ways, violate the principle of autonomy in the sport sector. Sport has traditionally argued it must be absent of political interference and governments should not be involved in how sport organisations are managed and governed (Geeraert, Alm & Groll, 2014). This belief is, in many ways, codified into the sport system as international federations will suspend national sport organisations when they determine government interference has occurred. The autonomous nature of sport organisations is also codified in their respective constitutions, where accountability is to members and their collective aims. To a large extent then, contemporary policies, programmes and funding regimes can be seen as means to render autonomous organisations more governable for the state. One issue of course, is that, despite the perceived superiority of a unitary model, it would be difficult for NSOs to sustain such a structure without some form of democratic legitimacy behind it. Indeed, if an NSO is to be only held accountable by the government agency (and not by provincial, regional or local interests), why have an NSO at all?

In addition to the "should" (i.e., autonomy of sport) and the "how" (i.e., change process), it is worth considering what elements of organisational governance have been and should be in the remit of government policy. Organisational governance involves structures (councils, boards, committees, term limits, etc.), composition (recruitment, diversity, tenure), dynamics, transparency, accountability and other considerations. Within each of these considerations, there are important questions but, overall, policy-makers should ask: What areas of organisational governance should we be concerned with?

At the forefront of these debates are Sport Australia's most recent governance papers focusing on the relationships between sport organisations (e.g., state and national bodies) and discussing federated and unitary models, voting rights and structures or shared management practices. This is in contrast to the agency's earlier focus on the board of directors. In many ways, this shift in focus mirrors the early trend in sport management governance research to topics related to the board (Doherty, Patterson & Van Bussel, 2004; Hoye & Cuskelly, 2003; Shilbury, 2001).

More recently, there has been a shift towards systemic perspectives in sport governance research (Dowling, Leopkey & Smith, 2018; Parent, Rouillard & Naraine, 2017; Shilbury, O'Boyle & Ferkins, 2016).

Furthermore, there may be concern that the government's increased interest in sport can result in government funding being tied to the policy goals of the government rather than the mission of a sport organisation. This new public management sees the government using sport to achieve its own policy goals. For example, the goal of Sport Australia's *Sport 2030* plan to build a more physically active Australia (including more social participation in sport) is laudable but does not necessarily fit with the traditional goals of sport bodies, which seek to increase the number of registered sport participants. The nuanced difference between physical activity and sport participation is significant enough to represent potentially different policy goals. Indeed, government aspirations for sport to achieve health outcomes frequently appear elsewhere, generating mixed responses from the organisations asked to deliver on these outcomes (e.g., Fahlén, Eliasson & Wickman, 2015; Stenling, 2014). Nevertheless, it is notable that in the last decade both Canada and New Zealand's respective central agencies have eschewed health promotion objectives, instead maintaining sport as their core business. One reason for this may simply be the governance challenges that arise from the need to coordinate/steer an even wider range of network partners across health, education and social welfare sectors (Sam, 2011).

In summary, the intersection between government policy and sport governance in Canada, New Zealand and Australia presents substantive tensions and challenges for sport organisations. While the increased attention by government and government agencies has resulted in resources designed to assist sport organisations with their governance, this attention also includes potential threats to sport. These threats include: 1) A decreased autonomy as funding becomes tied to governance practices, 2) an increased expectation on the part of state and provincial bodies to endorse a unitary model, and 3) a growing danger of mission creep or over-commitment as governments seek to steer sport organisations towards their own goals and agenda.

Future research

The general themes in the relationships between policy and governance in these three case countries highlight some potential future issues and areas worthy of research. Firstly, Sport Canada, Sport Australia and Sport New Zealand all advance policies and programmes aimed at coordinating and steering the broad network of organisations under their purview. Inasmuch as these policies aim for integration across the various sports' networks (state/provincial, regional and local), these efforts will undoubtedly have implications for organisational governance. While this chapter has described some high-level characteristics of each of the three cases, this is not a substitute for further empirical examination of the topic. Thus, close investigation of the relationship between policy and governance should continue to address the following research questions:

- How does policy impact the governance of sport organisations? What governance modes (hierarchies, markets or networks) are advanced through policy and how do these "travel" into the governance practices of national and sub-national sport organisations? From an organisational theory perspective, for example, how do sport organisations respond to, or transmit, mimetic, normative and coercive pressures regarding governance?
- Why do government agencies prescribe particular governance structures/practices over others? Indeed, what evidence is there for the efficacy of policy-suggested/mandated

reform? What is the effectiveness of government support resources (e.g., sample documents, evaluation templates, etc.) in helping governance?

The preceding questions help to establish a baseline understanding of the interplay between policy and governance in sport. Yet, as alluded to above, there are other research opportunities which may have broader impact into understanding the sport sector. These lines of questioning result from the increased interest in sport displayed by government and respective sport agencies. With this in mind, the following pertinent questions are posed:

- What are the intersections between the principle of autonomy of sport and government policy? How does increased codification and the introduction of mandatory practices affect the autonomy of sport organisations? In what instances and under what conditions might it be justified for government agencies to coerce governance reforms (e.g., around issues of diversity, gender quotas, etc.)?
- How responsive are NSOs to non-governmental meta-governance organisations (in Canada) versus the contractual funding conditions more heavily relied upon elsewhere (e.g., Australia and New Zealand)?

Conclusion

Government policy and governance are intertwined in the Canadian, Australian and New Zealand sport systems. The influence (or deployment) of particular governance structures such as hierarchies, markets and networks, holds implications for the overall structure of the sport sector and its accompanying relationships. Likewise, the mix of policy programmes, reports and funding regimes invariably influences the internal governance structures of organisations. Indeed, government policies have, in recent years, become more prescriptive regarding how sport organisations should govern themselves. The fact that sport policies serve as a tool for the government to advance a policy agenda continues to matter, not least, because this instrumental view of partnerships accords legitimacy to further governance reforms. In considering the future of sport governance, it is therefore critical to understand and account for the role and influence of government policy.

Notes

1 Māori are the indigenous people of New Zealand and constitute roughly 15% of the New Zealand population. Te Rōpū Manaaki is reflective of a broader *Kaupapa Māori* movement, an approach for action that expresses cultural aspirations, values and principles.
2 In 2018, the Australian Sport Commission was rebranded to Sport Australia. For the sake of simplicity, the organisation is referred to as Sport Australia in this chapter.

References

Bergsgard, N. A., Houlihan, B., Mangset, P., Nodland, S. I., & Rommetvedt, H. (2007). *Sport policy: A comparative analysis of stability and change*. Oxford: Butterworth-Heinemann.
Bevir, M. (2011). *The SAGE handbook of governance*. London: Sage.
Boston, J., Martin, J., Pallot, J., & Walsh, P. (1996). *Public management: The New Zealand model*. Auckland, NZ: Oxford University Press.
Doherty, A., Patterson, M., & Van Bussel, M. (2004). What do we expect? An examination of perceived committee norms in non-profit sport organisations. *Sport Management Review*, 7, 109–132.

Dowling, M., Leopkey, B., & Smith, L. (2018). Governance in sport: A scoping review. *Journal of Sport Management, 32,* 438–451.

Dowling, M., & Washington, M. (2018). The governing of governance: Metagovernance and the creation of new organizational forms within Canadian sport. *Managing Sport and Leisure, 22,* 458–471.

Fahlén, J., Eliasson, I., & Wickman, K. (2015). Resisting self-regulation: An analysis of sport policy programme making and implementation in Sweden. *International Journal of Sport Policy and Politics,* 7, 391–406.

Geeraert, A., Alm, J., & Groll, M. (2014). Good governance in international sport organizations: An analysis of the 35 Olympic sport governing bodies. *International Journal of Sport Policy and Politics, 6,* 281–306.

Grix, J., & Phillpots, L. (2011). Revisiting the 'governance narrative': 'Asymmetrical network governance' and the deviant case of the sports policy sector. *Public Policy and Administration, 26,* 3–19.

Havaris, E. P., & Danylchuk, K. E. (2007). An assessment of sport Canada's sport funding and accountabiltiy framework 1995–2004. *European Sport Management Quarterly, 7,* 31–53.

Héritier, A., & Lehmkuhl, D. (2008). The shadow of hierarchy and new modes of governance. *Journal of public Policy, 28,* 1–17.

High Performance Sport New Zealand. (2013). Targeted investment proves winning formula. Retrieved 12 August 2014, from http://www.hpsnz.org.nz/news-events/targeted-investment-proves-winning-formula

Hill, S., Kerr, R., & Kobayashi, K. (2016). Questioning the application of Policy Governance for small-scale sports clubs in New Zealand. *Managing Sport and Leisure, 21,* 203–217.

Hoye, R., & Cuskelly, G. (2003). Board power and performance within voluntary sport organisations. *European Sport Management Quarterly, 3,* 103–119.

Jessop, B. (2011). Metagovernance. In M. Bevir (Ed.), *Sage handbook of governance* (pp. 106–123). London: Sage.

Keat, R., & Sam, M. (2013). Regional implementation of New Zealand sport policy: New instrument, new challenges. *International Journal of Sport Policy and Politics, 5,* 39–54.

Levi-Faur, D. (2012). *The Oxford handbook of governance.* Oxford: Oxford University Press.

Macintosh, D., & Whitson, D. (1990). *The game planners: Transforming Canada's sport system.* Montreal & Kingston: McGill-Queen's University Press.

Moreland City Council. (2016). *Allocation and use of sporting facilities, grounds and pavilions policy.* Moreland: Moreland City Council.

Parent, M. M., Rouillard, C., & Naraine, M. L. (2017). Network governance of a multi-level, multi-sectoral sport event: Differences in coordinating ties and actors. *Sport Management Review, 20,* 497–509.

Pollitt, C., & Bouckaert, G. (2004). *Public management reform: A comparative analysis.* New York: Oxford University Press.

Rhodes, R. A. (1997). *Understanding governance: Policy networks, governance, reflexivity and accountability.* Buckingham, UK: Open University Press.

Sam, M. P. (2009). The public management of sport: Wicked problems, challenges and dilemmas. *Public Management Review, 11,* 499–513.

Sam, M. P. (2011). Building legitimacy at Sport Canada: Pitfalls of public value creation? *International Review of Administrative Sciences, 77,* 757–778.

Sam, M. P. (2012). Targeted investments in elite sport funding: Wiser, more innovative and strategic? *Managing Leisure, 17,* 206–219.

Sam, M. P. (2015). 'Big brother and caring sister': Performance management and the athlete's entourage. In S. S. Andersen, B. Houlihan, & L. T. Ronglan (Eds.), *Managing elite sport systems: Reseach and practice* (pp. 16–30). London: Routledge.

Sam, M. P. (2017). Sport development. In R. Hoye & M. M. Parent (Eds.), *Sage handbook of sport management* (pp. 227–240). London: Sage.

Sam, M. P., Batty, R., & Dean, R. G. K. (2005). A transaction cost approach to sport sponsorship. *Sport Management Review, 8,* 1–17.

Sam, M. P., & Macris, L. I. (2014). Performance regimes in sport policy: Exploring consequences, vulnerabilities and politics. *International Journal of Sport Policy and Politics, 6,* 513–532.

Sam, M. P., & Ronglan, L. T. (2016). Building sport policy's legitimacy in Norway and New Zealand. *International Review for the Sociology of Sport, 53,* 550–571.

Shilbury, D. (2001). Examining board member roles, functions and influence: A study of Victorian sporting organizations. *International Journal of Sport Management, 2,* 253–281.

Shilbury, D., O'Boyle, I., & Ferkins, L. (2016). Towards a research agenda in collaborative sport governance. *Sport Management Review, 19,* 479–491.

Sotiriadou, P., Gowthorp, L., & de Bosscher, V. (2013). Elite sport culture and policy interrelationships: The case of Sprint Canoe in Australia. *International Journal of Sport Policy and Politics*, *33*, 598–617.

Sport and Recreation Victoria. (2015). Inquiry into women and girls in sport and active recreation: A five year game plan for Victoria.

Sport Australia. (2012a). *Australia's winning edge*. Canberra: Author.

Sport Australia. (2012b). *Sports governance principles*. Canberra: Author.

Sport Australia. (2015). *Mandatory sports governance principles*. Canberra: Author.

Sport Australia. (2016). *Governance reform in sport*. Canberra: Author.

Sport Australia. (2018a). *Sport 2030*. Canberra: Author.

Sport Australia. (2018b). *Governance reform in sport: Discussion paper*. Canberra: Author.

Sport Canada. (2012). *Canadian sport policy 2012*. Ottawa: Sport Canada.

Sport Canada. (2018). Application guidelines - National Sport Organization. Retrieved 1 December 2018, from https://www.canada.ca/en/canadian-heritage/services/funding/sport-support/national-organization/application-guidelines.html

Sport New Zealand. (2012). *Strategic plan 2012–2015*. Wellington: Author.

Sport New Zealand. (2013a). *Sport NZ annual report*. Wellington: Author.

Sport New Zealand. (2013b). *Statement of intent 2013–2016*. Wellington: Author.

Sport New Zealand. (2017). *Governance mark for sport and recreation launched*. Retrieved 1 December 2018, from https://sportnz.org.nz/managing-sport/search-for-a-resource/news/governance-mark-for-sport-and-recreation-launched

Stenling, C. (2014). The emergence of a new logic? The theorizing of a new practice in the highly institutionalized context of Swedish voluntary sport. *Sport Management Review*, *17*, 507–519.

Te Rōpū Manaaki. (2005). *The strategic plan of Te Rōpū Manaaki: Sport and Recreation New Zealand ihi Aotearoa 2006–2009*. Wellington: Sport and Recreation New Zealand.

Torfing, J. (2012). Governance networks. In D. Levi-Faur (Ed.), *Oxford handbook of governance* (pp. 99–112). Oxford: Oxford University Press.

Winand, M., & Anagnostopoulos, C. (2019). *Research handbook on sport governance*. Cheltenham, UK: Edward Elgar.

Whitson, D., & Macintosh, D. (1989). Rational planning vs. regional interests: The professionalization of Canadian amateur sport. *Canadian Public Policy*, *15*, 436–449.

Williamson, O. E. (1985). *The economic institutions of capitalism*. New York: Free Press.

6

Government policy and principles of good governance in Latin America

Gonzalo A. Bravo and Luiz Haas

Introduction

The governance of sport across Latin America has been traditionally led and influenced by local governments' efforts as well as international non-governmental organisations. Examples of these organisations include the International Olympic Committee (IOC), the Fédération Internationale de Football Association (FIFA) and a number of other regional sport governing bodies affiliated with FIFA and the IOC that operate in the region. Some of these regional organisations are the South American Football Confederation (CONMEBOL), the Confederation of North, Central American and Caribbean Association Football (CONCACAF), the Pan American Sport Organisation (PASO), the Caribbean Association of National Olympic Committees (CANOC), the Central American and Caribbean Sport Organisations (CACSO) and the South American Sports Organisation (ODESUR), to name a few. Moreover, efforts to facilitate intergovernmental dialogue across nations in matters related to sport also led to the creation of organisations such as the Ibero-American Sports Council (CID) and the Confederation of South American Sports (CONSUDE). In the Caribbean, the Caribbean Community (CARICOM), a subregional association whose main focus is economic development, has also served as a platform to discuss issues related to sport among countries in the Caribbean (Bravo & Parrish, 2019).

Understanding the role of sport in the region is critical to understanding how sport is governed and why governments become deeply involved in it. Arguably, sport in Latin America has emerged as a powerful social phenomenon that has gone beyond pure entertainment and leisure to play a central role in shaping national identities (Alabarces, 2009). For many, the societal role of sport in Latin America seems unquestionable to the extent that across the region several nations have given sport a place in their respective constitutions, and some have even gone one step further by elevating sport to a constitutional rank (Bermejo Vera, Gamero Casado & Palomar Olmedo, 2003; Fernández, 2014). Table 6.1 provides an overview of these constitutional arrangements. Government attention to sport in Latin America is also illustrated by the fact that countries have created laws to govern, promote and fund sport initiatives.

In a region of more than 600 million people, few will argue against sport. Today, many believe that sport can bring numerous benefits, particularly in terms of providing exposure and international visibility (Latinobarómetro, 2016). Despite the popularity and positive perceptions of sport

Gonzalo A. Bravo and Luiz Haas

Table 6.1 Constitutional value of sport in Latina America

	Recognises the right of sport for its citizens
Brasil	Constitution of Brazil 1988
Colombia	Political Constitution of Colombia of 1991
Cuba	Constitution of Cuba of 2002
Ecuador	Political Constitution of the Republic of Ecuador of 2008
Nicaragua	Political Constitution of Nicaragua of 1986
Venezuela	Constitution of the Bolivarian Republic of Venezuela of 1999
	Recognises the importance of promoting sports
Guatemala	Political Constitution of the Republic of Guatemala of 2012
Honduras	Constitution of the Republic of Honduras of 1982
Mexico	Political Constitution of Mexico of 1917, Article 73
Panama	Political Constitution of the Republic of Panama of 1972
Paraguay	Constitution of the Republic of Paraguay of 1992
Perú	Political Constitution of Peru of 1993

Sources: Bermejo Vera, Gamero Casado and Palomar Olmedo (2003) and Fernández (2014).

in the region, many Latin American countries also face challenges. Some of these challenges include the lack of – or inadequate – policies towards the promotion of sport and physical activity with minimal evidence that existing policies and efforts might curb the high rates of sedentarism that currently affect the population in most countries of the region (Jaitman & Scartascini, 2017). In addition, the lack of safety at sporting events, particularly in football, continues to be an unresolved issue where football is the most popular sport. Efforts to eradicate this problem made by club officials, law enforcement and even legislatures have had minimal to no effect (Spaaij, 2005; Szlifman, 2014). Another major challenge has been the poor selection and lax hiring practices of unprepared human resources who work in the management of sport (Zuleta, 2017). In the absence of policies and accountability, these individuals promote clientelism, patronage and other forms of opportunistic behaviours that, in many instances, lead to mismanagement, fraud and corruption inside sport organisations (Cardenas, 2015; Rachman, 2007).

This chapter discusses trends and challenges of the governance of sport in Latin America with a focus on the Brazilian sport system. This chapter is organised in four sections. First, a brief description of Henry and Lee's (2004) sport governance analytical framework is provided. Then, in the following three sections, the focus shifts to how three approaches of governance – systemic, governmental and political – occur and have shaped the course of many sport organisations that are part of the Brazilian sport system. Finally, we offer a brief discussion on avenues for future research on the governance of sport organisations in Latin America.

Analytical framework

Although state and international non-governmental sport organisations have been the primary stakeholders that have shaped the governance of sport in most countries, the reality is that governance of sport is a much more complex process. Strictly speaking, governments – or the state – do not directly govern sports, but, instead, they influence or facilitate the process of governance. The need to establish and apply consistent rules in each sport has granted national sport federations (NSFs) and International Federations (IFs), the power and authority to rule each sport in a monopolistic manner (Geeraert, 2016). Although NSFs are voluntary non-profit private organisations that claim autonomy from the state, in reality these governing bodies need state support. This results in a complex relationship, whereby NSFs exert control over their own internal affairs, and governments influence the broader environment in which sport operates. Government influence is geared towards the sustainability, protection and growth of sport, whether by passing laws that protect sport fans or by providing tax exemptions for businesses that invest in sport programs. Despite government involvement and influence in the governance of sport, many stakeholders also influence this process. Therefore, the governance of sport is no longer hierarchical, but instead consists of a complex network of stakeholders who act and respond to different agendas with little or no coordination among them. This network and interaction occur at three levels and involves multiple stakeholders.

Henry and Lee (2004) referred to the three approaches of governance as *systemic, organisational* and *political*. According to these authors, *systemic governance* helps us to understand the interaction that occurs between and within multiple stakeholders who have a stake in the business of sport. This approach to governance "focuses on the relationship *between* organizations rather than directly over them" (Dowling, Leopkey & Smith, 2018, p. 6) and involves "the competition, cooperation and mutual adjustments between organizations in such systems" (Henry & Lee, 2004, p. 26). While the systemic governance of sport can be observed in a number of cases and contexts across the region, this approach is evident because of the transnational movement of players in some professional leagues in Latin America.

Carter (2016) illustrates the idea of systemic governance when discussing the complex dynamics of stakeholders involved with the movement of players from Latin American countries where multiple types of organisations (e.g., public agencies, voluntary and commercial organisations) influence the governance of players' migration. For baseball players aiming to sign for a Major League Baseball (MLB) team in the United States, their fate is not only decided when they receive an offer from a team; they also need to comply with MLB policies, agreements with their own domestic governing body and the migration policies imposed by the US Department of State. Interestingly, in most cases related to the transnational movement of players, the government agency related to sport (e.g., Sport Ministry or Secretary of Sport) has minimal say in this endeavour. Instead, the power and authority lie with other governmental bureaucracies, such as the Office of Labour or the Ministry of Foreign Affairs.

A second approach of governance is *organisational* or *corporate* governance, also referred to as "good governance" (Henry & Lee, 2004). This type of governance focuses on the rules, practices and processes that are used to govern each sport organisation. For national football federations in South America, each governing body follows not only their own specific rules and procedures but also CONMEBOL or FIFA rules and procedures that come from outside their territorial jurisdiction. Organisational governance is not just concerned with following the rules in terms of efficiency, but also following the spirit of the law that comes from normative principles that contribute to improving transparency and accountability. The 2015 FIFA scandal and particularly the involvement of several football associations from South and Central America serve to illustrate how the absence of normative principles, lack of accountability and a long history and culture of protectionism and impunity led to bypassing policies and rules. In turn, this allowed football leaders to improperly benefit through corruption and bribery. Certainly, this example does not demonstrate good governance, but it does show how the absence of good organisational governance principles and practices can have a devastating effect on the world of sport.

The third approach of governance is *political governance*. This refers to the way governments, the state and NSFs influence the governance of sport. According to Dowling, Leopkey and Smith (2018), this form of governance involves "achieving wider social and political objectives through strategic action involving direct and indirect mechanisms and interventions and control" (p. 7). Soria and Maldonado (2016) discuss political governance in light of professional football and the efforts made by the Chilean authorities to transform the fate of the football industry in that country. For decades, football in Chile suffered from poor financial practices, minimal investment in infrastructure, lack of safety in the stadiums and poor leadership from league officials. While these and other problems have not been new to the leaders of the Chilean Football Association, Soria and Maldonado (2016) contend that efforts to curb these problems have emerged not from league officials or club presidents but, instead, from people outside the football industry – specifically, from political appointees of different administrations who not only have witnessed the precarious conditions under which football clubs operated in Chile, but were also discontented with the performance of Chilean teams in the domestic as well as international levels. As a result, different laws have been approved to revitalise the football industry in Chile, including laws that transform clubs from non-profit associations to publicly listed companies, penalise vandalism in stadiums and rule labour relationships for professional footballers. While the transformation of football in Chile is still a work in progress, this case illustrates how the state governs matters related to sport, and, particularly, it shows the influence governments exert in the governance of Latin American football (Bravo, Parrish & López de D'Amico, 2016). The next section discusses how systemic, organisational and political governance have been manifested across different levels of the sport system in Brazil.

Systemic sport governance in Brazil

Sport has traditionally received significant attention in Brazilian society. Since 1988, the Brazilian constitution has granted the right to sport for every Brazilian citizen. According to article 217 of the constitution, it is the duty of the state to foster and fund the practice of sport among Brazilian people (Brasil, 1988). Similar to other countries in Latin America, sport in Brazil is highly influenced by the state. From 1995 to 2018, the Ministry of Sport represented the highest public cabinet in matters related to sport. Until recently, the Ministry's actions and coverage were national in scope, and from 2000 to 2016 the importance of this ministry reached an all-time high. This timeframe is when the country became the epicentre of a number of sport mega-events.[1] Likewise, during this time, the country experienced an array of economic, political and social problems. By 2016, in the aftermath of the 2016 Rio Olympics, Brazil moved to the opposite end of the spectrum from a prosperous and booming economy in the early 2000s to a country that experienced serious economic recession and political turmoil. In 2010, all seemed to suggest that Brazil was moving at a fast pace to become a developed nation. However, several factors in 2014 changed the fate of the country. Economic recession, corporate and political corruption including the infamous *Lava Jato*[2] case; the Zika epidemic of 2016; the rise of gangs and criminal activity due to drug trafficking; and the mass riots inside the penitentiary system (Ribeiro & Hartley, 2018; Zorovich, 2015) all contributed to change the course of politics in Brazil. Arguably, these events also affected the privileged role sport had played until then. The timing of these events also coincided with the end of the golden age of large sport mega-events and the allocation of public money to finance the operations and infrastructure of these mega ventures. In January of 2019, the new Brazilian administration repositioned the role of sport. The election of Jair Bolsonaro as President of Brazil redefined the administration of the country by downsizing the role of the federal government. One of these outcomes resulted in "lowering" the rank sport has inside the Brazilian administration to become a special secretariat linked to the Ministry of Citizenship (Brasil, 2019). The extent to which this change will affect both the delivery of sport programming and the governance of sport is too early to predict. However, one thing is known: Sport in Brazil still maintains a constitutional right.

The Brazilian sport system is comprised of a number of public, private and voluntary non-profit stakeholders that interact throughout a complex network and exert different degrees of power in the governance of sport. Some of these stakeholders and legal requirements include the federal government, the Constitution of Brazil, the Brazilian Olympic Committee, the Brazilian Paralympic Committee and the Brazilian Football Confederation, to list the most influential. Following is a description of the role played by some of these stakeholders and the influence they exert in shaping the governance of sport within the system.

The Constitution of 1988

Although the Constitution of Brazil mandates that the allocation of public resources to sport should prioritise the support of educational sport programs over recreational and high-performance sport, the reality is that high-performance sport has been historically prioritised by the Brazilian State (Bueno, 2008). This means programs that contribute to support the development of Olympic medallists or world-class champions have received more funding than programs that aim to develop sport in the school system (Almeida, Coakley, Marchi Júnior & Starepravo, 2012). It is important to remember that high-performance sport in Brazil refers mostly to sport and programs that are not professional. Therefore, the football industry, including professional teams, are not technically considered part of this category. As a result, football is treated apart from this system. However, this does not prevent football from receiving public funding. The Brazilian Football Confederation (CBF, in Portuguese), which rules football at the national level, the state football federations and major football clubs have all received some form of subsidisation and help from the federal government. In 2015, the federal government opened a national secretariat to deal exclusively with matters related to football (Brasil, 2015). Also, the government has allowed debt refinancing for football clubs that have gone into bankruptcy.

The National Lottery

Since 2002, systemic governance in Brazilian sport has been highly influenced by the National Lottery. Law N° 10264/2001, which mandates the distribution of these lottery resources among sport organisations (Brasil, 2001), has not only provided a significant amount of resources to sport organisations but also has changed the power within the Brazilian sport system by granting the Brazilian Olympic Committee (COB, in Portuguese) and the Brazilian Paralympic Committee (CPB, in Portuguese) the distribution of 85% and 15% of these lottery resources. Therefore, with the power to distribute funds, COB and CPB establish goals for each NSF.[3] For many NSFs, lottery resources, via COB or CPB, represent the only source of funding in their budgets.

The Brazilian Clubs Committee

In 2014 and 2018, changes in legislation (Brasil, 2011; Brasil, 2018) have resulted in umbrella sport organisations, such as the Brazilian Clubs Committee (CBC in Portuguese), the Brazilian Confederation of School Sports and the Brazilian Confederation of University Sports, being granted the right to receive direct funding from the National Lottery. This also resulted in creating a new shift in the balance of power within the Brazilian sport system. Of these three organisations, undoubtedly the most powerful is the CBC, which acts as an umbrella organisation that represents the interests of thousands of sport clubs that exist all over the country. With the formal entry into the sport system, the CBC began to distribute public money directly to the clubs. Prior to 2014, resources transferred to the NSFs hardly reached these clubs.

Athletes, non-governmental organisations and advocacy groups

Pressure from external stakeholders in sport organisations to increase transparency and account-ability are now more intense than ever. This pressure is no longer hierarchical (top-down). Instead, it occurs in the form of an elliptical network where stakeholders that are not formally part of the system also exert influence over sport organisations (Henry & Lee, 2004; Hoye & Cuskelly, 2007). Over the last decade, the role and the voice of athletes has grown significantly in power. Athletes have grown in power to influence sport policies, especially on questions related to the governance of sport. Just as has occurred in the international context, athletes in Brazil have begun to play a greater role on issues related to the development of sport policies (Kihl, Kikulis & Thibault, 2007; Thibault, Kihl & Babiak, 2010).

In Brazil, the influence of athletes on the sport system takes place in an organised manner through the NGO *Atletas pelo Brasil* (Athletes for Brazil), a nonprofit organisation founded in 2006. This organisation, formed by current and former athletes and which works for the advancement of sport, has called for changes in the current sport legislation to pressure NSFs to meet tougher demands on issues related to transparency, democracy and accountability in order to obtain public funding.

Two other initiatives, the *Sport Governance Award* and the *Pact for Sport* have also influenced sport organisations to adopt better governance practices. Both of these initiatives were born outside of the formal sport system. The *Sport Governance Award* initiative, created in 2015 by the NGO *Sou do Esporte,* recognises good governance practices among NSFs. To do this, *Sou do Esporte* conducts an annual survey with all Brazilian NSFs to assess their degree of compliance with five dimensions of good governance (e.g., transparency, equity, accountability, institutional integrity and modernisation). The survey is drawn from the Sport Governance Observer project run by Play the Game (Geeraert, 2015). From 2015 to 2017, the Brazilian Rugby Confederation received first place in the *Sport Governance Award*. Meanwhile, in 2018, first place was awarded to the Brazilian Sailing Confederation. Other NSFs ranked among the top five included volleyball, tennis table, handball and athletics.

The initiative *Pact for Sport*, promoted by the NGOs *Atletas pelo Brasil*, Ethos Institute and LIDE Sport, promotes good governance between corporate sponsors and sport organisations (NSFs and clubs) by establishing the rules and mechanisms that operate in the agreements between sponsors and sport organisations. Before an agreement is either signed or renewed, a sport organisation is thoroughly evaluated by two independent organisations. The goal is to provide self-regulation tools to enhance best practices in governance, integrity and transparency (Pacto pelo Esporte, n.d.).

With the increase of commercial relationships between sport and corporate sponsors and the significant allocation of public resources, sport organisations have exposed some of the failures that have influenced the governance of sport (Geeraert, Alm & Groll, 2014). For some organisa-tions, these failures have created external pressures in search for better governance, which have forced sport leaders to perform better on issues related to transparency, democracy and inter-nal accountability. The next section examines how the different stakeholders have influenced changes in the *organisational governance* inside sport organisations in Brazil.

Organisational sport governance in Brazil

Hoye and Cuskelly (2007) identified six environmental influences that pressure nonprofit sport organisations to adopt good governance practices. These influences are the relationship between government and the nonprofit sector, the regulatory environment, globalisation trends, government sport policies, governance guidelines from national sport agencies, and influences from other stakeholder groups. In Brazil, it is possible to identify at least three environmental influences as plausible reasons that triggered the need to implement changes in the organisational governance of sport. These influences are (a) government sport policies implemented from the early 2000s to 2016; (b) governance guidelines; and (c) the response of stakeholder groups to issues inside the governance of Brazilian NSFs.

Government sport policies

From 2002 to 2016, government policies allowed the allocation of massive public funding to pay the expenses of the 2007 Rio Pan American Games, the 2013 Confederation Cup, the 2014 FIFA World Cup and the 2016 Rio Olympics and Paralympics Games. In the beginning, the awarding and hosting of these events received positive public perception. However, by 2013 the public had begun to express dislike with the direction of some of the country's policies, thus resulting in massive protests in the streets of major cities in Brazil. While the main reasons for these protests focused on people's discontent with corruption, police brutality and the abandonment of the government's responsibility to improve public services like health and transportation, these demonstrations also served as a platform to show people's discontent with the large-scale spending on sport mega-events (Saad-Filho, 2013). By the end of 2018, three administrations had spent close to 24 billion Brazilian reais, or approximately USD$ 7.4 billion, on sport (Universidade de Brasilia, n.d.). Although most of the money spent during this time went to pay expenses to build the sport infrastructure for the sport mega-events, the federal government also authorised increased spending to support athletes' preparation towards the same events.

With the aim of placing Brazil among the top 10 countries in the 2016 Rio Olympic Games, and among the top five in the Paralympics, the Sport Ministry launched the *Brazil Medals Plan* in 2012. This plan resulted in a huge allocation of public money towards the Brazilian Olympic Committee, Brazilian Paralympic Committee and other NSFs. All this funding was justified not only as a part of the Brazilian sport policies but also as a part of a larger and more ambitious plan aimed to raise Brazil's global visibility (Almeida, Marchi Júnior & Pike, 2014). Policies that allowed massive funding for sport not only served to improve the training conditions and performance of Brazilian athletes, helped build and modernise sport venues and developed large urban projects (Filho, Damiani & Fontana, 2018), they also served to raise awareness and questioning of the actual benefit some of these sport mega-events provided for Brazil (Zimbalist, 2017).

Sport public policies exert influence over the organisational governance of sport entities via laws that mandate sport organisations to follow procedures and/or comply with specific requirements to operate. Sport policies can also influence the internal governance of sport organisations in an indirect way. This happens when existing policies are insufficient to tackle a problem, or when the policy does not reach the expected outcome for what it was designed for, or when there is an absence of policies. In all cases, sport organisations and stakeholders can react to these deficiencies or absences of policies by adopting governance practices that contribute to curb some of these problems. Arguably, the accumulated experiences in Brazil throughout the last two decades, particularly those associated with the hosting of large sporting events, contributed to educating government bureaucrats and sport officials that the organisational governance of many sport entities was in need of attention. One of the organisations that went through major transformations in their corporate governance was the Brazilian Olympic Committee (COB).

In October of 2017, 14 months after the Rio 2016 Olympic Games ended, the Federal Police and the Federal Public Ministry unleashed the so called *"unfair play operation"*[4] which resulted in the arrest of COB President Carlos Nuzman. This incident triggered not only the immediate resignation of Nuzman, but also resulted in the suspension of the COB from the IOC. In order to reduce the pressure from multiple stakeholders and improve the image of COB, the new board embarked on a large reform of its statutes. This reform resulted in the adoption of a series of good governance principles that transformed the day-to-day operations of the COB, particularly on issues related to democracy, internal accountability and control (Comitê Olímpico do Brasil, 2014, 2017) (see Tables 6.2 and 6.3).

Governance guidelines

Another example where external influences induce the adoption of good governance practices is the governance guidelines that are developed by sport agencies. National sport agencies across the world have developed their own sets of guidelines dedicated to improve the governance of sports organisations (i.e., UK Sport, 2004; Australian Sports Commission, 2005; Sport and Recreation New Zealand, 2004). In 2018, the Sport Ministry of Brazil developed and published the first official document to assist Brazilian sport NSFs to improve their organisational governance. Despite this being a "guide for governance", the document focused almost exclusively on the compliance aspects of the Pele Law without addressing any other aspect beyond those that

Table 6.2 Organisational governance of the Brazilian Olympic Committee – Democratic process

Area	Until September 2017	After November 2017
• Composition of the General Assembly	• NGBs representatives (30 members) • Only one athlete representative (president of Athlete's Commission • Two lifetime members • Eight elected members with the presidency • One Brazilian IOC member	• NGBs representatives (35 members) • 11 athlete representatives (1/3 of NGBs representatives) • One Brazilian IOC member

• Composition of the Board	• Seven members: president, vice-president and five members appointed by the president	• Fifteen members with representatives of various stakeholders:
		  • One Brazilian IOC member
		  • COB president and vice-president
		  • Two members of the Athletes' Commission
		  • Eight representatives of the NGBs
		  • Two independent members.

• Eligibility of president and vice-president	• Barrier clauses (At least five years as a COB member and signatures of a minimum of ten members of the General Assembly to apply for presidential election)	• No barrier clauses: Any Brazilian citizen over 18 years of age with the signatures of three Assembly members can apply for presidency election • Integrity of candidates checked by the Ethics Committee

Source: Comitê Olimpico do Brasil (2014, 2017).

Table 6.3 Organisational governance Brazilian Olympic Committee – Internal accountability and control

Area	Until September 2017	After November 2017
• Internal Financial Committee	• Six members (three effective and three substitute) elected jointly with the presidency	• Six members (three effective and three substitute) elected separately from the presidency in an open election process and with the monitoring of the Ethics Committee.
• Ethics Committee	• No Ethics Committee	• Five members of Ethics Committee elected in an open election by the General Assembly. Obligatory presence of independent members. Responsible for checking the integrity of candidates for elected and executive positions. Checks the conformity of internal processes and identifies possible conflicts of interest.
• Board Management Advisory Committees	• No Management Advisory Committees	• The Board can convene an Advisory Management Board Committee to help in decision-making in management and administrative related issues. • Athletes, coaches, referees, sponsors and/or journalists who are not members of the General Assembly can be part of this group.
• General Director (CEO)	• The Secretary General was the CEO and was freely appointed by the president	• The president, with approval of the Board and Ethics Committee, appoints the CEO.
• Compliance Officer	• No compliance officer	• Professional appointed by the CEO who responds to the Ethics Committee.
• Revision of the Statutes	• No pre-established period for revision	• A revision of the statutes is carried out every two years to ensure permanent and continuous up-dating

Source: Comitê Olimpico do Brasil (2014, 2017).

are legally required. In Brazil, much of the conversation related to sport governance started after the cycle of sport mega-events ended in 2016. Major changes in sport organisations have led to the gradual increase in the adoption of good governance practices since then.

In 2017, a group of Brazilian researchers were invited to join the National Sport Governance Observer (NSGO) project. The purpose of this project was to "assist and inspire national sport federations to enhance the quality of their governance by measuring governance and building capacity" (Geeraert, 2018 p. 11). Results of the NSGO project allows researchers and practitioners to compare and discuss the strengths and weaknesses of good governance practices in national sport federations from around the world. Results from the NSGO report revealed that Brazilian NSFs achieved a mere 32% in the NSGO overall index score. Although this is considered a weak score, it puts Brazil in a similar level to many other European countries. Brazilian NSFs reached 40% in accountability, 36% in transparency, 33% in democratic processes and 20% in societal responsibility (Geeraert, 2018). In terms of transparency, despite the Brazilian NSFs having made all constitutional documents (statutes and agendas of general meetings) available, there was less transparency in the disclosure of internal documents, such as minutes of general meetings and board meetings, and other documents, such as the strategic planning or biographical information of current leaders. This suggests that board members are more concerned with complying with the law (i.e., publishing annual financial statements and statutes) than disclosing internal information regarding decision-making processes or the accountability of board members (Haas & Barros, 2018).

Similarly, results regarding internal accountability showed that some indicators received higher scores due to the obligations imposed by the law. In terms of democratic participation, Brazilian NSFs received higher scores regarding athletes' involvement but results revealed minimal participation of coaches, referees and volunteers (Haas & Barros, 2018). Finally, results of societal responsibility indicated that Brazilian NSFs are not devoting much attention to address issues such as sexual harassment, promoting social inclusion, anti-discrimination, gender equality and environmental sustainability (Haas & Barros, 2018).

Stakeholder groups

Political pressure exerted by athletes through the organisation *Atletas pelo Brasil* has also been a major influence contributing to change the sport legislation of Brazil as well as the way sport organisations are run. Athletes are key stakeholders of the sport organisations they represent. Even though athletes do not hold the power to control the destiny of the NSFs, they possess legitimacy and can create urgency that mobilises other stakeholders to change their environment (Agyemang, 2014; Ferkins & Shilbury, 2015; Mitchell, Agle & Wood, 1997).

The work and influence exerted by *Atletas pelo Brasil* influenced important changes in existing legislation and resulted in stricter rules for NSFs. While previous legislation (Pelé Law of 1998) required sport organisations minimal compliance with financial and other administrative rules, current laws[5] are much more stringent, particularly in order to receive public funding. Some of these requirements include establishing fixed term limits for board of directors; transparency in financial information; establishing an independent internal audit committee; guaranteed members' access to information related to the rendering of accounts; and guaranteed representation of athletes on the boards of directors, in technical meetings and participation in the election process of the NSF. The next section considers the role of the Brazilian state and how it has influenced the political governance of sport, particularly the governance of football.

Political sport governance in Brazil

As noted throughout this chapter, state involvement in Brazilian sport is best illustrated by the number of laws and decrees that have been enacted over the decades. The first sport legislation used by the federal government to control the sport system was Decree Law 3199 of 1941. Until that date, sport in Brazil was characterised by little government interference, and the organisation, structuring and functioning was run by entities organised in the civil society (Bueno, 2008; Pimentel, 2007). Perhaps the most significant legislation was article 217 of the Brazilian Constitution of 1988, which gives sport constitutional status. Although the constitution establishes that the state must promote the practice of sport at all levels, most legislation until today has been related to professional football. The social significance of football in Brazil is undisputable and goes beyond the commercial value of an industry to be best described as a national passion that is fully engrained into the fabric of the Brazilian society (Mezzadri, Maoski & Donha, 2016).

The first legislation related to football was passed in 1943 when the state officially recognised football as a professional activity. Since the late 1990s, the Brazilian state has enacted more than 60 laws related to football (Matias & Mascarenhas, 2017). Most of these laws have not focused on access to play but rather in establishing rules and norms to improve the business side of the sport. Of these, the most common theme has been club finances, particularly the creation of lotteries to subsidise clubs in debt. Other themes included creating norms to regulate club expenditures and accountability; adjustment of existing laws to accommodate FIFA requirements during the 2014 World Cup; regulating the relations of players and clubs and establishing rules regarding the social security rights of players; and approving laws regarding the infrastructure and safety of stadiums.

As previously mentioned, sport policies in Brazil have undergone several changes after the Rio 2016 Olympic Games. Moreover, with the changes that took place in the political scene after the 2018 presidential election, the Sport Ministry lost power and was turned into a special secretariat with three divisions: Division of high-performance sport; division of sport, education, leisure and social inclusion; and division of football and supporters. Furthermore, at the federal level there are two regulatory agencies: The Brazilian Doping Control Authority, responsible for doping control; and the Public Authority of Football Governance, responsible for overseeing, regulating and disciplining the fiscal responsibility program of Brazilian football.

Future directions on sport on governance in Latin America

Over the last decade, scholarly work on sport governance in Latin America has grown slowly despite many of these studies being almost unknown to the English-speaking academic world. Most of these studies have been published in Portuguese or Spanish, and a number of these are master theses or doctoral dissertations. The focus of many of these studies has been on the governance of football, sport policy and, more recently, on the impact of sport mega-events. Despite the surge of interest in sport governance, empirical and more rigorous research on the subject still remains a work in progress. This dearth of research not only gives ample room to study governance issues pertaining to any of the three types of governance described throughout this chapter, but also to explore many of the themes/topic areas described by Dowling et al. (2018). Based on what has been presented in this chapter, and more specifically in the case of NSFs in Brazil, one area that needs attention is the role the board plays in the governance of sport organisations – particularly the roles of president, athletes and other stakeholders like coaches and referees.

As noted in the previous sections, the Brazilian State as well as sport organisations have approved changes to their current sport policies in an attempt to bring accountability and transparency to the governance of those organisations. One question that remains unanswered is the impact that legislation has had on the structure of NSFs, specifically regarding the governing boards. While many boards have become more inclusive by incorporating other stakeholders to its organisational apex, it seems that most of these NSFs still function as they did in the past. For many NSFs, the presence and voice of the President remains the most influential as many NSFs still remain Presidential-dependent. For those NSFs that have separated the powers into political (the assembly) and executive (the CEO), it is important to examine the effectiveness of this change.

In Brazil, athletes have gained a unique status inside the governance of many NSFs. However, the role and contribution that athletes make in the governance of these organisations is unknown. The presence of athletes brings a seal of legitimacy to the NSF. Athletes have developed an empirical knowledge of the problems that affect their organisations and bring their own unique understanding of why things are the way they are. But despite their inclusion, it is not clear how active or involved athletes are once they become part of the board, or what understanding they have in their role as a director of a sport organisation. Therefore, some questions arise in terms of the effectiveness of their inclusion. Thus, possible research questions in this regard are: Do athletes understand the role they play in the governance of their NSF? Specifically, it is important to investigate if athletes are and feel prepared to fulfil the political and leadership role that is needed once they become part of the governing board. Also, it is important to understand if athletes are prepared to challenge the status quo. How much do they know about the issues inside their NSF or about broader issues outside their sport that impact the sport industry? Do they understand the big picture? In other words, how prepared are they to be the agents of change?

Finally, it is important to examine the possible impact other stakeholders might have inside the NSF and why coaches and referees still represent a minority number in many NSFs. In addition, results from the National Sport Governance Observer project (Geeraert, 2018) on the state of sport governance in ten countries including Brazil, can also shed light on issues not only related to the governing boards but also on other broader areas of governance such as accountability, transparency, democratic processes and societal responsibility.

Conclusion

The process and dynamics of how sport is governed in Latin American countries is not much different from how it occurs in others regions of the world. On the one hand, the governance of each sport is mandated by the rules of the respective international governing body and the regional or global governing body that govern a sport mega-event like the Pan American Games or Copa América in Football. On the other hand, government initiatives, specifically the enactment of legislation, facilitate and influence the governance of each sport or multisport megaevent. Governments also subsidise sport activities in a given territory. In Latin America, this is true for most countries. The extent of influence that international governing bodies rules and procedures have on a specific country's sport policies often depends on how much needs to be negotiated between the country and the sport ruling body. Considering that many countries in the region aspire to achieve international visibility through sport, whether this is by achieving success with their national teams or by hosting international sport events, compliance with the governing body and even adjusting existing country's policies and laws is a must. Such was the case in Brazil when the country hosted the FIFA World Cup in 2014. A number of existing laws were temporarily adjusted and new laws were introduced to comply with FIFA requirements (Matias & Mascharenas, 2017; Mezzadri et al., 2016).

A number of stakeholders influence the governance of sport in Latin America. From a systemic point of view, national sport federations and government agencies represent just two players within the system. Although these two stakeholders are the most influential, other less visible groups also play a critical role in shaping the way sport is governed. Among these groups are the funding agencies and the mechanism employed to distribute the resources; non-governmental organisations that are part of the sport system; and advocacy groups that push for reform and change inside sport organisations. Similarly, changes in the organisational governance of sport organisations have been influenced by the broader socio-political climate as well as outside global trends. In the case of Latin America, and specifically Brazil, cases of corruption occurring both inside and outside sport organisations have been identified as some of the forces that triggered the need for change in the regulatory environment of sport organisations. As noted previously in the chapter, current transformations inside the Brazilian Olympic Committee (COB) occurred as a result of the sanctions imposed by the International Olympic Committee due to allegations of corruption inside the COB.

Historically, the governance of sport in Latin American countries has been greatly influenced by political initiatives that have been channelled through government agencies. Over the last two decades, government involvement in sport has not ceased, nor has it decreased. Instead, government involvement in sport has been on the rise. With the aim of achieving global visibility, countries across the region have not only allocated more resources to fund sport, but many countries have also entered the race to host sport mega-events. Brazil, the focus of analysis in this chapter, has been the leading country in the region in regard to this trend. While overall, the majority of sport organisations in Brazil have not achieved a level of "good organisational governance", serious efforts have been made to get there. The process has been difficult and has included trial and error. Brazil represents an interesting case – the examination of the evolution and transformation that follows the governance of sport in a large country experiencing severe economic and political change. The challenge of achieving good sport governance inside sport organisations will not be attained just by increasing government control but rather by developing more effective mechanisms and understanding of governance and coordination among the many stakeholders that participate and affect the sport system.

Notes

1 From 2000 to 2016, Brazil hosted the 2002 South American Games; 2007 Pan American Games; 2011 Military World Games; 2013 FIFA Confederations Cup; 2014 FIFA World Cup; Rio 2016 Summer Olympic and Paralympic Games.
2 The *Lava Jato* or 'Car Wash' operation is the largest case of corruption and money laundering that Brazil has ever had. It is estimated that billions of Brazilian reais were diverted from Petrobras, the country's largest state-owned company. Although initially this was a laundering money operation of small businesses, the scheme grew much larger to involve large contracting firms organised into cartels which paid bribes to senior state executives and other public officials for awarding construction projects at inflated costs (Watts, 2017).
3 In Brazil, the higher national governing body in each sport is called "sport confederation". In this chapter, we refer to these governing bodies as National Sport Federations (NSFs).
4 The Unfair Play Operation was a cooperative project between the prosecutorial bodies of Brazil, France, Antigua and Barbuda, the United Sates and the United Kingdom that investigated allegations of corruption in the process of choosing Rio de Janeiro as the venue for the 2016 Olympic Games. The investigation culminated in the arrest of several public and sports officials in Brazil and other countries, including Carlos Nuzman, former president of the Brazilian Olympic Committee and the Organising Committee of the 2016 Olympic Games (Ministério Público Federal Rio de Janeiro, 2017).
5 The Pelé Law from 1998 was amended in 2013, 2015 and 2018 with the purpose of mandate sports organisations, which receive public funding, to adopt good governance practices.

References

Alabarces, P. (2009). El deporte en América Latina. *Razón y Palabra, 14*(69), 1–19.
Almeida, B. S., Coakley, J., Marchi Júnior, W., & Starepravo, F. A. (2012). Federal government funding and sport: The case of Brazil, 2004–2009. *International Journal of Sport Policy and Politics, 4,* 411–426.
Almeida, B. S. D., Marchi Júnior, W., & Pike, E. (2014). The 2016 Olympic and Paralympic Games and Brazil's soft power. *Contemporary Social Science, 9,* 271–283.
Agyemang, K. J. A. (2014). Toward a framework of "athlete citizenship" in professional sport through authentic community stakeholder engagement. *Sport, Business and Management: An International Journal, 4*(1), 26–37.
Australian Sports Commission. (2005). *Governing sport: The role of the board, a good practice guide for sporting organizations.* Canberra, Australia: Author.
Bermejo Vera, J., Gamero Casado, E., & Palomar Olmedo, A. (2003). *Poderes públicos y deporte.* Seville, Spain: Consejería de Turismo y Deporte.

Brasil. (1988). *Constituição da República Federativa do Brasil* [online]. Brasília: Senado Federal. Retrieved 12 November 2018, from http://www.planalto.gov.br/ccivil_03/constituicao/ConstituicaoCompilado.htm

Brasil. (2001, July 17). Decreto Lei nº 10264. *Diário Oficial da República Federativa do Brasil* [online]. Brasília DF. Retrieved from http://www.planalto.gov.br/ccivil_03/LEIS/LEIS_2001/L10264.htm

Brasil. (2011, December 16). Lei nº 12395. *Diário Oficial da República Federativa do Brasil* [online]. Brasília DF. Retrieved from http://www.planalto.gov.br/ccivil_03/_Ato2011-2014/2011/Lei/L12395.htm

Brasil. (2015, August 15). Lei nº 13155. *Diário Oficial da República Federativa do Brasil* [online]. Brasília DF. Retrieved from http://www.planalto.gov.br/ccivil_03/_Ato2015-2018/2015/Lei/L13155.htm

Brasil. (2018, December 12). Decreto Lei nº 13756. *Diário Oficial da República Federativa do Brasil* [online]. Brasília DF. Retrieved from http://www.planalto.gov.br/ccivil_03/_Ato2015-2018/2018/Lei/L13756.htm

Brasil. (2019). Decreto Lei nº 9674. *Diário Oficial da República Federativa do Brasil* [online]. Brasília DF. Retrieved 2 February 2019, from http://www.planalto.gov.br/ccivil_03/_ato2019-2022/2019/decreto/D9674.htm

Bravo, G., & Parrish, C. (2019). Sport in Latin America and the Caribbean. In E. MacIntosh, G. Bravo & M. Li (Eds.), *International sport management* (2nd ed. pp. 47–60). Champaign, IL: Human Kinetics.

Bravo, G., Parrish, S., & López de D'Amico, R. (2016). Introduction. Sport in Latin America. In G. Bravo, R. López de D'Amico & C. Parrish (Eds.), *Sport in Latin America. Policy, organization, management* (pp. 1–17). London and New York: Routledge.

Bueno, L. (2008). *Políticas públicas no esporte no Brasil: razões para o predomínio do alto rendimento* [Public policies in sport in Brazil: Reasons for the predominance of high performance]. (Unpublished Doctoral dissertation). Fundação Getúlio Vargas, Sao Paulo, Brazil.

Cardenas, J. R. (2015, June 3). How the FIFA scandal put Latin American corruption under the microscope. *Foreign Policy*. Retrieved from https://foreignpolicy.com/2015/06/03/how-the-fifa-scandal-put-latin-american-corruption-under-the-microscope/

Carter, T. (2016). Labor migration, international politics and the governance of Latin American sport. In G. Bravo, R. López de D'Amico & C. Parrish (Eds.), *Sport in Latin America. Policy, organization, management* (pp. 135–147). London and New York: Routledge.

Comitê Olímpico do Brasil. (2014, February 18). *Estatuto do Comitê Olímpico Brasileiro.* Retrieved from http://memoriadasolimpiadas.rb.gov.br/jspui/bitstream/123456789/807/1/COB.Estatuto.2014.pdf

Comitê Olímpico do Brasil. (2017, November 22). *Estatuto do Comitê Olímpico do Brasil.* Retrieved from https://www.cob.org.br/public/uploads/documentos/201904111512463.pdf

Dowling, M., Leopkey, B., & Smith, L. (2018). Governance in sport: A scoping review. *Journal of Sport Management, 32*, 438–445.

Ferkins, L., & Shilbury, D. (2015). The stakeholder dilemma in sport governance: Toward the notion of "stakeowner". *Journal of Sport Management, 29*, 93–108.

Fernández, Z. F. (2014). El Contenido esencial del Derecho al Deporte. Perspectiva constitucional en Latinoamérica. *Lex Social: Revista de Derechos Sociales, 4*(2), 105–120.

Filho, A. R. R., Damiani, C., & Fontana, P. S. (2018). Sports mega-events in Brazil: An account of the Brazilian government's actions. *Acta Universitatis Carolinae: Kinanthropologica, 54*(1), 28–40.

Geeraert, A. (2015). *Sports governance observer 2015: The legitimacy crisis in international sports governance.* Copenhagen: Play the Game.

Geeraert, A. (2016). *The EU in international sports governance: A principal-agent perspective on EU control of FIFA and UEFA.* New York: Palgrave MacMillan.

Geeraert, A. (Ed.). (2018). *National sport governance observer. Final report.* Aarhus, Denmark: Play the Game.

Geeraert, A., Alm, J., & Groll, M. (2014). Good governance in international sport organizations: An analysis of the 35 Olympic sport governing bodies. *International Journal of Sport Policy and Politics, 6*, 281–306.

Haas, L., & Barros, L. F. (2018). National sport governance observer. Country report: Brazil. In A. Geeraert (Ed.), *National sport governance observer. Final report* (pp. 222–244). Aarhus, Denmark: Play the Game.

Henry, I., & Lee, P. C. (2004). Governance and ethics in sport. In S. Chadwick & J. Beech (Eds.), *The business of sport management* (pp. 25–41). Harlow, UK: Pearson Education.

Hoye, R., & Cuskelly, G. (2007). *Sport governance.* Sydney: Elsevier.

Jaitman, L., & Scartascini, C. (2017). *Deporte para el desarrollo.* New York: Banco Interamericano.

Kihl, L., Kikulis, L., & Thibault, L. (2007). A deliberative democratic approach to athlete-centred sport: The dynamics of administrative and communicative power. *European Sport Management Quarterly, 7*, 1–30.

Latinobarómetro. (2016). *¿Características que cree Ud. que hacen conocido a [País]?* [Survey results]. Retrieved from http://www.latinobarometro.org/latOnline.jsp

Matias, W., & Mascarenhas, F. (2017). Caracterização histórica e a legislação sobre o futebol no Brasil. *LICERE, 20*(4), 372–400.

Mezzadri, F. M., Maoski, A. P. C., & Donha, E. L. (2016). The Brazilian state and its involvement with the football industry. In G. Bravo, R. López de D'Amico & C. Parrish (Eds.), *Sport in Latin America. Policy, organization & management* (pp. 215–228). London and New York: Routledge.

Ministério Público Federal, Rio de Janeiro. (2017, October 5). *Lava Jato/RJ: MPF pede a prisão do presidente do COB*. Procuradoria da República no Rio de Janeiro. Retrieved from http://www.mpf.mp.br/rj/s ala-de-imprensa/noticias-rj/lava-jato-rj-mpf-pede-a-prisao-do-presidente-do-cob

Mitchell, R. K., Agle, B. R., & Wood, D. J. (1997). Toward a theory of stakeholder identification and salience: Defining the principle of who and what really counts. *Academy of Management Review, 22*, 853–886.

Pacto pelo Esporte. (n.d.). *O Pacto*. Retrieved from http://www.pactopeloesporte.org.br/o-pacto

Pimentel, E. D. S. (2007). *O conceito de esporte no interior da legislação esportiva brasileira: de 1941 até 1998* (Unpublished master's thesis). Universidade Federal do Paraná, Curitiba, Brasil.

Rachman, G. (2007). Beautiful game, lousy business: The problems of Latin American football. In R. M. Miller & L. Crolley (Eds.), *Football in the Americas: Fútbol, futebol, soccer* (pp. 161–173). London: Institute for the Study of the Americas.

Ribeiro, B., & Hartley, S. (2018, February 16). Why Brazil's Zika virus requires a political treatment. *The Conversation*. Retrieved from https://theconversation.com/why-brazils-zika-virus-requires-a-politica l-treatment-91955

Saad-Filho, A. (2013). Mass protests under 'left neoliberalism': Brazil, June–July 2013. *Critical Sociology, 39*, 657–669.

Soria, S., & Maldonado, A. (2016). The long and winding road of the football industry in Chile. In G. Bravo, R. López de D'Amico & C. Parrish (Eds.), *Sport in Latin America. Policy, organization, management* (pp. 253–269). London and New York: Routledge.

Spaaij, R. (2005). The prevention of football hooliganism: A transnational perspective. In *Actas del X Congreso Internacional de Historia del Deporte* (pp. 1–10). Seville, Spain: CESH.

Sport and Recreation New Zealand. (2004). *Nine steps to effective governance: Building high performing organizations*. Wellington, New Zealand: Author.

Szlifman, J. (2014, May 6). Safety in stadiums. A wave of violence among South America's football fans. *Play the Game*. Retrieved from https://www.playthegame.org/news/news-articles/2014/a-wave-of-vio lence-among-south-america%E2%80%99s-football-fans/

Thibault, L., Kihl, L., & Babiak, K. (2010). Democratization and governance in international sport: Addressing issues with athlete involvement in organizational policy. *International Journal of Sport Policy and Politics, 2*, 275–302.

UK Sport. (2004). *Good governance guide for national governing bodies*. London: UK Sport.

Universidade de Brasilia. (n.d.). Transparência no esporte. Retrieved 2 February 2019, from http://www. transparencianoesporte.unb.br

Watts, J. (2017, June 1). Operation Car Wash: Is this the biggest corruption scandal in history? *The Guardian*. Retrieved from https://www.theguardian.com/world/2017/jun/01/brazil-operation-car-wash-is-this-the-biggest-corruption-scandal-in-history

Zimbalist, A. (Ed.). (2017). *Rio 2016: Olympic myths, hard realities*. Washington, DC: Brookings Institution Press.

Zorovich, M. R. S. (2015). Trends in drug trafficking and organized crime in Brazil. In M. W. Brienen & J. D. Rosen (Eds.), *New approaches to drug policies: A time for change* (pp. 35–57). London: Palgrave Macmillan.

Zuleta, E. (2017). Entendiendo la crisis en el sector deportivo: Reflexiones para entender el comportamiento del sector en América Latina. *Ensayos de Gerencia Deportiva*. Retrieved from https://medium.com/@ andreszuleta/entendiendo-la-crisis-en-el-sector-deportivo-reflexiones-para-entender-el-comporta miento-del-5db357b96fe5

7

Sport systems, national sport organisations and the governance of sport codes

Ian O'Boyle and David Shilbury

Introduction

Sport governance exists in many different forms and guises, in different codes and within different nations around the world. There are a number of instances where similar, if not identical, governing structures exist in various nations; the federal model of governance is one of those. Federation refers to the delegation of power and authority from a central (national) authority to various regions usually within a bounded geographical context. In Australia, for example, federation exists as a direct result of British colonisation. Unsurprisingly, the evolution of sport governance in nations that have adopted federal political models reflects the systems and ideologies of federation. As sport has entered a new era of growth of commercialisation and professionalisation, the federal model has come under strain with many codes experiencing issues relating to distrust and conflict within their networks.

This chapter documents the evolution of the federal model and describes the mechanisms traditionally in place to elect and appoint individuals charged to govern in these federally based networks. A key issue at the individual level in federal sport governance is that the majority of boards are volunteer-led resulting in time and resource pressures being placed on those charged to govern. The change from a pure delegate system of board composition to more independent and "hybrid" boards is discussed in this chapter.

Given the challenges of governing in a federal model in the contemporary sporting environment (as detailed later), alternative governing arrangements are attracting increased attention with the notable example of unitary governance coming to the fore (Confederation of Australian Motorsport [CAMS], 2015). Unitary nations and unitary models are therefore afforded attention as a comparative to the federal model of sport governance, and the potential for transitioning towards a unitary model (if desirable) within existing federal networks is explored in this chapter.

As noted previously, sport governance exists in a variety of forms throughout the world. One of the more recent and unique iterations of sport governance is that of professional sport governance. Governance in professional sport codes is inherently different to that of governance within the common nonprofit network. Shareholder value is often a driving force in these systems contrasting the multitude of stakeholders (such as club members) that can have varying degrees of power within the nonprofit sport governance arena. An exploration of this unique professional sport governance environment with specific focus on the shareholder/stakeholder dynamic rounds out this chapter.

The federal model

Sport governance has been receiving increased attention in recent times often due to high-profile scandals such as those involving global sport organisations (GSOs) like Fédération Internationale de Football Association (FIFA) and the International Olympic Committee (IOC). Poor governance practice has also been highlighted on a domestic level where many existing structures are now outdated and no longer fit-for-purpose within the contemporary sporting environment (ASC, 2013). The federal model of sport governance has long been associated with the way in which sport is organised within a number of countries throughout the world including Australia, New Zealand, Canada and a host of European nations (Shilbury, Ferkins & Smythe, 2013). Within Australia in particular, this model is a direct reflection of the governance system established by the British Parliament in 1901 following the passing of the Commonwealth of Australia Act, which recognised six separate colonies (now states) and allowed each to govern in its own right. Now, over 100 years later, this governance system prevails in modern-day Australia and has been adopted by almost all other sectors in the country including the nonprofit sport context. Mirroring the federal governance system established by the British, sport in modern day Australia is governed through a mix of national sport organisations (NSOs) and state sport organisations (SSOs) which ultimately share power and responsibility for fostering the development of a sport, both in terms of participation and high-performance (O'Boyle & Shilbury, 2016; Shilbury & Ferkins, 2015).

Staying within the Australian context, Sport Australia (formerly The Australian Sports Commission [ASC]) has recognised the need to address governance deficiencies within the industry and have gone as far as introducing the *Mandatory Sport Governance Principles* document that all Sport Australia funded NSOs must adhere to. Lack of engagement or compliance with these principles may result in withdrawal of all or part of the funding allocated to these entities by this government agency (ASC, 2013). Although this document does not specifically advocate for either a unitary or federal model, the following extract is included as the opening section to these principles:

> Different sporting organisations operate under different governance structures. While not requiring the adoption of any single model, the ASC will consider closely whether sport governance models are likely to enable them to achieve their core participation and high-performance objectives in the most cost-effective fashion. Each structure should be clearly documented with a clear delineation of the roles, responsibilities and powers of the Board, management and each body involved. Further, there should be no overlap in the powers of any two bodies or individuals in a governance structure. (p. 2)

Perhaps the most interesting element of the extract above is contained in the last sentence where Sport Australia refer to overlap in the powers between entities and individuals within a sporting network. The nature of the federal model often results in an overlap of power and responsibility as each state, although attempting to achieve similar objectives, can often have different strategic and operational plans that may not facilitate a whole-of-sport perspective in relation to decision-making and the creation of shared understandings across a sporting network. As such, it becomes apparent that the federal model is not without its challenges and limitations.

The sharing of power and responsibility in these networks has often resulted in tension between affiliated entities that has presented itself in the form of distrust, fragmentation and occasionally even legal action (Shilbury & Ferkins, 2015). Further, the federal model arguably creates a situation where there is duplication of resources across the network given that multiple organisations are attempting to achieve similar objectives with potentially little collaboration or coordination (Shilbury et al., 2013).

Of the 21 principles included in the Sport Australia document, a number directly relate to the federal model, such as Principle 1.2, where Sport Australia clearly acknowledge one of the major complexities embedded within the federal model: "Where sports have a federated structure, all parts of the federation must demonstrate they are working in cohesion and adhere to a strategic direction set by the national entity to maximise the interests of the sport" (Principle 1.2, p. 2). The challenge for NSOs in this regard is to facilitate cooperation with their affiliated entities which may involve overcoming issues such as prehistories of conflict, personality clashes or a lack of trust within the federated network.

Academic discourse relating to the federal model

In academia, recent scholarly works have explored a variety of issues in the sport governance domain, including those that relate directly to the nature of the federal sport governance model (Adriaanse & Schofield, 2013; Ferkins, Shilbury & McDonald, 2009; Hoye & Doherty, 2011; O'Boyle & Bradbury, 2013; Shilbury, 2001; Taylor & O'Sullivan, 2009). Research in the sport governance domain has typically adopted theoretical frameworks from more established fields of enquiry. For instance, institutional theory, resource dependence theory (Dickson, Arnold & Chalip, 2005; Ferkins & Shilbury, 2010), agency theory (Hoye & Cuskelly, 2007), inter-organisational relationships and network theory (Henry & Lee, 2004) have all been adopted by researchers in the field and have provided useful results. However, there have also been calls for greater use of multi-theoretical approaches, where a number of established theories are explored simultaneously to better understand particular phenomena in the sport governance field (Cornforth, 2003; Hoye & Doherty, 2011; Pye & Pettigrew, 2005; Shilbury et al., 2013).

Further to the point above, much governance research in the traditional sense has been in reference to how a singular organisation adopts processes and practices to allocate resources and exercise control and coordination between entities (Rhodes, 1997; Rosenau, 1995; Shilbury et al., 2013). Governance in a singular organisation is, therefore, inherently different from governance in a network of organisations as, in the latter, additional complexities arise related to control and power in the interrelationships of the entities in such a system. Sport governance research to date has largely focussed on issues within the singular organisation such as the role of the board, volunteer motivations for serving as a board member, board performance, CEO-chairperson relationships and strategic capability of boards (Cuskelly & Boag, 2001; Ferkins et al., 2009; Hoye & Doherty, 2011; Inglis, 1997; Shilbury & Ferkins, 2011; Soares, Correia & Rosado, 2010). Although it is accepted in a number of these studies that the federal model influences the governance function in these systems, specific exploration and focus on the federal model itself is generally absent from the research cited above. However, more recent studies have begun to explore governance "between" organisations often referred to as systemic, network and federated governance in the literature (Shilbury et al., 2013; Shilbury & Ferkins, 2015).

O'Boyle and Shilbury's (2016) study explored the issue of trust in federal sporting networks and found that low levels of trust between boards were severely impacting the ability of these networks to enact a collaborative approach to governance. Likewise, Shilbury and Ferkins'

(2015) work highlighted how board leadership was a crucial component of resolving conflict and facilitating closer working relationships between the various entities that comprise federal sporting networks.

In another study, Henry and Lee (2004) explored the skills and traits required of leaders in sporting networks. They argued that mutual adjustment and negotiation skills were more important than the ability to control, if the goal of a network was to increase the levels of collaboration and harmony in order to achieve enhanced outcomes. Although not directly related to the field of sport governance, Henry and Lee's (2004) use of network theory again highlights the complexities inherent within sporting networks based on a federal model.

One of the key features synonymous with the federal model in the past has been its reliance on the delegate model of board composition which until recently was in place in the majority of NSOs operating under federation (Cricket Australia, 2011; Hoye & Cuskelly, 2007). Many NSOs have now made the transition to wholly independent models or, at a minimum, a greater inclusion of independent directors in the composition of their boards who are often appointed based on a particular skill set they possess that may be lacking in the current board makeup.

Volunteerism and board composition

As previously noted, a critical factor in nonprofit sport governance practice is the volunteer nature of the majority of boards in federated sporting systems. This voluntary involvement complicates the issue of governing in these systems as the skills, knowledge and characteristics that are required to govern effectively and collectively cannot always be guaranteed to be present in voluntary boards (Shilbury et al., 2013). We expand further on this point in the following section.

The volunteer nature of these boards is reflective of the delegate representative model of board composition noted previously that has been traditionally synonymous with federal governing structures (Hoye & Cuskelly, 2007). This representative model can somewhat explain the levels of parochialism and (mis)trust that are built in networks (O'Boyle & Shilbury, 2016) as delegates are generally elected to represent the interests of their own affiliations and not necessarily those of the sport (or a network) as a whole (Shilbury et al., 2013). Furthermore, the selection of essential skill-sets potentially required to foster trusting relationships, such as high-level leadership skills and communication and negotiation skills, is difficult, given the nature of the nomination process in delegate models. In the nonprofit context in general, Kearns (1995) suggested that board members should possess specific talents that add value to the board, a clear understanding of their role and selflessness, all of which would appear to be useful for governing and leading effectively in sporting networks. It can be seen how a delegate representative model may not necessarily facilitate this situation and, hence, the inclusion of these qualities in nonprofit sporting boards. All of these issues are further complicated by the limitations on time that volunteer board members may have to interact with other governing powers in a network.

The traditional delegate model has been heavily criticised in the past due to cases of perceived conflicts of interest and a board not acting in the best interest of the sport body as a whole (Shilbury et al., 2013). A further criticism has been that the skill-set of an elected board within the delegate model can vary from year to year depending on who has been chosen to lead the sport organisation at the board level, potentially jeopardising the overall performance of the entity. As referenced previously, there is no guarantee within this system that individuals with the appropriate skill-set will be elected and therefore the delegate system may put an organisation at risk of having a board that may not have to ability to control and influence the governance functions required to the full extent. In addition, these individuals commonly serve terms of up to three years or longer in the entity and often have the potential to be re-elected for consecutive terms (O'Boyle & Bradbury, 2013).

As a contrast to the traditional delegate model, an independent board model consists of a board that does not contain representatives who have current direct involvement in other federated bodies (regional/club) within the sport, and thus do not represent a specific alliance, such as those from affiliated regional associations. The logic behind an independent board is that it will represent the best interests of the sport itself and not the concerns of an affiliated association, thereby removing the issue of self-interest that has been a criticism of some boards in the past.

A major challenge to the implementation of the independent board is that some organisations can be wary of a backlash from current board members when an independent board structure is suggested over the delegate system. The hybrid model is essentially a mix of the delegate system and the independent board structure whereby up to half the members are appointed external independents and approximately half are elected from the regional affiliates (delegates). Ferkins and Shilbury (2012) suggested "board composition of this nature is considered to be 'hybrid' which allows for the democratic ideals of an election process to remain, supplemented by individuals chosen for their professional expertise, as well as 'outsider' perspectives" (p. 72). The central concept behind the hybrid model is that member-affiliated representatives and non-member directors sit on the board with the intention of achieving more independent and "best interest" governance decisions.

As already noted, self-interest has been identified as a major issue that influences the performance of many nonprofit sport boards. The selection of independent board members may help to overcome this challenge within sport governance. Another potential benefit from selecting board members from the external environment is that they may bring an understanding and "voice" to stakeholders of the organisation who may not have been previously heard (Yeh & Taylor, 2008). Furthermore, the adoption of a fully independent board should (in theory) ensure that appropriate knowledge and expertise is present within the board in order to deliver on strategic imperatives; a situation that cannot always be guaranteed with the delegate, and to a lesser extent, the hybrid model.

Unitary States and the unitary model

In countries such as Australia, New Zealand, Canada and some European nations, the federal model dominates the sport governance landscape reflecting the political systems in place within those countries. Conversely, the same can be said for unitary states where a centralised and "all-powerful" single governing entity exists. Unitary nations such as Russia, China, Japan, Italy, France and Greece all have sport governance structures that closely resemble the unitary model in which their political systems operate. This means that the national governing body (or equivalent) for a sport in those countries holds the balance of power in terms of fostering the development of that sport through the means of growing participation and investing in high-performance elite competition. Delegation of responsibility clearly occurs, particularly in those countries with expansive geographical footprints, yet this delegation only occurs at the decision of the national entity, and polices and practice align with those of that authority.

What is an evolving transition in the domain of sport governance is when a sport code that has been traditionally based in a federal model seeks to enact major structural change to align its various affiliated bodies in a more formalised arrangement closely resembling a unitary model. There are recent examples of this occurring in the sports of triathlon, golf, touch football and motorsport to name a few within the federally based Australian context. From a research perspective, we know little of the direct benefits, challenges and governance improvements that a transition from a federal model to a unitary model can offer, certainly from an evidenced-based perspective. One of the few studies that has afforded specific attention to this area is the work of O'Boyle and Shilbury (2017). They were able to provide an overview of the differences between these models at the broader level (see Table 7.1) and noted that a significant barrier to enacting a unitary model in an existing federal network was that affiliated bodies to the national entity would be required to absolve their authority and, indeed, their assets to the centralised

Table 7.1 Comparing federal and unitary sport governance models

	Federal model	Unitary model
Board structure	Independent from NSO retaining power and control of decisions made at state level	Advisory Board with no power or control over decisions made at state level
Board composition	Often state delegates assume positions on national board	Independent board with no delegate representation
Financial management and auditing	Responsibility of state organisation	NSO responsibility along with carrying out a national audit
Duplication of resources	Often duplication exists between a number of federated bodies	Reduction or elimination in duplication of resources
Resource allocation (financial/ non-financial)	Little or no sharing of resources between federated bodies	Regular sharing of resources between state offices and the NSO
Roles and responsibilities	Often confusion about specific roles and responsibilities	Clear delineation of roles and responsibilities across the network
Reporting structures	State board is not required to report to NSO	General manager of each state office reports directly to NSO CEO/board
Strategic planning	Individual strategic plan within each federated body that may not be consistent with NSO strategy	One strategic plan for all unified bodies developed at NSO level
CEO	Individual CEOs for each federated body	One CEO representing all unified bodies. General or state manager in place in each state office
High-performance and participation strategies	Individual strategies in each federated body	More consistent set of high-performance and participation strategies across the network
Governing responsibility	Each state responsible for governing the sport only within state boundaries	NSO responsible for governing the sport in each state as well as nationally
Soliciting sponsorship	Each federated body solicits individual, often small-scale sponsorship	Potential ability to market a sport to a national sponsor given unified approach
Insurance	Individual insurance policies in each federated body	Reduction in overall insurance premium within the network due to a single policy

Source: Adapted from O'Boyle and Shilbury (2017).

governing organisation. Further, what role if any a regional board should occupy following the transition to a unitary model remains unclear, even though O'Boyle and Shilbury attempted to investigate this specific issue.

In the absence of studies affording attention to unitary models of sport governance in the field of sport management, to inform thinking in this space, it is necessary to explore unitary models or similar descriptions where extensive work *has* been carried out in a closely related discipline. The majority of this work appears in research that relates to private sector entities and, namely, those that operate with international subsidiaries, divisions or units of a parent company (Toms & Filatotchev, 2004; Windsor, 2009). Surprisingly, there is a lack of research that focusses on issues related to sub-units of companies or similar descriptions in a domestic environment, even given the extent of private sector research. Exploring the body of research related to governance in business divisions/units and subsidiaries is relevant as, ultimately, in unitary nations and unitary sport governance models in federal nations, the state branches or offices of the NSO can be considered divisions/units of that organisation and are directly accountable to the NSO board through the CEO.

As noted previously, when discussing the unitary model of sport governance, one of the major issues to be addressed is the role of the board in an SSO once the federal model ceases to exist (O'Boyle & Shilbury, 2017). Kiel, Hendry and Nicholson (2006) examined corporate governance options for a unitary model of governance involving local subsidiaries of a multinational parent company. They suggested four frameworks for how a unitary governance model could be implemented: (1) Direct control, where there is essentially no board at the subsidiary level, and all responsibility and decision-making ability rests with the parent company; (2) Dual reporting, where the subsidiary CEO has a dual reporting line to the local board and the parent company management structure. The local board also has a communication line to the parent company governance structure; (3) Advisory board, where local individuals are not formally registered as directors but are given limited responsibility and mirror some of the roles of formal boards; (4) Local board, where the subsidiary's corporate governance is entirely the responsibility of a legally recognised local board. In this instance, the parent company essentially acts as a shareholder of the local subsidiary. These four different scenarios present interesting options for the potential adoption of a unitary model of governance in an existing federal sporting context, each presenting a variety of advantages and disadvantages.

In the sporting context, option (1) above presents the purest form of a unitary system where there is a complete absence of a board at a local (regional) level, and, therefore, there is direct control by the governing entity without any ambiguity. One of the few sports to transition to a partial unitary model in Australia is the sport of touch football. In that case, boards at the regional level remain in place, albeit only in an advisory capacity. The advisory-only status of these boards may result in cases of role ambiguity in relation to an understanding of what exactly they are responsible and not responsible for in a unitary governance model. Role ambiguity has previously been examined by Doherty and Hoye (2011), who found it was a significant factor in determining individual board member performance for voluntary board positions. They contend "that knowing what to do is fundamental to one's performance, and more critical than knowing how to do it, and what difference it makes" (p. 107).

This issue is further complicated by the voluntary nature of the majority of boards in Australian NSOs and SSOs (Cuskelly, Hoye & Auld, 2006) which was previously noted. The removal of a board (or its authority) at the regional level ultimately changes the human resource dynamic within a federal network by removing board-to-board relations, especially where distrust and prehistories of conflict may have been limiting the capacity of a sport to move forward in a given direction (O'Boyle & Shilbury, 2016). It also may facilitate a situation where NSO boards can focus on fulfilment of their strategic roles in accordance with their mandate, and management of the sporting network can be entirely the responsibility of the CEO and top level management (Ferkins & Shilbury, 2012). It could also be argued that this places increased pressure on the board of an NSO who would now ultimately be responsible for all aspects of the sport throughout the entire country with no delegation of power or responsibility to regional level affiliates. Given the voluntary nature of these boards, board composition potentially becomes an integral issue.

In private-sector research, an early study by Leksell and Lindgren (1982) explored the role of subsidiary boards in parent companies and suggested that boards had three major roles: External role – to foster external relations and provide advice; internal role – monitoring performance and strategy implementation; and a legal role. They also found that the parent company would appoint experienced directors to subsidiary boards that were deemed to be more strategically important to the organisation. In the sporting context, if boards at the regional level were to remain in some capacity, such as in option (2) or (3) in Kiel and colleagues' (2006) previously mentioned typology, then this point may have particular relevance given the popularity of different sports in certain regions. In the touch football case, the states of New South Wales and Queensland alone hold the majority of membership across the entire the sport and are "outside" the unitary system.

Kriger and Rich (1987), also focussing on the role of the board in local subsidiaries of multinational companies, found that only a minority of these organisations used their boards proactively and that they existed merely to fulfil a legal obligation. Building on this work and supporting the findings of Leksell and Lindgren (1982) above, Kriger (1988) showed that the importance of local boards in his study was a direct reflection of the parent corporation's strategy in that location. In contrast to these findings, Björkman (1994) found that subsidiary boards of multinational enterprises were actively involved in strategy and budget approval. Björkman's (1994) findings and option (4) in Kiel and colleagues' (2006) typology more closely reflect the federal model of governance where the local board remains intact and retains significant degrees of power and authority.

Gillies and Dickinson (1999) suggested that strong, relatively independent subsidiaries could bring significant benefits to a parent company but also found that "the role of subsidiary boards is rapidly decreasing" (p. 242) in the private sector. This point may help to explain the perceived reluctance of many regional boards to relinquish power and control in favour of a unitary model if they believe that, through time, their role in the governance of the sport will continue to diminish until it is no longer relevant at all.

Of course, it must be acknowledged with all of the cited research that private sector governance is inherently different from governance in a nonprofit sporting context where, generally, compliance "cannot be bought" and resistance to change from a traditional federal structure, along with other antecedents, are powerful forces that are perhaps contributing to the scarcity of unitary models of governance in nonprofit sporting networks (CAMS, 2015). Further, and of significant importance, is the fact that sport governance networks in general operate under a bottom-up approach. That is to say that power and decision-making authority has traditionally been vested with the levels "below" in the traditional pyramid structure of organised sport (Club – Regional – State – National). The owners of a sport, such as touch football in Australia, are the members who are represented by all of these entities and not just the national body. This presents a challenge when transitioning to a unitary system in sport, as ensuring that members retain a degree of power and authority is necessary; whereas, in the corporate environment, subsidiaries and business units many not necessarily encounter this complex issue as intensely.

Sport governance in the professional (for profit) environment

Notwithstanding the importance of governance within federal (and unitary) networks and the importance of boards in these environments as described previously, governance in this domain is largely limited to those organisations that operate on a nonprofit basis. Many face different challenges and pressures in comparison to those sport organisations which operate in an environment of private franchise/club ownership. This is seen in a number of professional sporting leagues throughout the world like the majority of professional soccer leagues and the dominant American sports in the United States. In the United States, specifically, although federalism exists in terms of the nation's political makeup, a reflection of this federal system is absent from the sporting context with a large disconnect between mass participation sport and professional sport. The combination of a federalist system of government and an avowedly free-market economy has resulted in a plethora of sport organisations claiming governance over the same sport (Green, Chalip & Bowers, 2013). Furthermore, the lack of a nationalised governance framework in any sports in the United States has created an opportunity for entrepreneurs who own professional sport franchises and who run the leagues in which their teams compete. These groups and individuals can operate their teams and leagues in any manner they see fit as long as those activities do not contravene American corporate law. Consequently, each of the major leagues in the United States, such as the National Basketball Association (NBA), National Football League (NFL) and Major League Baseball (MLB) has their own rules and systems of governance.

Taking the NFL as a prime example of the contrast between governance in the traditional nonprofit and for-profit sporting environments, it is clear to see the difference in governance challenges facing these alternative governance systems. The NFL is a private, for-profit enterprise. The stated mission of the organisation is: "To present the National Football League and its teams at a level that attracts the broadest audience and makes NFL football the best sports entertainment in the world" (NFL, 2012). Much like a traditional corporate entity, the league is headed by a Commissioner (equivalent to a CEO) who reports to the Executive Committee (equivalent to a board). A delegate system of board composition operates here with representation from each of the 32 NFL teams. League policies are brought into effect based on a three-quarters majority of team owners with the majority of teams owned by individuals or a consortium. Senaux (2008) discussed the contrast between European and American professional sport in particular where the European nonprofit sporting networks have members at grassroots level and are often referred to as the owners of the sport. Senaux (2008) noted the absence of this stakeholder group from the governance systems that operate in professional sporting networks in America and elsewhere. Corporate governance in these types of professional leagues and teams generally involves the adoption of a shareholder perspective – that is to maximise the economic performance of the team/organisation (Senaux, 2008).

In professional sport governance codes such as the NFL, broadcasting revenues are shared across the network, recruitment strategies are policed through the draft pick system, and entry into the market is monopolised by the league itself where a limited number of franchises exist with rare instances of expansion. Amara, Henry, Liang and Uchiumi (2005) noted how these "equalisation" measures exist in large part to protect the principle of "uncertainty of outcome" to sustain interest in the league from fans and, therefore, media. In contrast, the English Premier League (EPL), with no salary cap and few equalisation measures, has seen a wide disparity in the income levels of top and bottom teams in recent times and has led to somewhat of a reduction in the uncertainty of outcome with the competition. Although Gratton (2000) suggested there is a lack of empirical evidence to argue a causal relationship, the EPL should adopt a more "equalised" approach. Szymanski and Hoehn (1999) amongst others, have suggested that a European-wide league (different from the existing Champions League) with limited entry be established, as the various national leagues become increasingly predictable which could impact spectator interest.

As noted previously, maximising shareholder return is a key driver for the governance mechanisms in place within many professional sport governance codes. In contrast to this shareholder perspective, the nonprofit sporting environment can be seen to adopt a stakeholder view – and indeed Foreman (2006) and Senaux (2008) have shown that a number of for-profit professional teams and leagues also adopt this perspective.

The concept of a stakeholder and the development of the stakeholder model are attributed to Freeman's landmark publication *Strategic management: A stakeholder approach* (1984). He suggested that the stakeholder is "any group or individual who can affect or is affected by the achievement of the organisation's objectives" (p. 46). Further definitions and descriptions of stakeholders have been offered by numerous other scholars including Clarkson (1995) who labelled stakeholders as individuals or groups who have put something at risk in their relationship with the organisation. Both definitions, those by Freeman and Clarkson clearly insist on high levels of dependency between organisations and their stakeholders. However, Donaldson and Preston (1995) also added that it is important to establish a clear contrast between true stakeholders and those that simply influence the organisation. The media, for example, may influence the actions of a sport organisation but one could argue are not stakeholders in the truest sense of the word. Supporters, players, coaches, administrators and competitors on the other hand are more closely linked to the definition of a stakeholder from a sporting perceptive.

This stakeholder perspective from a governance viewpoint has its roots in the history of European sport specifically, where the majority of professional teams today evolved after originally being developed as community associations, in contrast to the professional sport governance context in the United States. Although professional sport governance in Europe also now reflects a strong emphasis on economic activity as one might expect, "there are still deep heritages which profoundly structured the organisation of sport in Europe and somehow explain the existence of complex power games" (Senaux, 2008, p. 9) between professional sport organisations and their stakeholders. The stakeholder perspective in relation to sport governance is therefore very relevant to professional sport in this context where there may be a variety of interests and goals competing and in conflict with each other. Similarly, shareholders in professional sport teams can have a number of interests and agendas as owners of the capital in the organisation. These interests may include financial returns, reputation, self-promotion and on-field success of the organisation as a result of a sporting passion. One could assume that the interests of shareholders in professional sport are often mixed and not necessarily explicit. Nonetheless, they clearly remain an integral stakeholder within the governance structure.

There are other primary stakeholders in professional sport governance including players, coaches, administrators, supporters and various sporting bodies that influence the activities of this unique sector. Players in particular have become an important group within the stakeholder model of professional sport governance as player associations and lobbying groups continue to exert an increased influence on the manner in which professional sport is organised and governed (Australian Athletes' Alliance, 2019). The same can be said for supporter groups who, in some instances, have even assumed capital ownership positions in professional sporting teams. This array of stakeholders makes professional sport an interesting context within which to examine corporate governance especially in the European model. Furthermore, within the nonprofit sporting environment, it is accepted with little dissent that the "owners" of a sport in these systems are the wider membership base. The entities that comprise the governance framework in nonprofit sport are seen as service organisations to their members in this regard. Within the professional sport governance context, sport organisations are rarely described as "service organisations" and, given the multitude of stakeholders and influencers in this environment, it raises an important question in relation to sport governance: Who owns professional sport?

Summary

It is unlikely that there will be wholesale change in the structure of sport governance codes in Australia and in other nations in the near future. Achieving structural change in a network where established traditions, cultures and ways of operating already exist is a daunting task. In any event, this is not to say that wholesale change is required in all sporting codes. Certainly, the federal model presents challenges to enacting contemporary sport governance practice, but it also offers significant benefits by enabling local delivery and resources to be acutely focussed within various geographic regions. The positive change that has occurred over the past decade is the acceptance that a delegate model of board composition is no longer a fit-for-purpose mechanism to allow for whole-of-sport governance. The majority of NSO boards operating in federal models are now generally comprised of individuals with specific skill sets relevant to the strategic direction of those organisations and a better understanding of the role, and requirements to govern and lead efficiently within these networks appears to be in place.

For those sports which can overcome the significant barriers to enacting structural change in their governance, the option of replacing a federal model in favour of a unitary system may provide significant benefit. However, due to the relative dearth of real-life examples and research exploring this area, it is a risk that requires significant planning and delivery to ensure it is the right change for any given sport. Further research is required to investigate the manner in which a unitary model should be adopted including the role of regional boards that previously would have held significant power and authority under a federal model.

Finally, the unique and evolving domain of professional sport governance is an under-researched area and would benefit from increased academic attention. Much like the nonprofit sport governance environment, sport governance in professional sport presents itself in a variety of guises. It is also subject to increased pressure from powerful player associations, ownership groups, fans and other stakeholders. Sport governance in professional sport will continue to pose questions of best practice and fit-for-purpose structures that researchers should be able to address and for which they may provide future direction.

References

Adriaanse, J. A., & Schofield, T. (2013). Analyzing gender dynamics in sport governance: A new regimes-based approach. *Sport Management Review, 16*, 498–513.

Amara, M., Henry, I., Liang, J., & Uchiumi, K. (2005). The governance of professional soccer: Five case studies: Algeria, China, England, France and Japan. *European Journal of Sport Science, 5*, 189–206.

Australian Athletes' Alliance. (2019). *About Us*. Retrieved 8 April 2019, from https://ausathletesall.com.au/who-we-are

Australian Sports Commission (ASC). (2013). *Mandatory sports governance principles*. Canberra: Author.

Björkman, I. (1994). Managing Swedish and Finnish multinational corporations: The role of the board of directors in French and Norwegian subsidiaries. *International Business Review, 3*, 47–69.

Clarkson, M. (1995). A stakeholder framework for analysing and evaluating corporate social performance. *Academy of Management Review, 20*, 92–117.

Confederation of Australian Motorsport. (2015). *Structure*. Retrieved 25 August 2015, from https://www.cams.com.au/about/structure

Cornforth, C. (Ed.). (2003). *The governance of public and non-profit organizations: What do boards do?* London, UK: Routledge.

Cricket Australia. (2011). *Cricket Australia governance review*. Melbourne: Author.

Cuskelly, G., & Boag, A. (2001). Organisational commitment as a predictor of committee member turnover among volunteer sport administrators: Results from a time-lagged study. *Sport Management Review*, *4*, 65–86.

Cuskelly, G., Hoye, R., & Auld, C. (2006). *Working with volunteers in sport: Theory and practice*. London, UK: Routledge.

Dickson, G., Arnold, T., & Chalip, L. (2005). League expansion and interorganisational power. *Sport Management Review*, *8*, 145–165.

Doherty, A., & Hoye, R. (2011). Role ambiguity and volunteer board member performance in nonprofit sport organizations. *Nonprofit Management and Leadership*, *22*, 107–128.

Donaldson, T., & Preston, L. (1995). The stakeholder theory of the corporation: Concepts, evidence, and implications. *Academy of Management Review*, *20*, 65–92.

Ferkins, L., & Shilbury, D. (2010). Developing board strategic capability in sport organisations: The national–regional governing relationship. *Sport Management Review*, *13*, 235–254.

Ferkins, L., & Shilbury, D. (2012). Good boards are strategic: What does that mean for sport governance? *Journal of Sport Management*, *26*, 67–80.

Ferkins, L., Shilbury, D., & McDonald, G. (2009). Board involvement in strategy: Advancing the governance of sport organizations. *Journal of Sport Management*, *23*, 245–277.

Foreman, J. (2006). *Corporate governance in the Australian football league: A critical evaluation* (PhD). Victoria University, Melbourne, Australia.

Gillies, J., & Dickinson, M. (1999). The governance of transnational firms: Some preliminary hypotheses. *Corporate Governance: An International Review*, *7*, 237–247.

Gratton, C. (2000). The peculiar economics of English professional football. In J. Garland, D. Malcolm, & M. Rowe (Eds.), *The future of football: Challenges for the twenty-first century*. London: Frank Cass.

Green, C., Chalip, L., & Bowers, M. (2013). United States of America. In I. O'Boyle & T. Bradbury (Eds.), *Sport Governance: International case studies* (pp. 20–36). London, UK: Routledge.

Henry, I., & Lee, P. C. (2004). Governance and ethics in sport. In J. Beech & S. Chadwick (Eds.), *The business of sport management* (pp. 25–41). Essex, UK: Pearson Education.

Hoye, R., & Cuskelly, G. (2007). *Sport governance*. Sydney: Elsevier.

Hoye, R., & Doherty, A. (2011). Nonprofit sport board performance: A review and directions for future research. *Journal of Sport Management*, *25*, 272–285.

Inglis, S. (1997). Roles of the board in amateur sport organizations. *Journal of Sport Management*, *11*, 160–176.

Kearns, K. P. (1995). Effective nonprofit board members as seen by executives and board chairs. *Nonprofit Management and Leadership*, *5*, 337–358.

Kiel, G. C., Hendry, K., & Nicholson, G. J. (2006). Corporate governance options for the local subsidiaries of multinational enterprises. *Corporate Governance: An International Review*, *14*, 568–576.

Kriger, M. P. (1988). The increasing role of subsidiary boards in MNCs: An empirical study. *Strategic Management Journal*, *9*, 347–360.

Kriger, M. P., & Rich, P. J. (1987). Strategic governance: Why and how MNCs are using boards of directors in foreign subsidiaries. *Columbia Journal of World Business*, *22*, 39–46.

Leksell, L., & Lindgren, U. (1982). The board of directors in foreign subsidiaries. *Journal of International Business Studies*, *13*, 27–39.

NFL. (2012). *Values*. Retrieved 8 April 2019, from http://www.nfl.com/careers/values

O'Boyle, I., & Bradbury, T. (Eds.). (2013). *Sport governance: International case studies*. London, UK: Routledge.

O'Boyle, I., & Shilbury, D. (2016). Exploring issues of trust in collaborative sport governance. *Journal of Sport Management*, *30*, 52–69.

O'Boyle, I., & Shilbury, D. (2017). Comparing federal versus unitary models of sport governance: A case study investigation. *Managing Sport and Leisure*, *21*, 353–374.

Pye, A., & Pettigrew, A. (2005). Studying board context, process and dynamics: Some challenges for the future. *British Journal of Management*, *16*, S27–S38.

Rhodes, R. A. W. (1997). *Understanding governance*. Buckingham, UK: Open University Press.

Rosenau, J. N. (1995). Governance in the twenty-first century. *Global Governance*, *1*, 13–43.

Senaux, B. (2008). A stakeholder approach to football club governance. *International Journal of Sport Management and Marketing*, *4*, 4–17.

Shilbury, D. (2001). Examining board member roles, functions and influence: A study of Victorian sporting organisations. *International Journal of Sport Management*, *2*, 253–281.

Shilbury, D., & Ferkins, L. (2011). Professionalisation, sport governance and strategic capability. *Managing Leisure*, *16*, 108–127.

Shilbury, D., & Ferkins, L. (2015). Exploring the utility of collaborative governance in a national sport organization. *Journal of Sport Management*, *29*, 380–397.

Shilbury, D., Ferkins, L., & Smythe, L. (2013). Sport governance encounters: Insights from lived experiences. *Sport Management Review*, *16*, 349–363.

Soares, J., Correia, A., & Rosado, A. (2010). Political factors in the decision making process in voluntary sports associations. *European Sport Management Quarterly*, *10*, 5–29.

Szymanski, S., & Hoehn, T. (1999). The Americanization of European Football. *Economic Policy*, *14*, 205–233.

Taylor, M., & O'Sullivan, N. (2009). How should national governing bodies of sport be governed in the UK? An exploratory study of board structure. *Corporate Governance: An International Review*, *17*, 681–693.

Toms, S., & Filatotchev, I. (2004). Corporate governance, business strategy, and the dynamics of networks: A theoretical model and application to the British cotton industry, 1830–1980. *Organization Studies*, *25*, 629–651.

Windsor, D. (2009). Tightening corporate governance. *Journal of International Management*, *15*, 306–316.

Yeh, C., & Taylor, T. L. (2008). Issues of governance in sport organisations: A question of board size, structure and roles. *World Leisure Journal*, *50*(1), 33–45.

8

The role of non-traditional sport structures in systemic sport governance

Spencer Harris and Pamm Phillips

Introduction

One of the unique contextual issues in sport is that, in some cases, sport organisations rely on the collaboration, and, in many instances, compliance of non-traditional sport stakeholders in order to effectively manage and deliver their sports. For example, in the Australian setting, many of the major sport facilities that host major international and professional sport events, as well as other entertainment events, are managed and operated by non-traditional sport entities. In other words, organisations such as these non-traditional sport entities are focused on running a business that hosts events, but are not necessarily sport-focused, nor are they governed or staffed by individuals who are qualified in the management of sport, or perhaps even interested in sport per se. Non-traditional sporting structures in England are typically sport-focused (in the broadest possible sense) and are governed by sport enthusiasts. For example, the strategic-level county coordination of sport and physical activity is led by a network of Active Partnerships (APs), organisations that are described as non-traditional sporting structures insofar as they do not represent traditional sporting structures.

This chapter explores the role that non-traditional sporting structures play in the governance of sport in their respective contexts. The chapter begins with a brief conceptualisation of the literature related to system-wide governance and the relevance of a range of perspectives to the cases. The chapter continues with an overview focused on Policy Network Theory (PNT), a lens which is useful insofar as it examines the range of variables that are considered critical to the effective performance of systems or networks and the non-traditional sporting structures that are typically part of a network or delivery system with specific responsibilities which contribute to the overall supply of sport. The chapter then applies the PNT to specific cases of non-traditional sporting structures in Australia and England. The case studies are intended to provide the reader with a grounding in the complexities of the structure of sport governance and the range of factors that have influenced the development of non-traditional sporting structures as an integral part of the sport governance landscape. The chapter concludes with some key observations about the practices of non-traditional sporting structures as presented in the cases, the implications for sport governance and also identifies the potential for future research in order to better understand the influences and impacts inherent in complex network governance structures.

Systemic, collaborative, network, stakeholder governance and policy networks

Henry and Lee (2004) categorise governance into three types: Corporate, political and systemic. Corporate governance is primarily concerned with the norms, practices and processes associated with the management of organisations. Political governance is focused on governments or governing authorities and their steering of systems to achieve certain outcomes through the use of pressure, financial incentives or regulation. Systemic governance reflects the shift in the way in which sport is controlled away from government, hierarchy and direct control and towards systemic governance (Henry & Lee, 2004). In particular, systemic governance emphasises the interrelationships between stakeholders in which different groups exert power in different ways and in different contexts by drawing on alliances with other stakeholders (Henry & Lee, 2004, p. 6). Unsurprisingly, the academic literature is not settled on this one conceptualisation of system-wide governance. Instead, there are at least four additional ideas that overlap, mirror or represent a very similar notion. The first of these is collaborative governance, which emanates from the public administration literature.

Collaborative governance is defined as "A governance arrangement where one or more public agencies directly engage non-state stakeholders in a collective decision-making process that is formal, consensus-oriented and deliberative and that aims to make or implement public policy or manage public programs or assets" (Ansell & Gash, 2008, p. 544). Collaborative governance offers a more exacting concept of system-governance with its focus on network interactions between state and non-state entities and their intentional role in the policy process (Shilbury & Ferkins, 2015). The second concept relates to stakeholder governance whereby governing authorities seek to focus on and involve key stakeholders in the decisions that are important to the future direction of the organisation. While, on first sight, this concept may appear to be focused on single organisations, it is possible to apply it to the range of stakeholders involved in broader networks or systems. Of particular value is Fassin's (2012) work in distinguishing between stakeholders on the basis of reciprocity (i.e., their role and involvement in governance) (cf. Ferkins & Shilbury, 2015 for a sport-related example). Here, Fassin identified stakeowners as the loyal and genuine stakeholders (e.g., key sports organisations such as IOC, IFs, NOCs, etc.); stakewatchers as those who might observe, report or pressure (e.g., media, players associations); and stakekeepers, who play a role in monitoring and regulating the system but play no direct role in it (e.g., Transparency International, Play the Game). The third idea is network governance. This has been used to articulate the complex network made up of 24 types of stakeholders involved in the Olympic system…and thus requiring "a more global form of governance capable of taking into account each stakeholder's own interests and the relations between stakeholders, including national and supranational governments" (Chappelet, 2016, p. 10). The final concept relates to policy networks – a term used to explain the links and interdependence between governments and societal actors in numerous areas of policy. The very conceptualisation of a policy network could be argued to mirror the aforementioned approaches to system-wide governance insofar as the policy network is involved in numerous and diverse areas of policy and not only involved in the policy making process but also the steering, allocation of resources and making of key decisions regarding the implementation of policy.

The main problem with the application of the policy network theory to governance studies appears to be associated with the use of the word *policy* as the network is a *policy network* and therefore involved exclusively in policy, not governance. However, almost all forms of governance are inextricably related to policies that influence, regulate or distribute resources, thereby influencing systems or networks (such as international or national sport) and individual organisations. Here, it is important to consider that policy represents a deliberate system of principles to guide decisions and achieve outcomes. Policies apply to government, private and not-for-profit sectors – to individual organisations and to entire systems. In this way, policy provides the guiding framework for governance action. The stakeholders involved in policy networks – that is, the network that is responsible for negotiating and agreeing policy – are typically the same set of stakeholders involved in the governance and implementation of policy. Similarly, the very definition of collaborative governance directly references the role of multiple stakeholders in policy and programmes (which typically flow from policy). Thus, this chapter argues that, with its focus on resources, skills, stakeholders, network interactions and outcomes, the conceptualisation of policy networks mirrors that of systemic or collaborative governance; and while the concept has not been frequently applied to the governance field, it is highly relevant to governance-related studies. Moreover, a diversity of theoretical approaches to a particular issue defends against the problems associated with the use of a singular lens and demonstrates a commitment to theoretical pluralism. Such diversity in specific fields of study such as governance is important, as it provides the opportunity to glean new insights through the use of new or adapted theoretical lenses (Cairney, 2011; van der Heijden, 2012).

Conceptualising policy networks

The development of policy network theory was, in part, a response to the overly rational view of policy making being controlled by government, thereby disregarding the influence of the numerous organisations that exist in between organisations and beyond formal rules (Heclo, 1978; Miller & Demir, 2006). The rejection of this rational view underpins the creation of network theory. Instead of rational or normative views of policy, network theory emphasises the fluid nature of relations between state and societal actors and the way in which this is bound by specific interests and resources (Howlett, 1998). As might be noted in the examples above, despite the outwards and perhaps convenient way of thinking about the sport systems in Australia, there are key actors (such as Sport Australia [formerly the Australian Sports Commission], government departments responsible for sport, as well as various facilities trusts and oversight bodies) that disrupt these seemingly rational systems and relationships.

One of the challenges of the network theory approach is the lack of a single, accepted definition (John, 1998), although this may be considered a norm within the political sciences, and is therefore neither exceptional nor overly problematic. In an attempt to illuminate the approach, Benson (1982) defined policy networks as "dependency relationships that emerge between both organisations and individuals who are in frequent contact with each other in particular policy areas" (p. 148). Adding to this, policy networks have been defined as "stable patterns of social relations existing between interdependent actors, which take shape around policy problems and/or programmes" (Kickert, Klijn & Koppenjan, 1996, p. 6). A particular challenge associated with the definition of a network approach is the use of a plethora of concepts within the policy network field, including policy communities, policy networks, iron triangles and issue networks (Miller & Demir, 2006). Here, Marsh and Rhodes' (1992) typology is instructive in helping to organise networks by key characteristics such as membership, integration, resources and power. This provides the analyst with a spectrum to plot various networks depending on their features. Policy communities are characterised by their close-knit, integrated structure with members sharing a common set of values (Marsh & Rhodes, 1992; Miller & Demir, 2006).

Government is often the key agency in a policy community, with other agencies often consciously excluded (Marsh & Rhodes, 1992). In contrast, issue networks are characterised by their large memberships with diverse affected interests. Issue networks are often viewed as "unstable",

109

being seen to lack stability over time and are frequently associated with policy consultation rather than being directly involved in the development of policy (Marsh & Rhodes, 1992). This categorisation of network types is useful in demonstrating the various forms of partnerships across traditional and non-traditional sporting structures that exist at different levels of the policy process (i.e., international, multi-national, national, regional, sub-regional and local).

In reviewing various policy network approaches, Marsh and Smith (2000) found that whilst each had particular strengths, common failures included a lack of detailed examination of two-way relationships among variables and little, if any, attempt to use networks as an explanatory variable. Thus, they developed a dialectical model of policy networks which aimed to illuminate the two-way relationship between variables and the way in which one variable might affect the other in a continuing, iterative process (Marsh & Smith, 2000). This approach has helped to develop a greater understanding of the way structural context affects networks, especially the explicit representation and consideration of agent as well as analysing the interrelationship between structure and agency, network and context and network and outcome (Marsh & Smith, 2000). With regard to structure and agency, Marsh and Smith (2000) stressed the need for a model that considers both structure and agency as although "structures matter, it is agents who interpret these structures and make decisions" (p. 5). The dialectical model highlighted that broader structural context influences both the network structure and the resources that agents have at their disposal. It also stressed the innate skill and learning that shape the agent and their ability to influence network interaction. Network interaction is not only shaped by the actors' skills and resources, but also by the network structure including consideration of the type of interaction within networks and the patterns of power that underpin such interactions. In addition, network interaction is affected by policy outcomes; in particular, policy learning and the realisation that network interaction influences policy implementation (Adam & Kriesi, 2007). Similarly, policy outcomes shape network structures as do the interaction amongst networks, the skills and resources of actors and the structural context. The model also considers the critical drivers of policy outcomes, namely, network structures and network interaction. In addition to the focus on agency, the model offers greater utility in examining the role of structure and agency as well as the interrelationship between context, agents, network structures, interaction and outcomes. In short, the policy network approach provides a rich vein of information that is useful in highlighting a range of variables that are integral to policy change within sport and, more generally, the sport-related policymaking process (cf. Lindsey, 2006).

Although the policy network approach has utility, it is important to clarify other criticisms of the theory beyond the problems of definitions and types. Some notable authors have criticised network approaches for lacking a theoretical basis, referring to it more as a "theoretical toolbox" than a theory per se (cf. Borzel, 1998; Dowding, 1995; Miller & Demir, 2006). It has also been criticised for developing informal models that lack formal modelling robustness and do little to explain the policy process beyond that which could be achieved by good quality empirical work (Dowding, 1995). In addition, the policy network approach is viewed by some to lack consideration of institutions or the role of the state in particular in the interactions of policy networks (John, 1998). In this chapter it is argued that the dialectical approach explicitly addresses such criticisms by recognising the network structure, network interactions and structural context affecting these factors. Despite these criticisms, Lindsey's (2006) application of the dialectical model to the sport policy domain illustrates its utility, specifically its analytical value, in explicitly considering structure and agency as well as the interrelationship between network structure and agents, the network and the context it operates in and the network and policy outcomes.

In sum, whilst the network approach is not without its limitations, it offers a helpful analytic framework in constructing specific empirical work to review the governance and policy context of non-traditional sporting structures. It addresses the limitations of previous work specifically noted by Marsh and Rhodes (1992) which focuses more specifically on structure, paying insufficient attention to agency (Dowding, 1995) by placing specific emphasis on the role of agency and demonstrates that policy outcomes are "the result of the actions of strategically calculating subjects" (Marsh & Smith, 2000, p. 6). Most importantly, for the focus of this chapter, the dialectical network approach emphasises the place of all agents involved in policy networks and does not give priority treatment to government or any other single entity involved in the policy process.

Non-traditional sporting structures in England

While sport in England has endured the political whim and caprice of various ministers over the years (Houlihan & White, 2002), it has more recently settled around the formalisation of two primary sport policies, namely, community sport and elite sport. Within the community sport policy arena, the principles of network governance are clearly visible in the range, roles and responsibilities of key stakeholders involved in the delivery of community sport policy. As a non-traditional sporting structure, Active Partnerships play a central coordinating role in the planning, delivery and evaluation of community sport policy. Active Partnerships originated in England as County Sport Partnerships (CSPs) in the mid-2000s. In February 2019, CSPs were rebranded to Active Partnerships (APs) in order to better reflect the core purpose of the networks of organisations, which is to create an active nation by engaging communities, building understanding and insight, brokering cross-sector partnerships and influencing policy and practice (Knaggs, 2019). The following section applies the dialectical policy network model to the development of APs and their place in the systemic governance of community sport policy in England.

Structural context

The initial creation of CSPs was largely a response to two significant policy developments. The first development was the government strategy for sport *Game Plan* which emphasised the need for a more efficient single system for the planning and delivery of community sport (Department of Culture, Media & Sport, 2002). The second development was the government commissioned Carter Review of sport in England. This review was focused on modernising the sport infrastructure and creating more efficient, performance-motivated and business-like sporting structures and processes in England (Carter, 2005). The apparent impetus for these policy initiatives was the growing frustration of working with local government who were the preferred policy implementation agents of central government up to the early 2000s. The frustrations included frequent policy implementation failures, replacing or overlaying central government policy objectives with local government priorities, and the practical difficulties of working with more than 350 local authorities (Harris & Houlihan, 2014). Subsequently, CSPs emerged as a new, central hub in the delivery system for community sport, with a critical role in the sub-regional coordination of community sport policy implementation resulting in the initial creation of 49 partnerships along the same or similar boundaries as English counties.

More recently, CSPs have rebranded as APs. This reflects two changes in the structural context. First, the change mirrors the pendulum-like shift in community sport policy from previous policy focused on sport-for-sport and increased sports participation to the most recent iteration of policy focused on sport for broader, social outcomes. The rebranding of CSPs to a broader notion of physical activity, with a focus on changing behaviour and demonstrating wider societal impact aligns with these policy-based changes. Second, and a significant influence in the change to sport policy, the rebranding can be seen as both a reaction to the growing public concern about obesity rates, mental health and sedentary behaviour particularly among young people, and the growing political challenge associated with a lack of street-level agents who are perceived to be well-equipped to deliver interventions to address such problems. As of 2019, there are a total of 43 APs across England with each being responsible for aspiring to increase levels of engagement in sport and physical activity, reduce levels of inactivity, tackle stubborn inequality and use the power of sport and physical activity to transform lives in each of the 48 counties across England (Active Partnerships, 2019).

Actors' resources, skills and learning

The role and ability of APs to fulfil their responsibilities in the systemic governance of community sport in England is, at least in part, predicated on the resources and skills of the partnership. All APs receive core funding from Sport England. The core funding for APs ranges from £200,000 to over £1 million, with variances being dependent on population. Further funding is commonly sourced through local government, local health authorities, donations and sponsorship from corporations. Importantly, previous research has indicated that while policy agents such as APs are satisfied with the level of funding invested into community sport, they are challenged by the funding bottleneck, a term used to describe a lack of funding allocated to implementation of policy (Harris & Houlihan, 2016). The inference here is that while there is ample funding in the system, the majority of this funding is allocated to the development of structures and the employment of new staff rather than to projects or activities that are delivered to inspire behaviour change or promotional campaigns to make people more aware of opportunities. More recently, this appears to be a challenge which Sport England have addressed through the provision of more targeted programmatic funding. This funding varies according to the programmes, geographical area and outcomes, but it is not unusual for the annual programmatic funding from Sport England to each AP to be in the range of £300,000–£500,000 per year.

With regard to the skills and learning, the majority of staff working in APs are sport enthusiasts and have formal higher education qualifications in sport management or sport development together with background experience in sport administration. On this point, previous research has highlighted views from within the system where such a sport-centric workforce may be beneficial but also problematic: "Whilst highly engaged and passionate about sport [the workforce] lack the softer skills of collaboration and strategic leadership" (Harris & Houlihan, 2016, p. 14). That said, there is perhaps an opportunity to address such challenges in the annual workforce development plans that are implemented by APs annually. Further, there is a suggestion that APs have learned important lessons regarding advocacy and collaboration from previous community sport policy, insofar as they are collaborating with other important strategic-level partners, working collectively across all 43 geographical APs and speaking with one voice through the national APs leadership group. Such learning has undoubtedly helped to elevate the status of APs locally and nationally and has given them a notable platform upon which they are better able to influence future policy decisions.

Network structures

The network structures of community sport – and the patterns of power across these structures – has been subject to considerable change over recent years. During the 1990s, local government led the charge. In the pre- and post-London 2012 Games period (2008–2015) national governing bodies (NGBs) of sport were the lead agency with CSPs playing a support role by assisting NGBs in the delivery of their whole-of-sport. In the face of widespread policy failure, the UK government ushered in a new policy directive and a revised approach to the network of structures involved in policy implementation. The Department of Culture, Media and Sport strategy stated that:

> Much local partnership work in sport has for many years been organised by the national network of County Sports Partnerships (CSPs). They play an important role across the country in promoting sport and physical activity, working closely with local authorities, schools and others. (2015, p. 14)

The re-positioning of CSPs was reinforced by Sport England when they emphasised the importance of local delivery and how this was critical in order to tackle inactivity across communities and especially among under-represented groups. The strategy, though, also shifted away from previous explicit attempts to define a delivery system for community sport and instead focused on the creation of investment programmes (discussed in more detail later). The overall principle driving this change is the requirement to emphasise Sport England's place as an investment agency and its aspiration to invest its resources in organisations that are able to demonstrate a financially responsible and practically feasible return on investment for Sport England. However, while there is no explicit delivery system for community sport, the network of key stakeholders that are involved in community sport policy (see Figure 8.1) remains relatively stable although the roles, resources, responsibilities and interaction across stakeholders has changed considerably.

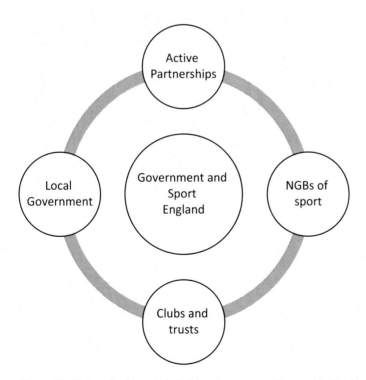

Figure 8.1 Network of key stakeholders in community sport in England.

Spencer Harris and Pamm Phillips

Network interaction

Partnerships in community sport in England have, since the 1990s, been portrayed normatively both as a social good and a way of working that will more likely be effective in delivering social policy outcomes. The interaction across the community sport network or organisations and partnerships can be understood through a consideration of policy discourse as stated in policy statements, strategies, annual reports and promotional literature (website, social media posts). From such discourse, it is possible to identity a core network made up of the Sport England central office, Sport England regional offices, APs and NGBs of Sport. Here, interaction is heavily influenced by resources. Sport England allocates significant monies into APs and NGBs of Sport in return for delivering key outputs and outcomes of the governments community sport policy goals. More specifically, policy makers, such as Sport England, advocate and influence policy and advise implementers, such as APs, on participation trends, provide insights on the processes of behaviour change and invest funding into a range of priority issues.

APs work alongside key partners, such as NGBs of Sport, to apply these insights and resources to the employment of key personnel and the implementation of targeted programmes to achieve specific outcomes. It is here where policy discourse perpetuates efficiency and win-win collaborations as core ideals and where society gets more for less through working together. Additionally, policy discourse suggests that power is unapologetically centralised and hierarchical; particularly in the role of the NSA in investing significant funding into a range of funded agencies in order to achieve specific policy goals; and with a raft of new public management techniques being used to identify, track and respond to (reward or penalise) performance. Thus, a cursory look at some key documentation reveals a top-down policy process whereby power is retained by the governing authority (DCMS, Sport England) and resources are allocated on the transactional basis of the outputs and outcomes being achieved. However, such insights could be argued to offer a relatively shallow understanding of network interactions, as they tend to frame and articulate the network and relationships within them as they would like them to be seen rather than reflecting the reality of their nature.

Deeper level empirical insights into community sport policy system reveal a more nuanced view of the nature of network interactions between key stakeholders. In particular, previous research has demonstrated the complexities associated with partnership work (Phillpots, Grix & Quarmby, 2010), the problems of differing values across partnerships (McDonald, 2005) and the importance of understanding the asymmetrical patterns of power that underpin partnerships (Harris & Houlihan, 2016). On this latter point, the impetus for APs to work with others such as NGBs of Sport is not the possibility of mutual dependence but rather the contractual requirement or conditions of funding that requires such interaction. Thus, on the one hand, centralised power is manifest in the core funding of APs. On the other hand, APs have worked strategically to ensure that the power in the interactions of DCMS, Sport England and APs is more balanced than it otherwise might be. This has been achieved through four key tactics. First, APs have positioned themselves as a policy implementation agency – an organisation that is competent and effective in designing, delivering and evaluating community-based sport and physical activity programmes. Second, the majority of APs have diversified their business model around the central focus on sport and physical activity, so that they can secure funding from a wider variety of sources. This has enabled partnerships to increase total funding, lessen the ratio of government funds to overall funds and thereby lessen their dependence on central government. Third, many APs have made shrewd board appointments including local councillors, business leaders and Members of Parliament, which has helped to grow the influence of APs at the local, regional and national level. Finally, the 40+ local-level partnerships recognised that they were politically stronger together than they were apart. This realisation led to the creation of a national-level AP umbrella organisation to represent, support and lead local-level APs. Since its creation, this organisation has been particularly effective at providing a representative voice for APs, raising the profile of APs on the political agenda and influencing future sport and physical activity policy.

In short, the hierarchical funding of government and the collective efforts of APs result in a policy community where power is not a reflection of a zero-sum game; rather, it reflects a space where negotiation and compromise are necessary in order to ensure the medium- to longer-term survival of APs and to improve the prospects of achieving specific policy outcomes.

Policy outcomes

The role and function of APs has been heavily influenced by policy outcomes. Previous community sport policy was focused on increased sports participation. NGBs of Sport led the implementation of policy with support from CSPs. Between 2008–2015 over £1 billion was invested into community sport policy. By 2016, there were no significant increases in sports participation, when compared to the baseline taken in 2008, with the exception of informal pursuits such as road running, recreational cycling, gym and fitness and conditioning classes. The 2008–2015 community sport policy is a clear representation of policy failure, and, as a result, the failure to achieve policy outcomes influenced the structural context and learning which in turn influenced decisions about future policy aspirations and the network structures to implement against such aspirations.

Community sport policy changed to focus on the instrumental use of sport to achieve social outcomes, specifically mental and physical health, individual development, as well as community, social and economic development. Simultaneously, CSPs repositioned themselves to focus on competent and well-placed agents to implement policy. CSPs were generally viewed as competent for their work in delivering bespoke policy programmes such as the Youth Games, the School Games and Sportivate. They also escaped direct responsibility for the failures associated with previous policy failure, as this was largely seen to be a problem owned by NGBs of Sport. CSPs were well-placed as they had skilled capacity, were regionally dispersed, and were locally well-connected. CSPs were readily able to articulate the needs and priorities of the local communities that they served. Consequently, the shift in policy from sport-for-sport to sport-for-social outcomes provided CSPs with the opportunity to lead the implementation of policy. In their renewal of community sport policy from 2016 onwards, the DCMS developed a number of high-level performance indicators that relate to each specific policy output which, in turn, directly impacts policy outcomes. Table 8.1 provides a detailed overview of the key performance indicators as they relate to each of the three policy outputs. While the responsibility for and measurement of key areas of work goes beyond APs, they will clearly be expected to play an important role in increasing sports participation, increasing and addressing inequality in sport volunteering, planning and implementing workforce development, as well as ensuring that principles of good governance are enacted.

When examined more clearly in this way, the extent to which community sport policy objectives have really changed from previous iterations is a matter open to debate. What has changed is the extent to which inequality, good governance and the impact of sport on social outcomes is an explicit priority. The success and future role of non-traditional sport structure codes, such as APs, will largely depend on their ability to deliver against these priorities or at least shape perceptions so that they are generally believed to be the implementation agent who had the best chances of effectively implementing such policies.

Table 8.1 Key performance indicators and policy outputs in the UK

Policy outputs	High-level indicators
More people taking part in sport, more people volunteering in sport, and more people experiencing live sport	• Increase in the percentage of the population in England meeting the CMO guidelines for physical activity; • Decrease in the percentage of the population in England that are physically inactive; • Increase in the percentage of adults utilising outdoor space for exercise; • Increase in the percentage of children achieving physical literacy standards; • Increase in the percentage of children achieving swimming proficiency and Bikeability levels 1–3; • Increase in the percentage of young people (11–18) with a positive attitude towards sport and being active; • Increase in the number of people volunteering at least twice in the last year; • The demographics of volunteers in sport to become more representative of society as a whole; • Number of people who have attended a loved sporting event more than once in the past year;
A more productive, sustainable and responsible sport sector	• Employment in the sport sector; • Position of the UK in the Nation Brands Index (overall and UK excelling at sport); • Increase in the amount of non-public investment into sport bodies which are in receipt of public investment; • Increase in the number of publicly funded bodies that meet the new UK Sports Governance Code; • Number of sports that meet the voluntary code to reinvest 30% of their net UK television broadcasting revenues into grassroots sport; • Results of the new sport workforce people survey (indicator to be developed); • The percentage of stakeholders who believe that duty of care policies are working effectively (relates to duty of care review…indicator to be developed);
Maximising international and domestic sporting success and the impact of major events	• Number of medals won at summer and winter Games; • Position in summer and winter medal tables; • UK/Home Nation performance in World, European, or Commonwealth competitions; • Average attendance levels at national-domestic sport; • Attendance at events supported through government and UK Sport major events programmes; • Economic impact of events supported through government and UK Sport major events programmes;

The governance of sport in Australia: A case study of the State of Victoria

The governance of sport in Australia has been covered elsewhere in this book. In Chapter 7, the reader is provided with detailed information about the federated model through which sport in Australia is organised. Chapter 5 introduced Sport Australia, the statutory agency of the federal government with an independent board of directors which is appointed by the Minister for

Sport. There it was noted that Sport Australia is the primary pathway for government influence in sport, and is the principal policy-maker at the national level. However, as noted, state and local government sport policy can also influence the governance of sport.

The Federal government have only seriously become interested in Australian sport since the early 1970s. The same is true for state government involvement in sport. Today, each of Australia's states and territories have a department that is responsible for sport and recreation. Thus, there are eight state/territory government departments, each of which aim to increase opportunities for participation in sport and recreation at all levels of performance. Underpinning state government involvement in sport (which is consistent with Sport Australia at the national level of the sport) is that participation has the potential to enrich the quality of life in all communities. The scope of this section is to discuss non-traditional sporting structures in the Australian context; and to do this, and augment the information already presented about the governance of sport in Australia, a case study of one state – Victoria – examines the non-traditional sporting structures that are intricately involved in the management, delivery and governance of sport in Victoria; and ultimately, influence national sport policy.

In the state of Victoria, the government (or public sector) is made up of two distinct groupings – the Victorian Public Service (which refers to state government departments and offices) and Victorian Public Entities. Public entities are organisations that exercise a public function and are established outside the public service, hence operating at "arm's length" from government. It is the public entities which service sport that are the focus of this chapter.

The government agency responsible for sport and recreation in Victoria is Sport and Recreation Victoria, which is part of the Department of Health and Human Services. Sport and Recreation Victoria seek to work collaboratively with not-for-profit, private and government sectors to use sport in ways that: Improve the health and wellbeing of Victorians, build stronger and more connected communities, deliver economic growth and jobs and enhance liveability (Victoria State Government, 2019a). Thus, Sport and Recreation Victoria have a broad role in increasing opportunities for participation in sport and recreation and, in doing so, contribute to the quality of life in communities through the creation of employment, as well as enhancing experiences that people have in the state (whether they reside in Victoria or are visiting). While it is not the aim of this chapter to describe and explain all of the functions and roles of Sport and Recreation Victoria, an investigation of the public entities that function to serve the sport and recreation sector provide an excellent lens to better understand the strategic efforts that are at the core of Sport and Recreation Victoria's existence. Those public entities, therefore, form the non-traditional sporting entities that are the focus of this chapter.

Structural context

State governments in Australia are not formally required to have policies that mirror federal government policy or policies of other states. The degree to which power and responsibility for a whole range of issues in Australian society are vested in state and local governments has been debated since Federation in 1901, and sport is no exception (Shilbury, Phillips, Karg & Rowe, 2017). The roles and responsibilities of federal versus state government in delivering, managing and catering for sport is often an area of tension.

Sport and Recreation Victoria is a crucial organisation that supports the complex and interconnected sport system that facilitates nearly four million Victorians who play sport and/or are engaged in active recreation. Victoria has 100 state sports associations and houses one third of Australia's national sport organisations and has more than 16,000 sport clubs in communities across the state. Further, there are 9,500 community sport facilities, leisure and recreation centres, a network of over 2,000 trails and thousands of playgrounds, parks and sport reserves. Most importantly, these facilities and organisations would not be viable without Sport and Recreation Victoria in terms of funding as well as administrative and governance support.

Moreover, Victoria has developed a global reputation as a major sporting events capital. World-class sporting infrastructure supports a calendar of events that adds over $AUD 1.8 billion per annum to the State's economy. In fact, Melbourne (the capital city of Victoria) is the only city in the world that has six international standard sporting facilities (including five with retractable roofing) on the fringe of its central business district. The state also boasts world-class expertise in high-performance with its own institute of sport that offers coaching services, sport analytics and the management of high-performance athletes for over 25 sports. Of interest for the current chapter is that Sport and Recreation Victoria is structured in a way that it has six public entities that function to service sport in various ways; these are the core of what Sport and Recreation Victoria do and, therefore, are central to the delivery and management of sport in the state. The network structures of the sport system have changed to include six public entities that function to serve sport. In this section, these network structures will be introduced and examined.

In the state of Victoria, public entities are statutory authorities, state-owned corporations that include professional registration boards, advisory organisations, service providers and industry regulators. They are established by government legislation to undertake a public purpose. Victoria's public entities serve a range of sectors including the public health sector, government schools, higher education institutions, police and emergency services, water and land management, as well as arts, finance, sport and other sectors.

In Victoria, there are six public entities that function to serve sport. These are:

- The Professional Boxing and Combat Sports Board of Victoria;
- The Victorian Institute of Sport;
- Melbourne and Olympic Parks Trust;
- The State Sport Centres Trust;
- The Melbourne Cricket Ground Trust; and
- Kardinia Park Stadium Trust (Victoria State Government, 2019b).

All six public entities for sport report to Victoria's Minister for Sport (Victoria State Government, 2019b). The Minister for Sport holds a range of portfolios and is currently also Victoria's Minister for Tourism and Major Events; Minister for Jobs, Innovation and Trade; and the Minister for Racing. What is interesting for the reader to note is that four of six public entities exist for the management of Victoria's major international standard sporting facilities in which major events are hosted, and that the Minister's portfolio includes sport, events and tourism. Although some of the facilities also host participation, the main role of these is in international standard events. These will be the focus of the following sections of this chapter.

Like many cities and states around the globe, Victoria experienced a state government-led push for the state to be an event destination – and this was the catalyst for the development of a network structure that put the management of the major facilities (through the four trusts listed above) in the hands of state government. International events hosted at the facilities managed under the trusts have included the Olympic Games (in 1956); the Commonwealth Games (2006); FINA World Swimming Championships (2007); AFC Asian Cup (2014), the ICC Cricket World Cup (2015); the Formula 1 Grand Prix (annually); the Australian Open Tennis Championships (annually) as well as a host of national events of significance.

It may come as no surprise to the reader, then, that the facilities (essentially under governance by the state government) have been critical to Victoria's ability to implement strategies to secure events, teams and sport activities that have resulted in it being named an Ultimate Sport City in 2006, 2008 and 2010. Further, events and accessibility to them is a highly weighted criteria used to judge the world's most liveable cities – and Melbourne has consistently ranked in the top three globally since 2002 – second to Vienna in 2019 (Visit Victoria, 2019). With facilities under the auspices of government, there is some level of stability that is provided for the standard of access to, maintenance and use of facilities as central to an ongoing event strategy for the state of Victoria. The international facilities that are governed through the various trusts provide the cornerstone for continued investment in sport and events.

That is, facilities are central to the delivery of most organised sports, and, in particular, stadiums and large event venues are crucial for professional or corporate sport leagues. Facilities provide sport organisations who play at them, lease them, or are in partnership with a local government or public entity that might own them a stream of revenue (through ticket sales), sponsorship and advertising revenue, a home venue to play and/or train, and revenue through concessions sales.

However, state-of-the-art stadiums and event venues that are critical to sport organisations, are increasingly used as a tool for governments and other stakeholders as a key part of a social health agenda, social cohesion and capital, peace and financial agendas. Without facilities, sport, whether at the grass roots level or professional levels, cannot exist – and therefore the outcomes of sport that governments desire (health, social, peace, economic) might not be realised – particularly if the stakeholders are not in a position of power to make decisions about their use.

Network interaction: The case of Melbourne and Olympic Parks Trust

Within walking distance of the Melbourne City Centre (known as the CBD), in the state of Victoria, are a range of sporting facilities that are all governed under the Melbourne and Olympic Parks Trust (MOPT) (Melbourne Olympic Parks Trust, 2019). The MOPT is a statutory authority established to be the custodians and managers of the Melbourne and Olympic Parks precinct. The precinct covers 40 hectares of land and includes facilities that host some of the city's professional sport teams and hosts some of the city's major events. The precinct hosted the 1956 Olympic Games, but has since been renovated substantially and has been a central pillar in Melbourne's successful hosting of the 2006 Commonwealth Games as well as the 2007 FINA World Swimming Championships. The Australian Open Tennis Championships (Australia's Grand Slam event) is also hosted in the Melbourne and Olympic Parks precinct and a series of stadiums and facilities host rugby league, soccer, netball, cycling, basketball and Australian rules football training and professional league competitions. It also includes a high-performance centre for the Collingwood Football Club and Netball team.

The MOPT was established in 1995 and was a merger of the National Tennis Centre Trust (now called Melbourne Park, where the Australian Open Tennis Championship is held) and the Olympic Park Committee of Management (formed originally in 1909) under the Melbourne & Olympic Parks Act 1985 (as amended). It was created by the merger of the National Tennis Centre Trust (established 13 November 1985) and the Olympic Park Committee of Management (formed originally in 1909). Under the Act, the Victorian state government Minister – the Minister for Tourism, Sport and Major Events – oversees its management and operations.

The Melbourne and Olympic Parks Trust has five main goals which include maintaining the financial viability of the precinct; increasing the benefits of the precinct to the state of Victoria; improving value that customers get when they visit the precinct; more effective and efficient business processes within MOPT; and organisational effectiveness (Melbourne Olympic Parks Trust, 2019). The Trust consists of 12 members appointed by the governor of the

State of Victoria. Of the 12 members, nine are to be appointed by nomination of the Minister. Two are to be appointed by nomination of the Lawn Tennis Association of Australia (which is, as of 1986, trading as Tennis Australia, the national governing body of the sport in Australia, under which the Australian Open is run); and one person is to be appointed by nomination of the Victorian Tennis Association (the state governing body of the sport of tennis, Tennis Victoria). Interestingly, the current chair of MOPT has a long history in the oil and gas industry, a 42-year career with Shell Oil Company and relatively little experience in the business of sport, event or facility management.

The importance of tennis to MOPT is certainly illustrated by board membership – with two representatives from Tennis Australia and one further representative from Tennis Victoria (the state governing body for the sport). A state-of-the-art $AUD 972 million redevelopment for Melbourne Park (the home of the Grand Slam event) is currently being carried out by the Victorian government. The redevelopment has been aimed at catering to the precinct's growing popularity and to enhance Victoria's sport and entertainment legacy for generations to come. The Australian Open injects nearly $AUD 300 million (https://www.premier.vic.gov.au/mel bourne-set-to-serve-up-the-worlds-best-tennis/) into the Victorian economy each year, and the state government has been eager to ensure the event facilities are some of the best in the world. Works have included Rod Laver Arena's first makeover in 30 years. From the perspective of MOPT, the redevelopment directly impacts one of their stated goals, and they suggest the redevelopment will significantly enrich every aspect of the customer experience at the facility, while providing exciting innovations and sustainability for the iconic venue.

While the redevelopment of Melbourne Park – the home of the Australian Open Tennis Championships – has undoubtedly been a major success for the sport, it also has been a success for the state government economically and socially. Indeed, one of the reasons that the state government committed money to the redevelopment of the facilities in the first place was so that it could meet their needs of ensuring that more people get to enjoy and have value from the public spaces encompassed in the precinct. Importantly, although there is 40 hectares of land in the precinct, very little of the land is open to public access. For the larger stadiums, the public needs to pay for tickets to events or other activities that might be hosted within them. Further, other facilities are for the use of professional sport teams and organisations.

Therefore, any redevelopment of land, by the very nature and objectives of government would need to cater to public access and use. In 2019, the Australian Open had record crowds with almost 800,000 attendees. It continues to be the most attended Grand Slam event. The 2019 event included top music acts from around the world, as well as a film festival. The change from a largely tennis event venue to a cultural festival venue beyond the sport of tennis has been a large part of this growth. Of course, without the impetus to build spaces appropriate for extensions such as those beyond the sport of tennis (which is largely a result of the state govern-ment governance and funding of the facility itself) these attendance records may not have been reached. The ticket packages offered also are aimed at those who want to attend the extension events rather than purely the sport of tennis. Perhaps the influence of the facilities management arrangements or structures, and governance through the MOPT has led to the event being broadened from purely sport to a sport and cultural festival and policy outcomes.

There are some hints in the empirical literature that might suggest that the governance of facilities has led sports down the pathway where there is a compromise between the sport and the government to fund and build a facility in a precinct that meets both sport needs (sustaining and redeveloping the facility to host the sport event into the future) as well as the broader needs of the government in providing a space and facility that is relevant and accessible to the public. Indeed, the 2006 Commonwealth Games (largely hosted in the MOPT precinct) marked the first time that the combined sport and cultural events were envisioned. The network interaction has been clearly documented as a way for the state government (through social policy and the development and governance of the MOPT precinct) to attract more visitors to the city and the precinct areas (Kellett, Hede & Chalip, 2008). It is also clear that stakeholder involvement in governance processes are central to obtaining the best policy outcomes. In this instance, policy networks are reflected through stakeholder governance.

Policy outcomes

The example above provides insights into the complexities of the structure of sport governance at least as it pertains to facilities in Victoria, as well as the range of factors that have influenced the development of non-traditional sport entities as an integral part of the sport governance landscape. Policy outcomes are also apparent in this case. In 2009, the state government developed the Major Sporting Events Act to provide protections to event organisers and the public to assist with safe and efficient staging of events. The Act includes providing power to enhance crowd management, prevent ambush marketing, protect event logos and images, safeguard events from unauthorised broadcasting and ensure compliant ticket sales.

Concluding remarks

This final section sums up key insights relating to the reasons why non-traditional sporting structures exist and the power of these structures in sporting systems. Following this, ideas for future research into non-traditional sporting structures will be presented.

In short, the first key insight is somewhat philosophical in reflecting on why non-traditional sporting structures have been intentionally created within systems that are sport-focussed. In this respect, opportunity, bespoke organisational design and – linked to this – their specialised nature and ability to reach agendas where sport has traditionally struggled are all reasonable explanations. Non-traditional sporting structures tend to address specific areas of work that traditional sports organisations either do not, cannot, or have proven to be ill-equipped to address. For example, few traditional sport organisations have the capacity or expertise to manage major regional-level sport facilities or international standard facilities as seen in the case from the state of Victoria. Similarly, few sport organisations have the resources, reach or community-based insights to design and deliver community-based sport across the entire country. Furthermore, non-traditional sporting structures can be seen to act as a bridge that connects conventional sport organisations with other sub-sectors, thereby opening up the prospect of new ways of working and new collaborative opportunities as well as additional funding opportunities. An example here is the work of APs in developing stronger local-level relations with health and wellbeing agencies in order to address sedentary behaviour, an issue that traditional sport organisations have struggled to effectively address.

The non-traditional classification of the agency neutralises adverse judgements that may historically be aimed at sport and also aligns the organisation more with a broader goal for a specific community (i.e., Active Suffolk) rather than a narrower focus on sport which may be viewed as only being accessible for certain sport types. The case of MOPT and, in particular, the way in which they have brokered agreements with key stakeholders Tennis Australia and Tennis Victoria – the tenants of one of the largest facilities within that Trust – is also an example of the ways in which the specialist knowledge of MOPT board and management have worked with the sport to create a space and an event that extends well beyond the sport itself and has relevance, accessibility and inclusion for residents and tourists alike.

A second key issue emanating from the cases is power. Here, the cases demonstrate the varied and increasingly important role that non-traditional sporting structures play in sport. They also reinforce the continued trend away from hierarchical structures towards networks or systems that share responsibility in delivering specific areas of public policy. This is not to suggest that there is no hierarchy and no transactional relationship evident in such networks. For example, there is clearly a hierarchy and a transactional relationship in the way in which DCMS fund Sport England in return for specific outcomes and so too Sport England and their relationship with the APs. The same is true for facility trusts and the sports that are tenants within their facilities. However, the relationship and shared responsibility for community sport and for sport events is more complex and nuanced than can be understood merely by hierarchical relations.

In the case of Sport England, this complexity is in part the result of the range and nature of relationships with other stakeholders in the network. Community sport is not only reliant upon the DCMS, Sport England and APs, but also a range of other stakeholders. The nature of these relationships has an effect on the overall credibility of each stakeholder and their ability to interact and negotiate with other stakeholders involved in the network. In this way, local-level partnerships and the credibility gained through such partnerships can empower non-traditional sporting structures, particularly when additional resources are part of such collaborations. This has the effect of reducing the APs dependence on government funding and bolsters the impression that government and Sport England have towards APs. Such collaborations help to change the outdated view of APs as simply a part of the government sport policy apparatus to an elevated conception of the APs as local-level, independent organisations that aspire to create a more active nation.

While this chapter has focused on the system-wide governance of sport and the role of non-traditional sporting structures within such systems, this is by no means intended to be a definitive account. Indeed, broader conceptualisations of governance should be applied to such structures to advance our understanding of their role, strategy and practices as well as how such issues could be enhanced to support efficient and effective policy making and implementation. To this end, future research could examine the current organisational practices of non-traditional sporting structures and how such practices compare with a view to providing a summary of good practices in the governance of such structures. Related to this, a comparative analysis of the workforce skills of non-traditional sporting structures as compared to traditional sporting structures would help to add to the literature on previous questions about the extent to which sport is hindered by an overly passionate workforce that lacks objective analytical decision-making skills (Harris, 2013). Additionally, good governance principles could be applied to non-traditional sporting structures to benchmark and assess the extent to which such structures address good governance principles as well as identify areas for further development.

It would also be of some interest, specifically in England, to analyse the impact of governance code on the administration of APs. This is because APs are required to meet certain conditions set out in the governance code as a requirement for government funding. While it is known that APs go through the process and report how they meet certain conditions, little is known about how such requirements shape interactions among stakeholders, whether such processes are effective in delivering better governance, or any of the broader impacts that the governance code may have on APs. Finally, given the amount of attention focused on organisational culture and its relationship with notable governance failures, it would be useful to have more focused empirical insights relating to organisational culture studied through a governance lens in order to better understand how organisational culture can be changed and cultivated through governance structures and the behaviours of those involved in governing at all levels of the organisation.

The relationship between various aspects of the political governance of sport and non-traditional sporting structures would also benefit from further research. In particular, there would be considerable value in having clearer insights into the attitudes and perspectives of traditional stakeholders (state agencies, umbrella sport organisations, NGBs) towards non-traditional structures. Such research could, at minimum, help to raise awareness of how the opportunities and challenges that confront such systems could be managed to enhance the governance of sport. Similarly, a clearer understanding of the work of non-sport codes in policy advocacy and how such structures enhance and sustain influence over time would be helpful in creating a fuller picture of the patterns of power that exist across governance networks and of how agents that are perceived to be traditionally weak gain influence and power. Linked to the previous point, it would also be interesting to examine the direct and indirect role of elected politicians in the governance of non-sport codes, particularly given the geographically representative nature of elected politicians and non-traditional sporting structures which tend to be geographically embedded – a point of particular distinction when compare to traditional national sporting structures. To be clear, the inference here lay in the extent to which politicians support non-traditional sporting structures due to populism, parochialism and the need to be seen as supportive of local causes.

The final, somewhat obvious, strand of research would extend insights into the role, function and performance of non-traditional sporting structures within systemic governance. Here, as Dowling and colleagues (2018) suggest, it may be useful to consider the relationship between governance approaches; for example, the degree to which organisational governance and performance affects systemic governance. Another area of research that would be apposite for sport given the importance of Lex Sportiva and the notion of autonomy of sport, is the role and function that international-level non-traditional sporting entities could play in providing oversight and reporting on ethical issues and governance failures in international sport. Here, notable developments in the engagement of the various UN-related agencies in sport and in the developments of not-for-profit organisations, such as Transparency International and Play the Game, are evident. However, more published work on the overall impact of such agencies in enhancing governance practices would be a useful addition to the literature. A final area of research within the area of systemic governance could look to add greater contextual richness to the collaborative capacity literature and how such capacity can be developed and sustained within the sport system. Here, it would be particularly helpful to identity the antecedents of collaborative capacity as well as the extent to which antecedents vary according to structure. To conclude, this chapter re-asserts the growing prominence of non-traditional sporting structures within domestic and international sport systems and, thus, the need to include such structures in the analyses of sport governance. The research ideas detailed above should help to address the lack of enquiry and therefore build our understanding of the performance of non-traditional sport structures and their role, responsibilities and relationships within the systemic governance of sport.

References

Active Partnerships. (2019). Active partnerships *About us*. Retrieved 3 June 2019, from https://www.activepartnerships.org/

Adam, S., & Kriesi, H. (2007). The network approach. In P. Sabatier (Ed.), *Theories of the policy process* (pp. 129–155). Boulder, CO: Westview Press.

Ansell, C., & Gash, A. (2008). Collaborative governance in theory and practice. *Journal of Public Administration Research and Theory, 18*, 543–571.

Benson, K. J. (1982). A Framework for policy analysis. In D. Rogers & D. Whitten (Eds.), *Interorganizational co-ordination: Theory, research and implementation* (pp. 137–176). Ames, IO: Iowa State University Press.

Borzel, T. (1998). Organizing Babylon: On the different conceptions of policy networks. *Public Administration, 26*, 253–273.

Cairney, P. (2011). *Understanding public policy*. Basingstoke: Palgrave Macmillan.

Carter, P. (2005). *Review of national sport effort and resources*. London: Dept. of Culture, Media & Sport.

Chappelet, J. L. (2016). From Olympic administration to Olympic governance. *Sport in Society, 19*, 739–751.

Department for Culture, Media and Sport. (2002). *Game plan: A strategy for delivering Government's sport and physical activity objectives*. London: Author.

Department for Culture, Media and Sport. (2015). *Sporting future*. London: Author.

Dowding, K. (1995). Model or metaphor? A critical review of the policy network approach. *Political Studies, 45*, 136–158.

Dowling, M., Leopkey, B., & Smith, L. (2018). Governance in sport: A scoping review. *Journal of Sport Management, 32*, 438–451.

Fassin, Y. (2012). Stakeholder management, reciprocity and stakeholder responsibility. *Journal of Business Ethics, 109*, 83–96.

Ferkins, L., & Shilbury, D. (2015). Board strategic balance: An emerging sport governance theory. *Sport Management Review, 18*, 489–500.

Harris, S. (2013). *An analysis of the significance of sub-regional partnerships in the community sport policy process* (Ph.D. Thesis). Loughborough University: Loughborough, UK.

Harris, S., & Houlihan, B. (2014). Delivery networks and community sport in England. *International Journal of Public Sector Management, 2*, 113–127.

Harris, S., & Houlihan, B. (2016). Implementing the community sport legacy: The limits of partnerships, contracts, and performance management. *European Sport Management Quarterly, 4*, 433–458.

Heclo, H. (1978). Issue networks and the executive establishment. In A. Kind (Ed.), *The new American political system* (pp. 87–107). Washington, DC: American Enterprise Institute.

Henry, I., & Lee, P. C. (2004). Governance and ethics in sport. In S. Chadwick & J. Beech (Eds.), *The business of sport management* (pp. 25–42). Harlow: Pearson Education.

Houlihan, B., & White, A. (2002). *The politics of sport development: Development of sport or development through sport?* London: Routledge.

Howlett, M. (1998). Predictable and unpredictable policy windows: Institutional and exogenous correlates of Canadian federal agenda setting. *Canadian Journal of Political Science, XXI*, 495–525.

John, P. (1998). *Analysing public policy*. London: Pinter.

Kellett, P., Hede, A. M., & Chalip, L. (2008). Social policy for sport events: Leveraging (relationships with) teams from other nations for community benefit. *European Sport Management Quarterly, 8*, 101–121.

Kickert, W., Klijn, E., & Koppenjan, J. (1996). *Managing complex networks: Strategies for the Public Sector.* London: Sage.

Knaggs, A. (2019, March 13). Rebrand sees CSP become active partnerships. *Sport Management magazine, No pagination.*

Lindsey, I. (2006). Local partnerships in the United Kingdom for the New Opportunities for P.E. and sport initiative: A policy network analysis. *European Sport Management Quarterly, 6*, 167–184.

Marsh, D., & Rhodes, R. A. W. (Eds.). (1992). *Policy networks in British government*. Oxford: Clarendon.

Marsh, D., & Smith, M. (2000). Understanding policy networks: Towards a dialectical approach. *Political studies, 48*, 4–21.

McDonald, I. (2005). Theorising partnerships: Governance, communicative action and sport policy. *Journal of Social Policy, 34*, 579–600.

Melbourne Olympic Parks Trust. (2019). Overview. Retrieved 3 May 2019, from https://mopt.com.au/about/overview/

Miller, H. T., & Demir, T. (2006). Policy communities. In F. Fischer, G. Miller & M. Sidney (Eds.), *Handbook of public policy analysis: Theory, politics, and methods* (pp. 137–149). London: Taylor and Francis.

Phillpots, L., Grix, J., & Quarmby, T. (2010). Centralized grassroots sport policy and new governance: A case study of County Sports Partnerships in the UK - unpacking the paradox. *International Review for the Sociology of Sport, 46*, 265–281.

Shilbury, D., & Ferkins, L. (2015). Exploring the utility of collaborative governance in a National Sport Organization. *Journal of Sport Management, 29*, 380–397.

Shilbury, D., Phillips, P., Karg., A., & Rowe, K. (2017). *Sport management in Australia: An Overview*. Crows Nest: Allen & Unwin.

Van der Heijden, J. (2012). Different but equally plausible narratives of policy transformation: A plea for theoretical pluralism. *International Political Science Review, 34*(1), 57–73.

Victoria State Government. (2019a). About us. Retrieved 2 May 2019, from https://sport.vic.gov.au/about-us

Victoria State Government. (2019b). Public entities. Retrieved 2 May 2019, from https://sport.vic.gov.au/about-us/public-entities

Visit Victoria. (2019). Sport business honours Melbourne. Retrieved 2 May 2019, from https://corporate.visitvictoria.com/news/sportbusiness-honours-melbourne

Part III

Ownership structures and governance models: Implications for sport governance

9

Professional team ownership models in North America

Norm O'Reilly

Introduction

Club ownership in professional team sport in North America is characterised by wealth, syndicates and collective bargaining with the players. Much of this characterisation has to do with the ownership models that have been developed as a result of these dynamics. Although there is considerable discussion on governance-related topics of club ownership in North America in trade journals, newspapers, blogs and books, there exists limited academic research specific to ownership models. The existing body of academic research on ownership in North American major team sport has typically focussed on management aspects, as opposed to overall models – with a lot of work done in the area. For instance, published work that includes ownership as a variable or a key concept include work on club profitability (Nadeau & O'Reilly, 2006), linking ownership structure and perception to team performance (Wilson, Plumley & Ramchandani, 2013), the acceptance of foreign owners by fans (Coombs & Osborne, 2012), perception of team ownership in securing government and community support for urban development projects (Mason, Sant & Soebbing, 2017; Mitrook, Parish & Seltzer, 2008), merchandise sales (O'Reilly, Foster, Murray & Shimizu, 2015), corporate social responsibility (Sheth & Babiak, 2010), legitimacy (Lock, Filo, Kunkel & Skinner, 2015), managing uncertainty (Soebbing & Mason, 2009), brand management (Agyemang & Williams, 2013), relationship management (Hambrick & Kang, 2015) and social media (Abeza, O'Reilly, Seguin & Nzindukiyimana, 2015; Watanabe, Yan & Soebbing, 2015).

For those undertaking research in this area, it is well known that there is a limited amount of scholarship specific to ownership models and that it has more has more to do with access to information than the prevalence of leadership, governance and decision-making for owners of clubs. However, given the intensive media and fan interest, along with the considerable attention paid in the media, one could argue that leadership, the governance process and the structure of ownership in professional team sport in North America, is more important than in other areas of the sport industry. Perhaps the most illustrative of this difference from other parts of the sport industry is the model of eight forms of professional sport ownership intent (i.e., rationales to own, or partially own, a professional sport club) articulated by Foster, O'Reilly and Davila (2016), which outlined eight specific reasons why – based on the authors' experiences – an entity would purchase ownership in a club.

Unlike many other parts of the sport industry, major professional team sport has relied on professional staff and procedures for many years, as opposed to the volunteer kitchen-table style of management and governance historically observed in amateur sport (Thibault, Slack & Hinings, 1991). However, similar to the rest of the industry, professional team sport in North America has been professionalising in recent years becoming more formalised, commercially focussed and savvy (Siegfried, Schlesinger, Bayle & Giauque, 2015). Elements of this trend includes the hiring of more trained staff (i.e., sport management professionals rather than untrained former athletes), the use of specialised third-party agencies (e.g., outsourcing marketing efforts to a specialised agency, such as IMG, GMR or Octagon) and the creation of owned assets by the leagues and/ or clubs (e.g., the NHL's creation of outdoor ice hockey games played at large venues) (Foster, O'Reilly & Davila, 2016).

In recent decades, the major North American professional leagues have also been characterised by an ongoing and significant growth in both club revenues and club values (i.e., sale price to change ownership) across all the five major leagues. A review of the annual estimates by Forbes Magazine[1] finds that club values, across the leagues, have increased at a rate greater than inflation for many years but with a noticeable spike upwards recently, such as the 2018 estimates for the NBA, which show that all clubs are worth more than US$1 billion, an average increase of 22% over the previous year estimate by Forbes. As club values have appreciated and revenues have grown, interest in ownership of a club has also changed to be limited to very wealthy individuals and corporations, those seeking commercial benefit, some with alternate business objectives and, although it is largely agreed to not be the primary purpose of ownership of a club (Foster, O'Reilly & Davila, 2016), profit-seekers.

As outlined, club ownership is an important area, but with limited specific published work. Thus, the purpose of this chapter is to outline the governance of major North American professional team sport by providing conceptual background and secondary data on ownership, with the aim to provide a basic understanding of the context and to suggest future research needs in the area.

Professional sporting clubs in major North American team sport

The club, or team, is the most recognised property in professional sport. Club brands endure poor on-field results, player scandals, roster changes, coaching problems and ownership switches. Fan affinity, in many cases, is with the club and mega-clubs such as the Montreal Canadiens (NHL), New York Yankees (MLB), Boston Celtics (NBA), Los Angeles Galaxy (MLS) and Dallas Cowboys (NFL) have fan bases of all ages, backgrounds and locations. Importantly, clubs within any league differ across financial (e.g., local revenues), pricing (e.g., average ticket price, cost of a hot dog), market (e.g., size of market, average household income), promotions (e.g., strength of regional sport network) and other factors (e.g., presence of a star player or local hero) (Foster, O'Reilly & Davila, 2016; O'Reilly & Nadeau, 2006).

The current environment of professional sport clubs in the five major leagues in North America that are the topic of this chapter, includes 146 clubs, of which 133 are based in the United States and 13 in Canada. The NFL has 32, clubs, the NHL 31 (The NHL's 32nd club, based in Seattle, will commence in 2022), MLB and NBA 30 each and MLS 23. With only a few exceptions (e.g., Green Bay), clubs are located in large urban markets and are owned by wealthy individuals or syndicates. Most clubs are the only club for their league in their market, with the exception of New York, Los Angeles and Chicago, where some leagues have more than a single club. For example, there are three NHL clubs in the New York City metropolitan area (New York Rangers, New York Islanders, New Jersey Devils).

Clubs are members of leagues and adhere to the rules of the league which are determined by the league's Board of Governors, comprised of one representative of the ownership of each club and executed by the league Commissioner, who is hired by the Board of Governors. Typically, the commissioner of a league is the "public face" of the league and represents the club ownership/board of governors on most issues. The league regulates the competition of the clubs who compete for the league championship. This regulation includes both on-field (e.g., technical rules of the game) and off-the-field elements (e.g., player drafts/movements) related to the competition. As outlined by Foster, O'Reilly and Davila (2016), most clubs function as two silos with the sport side and the business side not interacting a great deal, with the exception of a few general managers (i.e., the club executive who selects, drafts, hires and negotiates with players and coaches) who span both sides and the evolution of analytics departments who do work for both sides (e.g., ticket pricing, athletic performance).

The role of the league in club ownership and governance

Amongst many factors, professional sport leagues differ by architecture, composition, scope, governance approach and view on competitive balance (Foster, O'Reilly & Davila, 2016). In turn, the varying characteristics of any league will influence the ownership and governance of any club in any league. By definition, the league is the lead organiser of professional sport. The league regulates the structure of competition (e.g., number of games, playoff format), decides on resource allocation (i.e., revenue-sharing rules), determines how to structure its relationship with its players (i.e., collective bargaining), determines the rules of the game (e.g., penalties, instant replay use, referee behaviour), outlines the jurisdiction of operation (i.e., expansion, global development), leads league-level marketing (e.g., sponsorship, merchandising) and manages media relationships for the league (e.g., national television contracts).

Since the focus of this chapter is professional team sport where members are sporting clubs, it is important to note that leagues also exist that manage professional individual sports, such as golf, tennis, auto racing and skiing. In motorsports, for example, the professional sport of "stock car driving" is managed by NASCAR, a league whose members are individual drivers (e.g., Dale Earnhardt Jr., Danika Patrick) who are supported by teams but compete as individuals.

The major North American clubs govern based on an approach that is very different than what is observed in clubs in other parts of the worlds (see Chapters 10, 11 and 12), individual sports and minor North American professional sports. A few of the key differentiating concepts are presented here to aid in understanding the governance context of these major clubs.

First, for these leagues, the principles of value creation and value sharing are closely linked – some would even say intertwined. Indeed, these leagues are dual focussed on building value for the league *and* sharing that value equally amongst the clubs. For example, when the leagues create new revenues through league-wide sponsorship, digital marketing efforts, new asset creation or other league-led efforts, the proceeds are shared equally amongst the member clubs. In determining how to share its revenues, leagues consider both what should be included in the pool of revenues to be shared and how the sharing between the clubs will occur. The structure of revenue-sharing is determined in consultation with the players and outlined in a document called the collective bargaining agreement (CBA), which outlines all the specifics. As an example of a revenue-sharing initiative, the NFL collects and manages all media contracts at the league level, while MLB, NBA and NHL have media revenues at both the league and the club levels. Typically, a league covers its costs and keeps a percentage of the total revenues, with the balance shared equally amongst the clubs. However, there are additional rules applied in certain cases around revenue-sharing. For instance, some leagues will allocate higher proportions to low-revenue/small market clubs from high-revenue/large market clubs through rules such as the luxury tax that MLB uses, where clubs who spend more than a set threshold are charged a tax that is then re-allocated to the lowest revenue clubs in the league. The specific details of these rules are renegotiated in each round of collective bargaining (typically every ten years).

Second, these leagues seek a structure that is competitively balanced, where – from a resource perspective – each club has an equal chance to compete for a championship at the start of each season. This has led to these leagues implementing a number of league-level measures to eliminate situations where some clubs are spending many times more on players than other clubs or where all of the best talent in the league plays with one or two clubs. There are many such measures used by these clubs, including (i) salary caps (i.e., maximum spend allowed by a club) and floors (i.e., minimum spend allowed by a club), (ii) an entry draft system for young talent that allow the poorer performing clubs to select first with selection order set on a worst-to-best criteria and (iii) agreed upon limits as to what benefits clubs can provide beyond salary to players (e.g., off season training support, extra benefits to families, etc.) to limit player movement based on such factors. These measures are put in place to allow for a broader spectrum of star players across clubs rather than stockpiled on a few clubs.

Third, these leagues operate in a "closed" league structure where there is no promotion or relegation, unlike many other major global leagues (Davila, O'Reilly & Foster, 2009). This means that club membership in a league is a set group (e.g., NFL as 32 clubs) and it is the owners (board of governors) who decide whether a new club (typically called an expansion team) is allowed to join and whether a current club can move to a new market (typically referred to as a relocation) . Contrarily, in an "open" league structure such as the premier leagues in Europe (e.g., La Liga in Spain), the lowest performing clubs will be relegated to a lower level league to be replaced by the highest performing clubs in the lower league, who move up. Thus, given the closed structure in major North American professional team sport, these leagues are able to keep close control of the criteria and decisions around which clubs can compete in the league and what criteria a new club needs to meet to join. This is particularly important as these leagues consider future domestic and/or global expansion.

How does a league structure club ownership at start-up?

An important phase in the development of any organisation is its start-up. This is no different with professional team sport leagues, including those in North America. The four major leagues are all very well established with the MLB (founded 1903), NHL (founded 1917), NFL (founded 1920) and NBA (founded 1946) all in existence for more than 70 years. More recently, MLS, now largely considered to be the fifth major league was founded in 1993, being the first soccer league to achieve success in North America following a number of failed attempts by other soccer leagues. The failure of leagues is common and a key learning point about the structure of club ownership within a league. In fact, the majority of the professional leagues started in North America fail (Foster, O'Reilly & Davila, 2016), with recent examples including the Association of American Football (AAF), the Canadian Women's Hockey League (CWHL) and the United Football League (UFL). At start-up, a league has an opportunity to set its ownership structure without any history or limits. A number of models are available to new leagues ranging from the distributed club ownership model to the single-entity model with a number of alternatives possible in between (Foster, O'Reilly & Davila, 2016).

The *distributed club ownership model* is what characterises the majority of club ownership in each of the major North American leagues today, with some slight alterations league by league. In this model, each league has its own distinct ownership group, with no owner allowed to hold ownership in more than one club in that league. Most of the ownership groups are syndicates, comprised of multiple individuals or organisations (e.g., a media company) who all have varying levels of ownership interest in the club, normally defined by the number of shares they own/control (Foster, O'Reilly & Davila, 2016). Due to the increasing cost to own all or part of a club, the syndicate has become more common. As noted, one owner is designated the "governor" who represents the club at the league's Board of Governors level. Each club also designates an "alternate governor". The club owners, as part of the Board of Governors, are active in league decision-making in a number of capacities including auditing, appointing and monitoring the commissioner, exploring and approving league expansion (new clubs), approving club relocation, new ventures (e.g., NFL Europe), collective bargaining with the players and sitting on a variety of standing committees for league work.

The *single-entity ownership model* is a structure of club ownership normally only observed at the start-up phase of a new league. This model occurs when a single entity (individual or group) owns the entire league and *all* of its teams. A classic example from the North American context is the Women's National Basketball Association (WNBA) which has evolved to be a distributed club ownership model today, but began as a single-entity ownership model in 1997 with the entire league and all the clubs owned by the NBA. The Extreme Football League (XFL) is another example from North America. Its initial (2001) launch, which failed after one season, had the league and all its clubs jointly owned by National Broadcasting Corporation (NBC) and World Wrestling Entertainment (WWE), with a second attempt planned for 2020 and fully owned by WWE.

From a governance perspective, the single-entity club ownership model provides a few important benefits when compared to the distributed model. First, the single-entity model provides the league with the ability to ensure competitive balance as they can strategically allocate players to clubs across the league. Second, the league has full control from a club ownership view, where the clubs can be placed where the league would like, and the league can subsidise certain clubs in certain key markets. Third, the league can be strategic in its allocation of players and markets. For instance, while a single-entity ownership model, the WNBA assigned superstar player Sheryl Swoopes to the Houston Comets following her graduation from nearby Texas Tech University. Finally, the single-entity model allows ownership to control costs and limit legal disputes, such as player salaries, since there are no clubs competing for talent. There are also a number of drawbacks to this model, namely that it has many inherent conflicts of interest that do not favour certain individual clubs and some players. Notably, a player has no mobility to move to another club or to negotiate for a salary at their market value.

Who owns a major professional sport club in North America and why?

The 146 clubs who currently make up the five major North American team sport professional leagues are very different. They differ in terms of financial metrics (e.g., revenues, ticket prices, local television contract) and non-financial metrics (e.g., population size of home market, brand strength, age of club), as well as by their performance on the field (Foster, O'Reilly & Davila, 2016). The ownership of a club has much to do with these outcomes, as do the league rules in which the clubs operate.

Who are these owners?

By definition, a club owner is any group of individuals that has equity in the club. Some clubs have a single owner (i.e., 100% ownership) who is typically a wealthy individual who has wealth from family or business success and as opted to purchase the entirety of a club. Others are also owned privately but by a group of two or more owners. As noted, these multiple-owner scenarios are called "ownership syndicates" and are becoming more common in clubs in North American major leagues. A syndicate is inherently more complicated to govern than a single-owner model as individual members will have different priorities, voting rights, decisions rights and roles to occupy. There are other alternatives to club ownership within leagues. One is exemplified by the NFL club, the Green Bay Packers, who are a publicly-owned, not-for-profit organisation where the club's owners are more than 300,000 fans/investors who purchased shares in the club and who elect a board of directors to manage the club. Table 9.1 shows the ownership and a few details about the 32 NFL clubs. As outlined in Table 9.1, all of the lead owners for the clubs listed are individuals since the NFL is the one league that does not allow corporate ownership. The extreme billionaire-level wealth of the owners across the league is also shared, as is the strong revenues and valuations of clubs. Next, Table 9.2 describes the current ownership of MLB and its 30 clubs.

Similar to the NFL, MLB clubs are in a period of high value and strong revenues. Although most of their ownership groups are also private individuals, corporate ownership is observed in MLB. For example, Rogers Communications (a large telecommunications company) owns the Toronto Blue Jays and Liberty Mutual (a financial investment firm) owns the Atlanta Braves. In the case of corporate ownership, it is typically classified as either independent (i.e., no relationship to the sport being played) or convergent (i.e., directly integrated with the sport being played) (Nadeau & O'Reilly, 2006). In the examples from MLB, Rogers would be classified as converged, while Liberty as independent. The ownership of the Los Angeles Dodgers is a great example of a syndicate, as the Guggenheim group includes a number of key ownership members as part of a consortium that includes a number of wealthy investors and a celebrity owner (Magic Johnson).

Tables 9.3 and 9.4 show the current ownership in the NBA and NHL, respectively. These ownership groups are similar in that their wealth, club values and club revenues are lower than the NFL and MLB. Tables 9.3 and 9.4 include many individual private owners but also a number of syndicates (e.g., Aquilini Investment Group, Boston Celtics Syndicate, Calgary Flames LP and True North Sports & Entertainment) and converged corporate ownership (e.g., Comcast, Madison Square and Rogers/Bell). Table 9.5 presents the ownership of the MLS. MLS, as the newest and lowest value league of the five, also has owners with the least wealth and the clubs are the lowest value/revenue drivers. The large number of owners who are also owners in other leagues is observed as well (e.g., Arthur Blank, Robert Kraft, Maple Leaf Sport & Entertainment and Kroenke Sports & Entertainment), perhaps supporting owner interest in adding tenants to NFL football venues and maximising use of staff to support other properties, both efforts known to support the business success of clubs (Nadeau & O'Reilly, 2006).

Ownership intent

As noted in Tables 9.1 through 9.5, owners are a diverse group of individuals and syndicates, who are independent or converged, with varying levels of wealth, who invest in clubs of different values, revenues and market sizes. Foster, O'Reilly and Davila (2016) reported that these groups decide to invest to become owners for a number of reasons, which are presented as the 8 P's of ownership intent: Performance, Profit, Platform, Preemptive, Purpose, Profile, Power and Passion.

Performance is about winning a championship (or many), contending, making the play-offs and/or having a successful regular season, and the owner's desire for such. **Profit** is when an owner prioritises revenue generation, loss avoidance and/or asset appreciation. **Platform** is

Table 9.1 National Football League (NFL)

Team	Home City	Owner(s)	Owner – Who Sits on Board of Governors	Wealth of the Owner on Board ($B)	Current Value ($B)	Revenue ($M)	Metro Area Population (M)
Arizona Cardinals	Phoenix	William (Bill) Bidwill	William (Bill) Bidwill	$1.4	$2.15	$380	4.7
Atlanta Falcons	Atlanta	Arthur Blank	Arthur Blank	$4.3	$2.60	$451	5.8
Baltimore Ravens	Baltimore	Steve Bisciotti	Richard W. Cass	$4.4	$2.59	$417	2.8
Buffalo Bills	Buffalo	Kim and Terry Pegula	Terry Pegula	$4.3	$1.60	$364	1.1
Carolina Panthers	Charlotte	David Tepper	David Tepper	$11	$2.30	$396	2.5
Chicago Bears	Chicago	Virginia Halas McCaskey	George Halas McCaskey	$1.3	$2.90	$431	9.5
Cincinnati Bengals	Cincinnati	Mike Brown	Mike Brown	$0.925	$1.80	$359	2.1
Cleveland Browns	Cleveland	Jimmy and Dee Haslam	Jimmy and Dee Haslam	$3.7	$1.95	$375	2
Dallas Cowboys	Dallas	Jerry Jones	Jerry Jones	$5.6	$5	$864	7.2
Denver Broncos	Denver	Pat Bowlen and The Bowlen Family Trust	Joe Ellis		$2.65	$427	2.9
Detroit Lions	Detroit	Martha Firestone Ford	Martha Firestone Ford	$1.5	$1.70	$361	4.3
Green Bay Packers	Green Bay	Green Bay Packers, INC	Mark Murphy		$2.63	$434	0.3
Houston Texans	Houston	Janice McNair and Family	Janice McNair	$3.8	$2.80	$464	6.3
Indianapolis Colts	Indianapolis	Jim Irsay	Jim Irsay	$2.7	$2.38	$373	2
Jacksonville Jaguars	Jacksonville	Shahid Khan	Shahid Khan		$2.08	$391	1.5
Kansas City Chiefs	Kansas City	Clark Hunt and Hunt Family	Clark Hunt	$13.7	$2.10	$380	2.2
Los Angeles Chargers	Los Angeles	Dean Spanos	Dean Spanos		$2.28	$346	13.1
Los Angeles Rams	Los Angeles	Kroenke Sports & Entertainment, Stan Kroenke	Stan Kroenke	$8.3	$3.20	$366	13.1
Miami Dolphins	Miami	Stephen M. Ross	Stephen M. Ross	$7.6	$2.58	$414	5.6

(Continued)

Table 9.1 Continued

Team	Home City	Owner(s)	Owner – Who Sits on Board of Governors	Wealth of the Owner on Board ($B)	Current Value ($B)	Revenue ($M)	Metro Area Population (M)
Minnesota Vikings	Minneapolis	Zygi Wilf, Mark Wilf, Leonard Wilf	Mark Wilf		$2.40	$408	3.6
New England Patriots	Boston	Robert Kraft	Robert Kraft	$6.2	$3.80	$593	4.6
New Orleans Saints	New Orleans	Gayle Benson	Dennis Lauscha		$2.08	$413	1.3
New York Giants	New York	John K. Mara, Steve Tisch	Steve Tisch	$1.2	$3.30	$493	20.1
New York Jets	New York	Woody and Christopher Johnson	Christopher Johnson	$4.19	$2.85	$443	20.1
Oakland Raiders	Oakland	Mark Davis	Marc Badain		$2.42	$335	4.7
Philadelphia Eagles	Philadelphia	Jeffrey Lurie and Christina Weiss Lurie	Jeffrey Lurie	$2	$2.75	$458	6.1
Pittsburgh Steelers	Pittsburgh	Art Rooney II and Family	Art Rooney II	$1.2	$2.59	$415	2.4
San Francisco 49ers	San Francisco	Jed York, Denise Debartolo York, John York	Denise York, John York	$2.5	$3.05	$470	4.7
Seattle Seahawks	Seattle	Estate of Paul Allen	Bert Kolde		$2.58	$413	3.7
Tampa Bay Buccaneers	Tampa Bay	Bryan Glazer, Edward Glazer, Joel Glazer	Bryan Glazer, Edward Glazer, Joel Glazer	$4.7	$2	$383	3
Tennessee Titans	Nashville	Amy Adams Strunk	Amy Adams Strunk	$1.3	$2.05	$371	1.8
Washington Redskins	Washington	Dan Snyder	Bruce Allen	$2.3	$3.10	$491	6.1

Source:
https://www.forbes.com/nfl-valuations/list/#tab:overall
https://www.si.com/nfl/2018/nfl-owners-guide-32-teams-franchises
https://www.nfl.com/

Table 9.2 Major League Baseball (MLB)

Team	Home City	Owner(s)	Owner – Who Sits on Board of Governors	Wealth of the Owner on Board ($B)	Current Value ($B)	Revenue ($M)	Metro Area Population (M)
Arizona Diamondbacks	Phoenix	Ken Kendrick	Derrick Hall		$1.21	$258	4.6
Atlanta Braves	Atlanta	Liberty Media	Terence McGuirk	$5.1	$1.63	$336	5.7
Baltimore Orioles	Baltimore	Peter Angelos	Peter Angelos	$2.1	$1.20	$252	2.8
Boston Red Sox	Boston	John Henry	Thomas Werner	$2.5	$2.80	$453	4.6
Chicago Cubs	Chicago	Ricketts Family	Tom Ricketts	$2.1	$2.90	$457	9.5
Chicago White Sox	Chicago	Jerry Reinsdorf	Jerry Reinsdorf	$1.4	$1.50	$266	9.5
Cincinnati Reds	Cincinnati	Robert Castellini	Robert Castellini	$0.4	$1.01	$243	2.1
Cleveland Indians	Cleveland	Lawrence Dolan, Paul Dolan	Paul Dolan		$1.05	$284	2.1
Colorado Rockies	Denver	Charles Monfort, Richard Monfort	Richard Monfort		$1.10	$266	2.8
Detroit Tigers	Detroit	Christopher Ilitch	Christopher Ilitch	$2.4	$1.23	$277	4.3
Houston Astros	Houston	Jim Crane	Jim Crane	$2	$1.65	$347	6.3
Kansas City Royals	Kansas City	David Glass	David Glass		$1.02	$245	2.2
Los Angeles Angels	Anaheim	Arte & Carole Moreno	Arturo Moreno	$2.5	$1.80	$334	13.1
Los Angeles Dodgers	Los Angeles	Guggenheim Baseball Management, Mark Walter	Mark Walter	$3.2	$3	$522	13.1
Miami Marlins	Miami	Bruce Sherman	Bruce Sherman		$1	$219	5.6
Milwaukee Brewers	Milwaukee	Mark Attanasio	Mark Attanasio	$0.7	$1.03	$255	1.6
Minnesota Twins	Minneapolis	James Pohlad	Jim Pohlad	$3.6	$1.15	$261	3.5
New York Mets	Corona	Fred & Jeff Wilpon, Saul Katz	Fred Wilpon	$0.5	$2.10	$336	20.2
New York Yankees	Bronx	Hal Steinbrenner	Hal Steinbrenner	$3.2	$4	$619	20.2
Oakland Athletics	Oakland	John Fisher	John Fisher	$2	$1.02	$210	4.7
Philadelphia Phillies	Philadelphia	John Middleton, Buck Family, David Montgomery	John Middleton		$1.70	$329	6.1
Pittsburgh Pirates	Pittsburgh	Nutting Family	Robert Nutting	$1.1	$1.26	$258	2.4
San Diego Padres	San Diego	Ron Fowler, Peter Seidler	Ron Fowler		$1.27	$266	3.1

(Continued)

Table 9.2 Continued

Team	Home City	Owner(s)	Owner – Who Sits on Board of Governors	Wealth of the Owner on Board ($B)	Current Value ($B)	Revenue ($M)	Metro Area Population (M)
San Francisco Giants	San Francisco	Charles Johnson	Laurence M. Baer	$6.4	$2.85	$445	4.6
Seattle Mariners	Seattle	John Stanton, Chris Larson	John Stanton	$1.1	$1.45	$288	3.7
St Louis Cardinals	St. Louis	William DeWitt Jr	William DeWitt Jr	$4	$1.90	$319	2.8
Tampa Bay Rays	St. Petersburg	Stuart Sternberg	Stuart Sternberg	$0.8	$900	$219	3
Texas Rangers	Arlington	Ray Davis, Bob Simpson	Ray Davis	$2.5	$1.60	$311	7.1
Toronto Blue Jays	Toronto	Rogers Communications, Edward S. Rogers III	Edward Rogers		$1.35	$274	5.9
Washington Nationals	Washington	Lerner Family	Mark D. Lerner		$1.68	$311	6

Source:
https://www.forbes.com/mlb-valuations/list/#tab:overall
https://www.bloomberg.com/research/stocks/private/person.asp?personId=866783&privcapId=4319252
https://www.celebritynetworth.com/

Table 9.3 National Basketball Association (NBA)

Team	Home City	Owner(s)	Owner – Who Sits on Board of Governors	Wealth of the Owner on Board ($B)	Current Value ($B)	Revenue ($M)	Metro Area Population (M)
Atlanta Hawks	Atlanta	Tony Ressler, Grant Hill, Steven Prince, Rick Schnall, Sara Blakely, Jesse Itzler	Tony Ressler	$2	$1.15	$209	5.7
Boston Celtics	Boston	Wycliffe Grousbeck, Robert Epstein, Irving Grousbeck, Stephen Pagliuca	Wycliffe Grousbeck	$0.4	$2.50	$257	4.6
Brooklyn Nets	Brooklyn	Mikhail Prokhorov	Mikhail Prokhorov	$9.6	$2.30	$273	20.1
Charlotte Hornets	Charlotte	Michael Jordan	Michael Jordan	$1.6	$1.05	$202	2.5
Chicago Bulls	Chicago	Jerry Reinsdorf	Jerry Reinsdorf	$1.4	$2.60	$281	9.5
Cleveland Cavaliers	Cleveland	Dan Gilbert	Dan Gilbert	$6.5	$1.33	$280	2.1
Dallas Mavericks	Dallas	Mark Cuban	Floyd Jahner		$1.90	$233	7.2
Denver Nuggets	Denver	Ann Walton Kroenke, Kroenke Sports & Entertainment	Josh Kroenke		$1.13	$202	2.8
Detroit Pistons	Detroit	Tom Gores	Tom Gores	$3.9	$1.10	$221	4.3
Golden State Warriors	Oakland	Joe Lacob, Peter Guber	Joe Lacob	$1.5	$3.10	$359	4.3
Houston Rockets	Houston	Tilman Fertitta	Tilman Fertitta	$4.3	$2.20	$296	6.3
Indiana Pacers	Indianapolis	Herbert Simon, Stephen Simon	Herb Simon	$3	$1.18	$205	2
Los Angeles Clippers	Los Angeles	Steve Ballmer	Steve Ballmer	$38.4	$2.15	$257	13.1
Los Angeles Lakers	Los Angeles	Jerry Buss Family Trusts, Philip Anschutz	Jeanie Buss		$3.30	$371	13.1
Memphis Grizzlies	Memphis	Robert Pera	Robert Pera	$4.3	$1.03	$206	1.3
Miami Heat	Miami	Micky Arison	Micky Arison	$9.7	$1.70	$253	5.6
Milwaukee Bucks	Milwaukee	Wes Edens, Jamie Dinan, Marc Lasry	Peter Feigin		$1.08	$179	1.6

(Continued)

Table 9.3 Continued

Team	Home City	Owner(s)	Owner – Who Sits on Board of Governors	Wealth of the Owner on Board ($B)	Current Value ($B)	Revenue ($M)	Metro Area Population (M)
Minnesota Timberwolves	Minneapolis	Glen Taylor	Glen Taylor	$2.6	$1.06	$204	3.5
New Orleans Pelicans	New Orleans	Gayle Benson	Gayle Benson	$2.8	$1	$204	1.3
New York Knicks	New York City	Madison Square Garden Company, James L. Dolan	James L. Dolan	$1.5	$3.60	$426	20.1
Oklahoma City Thunder	Oklahoma City	Clayton Bennett, Aubrey McClendon estate	Clayton Bennett	$0.4	$1.25	$222	1.4
Orlando Magic	Orlando	DeVos Family	Daniel DeVos		$1.23	$211	2.4
Philadelphia 76ers	Philadelphia	Joshua Harris, David Blitzer	Scott O'Neil		$1.18	$184	6.1
Phoenix Suns	Phoenix	Robert Sarver	Kelly Norton		$1.28	$218	4.5
Portland Trail Blazers	Portland	Estate of Paul Allen	Chris McGowan	$21.7	$1.30	$223	2.4
Sacramento Kings	Sacramento	Vivek Ranadive	Vivek Ranadive		$1.38	$240	2.1
San Antonio Spurs	San Antonio	Peter Holt, Julianna Hawn Holt	Peter Holt		$1.55	$259	2.5
Toronto Raptors	Toronto	Maple Leaf Sports & Entertainment	Masai Ujiri		$1.40	$250	5.9
Utah Jazz	Salt Lake City	Miller Family Trust	Gail Miller	$1.2	$1.20	$221	1.1
Washington Wizards	Washington	Ted Leonsis	Ted Leonsis	$1.1	$1.35	$222	6.1

Source:
https://www.forbes.com/nba-valuations/list/
https://www.celebritynetworth.com/
https://www.nba.com/

Table 9.4 National Hockey League (NHL)

Team	Home City	Owner(s)	Owner – Who Sits on Board of Governors	Wealth of the Owner on Board ($B)	Current Value ($B)	Revenue ($M)	Metro Area Population (M)
Anaheim Ducks	Anaheim	Henry Samueli, Susan Samueli			$0.460	$136	13.1
Arizona Coyotes	Glendale	Andrew Barroway	Andrew Barroway		$0.300	$98	4.6
Boston Bruins	Boston	Jeremy Jacobs	Jeremy Jacobs	$4.6	$0.89	$176	4.6
Buffalo Sabres	Buffalo	Terrence Pegula	Terrence Pegula	$4.3	$0.350	$120	1.1
Calgary Flames	Calgary	Calgary Flames LP, N. Murray Edwards	Ken King		$0.430	$129	1.4
Carolina Hurricanes	Raleigh	Tom Dundon, Peter Karmanos Jr	Tom Dundon		$0.370	$108	1.3
Chicago Blackhawks	Chicago	Rocky Wirtz	Rocky Wirtz	$4.4	$1.00	$183	9.5
Colorado Avalanche	Denver	Ann Walton Kroenke, Kroenke Sports & Entertainment	Stan Kroenke	$8.3	$0.385	$113	2.8
Columbus Blue Jackets	Columbus	John P. McConnell, Nationwide	John P. McConnell	$3	$0.315	$106	2
Dallas Stars	Dallas	Tom Gaglardi	Tom Gaglardi	$3.92	$0.515	$140	7.2
Detroit Red Wings	Detroit	Marian Ilitch, Ilitch Holdings	Chris Ilitch	$5.3	$0.700	$141	4.3
Edmonton Oilers	Edmonton	Daryl Katz	Daryl Katz	$3.1	$0.520	$151	1.2
Florida Panthers	Sunrise	Vincent Viola	Vincent Viola	$2.9	$0.305	$100	5.6
Los Angeles Kings	Los Angeles	Philip Anschutz, Anschutz Entertainment Group	Philip Anschutz	$13	$0.750	$175	13.1
Minnesota Wild	Saint Paul	Craig Leipold	Craig Leipold	$3.6	$0.440	$139	3.5
Montreal Canadiens	Montreal	Molson Family	Geoff Molson	$1.75	$1.25	$236	4.1
Nashville Predators	Nashville	Predators Holdings, Thomas Cigarran	Thomas Cigarran		$0.380	$141	1.8
New Jersey Devils	Newark	Joshua Harris, David Blitzer	Scott O'Neil		$0.400	$137	20.1
New York Islanders	New York City	Jon Ledecky, Scott Malkin	Scott Malkin		$0.395	$110	20.1

(Continued)

Table 9.4 Continued

Team	Home City	Owner(s)	Owner – Who Sits on Board of Governors	Wealth of the Owner on Board ($B)	Current Value ($B)	Revenue ($M)	Metro Area Population (M)
New York Rangers	New York City	Madison Square Garden Company, James L. Dolan	James L. Dolan	$1.5	$1.50	$246	20.1
Ottawa Senators	Ottawa	Eugene Melnyk	Eugene Melnyk	$1.15	$0.420	$135	1.2
Philadelphia Flyers	Philadelphia	Comcast Spectacor, Brian L. Roberts	Dave Scott		$0.740	$170	6
Pittsburgh Penguins	Pittsburgh	Mario Lemieux, Ron Burkle	Mario Lemieux	$0.15	$0.650	$196	2.4
San Jose Sharks	San Jose	Hasso Plattner	Hasso Plattner	$12.7	$0.490	$137	2
St Louis Blues	St Louis	Tom Stillman	Tom Stillman		$0.450	$150	2.8
Tampa Bay Lightning	Tampa	Jeffrey Vinik	Jeffrey Vinik	$0.515	$0.390	$124	3
Toronto Maple Leafs	Toronto	Maple Leaf Sports & Entertainment, Larry Tanenbaum	Brendan Shanahan		$1.40	$211	5.9
Vancouver Canucks	Vancouver	Aquilini Investment Group, Francesco Aquilini	Francesco Aquilini	$3.3	$0.730	$156	2.5
Vegas Golden Knights	Paradise	Bill Foley, Maloof family	Bill Foley	$0.6	$0.500	-	2
Washington Capitals	Washington	Ted Leonsis	Ted Leonsis	$1.1	$0.625	$146	6
Winnipeg Jets	Winnipeg	True North Sports & Entertainment, David Thomson, Mark Chipman	Mark Chipman		$0.375	$119	0.8

Source:
https://www.forbes.com/nhl-valuations/list/
http://www.nhl.com/ice/teams.htm
https://www.thesquander.com/net-worth-jeffrey-vinik-owner-tampa-bay-lightning
https://www.celebritynetworth.com/

Table 9.5 Major League Soccer (MLS)

Team	Home City	Owner(s)	Owner – Who Sits on Board of Governors	Wealth of the Owner on Board ($B)	Current Value ($B)	Revenue ($M)	Metro Area Population (M)
Atlanta United	Atlanta	Arthur Blank	Arthur Blank	$4.50	$0.330	$47	5.7
Chicago Fire	Bridgeview	Andrew Hauptman, Andell Holdings	Andrew Hauptman		$0.245	$27	9.5
Colorado Rapids	Commerce City	Kroenke Sports & Entertainment, Stanley Kroenke	Stanley Kroenke	$8.30	$0.155	$18	2.8
Columbus Crew	Columbus	Anthony Precourt, Precourt Sports Ventures LLC	Anthony Precourt		$0.160	$24	2
D.C. United	Washington	Jason Levien and Steven Kaplan	Jason Levien and Steven Kaplan		$0.265	$26	6
FC Dallas	Dallas	Clark Hunt	Clark Hunt	$13.70	$0.190	$34	7.2
Houston Dynamo	Houston	Gabriel Brener, Oscar De La Hoya, Jake Silverstein, Ben Guill			$0.220	$28	6.3
Los Angeles FC	Los Angeles	Peter Guber (Executive Chairman), Henry Nguyen, Tom Penn, Ruben Gnanalingam, Vincent Tan, Brandon Beck, Larry Berg, Will Ferrell, Nomar Garciaparra, Mia Hamm, Chad Hurley, Magic Johnson, Tucker Kain, Kirk Lacob, Mark Leschly, Mike Mahan, Irwin Raij, Tony Robbins, Lon Rosen, Bennett Rosenthal, Paul Schaeffer, Brandon Schneider, Mark Shapiro, Allen Shapiro, Jason Sugarman, Harry Tsao	Peter Guber	$0.80	$0.305	n/a	13.1
Los Angeles Galaxy	Carson	Philip F. Anschutz, Anschutz Entertainment Group	Philip F. Anschutz		$0.320	$63	13.1
Minnesota United	Minneapolis	Bill McGuire, Jim Pohlad, Robert Pohlad, Glen Taylor, Wendy Carlson Nelson			$0.248	$24	3.5
Montreal Impact	Montreal	Joey Saputo	Joey Saputo		$0.168	$24	4.1
New England Revolution	Foxborough	Robert Kraft	Robert Kraft	$2.90	$0.225	$28	

(Continued)

Table 9.5 Continued

Team	Home City	Owner(s)	Owner – Who Sits on Board of Governors	Wealth of the Owner on Board ($B)	Current Value ($B)	Revenue ($M)	Metro Area Population (M)
New York City FC	New York City	City Football Group (majority) & Yankee Global Enterprises (minority)			$0.278	$42	20.1
New York Red Bulls	Newark	Red Bull GmbH	Dietrich Mateschitz	$7.10	$0.250	$38	20.1
Orlando City SC	Orlando	Flávio Augusto da Silva	Flávio Augusto da Silva		$0.275	$44	2.4
Philadelphia Union	Chester	Jay Sugarman, Keystone Sports & Entertainment, LLC	Jay Sugarman		$0.175	$26	
Portland Timbers	Portland	Henry Merritt Paulson III, Peregrine Sports, LLC	Henry Merritt Paulson III		$0.280	$48	2.4
Real Salt Lake	Salt Lake City	Dell Loy Hansen	Dell Loy Hansen		$0.170	$22	1.2
San Jose Earthquakes	San Jose	Lewis Wolff and John J. Fisher (Earthquakes Soccer, LLC)			$0.235	$36	2
Seattle Sounders	Seattle	Adrian Hanauer (majority), Paul Allen, Drew Carey, and Joe Roth (minority)	Paul Allen	$15.80	$0.310	$52	3.7
Sporting Kansas City	Kansas City	Sporting Club, the Patterson Family, Cliff Illig, Robb Heineman, Greg Maday, Pat Curran	Neal Patterson	$1.50	$0.270	$41	2.2
Toronto FC	Toronto	Maple Leaf Sports & Entertainment	Larry Tanenbaum		$0.290	$49	5.9
Vancouver Whitecaps	Vancouver	Greg Kerfoot, Steve Luczo, Jeff Mallett, Steve Nash	Greg Kerfoot		$0.165	$22	2.5

Source:
https://www.forbes.com/sites/chrissmith/2018/11/14/mls-most-valuable-teams-2018/#786e10352ee9
https://www.revolvy.com/page/Major-League-Soccer-owners
https://www.forbes.com/pictures/emdm45efhhd/philip-anschutz/#5c6cb97f7808
https://www.celebritynetworth.com/
https://www.mlssoccer.com/

common in the previously mentioned converged ownership model, where the purpose of the ownership is to enhance the value of other assets. **Preemptive** is where the ownership purchase is a strategy play to prevent a competitor (e.g., media company) from acquiring a club. **Purpose** is where an owner, typically an independent one, invests to keep a club in a community and prevent relocation. **Profile** is a personal motivation where the intention of the owner is to boost their profile, often globally. **Power** is similarly individually driven and is related to the owner accessing new networks and positioning themselves for other opportunities. Finally, **passion** is an intention that captures those owners whose purchase is motivated by their love for the sport, the club or the city in which it plays. When considering ownership intention, it is important to note that most owners have more than a single motive and that each covers a range of possible motivations within the theme (Foster, O'Reilly & Davila, 2016).

Ownership models

The ownership situations described in Tables 9.1 through 9.5, can be organised into a few different models. First, is the *private or single individual/family owner* where 100% ownership is by a single person or family. Often this type of ownership is found in the original clubs in the league or from purchases before the turn of the millennium when club values were lower. An example is the Buffalo Bills of the NFL, owned by Terry and Kim Pegula. One aspect of this ownership model is that sometimes the owner can take a very active role in decision-making at the club level, or opt for a hands-off approach.

The second model is the *private company or investment syndicate ownership* model. In this situation, a group of two or more individuals share ownership of the club. This is a very common structure today and can vary significantly in terms of membership. Structurally, syndicate members will adhere to shared governance rules related to equity (e.g., what happens when an owner wants to sell their shares), annual sharing of profits/losses and risk management (e.g., decisions related to a new investment, such as a new stadium or free agent).

Third, is the *publicly traded corporation* model. Although this model is more common to professional sport in other parts of the world, a "quasi" version of the model (Foster, O'Reilly & Davila, 2016) is found in the NFL's Green Bay Packers, who issue shares that individuals can purchase but operates as a nonprofit company (i.e., shareholders do not receive dividends but the club makes donations to charities near Green Bay). Each shareholder has a basic set of rights, including the right to vote in elections to elect the board of the not-for-profit organisation.

Fourth is another model that is rarely observed in North America, the *subsidiary of a publicly traded corporation* model, where the club is majority-owned by a larger company that is publicly traded (Foster, O'Reilly & Davila, 2016). This often fits with the "platform" P of ownership intent, as ownership of the club allows for benefit to other assets of the larger company. This approach was more common in the 1990s and early 2000s, but a few examples remain today, including telecommunications giant Comcast who founded the NHL's Philadelphia flyers in 1967 and still retain ownership today.

What drives the governance structure of a major professional sport club in North America?

There are many combinations of club ownership, intentions and structures amongst the 146 clubs as was made clear in the previous sections and supported in Tables 9.1 through 9.5. Despite these varying structures and intents, however, there are many commonalities amongst individual clubs in terms of how they operate. Ten of these common themes and drivers are outlined below.

These common themes are strong descriptors of the governance reality of these clubs and each represents an area of significant research need.

1. *For most owners, profit is not the primary objective.* Counter to most industries (and with a few exceptions of particular owners of clubs in large markets where the sport is very popular), owners express that profit is not the primary objective of the club, and that if owners really wanted profit, they would invest in assets outside of professional sport (Foster, O'Reilly & Davila, 2016). Note that the argument for asset appreciation (club value growth over time) may be a key objective to some owners/syndicates over annual profitability.

2. *Club ownership is, in fact, a "club".* Fellow owners (in their capacity as league managers) often exclude potential owners or ownership groups for "integrity reasons" or conflicting objectives. Potential owners have been declined for reasons such as image, political affiliation, interest in moving a club, gambling background, wealth and more (Foster, O'Reilly & Davila, 2016).

3. *Integration is an important ownership consideration.* This is an ongoing theme in the discussions at both the league and the club level. One key element of these discussions is the question of horizontal integration (i.e., should the owner of a club in a given market purchase a club in another league in that same market?). At the club level, if the owner of an NHL club is able to purchase an NBA club in the same market, they can share their venue, staff and benefit from economies of scale (Nadeau & O'Reilly, 2006). At the league level, a board of governors may be concerned about the focus of an owner who has interests in multiple leagues. A second important question is vertical integration (i.e., should a club owner purchase a business that is part of their supply chain? [e.g., regional sport network, arena/stadium]) (Foster, O'Reilly, Shimizu, Khosia & Murray, 2014). For example, there have been many examples of efforts by large media organisations to own clubs (e.g., Comcast, Disney, Cablevision, News Corp., TSN, Rogers, Time Warner) (Nadeau & O'Reilly, 2006).

4. *Leadership models vary.* Professional sport clubs have very strong personalities involved in their operation, leading to four (or even 5) potential models of who is driving the key decisions in governing the club. These include (i) owner-led, (ii) CEO-led, (iii) general manager-led, (iv) coach-led or even (v) star player-led, all referring to the individual who is most central in the key decisions pertaining to the club.

5. *Club brand power.* Agyemang and Williams (2013) outlined the ability of professional sport clubs to manage their brand and their images through what they call "brandpression". Regardless of ownership group, club history, club revenues or market, their brand can be managed and built. The strength of "brand power" is evident in the financial values provided in Tables 9.1 to 9.4, where established, long-standing clubs in strong markets have higher values than most of the others. In the NHL, for example, the "Original Six" franchises − Boston, Chicago, Detroit, Montreal, New York, Toronto − all would fit this situation (see Table 9.4).

6. *Available resources.* The owner(s) ability to invest in players, facilities, coaches and management is a key determinant to the club's ability to achieve its objectives. This ability is based on both the available resources that the owner(s) have and their willingness to invest those resources in the club. Notably, in sports where there are limited restrictions regarding spending on player salaries, a positive correlation exists between spending and on-field performance, as clubs can both retain and acquire talent through an advantage in spending ability (Foster, O'Reilly & Davila, 2016). Research into the full range of stakeholders here, particularly coaches and management, is needed.

7. *League infrastructure.* The league in which the club operates will have its own set of rules and regulations that will determine how the club can operate (O'Reilly & Nadeau, 2006). The most important document to this effect is the aforementioned typically ten-year CBA deal between the owners and the players' associations (the union representing the interests of the players in the league), that outlines the specifics of the financial and non-financial relationships between the clubs and the players. As noted, a CBA will include specific details on the salary cap, the process by which to call up a player from the minor leagues, revenue-sharing and player benefits off-the-field. In practice, all clubs now have "capologists" to help the team navigate the many rules within, another area where research is needed.

8. *Market size and arena location.* The place-related variables of a major North American professional sport club, including both the size of the market in which a club operates and the quality of its stadium or arena, even in a league revenue-sharing situation, has a considerable impact on the club's resources, fan base, local television market size and operations (O'Reilly & Nadeau, 2006). Governance approaches need to consider market size and competitive dynamics. Geo-demographic-based research on clubs would be an important contribution to the sport management literature.

9. *Regional sport network strength.* With the exception of the NFL, which has national television deals only, the other four leagues rely on deals with regional sport networks (RSN) to drive revenues and deliver their content to their own market (Foster et al., 2014). Starting with the New York Yankees and the YES Network, clubs having ownership stake in an RSN has become an attractive aspect of club ownership (Foster, O'Reilly & Davila, 2016).

10. *Player salary structure.* In the major North American professional team sports, a controlled salary structure has been agreed to in the NFL, NHL and NBA, to varying degrees. MLB and MLS have some controls but can be characterised as "open markets" more like the premier leagues in Europe. The controlled salary structure can be described as having restraints on spending at each of the league, club and player levels. At the league level, via collective bargaining, a certain amount is agreed upon (e.g., 51% of total league basketball-related revenues) that will comprise the total salaries of the players. At the club level, the aforementioned salary cap and salary floor provide a band (or range) within which every club must spend each year. Finally, at the player level, minimum and maximum salaries, guaranteed contracts (or not), signing bonuses, performance bonuses, rookie contracts and exceptions are common in some of the agreements.

Future research on major North American professional sport clubs

This chapter set out to provide background on ownership, governance and decision-making in the major North American professional sport clubs. It articulates the key governance documents, details ownership across the five major leagues, the drivers of governance decisions and the 10 common themes in governing the five leagues. In order to provide a "map" for future research in this area (Shilbury, O'Boyle & Ferkins, 2016), a series of suggested research questions and potential methods to address them are provided here by topic area.

First, very little is known about the inner workings of the governance of leagues, leading to a number of potential research questions. How do commissioners make decisions? What is the role of owners? What is the nature of the league–club relationship on decisions and governance? Although it is acknowledged that access to this data will be very challenging (if not fully restricted), in an ideal world an ethnographic approach where a researcher would have access to the boardrooms of league governors and owners, or expert interviews with commissioners and/or owners would be useful. An important element of this line of research would be to delve qualitatively into the governance of clubs in each of the contexts of ownership (single owner, family owner, corporate owner, etc.) and the implications on club governance as such. Possible areas of benefit to the field would include application of various theories (e.g., Agency Theory, Resource-Based View of the firm, etc.) and concepts (e.g., performance management, compliance, club strategy, player recruitment, salary cap management, etc.).

Second, in building on the 8 P's of owner intention (Foster, O'Reilly & Davila, 2016), survey research of owners and minority owners of clubs would be very interesting to assess the priority of these intentions and to uncover additional motivations, ideally leading to a theory-based view of owner intention in professional sport. Research on fans of clubs to ascertain their views or impressions of the intentions of the ownership of their club would also be beneficial.

Third, future research in the areas of horizontal and vertical integration in professional sport clubs would be of considerable benefit to the sport management literature on strategy, where case studies of successful and unsuccessful integrations would inform both our understanding of how governance works and how ownership decisions are made. Further, practical value to those working in the organisations involved would likely emerge. A specific example would be using these case studies to articulate the supply chain (including both horizontal and vertical elements) of ownership in major North American professional sport.

Fourth, research related to the brandpression (Agyemang & Williams, 2013) elements of professional sport clubs would be interesting. Governing a club in a brand-focussed way could be tested in a similar manner as marketing a sport property based on a sponsorship focus (i.e., sponsorship-linked marketing (Cornwell, Weeks & Roy, 2005). As brand is based in the perceptions of consumers (fans), this research could be done using surveys, social media methods or other techniques that gather data related to fan views on the club but linked back to ownership and governance decisions.

Finally, a research program based on content analysis and follow-up expert interviews on the CBA's of each of the major leagues would enable learning from a comparative level (league-to-league) and a governance level (owner decision). The fact that CBA's are published in their full form publicly facilitates access to this data. Linking these results back to previous work on governance (e.g., Ferkins, Shilbury & McDonald, 2009) and club profitability (Nadeau & O'Reilly, 2006) could be important contributions.

Note

1 See www.forbes.com/lists

References

Abeza, G., O'Reilly, N., Seguin, B., & Nzindukiyimana, O. (2015). Social media scholarship in sport management research: A critical review. *Journal of Sport Management, 29*, 601–618.

Agyemang, K. J., & Williams, A. S. (2013). Creating revenue via organisational 'brandpression' management (OBpM): A marriage of brand management and impression management in professional sport. *International Journal of Revenue Management, 7*, 171–181.

Coombs, D. S., & Osborne, A. (2012). A case study of Aston Villa Football Club. *Journal of Public Relations Research, 24*, 201–221.

Cornwell, T. B., Weeks, C. S., & Roy, D. P. (2005). Sponsorship linked marketing: Opening the black box. *Journal of Advertising, 34*(2), 21–42.

Davila, T., O'Reilly, N., & Foster, G. (2009, November). Professional sport Leagues: Contrasting views on how to structure the business side, Armand Carabén Workshop on Football Economics, IESE Business School, Barcelona, Spain.

Ferkins, L., Shilbury, D., & McDonald, G. (2009). Board involvement in strategy: Advancing the governance of sport organizations. *Journal of Sport Management*, *23*, 245–277.

Foster, G., O'Reilly, N., & Davila, T. (2016). *Sports business management: Decision-making around the globe*. New York: Routledge.

Foster, G., O'Reilly, N., Shimizu, C., Khosia, N., & Murray, R. (2014). Determinants of regional sport network television ratings in MLB, NBA and NHL. *Journal of Sport Management*, *28*, 356–375.

Hambrick, M. E., & Kang, S. J. (2015). Pin it: Exploring how professional sports organizations use Pinterest as a communications and relationship-marketing tool. *Communication & Sport*, *3*, 434–457.

Lock, D., Filo, K., Kunkel, T., & Skinner, J. L. (2015). The development of a framework to capture perceptions of sport organizations legitimacy. *Journal of Sport Management*, *29*, 362–379.

Mason, D., Sant, S. L., & Soebbing, B. (2017). The peculiar economics of sports team ownership: Pursuing urban development in North American cities. *Sport, Business and Management: An International Journal*, *7*, 358–374.

Mitrook, M. A., Parish, N. B., & Seltzer, T. (2008). From advocacy to accommodation: A case study of the Orlando Magic's public relations efforts to secure a new arena. *Public Relations Review*, *34*, 161–168.

Nadeau, J., & O'Reilly, N. (2006). Developing a profitability model for professional sport leagues: The case of the National Hockey League. *International Journal of Sport Finance*, *1*(1), 46–52.

O'Reilly, N., Foster, G., Murray, R., & Shimizu, C. (2015). Merchandise sales rank in professional sport: Purchase drivers and implications for National Hockey League Clubs. *Sport, Business, Management: An International Journal*, *5*, 307–324.

O'Reilly, N., & Nadeau, J. (2006). Revenue generation in professional sport: A diagnostic analysis. *International Journal of Sport Management and Marketing*, *1*, 311–330.

Sheth, H., & Babiak, K. M. (2010). Beyond the game: Perceptions and practices of corporate social responsibility in the professional sport industry. *Journal of Business Ethics*, *91*, 433–450.

Shilbury, D., O'Boyle, I., & Ferkins, L. (2016). A research agenda for collaborative sport governance. *Sport Management Review*, *19*, 479–491.

Siegfried, N., Schlesinger, T., Bayle, E., & Giauque, D. (2015). Professionalisation of sport federations – a multi-level framework for analysing forms, causes and consequences. *European Sport Management Quarterly*, *15*, 407–433.

Soebbing, B. P., & Mason, D. S. (2009). Managing legitimacy and uncertainty in professional team sport: The NBA's draft lottery. *Team Performance Management: An International Journal*, *15*(3/4), 141–157.

Thibault, L., Slack, T., & Hinings, B. (1991). Professionalism, structures and systems: The impact of professional staff on voluntary sport organizations. *International Review for the Sociology of Sport*, *26*, 83–98.

Watanabe, N., Yan, G., & Soebbing, B. P. (2015). Major league baseball and Twitter usage: The economics of social media use. *Journal of Sport Management*, *29*, 619–632.

Wilson, R., Plumley, D., & Ramchandani, G. (2013). The relationship between ownership structure and club performance in the English Premier League. *Sport, Business and Management: An International Journal*, *3*, 19–36.

10

Ownership and governance in men's professional football in Europe

Hallgeir Gammelsæter and Geoff Walters

Academic literature on ownership in European professional sport is limited, and almost entirely confined, to men's football. The ownership of professional football clubs has become a prominent issue with a heightened level of media attention, perhaps because it is a way for individuals (or nation-states) to buy respectability and enhance legitimacy and soft power (Franck, 2010). Other concerns have centred on how ownership has increasingly become detached from the communities in which football clubs have their historical roots and traditional fan base (Morrow, 2003). More recently, scholars have sought to understand how ownership models impact on the business models of clubs (e.g., Franck, 2010; Rohde & Breuer, 2017) and whether there is a link between ownership structure and organisational performance (Wilson, Plumley & Ramchandani, 2013).

The purpose of this chapter is to provide an understanding of how ownership in professional football links to governance. To this effort, the chapter is organised in three main sections. The first provides an overview of the emergence of the pyramidal structure of European football, the ownership of leagues and clubs and the recent challenges to the system posed by shifting ownership. The next outlines the institutional logics perspective used to analyse the changes in the field. It argues that these developments can be understood as a shift towards a more market-driven logic that reduces the impact of the logics of sport and community. The move towards a more network system of governance is both the result of and the driver towards defining and governing football in market terms. The chapter concludes by highlighting some of the future challenges that may arise due to these shifting logics.

The rise of the football pyramid and its recent challenges

Historically, within Europe, football clubs were formed as member associations that represented geographical locations, emerging from institutions such as schools, churches and workplaces. Then, owing to the need for regular competitive fixtures, regional leagues were formed that later reorganised to national leagues, usually with a relegation–promotion rule between the tiers. National leagues presupposed national associations (FAs), which were established across Europe throughout the first half of the 19th century, following the early pioneers in the British

Isles, the first being the English Football Association founded in 1863. In 1954, the Union des Associations Européennes de Football (UEFA) was set up to organise pan-European competitions.[1] Hence, the organisational structure developed into a pyramid system in which football was organised from the local to the pan-European level.

Notably, the system contains a competition pyramid that is inextricably bound with an organisation pyramid based on collaboration – both presupposing the other. In one sense, the organisation pyramid promotes a "top-down" approach to decision-making and governance, with UEFA making decisions regarding its competitions, national FAs taking decisions governing the sport and the competitions in their respective country and clubs focusing on the day-to-day running of their organisation. However, the organisation pyramid was set up with a "bottom-up" democratic structure where individuals were voting members in clubs, clubs were voting members of their national FAs and the FAs making up the general assembly of UEFA. Up until the 1980s, there were relatively few additional stakeholders in this system, an exception being leagues organising top competition in a few countries.

Whilst UEFA competitions used to be based on a one-club-per-national-FA principle, this has gradually been replaced by a ranking system that, although based on club and national team performances, effectively favours entries from the bigger nations, which ensure more teams from the largest commercial markets. This change was underpinned by the developing television (TV) market in the 1980s and the observation that the UEFA cup gradually turned out to be more lucrative than the champions' and cup winners' tournaments (Olsson, 2011). The clubs were responsible for selling their own broadcasting rights; hence, the draw of opponent was a determining factor in the corresponding value of TV income. As the UEFA cup contained more clubs from bigger markets, TV revenues would often exceed that of the more prestigious cups. The effect was that national league and cup champions made less income than the lower-ranked teams in the UEFA cup.

Simultaneously, clubs mistreated UEFA's income distribution system by under-reporting gate and TV revenue, thus reducing their payment to UEFA. Although many clubs were heavily fined, UEFA gradually found the system unsustainable. This prompted the revamping of the European Cup, resulting in the creation of the UEFA Champions League in 1991, a tournament adopting the entry principle of the UEFA Cup and introducing a group stage to play more games among the best teams (Olsson, 2011). Furthermore, UEFA tightened its grip over the competition by centralising marketing and TV rights. In 1999–2000, UEFA expanded the tournament by allowing more teams and ran two group stages, which left more games (and revenue) for the best teams (Holt, 2005). The restructuring came about following revelations that Italian Media Partners and 18 of Europe's biggest clubs (who called themselves the G14) had been working towards establishing a European breakaway league. This pressured UEFA to negotiate a compromise that ensured the top European teams more revenues through UEFA competitions. This also demonstrated that the clubs went outside their national FAs to enhance their collective power. Accordingly, over the past 15 years, UEFA has had to establish a governance structure that allows powerful interest groups direct access to its consultative bodies. These groups are European Leagues (previously European Professional Football Leagues), European Club Association (ECA, previously G14) and FIFPro, World Players' Union.

While UEFA still controls and runs the European tournaments, the increasing power of rich clubs within the European football network (alongside commercial and broadcasting stakeholders) continues to further destabilise the governance structures of European football (Holt, 2005; Spiegel, 2018). The ECA, who have two seats on the UEFA Executive Committee, thus having institutionalised their power within UEFA's internal organisational structure, continues to support changes to the UEFA Champions League that will increase the number of group matches. European Leagues are against this, as they fear it will damage domestic leagues across Europe. This has all the hallmarks of the long-standing concerns over a breakaway super league, something that Hoehn and Szymanski (1999) argued for 20 years ago. Up until now, the commercial success of the UEFA Champions League has prevented breakaway. It has, however, accelerated the financial gap between clubs and leagues (and nations), negatively affected the competitive balance within the leagues (e.g., Plumley, Ramchandani & Wilson, 2018; Poli, Ravenel & Besson, 2018) and never fully appeased the desire of the most powerful clubs in European football.

Thus, in 2019, the wider system of governance within European football has become more complex, with key stakeholders having more power on UEFA through the integration into the internal organisational governance structures of the organisation. This demonstrates a shift from pyramid to network governance (Henry & Lee, 2004), and as a result, UEFA's ability to make changes to its own competitions are now dependent upon trade-off and negotiation amongst key stakeholders.

The control of professional football leagues

It is notable that by taking ownership of the Champions League, UEFA was diverging from the tendency of many premier leagues across Europe that were seeking greater independence from their FAs to take over the responsibilities and ownership of the league. One fundamental reason for this move was to allow the leagues (and the member clubs) more independence and, in many cases, more ability to ensure that growing commercial revenues stay within the league and the member clubs. For example, the formation of the Premier League in 1992 in England was to ensure that the top division clubs were able to negotiate their own broadcasting deal and would not have to redistribute revenue amongst the remaining 72 members of the Football League.

This model of league self-subsistence spread across Europe. By 2004, the majority of the UEFA member countries had separate league organisations (Holt, 2005). Today an unknown number of these have taken some or full responsibility for running the competition in their country. In England and Scotland (Morrow, 2011) and the Netherlands, the premier leagues are organised as corporate entities (Marston, Boillat & Roitman, 2017). In Belgium (Balduck & Lucidarme, 2011), France (Senaux, 2011), Germany (Wilkesmann, Butner & Müller, 2011), Greece (Anagnostopolos, 2011), Italy (Baroncelli & Caruso, 2011), Portugal (Relvas, 2011), Spain (Ascari & Gagnepain, 2006; Gómez, Martí & Mollo, 2011) and Denmark and Romania (Marston et al., 2017), the leagues are financially independent associations. As well as being financially independent, these leagues have their own statutes, regulations and administration; although, to be approved by UEFA, they have to be affiliated to their respective national FA. Their relationship is regulated by an agreement which often stipulates some financial contribution to grassroots and youth football – for instance, an agreed percentage from TV deals (i.e., Gómez et al., 2011).

The growing independence of professional leagues has led to increasing tensions with national FAs. They have differing priorities, for example, promoting the growth of grassroots football and national team performance versus developing and enhancing the league competition. The increasing commercial power of the top leagues also means that the pyramidal model within individual nations has been under threat causing a movement towards a network governance model. At the pan-European level, the European Leagues represents an increasing number of football clubs and engages in dialogue with UEFA and FIFA to further the interests of the leagues. Originally formed in 1997 by 14 members, it has grown to represent 35 professional football leagues from 28 countries and more than 900 clubs, thus broadening its base as a representative stakeholder. This includes most premier leagues in Western Europe and the bigger countries in Eastern Europe such as Azerbaijan, the Czech Republic, Kazakhstan, Poland, Romania, Russia and Ukraine. European Leagues stated that its "main goal is to enhance and protect competitive balance in league competitions" (https://europeanleagues.com). When recently voicing its strong opposition to a European breakaway league, it argued that "the European sports model is based on a pyramid structure where the mechanisms of promotion and relegation and the sporting merits of clubs are at the core of any competition" (https://europeanleagues.com).

The control and ownership of professional football clubs

On the European continent, the association club model dominated until it was dismissed in Eastern Europe by the Communist regimes after World War II, paving the way for control by industrial sectors (e.g., mining, iron and steel) or institutions (e.g., the police, the railway, arms of the military) controlled by the Communist state. In Western Europe, there were industry families that controlled clubs for decades, if indirectly, through financial support and board membership in association clubs, but also holding companies as in Italy (Morrow, 2003). However, the dominant pattern of association control survived the past century. Until the 1990s, organising football clubs as corporations with shareholdings was uncommon in Europe (notably with the exception of the professional clubs in the UK – see below).

Over the past three decades, the association model of ownership has become less dominant due to two particular phases that have occurred at different points in time in different European nations. The first phase, professionalisation, is characterised by clubs transforming to legal entities owned by shareholders with limited liability status (Rohde & Breuer, 2017). English football clubs were early adopters of corporatisation. Small Heath (Birmingham City) was the first club to take advantage of this in 1888 (Buraimo, Simmons & Szymanski, 2006). Eighty-four out of 86 Football League clubs had converted to limited liability status by 1921 (Dobson & Goddard, 2001).

In France, Germany, Italy and Spain, clubs could not make the transition to private limited companies until the last decade of the twentieth century, and, even then, there were restrictions (Gammelsæter & Senaux, 2011; Rohde & Breuer, 2017). While German clubs were traditionally constituted as not-for-profit member associations, in 1998 they were permitted to incorporate the professional football club as a subsidiary of the member association because it permitted a more professional hierarchical structure. This ruling provided that the association retain at least 50 percent of the shares plus one voting right (Wilkesmann & Blutner, 2002). In 2009 (Ward & Hines, 2017), and as late as March 2018, the German Bundesliga voted to retain the "50+1" scheme (Deloitte, 2018). However, analysis of the UEFA Licensing Benchmarking Reports (UEFA, 2008, 2017) demonstrated increasing incorporations. In 2008, 54 percent of all UEFA licensed clubs had a company-based ownership model. This increased to 60 percent of the 237 clubs that competed in the 2013/14 UEFA competitions, with 25 percent structured as associations, nine percent not-for-profit and three percent state-funded.

The second phase, commercialisation, is characterised by the entry of private majority investors (Rohde & Breuer, 2017). UEFA (2017) documents that in 2016, 63 percent of clubs in 15 of Europe's major leagues had a controlling party. However, it is not necessarily the case that when private investors owned clubs, they became more commercial in focus: Poor financial performance has historically plagued English football (Buraimo et al., 2006). Clubs in the UK entered into this phase earlier than many counterparts across Europe, but, due to the model of utility maximisation (Sloane, 1971), many struggled financially. They were only able to remain financially viable due to investment from their owners, local businesspersons who bought into football clubs as a reflection of their social role alongside notions of community, tradition, social solidarity and local distinctiveness (Sugden, 2002). Starting in the 1980s, many majority owners of football clubs in the UK looked to the stock market to raise additional funds.

The move to stock market listing was enabled by the circumvention of the historic FA Rule 34, introduced in 1912 to restrict the amount payable in dividends to five percent of the face value of the shares (Michie & Oughton, 2005). It also prevented directors from being paid for their role at the club and ensured that owners could not wind up a club and profit from the sale of the ground; instead, all proceeds had to be distributed to local sporting institutions. However, in 1983, Tottenham Hotspur sidestepped this rule by creating a holding company, with the football club a subsidiary company, and subsequently floated the holding company on the stock exchange arguing that FA rules did not apply. At the time, FA did nothing to prevent this. By allowing clubs to form a holding company and for them to bypass Rule 34 was an abdication of their role as a governing body; in 1998 the FA ceased with Rule 34 altogether.

By 2000, there were 22 listed clubs in the UK and a total of £167 million had been raised through stock market floatation (Morrow, 1999). However, the concentrated ownership structure, where power lies with one or a few individuals, was still dominant (Morrow, 2003). The majority of the clubs that had once been listed have now de-listed due to poor levels of dividends and capital gains through share price increases.

The rise of foreign ownership in European football

The foreign-investor model of ownership has been a prominent trend over the last ten years (Rohde & Breuer, 2017). This is particularly apparent in the English Premier League, where 70 percent (14 clubs) are now owned by foreign investors with a further 12 clubs (50%) also owned by foreign investors in the Championship. Foreign ownership is also seen in France (5 clubs), Italy (4 clubs), Belgium (3 clubs) and Spain (3 clubs). By 2017, altogether 47 clubs (18%) in 15 European leagues have foreign owners, the biggest proportion of owners originating in Asia (17 clubs), Europe (12 clubs) and North America (11 clubs). Of the changes in club ownership since 2016, the majority have been Chinese investors (UEFA, 2017).

One reason to help explain the rise in foreign investment is that the costs required to purchase a club in the top European leagues have increased substantially. Whilst this does not preclude domestic ownership, it does reduce the number able to invest, opening up the opportunity for wealthy overseas investors who regard ownership of a top club as an attractive political tool. The "trophy asset" character of top clubs (Hamil & Walters, 2010) motivates individuals or nation-states to buy respectability, legitimacy and soft power (Brannagan & Giulianotti, 2014). Others, in particular American investors, may see the opportunities to seek a return on their investment given the increased value of domestic and international broadcasting rights within European football. The growing influx of foreign investors, who often appear motivated by the desire to maximise revenues and to ensure that they receive a financial return on their investment, further complicates the system of network governance. Teams owned by extremely wealthy individuals or nation-states have increasing power, authority and influence. The recent exposé of allegations surrounding Manchester City's circumvention of UEFA Financial Fair Play rules and subsequent settlement with UEFA is an example (Spiegel, 2018). These new types of foreign investors are arguably seeking to use their power to influence the wider institutional structures (Holt, 2005), which further threatens the governance system in European football.

The rise of supporter ownership

The commercialisation phase is arguably underpinned by a commercial logic with the top level of professional sports now widely recognised as part of the global entertainment industry. However, what we have also witnessed is a resistance to this, particularly through the emergence of the Supporter Trust movement that began in the UK (García & Welford, 2015) and spread to Europe with supporters taking action in individual clubs elsewhere (e.g., Cocieru, Delia & Katz, 2019; Hodges & Brentin, 2018; Totten, 2016). The supporters advocate a cooperative form of ownership underpinned by an emphasis on the community role of a sports club.

The concept of supporter ownership was initiated at Northampton Town FC with the formation of a Supporters Trust, an independent, not-for-profit democratic organisation that seeks to influence the club through improved supporter representation and develop stronger links between a club, community and supporter base. Two ways that trusts are able to increase their influence is through shareholding and board representation. In 1997, the government launched the Football Task Force to look into the industry given the growing commercialisation. The report, "Investing in the Community" (http://www.sportdevelopment.org.uk/), recommended that more encouragement should be given to supporter involvement in clubs. Subsequently, in 2000, the government provided £250,000 per year for an initial three-year period to support the creation of Supporters Direct. The organisation expanded, with the creation of Supporters Direct Scotland and Supporters Direct Europe, who promote this form of ownership model across Europe.

Whilst this was generally seen as a success, it has been recognised that mutual ownership does not work for clubs in the Premier League. For instance, Brown (2007) argued that the supporters trust model has "totally failed to demonstrate how it can work in a company of the size of Manchester United, where major corporate finance is needed to create a meaningful stake" (p. 617). Moreover, D. Kennedy and Kennedy (2007) argued that Supporters Direct represents an integral part of the Labour Government's social policy that aimed to preserve and extend the commodification of social relations. In the context of New Labour and the "Third Way" philosophy, whereby free-market enterprise was coupled with regulation to address issues such as social inclusion and community involvement, they argue that there were limits to the extent that Supporters Direct can be seen as a challenge to the increasing commercialisation and commodification of football.

Despite these criticisms, Supporters Direct helped to set up over 150 supporters trusts (including many in rugby and cricket), some of whom took majority shareholdings in their club. Within the football league, at one stage Brentford, AFC Wimbledon, Exeter City, Portsmouth and Swansea City were all owned by their Supporters Trust. However, in all but two of these cases, the members of the Supporters Trust voted to sell their shares to a private owner, thus reverting the club back to private ownership. More recently, Supporters Direct (England) merged with the Football Supporters Federation to form a new organisation, with concerns that this will dilute the mission to achieve supporter representation in club governance owing to the broader remit of the new organisation.

A glimpse into the board "black box"

The Centre International d'Etude du Sport (CIES, 2019) recently published a report on the governance and finance of 12 prominent European football clubs, providing one of very few descriptions of the boards of directors (BoDs) in football. While the report tells us little about what goes on in the boards and how they relate to other governing bodies in the club, what is interesting to note is the significant diversity across the clubs. In *socios*-governed Spanish clubs (Barcelona and Real Madrid), the BoDs contains 17–19 members, contrasting with German 50+1 clubs, Bayern Munich and Borossia Dortmund, which have three to four members. In the German two-tier system, BoDs report to a supervisory board, which may level out the difference. However, what these four clubs share is that all directors are domestic citizens. Among the other clubs, BoD size ranges between four (Chelsea) and 12 (Manchester United), and foreign BoD majority is found in Inter Milan (7 of 9), Chelsea (3 of 4), Manchester City (6 of 8), Paris SG (4 of 6), Liverpool (4 of 7) and Manchester United (7 of 12). Manchester United and Juventus are the only listed clubs. Only nine of 107 directors are women (eight percent), and the age range is 45–57.

This section has shown that diverging interests within European football have intensified, and that the influence of UEFA as a governing body has been eroded. The emergence of different types of ownership and foreign profit-seeking investors has complicated the system of network governance. Nevertheless, even at club level, there are still a number of different ownership and BoD models. Variety persists, despite the unequivocal trends of corporatisation and commercialization.

Institutional logics and governance: Converging towards a market logic?

Why has the control of so many clubs shifted from the community in which they are located to distant, increasingly overseas, commercial and quasi-commercial owners? How can we make sense of the transition towards the hybrid governance structures observed in European football? At face value, these questions may look quite diverse, but, as will be shown, they are interconnected.

When it is not down to pure accident, change is often the outcome of ideological or mental models that prompt key decisions which change structures and premises for the actors in the field. In the course of change, actors may also change as they possibly drive the development further. Institutional sociology, broadly defined, addresses this phenomenon by seeing systems as not merely composed of formal structures, rules and procedures, but also cultural and symbolic elements (i.e., Greenwood, Oliver, Sahlin-Andersson & Suddaby, 2008; Powell & DiMaggio, 1991). In this perspective, the withering of ideologies and symbols that bolstered the pyramid structure of the past must have preceded new ideas that paved the way for increased network governance in European football.

The institutional logics perspective (Friedland & Alford, 1991; Thornton, Ocasio & Lounsbury, 2012) offers a conceptual framework to analyse the historical changes outlined above. This perspective departs from the idea that multiple interdependent institutions meaningfully constitute society and powerfully affect change in and between organisations, horizontally as well as vertically. These authors suggest each institution assumes different logics of what is rational, right and good, and that each logic constrains the cognition as well as the means and ends of social action. Institutional logics provide root symbols, metaphors and categories that give meaning and value to the experiences and perception of organisation members. For instance, public agencies (and their servants) would carry the logic of the bureaucratic state; professionals, the logic of the profession; and business firms (and their managers), the logic of the market. It is also common to see the persistence of institutional logics when symbols, metaphors, categories and rules that give meaning and value in one institutional context occur as misplaced and counterproductive in another. Thus if public servants or politicians apply the logic of the market and trade with public goods or votes, their actions can be viewed as corrupt. If corporations coordinate prices between them rather than competing, it is seen as a violation of the market logic. Accordingly, businesses are subject to regulation from the bureaucratic state.

Whereas typologies (i.e., ideal types) do not fully capture the empirical nature of social phenomena, they can aid scientific inquiry by highlighting the diversity of drivers that lead to specific structures. In this case, it may be useful to conceptualise (European) sport as an institution to outline specific dynamics. Sport can be seen as an institution alongside other institutions that make influential claims on the football field.[2] For example, sport bodies depend on state authorities to provide sport facilities and security measures at big events, yet they forcefully exclude political figures or state executives from their national governance bodies (Meier & Garcia, 2015). Sport's logic prescribes to avoid entanglement in political rivalries that might undermine sports' integrity. This is illustrated in the case of the state-assisted doping in the 2014 Sochi Olympic Games and the subsequent ripple effects on the international sport world. While the Russian state accepts interference in sport, it is rejected in the European sport template that predicates sport governance autonomy (and accordingly, Russian state authorities reject any allegation of collusion).[3] As the examples show, governance is not a given but subjected to social construction. Actors may create, define and translate constructs, norms and rules anew, borrowing from several institutional logics in their re-creation of the field (Friedland & Alford, 1991). Unless this was the case, the topic of this chapter, ownership in European football, would be nonsensical, because the idea of someone "owning football" and exchanging their ownership to another is a recent one (cf. Hassan & Hamil, 2011) and an example of how the field of football is re-created amid claims from diverse logics.

The field of football: A definition game

The social construction of European football relies, particularly, on four institutional logics: sport, community, state and market (cf. Figure 10.1). In theory, these logics are represented by diverse sectors, but re-creation also means that the borders between them are sometimes blurred, notably, because actors mix roles (a fan and voluntary sport officer may also be a businessman or civil servant).

Building on these ideas, the historical pyramid of international football embodies a *sport logic* that departs from the meaning of doing sport and that there is a need for bodies that can organise tournaments and standardise as well as enforce rules. While the spread and popularity of the sport attracted commercial activities, sport activity was not seen as a means to profit. It is well established in psychological research that athletes and sport officials are motivated primarily by intrinsic rewards, not commercial or political aims (e.g., Andersen & Hagger, 2010; Hancock, Dawson & Auger, 2015). The pyramid of football relied heavily on a logic where sporting mastery, development, excellence and spectacle were the end of the activity. For professional football, this logic is echoed in Sloane (1971) who declared that the objective of a football club was to maximise utility (playing success, average attendance, league health, recorded profit and after-tax profit) whilst remaining financially solvent.

It is also noteworthy that the sporting pyramid is democratic. It relies on membership and the one-member-one-vote principle. Athletes, umpires, support staff and sport officials are conceptualised as members with equal rights of vote and representation, and, at the next tiers, the same holds for clubs and national association. Scholars writing on the topic have ignored this nature of the system, naming it "undemocratic" (i.e., Geeraert, Scheerder & Bruyninckx, 2013) and highlighting its hierarchical structure where "rules and regulations adopted at their [FIFA/

Sport   **Community**

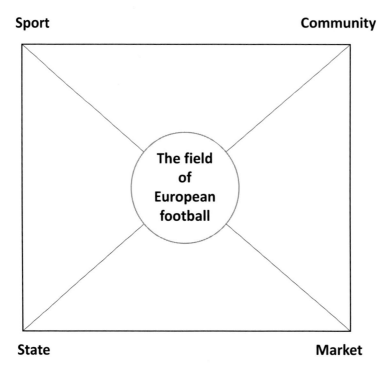

State   **Market**

Figure 10.1 Institutional logics defining European football governance.

UEFA] level are filtered down the pyramid and abided by those stakeholders in the lower echelons" (García & Meier, 2012, p. 360). It is obvious that members towards the bottom of the pyramid feel powerless in the same way citizens in democratic states may feel powerless. However, the pyramid of European football was created from the bottom up, and stakeholders at the lower echelons may still mobilise and overturn proposals from the apex of the pyramid.

Some actors also claim to define football utilising a *community logic*. Whereas football as a sport is "placeless" (it can be played everywhere), football clubs have historically been a source of pride within their geographical locality with various communities demonstrating strong levels of commitment, solidarity and emotional attachment to their club. It is based around a highly significant social role reflected in the representation of notions of community, tradition, social solidarity and local and national distinctiveness (Sugden, 2002). The local football fan typically sees themselves as the true owners of the club (Cocieru, Delia & Katz, 2019) and are hostile to investors that do not represent the region (e.g., Llopis-Goig, 2014; Totten, 2016).

State and sport interaction is widespread but not much studied (Bairner et al., 2016). As already mentioned, after World War II, football clubs in Eastern Europe were subordinated to the totalitarian communist state (e.g., Molnar, 2007). In the southern regions of Europe, the state is more actively regulating the governance of the game compared to the British Isles and Northern Europe (Gammelsæter & Senaux, 2011). In Mediterranean Europe, while clubs are historically rooted in nonprofit traditions, sport has long been perceived as the responsibility of the state with sport associations as an ally, forming a bureaucratic sport policy configuration (Vocasport Research Group, 2004).

The *logic of the state* is also evident at the super state, or the European Union (EU) level (e.g., Geeraert et al., 2013). In a sense, the 1995 Bosman ruling defined professional football as working life subjected to EU regulation (Gammelsæter, 2019). Whereas EU court decisions have acknowledged that there are features of sport that are specific, the EU has also insisted that sport as an economic activity falls within the scope of its constitution. In the Lisbon Treaty, the EU committed to the promotion of European sporting issues, recognising sport's social and educational functions (García & Weatherill, 2012). For the EU and nations alike, sport is associated with a large number of welfare policy areas including public health, education, youth, equal opportunities and other areas that fall within the logic of what a modern state should promote.

The impact of a *market logic* on professional men's football is unmistakeable. Against the background that the raison d'être of the market is profit maximisation, it is notable that professional football was unprofitable despite a massive revenue increase from 1996 to 2016, rising from €2.8bn to €18.5bn (UEFA, 2017). Recently, UEFA (2018) issued a statement that European club football made a profit of €600m for 2017, compared to cumulative losses of €1.7bn seven years earlier, relating the improvement to the introduction of the Financial Fair Play regulation. In similarly optimistic parlance, Deloitte (2018) reported on the English Premier League financial year 2016/17 as record-breaking because for the first time no clubs reported an operating loss. Therefore it "feels increasingly as if we have now entered a new financial era for the Premier League clubs and their owners and investors" (Deloitte, 2018, p. 20). However, in the league below, the Championship, owners and investors have less reason to rejoice as the clubs continue to report operating and pre-tax loss. Similarly, the premiere leagues in France and Italy do not yet break even (Deloitte, 2018).

The four institutional logics of sport, community, state and market capture many of the drivers that transform the governance of football and will continue to do so. This take on analysing the field has the advantage that it directs attention to how logics can coexist and interweave in different forms, without collapsing into one, while at the same time being inherently in conflict and a threat to each other. It sensitises us to the fact that the pyramid of sport governance is premised on the idea inherent in competition sport that athletes are driven by intrinsic autotelic motivation, the value that arises in sport participation and the competition itself (Gammelsæter 2010; Walsh & Giulianotti, 2007). A pyramidal association-based structure is a rational means to cultivate this passion. It further sensitises us to the meaning of historical and local roots of European football, to the impelling force of states to capitalise on any externality of athlete's sport activity that fits their aims and to commercial actors' desire to exploit the popularity of sport for profit purposes. State and business stakeholders, local fans and the supporters of sport purism all seek to employ governance structures that promise to realise their ideas about how things should work. States have the power to finance sport and to issue sport regulation as part of their sport policies. Commercial actors channel excess capital into models that are known to them and where they, as far as possible, can control the return on their investment. Ownership through shareholding and limited responsibility is their preferred model, in sport as well as in other sectors. However, committed fans are seen as the backbone of football's attraction, hence uprooting football from its local communities may violate commercial aims. Despite this "cultural restriction", it is obvious from the ownership changes in clubs and leagues and the impetus for the bigger clubs and leagues to form interest organisations at the European level, that the market logic increasingly has gained ground in European football. The emergence of ownership as a topic in the field is witness of the same.

Looking to the future

What this chapter has tried to show is that the issue of ownership needs to be placed in the broader environment and that we cannot separate club ownership from changes that are taking place within the ecosystem of professional sport. It should be clear from the above that market logic has infused European football over the past three decades. What is more difficult to conclude is that the stakeholders pursuing this logic have, on average, over the past three decades actually made a profit. It is assumed here that the more recent international investors seek soft power or trophy assets, but that they also pursue profits – certainly in the long run. If this is correct, what will the future of European men's football look like? How will increased pressure for profit influence the governance structure?

The research literature has established that the "winner's curse" problem causes a challenge to profitability in European football. Because of the importance of trophies and entry to the most prestigious tournaments, clubs will tend to increase their costs beyond what is profitable, even if revenues continue to increase. To realise their logic, commercial owners will therefore continue to pursue governance structures that increase profit. For this reason, the oligarchic closed league format, governed outside of UEFA, is appealing to commercial owners. This model keeps a better control of expenses and secures profit. However, if this is the aim of commercial owners, why has it not yet materialised, after two decades of threats of a super league? The answer may be that the other logics still have power. In Europe, the sport logic is tightly related to the competition pyramid, the promotion–relegation formula and the organisation pyramid that connects elite football with grassroots and youth football. European Leagues has recently committed to the pyramid structure, and UEFA has done its utmost to keep it. What will UEFA do if its most important tournament, the Champions League, is undermined? UEFA may ban players performing in a super league from national teams and, perhaps, from teams playing in the European club tournaments. If this happens, will there be a reaction from the EU? It is notable that the system below the elite, which supplies the top teams with talent, is very different in Europe compared to the USA. Does this pose a problem? Will the EU go back to revise its sport policy and defend the European sport model, or will it leave it to the Court and Commission, as it has before?

The community logic still has a strong grip on dedicated fans in Europe. Inherent in this logic is rivalry across teams and cities and historical derbies, often between teams from the same city. A super league may threaten derbies in Liverpool, Manchester, London, Madrid, Barcelona and Torino, for example, but also between rivalling cities. The statistics show that some clubs (e.g., Barcelona, Real Madrid, Atletico Madrid, Borussia Dortmund) have higher average attendances in the domestic league than in the Champions League (European Football Statistics, 2019). Even though a super league would be based more on worldwide TV deals than gate revenues, could it be sure to be a success unless it sells out the stadia? Hence, is there a risk that a club-owned super league will decouple not merely from the pyramid of European football, but also from the logics that underpin football's popularity? The future is composed of many questions, and we believe that the institutional logics perspective provides a guide to help us unpack some of these questions as regards the future of European football.

When considering the impact of the varieties of institutional logics on organisational governance, there are challenges that scholars face in better understanding what is happening. The closed nature of the world of professional football (e.g., Kelly & Harris, 2010; Roderick, 2006) makes access to boards difficult, hence research on board structures and decision-making processes in clubs are lacking. It has long been recognised that to understand what goes on at an organisational governance level requires access to boards of directors to be able to shed light on how boards work and make decisions. Pettigrew (1997) argued that organisational governance can (or should) be empirically examined through "processual analysis" that pays close attention to governance talk. When looking to understand how the broader environmental changes within the professional sporting landscape impact on organisational governance, it is important to adopt a process approach (e.g., Langley, 1999) that allows access to the "black-box" of the board (Leblanc & Schwartz, 2007). To get to the heart of how boards work and to really understand the impact of changing institutional logics on organisational governance, researchers need to be aware of the methodological challenges involved in getting access to relevant data. This is a long-standing challenge – and one that holds for the sporting field just as it does in any other organisational context.

Notes

1 The first European competition, the Inter-Cities Fairs Cup, was, in fact, set up by private organisers in 1955; but since the first competition ran over three years, its first final took place the same year that the first UEFA tournament, the European Cup, also set up in 1955, celebrated its third winner (Week, 2017).
2 From a European perspective, it is interesting that North-American sociologists long ignored civil society (other than religion and families) and sport as social institutions (cf. Friedland & Alford, 1991; Thornton et al., 2012). This testifies that the constraining powers of institutional logics also applies to researchers, as sport in the USA can be subsumed within the market, corporations, the state (inter-collegiate sport) and the family. In contrast, in Europe, sport is more closely associated with the nonprofit sector.
3 The sport-politics interaction is, of course, not an East–West issue. Sport and politics are inextricably bound together despite many sport people claims that sport and politics do not mix (Bairner, Kelly & Lee, 2016; Gammelsæter, 2019).

References

Anagnostopoulos, C. (2011). The battlefield of Greek football. Organising top-tier Football in Greece. In H. Gammelsæter & B. Senaux (Eds.), *The organisation and governance of top football across Europe: An institutional perspective* (pp. 209–223). New York: Routledge.

Andersen, M. B., & Hagger, M. (2010). Debate: Should sport psychologists try to help athletes and exercisers become more intrinsically motivated? *Sport & Exercise Psychology Review, 6*, 47–51

Ascari, G., & Gagnepain, P. (2006). Spanish football. *Journal of Sports Economics, 7*, 76–89.

Bairner, A., Kelly, J., & Lee, J. W. (2016). Editors' introduction. In A. Bairner, J. Kelly & J. W. Lee (Eds.), *Routledge handbook of sport and politics* (pp. xxxxviii). London: Routledge.

Balduck, A-L., & Lucidarme, S. (2011). Belgian football. A uniting force in a two-track policy. In H. Gammelsæter & B. Senaux (Eds.), *The organisation and governance of top football across Europe: An institutional perspective* (pp. 107–122). New York: Routledge.

Baroncelli, A., & Caruso, R. (2011). The organization and economics of Italian top football. In H. Gammelsæter & B. Senaux (Eds.), *The organisation and governance of top football across Europe: An institutional perspective* (pp. 168–181). New York: Routledge.

Brannagan, P. M., & Giulianotti, R. (2014). Soft power and soft disempowerment: Qatar, global sport and football's 2022 World Cup finals. *Leisure Studies, 34*, 703–719.

Brown, A. (2007). "Not for sale?" The Destruction and reformation of football communities in the Glazer takeover of Manchester United. *Soccer and Society, 8*, 614–635.

Buraimo, B., Simmons, R., & Szymanski, S. (2006). English football. *Journal of Sports Economics, 7*(1), 29–46.

CIES. (2019). Governance and financial landscape of top European football clubs. Retrieved 25 May 2019, from https://www.cies.ch/fileadmin/documents/News_Agenda_Publications/Governance_and_Financial_Landscape_of_Top_European_Football_Clubs_Final_.pdf

Cocieru, O. C, Delia, E. B., & Katz, M. (2019). It's our club! From supporter psychological ownership to supporter formal ownership. *Sport Management Review, 22*, 322–334.

Deloitte. (2018). Roar power. Annual review of football finance 2018. Retrieved 5 June 2019, from https://www2.deloitte.com/content/dam/Deloitte/uk/Documents/sports-business-group/deloitte-uk-sbg-annual-review-of-football-finance-2018.PDF

Dobson, S., & Goddard, J. (2001). *The economics of football.* Cambridge: Cambridge University Press.

European Football Statistics. (2019). Retrieved 15 November 2018, from https://www.european-football-statistics.co.uk/

Franck, E. (2010). Private firm, public corporation or member's association governance structures in European Football. *International Journal of Sport Finance, 5*, 108–127.

Friedland, R., & Alford, R. R. (1991). Bringing society back. In W. W. Powell & P. DiMaggio (Eds.), *The new institutionalism in organizational theory* (pp. 232–263). Chicago, IL: The University of Chicago Press.

Gammelsæter, H. (2010). Institutional pluralism and governance in "commercialized" sport clubs. *European Sport Management Quarterly, 10*, 569–594.

Gammelsæter, H. (2019). Points, pounds and politics in the governance of football. In S. Chadwick, D. Parnell, P. Widdop & C. Anagnostopoulos (Eds.), *Routledge handbook of football business and management* (pp. 44–55). London: Routledge.

Gammelsæter, H., & Senaux, B. (2011). Understanding the governance of football across Europe. In H. Gammelsæter & B. Senaux (Eds.), *The organisation and governance of top football across Europe: An institutional perspective* (pp. 268–291). New York: Routledge.

García, B., & Meier, H. E. (2012). Limits of interest empowerment in the European Union: The case of football. *Journal of European Integration, 34*, 359–378.

García, B., & Weatherill, S. (2012). Engaging with the EU in order to minimize its impact: Sport and the negotiation of the Treaty of Lisbon. *Journal of European Public Policy, 19*, 238–256.

García, B., & Welford, J. (2015). Supporters and football governance, from customers to stakeholders: A literature review and agenda for research. *Sport Management Review, 18*, 517–528.

Geeraert, A., Scheerder, J., & Bruyninckx, H. (2013). The governance network of European football: Introducing new governance approaches to steer football at the EU level. *International Journal of Sport Policy and Politics, 5*, 113–132.

Gómez, S., Martí, C., & Mollo, C. B. (2011). Commercialization and transformation in Spanish top football. In H. Gammelsæter & B. Senaux (Eds.), *The organisation and governance of top football across Europe: An institutional perspective* (pp. 182–194). New York: Routledge.

Greenwood, R., Oliver, C., Sahlin-Andersson, K., & Suddaby, R. (Eds.). (2008). *The handbook of organizational institutionalism*. Thousand Oaks, CA: Sage.

Hamil, S., & Walters, G. (2010). Ownership and governance. In S. Hamil & S. Chadwick (Eds.), *Managing football: An international perspective* (pp. 17–36). Oxford: Butterworth-Heinemann.

Hancock, D. J., Dawson, D. J., & Auger, D. (2015). Why Ref? Understanding sport officials' motivations to begin, continue, and quit. *Movement & Sport Sciences – Science & Motricité, 87*, 31–39

Hassan, D., & Hamil, S. (2011). *Who owns football? The governance and management of the club game worldwide*. Oxford: Routledge.

Henry I., & Lee, P. C. (2004). Governance and ethics. In J. Beech & S. Chadwick (Eds.), *The business of sport management* (pp. 25–42). Harlow: Prentice Hall.

Hodges, A., & Brentin, D. (2018). Fan protest and activism: Football from below in South-Eastern Europe. *Soccer & Society, 19*, 329–336.

Hoehn, T., & Szymanski, S. (1999). The Americanization of European football. *Economic Policy, 14*, 203–240

Holt, M. (2005). *UEFA, governance and the control of club competition in European football*. London: Football Governance Research Centre, Birkbeck College.

Kelly, S., & Harris, J. (2010). Managers, directors and trust in professional football. *Sport in Society, 13*, 489–502

Kennedy, D., & Kennedy, P. (2007). Supporter trusts and third way politics. *Sport in Society, 10*, 285–303

Langley, A. (1999). Strategies for theorizing from process data. *The Academy of Management Review, 24*, 691–710.

Leblanc, R. W., & Schwartz, M. S. (2007). The black box of board process: Gaining access to a difficult subject. *Corporate Governance: An International Review, 15*, 843–851.

Llopis-Goig, R. (2014). Football clubs ownership and management. The fans perspective. *International Journal of Sport Science, 10*, 16–33.

Marston, K. T, Boillat, C., & Roitman, F. (2017). *Governance relationships in football between management and labour. Players, clubs, leagues & national associations*. Neuchâtel: Centre International D'Etude du Sport.

Meier, H. E., & García, B. (2015). Protecting private transnational authority against public intervention: FIFA's power over national governments. *Public Administration, 93*, 890–906.

Michie, J., & Oughton, C. (2005). *The FA: Fit for purpose?* A report for the Sports Nexus. The Sport Nexus.

Molnar, G. (2007). Hungarian football: A socio-historical overview. *Sport in History, 27*, 293–317.

Morrow, S. (1999). *The new business of football: Accountability and finance in football*. Hampshire: MacMillan Business.

Morrow, S. (2003). *The people's game? Football, finance and society*. Hampshire: Palgrave Macmillan.

Morrow, S. (2011). History, longevity and change: Football in England and Scotland. In H. Gammelsæter & B. Senaux (Eds.), *The organisation and governance of top football across Europe: An institutional perspective* (pp. 46–61). New York: Routledge.

Olsson, L.-C. (2011). Decisive moment in UEFA. In H. Gammelsæter & B. Senaux (Eds.), *The organisation and governance of top football across Europe: An institutional perspective* (pp. 17–31). New York: Routledge.

Pettigrew, A. M. (1997). What is a processual analysis? *Scandinavian Management Journal, 13*, 337–348.

Plumley, D. J., Ramchandani, G., & Wilson, R. (2018). Mind the gap: An analysis of competitive balance in the English football league system. *International Journal of Sport Management and Marketing, 18*, 357–375.

Poli, R., Ravenel, L., & Besson, R. (2018). Competitive balance: A spatio-temporal comparison. *CIES Football Observatory Monthly Report, 40* - December 2018.

Powell W. W., & DiMaggio P. J. (1991). *The New institutionalism in organizational analysis.* Chicago, IL: The University of Chicago Press.

Relvas, H. (2011). The organization of football in Portugal. In H. Gammelsæter & B. Senaux (Eds.), *The organisation and governance of top football across Europe: An institutional perspective* (pp. 195–208). New York: Routledge.

Roderick, M. (2006). *The work of professional football: A labour of love?* Oxford: Routledge

Rohde, M. & Breuer, C. (2017). The market for football club investors: A review of theory and empirical evidence from professional European football. *European Sport Management Quarterly, 17*, 265–289.

Senaux, B. (2011). The regulated commercialisation of French football. In H. Gammelsæter & B. Senaux (Eds.), *The organisation and governance of top football Across Europe: An institutional perspective* (pp. 123–137). New York: Routledge.

Sloane, P. (1971). The economics of professional football: The football club as a utility maximiser. *Scottish Journal of Political Economy, 18*, 121–146.

Spiegel. (2018). American gold rush: How financial incentives dictate teams' U.S. Games. Retrieved 15 November 2018, from http://www.spiegel.de/international/world/international-champions-cup-driven-by-financial-incentives-a-1236556.html

Sugden, J. (2002). Network football. In J. Sugden & A. Tomlinson (Eds.), *Power games: A critical sociology of sport* (pp. 61–80). London: Routledge.

Thornton, P. H., Ocasio, W., & Lounsbury, M. (2012). *The institutional logics perspective. A new approach to culture, structure, and process.* Oxford: Oxford University Press.

Totten, M. (2016). Football and community empowerment: How FC Sankt Pauli fans organize to influence. *Soccer & Society, 17*, 703–720.

UEFA. (2008). *The European club footballing landscape, club licencing benchmarking report. Financial Year 2008.* Retrieved 6 June 2019, from https://www.cies-uni.org/sites/default/files/2008_UEFA_Club_Licensing_Benchmarking.pdf

UEFA. (2017). *The European club footballing landscape, club licencing benchmarking report. Financial Year 2016.* Retrieved 5 June 2019, from https://www.uefa.com/MultimediaFiles/Download/OfficialDocument/uefaorg/Clublicensing/02/58/98/12/2589812_DOWNLOAD.pdf

UEFA. (2018). *UEFA statement on Financial Fair Play,* Retrieved 12 November 2018, from https://www.uefa.com/insideuefa/protecting-the-game/club-licensing-and-financial-fair-play/news/newsid=2581760.html

Vocasport Research Group. (2004). *Vocational education and training in the field of sport in the European Union: Situation, trends and outlook.* Lyon: European Observatoire of Sport and Employment.

Walsh, A., & Giulianotti, R. (2007). *Ethics, money and sport. This sporting mammon,* London: Routledge.

Ward, S., & Hines, A. (2017). The demise of the members' association ownership model in German professional football. *Managing Sport and Leisure, 22*, 358–373.

Week, J. (2017). The Inter-Cities fairs cup: European football's strange and forgotten grandfather. Retrieved 30 October 2018, from https://sports.vice.com/en_uk/article/wnmgw5/the-inter-cities-fairs-cup-european-footballs-strange-and-forgotten-grandfather

Wilkesmann, U., & Blutner, D. (2002). Going public. The organizational restructuring of German football clubs. *Soccer and Society, 3*, 19–37.

Wilkesmann, U., Blutner, D., & Müller, C. (2011). German football: Organizing for the European top. In H. Gammelsæter & B. Senaux (Eds.), *The organisation and governance of top football across Europe: An institutional perspective* (pp. 138–153). New York: Routledge.

Wilson, R., Plumley, D., & Ramchandani, G. (2013). The relationship between ownership structure and club performance in the English Premier League. *Sport, Business and Management: An international Journal, 3*, 19–36.

11

Professional team ownership models in Australia, New Zealand and South Africa

Adam Karg and Coral Ingley

Introduction

This chapter examines the ownership and governance of professional sport teams in Australia, New Zealand and South Africa. It provides a detailed analysis of how sport leagues and teams are structured and managed in each region and how ownership and governance can challenge efficient sport outcomes. While we provide coverage of a wide range of corporate sports in all regions, we limit the comparative analysis to professional or corporate sport leagues and to the sports of cricket, rugby union and association football (soccer), given the commonality of these sports as dominant sports with professional leagues in each country. As well as the size and popularity of the sports, study of the professional leagues and teams in the region provide evidence of recent environmental and structural changes in many instances, presenting a range of diverse ownership designs and issues.

The chapter first provides a descriptive comparison of ownership models for leagues and teams in each region. Dominant ownership designs for the region include public, private and emerging hybrid ownership models. This is followed by a summary and analysis of the implications of different models for governance, focusing on motivation for sport team ownership, drivers and the impact for change as well as the implications of ownership design for established principles of governance. While governance of both corporate and nonprofit organisations are well-developed research areas, empirical findings linking ownership models and governance of sport teams remain very limited. The nations studied present a rich research context for future research spanning: a) the study of ownership change, b) motivations and implications of private or equity ownership and c) operation of diverse networks and collaborative settings. These regions therefore provide a unique context to advance the understanding of how ownership impacts governance and the efficient and effective operation of professional sport leagues and teams.

A focus on three sports: Football, rugby and cricket

In this section, a justification and focus on the three sports common to the region is provided noting a distinct focus on football, rugby and cricket. The sport of football has long been commercialised and globally provides a setting where private ownership models are evident in most major markets. The sport is governed globally by FIFA and has the largest global sporting event outside of the Olympics with over 200 countries competing to qualify for the World Cup. Each of the three subject countries have participated in recent World Cups although South Africa, Australia and New Zealand are aligned with, and qualify through, different continental federations. Professional football leagues are established in most countries, providing diverse levels of commercial opportunities for athletes and, in turn, leading to significant movement of players internationally. In the case of Australia and New Zealand, professional teams from both countries compete in the same league (the A-League), while South African football is headed by a two-division professional structure. The setting of the sport and cases of private ownership provide the basis for discussion on ownership models and governance.

The second featured sport, rugby union, is a sport with a lesser history of commercialisation, existing as a professional sport only since 1995. Governed by World Rugby, the sport's centrepiece, its World Cup, is the second largest single sport event in the world. There has been significant growth with the number of countries entering the sport competitively, with over 120 member–nations and a number of professional leagues spanning both hemispheres. The focus of the southern hemisphere has traditionally centred on Australia, South Africa and New Zealand with, intriguingly for the setting of this chapter, all three of the countries having competing clubs in the same Super Rugby competition. South African, New Zealand and Australian Rugby (SANZAR) is the organisation responsible for administering the competition, formed as a collaboration between administrations of the Australian, New Zealand, South African and Argentine rugby unions. Arguably, rugby presents the most complex professional sport setting in the region; the examination of teams across the three countries existing in an environment of change between community and public ownership, together with the transition towards hybrid models incorporating private ownership, present a range of tensions for exploration in the chapter.

The final sport is cricket. Headed by the International Cricket Council (ICC), there are 105 member–nations, but only 12 countries hold full membership. Traditionally, commercial interest has been most dominant at the international level, where broadcast rights, gate and sponsorship revenue have centred on competitions where nations played against each other. Domestic leagues and competitions were active but existed primarily as "feeder" competitions (i.e., a competition where the best players could be selected to participate in their national teams). However, in the last decade, the relevance of cricket as a professional league product has grown as a result of the creation of Twenty20 (T20) cricket leagues. This emerging version of the game provides a faster-paced product which is shorter in time, compacts the excitement and action of the game and merges sport and entertainment in an attempt to attract new audiences and commercial investment. In line with this approach, new T20 leagues have been created over the last decade with the Indian Premier League (IPL) the most successful. The three countries reported here all provide cases of new T20 leagues being created to leverage this potential. While private ownership of teams has been explored for cricket in the three countries, public or association team ownership remains the dominant model for professional teams in each country.

Importantly, in all countries, professional league products evolved from sports which all operate under traditional international and national governance models (i.e., sports are controlled by a national governing body [NGB] in each region). Hence, the way that diverse ownership designs for professional teams impact sport governance provides visible and critical discussion points for the intersection of ownership and governance. In the case of change or pressure towards change, this chapter will focus on what has driven the changes in different markets and settings. While the comparative focus is limited to three core sports, some additional context for popular sports in each market (i.e., the case of the Australia Football League and National Rugby League in Australia and the sport of basketball in New Zealand and Australia) is provided. From here, the chapter focuses on addressing ownership design in each of the three countries followed by a discussion of critical issues stemming from ownership and implications for governance.

Corporate sport and ownership design

In the following sections, ownership design is considered in each of our three national settings. The purpose here is to present divergent cases of ownership and introduce material relevant to the critical issues developed later in the chapter.

Australia

The setting of Australian sport represents the most competitive market of the three sports. While the professional sport market is dominated by Australian Rules Football and Rugby League, the three subject sports introduced below remain prominent professional leagues for exploration.

In the case of football, the history of professional leagues dates back to the 1970s with the National Soccer League (NSL). The league was operated by the NGB for the sport and provided scope for competition between teams, which had progressed from member- or community-owned clubs. The league underwent a complete restructure in the mid-2000s when the NGB changed the league model. The current A-League consists of 10 teams (including one from New Zealand) with all teams privately owned and the league aligned with the Asian Football Confederation. Foreign investment is common, with only three teams fully owned by Australian investors. Further, 62 percent of the aggregate share of owners or ownership groups are based overseas, including China, Indonesia, the UAE, England, The Netherlands and The Philippines (Mersiades, 2018). Historically, private ownership of A-League teams has brought instability, with multiple cases of ownership change in the last decade, driven by team performance, financial issues and other business opportunities. Ownership change has involved new investment from corporate and sporting organisations and, for example, includes acquisition and ownership of one team (Melbourne City) by City Football Group, the parent entity which owns Manchester City and related sister teams in North American and Japanese leagues. Recently, expansion has created opportunities for new investment into the sport and the league. Despite few cases of success (more expansion teams folded in the first decade than survived), the league offered new licences to two new teams in late 2018 (Gatt, 2018). There has been recent conflict between private owners and the league, which has in part led to FIFA intervention, but, in sum, the league has stabilised entering its second decade and enjoys solid commercial performance mainly driven by media-rights fees.

The setting for cricket as a professional league product has evolved in the last decade. The Big Bash League (BBL) was created in 2011 and is owned and run by the sport's NGB, Cricket Australia (CA). The eight-team league was created to leverage the popularity of T20 cricket, to widen the sport's supporter base and attract new audiences to the game (Shilbury, Westerbeek, Quick, Funk & Karg, 2015). Teams are owned by organisations linked within the sports federated structure. For example, CA represents six state-based associations which each controlling the sport in their respective region and having up to two teams that compete in the BBL. At the league inception, CA considered offering private ownership shares in teams, but no private or equity investment was sold at the time (Barrett, 2016). Commercial performance has been strong, with increasing media rights and, at one stage, the league being recognised as one of the top 10 most attended professional sport leagues in the world. The case of cricket provides (like the A-League) an NGB-controlled league but with public or state association ownership and operation of teams.

Rugby Union is one of four football codes with a strong following in Australia. Australia has entered between three and five teams since the inception of the SANZAR-operated Super Rugby format in 1995. Where interest in the sport has traditionally been concentrated in north-eastern markets of New South Wales and Queensland, expansion of the sport has allowed growth into other markets, with Perth (Western Australia) and Melbourne (Victoria) hosting expansion teams. However, expansion teams have led to mixed results regarding sustainability and perfor-mance, distribution of the limited talent pool and, ultimately, the on- and off-field strength of teams. In sum, the capacity to support five teams appeared stretched, with the Perth-based team removed from the league in 2017, in part, to allow for league expansion in new international markets (e.g., a Japan-based team). Teams in the Australian market have largely been publicly owned, with licences operated by state bodies in each region. For example, the NSW Waratah's licence is owned and operated by NSW Rugby, with similar arrangements of licence owner-ship existing for other teams. The exception is the Melbourne Rebels, who have bridged public control (i.e., by the Victorian Rugby Union (VRU), the state body for the sport) and equity ownership via two stints of privatisation. In each period, different owners funded and led the team before returning the licence to the state body. In these cases, the need for external owner-ship was driven more by a need to provide sustainability and investment, as opposed to attracting owners to leverage the commercial success of the team. The team licence was returned to the VRU in 2017 (Windley, 2018). While there have been limited examples of private or alternative investment in Super Rugby teams in Australia, this has been challenged recently with teams cit-ing interest from private investment groups or exploring options for share offerings in teams to generate capital from investors and supporters.

In sum, the three sport cases are unique, with two where the league is owned and operated by the NGB. However, these two are distinct with teams privately owned in football's A-League but publicly owned via licences operated by state or regional sport governing bodies for Cricket's BBL). While SANZAR's quad-national structure (where four NGBs are represented) provides a common league-level ownership setting, teams in Australia are unique from the other two countries, given limited private investment in team ownership. It should be noted that, uniquely in the case of Australia, the sports we profile do not represent the largest commercial sports (as they do in each of our other countries). For example, the Australian Football League (AFL) (the professional league for Australian Rules Football) and the National Rugby League (NRL) represent the sports with the highest national interest. Here, the AFL has member-owned and -run teams, where clubs are awarded licences but are essentially owned by, and report to, public member bases. In the case of the NRL and other leagues (including the National Basketball League) private ownership of teams exists in a range of cases.

New Zealand

In the case of New Zealand football, one fully professional team (the Wellington Phoenix) plays in the A-League, the Australian-run league established in 2005. The team entered in 2007, replacing the New Zealand Knights after a range of on- and off-field struggles. At that time, the licence was transferred to New Zealand Football (the NGB) who sub-licenced it to private owners. The original Wellington Phoenix owners relinquished ownership in 2011 following financial troubles and the licence was passed to a new consortium (Rugari, 2018). As such, the club, via private ownership, is aligned with the other A-League teams with which it competes.

As well as the A-League, a 10-team national Football Championship (ISPS Handa Premiership) operates as a semi-professional league limited to New Zealand participation and is aligned with the Oceania Football Confederation (OFC). The semi-professional league has run since 2004 when it accepted bids from eight new teams to enter a new league structure.

The case of cricket provides a very similar model to Australia. While New Zealand Cricket, as the NGB, facilitates the development and administration of all aspects of the sport, they also operate the T20 competition which, since 2014, has been known as the Super Smash. Aligned with the BBL, the competing teams represent and are owned by the six regional cricket associations across the country. Each of the six associations has a first-class cricket team structure and provides teams that compete in a range of different national competitions. In most cases, the regional teams maintain the same branding for the Super Smash as the teams that represent the associations in other cricket competitions. The exceptions are Canterbury and Northern Districts, where T20 teams have alternate brands. While a minor difference, it is meaningfully distinct from the case of the BBL in Australia, where franchises were created specifically to represent cities, with distinct branding and monikers created for the teams to distinguish them from state-governed teams competing in other competitions.

New Zealand contributes five teams to the SANZAR Super Rugby competition, each of which was created and licenced by New Zealand Rugby Union (NZRU) in 1995. Rugby represents New Zealand's major sport; hence the profile and visibility of the teams and commercial opportunities are strong. From inception, teams were owned subsidiaries of NZRU, structured on a geographic basis to represent provincial unions across the country and operated by regional associations. Changes to ownership unfolded from 2012, where NZRU facilitated a program of privatisation (SBS News, 2018). While the NGB retains ownership of the team and brand, it provided a licence to new entities to run teams. Where operationalised, shares have generally been divided between regional associations with up to 50 percent ownership being transferred to private investors. This has provided additional capital for teams, as well as opportunities for greater diversity and business acumen in the leadership and operations of teams. However, the movement to privatisation has not always been smooth, with NZRU called in to assist in a buy-out of the Auckland Blues' 40 percent allocation by private investors after a range of management and governance issues (SBS News, 2018).

In sum, ownership of football and cricket largely mirror Australian settings, where fully professional football teams are privately owned since inception of the A-League, while cricket's T20 teams are operated and owned by regional associations. Within the Super Rugby setting, teams display progression towards privatisation via hybrid models of ownership, distinct from the Australian setting. In other popular sports, similarities can be observed, where New Zealand teams compete in other Australian-governed competitions. For example, the New Zealand Breakers compete in the National Basketball League, a league where all other teams reside in Australia. The team is privately owned, with transition to a new group of investors including former NBA players and private businessmen (NZ Herald, 2018). The New Zealand Warriors of the National Rugby League have, likewise, been funded by private investment for much of the past few decades with recent changes resulting in shares being distributed across the governing body for the sport in Auckland and corporate interests (NZ Warriors, 2018).

South Africa

In the case of South Africa, our three profiled sports cover the consensus top three sports and, hence, the most professional and developed sports in the region. The structure of football in South Africa is a two-tier Premier Soccer League (PSL) comprising Premier and National

First Divisions. It was founded in 1996, with a total of 32 teams and is controlled and operated independently from the NGB, by the South African Football Association (SAFA). SAFA was formed in 1991 and operates lower levels of the sport's competition structure for an additional 140 teams. PSL teams are privately owned, including backing from individual and corporate owners, as well as examples of ownership by professional teams from other countries (e.g., Ajax Amsterdam [a successful Dutch team] is a shareholder of the Cape Town-based team). Team owners form a committee and elect an executive to run the league, in a similar way to commission structures in North American leagues. Despite some stable teams, recent reports suggest that many teams and owners struggle financially (Molobi, 2017).

Cricket in South Africa and its foray into a new professional league presents a curious recent case. Until 2017, a domestic competition had run in South Africa, with six teams representing different provinces or regions. In mid-2017, Cricket South Africa (CSA) announced plans for a new Global T20 League (GT20) to be established. Initially, it planned to attract private ownership for eight teams, with bidders acquiring teams and paying franchise fees ahead of a planned 2017 debut season. However, difficulties in attracting commercial revenue for the planned new league meant the inaugural season was postponed. In a 2018 change of approach, CSA launched an alternative competition, the Mzansi Super League, a T20 competition owned and run by the NGB, with six teams (essentially representing existing provinces) participating in the inaugural version of the league in late 2018 (South Africa Cricket Magazine, 2018). The change from an equity-based model with much foreign, private investment, to a public or NGB-owned venture represented a significant shift. Both the initially planned and later established league struggled to find a title sponsor or broadcaster, and the inaugural competition was met with moderate attendance.

Ownership design of rugby teams mirrors New Zealand, with professional teams representing a range of unions across the country. Currently, four South African teams compete in the Super Rugby competition, with each representing a range of provinces (between two and six per team). SANZAR reduced the number of South African teams from six to four for the 2018 season, with the Cheetahs and Kings omitted from the 2018 competition. Since the late 1990s, Super Rugby franchises have attracted equity investment, with private ownership originally capped at 49.9 percent. This ensured that the South African Rugby Union (SARU) and its associations had control over franchises. However, recent changes have allowed greater private ownership, with "participation of private equity in the commercial arms of unions (increased) to a maximum of 74 percent to ensure continued financial sustainability in the unions" (SARU, 2017). Changes to ownership and equity have been reported since 2017 (Rugby 365, 2018) but reports of financial struggles within franchises continue.

In sum, South Africa provides the most progressed case of private team ownership in the subject sports. Football ownership largely mirrors the international setting, with private ownership dominant for club teams. Super Rugby sees hybrid ownership encouraged between private equity investors and associations (albeit with a higher equity share than is allowed in NZ), while the case of cricket highlights consideration of both equity and public ownership design prior to the new T20 league.

Ownership and implications for governance

Summary of ownership models

The above national profiles considered three sports and professional team ownership designs in each. Pertinent in each setting is change, largely driven by environmental themes of professionalisation and commercialisation (Gomez, Opazo & Marti, 2008) in each of the sports in each region. This has led to the formation of new leagues, as well as changes within existing leagues to offer different models for ownership and equity investment. Critically, it is recognised that prominent international competitions take place outside the professional or corporate leagues profiled in this chapter. Aligned with this, NGBs (who have both commercial and sporting responsibilities) remain highly involved in most cases, either operating leagues (e.g., cricket league in all countries and the football league in Australia and NZ), or with the NGB being a partner to the organising body of the competition (e.g., SANZAR in the case of rugby).

In aggregating findings, it is clear that three different team ownership models exist for professional sport in the region, namely, a) "public" owned teams which are NGB- or association-owned and/or operated; b) privately owned teams; and c) "hybrid" or mixed ownership or licence models with both private and public interests. In the absence of other ownership models in the region, these three (summarised in Table 11.1) can be considered on a continuum from public to private (with hybrid bridging the two) and present cases and tensions related to motivation for ownership, as well as operational and financial implications that are addressed at the end of the chapter.

Most commonly – and seen particularly in cricket in all three regions – are public- or NGB-operated professional teams. NGBs in each case have all started new leagues in the last decade. Here, cricket bodies in both Australia and South Africa explored forms of private ownership but ultimately retained full control over teams; these are operated largely by, or on behalf of, state, regional or provincial associations that sit within the sport's governing structure. This is distinct from the successful Indian Premier League and other new global T20 cricket leagues, which have attracted significant levels of private investment since their inception. Rugby teams in Australia are also predominantly owned and operated by national and state bodies.

Private ownership models are common to football, where professional teams are privately owned in all countries. League structures are differentiated in South Africa where there is clear separation between the national league structure and the NGB. This structure is typical of most FIFA-sanctioned nations. In the case of Australia, the NGB (Football Federation Australia) still operates the league but change towards greater independence seems to be favoured by FIFA and other stakeholders. Private ownership is also seen in other sports (e.g., Rugby League and basketball in Australia and New Zealand).

As an alternative that most highlights both the opportunities and potential hazards of private or equity ownership, hybrid or mixed ownership models have arisen in Rugby in South Africa and, more recently, New Zealand. Here, the commercial arms of the sport (Super Rugby teams)

Table 11.1 Summary of club/team ownership (3 sports × 3 countries)

Sport	Australia		New Zealand		South Africa	
	League	*Club/team ownership*	*League*	*Club/team ownership*	*League*	*Club/team ownership*
Cricket	Big Bash League	Public/ NGB and associations	Super Smash League	Public/NGB and associations	Mzansi Super League	Public/NGB and associations
Football	A-League	Private	A-League	Private	Premier Soccer League	Private
Rugby	Super Rugby	Public/ NGB and associations	Super Rugby	Hybrid – Private Equity up to 50%	Super Rugby	Hybrid – Private Equity up to 74%

have been divided as separate or licence-based entities, with portions sold to generate investment while looking to professionalise and bring diverse business acumen and opportunities to the running of teams. The level of equity that can be sold privately is capped in both markets with portions of ownership retained by the provinces or regional unions.

Ownership and governance implications

In assessing recent development of leagues and teams, the impact of commercialisation (Gomez et al., 2008) within our subject nations is clear. Commercialisation is, alongside other metrics, highlighted by the development of new corporate leagues and teams in each market and movement towards greater engagement with private and hybrid ownership models. In analysing the region, multiple aspects of, and implications for, governance and future research are considered in the remaining sections of this chapter.

First, the critical issue of the motivation for different ownership of teams arises as a key initial issue. Hence, the benefits and opportunities of different ownership designs are considered, demonstrating the tensions and limitations that privatisation of teams has presented or may present. Second, how these tensions and implications might impact core principles of governance are addressed, which are increasingly conceptualised in research on sport organisations (e.g., Chappelet, 2018; Parent & Hoye, 2018). The development of such principles is suggested in a range of work on NGBs and nonprofit sport settings (Chappelet & Mrkonjic, 2013) and are introduced and applied here for professional teams. Following this, given that empirical findings specifically linking ownership models and governance remain limited, future research options that leverage the ownership design and governance issues of the region are discussed.

Motivations for ownership

Consideration in the literature on sport teams of what attracts individuals and companies to undertake private ownership is limited, but diverse motivations relative to professional sport league settings are evident (e.g., Conn, 2015; Fort, 2000; Lang, Grossman & Theiler, 2011; Mason, Sant & Soebbing, 2017). At a personal level, sport team ownership comes with great profile, with "ego" factors being a rationale for ownership of teams. At a corporate level, the ability to create synergies with existing business pillars, leverage the emotional connections consumers have with sport teams and build better business and government relationships may be viewed as rationales for equity-level involvement. Other strategic reasons, for example, capturing additional aspects of the value chain within a sport, can be relevant. Here, the involvement of media companies or brands purchasing teams and leagues highlight horizontal or vertical integration strategies (Gratton & Solberg, 2007), providing capacity to generate and own content or enhance brands (Mills & Winfree, 2016). Where "networks" of teams have been created within a sport (e.g., where global brands, such as City Football Group or Ajax Amsterdam, have invested in teams in the profiled regions), brand growth, increasing asset bases and access to player pools can form specific motivations.

Certainly, there can be more altruistic rationales for private ownership; building interest in a sport, giving back to a community and using the profile of the team to assist transformation in a region have all been cited as rationales for investment. Counter to this, more fiscally-dominant rationales are evident for corporate investment. For the time being, these rationales – and their consequences – are more prominent in European and North American markets. Here, financially oriented ownership of teams in larger professional leagues has sought to hold the team as an asset and capitalise on the growth of revenue and value of the team over time (Conn, 2015, 2018).

In sum, the motivations of private owners can be diverse and, at times, clearly conflict with what might be considered the sporting or community outcomes and priorities by stakeholders, such as NGBs, participants of the sports in a region and fans of professional teams.

For teams looking to attract private equity or ownership, often the rationale is new or additional capital investment and equity which can aid investment in the team or, more widely, the operations and development of the league, association or province which is selling the equity share or licence fee. Licence fees cited to be paid for expansion of A-League teams, and those originally proposed to be paid for teams entering South Africa's (now defunct) GT20 cricket competition in 2017, are examples of opportunities to generate substantial new capital investment for leagues and teams. Arguably, such substantial local and global investment that has flowed into teams in football and rugby would be unlikely had teams be maintained as member or publicly owned and operated entities.

In addition to financial capital, private ownership creates models where risk is shared and the presence of new individuals and organisations can widen the expertise available to the team, diversify the skill set of organisations running teams and increase the resources or business networks available to teams. In making changes to the percentage of equity that could be owned in a South African Super Rugby team, the SARU and teams cited opportunities via private equity to inject capital into the franchises, professionalise the game and engage greater business and marketing expertise to develop franchises (Gedye, 2017). The ability to attract external investment also shows confidence in the brand of the league, which can have other flow-on effects. In sum, non-capital benefits acquired via private ownership can increase professionalisation of teams and, in turn, the efficiency and effectiveness of their governance and operations.

There are, therefore, short- and long-term benefits not only from financial or capital inflows of privatisation, but also from additional networks, brands, expertise and resources that the right type of private owner might bring. From here, it is possible to connect ownership design cases to governance principles to explore implications for governance and the functioning of sport organisations within different ownership models. To underpin this, as a base, the existing work on corporate and nonprofit governance is used, as well as existing theories and principles of governance.

Implications for governance principles

Initially, consideration of the motivations of different ownership models highlight differing lenses for the study of governance given different ownership designs. Under a corporate governance framework, the focus is on increasing efficiency, enhancing value and generating profit (Hoye & Doherty, 2011). The principles of corporate governance can be applied most closely to private ownership of professional teams, where profit maximisation or fiscal interests are more likely to influence the orientation of teams (Lang, Grossman & Theiler, 2011). Counter to this, nonprofit governance frameworks provide a setting for the study of sporting organisations as custodians or stewards of teams. This framework can be applied to community focused or nonprofit national or regional governing bodies. In this setting, these are owners and operators in our "publicly" owned team setting. Under such orientations, organisations represent, and are accountable to, a greater number of stakeholders than in the corporate context and exist for reasons beyond profit generation (Hoye, Smith, Westerbeek, Stewart & Nicholson, 2006). Comparing corporate (private) and nonprofit (public) ownership models of teams, the number of decision-makers, their relationships, their focus, orientation and management processes differ. Nevertheless, existing governance models help recognise and provide a setting for studying different motivations that private and public owners may hold in terms of orientation, stakeholders and perspectives which may in turn influence priorities and decision-making as well as organisational conflict, performance and efficiency.

There are myriad bases from which to explore examples of conflict and issues that may arise for organisations in their quest for efficiency. Previously, a wide range of potential motivations were noted for private ownership, many of which might focus on corporate, business or financial outcomes. However, NGBs, as public owners by definition, have and report to a complex range of stakeholders where financial sustainability presents only one of many performance objectives (Bayle & Madella, 2002; Bayle & Robinson, 2007). As examples, NGBs or public owners may utilise a league which they control, to fulfil a range of outcomes. These may include increased promotion of the sport, providing a competitive setting to develop players who can best represent and excel for national teams in international competitions, or to generate revenue and profit that can be reinvested into the sport. As such, retaining ownership and control of corporate sport leagues (and their teams) allows an NGB or member association to retain financial income and revenue while maintaining control of the league, teams and presentation of the sport and how it is leveraged. Conceptually and operationally, there exists diversity in the goals and priorities of public and private owners. Under private ownership orientations, profit-maximising principles suggest that owners will expect the asset (team or league) to increase in value and generate profit which may be returned to owners (i.e., not be retained in the sport). As such, scenarios for conflict or complex decisions within corporate sport settings as to what is best for the sport, versus what is best from a commercial perspective, may unfold (Shilbury, Phillips, Karg & Rowe, 2017).

Here, financial aspects are perhaps most clear where, for example, private owners are able to take revenue and profits generated by teams from the sport and reinvest as they wish. Public owners (i.e., NGBs or associations as owners), given a wider range of (non-financial) objectives and can be expected to act more as custodians. Therefore, they need to consider reinvestment in activities that both support the sustainability of the team while also considering other aspects such as junior development and sport pathways that may have a lower priority for a private owner. Given that, in sports like rugby, where (Super Rugby) team revenue represents a substantial, if not the, majority of state or provincial income, there are significant implications for how the constitutions, policies and decision-making of leagues and teams are established to ensure private-owner objectives are balanced against the needs of the sport. An example spanning league and team structure is seen in the role of national competitions and leagues as Super Rugby went through its review prior to the reduction of Australia teams in 2017. Here, the private owner of the Melbourne Rebels questioned the role of Super Rugby teams in relation to player-import restrictions for Australian clubs. NGB (Rugby Australia) rules restricted the number of international players a team could recruit, seeking to balance player quality with a mandate for teams to assist in developing talent for the national team. However, as an owner, greater freedom to recruit high-quality international players (at the expense of the development of local players) could arguably provide the most "entertaining, professional sporting package" and the best opportunity to win, as well as attract members and fans to drive revenue (Australian Associated Press, 2017). Such rules are set by the NGB but, in this case, impact both the composition of teams as well as talent development and national team representation issues that are the focus of NGBs. This is just one of many situations where a private owner and public custodian of a team may justifiably differ in approach to key issues.

While a range of differences are evident between public and private ownership designs, it appears that hybrid models, while for the most part positive, have nevertheless resulted in similar tensions and conflicts. Hybrid ownership, as seen in southern hemisphere rugby, translates to a need for hybrid or shared governance models between those representing components of private and public ownership for these teams. Given shared responsibility for strategic direction, decision-making can become a basis for conflict between public associations and private owners responsible for such tasks. As board cohesion (Doherty & Carron, 2003) and organisational functioning (Bayle & Madella, 2002) are critical aspects of sport organisation performance, such conflict presents strategic issues that can challenge efficiency and effectiveness. Importantly, New Zealand (and South Africa until 2017) enforced the requirement for majority ownership to be held by rugby associations, therefore allowing the NZRU and its associations to maintain control, limit risk and theoretically regulate the balance between the diverse needs of the NGB and its associations. However, while the majority of New Zealand's hybrid rugby ownership models have been retained, the case of the Auckland Blues highlights a dysfunctional case. While Bolton Equities Limited (BEL) purchased 40 percent of the Blues franchise, NZRU in 2018 took back the private shareholding following an independent review into poor on- and off-field performance. The review was not fully made public but concluded that the mix of existing shareholders was not sustainable, highlighting governance issues and clashes between BEL and rugby stakeholders who were said to be critical (SBS News, 2018).

Thus, while private ownership can bring benefits, diverse orientations of public and private owners can provide settings for conflict, resultant inefficiency and a lack of functionality which impact the core objectives and outcomes of governance and, in turn, organisational performance. The above raises the question of how opportunities for effective governance can be maximised via different structures. As noted, hybrid models, such as those seen in NZ and South Africa, largely have been sustainable to date and allow, conceptually, for inflow of capital and sharing of risk while limiting leakage of profit or revenue generated by the sport. Where hybrid models are used, this has been facilitated by clearly delineating the Super Rugby franchise or commercial aspects of the sport operations as an entity distinct from the other rugby operations governed by the association. Further, capping private ownership has helped sport organisations retain power and control. The SARU's 2017 removal of restrictions on the maximum private ownership (up to 74 percent can now be privately owned) presents an emerging opportunity to explore how hybrid models may operate where private owners have control.

As well as issues of ownership motivation and orientation that may lead to conflict and limit efficiency, private ownership can influence aspects of democracy, transparency and accountability that are core principles of governance (Chappelet, 2018; Parent & Hoye, 2018). For example, ownership or majority-control by private owners limits input and power to a smaller number of stakeholders and removes the influence of sport organisations in how teams are structured, financed and promoted. Here, the decision of cricket NGBs, in all three markets, not to privatise teams playing in newly created T20 competitions is relevant. Had teams been privatised, it would have removed the ability of stakeholders, including regional, provincial and state associations, to not only dictate how revenue was used, invested and distributed, but also their input into how teams were run, including the development of talent and promotion and positioning of teams. The role of multiple stakeholders within federated systems is instrumental in enforcing greater transparency and accountability of teams where team ownership and operations are retained by NGBs or associations. In considering the equivalent scenario under private ownership, transparency of ownership, club structure and reporting could be substantially different. In the case of some A-League clubs, some owners remain publicly anonymous, while across privately owned teams, financial and operational reporting processes and transparency are undertaken under principles of private practices, compared with the more public reporting standards of NGBs and publicly funded sport organisations. Again, when considering opportunities for effective governance via different structures, there are steps that can be taken. Mirroring European regulations, "fit and proper" ownership tests and financial reporting standards can be enforced. The nature of sporting leagues which are, by design, heavily regulated, can also enforce operational restrictions, these being particularly critical where private and public teams compete against each other.

Research opportunities and conclusion

Future research

Whereas much past research has centred on governance, including specific focus on board roles, performance, capability and collaboration (e.g., Ferkins & Shilbury, 2015; Hoye & Doherty, 2011; Taylor & O'Sullivan, 2009), less emphasis has been placed on team ownership design and its implications. This is especially the case when considering professional sport, given that the dominant focus of work has been on NGBs and event bodies (Parent & Hoye, 2018). The exploration of ownership in our context has uncovered different models of professional sport team ownership, highlighting examples of ownership change, new leagues and teams and implications and considerations that can inform future work and practice.

While scholars have explored diverse team models including member-owned (Hamil, Walters & Watson, 2010) and mutuality ownership models (Ward, Scanlon & Hines, 2012), as well as debt and capital structure (Dimitropoulos, 2014), a wider exploration of the design options, motivations for ownership and how they impact governance and organisational functioning is essential. Further, other work on professional teams has related to single cases and is dominated by views of football in the northern hemisphere. The exploration and comparison of multiple countries in this chapter suggests that concurrent exploration of multiple professional sport leagues can usefully inform understanding of ownership and governance. Critical aspects include the need for a greater understanding of the environmental pressures and opportunities created by different structures and how opportunities for effective governance can be maximised in different structures. The robust exploration of governance principles, as well as their impact on performance, remain a critical research gap (Parent & Hoye, 2018). Advancing this to the setting of professional teams, the exploration of such principles and performance in different ownership models provides an additional layer spanning both corporate and nonprofit governance settings.

As well as established private and public ownership models and their operation within federated structures, our exploration demonstrates increasing utilisation of hybrid ownership as an evolving design option. Contiguously is the exploration of the rationale for, and the process of, change in ownership models. The case of establishing new leagues and teams, as well as changing ownership designs, provides an opportunity to explore the impacts of increased commercial investment in professional teams and the consequent impacts on other aspects of the sport. In most cases, aligned with commercialisation and professionalisation, the move has been towards full or partial privatisation of teams, providing scope to explore the impact of change in guiding best practices.

As well as governance of and within sport organisations, systemic governance and exploration of increasing networks of organisations provide fruitful research areas. League and team structure, both within, as well as external to, existing federated models, provide a complex mix of governance settings. For example, football and rugby leagues (and teams) have, or are moving towards being structurally independent from NGBs. However, cricket leagues continue to be intrinsically owned and linked within NGB structures. Therefore, the role, orientation and outcomes of leagues in different ownership settings are worthy of exploration. Where teams have been partly privatised, the separation or division of franchises from associations of NGBs provides an opportunity to explore this understanding. Relatedly, we see increasing evidence of networks of teams and strategic partnerships becoming more prevalent. The emergence of global sport brands, such as City Football Group, and other brands, such as Red Bull, which have built "families" of sporting teams under central brands presents increasingly complex stakeholder structures. With hybrid models as one example, increased commercialisation across sports in this region should provide rich cases of increasing complexity. Already, we see evidence, in the context of New Zealand and South African teams and associations investing in European and North American teams, providing scope for exploration and increased understanding of the implications of such networked organisational settings.

Summary

The investigation of professional sport-team ownership design in cricket, football and rugby in the three countries has presented a range of public, private and hybrid ownership models. This chapter has summarised a critical junction in time, given the emergence of expansion leagues and teams, as well as recent changes in ownership of teams. Of the three sports, football appears the most stable and consistent, with private ownership the norm for professional levels in each country. Analysis of cricket focused mainly on T20 as the professional league product, where the NGB in each country has created and maintained publicly owned league structures and teams in the last decade. While both Australian and South African NGBs explored private team ownership at the inception of T20 leagues, more conservative or traditional models were employed, with team ownership maintained by associations representing states, regions or provinces in each country. Private ownership remains an option in the future for such leagues. Rugby provided a dynamic case, with recent change in all nations. For most Super Rugby teams, hybrid ownership models are in operation. Such ownership models provide increasingly complex stakeholder mixes and, hence, considerable challenges for governance effectiveness.

The range of ownership models provided scope to explore differing motivations, apply and compare corporate and nonprofit governance frameworks and examine evidence (and potential impact) of ownership design on governance principles. While a full review of all governance principles is outside the scope of this chapter, perspectives and examples relevant to governance efficiency and effectiveness, democracy and transparency have been highlighted. The region provides evidence of models, which are responding to environmental pressures, including professionalisation and commercialisation, while retaining a need to balance the demands of diverse stakeholders within existing federated models for each sport. Rich opportunities exist to study such change and thereby inform the efficacy of different ownership structures and their impact on governance effectiveness, sustainability and success in the context of sports in the regions.

References

Australian Associated Press. (2017). Melbourne Rebels owner confident about Super Future. Retrieved 8 May 2018, from https://www.foxsports.com.au/rugby/melbourne-rebels-owner-andrew-cox-confid ent-club-isnt-on-super-rugby-chopping-block

Barrett, C. (2016). Multi-million-dollar franchises. Now's the time to privatise. *Sydney Morning Herald.* Retrieved 8 May 2019, from https://www.smh.com.au/sport/cricket/big-bash-league-201516-multi milliondollar-franchises-nows-the-time-to-privatise-argues-players-chief-20160112-gm44ax.html

Bayle, E., & Madella, A. (2002). Development of a taxonomy of performance for national sport organizations. *European Journal of Sport Science, 2*(2), 1–21.

Bayle, E., & Robinson, L. (2007). A framework for understanding the performance of national governing bodies of sport. *European Sport Management Quarterly*, 7, 249–268.

Chappelet, J.-L. (2018). Beyond governance: The need to improve the regulation of international sport. *Sport in Society*, 21, 724–734.

Chappelet, J.-L., & Mrkonjic, M. (2013). Existing governance principles in sport: A review of published literature. In J. Alm (Ed.), *Action for good governance in international sports organisations*. Copenhagen: Danish Institute for Sports Studies.

Conn, D. (2015). What is it that attracts US investors to the multi-million-pound EPL? *The Guardian*. Retrieved 8 May 2019, from https://www.theguardian.com/football/blog/2015/dec/23/everton-us-investors-john-moores-charles-noell

Conn, D. (2018). Manchester United have been owned by the Glazers for 13 years. No wonder they're struggling. *The Guardian*. Retrieved 8 May 2019, from https://amp.theguardian.com/football/2018/oct/04/glazers-manchester-united

Dimitropoulos, P. (2014). Capital structure and corporate governance of soccer clubs: European evidence. *Management Research Review*, 37, 658–678.

Doherty, A., & Carron, A., (2003). Cohesion in volunteer sport executive committees. *Journal of Sport Management*, 17, 116–141.

Ferkins, L., & Shilbury, D. (2015). The stakeholder dilemma in sport governance: Toward the notion of 'stakeowner'. *Journal of Sport Management*, 29, 93–108.

Fort, R. (2000). European and North American sports differences? *Scottish Journal of Political Economy*, 47, 431–455.

Gatt, R. (2018). FFA bring in two new teams to A-League and a financial windfall. *The Australian*, Retrieved 8 May 2019, from https://www.theaustralian.com.au/sport/football/ffa-bring-in-two-new-teams-to-aleague-and-a-financial-windfall/news-story/227d81b80d90cff013117f79e95661b6

Gedye, L. (2017). Building the business of rugby. Retrieved 8 May 2019, from https://www.fin24.com/Finweek/Featured/building-the-business-of-rugby-20170426

Gomez, S., Opazo, M., & Marti, C. (2008). *Structural characteristics of sport organizations: Main trends in the academic discussion*. Pamplona, Spain: IESE Business School, Universidad de Navarra.

Gratton, C., & Solberg, H. (2007). *The economics of sports broadcasting*. London: Routledge.

Hamil, S., Walters, G., & Watson, L. (2010). The model of governance at FC Barcelona: Balancing member democracy, commercial strategy, corporate social responsibility and sporting performance. *Soccer & Society*, 11, 475–504.

Hoye, R., & Doherty, A. (2011). Nonprofit sport board performance: A review and directions for future research. *Journal of Sport Management*, 25, 272–285.

Hoye, R., Smith, A., Westerbeek, H., Stewart, B., & Nicholson, M. (2006). *Sport management: Principles and applications*. Oxford, UK: Elsevier.

Lang, M., Grossman, M., & Theiler, P. (2011). The sugar daddy game: How wealthy investors change competition in professional team sports. *Journal of Institutional and Theoretical Economics*, 167, 557–577.

Mason, D., Sant, S., & Soebbing, B. (2017). The peculiar economics of sports team ownership: Pursuing urban development in North American cities. *Sport, Business and Management: An International Journal*, 7, 358–374.

Mersiades, B. (2018). Know your A-League owners. *Football Today*. Retrieved 8 May 2019, from http://footballtoday.news/features/long-read-know-your-a-league-owners

Mills, B., & Winfree, J. (2016). Market power, exclusive rights, and substitution effects in sports. *The Antitrust Bulletin*, 61(3), 423–433.

Molobi, T. (2017). Take the money and walk. *Sport 24*. Retrieved 8 May 2019, from https://www.sport24.co.za/Soccer/South-Africa/take-the-money-and-walk-20170701

NZ Herald. (2018). New Breakers owners revealed. *New Zealand Herald*. Retrieved 8 May 2019, from https://www.nzherald.co.nz/sport/news/article.cfm?c_id=4&objectid=12002096

NZ Warriors. (2018). Vodafone Warriors announce ownership change. *New Zealand Warriors*. Retrieved 8 May 2019, from https://www.warriors.kiwi/news/2018/05/02/vodafone-warriors-announce-ownership-change/

Parent, M., & Hoye, R. (2018). The impact of governance principles on sport organisations' governance practices and performance: A systematic review. *Cogent Social Sciences*, 4, 1–25.

Rugari, V. (2018). Wellington Phoenix could be replaced as A-League formally confirms expansion plans. Retrieved 8 May 2019, from https://www.stuff.co.nz/sport/football/a-league/102795194/wellington-phoenix-set-to-be-replaced-as-aleague-expansion-looms

Rugby 365. (2018). SA Rugby: Equity changes abound. Retrieved 8 May 2019, from https://rugby36 5.com/tournaments/super-rugby/news-super-rugby/sa-rugby-equity-changes-abound

SARU. (2017). *Annual Report*. Retrieved 8 May 2019, from http://images.supersport.com/content/SA_ Rugby_Annual_Report_2017.pdf

SBS News. (2018). NZ Rugby take back ownership of misfiring Blues. Retrieved 8 May 2019, from https ://www.sbs.com.au/news/new-zealand-rugby-take-back-ownership-of-misfiring-blues

Shilbury, D., Phillips, P., Karg, A. & Rowe, K. (2017). *Sport in Australia: An organisational overview* (5th ed.). Sydney: Allen & Unwin.

Shilbury, D., Westerbeek, H., Funk, D., Quick, S., & Karg, A. (2015). *Strategic sport marketing* (4th edn.). Sydney: Allen & Unwin.

South Africa Cricket Magazine. (2018). Mzansi Super League unveiled. Retrieved 8 May 2019, from https ://www.sacricketmag.com/mzansi-super-league-unveiled-csa/

Taylor, M., & O'Sullivan, N. (2009). How should national governing bodies of sport be governed in the UK? An exploratory study of board structure. *Corporate Governance: An International Review*, 17, 681–693.

Ward, S., Scanlon, T. J., & Hines, T. (2012). Mutuality ownership form and professional sports: Football. *Nonprofit and Voluntary Sector Quarterly*, 42, 763–780.

Windley, M. (2018). How Melbourne Rebels survived Super Rugby axe — and are now trying to thrive. *Herald Sun*. Retrieved 8 May 2019, from https://www.news.com.au/sport/rugby/super-rugby/me lbourne-rebels/how-melbourne-rebels-survived-super-rugby-axe-and-are-now-trying-to-thrive/ news-story/a1863a065b7002c2b7539314ca79abf2

12

Professional team ownership models in Japan, South Korea and China

Joon-ho Kang, Masayuki Yoshida and Dongfeng Liu

Introduction

Japan, South Korea and China represent major professional sports markets in Far East Asia. They have different histories, cultures and systems. Nippon Professional Baseball (NPB), Korea Baseball Organisation (KBO) and the Chinese Football Association Super League (CSL) were launched as the first professional sports league of each country in 1936, 1982 and 1994, respectively. The similarities and differences among the three countries and the differences between Far East Asia and other continents may be substantially attributed to the respective governance structures. The governance of professional sports teams varies depending on the culture and the institution of each country and the context in which professional sports were introduced. Particularly, the ownership model is the key to understanding the governance of professional sports in the three countries.

In this chapter, the professional sports team ownerships of Japan, South Korea and China are examined for the purpose of understanding the governance of the respective country. First, Japanese professional sport governance is examined focusing on Nippon Professional Baseball (NPB) and the Japan Professional Football League (J.League). Second, Korean professional sports team ownership is addressed by focusing on the Korea Baseball Organisation (KBO), K-League, Korea Basketball League (KBL) and the Korean Volleyball Federation (KOVO). Finally, the Chinese model is explained using Chinese Football Association Super League (CSL) and Chinese Basketball Association (CBA).

Professional team ownership in Japan

History and structure of Nippon Professional Baseball and the J.League

NPB

In Japan, there are two major professional sport leagues: Nippon Professional Baseball (NPB) and the Japan Professional Football League (J.League). NPB was established in 1936 and initially included seven teams. In 1950, NPB formed the Central League and the Pacific League, with six teams in each league. Since then, NPB has been considered the most popular professional sport league in Japan. Much of its growth has been attributed to the member teams, which are owned by large newspaper media groups and railroad companies. This business model allowed the teams to gain lucrative broadcast rights deals and to increase ticket sales by building a strong fan base. In 2004, however, the NPB lost two teams. One was the Osaka Kintetsu Buffaloes, which were sold to ORIX Corp., a financial services group; the team merged with the ORIX Bluewave to form a new team called the ORIX Buffaloes. Another was the Fukuoka Daiei Hawks, which were acquired by SoftBank Group Corp., a multinational telecommunications and Internet corporation. Because the merger of the Buffaloes and the Bluewave decreased the number of the teams from twelve to eleven, NPB decided to add a new team, the Tohoku Rakuten Golden Eagles, to the Pacific League. The Golden Eagles are owned by Rakuten, Inc., which is a global online marketplace company and was an official jersey sponsor of Football Club (FC) Barcelona from the 2017–18 season until the 2020–21 season.

Figure 12.1 shows the organisational structure of NPB. NPB can be understood either as an association or as an organisation. On one hand, NPB follows the articles of an association, which are necessary to guide the business and affairs of the league (e.g., the membership, structure and appropriate behaviour that NPB promotes) towards the development of a sustainable baseball culture. On the other hand, as an organisation, NPB coordinates and facilitates baseball businesses among the twelve teams under an agreement that determines the working condition requirements (e.g., through an executive committee and investigating committee). While the two governing bodies (i.e., the association and organisation) of NPB have some overlapping functions (e.g., the commissioner's and owners' involvement), it is undeniable that this NPB structure increases the power and responsibility of the owners' meeting, in which the owners of the twelve teams discuss both cultural and business issues as the highest decision-making body.

J.League

The first season of the J.League took place in 1993 with ten clubs. In the five-year period between 1994 and 1998, eight clubs were added to the league. In 1999, the J.League switched to a two-division format, including sixteen Division 1 clubs and ten Division 2 clubs and started using a system of promotion and relegation between the two divisions. In the last decade, the J.League has continued to expand both in terms of the number of clubs and in the number of divisions. By 2018, the league had three divisions and 57 clubs (18 Division 1 clubs, 22 Division 2 clubs and 17 Division 3 clubs). Furthermore, it is important to note that, in 2012, the J.League

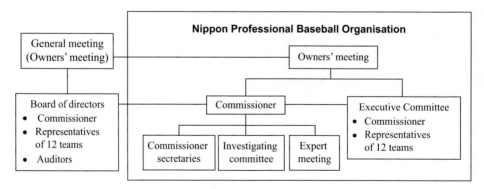

Figure 12.1 The NPB structure. The figure was created based on the Sport White Paper 2017 (Sasakawa Sport Foundation, 2017) and the Japan Professional Baseball Players Association (2016).

started the "club license system", which requires the member clubs to meet certain criteria in terms of sport development, stadium quality, professional staffing and finance in order to participate in the league. By the 2018 season, 40 clubs had obtained the Division 1 license, while seven clubs have qualified for Division 2.

The governing body of Japanese football is the Japan Football Association (JFA). The J.League and other amateur associations belong to the JFA (see Figure 12.2). The J.League is formed of the following components: (1) The general meeting of the member clubs and the chairman; (2) the board of directors, including external experts; (3) the executive committee, composed of the representatives of the member clubs; (4) the arbitration committee as an advisory body for the chairman; (5) four technical committee meetings pertaining to regulation, legal, the match commissioner and marketing; and (6) office workers to support the league businesses. Since the 2018 season, the board of directors includes 24 individuals. Among them, seven board members are external non-football professionals, such as an economist, college professor, certified public accountant, former Olympic athlete and vice president of a multinational electronics corporation.

Ownership structures of individual teams

NPB teams

In Japanese professional sport, teams can be characterised by how they are controlled by the parent companies. In most cases, Japanese professional baseball teams are owned by large conglomerates such as the Yomiuri Shimbun Holdings, SoftBank Group and Rakuten Group. For example, as shown in Figure 12.3, the Yomiuri Giants – the league's oldest team, established in 1934 – can be considered as a strategic business unit that focuses on the baseball business within the divisional structure of the Yomiuri Shimbun Holdings; this structure includes newspaper, magazine publisher and baseball divisions. "Divisional structure" is defined as the structure of an organisation according to individual products (Daft, 2004). This structure is often used by large organisations and allows units to adapt to the requirements of different customers and regions (Daft, 2004). However, while

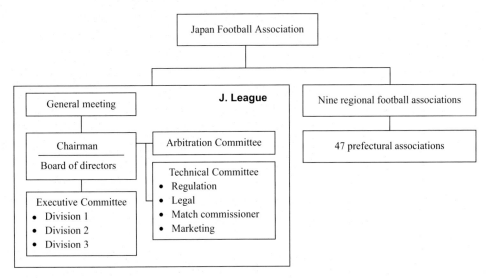

Figure 12.2 The J.League structure. The figure was created based on Sport White Paper 2017 (Sasakawa Sports foundation, 2017) and J. League Official website (2018).

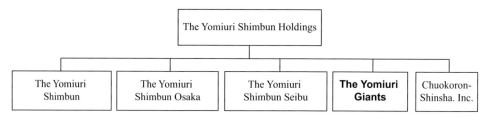

Figure 12.3 The ownership structure of the Yomiuri Giants. The figure was created based on the Yomiuri Shimbun Holdings website (Yomiuri Shimbun Holdings, 2018).

they are business experts, it is also true that most workers organised by the divisional structure of a non-sport company do not have a sport management degree, resulting in the restriction of technical competence and specialisation in baseball management.

Usually, professional baseball teams' stock is not traded publicly but is owned by the owners, parent companies and affiliated firms. In the case of NPB, the governing body of the team is the board of directors, which consists of senior executives, a legendary former head coach and auditors of the team, as well as the chairman of the parent company. For example, Fukuoka SoftBank Hawks Corp. is controlled and coordinated through the vertical hierarchy of management under the leadership of the board of directors. Most board members are firm insiders chosen by SoftBank Group and serve as the internal control system of the team. The organisational structure is flat, as the board of directors is directly linked to functional departments such as the sport operations, business operations, management team and brand management divisions. From a sport governance perspective, the most interesting aspect is that decision-making is centralised to the board of directors before any problems influencing several divisions are solved. This is common among many Japanese professional baseball teams because boards of directors have complete control over their organisations and can use their legitimate power to dominate decision-making. Thus, the managerial goals of these teams tend to be oriented towards coordinating activities between the top and bottom of the organisations to maximise profits rather than towards achieving adaptation and change in the face of the external social environment.

J.League clubs

The ownership structures of J.League clubs are different from those of NPB teams. For example, most J.League clubs sell their shares to a third party in their franchise areas. In the 2018 season, Albirex Niigata Inc., a professional football club based in Niigata is owned by 163 companies and investors who are mostly located in the Niigata Prefecture (Albirex Niigata, 2018). The club's board of directors includes five chief executive officers (CEOs) of local companies. Before the club joined the J.League in 1998, the club was capitalised at approximately USD$ 5 million, with 151 corporate and individual owners. This example suggests that the biggest difference between NPB teams and J.League clubs is the capital stock held by external stakeholders. Contrary to the NPB teams that were formed to commercialise certain large companies, the foundation of each J.League club was designed to promote the active participation of many local companies and investors when it was established.

Another trend among big clubs, such as the Urawa Red Diamonds and FC Tokyo, has led to a broadening of the role of J.League clubs in their local communities. Clubs have begun to encourage prefecture- and city-level governments to become shareholders and subsequently to participate in the annual shareholders' meeting. For instance, four percent of the shares of Urawa Red Diamonds Co., Ltd. were sold to Saitama Prefecture and four percent to the city of Saitama

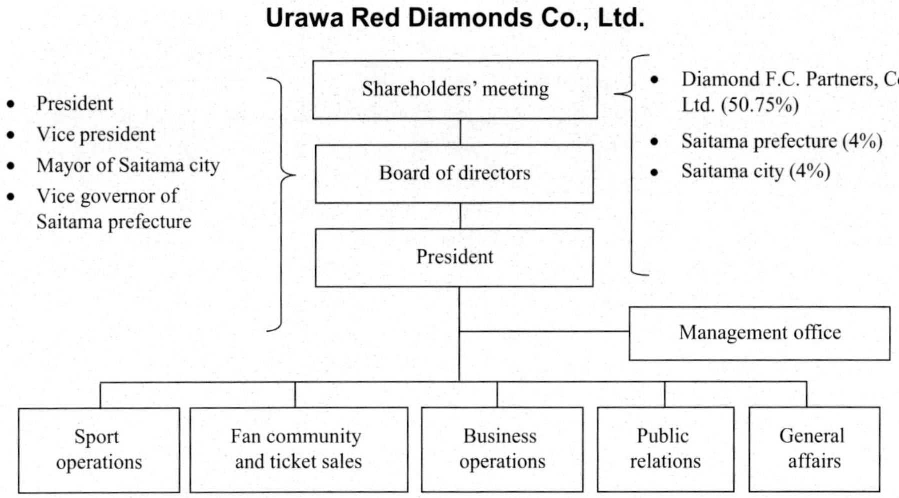

Urawa Red Diamonds Co., Ltd.

- President
- Vice president
- Mayor of Saitama city
- Vice governor of Saitama prefecture

| Shareholders' meeting |
| Board of directors |
| President |
| Management office |

- Diamond F.C. Partners, Co., Ltd. (50.75%)
- Saitama prefecture (4%)
- Saitama city (4%)

| Sport operations | Fan community and ticket sales | Business operations | Public relations | General affairs |

Figure 12.4 The organisational structure of Urawa Red Diamonds Co., Ltd. The figure was created based on the Urawa Red Diamonds Co., Ltd. website (Urawa Red Diamonds Co., Ltd., 2016). The percentages shown in the parentheses represent the percentages of equity held by the major shareholders.

(see Figure 12.4). This enables the club to receive higher levels of social support by creating a close formal relationship with local governments. While the affiliated company (Diamond F.C. Partners, Co., Ltd.) still has a much larger percentage of the shares, the governance of the club is rooted not only in the top management but also in their accountability to external shareholders. Clubs that use this type of ownership structure are typically those building strong relationships with their fans, local residents and society as a whole. Unlike the clubs compelled to obey only their parent companies, socially owned clubs are governed both by many local firms and by local governments, causing them to address current social and environmental challenges.

Sport governance themes in NPB and the J.League

According to Ferkins and Shilbury's (2016) theory of board strategic balance, there are four sport governance themes: (1) board structure, (2) board role, (3) board motivation and (4) shared leadership. Applying these themes to the realm of NPB and the J.League, important characteristics in each league can be identified. First, the board structure is different between NPB teams and J.League clubs. The board members of NPB teams are primarily the insiders of the teams and the parent companies, whereas the board of directors of J.League clubs includes many outsiders, such as the CEOs of local firms and the representatives of local governments.

The board role and board motivation are uniquely characterised either to control functional divisions under the top management team (i.e., in NPB) or to guide the organisation and its members towards goals shared by external stakeholders (i.e., in the J.League). For NPB teams, the board members' motivation is primarily business-oriented and influenced by the parent companies and other competing teams in the league. In contrast, the board members of J.League clubs are motivated to achieve both sustainable firm performance and local community development.

Finally, diverse leadership styles may exist and be shared with board members depending on the power of the owners and the complexity of the change. In NPB, charismatic leadership – that is, the leadership of those who have the ability to influence followers' enthusiasm and behaviour

183

(Conger & Kanungo, 1987) – is likely to be shared with board members because the CEOs of most teams are charismatic leaders of large conglomerates; at the same time, the relationship between the top and bottom of the organisations is primarily transactional in the vertical hierarchy as the CEOs and followers engage in an exchange for rewards. In the J.League, the board members of many clubs may choose both transformational leadership – to change followers' motivation to enhance organisational performance beyond self-interests (Avolio, Bass & Jung, 1999) – and ethical leadership – to demonstrate and promote normatively appropriate conduct to followers (Brown, Treviño & Harrison, 2005). This is because (1) the league structure is unstable due to the promotion and relegation system between the three divisions and (2) the clubs need to respond to the social pressure created by their external shareholders, local governments and the J.League.

Summary of Japanese professional sports team ownership models

Ownership structure has a significant impact on the sport governance themes (i.e., board structure, board role, board motivation and shared leadership) of Japanese professional sport teams. Particularly, professional ownership exerts two critical influences on the teams: (1) The emphasis of top management within the teams and (2) corporate social responsibility in the teams' local communities. Many J.League clubs are socially constructed entities that rely on social support from various external stakeholders in their hometowns. Even teams that are primarily owned by private companies are governed by business experts with a broader range of strategic capabilities developed in large conglomerates.

Ownership models of professional sport teams in South Korea

Overview of professional sports in Korea

Professional sports leagues in South Korea have a rather short history compared with those of other developed countries. Four major professional sports leagues of baseball, football, basketball and volleyball operate throughout a year. The professional baseball league, Korea Baseball Organisation (KBO), kicked off with six teams in 1982 and the Korean professional football league, renamed as K-League later, was launched with five teams in 1983. It was the government under then President Chun Doo Hwan that initiated the two professional sports leagues by asking large conglomerates such as Samsung, LG and Hyundai to run pro sports teams (Kang, 2017). The Korean Basketball League (KBL) was voluntarily founded in 1997 and the Women's Korean Basketball League (WKBL) was established the year after in 1998. Lastly, the Korean Volleyball Federation (KOVO) was formed to launch both men's and women's pro volleyball league, V-League in 2005. KBO and K-League compete with each other from spring to fall whereas KBL and KOVO compete from fall to spring (see Table 12.1).

Ownership models of KBO teams

The KBO is the first professional as well as and the most popular sports league in South Korea. The KBO has enjoyed unprecedented success at the gates in recent years and has set new regular-season attendance records (8.4 million) in 2017 (KBO, 2018a). The organisational structure of KBO consists of commissioner, secretary general, deputy secretary general, six administration teams (new business, management, finance, communication, operations planning and youth development), eight committees (referee, record, operations, youth development, disciplinary and technical) and one center (The Clean Baseball Center). KBO also has KBO Properties Co. Ltd. (KBOP), which is its subsidiary company managing media, sponsorship and merchandising businesses (KBO, 2018a). The KBO owns 100% of the shares of KBOP.

Table 12.1 Overview of professional sports leagues in Republic of Korea

Pro sports league	Founding year	Number of teams (2018)	Regular season	Post-season event
KBO (Baseball)	1982	10	Mar–Nov	Post-season (Oct–Nov)
K-League 1 (Football)	1983	12	Mar–Dec	Playoff (Dec)
K-League 2 (Football)	2013	10	Mar–Dec	Playoff (Dec)
Men's Basketball (KBL)	1997	10	Oct–Mar	Playoff (Mar–Apr)
Women's Basketball (WKBL)	1998	6	Nov–Mar	Playoff (Mar)
Men's Volleyball (KOVO)	2005	7	Oct–Mar	Post-season (Mar–Apr)
Women's Volleyball (KOVO)	2005	6	Oct–Mar	Post season (Mar–Apr)

Note: The table was created based on the public information available in the websites of KBO (2018b), K-League, KBL and KOVO.

All KBO teams except Nexen Heroes are unlisted subsidiary companies of large non-sports corporations. Seven out of nine teams (SK Wyverns, Doosan Bears, Hanwha Eagles, KIA Tigers, Samsung Lions, Lotte Giants and NC Dinos) are subsidiaries of parent corporations. Two teams (LG Twins and KT Wiz) are part of sports-related subsidiaries of parent corporations (LG and KT), called LG Sports Co. Ltd. and KT Sports Co. Ltd, respectively. These two sports subsidiaries own pro basketball teams as well.

Each parent corporation designates its chairman or top management as the owner of the team. The owners and the commissioner of KBO holds the owners' meeting, which is the symbolic, supreme body of the league. Parent corporations also appoint their executives as the CEO of their baseball team. The KBO commissioner and secretary general and the CEOs of ten teams compose the board of directors. Critical decisions such as recruiting the commissioner, accepting new team or relocating franchises are discussed in the owners' meeting whereas all the other important team and league-related regulations, management and operations agenda are examined during the board of director's meeting. The CEOs of the teams are not pro sports team management experts, but the executives from non-sport corporations. In KBO board of director's meetings they tend to speak for the best interest of their own teams or parent corporations, not for the best interest of KBO. This governance structure becomes one of the most fundamental obstacles to the advancement and innovation of KBO.

Nexen Heroes has a unique ownership model in KBO. Individual investors took over the Hyundai Unicorns that its parent corporation, Hyundai Group, ceded in 2007. They renamed the team Nexen Heroes after selling the title sponsorship to Nexen, a tyre company, in 2010. Nexen has been the title sponsor of the Heroes for nine years. However, Kiwoom Securities Co. replaced Nexen in 2019, and the name of the team was changed to Kiwoom Heroes. Unlike the other teams, Nexen Heroes have desperately tried to be financially independent, because there is no parent corporation on which to rely.

No team except the Nexen Heroes stands alone financially. Hence, the parent corporations cover the teams' financial losses accepting that this represents cause marketing communications or social responsibility. The teams are a vehicle for cause marketing or social responsibility activities on behalf of the parent corporations, which perceive them as cost centres from the financial perspective rather than sport business units. Because of the aforementioned governance structure and the financial dependence, the teams must receive approval from parent companies for most of the important management decisions.

Ownership models of K-League teams

The K-League consists of the first division, K-League 1 (founded in 1983), with 12 clubs and the second division, K-League 2 (founded in 2013), with10 clubs. After the regular season, the lowest team in K-League 1 and the highest team in K-League 2 play off to determine promotion and relegation. Unlike the KBO, the K-League has been struggling to establish a fan base. The average attendance for the first division reached only 6,486 in 2017, which was a drop from 7,866 in 2016 (Statistics Korea, 2018).

The K-League is composed of the general meeting, board of directors, audit, president, vice president, secretary general, general director, seven administration teams (communications, club support, marketing, strategy, youth, education and management planning) and five committees (games, referee, disciplinary, players and development) (K-League, 2018). The board of directors include three persons from K-League (president, vice president and secretary general), one person from Korea Football Association (executive director), four CEOs or general managers of K-League 1 clubs, two CEOs or general managers of K-League 2 clubs and three outside directors (e.g., lawyers, professors, etc.). Unlike the other leagues, the K-League is a separate entity to the Korea Football Association (KFA), which, as an umbrella organisation, influences the K-League's operations. As FIFA strongly controls the world of football, the relationships between national football associations and professional football leagues are quite similar in most countries.

There are primarily two types of ownership model in the K-League: Subsidiaries of large corporations and publicly owned companies. Like most of the KBO teams, seven clubs in K-League 1 and two clubs in K-League 2 are subsidiaries of non-sport corporations whereas five clubs in K-League 1 and eight clubs in K-League 2 are publicly owned companies. In K-League 1, each of five clubs (Suwon Samsung Bluewings FC, FC Seoul, Ulsan Hyundai, Jeonbuk Hyundai Motors and Jeju United FC) are owned by a single parent corporation (Cheil Worldwide Inc., GS Sports Co. Ltd., Hyundai Heavy Industries Co. Ltd., Hyundai Motor Company and SK Energy Co. Ltd.) while two clubs (Pohang Steelers, Jeonnam Dragons) are owned by POSCO Co. Ltd. and local companies. In K-League 2, Busan I-Park club and Seoul E-Land club are 100% owned by Hyundai Development Company and E-Land World Co., respectively. The governance structure of the subsidiaries of parent corporations in K-League is almost the same as that of the KBO. Parent companies appoint their executives and club CEOs and cover clubs' financial deficits using their own marketing budget.

The second type of ownership model in the K-League is the publicly owned company, which is found only in the K-League in Korea. The largest shareholders of publicly owned clubs are local sport councils. For example, in K-League 1, Gangwon-do sports council has 47.62 percent of Gangwon FC shares and Gyeongsangnam-do sports council holds 58.92 percent of Gyeongnam FC shares; whereas, in K-League 2, Daejeon Sports Council owns 40.61 percent of the Daejeon Citizen's share and Gwangju Sports Council possesses 65.02 percent of the Gwangju FC share. The remaining shareholders are a group of local companies and individuals.

It should be noted that the governors or mayors of the franchises become automatically the president of local sports councils, and local governments financially support local sports councils. As local sport councils become the largest shareholders, the governors or mayors are designated as "club owners", and local governments financially support the club. Therefore, they are similar to chairmen of parent corporations in the subsidiary ownership model. Due to this ownership structure, publicly owned clubs are strongly influenced by local governments, especially when recruiting senior management and making financial decisions. Most of the publicly owned clubs are under financial pressure because of the stagnant local economy.

One exceptional ownership model in the K-League is Sangju Sangmu, which is not a professional football club but part of Korean Armed Forces (KAF) Athletic Corps. Military service is mandatory for all men in Korea and the Korean Armed Forces runs athletic corps consisting of elite players in various sports. Sangmu is the Korean Armed Forces' football team with the city of Sangju as its franchise where the KAF Athletic Corps are located. The Ministry of Defense financially supports the club.

Ownership models of KBL & WKBL teams

The KBL was established with ten teams in 1997. Unlike the KBO and the K-League, the KBL was carefully planned before launching. In the early stages, the KBL could instantly and successfully position itself as a representative winter professional sport because in the 1990s the college basketball league had been very competitive thus making it easier for people to watch and follow basketball games. However, its popularity has declined since the pro volleyball league, the V-League, was launched in 2005 and both leagues' regular seasons overlapped.

The KBL consists of the general meeting of "team owners", board of directors, president, secretary general, general director, games department, four administration teams (management, marketing, communications and operations) and eight committees (finance, technical, games, referee, player welfare, anti-corruption and medical) (KBL, 2018). "Team owners" are the chairmen of parent corporations whereas board of directors include KBL president and secretary general and CEOs or general managers of ten teams.

The majority of KBL teams (eight out of ten) are not independent companies but part of the department within parent corporations while only two teams are subsidiaries of parent corporations. Changwon LG Sakers belongs to LG Sports Co. Ltd., which is solely owned by the LG group. Busan KT Sonicboom is part of KT Sports, which is owned by KT Co. Ltd. (66%), KT Skylife (18%), KTis Co. Ltd. (6%), KTcs Co. Ltd. (6%) and BC Card Co. Ltd. (4%), respectively.

The WKBL started with six teams in 1998 with a similar governance structure to that of the KBL (WKBL, 2018). The differences are that there are two teams (operations, communications and marketing) and six committees (finance, games, technical, anticorruption, player welfare and advisory) and there is no general director. Also, all six teams belong to their parent companies. Overall, the parent corporations' influence on team management is more direct and stronger in the KBL and the WKBL than in the KBO or the K-League.

Ownership models of KOVO teams

Unlike the KBL and the WKBL, the Korean Volleyball Federation (KOVO), established in 2005, launched and managed both men's and women's league, called the V-League, with seven and six teams, respectively. Although KOVO started last among the four leagues, it is currently in its prime competing with the KBL as a result of continuous innovation. While the KBL has been a mainstream relative to the WKBL, the popularity difference between the men's and women's volleyball league is relatively small.

The KOVO is composed of the general meeting of "team owners", board of directors, president, secretary general, two general managers, five administration teams (management, marketing, communication, games and league system innovation) and six committees (games, disciplinary, youth, league system innovation, human resources and fund management) (KOVO, 2018). The board of directors include KOVO president and secretary general and CEOs or general managers of both men's and women's teams. The popularity of women's volleyball compared to the WKBL may be partially attributed to the KOVO's governance structure.

All men's teams and four women's teams in the V–League are operated as part of its parent company. Two women's teams, GS Caltex Seoul Kixx Volleyball team and Korea Expressway Corporation Hi-pass Volleyball team, are categorised as the subsidiaries of parent corporations, but operated like a department of social responsibility or public relations. GS Holdings Co. Ltd. has invested in GS Sports Co. Ltd, to establish a sport-related subsidiary, and GS Sports Co. Ltd. manages FC Seoul (football team) and GS Caltex Seoul Kixx (volleyball team).

Summary of Korean professional sports team ownership models

Table 12.2 shows the number of pro sport teams by ownership model in Korea. The ownership structure can be broadly classified into subsidiaries of parent corporations, department within a corporation, publicly owned company, independent company and Korean Armed Forces Athletic Corps. The majority of the KBO teams are subsidiaries of large non-sports corporations except one independent company owned by a group of individual shareholders. K-league teams are either subsidiaries of parent corporations or a publicly owned company. Unlike the other three leagues, K-League has a team ownership model that local governments are allowed to directly own and financially support teams through local sports councils. Both basketball and volleyball teams are mostly part of a department within a non-sport corporation except two men's basketball teams and two women's volleyball teams.

Table 12.2 The number of professional sports teams by ownership model in Republic of Korea

	Subsidiary company of parent corporation	Department within corporation	Publicly owned company	Independent company	Korean Armed Forces Athletic Corps.
KBO (Baseball)	9	–	–	1	–
K-league 1 (Football)	7	–	5	–	1
K-league 2 (Football)	2	–	8	–	–
KBL (Men's Basketball)	2	8	–	–	–
WKBL (Women's Basketball)	–	6	–	–	–
KOVO (Men's Volleyball)	–	7	–	–	–
KOVO (Women's Volleyball)	2	4	–	–	–
Total	22 (35%)	25 (40%)	13 (21%)	1 (0.2%)	1 (0.2%)

Note: The table was created based on the interviews with team and league officers.

The most conspicuous characteristics of Korean pro sport team ownership is that non-sport parent conglomerates, which have dominated the Korean economy, have powerful influence on team governance and management. In the case of publicly owned teams in the K-League, local governments, instead of parent corporations, play a similar role. Overall, the league's management and operation have been centred on the individual teams' interest rather than the best interest of the whole league. Given the team ownership, it would be a big challenge for the leagues to push forward with long-term development efforts.

Ownership models of professional sport league clubs in China

A brief history of professionalisation of Chinese sport

Professional sport in China has a relatively short history. Up until the mid-1990s, sport in China remained the prerogative of the government. China was and still is one of the countries that have a ministry-level government department (National Sports Commission or NSC before 1998 and General Administration of Sports or GAS thereafter) that is solely responsible for sport affairs ranging from elite sports, to sports for all to sport business regulation and promotion. But the priority had long been on elite sports supported by a state-sponsored high-performance sport administration system, widely known as "Ju Guo Ti Zhi" (Chinese for a centralised system), by mobilising nationwide resources available in the country, with the ultimate goal of winning medals at international competitions, especially at the Olympics, to serve national pride (Liu, Zhang & Desbordes, 2017).

The situation began to change slowly as the macro-political-economic environment evolved. The year of 1992 marked a decisive year as the Communist Party of China decided to continue with its reform and "opening up" policy at its 14th National Congress, making it clear that the goal of China's economic reform is to establish a socialist market economy, after the late state leader Mr. Deng Xiaoping's inspection tour to South China. In effect, this meant a transformation from a planned economy to a market-based economy with the private sector playing an increasingly more important role in the national economy. Against this backdrop, the National Sports Commission (NSC), then ministry-level government department responsible for sports in China, started to explore the reform of sport administration and development. Socialisation, commercialisation and professionalisation were some of the major themes proposed by the NSC, meaning the society and private sector vis-à-vis government should play a more important role in terms of supply of sport products and services. In June 1992, at the National Football Conference, as a flagship of the sport reform, it was decided by the NSC that professional football clubs and leagues should be established (Liu, 2008).

On 17 April 1994, the first national professional football league was formally launched, with the top flight titled Series A League consisting of 12 clubs and second tier Series B consisting of 11 clubs. The Series A League was renamed China Football Association Super League or CSL in 2004. The professionalisation was soon extended to basketball, and the Chinese Basketball Association League, the first China Men's professional league in basketball, was launched in 1995. Today, football and basketball remain the two most popular professional sports in China.

Caution needs to be exercised when it comes to professional sports in China, as they are run very differently from the west with the government still playing a decisive role in league management. Most of the sports in China have national governing bodies called sports associations, as required by their respective international governing bodies (such as Chinese Basketball Association), but, in reality, these associations are only organisations in name, and are all considered quasi-governmental organisations. The 70 national sports associations exist in parallel with 22 sport management centres (governmental departments) controlled and managed by the same group of people. In other words, while a market economy has been largely established in China since the early 1990s, sport remains a government-controlled and planned system. As a result, tension between this planned system and a market-based professional and commercial sport is unavoidable. This centralised governing system itself has become one of the major obstacles that should be deregulated and reformed to release the huge market potential of the sport industry in China (Liu, 2008). On 24 February 2016, as a milestone in the reform of Chinese sport and football, China's Management Center for Football was dissolved and the China Football Association (CFA) was announced and was formally detached from the government (i.e., China Generational Administration of Sport or GAS). The fact that Mr. Cai, the Deputy Minister of GAS, has remained to serve as the President of the newly restructured CFA seems to question the autonomy the association could enjoy as an independent sport governing body (Liu, Zhang & Desbordes, 2017).

It is also worth noting the fast-growing sports market in China over the past several years partly driven by steady economic growth in China for more than three decades. It is reported that Chinese mergers and acquisitions in domestic and overseas sports markets have seen exponential growth since 2015, when it spent almost 40 billion yuan (around USD$ 5.99 billion) in total investments with 33 deals valuing over 10 million yuan (around USD$ 1.50 million) (Liu, Zhang & Desbordes, 2017). This rise of sport business in China has been widely attributed to the strong top-down government promotion with a series of high-profile policies released from the central government. Among other things, a national strategic policy entitled "Opinions on Accelerating the Development of Sports Industry and Promoting Sports Consumption" (the Decree, hereafter), issued by China's State Council on 20 October 2014, was widely cited as a milestone leading to the takeoff of the sport business. It predicted that Chinese sport business would develop into a market worth RMB 5 trillion (equivalent to approximately USD$ 815 billion), with an annual Gross Value Added of RMB 1.7 trillion or roughly between 1.2 percent and 1.5 percent of national GDP by 2025 (Liu, Zhang & Desbordes, 2017).

Ownership models of CSL clubs

There are 16 football clubs currently competing in the 2018 CSL, and, as required by the China Football Association, these clubs are all registered as corporate entities in the form of a limited company. Out of the 16 clubs, 8 are solely owned clubs, including five private clubs and three state-owned ones. Among the other eight clubs, two are controlled by state-owned companies and six are controlled by private companies (see Table 12.3). Generally speaking, the CSL clubs can be regarded as corporate ownership. In cases where there are more than one investor, the

Table 12.3 Ownership of CSL clubs

Ownership model	CSL clubs		CBA clubs	
	Number	Percentage	Number	Percentage
Sole state-owned company	3	19%	3	19%
Sole privately held company	4	31%	5	31%
Co-owned by state-owned companies	2	12%	2	12%
Co-owned by private companies	6	38%	6	38%

Note: The table was created based on the public information on the websites of CSL clubs.

board is normally composed of members coming from either the dominant shareholder or the few major shareholders. For example, Evergrande Real Estate Company and Alibaba own 56.71 percent and 37.81 percent shares of Guangzhou Evergrande Taobao FC, respectively, and the rest of the shareholders have 5.48 percent. As a result, three out of the five board members are appointed from Evergrande Real Estate Company, and the other two members are from Alibaba (see Figure 12.5). Guangzhou Evergrande Taobao FC is also the first CSL club that went public which has been listed on the domestic "New Three Board" stock exchange since November 2015. In the case of solely owned clubs, the board members are normally appointed by the owning company. Generally speaking, as the board members are not elected but rather appointed by the sole owners or controlling shareholders, these owners or shareholders have a decisive impact on the formation of the board and its decision-making.

The aforementioned takeoff of the sport industry in China also has had a profound impact on the development of professional sports in China. Widely seen as the new economic growth point for the coming decades, money has been pouring into the Chinese sports market, and CSL and CBA, the top two professional sports in China, have become the new "gold rush" for cash-rich Chinese investors. As a result, it's also becoming increasingly expensive to sustain a professional club at the top-flight level. In the CSL, loss making is the norm rather than the exception. This also explains why 70 percent of the CSL club investors are from the real estate sector, which is also one of the most lucrative sectors in China amassing huge wealth. For the 2016 financial year, 14 out of the 16 CSL clubs took losses, and, in total, the 16 clubs took losses of 4.645 billion RMB (about USD$ 700 million) (Sohu, 2017). Guangzhou Evergrande Taobao FC, the CSL champion and two-time Asian Champions League Winner, dubbed the most successful CSL club on the pitch, was also the champion on the loss-making tally, posting a loss 334 million RMB (Sohu, 2017). Since the clubs rely heavily on the parent company financially, it should come as no surprise that the sole or controlling investor would also dominate the governance of the club.

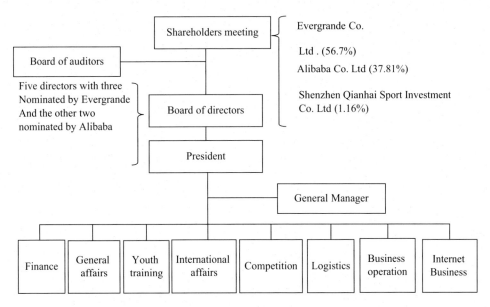

Figure 12.5 Guangzhou Evergrande Taobao Football Club Co., Ltd. This Figure was created based on Guangzhou Evergrande Taobao FC website (2015).

Ownership models of CBA clubs

There are 20 clubs competing in CBA league, the top-flight professional basketball league in China. Just like the CSL clubs, all the CBA clubs are registered as corporate entities as required by the CBA. But the ownership of these clubs is much more complicated than it appears. Over half of the clubs (11) are a partnership between the local government through the local sport authority or its affiliations and a company, and the remaining nine clubs are solely owned by a private or state-owned company (see Table 12.3).

One of the major sources of complexity lies in the fact that most of these clubs were originally established by the local sport administration representing the government, and, even though the past two decades witnessed growing investment from the private sector, most of the clubs still rely on local government in terms of youth training. In other words, even though basketball is one of the most professionalised sports in China next to football, it still maintains a strong tradition of the so-called state-sponsored elite sport system. Most of the Chinese CBA players still come from this government-sponsored system. They normally start training from an early age in government-funded sports schools and then join the local provincial team funded by the local sport administration as full time athletes. Even when they are good enough and drafted by a CBA professional club, most of them choose to maintain their employment relationship with the original local sport administration with budgeted posts. When there are basketball competitions at the national level (such as the Chinese National Games, which are held every four years just like the Olympics), these players would then play in their provincial team. As a result, even though 14 out of the 20 CBA clubs are owned or controlled by private companies, the majority of them still work in strong partnership with the local sport administrations. More than half of the CBA clubs are still co-owned by the local Sports Authority and a company (see Table 12.3).

Just like their football counterpart, the CBA clubs are also relying on their sole or controlling parent company for financial survival. The board, if it exists at all, is a structure in name only, and both the board president and general manager would normally be appointed by the parent company. While the board members are appointed mainly by the owning or controlling companies, the local governments still have a strong impact on the decision-making of the clubs, in particular when it comes to training and competition-related decisions. As a result, while all the clubs are registered as limited corporations, the governance of these clubs is far short of real corporate governance based on market principle. Using the Jiangsu Kentier Basketball Club as an example, it is a typical public–private partnership with Chinese characteristics as Kentier, the controlling private company, has a 70 percent of share and the Sports Authority of the host province retains the other 30 percent (see Figure 12.6). On the ground, the private company is mainly responsible for the finance and business operation of the club and the Sports Authority has a decisive say regarding team management. Sometimes, conflicts arise when the separation of rights and obligations is not clear between the Sports Authority and the investing company (Yang, Tao, Mao & Zhao, 2017).

Summary of Chinese professional sports club ownership models

- Both the CSL and the CBA clubs are registered as limited corporation entities controlled by a parent private or state-owned company, and none of these clubs are traditional member-based clubs or associations;
- In most cases, the clubs rely on the sole or controlling parent company financially and accordingly are also controlled by that parent company through appointment or nomination of a board of directors and senior management; as a result, minor shareholders or external stakeholders have little or no say in strategic decision-making;

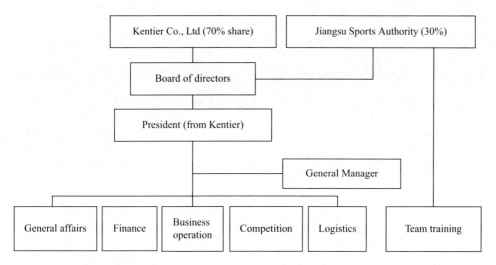

Figure 12.6 Jiangsu Kentier Basketball Club Co., Ltd.

- The development of corporate governance in both the CSL and the CBA clubs is in its infancy, as in most cases, there is a lack of clear-cut separation between shareholders meeting and board and senior management would be decided by the sole or controlling parent company;
- While, in general, local governments have strong influence on club governance in both the CSL and the CBA, CBA clubs are much more prone to government influence as governments either maintain shares in the club or work in partnership through youth training and facilities provision. In contrast, CSL clubs are relatively more independent from the government than CBA clubs;
- In addition to the influence from the local government, the governance of clubs in both the CSL and the CBA is also impacted by the Sport Authority at the national level, as in both cases, the CSL and the CBA at league level (i.e., Chinese Football Association and Chinese Basketball Association) are actually quasi-government organisations – for the moment, at least.

Conclusion

In this chapter, pro sports team ownership and its influence on governance were examined for Japan, South Korea and China. It is common to see that pro sports were launched or advanced primarily during economically fast-growing periods in each country. Although the pro baseball league started in 1936 in Japan, it has grown since 1950 following the downturn during World War II and the Pacific War. Japan rapidly rebuilt its economy leveraging US aid, the Korean War and 1964 Tokyo Olympic Games from the 1950s through to the 1970s. In the case of South Korea, the pro baseball league was launched in 1982 while Korea was experiencing "the Han River's miracle", the unprecedented economic growth in the world economy after the Korean War. The first Chinese pro sports league, the CSL, was initiated in 1994 after the Communist Party of China committed to enacting its policy reforms to "open up" to a market-based economy at its 14th National Congress. Then Chinese state leader, Mr. Deng Xiaoping, emphasised the need in 1992 to accelerate transformation from a planned economy to a market-based economy.

These backgrounds may contribute to understanding the similarities and differences among Japanese, Korean and Chinese professional sport governance. One of the most noticeable similarities across the three countries is that few professional sports teams stand as independent sport business entities that are able to make profits. Most of the teams except in the J-League are directly or indirectly under the control of non-sport parent corporations or local governments although there are some differences. Thus, the teams and the leagues tend to be operated and managed in the best interests of parent companies or local governments, not the best interests of sports leagues and teams. Given the governance structure, it may be difficult to implement league-centred development strategy.

Specifically, pro baseball team ownership is quite similar between Korea and Japan, whereas in football, there are differences. K-League team ownership models are split into subsidiaries of parent corporations and publicly owned companies, of which local government and various local companies are involved as shareholders. The J-League had pursued the franchise-centred ownership model when the league was designed in early 1990s. Thus, the teams' shareholders are primarily local companies and residents. In China, the central and local governments are very influential in team management because they have direct or indirect ownership through state-owned companies or partnerships with private companies. It should be remembered that China is governed by one party, the Communist Party, which stands above the government. It seems unavoidable that the Chinese centralised governing system may conflict with the development of the market-based professional sports system.

Overall, the strong financial and administrative support of parent corporations and governments have provided a solid foundation of successful development of pro sports so far in the three countries. However, it is hard to deny that the existing governance systems (except in the J-League) make it difficult for the leagues to innovate and hinder the teams from becoming more active sport business units. It is time to critically reevaluate the current ownership model and governance structure of professional sports in Japan, South Korea and China.

Through this examination of ownership structures, some areas of future research have emerged such as the analysis of the league vs. team combined with governance vs. management (Figure 12.7). The relationships between team ownership structures (e.g., privately owned,

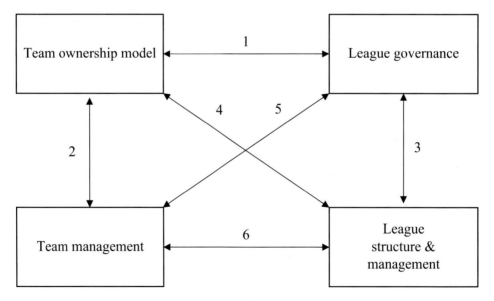

Figure 12.7 Research agenda for future research.

non-sport corporation owned, socially or publically owned or independent) and league governance (e.g., composition of board of directors) structures (e.g., competitive balance) and management (e.g., leadership, strategy, operation, marketing, corporate social responsibility, evaluation, etc.) is a set of interrelationships worth further investigation to better understand the implications for the governance of pro sports (see 1 & 4 in Figure 12.7).

The relationships between league governance and league management as well as those between league governance and team management (leadership, strategy, operation, marketing, community relations, evaluation, etc.) may also generate interesting research questions for further investigation (3 and 5 in Figure 12.7). Also, future research may come from an investigation of the relationships between team ownership structure and team management, as well as those between team management and league structure and management, given the team and league governance (2 and 6 in Figure 12.7). Finally, comparative studies could be conducted across the three countries, or between Far East Asia and other regions, such as North America or Europe, for each of the above agendas.

References

Albirex Niigata Inc. (2018). *Corporate profile*. Niigata City, Niigata. Retrieved 20 August 2018, from http://www.albirex.co.jp/pdf/corporate-profile2018.pdf

Avolio, B. J., Bass, B. M., & Jung, D. I. (1999). Re-examining the components of transformational and transactional leadership using the Multifactor Leadership Questionnaire. *Journal of Occupational and Organizational Psychology, 72*, 441–462.

Brown, M. E., Treviño, L. K., & Harrison, D. A. (2005). Ethical leadership: A social learning perspective for construct development and testing. *Organizational Behavior and Human Decision Processes, 97*, 117–134.

Conger, J. A., & Kanungo, R. A. (1987). Towards a behavioral theory of charismatic leadership in organizational settings. *Academy of Management Review, 12*, 637–647.

Daft, R. L. (2004). *Organization theory and design* (8th ed.). Mason, OH: Thompson Southwestern.

Ferkins, L., & Shilbury, D. (2016). Developing a theory of board strategic balance. In G. B. Cunningham, J. S. Fink, & A. Doherty (Eds.), *Routledge handbook of theory in sport management* (pp. 114–129). New York: Routledge.

Guangzhou Evergrande Taobao. FC. (2015). Public transfer statements of Guangzhou Evergrande Taobao Football Club Co. Ltd. Retrieved 28 August 2018, from https://max.book118.com/html/2017/0222/92956444.shtm

Japan Professional Baseball Players Association. (2016). *Japan professional baseball agreement*. Retrieved 20 August 2018, from http://jpbpa.net/up_pdf/1471951971-129176.pdf

J.League. (2018). *About J.League*. Retrieved 20 August 2018, from https://www.jleague.jp/aboutj/aboutj/soshiki.html

Kang, J. (2017). Sport market value network in Korea. In J. J. Zhang, H. Huang & J. Nauright (Eds.), *Sport business in leading economies* (pp. 34–381). Bingley, UK: Emerald Publishing Ltd.

KBL. (2018). *About KBL*. Retrieved 10 October 2018, from http://www.kbl.or.kr/about/organization.asp

KBO. (2018a). *About KBO*. Retrieved 10 October 2018, from https://www.koreabaseball.com/About/Group/Office.aspx

KBO. (2018b). *History*. Retrieved 10 October 2018, from https://www.koreabaseball.com/History/Crowd/GraphYear.aspx

K-League. (2018). *About K-League*. Retrieved 10 October 2018, from http://www.kleague.com/about/Organization

KOVO. (2018). *About KOVO*. Retrieved 10 October 2018, from https://www.kovo.co.kr/kovo/71200_kovo-info.asp

Liu, D. (2008). Review of national governing bodies' reform in China. *Academic Journal of Sport, 15*(9), 21–25.

Liu, D., Zhang, J., & Debordes, M. (2017). Sport business in China: Current state and prospect. *International Journal of Sports Marketing and Sponsorship, 18*(1), 3–12

Sasakawa Sports Foundation. (2017). *Sport white paper 2017*. Tokyo, Japan: Sasakawa Sports Foundation.

Sohu. (2017). CSL clubs made a total loss of 4.6 billion RMB with only two clubs making a profit in 2016. Retrieved 28 August 2018, from http://sports.sohu.com/20170609/n496312866.shtml

Statistics Korea. (2018). Pro sports attendance. Retrieved 10 October 2018, from http://www.index.go.kr/potal/main/EachDtlPageDetail.do?idx_cd=1662

Urawa Red Diamonds Co., Ltd. (2016). *The organizational structure of the Urawa Red Diamonds.* Retrieved 20 August 2018, from http://www.urawa-reds.co.jp/wp-content/uploads/2016/02/d59857378e59b72eadacfde3793855fc.pdf

WKBL. (2018). *About WKBL.* Retrieved 10 October 2018, from http://www.wkbl.or.kr/about/organization.asp

Yang, G., Tao, X. Mao, Z., & Zhao, L. (2017). Research on situation of management of Jiangsu Professional Sports Club and its optimization strategy. *Journal of Sports and Science, 38*(6), 36–42.

Yomiuri Shimbun Group. (2018). *Basic data: Organizational structure.* Retrieved 20 August 2018, from https://info.yomiuri.co.jp/group/about/data/index.html

13

Governance of international sports federations

Jean-Loup Chappelet, Josephine Clausen and Emmanuel Bayle

Introduction

International Sports Federations (IFs) govern global sport. There are more than 100 IFs (members of the Global Association of International Sports Federations [GAISF]), of which approximately 60 have their headquarters in Switzerland. IFs range from the powerful FIFA (Fédération Internationale de Football Association) which has been based in Zurich since 1932, to the International Wushu Federation (IWUF), which recently established its headquarters in Lausanne to govern the Chinese martial art also known as Kung Fu. IFs act as umbrella organisations for the national federations of their sport; in turn, national federations and state federations oversee clubs. IFs establish and control global rules, award championships to cities and countries, negotiate with sponsors and broadcasters and fight the excesses of sport such as doping and corruption. They are usually associations of associations and, from this point of view, their governance deserves to be studied separately from that of sports associations that comprise individuals, such as the IOC (International Olympic Committee) or clubs (Chappelet, 2016a).

IFs work with private and public actors that have embraced organisational (or corporate) governance and political (or democratic) governance since the 1990s and, increasingly, require that their sport partners be governed appropriately within the scope of a systemic governance that involves all actors (private, public and nonprofit third parties) in the sport (Henry & Lee, 2004). Many IFs are over a century old, but their governance – which is obliged to take up a position straddling corporate and political governance – has evolved little since the Belle Époque, whereas the challenges in terms of commercial issues and sports regulation have become much more complex (Chappelet, 2018). At the turn of the century, several IFs experienced problems that can be described as problems of governance (i.e., failings concerning transparency, accountability, democracy, integrity and the control of decision-making by stakeholders).

The IOC, which governs the Olympic Games in conjunction with a wide range of partners (mainly Organising Committees of the Olympic Games [OCOGs], National Olympic Committees [NOCs] and International Sports Federations [IFs]), itself experienced governance problems in 1998–1999 [concerning the award of the Olympic Games]. These issues obliged the IOC to embark on significant reforms, such as introducing term limits for IOC members (maximum 8 + 4), reducing the age limit of its active members (from 80 to 70) and publishing detailed financial accounts (Wenn, Barney & Martyn, 2011). Subsequent to what became known as the Salt Lake City Scandal (because it initially involved that city's bid committee for the 2002 Winter Games), other scandals that received less media coverage affected several IFs. These led to certain reforms of governance and the resignation of the presidents, who were also IOC members, of some IFs including the FIVB (volleyball), IJF (judo) and WTF (taekwondo).

Two of the largest IFs – FIFA for football and IAAF for athletics – experienced so-called "governance scandals" in 2015, which involved their respective former presidents. Following these scandals, in December 2015, the IOC asked the ASOIF to set up a working group on the governance of sport. This working group was established to study the issue in respect of IFs, while recognising their independence and autonomy and specifying that it would conduct an audit of its main subsidies to IFs (and also to NOCs and OCOGs) (IOC, 2015). More recently, the IOC (2018) called for reforms of the governance of the IFs overseeing boxing (AIBA) and biathlon (IBU) following the resignation of these IFs' presidents as the result of scandals.

This chapter focuses on the governance of IFs. It examines how ASOIF dealt with the IOC's request and what overall results were achieved (Section 1). The chapter then takes a closer look at the governance of a specific IF overseeing a major sport, namely cycling and the Union Cycliste Internationale (UCI) (Section 2). The UCI has had four presidents since the start of the 21st century. These changes in the presidency marked evolutions in the UCI's governance since 2000. Going beyond respect for the general principles of governance, Section 3 emphasises the importance to governance of the leadership of an IF and the relationship between the IF and the national federations. In conclusion, it is reiterated that the governance of an IF, beyond its own (organisational) governance, must absolutely address issues that arise from the political governance of its leaders and the systemic governance of its network.

The assessment of IF governance by ASOIF

In response to the IOC's request (IOC, 2015), ASOIF set up a working group known as the Governance Task Force (GTF). This task force, chaired by the ASOIF president – the former president of the ITF (International Tennis Federation) – consisted of three IF representatives (FEI – equestrian sport; FIBA – basketball; and FIVB – volleyball), an IOC member (former President of FISA – rowing), the IOC Chief Ethics and Compliance Officer, the FIBA Legal Director, an external expert and an academic (one of the authors), assisted by ASOIF staff and an independent "moderator". (Information on the GTF and its activities is available at www.asoif.com/governance-task-force.)

The GTF rapidly came up with a set of five major principles (transparency, integrity, democracy, sport development and solidarity and control mechanisms), each measured by ten indicators. This followed the example of the tool that had been proposed a few years earlier by Chappelet and Mrkonjic (2013) featuring Basic Indicators for Better Governance in International Sport (BIBGIS) (ASOIF, 2016a). The Council and General Assembly of ASOIF, (i.e., the association of the 28 IFs that govern sports on the programme of the Summer Olympic Games) (ASOIF, 2016b), adopted these principles and indicators in April 2016.

Following this approval, a questionnaire was sent to all IF members of ASOIF. Each question was based on a pre-defined indicator. The IFs were asked if the indicators were either not fulfilled at all (in which case a score of 0 was allocated) or fulfilled (in which case a score of 1 to 4 was allocated depending on the degree of fulfilment of the indicator. The scores were 1 = partially fulfilled; 2 = fulfilled; 3 = well fulfilled according to published rules/procedures; 4 = totally fulfilled in a state-of-the-art manner). The indicators were not weighted (i.e., all were considered equally important).

A predefined scale of scores between 1 and 4 was provided for each indicator/question and the IF was asked to self-assess. For example, for the question "Do you publish an annual activity report and main event reports?", the responses were scored in accordance with the quality of the reports (ASOIF, 2016c): 0 = No; 1 = Some news published on IF website; 2 = News published regularly and an annual report available on IF website; 3 = News published regularly and several years of annual reports, easy to find on IF website; 4 = Full publication, easy to find on IF website, with extra data or explanation from past reports (for comparison). The score given for each indicator had to be justified (for example, by a website URL or an official document) and could be modified by the GTF as IFs were sometimes too severe or generous with themselves on the assessment of a specific indicator.

This scoring system allows both a quantitative evaluation (based on a score of 0 or another value, i.e., no/yes) and a qualitative evaluation (a score between 1 and 4 depending on the degree of sophistication in achieving the indicator). Thus, an age limit (an indicator not considered by the GTF) for IF board members of 80 years or more could correspond, for example, to a score of 1, age up to 75 to a score of 2, age up to 70 to a score of 3, age of 65 or less to a score of 4. No age limit would give an IF a score of 0 for this indicator. The scale chosen is important in determining the governance requirement at a given time in history and in accordance with different cultures/countries. For example, an advanced age is (was) more valued in Eastern than in Western cultures.

Depending on the prevailing ethos and standards of fairness, an age restriction could be considered as discriminatory, illustrating the cultural and temporal relativity of an assessment of governance. The notion that "good governance" could permanently be "good", at any time, is a notion unfortunately very widely used by many authors. However, GTF indicators do constitute a "hard core" considered to be important for the bodies governing international sport (IFs) regardless of the country/culture in which they operate.

The five dimensions (each with 10 indicators) were complemented by a preliminary section entitled "Guiding Codes". It is composed of 10 questions on the degree to which the responding IF satisfied the main codes of the Olympic movement (Olympic Charter, Code of Ethics, World Anti-Doping Code, Universal Basic Principles, Agenda 2020, Code on the Prevention of the Manipulation of Competitions) and national and international laws on sport. The 28 ASOIF member federations responded to the questionnaire and the results were published in April 2017 at the ASOIF General Assembly (ASOIF, 2017a) after the GTF had checked the answers and evidence provided (monitoring). The Guiding Codes section turned out to be difficult to monitor as it was very subjective; therefore, it was not published. The IFs achieved a score for each of the five dimensions. All the indicator scores for each IF were summated to give total scores (ASOIF, 2017a). This allowed the IFs to be classified into three groups: Group A (8 IFs with a total score between 122 and 170); group B (11 IFs with a total score of 91–113); group C (9 IFs with a total score of 65–83). The maximum score achievable was 200 and the average was 100. It was noted that, as often happens with the introduction of an innovation (in this case governance), the targets affected (in this case the IFs) can be categorised into three groups: The early adopters and late adopters – groups that are numerically similar and well above or below the average respectively – and a slightly larger middle-of-the-road group, scoring around the average. The average score of the IFs for this first review was 104 (out of a maximum of 200). A margin of error exists as in all measurements. In the end, it is not the absolute value of the scores which mattered but the fact that each IF could position itself in one of the groups and see how it could be better governed. In other words, if the IFs were too lenient with themselves, it was fooling nobody but itself.

This monitored self-assessment exercise was repeated at the end of 2017 and published in April 2018. However, this time 40 IFs were included – the 28 ASOIF members plus its five observer members (the IFs of sports added to the programme of the Tokyo 2020 Olympic Games in addition to the 28 full Olympic sports), together with the seven IFs of the sports on the Winter Olympic Games programme. The questionnaire was almost the same as in the first exercise to allow year-on-year comparisons. There were only minor amendments of questions that had been poorly drafted or were the subject of debate (depending on the IFs' understanding) with the addition of general questions such as the IF's staff numbers, turnover and registered office (ASOIF, 2017b). The principle of five dimensions and ten indicators per dimension was retained, as was the Guiding Codes section, although this was renamed "Background".

The results for the 33 IFs that are members or observer members of ASOIF were published in April 2018 at the ASOIF General Assembly (ASOIF, 2018). This time the IFs were classified into four groups: A1 (6 IFs with scores between 152 and 177); A2 (8 IFs with scores of 120–142); B (10 IFs with scores from 96 to 112); C (9 IFs with scores of 46–89). These groups could be described respectively as strong, quite strong, average and weak in relation to the governance indicators used by ASOIF. The results of the seven winter sports IFs governance were published later by their association (AIOWF, 2018).

Compared to the results of the ASOIF 2017 review, the ASOIF 2018 review showed an improvement in the average score from 104 to 121. This suggests that, from one year to the next, the 33 IFs that are members or observer members of ASOIF have broadly improved their governance, with observer members (who want to remain on the Olympic programme after Tokyo 2020) achieving particularly high scores. Furthermore, half of the IFs evaluated in 2017 increased their total score by 20 points or more. The second review of governance of AIOWF members for 2017–2018 showed some progress since the first edition (mean scores improved from 93 to 109).

Each IF received its score from these reviews with a view to highlighting where their own governance could be improved. However, the IF individual scores were not published as this would inevitably have led to a classification of IFs which, according to the GTF, would be nonsensical given the very different sizes of the organisations (from over 500 to fewer than 10 employees). Two questions in the second questionnaire by the ASOIF GTF on the IFs' staff size and turnover did illustrate a strong correlation between large size or turnover and a good governance score (ASOIF, 2018).

Another system for measuring IF governance was published for the first time in 2015 as a result of the Action for Good Governance in International Sport (AGGIS) project funded by the European Commission within the scope of the Erasmus+ programme (Alm, 2013). The system, known as Sports Governance Observer (SGO), is based on a method similar to the GTF and features four dimensions: Transparency and public communication (12 indicators); democratic process (10 indicators); checks and balances (9 indicators); solidarity (7 indicators), namely a total of 38 indicators for the current version of the SGO (Play the Game, 2017). The SGO study originally concerned 35 IFs of sports that feature in the programmes of the Summer or Winter Olympic Games. Unfortunately, the report is no longer available on the Play the Game website (AGGIS consortium leader). It emphasised the overall need to improve IF governance and highlighted glaring deficiencies, particularly in terms of the non-publication of financial reports or officials' remuneration and the absence of a limit on the number of terms of office for IF presidents. The report produced a ranking of IFs, with FEI (equestrian) placed first and FIFA (football) second, even though FIFA was in the middle of a scandal concerning governance (Ingle, 2015).

In 2018, the SGO study considered just five IFs: FIFA (football), FINA (swimming), IAAF (athletics), IHF (handball) and ITF (tennis) (Geeraert, 2018). These five IFs do not reflect the diversity of the 40 organisations (33 if only those IFs governing sports on the programme of the

Summer Games are considered). It is also not clear why some IFs were chosen and others were not, irrespective of whether or not they were affected by governance scandals. In addition, the collection of the data necessary for the 2015 and 2018 SGO studies was largely conducted without the collaboration of the IFs in question. Information was taken from the available websites and did not benefit from comments made by the parties involved.

When the sports ministers of the Council of Europe met in Budapest in November 2016, the second resolution of the meeting encouraged all IFs to use the principles and indicators developed by the ASOIF GTF as a first step towards improving their governance (Council of Europe [CoE], 2016). In January 2018, the Parliamentary Assembly of the Council of Europe, following a report by Assembly member Jensen (not available on the organisation's website), acknowledged the efforts made by the ASOIF GTF while making two recommendations (PACE, 2018, p. 1) that a set of indicators for the governance of IFs should be certified, for example, by organisation such as ISO (International Organisation for Standardisation) (point 8 of Resolution 2199,2) that the sports movement should establish an "independent sport ethics rating system" similar to rating systems that exist in other areas such as environmental issues (point 12).

ASOIF launched a Governance Support Monitoring Unit (GSMU) in November 2018. This comprised the same members as the GTF but without IF representatives, in this way being more independent of IFs. This new unit is also chaired by the ASOIF president and is tasked with carrying out a further assessment of the governance of IFs, again based on the GTF questionnaire, for publication in 2020. Furthermore, the GSMU will assist IFs that want to improve their governance – in particular by means of quick wins that can be implemented by IF management without decisions by the board or general assembly. The GSMU will also study the proportion of IOC subsidies in IF budgets (originally requested by the IOC Executive Board in December 2015 – see above) and support risk assessment for IFs, an important dimension of governance. Moreover, the GTF example is to be followed by other IFs rather than just ASOIF or AIOWF members. In November 2018, the approximately 50 IF members of the GAISF, which are not part of ASOIF or AIOWF, announced their intention to use a reduced set of ASOIF GTF indicators (about 20) to improve their governance.

It should be noted that the IOC has gradually increased pressure on IFs to practice better governance. Evidence of this lies in the November 2018 decisions of the IOC Executive Board to continue monitoring the governance of the IWF (weightlifting), in particular with regard to its anti-doping programme and to open an investigation into the governance of the AIBA (boxing) which could lead to the removal of boxing from the Olympic programme (IOC, 2018) despite the efforts of this IF with its New Foundation Plan adopted in mid-2018 (AIBA, 2018). Similar pressures were exerted on the IBU at the time that it was changing its president. The previous president was under investigation in his own country (Norway) and in the country of the IBU's headquarters (Austria).

As can be seen, the work on the governance of IFs is far from complete, even though there has been significant progress. This is not just due to the GTF; there has also been an independent move by some IFs since the turn of the century, as is shown in the next section in relation to the UCI (cycling) (Section 2). However, it will also be shown (in Section 3) that much depends on the leadership of the IF president and the network of member national federations, in other words it is not enough for an IF to simply "tick the boxes". Stakeholders and observers should be able to undertake a qualitative assessment of the governance style of IFs leaders which cannot be assessed only by indicators such as those used by the GTF and which would take into consideration the effectiveness of boards in ensuring good governance and the achievement of organisational objectives.

The governance of the UCI (Union Cycliste Internationale)

The governance of IFs has become an all-consuming question not only in academic literature but also in the mainstream media. This reflects concerns about the limits of IFs' autonomy as closed, self-regulating organisations at the head of an inter-organisational network. Enjoying significant legal freedom despite their increasing commercialisation, IFs continue to function as quasi-monopolies (Forster, 2006; Geeraert, 2015). Waning public trust and the proliferation of scandals involving governance raises the question of whether IFs are still capable of self-regulation. The example of the UCI illustrates the shift from a governance model centred on the president to one that is increasingly influenced by external pressures. The following section describes and analyses the evolution of the UCI's governance model from 1991 to the present day by examining four presidencies (Hein Verbruggen, Pat McQuaid, Brian Cookson and David Lappartient) and the respective changes in governance that these presidents ordered/initiated on their own or were forced to implement. The data upon which this section is based comes from personal observations, discussions and interviews conducted by one of the authors who used to work at the UCI. Secondary sources are also used, such as the Regulations, Constitution and reports published on the UCI website, as well as journal articles.

Hein Verbruggen (1991–2005)

The presidency of Hein Verbruggen laid the foundation of the UCI's governance model. This period is characterised by three major, distinct issues, namely (1) the recognition of the UCI as the sole governing body of cycling, (2) control of the international cycling calendar and (3) corporate leadership. Hein Verbruggen became UCI president in 1991. Before this, from 1984 to 1991, he was president of the Fédération Internationale du Cyclisme Professionnel (FICP), one of cycling's three governing bodies in that era. Since 1965, cycling had been governed by the UCI, the FICP (mainly representing western capitalist countries) and the Fédération Internationale Amateur de Cyclisme (FIAC) (mainly representing communist countries). This separation had become compulsory when Avery Brundage, IOC president from 1952 to 1972, reinforced the amateur code in 1964. The amateur code excluded all athletes who had participated in sporting events for money or material advantage from the Olympic Games. The IOC only recognised the FIAC, cycling's amateur federation. In an attempt to ensure political balance, the UCI board was equally composed of FICP and FIAC members. However, persistent political and ideological differences between the FICP and the FIAC resulted in an unsurmountable impasse. This *de facto* deadlock paralysed the UCI for 27 years. Verbruggen's first major official act was therefore to confer all powers to the UCI. He achieved this goal through the dissolution of both the FICP and the FIAC in 1992. Two events facilitated these dissolutions. Firstly, the word amateur was removed from the Olympic Charter and, as of 1984, professional athletes could participate in the Olympic Games. Secondly, the demise of the USSR in 1989 simplified the fall of the Iron Curtain in cycling.

Verbruggen was convinced that, in order to control and govern its sport, an IF had to take charge of its international calendar and sporting rules. The UCI rulebook was very thin at the time. The actual regulatory power lay with race organisers, who established their own rules for their races. Verbruggen "saw very quickly that ASO[1] was the master of the international cycling calendar" (Hein Verbruggen, November 2014). In fact, the international cycling calendar represented a means to regulate and control race organisers, cycling teams and the sport itself and was also a source of revenue. Verbruggen's main political and economic challenge in 1991 was therefore to wrest control of the international cycling calendar from the all-powerful race organisers. As the UCI tried to take hold of the calendar, tensions with the most powerful race organisers increased, especially with the ASO. The launch of the ProTour in 2005, a UCI-owned circuit, marked the beginning of a power struggle between the UCI and ASO, which was to last until 2008 and required the intervention of the IOC as a mediator. In terms of the rules, the UCI set an example to other IFs and some even "revised their statutes in function of our statutes" (Hein Verbruggen, November 2014). For instance, as early as 1992, the remuneration of board members in the form of compensation for loss of earnings was openly introduced into the UCI Constitution.

Unlike multinationals, the shareholders of which seek a return on investment, IF members (i.e., continental confederations and national federations) generally lack common objectives. At least, this was Hein Verbruggen's point of view: "It's like a basket full of frogs. They go in all directions. [...] 150 or 200 members, all have their own interests and work against each other. You're not going to find optimal solutions with 200 people in a room" (Hein Verbruggen, November 2014). Verbruggen tried to overcome the political sclerosis of the UCI's system of governance by imposing strong (autocratic) leadership. Applying the principles of management that he had learned during his time at M&M/Mars (the confectionary company, which was a major cycling sponsor), Verbruggen was a pioneer with regard to the implementation of corporate management practices in IFs. The president became an executive president who, together with the 15 board members, determined the objectives and the strategy of the UCI. A small group made up of the president, director general and the legal and financial directors, took political decisions. The director general was in control of several departments (e.g., legal, financial, event, marketing and sports). One of Verbruggen's main concerns was to ensure a clear separation of powers to avoid staff becoming involved in politics and to prevent elected officials having an influence in day-to-day operations. However, Verbruggen was said to be involved in both – and to have acted with an iron fist. As the UCI Constitution had to be revised after the dissolution of the FICP and FIAC, Verbruggen used this opportunity to reduce the power of the continental confederations, considering them a political and financial burden and responsible for draining money from the IF. Continental confederations were mainly represented in their role as voting delegates. Instead of a one-nation-one-vote system, the UCI adopted a representative democracy under Verbruggen. This system consisted of 42 voting delegates distributed among the five continental confederations. This weighted system of votes was supposed to reflect the geographical representation of cycling worldwide and was therefore very Eurocentric. The system is still in place today, as Article 36 of the UCI Constitution testifies, although now consisting of 45 voting delegates (UCI, 2018a).

Hein Verbruggen was much praised during his presidency for the UCI's growing prosperity, improved structure and professionalisation. In 2004, the UCI was one of the first IFs to adopt Rules of governance based on 11 principles: Identity, objectives, representation, decision-making process, transparency, communication, sport management, roles, commercial activities, finances and solidarity (Chappelet & Mrkonjic, 2013). Hein Verbruggen became an IOC member in 1996 in his capacity as an IF president. However, a string of allegations against Verbruggen emerged from 2008. Although a report commissioned by the UCI and published in 2015 could not establish clear proof of corrupt behaviour, Verbruggen was accused of preferential treatment in specific cases, autocratic leadership and a lack of checks and balances during his time as UCI president. He robustly defended his achievements as UCI president and refuted these allegations until his death in June 2017.

Pat McQuaid (2005–2013)

Pat McQuaid's presidency represented somewhat of a continuity of Verbruggen's agenda. According to former staff members, McQuaid often called Verbruggen for advice. McQuaid did not have the charisma of Verbruggen – nor his skills in politics, management or visionary thinking. Nevertheless, his presidency is associated with two main achievements. Firstly, the creation of the Cycling Anti-Doping Foundation (CADF) in 2008 to manage the UCI's anti-doping programme (e.g., to define and implement the UCI's doping control strategy and conduct in- and out-of-competition testing). Secondly, after a power struggle that started with the announcement of the ProTour in 2004, ASO and the UCI finally came to an agreement in 2008. Throughout McQuaid's presidency, the pervasive influence of Verbruggen on the governance of cycling persisted. (Verbruggen was re-elected as an IOC member in 2006 in his capacity as Honorary UCI president; he was also a close friend of Jacques Rogge, the IOC president at the time.) McQuaid was defeated by Brian Cookson in the 2013 presidential election after a hard-fought campaign. Cookson and his team did everything they could to discredit Verbruggen and McQuaid in order to present Cookson as the leader of a campaign to restore the UCI's credibility and distance the new president from allegations against the UCI.

Freeburn (2013), who examined the allegations against the UCI in the investigation into doping concerning Lance Armstrong and the US Postal Service Pro Cycling Team, argued that although Pat McQuaid was not an instigator, he did maintain a defective structure of governance that ultimately resulted in many calls for the reform of the UCI.

Brian Cookson (2013–2017)

Brian Cookson took over the UCI presidency at a time when its credibility had suffered a considerable blow as a result of the Lance Armstrong affair. This had severely discredited the UCI's governance. Cookson's 2013 electoral manifesto had two priorities: An overhaul of cycling's anti-doping policies and the development of women's cycling. The first aimed to come to terms with the past (i.e., UCI anti-doping practices and allegations of laxity regarding Verbruggen and McQuaid) and restore credibility (notably vis-à-vis the IOC and cycling's stakeholders). The objective of the second priority (the development of women's cycling) was to create a forward-looking, progressive image for the UCI. Soon after his election, Cookson established the Cycling Independent Reform Commission (CIRC), which published a damning 227-page report in 2015 accusing Verbruggen and McQuaid of colluding with Lance Armstrong (Mackay, 2015).

Despite his ambitious objectives and desire for governance reform, Cookson's short presidency was contested for various reasons. He was accused by both staff and board members of being too hesitant, of lacking the necessary leadership skills and of delegating too many responsibilities to his director general (Pavitt, 2016; Roan, 2017). Cookson further ignored the growing dissatisfaction of the board with the leadership imbalance that arose from the director general's prominence and Cookson's absence. He was not an executive president as his predecessors. Furthermore, after just 18 months, the turnover of UCI staff had exceeded 50 percent (due to dismissals and voluntary departures) with no strategy in place for knowledge transfer. Cookson suffered a humiliating defeat to David Lappartient in the 2017 presidential election (37 votes to 8). He thus became the first UCI president to serve just one term. Despite Cookson's defeat and repeated criticism of his leadership, he and his team achieved many important governance reforms during the four years of his mandate. Table 13.1 gives details of three of the five GTF dimensions.

David Lappartient (since September 2017)

While Brian Cookson's main challenge was to restore trust in the UCI's governance, which he notably tackled by reforming anti-doping policies, governance was no longer a critical issue when David Lappartient was elected to the UCI presidency in September 2017. On the contrary, the UCI was even considered a model of governance in many respects. According to

Table 13.1 The UCI's governance reforms under President Brian Cookson

Democracy	A term limit (12 years) was introduced for the president in 2016 – UCI Constitution, Art. 62 (UCI, 2018a).
Transparency	The president's remuneration and the overall remuneration of all board members have been disclosed in the UCI's financial report since 2013.
	A transparent bidding process for the award of major cycling events was introduced in 2015[2].
Integrity	The UCI Ethics Commission was completely revamped in 2016. It now has to be composed of five members, including a minimum of one woman. As per Article 12 of the UCI Code of Ethics, the chair and two further members have to be independent of the world of cycling. The secretariat of the Ethics Commission is independent of the UCI administration (UCI Code of Ethics, Art. 13.1). The Ethics Commission can sanction behaviour (UCI, 2018b).
	Until 2013, the UCI president was a member of the Cycling Anti-Doping Foundation (CADF) board. Under Cookson, the CADF became a separate legal entity, completely independent of the UCI. Furthermore, Legal Anti-Doping Services (LADS) was created, overseen by an external lawyer (CADF, 2018).
	In 2014 and 2015, the Cycling Independent Reform Committee, an independent entity, conducted "a wide-ranging independent investigation into the causes of the pattern of doping that developed within cycling and allegations which implicate the UCI and other governing bodies and officials over ineffective investigation of such doping practices" (Rebeggiani, 2016).
	State-of-the-art confidential reporting mechanisms were created for whistle-blowers.
	A Women's Commission was established.
	Every commission/committee must have at least one female member (although this is not yet formalised in the Constitution).
	All UCI World Championships offered equal prize money for men and women by 2016 (Clarke, 2016).

a staff member, this has left Lappartient in the comfortable position of being able to focus on sporting projects, such as the reform of the WorldTour, which features cycling's most prestigious cycling races (e.g., Tour de France, Giro d'Italia, Vuelta a España). Lappartient's impact in terms of shaping and improving the UCI's governance will have to be measured against the promises he set out in his election manifesto in which he emphasised his commitment to improving the governance of cycling, notably with regard to technological fraud, doping and potential manipulation through betting. Since his election, Lappartient's manifesto has been developed into a strategic vision known as UCI Agenda 2022 (UCI, 2018c), bringing to mind the IOC's Agenda 2020. In the UCI Agenda 2022, Lappartient reiterates the need for "real and effective leadership" (p. 6), reaffirms the role of the president and stresses rebuilding the "badly damaged relationship" (p. 7) between the president and the Management Committee. The principles of modern governance will be further improved in the following areas: 1) The processes of managing solidarity funds and the transparency of allocations to stakeholders, 2) regular audits by independent external entities and gender parity at all levels. Greater transparency on allocations and working towards gender parity seem to be direct responses to the weaknesses in the UCI's governance revealed by the ASOIF governance reviews. Some aspects that may require further improvement are listed below by GTF dimension (see Table 13.2).

Table 13.2 Possible future improvements to the UCI's governance

Democracy	A term limit was introduced for the president in 2016, but not for members of the Management Committee or Commissions[3].
Transparency	No independent reporting mechanisms exist regarding the allocation of resources for development.
Integrity	The UCI performs poorly at decision-making level in terms of gender balance (11% female board members in May 2018). On a more positive note, the UCI is seeking to implement equal pay at the administrative level.
Checks & balances/ control mechanisms	An Internal Audit Committee was established under Cookson, fulfilling a strategic promise (the consolidated financial statements of the UCI were audited by KPMG). However, since the UCI replaced the financial consultant with a full-time chief financial officer under Lappartient, the Internal Audit Committee is not independent of the UCI administration.

The announcement by broadcast giant Sky in December 2018 that it would end its sponsorship deal with Team Sky, worth £30 million a year, after the 2019 season brought another recurring issue to the fore; namely, the financial precariousness of the economic model of cycling in general, and professional road cycling teams and riders in particular, given the considerable dependence on sponsor investment (Pavitt, 2018). Verbruggen had already tried to tackle the issue of teams' vulnerability by creating the ProTour/WorldTour in 2005. The objective of the UCI-owned circuit was to stabilise the teams' financial situation by guaranteeing top-level participation. "We wanted to open new sources of revenues for the teams and bind sponsors via participation guarantees" (Hein Verbruggen, April 2015). However, cycling's economic model continues to be fragile and many professional road cycling teams disband once the main sponsor leaves. Probably the most dangerous downside of this situation is the professional instability for riders and the increased risk of them using prohibited substances to improve their results to secure a contract (Aubel & Ohl, 2015; Ohl, Fincoeur, Lentillon-Kaestner, Defrance & Brissonneau, 2015). If teams rely almost entirely on their main sponsors this is also because there is no redistribution of TV rights to them. The withdrawal of Sky as the sponsor of the team that has dominated road cycling over recent years shows that "no team is immune from potential difficulties under the current model" (Pavitt, 2018). The issue of the precariousness of cycling's economic model needs to be addressed in future reforms of the UCI, especially as event organisers and teams are seeking more involvement. While Verbruggen's presidency was very autocratic and built around his personality, Lappartient has to involve cycling's main stakeholders in decision-making.

The example of the UCI illustrates the importance of the president's leadership in the governance of an IF. It also shows the power of the national federations that elect (or sometimes do not re-elect) the president and that must vote on significant reforms of governance while being beneficiaries, or not, of a redistribution of IF resources.

Two underestimated key factors of IF governance

According to Henry and Lee (2004), three dimensions of governance that have an impact on the operation of organisations can be distinguished; these specifically apply in the case of IFs and shine a light on the levels of reflection and action and associated key factors. These three dimensions are the organisational, political and systemic dimensions. The organisational (corporate) dimension concerns the exercise of the power of management and control within IFs, in other words the decision-making processes and the conduct of strategy in order to improve the performance of the organisation and the achievement of its objectives.

The political dimension concerns the relationship that IFs maintain in the political field. It reports on the manner in which political institutions (states, European Union, United Nations, etc.) seek to influence, or indeed regulate, international sport by means of the mobilisation of regulatory, financial and moral mechanisms or by various political influences. The question of power is no longer analysed in its intra-organisational dimension but rather in its inter-organisational dimension. This political governance is less significant for IFs than for national federations, which generally maintain strong partnership relationships with their ministries of sport.

The systemic dimension aims to describe situations of interdependence and the forms of regulation of inter-organisational relations as well as the coordination of actions within a complex system such as the total Olympic system (Chappelet, 2016b). The concept of the complexity of the sporting and Olympic system refers to the uncertainty of the environment, the wide range of stakeholders – often with differing interests (public, community, commercial) – and the multiplicity of levels of coordination (from local to global). In dynamic terms, the notion of systemic governance marks the transition from a regulation/coordination of actions that is centralised, hierarchical and vertical (government) to a horizontal regulation/coordination in terms of networks based on consensus/compromise and power shared with several actors (governance). This new type of regulation is well expressed in the implementation of public–private partnerships, as demonstrated by the regulation of the global fight against doping through the operations of the World Anti-Doping Agency (Chappelet & van Luijk, 2018).

These three levels of governance are complementary, interrelated and must be integrated and implemented in the governance of an IF in order to improve their efficacy and legitimacy. There seem to be two key points. The first point relates to the exercise of power and leadership in the IFs and at the administrative headquarters. This concerns a good definition within the IFs, going beyond statutory formalism, of questions such as: Who decides? Who implements? Who checks and reports on the results and to whom? In this respect, it is necessary to analyse the roles of the president, the director general, the Board of Directors (BoD) and the general assembly (GA). There are four main types of configuration of power in IFs, namely 1) a strong presidency (an executive president generally relying on two key employees, the administrative/financial director and the sports director, in order to lead the federation); 2) a dispersed presidency (a powerful executive president surrounded by five or six main key actors, whether paid or not); 3) a tandem presidency (also termed the president/director tandem); and 4) managerial power (managerial and political power to a paid CEO) over elected officials (Bayle & Robinson, 2007).

Four cases of IFs (UCI, FIFA, FISA, International Hockey Federation [FIH]) of different sizes and levels of professionalisation serve to illustrate these power configurations. As seen above, the UCI has traditionally had a strong presidency (type 1) (followed by managerial power around the CEO and a reluctant board during the Cookson presidency - type 4). FIFA is a dispersed presidency (type 2) that had autocratic leadership by the president during the Blatter era. This situation recurred after Infantino's election despite governance reforms and the reinforcement of the secretary general's position to oversee the administrative headquarters (the FIFA Board is more dedicated to ensuring political equilibrium between representatives of continental confederations). FISA has a tradition of a president with a strong rowing background (obligatory in the constitution) and has achieved greater professionalisation through a tandem presidency (type 3) of the president/director general. FIH built a managerial model around a strong CEO between 2010 and 2015 (type 4).

In reality, the doctrine by which elected officials (board) decide, employees (the IF's secretariat or administration) implement and the GA monitors is often poorly observed. Presidents are increasingly executive or compensated presidents and other elected officials are less prominent at the headquarters; boards of directors rarely play an executive role and act as a genuine counterweight to presidential power. Furthermore, the GA monitors the results obtained in a rather distant and very formal manner. While IF reporting methods are evolving and becoming more professional (with the emergence of more detailed financial and activity reports that are publicly accessible on the Internet), checks of performance measurements and countervailing powers are still weak (states, the media and NGOs have little influence in regulating any excesses of governance).

The IOC has a significant right of scrutiny as a result of the redistribution of a part of the broadcasting and marketing rights for the Olympic Games to IFs (via ASOIF). The magnitude of this has increased substantially since 2012 (approximately USD$600 million over four years shared between the 28 Summer Olympic IFs for 2013–2016) and one of the evaluation criteria for sport to remain on the Olympic programme is IF governance (IOC, 2012). However, the effectiveness of this evaluation can be queried. After the Rio Games, the largest sum was allocated to the IAAF[4] despite the 2015 governance scandal involving its former president. Changes in systemic governance also sometimes imply consequences for organisational governance, as illustrated by the advent of directorships on the BoD reserved for stakeholders (athletes, officials, representatives of the professional sport, doctors and women) and/or qualified or independent individuals. Independent ethics committees (e.g., for the UCI) and/or governance committees (for FIFA) have also been established with the aspiration of ensuring better governance.

The second key point for the governance of IFs concerns the support of continental and national structures and, more broadly, the improvement of the federal network. In other words, the governance of the federal pyramid and the quality of collaboration between the five levels of intervention (international, continental, national, regional and local) are important to create the optimal conditions for the organisation and development of the sport. Mrkonjic's work (2015) on European federations shows that three models of continental IF organisation can be distinguished. The first is the legal (and sometimes political, although rarely economic) autonomy of continental confederations with a European federation that is often stronger than the others (a clear example is the case of the European Football Confederation (UEFA). This model is very rare; continental confederations are generally weak and their connections are sometimes ineffective in the implementation of IF development policies. Two other organisational models exist, namely a) the very common institutional absence of continental confederations (e.g., FISA) and b) the unique case, potentially offering inspiration for the future, of the creation of continental offices under the control of the international headquarters in line with the one FIBA strategy (FIBA Europe, FIBA Americas, etc.).

IFs that are seeking to give impetus to their federal network of national federations have a range of choices and resources depending on whether or not they can fund the development and structuring of the network. FIFA has connections through its six confederations and offers strong support to national federations with overall annual contributions both to operations and in accordance with national federation projects. Each national federation has the same influence as the GA (one-country-one-vote system). The FIH instead relies on a collaboration with its strongest national federations (England, the Netherlands, India, etc.) and through knowledge-sharing with others. The UCI tries to support its national federations through a knowledge-sharing platform for each continent. FISA is more focused on institutional and sport relationships with its national federations.

The management of the organisational governance of the administrative headquarters and the federal network is a challenge due to the very strong heterogeneity of continental and national structures in terms of professionalisation. Systemic governance must therefore be more strongly integrated into the reflections of IFs in the future through the relationships that they must form with the IOC, other IFs, states (often co-organising their events), intergovernmental organisations (EU, UN), private partners, the media, NGOs and even civil society. This increased complexity requires high-level organisational governance, bringing together professionalism and responsiveness while preserving democratic principles (efficacy and democracy can sometimes appear to be contradictory). The qualities of leaders (skills, managerial expertise, strategic vision, involvement, values) and, more specifically, of IF presidents, are put directly to the test on this subject.

In this respect, it should be noted that the accession of an IF president to power is not only achieved through professional skills but also, and especially, by a political capacity to achieve and retain power. The media and soft power platforms that international sport and the Olympic Games offer explain why countries (such as Russia, the Gulf States, China, United States, etc.) are developing genuine strategies to encourage their citizens to attain these presidential functions. However, despite everything, these positions are overwhelmingly occupied by men from Western Europe.

Conclusion

This chapter summarises the efforts made by the IFs of sports of the summer and winter Olympic programmes to achieve better governance under the auspices of a system of indicators drawn up by ASOIF in 2015 at the IOC's request. In particular, it focuses on the case of the UCI, which governs cycling and has had a series of four presidents since the turn of the century. These presidents have initiated, and then confronted, major governance reforms that have not yet been fully accomplished. The chapter then emphasises two important factors for improved IF governance. Firstly, it is essential for the organisational and political governance of an IF for the elected president to demonstrate leadership, in particular for the day-to-day operation of its administrative headquarters. This leadership is also key to the chemistry of the duo formed by the president and the IF's number two, whether he or she is known as the director or secretary (general or executive) or chief executive officer (CEO) and whether elected or appointed, with a greater or lesser degree of autonomy. Secondly, the governance of the network of national and continental federations and, more broadly speaking, stakeholders, is crucial to the governance of the IF and the systemic governance of the ecosystem of its sport through the redistribution of sometimes significant resources and the democratic principle that almost always gives one vote to each member–national federation of the IF. Future research should be carried out examining the leadership styles and national networks of IFs as they can both impact negatively the overall governance of an IF and can destroy the best efforts towards better governance at the international level through scandals linked to a person or a country at a local level. To what extent, for example, can an IF impose its governance standards on its national sport federations or push its national leaders towards improved governance?

Many IFs are over 100 years old and operate with substantial budgets. However, there are now many new players interested in sport that want to take advantage of its benefits. These are, of course, primarily athletes of the sport in question. There are also commercial players such as sponsors, broadcasters and professional leagues, as well as public actors, such as local or national governments, becoming increasingly involved in the organisation of sporting events and the fight against the scourges afflicting sport; or, quite simply, they are seeking to get their populations moving to enjoy the benefits of movement through sport. The basics of the governance of IFs dates back to the foundation of many of these federations in the early 20th century. Governance practises must now adapt to the current situation in which commercialisation and professionalisation of the IFs demand a more transparent culture.

Notes

1 Amaury Sport Organisation (ASO) is the company that organises the Tour de France, the Vuelta a España, Paris–Nice, as well as other major cycling races and sporting events (e.g., Dakar, Paris Marathon), totalling 75 events in 25 countries in 2018 (aso.fr, 2018).
2 The 2016 UCI Road World Championships in Qatar (awarded during the presidency of Pat McQuaid) was an example of a contrary approach; the event was awarded to Qatar as the highest bidder.
3 According to a staff member, term limits for members of the Management Committee were rejected in 2016.
4 FINA (swimming) and FIG (gymnastics) receive the same amount as the IAAF.

References

AIBA. (2018). *New foundation plan.* Lausanne: Amateur International Boxing Association.
AIOWF. (2018). Second review of governance of AIOWF IF members, a study by I Trust Sport. Retrieved 30 March, from www.fis-ski.com/en/international-ski-federation/news-multimedia/news/article=fis-governance-survey-and-aiowf-report-2018-published
Alm, J. (2013). *Action for good governance in international sports organizations.* Copenhagen: Play The Game.
ASOIF. (2016a, December 1). *ASOIF taskforce agrees new sports governance principles and indicators.* 28 January 2016. Retrieved from www.asoif.com/news/asoif-taskforce-agrees-new-sports-governance-principles-and-indicators (consulted on 2018 December, 1).
ASOIF. (2016b, December 1). *ASOIF governance task force (GTF) first report to ASOIF Council.* Retrieved from https://asoif.my.salesforce.com/sfc/p/#D0000000lcuP/a/57000000Hjuz/kwc6VBCB6HE3pxgEhuBHJI_89MiQ1AIyrdr2nJ57UeM
ASOIF. (2016c, December 1). *ASOIF governance task force (GTF) international federation (IF) self-assessment questionnaire, to be returned by 27 February 2017.* Retrieved from www.asoif.com/sites/default/files/basic_page/if_governance_questionnaire.pdf
ASOIF. (2017a, December 1). *First review of IF governance, 2017 ASOIF General Assembly.* Lausanne: ASOIF GTF. Retrieved from www.asoif.com/sites/default/files/basic_page/first_review:of_if_governance_2017.pdf
ASOIF. (2017b, December 1). *ASOIF Governance Task Force (GTF) International Federation (IF) Self-Assessment Questionnaire, to be returned by 19 January 2018.* Retrieved from www.asoif.com/sites/default/files/download/if_governance_questionnaire-stage_2.pdf
ASOIF. (2018, December 1). *Second review of international federation governance.* Lausanne: ASOIF. Retrieved from www.asoif.com/sites/default/files/download/asoif_2018_second_review:v4_interactive.pdf
Aubel, O., & Ohl, F. (2015). From the precariousness of professional bicycle racers to doping practices. *Actes de la recherche en sciences sociales, 4,* 28–41.
Bayle E., & Robinson L. (2007). A Framework for understanding the performance of national governing bodies of sport. *European Sport Management Quarterly, 7,* 249–268.
CADF. (2018, December 14). *Cycling anti-doping foundation - governance.* Retrieved from https://www.cadf.ch/governance/
Chappelet, J.-L. & Mrkonjic, M. (2013). *Basic indicators for better governance in international sport* (IDHEAP Working Paper, 1/2013). Lausanne: Swiss Graduate School of Public Administration, University of Lausanne.
Chappelet, J.-L. (2016a). Which governance for which Olympic sport organization? *Sport in Society, 19,* 838–840.
Chappelet, J.-L. (2016b). From Olympic administration to Olympic governance. *Sport in Society, 19,* 739–751.

Chappelet J.-L. (2018.) Beyond governance: The need to improve the regulation of international sport. *Sport in Society*, *21*, 724–734.

Chappelet, J.-L. & Van Luijk, N. (2018). The institutional governance of global hybrid bodies: The case of the World-Anti Doping Agency, In A. Bonomi Savignon, L. Gnan, A. Hinna, & F. Monteduro, (Eds.), *Hybridity in the governance and delivery of public services* (pp. 167–191). London: Emerald Publishing.

Clarke, S. (2016, December 14). *All UCI World Championships Road Races will have equal prize money in 2016*. Retrieved from https://www.cyclingweekly.com/news/racing/uci-world-championships-road -races-will-equal-prize-money-2016-231952

Council of Europe (CoE). (2016, November 29). *14th Council of Europe Conference of Ministers responsible for sport, final resolutions. MSL14*. Budapest, Hungary, Resolution 2.

Forster, J. (2006). Global sports organisations and their governance. *Corporate Governance: The International Journal of Business in Society*, *6*(1), 72–83.

Freeburn, L. (2013). The Union Cycliste Internationale: A study in the failure of organizational governance of an International Federation. *International Sports Law Journal*, *13*, 71–81.

Geeraert, A. (2015). *Sports governance observer 2015: The legitimacy crisis in international sports governance*. Copenhagen: Play the Game.

Geeraert, A. (2018). *Sports governance observer 2018. An assessment of good governance in five international sports federations*. Copenhagen: Play The Game.

Henry, I., & Lee, P. C. (2004). Governance and ethics in sport. In J. Beech & S. Chadwick (Eds.), *The business of sport management* (pp. 25–42). Harlow: Pearson Ed.

IOC. (2012, November 1). *Evaluation criteria for sports and disciplines − 2012*. Lausanne: International Olympic Committee Olympic Programme Commission. Retrieved from https://stillmed.olympic. org/media/Document%20Library/OlympicOrg/IOC/Who-We-Are/Commissions/Olympic-Progr amme-Commission/EN-2012-06-IOC-evaluation-criteria-for-sports-and-disciplines.pdf#_ga=2.87 034718.738294805.1544901384-2146452662.1542277806

IOC. (2015, December 10). *IOC executive board adopts declaration on good governance in sport and the protection of clean athletes*. Lausanne: Press Release.

IOC. (2018, December 1). *IOC executive board initiatives an inquiry into AIBA*. Press Release. 30 November. Retrieved from www.olympic.org/news/ioc-executive-board-initiates-an-inquiry-into-aiba

Ingle, S. (2015, November 27). Solving FIFA's and IOC's problems is easier said than done. *The Guardian*.

Mackay, D. (2015, December 1). *Verbruggen and McQuaid accused by new UCI report of colluding with Armstrong to cover up doping, Inside the Games*. 9 March. Retrieved from www.insidethegames.biz/articles/1026027

Mrkonjic, M. (2015). *L'état de la gouvernance des fédérations sportives européennes : enseignements et recommandations pour une « meilleure » gouvernance du sport en Europe* (Unpublished doctoral thesis) Lausanne: IDHEAP-UNIL.

Ohl, F., Fincoeur, B., Lentillon-Kaestner, V., Defrance, J., & Brissonneau, C. (2015). The socialization of young cyclists and the culture of doping. *International Review for the Sociology of Sport*, *50*, 865–882.

PACE. (2018, December 1). *Resolution 2199 (2018) towards a framework for modern sports governance*. Paris: Parliamentary Assembly of the Council of Europe. Retrieved from http://assembly.coe.int/nw/xml/ XRef/Xref-XML2HTML-EN.asp?fileid=24443&lang=en

Pavitt, M. (2016, December 10). *Cookson's leadership of UCI reportedly criticised in letter by UEC president*. Retrieved from https://www.insidethegames.biz/articles/1038724/cooksons-leadership-of-uci-repor tedly-criticised-in-letter-by-uec-president

Pavitt, M. (2018, December 17). *Is Sky withdrawal both an opportunity for road cycling and sign of its problems?* Retrieved from https://www.insidethegames.biz/articles/1073395/michael-pavitt-is-sky-withdrawal -both-an-opportunity-for-road-cycling-and-sign-of-its-problems

Play the Game. (2017, December 1). *Sports Governance Observer indicators*. Retrieved from www.playth egame.org/theme-pages/the-sports-governance-observer/indicators

Rebeggiani, L. (2016). The organizational structure of professional road cycling. In D. Van Reeth & J. Larson (Eds.), *The economics of professional road cycling* (pp. 33–54). Cham: Springer.

Roan, D. (2017, December 10). *Brian Cookson: World cycling chief criticised by UCI vice-president*. Retrieved from https://www.bbc.com/sport/cycling/40663467

UCI. (2018a, December 14). *UCI Constitution*. Retrieved from https://www.uci.org/docs/default-source/ rules-and-regulations/uci-constitution-and-standing-orders.pdf?sfvrsn=c7d56a45_8

UCI. (2018b, December 14). *UCI Code of Ethics*. Retrieved from https://www.uci.org/docs/default-so urce/rules-and-regulations/uci-code-of-ethics.pdf?sfvrsn=6fa3e274_12

Jean-Loup Chappelet, Josephine Clausen and Emmanuel Bayle

UCI. (2018c, December 5). *UCI Agenda 2022*. Retrieved from https://www.uci.org/docs/default-source/agenda-2022/2018-uci-agenda2022-en-web.pdf?sfvrsn=56b641e7_6

Verbruggen, H. (2014, November). *Personal interview with two of the authors.*

Verbruggen, H. (2015, April). *Personal interview with two of the authors.*

Wenn, S., Barney, R., & Martyn, S. (2011). *Tarnished rings, the International Olympic Committee and the Salt Lake City bid scandal.* Syracuse, NY: Syracuse University Press.

14

Governance of intercollegiate athletics in the USA

Barbara Osborne and Erianne A. Weight

Introduction

Intercollegiate athletics is a $14 billion industry (US dollars) and relatively unique to the United States (Murphy, 2019). Colleges and universities offering athletics programs may choose, but are not required, to affiliate with a national governance organisation. There are five national voluntary membership organisations that provide championships opportunities and regulate intercollegiate athletics. The National Collegiate Athletic Association (NCAA) is the oldest organisation with the largest membership – over 1,110 colleges and universities and 100 athletics conferences. The National Association of Intercollegiate Athletics (NAIA) is another governing body and is best known for its sponsorship of the longest-running national basketball tournament in the United States. The NAIA was also the first national intercollegiate athletics governing body to invite historically black institutions into membership (in 1953) and to sponsor both men's and women's national championships (in 1980). The NAIA is currently home to almost 300 colleges and universities and some 60,000 student-athletes competing in 13 sports. The National Junior College Athletic Association, established in 1938, promotes competition between institutions granting two-year or associate degrees. The National Christian College Athletic Association was incorporated in 1968 and emphasises a unique mission of promoting Christian outreach and ministry through sponsorship of national championships in 23 sports. The newest national governing body for intercollegiate athletics is the United States Collegiate Athletic Association, established in 2009, which provides national competitive experiences for small-enrollment schools offering four-year and associate degrees and nontraditional or trade programs.

This chapter will focus on the NCAA as the most internationally recognised intercollegiate governing body. A brief history of the evolution the NCAA highlighting the major changes in the governance structure provides a frame of reference. Then an overview of the current governance structure is provided including the roles of the national office, conferences, institutions, student-athletes and external stakeholders. Finally, the need for independent research on the governance of college athletics is identified and described.

Historical evolution of college sport in the US

Intercollegiate athletics were created by students at exclusive private universities in the north-eastern United States. The first recognised intercollegiate athletic contest was a rowing competition between Harvard University and Yale University on 3 August 1852 (Lewis, 1970). Students organised intercollegiate baseball games in 1859 and soccer games in 1869. Disputes concerning competition rules and the eligibility of players were common. Student-run teams recruited graduate students, alumni, part-time students and even professionals to gain competitive advantage and bragging rights without concern for ethics or the integrity of the universities. Students attempted to address issues by organising sport associations, such as the Rowing Association of American Colleges in 1871, the Intercollegiate Football Association in 1876 and the Baseball Association in 1879. The Intercollegiate Football Association's annual Thanksgiving Day game, played in New York City for 20 years, was a huge commercial success (Smith, 2011).

Intercollegiate athletics became popular social events on campuses, and the visibility of athletic teams became associated with the identity of the institution. Faculty were concerned about academic integrity and believed that students should be focused on academics and not athletics. Princeton University was the first institution to establish faculty governance through its Committee on Athletics and Music, on 29 April 1881. Missed class time for competition was the primary faculty concern, and limitations on the number of games played were instituted. The next issue addressed was faculty approval of student-chosen coaches in an effort to limit professionalism (Smith, 2011). The goals of faculty were often at odds with the desires of the student body, so Brown University held a conference on 18 February 1898. Students, faculty and alumni were invited to

> ...purge professionalism and commercialism by eliminating recruiting and the paying of athletes, hired coaches, participation by freshmen, students not in good academic standing, part-time students, transferring of students for immediate participation, free training tables and playing contests on other than college grounds. (Smith, 2011, p. 215)

While well intentioned, most proposals failed. The NCAA became the first national governing body for intercollegiate athletics in 1905, and the organisation held its first annual convention on 29 December 1906. Membership was made up of colleges and universities, and volunteers from the schools were elected to leadership roles and to serve on committees. Each member institution had a vote. The NCAA Constitution required member institutions and conferences to enact and enforce rules governing college athletics. This concept of institutional autonomy was known as Home Rule. The next year, 1907, the major issue at the annual convention was violations of the principles of amateurism in college baseball. It was not until the 1916 annual convention that the membership agreed on the definition of an amateur as "one who participates only for pleasure and the physical, mental, moral and social benefits gained" (Smith, 2011, p. 217).

Rules compliance remained a major concern for the NCAA membership, as many members were suspected of intentionally or negligently violating the rules. At the 1948 annual convention, the NCAA became a regulatory body by instituting the Sanity Code, strict regulations on recruiting, amateurism, financial aid, academic standards and institutional control. A committee was established to investigate potential violations and a penalty established. Those found in violation would be expelled from the NCAA with the approval of two-thirds of annual convention delegates. While seven institutions were found to be in violation, none were expelled as the membership failed to reach a two-thirds majority with a 111-93 vote. The Sanity Code was repealed at the 1951 annual convention (Smith, 2000).

In 1951, the NCAA hired Walter Byers as its first full-time executive director. Over the next year, Byers set up a national office in Kansas City, Missouri and began hiring staff. Under Byers' leadership, the NCAA established new procedures for examining and investigating complaints of rules violations. Findings were reported to the NCAA Council, who would then place the institution on probation or suspend it. The system was tested in 1952 when the University of Kentucky was found to have provided impermissible financial aid to ten basketball players. The NCAA Council suspended the entire Kentucky athletics program for one year. The enforcement process continued to evolve with the establishment of the Committee on Infractions in 1954 and hiring a full-time staff at the national office to support it (Smith, 2011).

As the NCAA membership continued to grow there was significant diversity among the sizes and missions of the institutions and their philosophies regarding athletics. The first special convention of the NCAA was held in August 1973 to discuss dramatic change to the governance structure. The membership voted to federate into three divisions, self-determined and differentiated by philosophy. The most significant differentiating factor between the three divisions was providing athletics scholarships: Division I schools provided significant levels of scholarship funding for athletes in all sports, with preference for football and men's basketball; Division II provided athletics scholarships on a more limited basis seeking balance between athletic and academic priorities; and Division III embraced a non-scholarship model where academics were a priority and athletes participated for the love of the game. Table 14.1 highlights the differences in Division I, II and III. The Association was still led by an Executive Committee, with equal representation for all three divisions and elected by the entire membership following the democratic one-school, one-vote system. A President's Council was created for each division, and business matters were designated as association-wide or division-specific. At the annual convention, the entire membership convened for association-wide matters, and then each division met separately to discuss and enact regulations relevant to their philosophy.

While the NCAA had established a Special Committee on Women's Sports in April 1964, there was little interest from the membership in sponsoring women's varsity athletic programs or NCAA championships for women. The Association for Intercollegiate Athletics for Women

Table 14.1 Defining characteristics of NCAA membership divisions

	Division I	*Division II*	*Division III*
Sport Sponsorship	Minimum 7 men's and 7 women's teams OR 6 men's and 8 women's	Minimum 5 men's and 5 women's teams OR 4 men's and 6 women's	Minimum 5 men's and 5 women's teams OR 4 men's and 6 women's
	Both genders play in all 3 seasons	Two team sports per gender. Both genders play in all 3 seasons	Two team sports per gender. Both genders play in all 3 seasons
Athletic scholarships	Must meet minimum standards per sport; cannot exceed maximum levels	Cannot exceed maximum levels; athletes may also receive grants, loans, and employment earnings	No athletics-related scholarships; student-athletes may receive need-based financial aid and/or academic merit grants
Scheduling	100% minimum contests per sport played against DI opponents 1/3 of all contests per sport played at home	50% minimum contests in football and men's basketball against DII or higher level opponents	n/a

became the national governing body for women's college athletics in 1972, not coincidentally the same year Title IX of the Education Amendments was passed preventing sex discrimination in programs or activities at educational institutions. The NCAA still did not act, and the NAIA was the first collegiate athletics governing body to go co-ed, sponsoring the first women's championship (cross country) in 1980 (Wilson, 2005). On 13 January 1981 the NCAA membership voted to offer national championships for women's athletics, effectively initiating the death of the AIAW in 1982 as most NCAA members shifted their women's athletics affiliation to the NCAA (Carpenter, 1993).

The federated governance structure worked fairly well, with the majority of regulation occurring within each division consistent with their priorities. Division I schools were typically the "face" of the NCAA, with games regularly televised and the NCAA men's basketball tournament generating the majority of the association's income. However, the one-school, one-vote governance structure allowed Division II and III to easily out-vote Division I in association-wide matters. At the 1996 annual convention, the NCAA membership voted to dramatically change the association-wide governance structure. Instead of equal representation on the Executive Committee, the new structure heavily favored Division I, with eight members from the re-named Division I Board of Directors, two members from the Division II President's Council and two members from the Division III President's Council. Instead of maintaining the one-school, one-vote structure, Division I moved to governance represented by the conferences. Rules were also changed to limit association-wide voting matters; since 1997, almost all NCAA matters are decided within the division business meetings and there have been only three association-wide voting matters.

While the 1997 changes allowed Division I to address most issues without interference from the Division II or III membership, the conference representation governance system needed a few adjustments. Division I membership had grown to almost 350 institutions which varied significantly in resources. The member institutions of conferences with the most resources and generally reaping the benefits through high-profile visibility and competitive success were still being out-voted by the smaller conferences. In 2008, Division I restructured its governance instituting weighted voting based on whether the conferences were in the Football Bowl Subdivision (FBS), Football Championships Subdivision (FCS) or were conferences not offering football (NCAA, 2009). Under the new weighted system, FBS conferences collectively could out-vote the combined votes of the FCS and non-football playing conferences. The FCS and non-football playing conferences supported the change, as there was an opportunity to override legislation on an institutional roll call vote and for fear of the FBS schools breaking away from the NCAA.

The roll call override was quite effective, as the most successful FBS conferences enacted legislation only to have it repealed months later. This led to the most recent restructuring of Division I governance, when the NCAA Division I Board of Directors approved an even more weighted system on 7 August 2014 favoring the five most powerful athletics conferences – the Atlantic Coast Conference, Big 12, Big Ten, Pac-12 and Southeastern Conference – commonly known as the Autonomy 5 or the Power 5 conferences (Division I Governance, n.d.).

Current NCAA governance structure

The NCAA's core values are listed below.

- The collegiate model of athletics in which students participate as an avocation, balancing their academic, social and athletics experiences.
- The highest levels of integrity and sportsmanship.

- The pursuit of excellence in both academics and athletics.
- The supporting role that intercollegiate athletics plays in the higher education mission and in enhancing the sense of community and strengthening the identity of member institutions.
- An inclusive culture that fosters equitable participation for student-athletes and career opportunities for coaches and administrators from diverse backgrounds.
- Respect for institutional autonomy and philosophical differences.
- Presidential leadership of intercollegiate athletics at the campus, conference and national levels. (247 Sports, 2019)

Association-wide governance

The highest level of association-wide leadership is the Board of Governors. Sixteen university chancellors or presidents are voting members, with weighted representation as follows: eight FBS institutions, two FCS institutions, two non-football institutions in Division I, two Division II President's Council members and two Division III President's Council members. The chairs of the Division I Council and the Division II and III Management Councils serve as *ex officio* non-voting members. The President of the NCAA is also *ex officio*, but casts the deciding vote in the event of a tie (NCAA, 2018a, Bylaw 4.1). The Board of Governors provides strategic planning for the Association, including identifying core issues and adopting and implementing measures to resolve those issues. The board also provides oversight of the NCAA budget, employs the NCAA president and initiates and settles litigation (NCAA, 2018a, Bylaw 4.1.2). Representatives on the Board of Governors are appointed by the Division I Board of Directors and Division II and III Presidents Councils.

Divisional governance

The next layer of NCAA governance are the divisional boards that establish the strategic vision, policies and regulations for each division. While Division II and III are represented solely by institutional presidents or chancellors, Division I representation includes two athletics administrators, a faculty athletics representative and a student-athlete. Diversity and inclusion are required for the governing boards and for committees other than sport committees. A minimum of one person who is an ethnic minority and one person of each gender is required, with a combined leadership goal of 20 percent ethnic minority and 35 percent women representation (NCAA, 2018a, Bylaw 4.02.5).

The Division I Board of Directors is made up of 24 representatives: 20 presidents or chancellors, one athletics director, one senior woman administrator, one faculty athletics representative and one student athlete. The group of presidents or chancellors are heavily weighted, with one representative chosen by each of the ten largest conferences, five chosen from the top 11 FCS conferences and the remaining five from the top 11 non-football conferences (NCAA, 2018a, Bylaw 4.2).

The Division II Presidents Council is based on a weighted regional representation system with one president or chancellor for every 22 institutions in that region. Two at-large positions were added to represent independent institutions and enhance diversity. To include more institutional representation, an institution cannot have more than one representative on either the DII Presidents Council or the DII Management Council. The role of the DII Presidents Council is to implement association-wide policies in Division II and establish a strategic plan and direct the general policy for the division. The Division II Presidents Council can adopt non-controversial legislation, can sponsor legislation to be voted upon by the membership and can grant exemptions from legislation in exceptional circumstances. The Division II Presidents Council also develops and approves the budget and administration of Division II Championships among other tasks. Members of the DII Presidents Council serve four-year terms, are not immediately eligible for re-election and cannot serve more than two terms total (NCAA, 2018b).

The Division III Presidents Council includes 18 presidents or chancellors, with a minimum of two representatives from each of the geographic divisions and seven at-large members. With the largest number of institutional members, Division III assures representation based on institutional diversity with a minimum of three presidents or chancellors from institutions with undergraduate enrollments of 2,400 or more; three from institutions with undergraduate enrollments between 1,400 and 2,400; three from institutions with less than 1,400 undergraduate students and a minimum of three representative each from public and private schools. Gender and ethnic minority diversity is also considered with a minimum of four male and four female representatives and at least two ethnic minorities. The role of the DIII Presidents Council is to implement association-wide policies in Division III and establish a strategic plan and direct the general policy for the division. The Division III Presidents Council can adopt non-controversial legislation and can sponsor legislation to be voted upon by the membership. The Division II Presidents Council may ratify, amend or rescind actions of the DIII Management Council. Division III budget recommendations and administration of championships are included among other tasks. Members of the Division III Presidents Council serve four-year terms, cannot be re-elected for at least two years after their initial term expires and cannot serve more than two total terms (NCAA, 2018c).

Management councils

The third layer of NCAA governance consists of the Division I Council and the Division II and III Management Councils. The Division I Council has 40 members including athletics administrators, faculty athletics representatives and conference administrators. Each conference is represented by one individual. Additionally, four conference commissioners are included, with two representing the ten strongest Division I conferences and the other two representing the 24 remaining conferences. The two faculty athletics representatives are designated by the 1A Faculty Athletics Representatives group and the Faculty Athletics Representatives Association. Student-athletes fill the remaining two positions. The primary responsibility of the DI Council is as the legislative authority and supervising qualification procedures for the NCAA Division I post-season championships. The DI Council utilises weighted voting: Representatives of the Autonomy 5 conferences and associated conference commissioners have 4 votes each; representatives of the next five conferences and associated conference commissioners have two votes each; and all remaining representatives, conference commissioners, faculty athletics representatives and student-athlete representatives have one vote each. Football-related matters are addressed separately by FBS or FCS division and also employ weighted voting (NCAA, 2018a, Bylaw 4.3).

The Division II Management Council includes athletics administrators, faculty athletics representatives and student-athletes. Each of the DII multisport voting conferences is represented by an administrator, with two at-large positions for diversity and two student-athletes from the DII Student-Athlete Advisory committee. Diversity efforts include a minimum of four athletics directors, four senior woman administrators, four faculty athletics representatives and one conference administrator. The primary duties of the DII Management Council involve implementing the policies of the Association, interpreting Division II bylaws, supervising the DII committees and acting on enforcement appeals (NCAA, 2018b).

The Division III Management Council is comprised of 21 members with inclusive representation from various perspectives and the minimum number of each type: Two presidents or chancellors, two other administrators serving in a direct-report role over athletics, two faculty athletics representatives, nine athletics directors or senior woman administrators, two student-athletes and conference representatives. At least two members are from each Division III-designated geographic region, three ethnic minorities and eight men and eight women. The primary duties of the Division III Management Council are to implement policies adopted by the Association, make recommendations on Division III matters, supervise budgets and championships and resolve Division III issues (NCAA DIII Manual, 2018, Bylaw 4.8).

Annual convention

As noted in the brief history of the NCAA, members meet annually to discuss the business of the NCAA, vote on legislation and engage in round-table discussions of matters of general interest. Legislation that applies to all NCAA members requires a two-thirds majority vote of all delegates present at the annual convention. Otherwise, members of Divisions II and III address their respective legislative proposals and amendments in their business sessions. Division I members vote only for Association-wide matters, as legislation is enacted through the Council and Board of Directors, with special provisions for the Autonomy 5 conferences. Autonomy legislation must align with the values of higher education and advance the educational and athletics-related needs of student-athletes. This allows flexibility for these conferences to utilise their resources to enact legislation for student-athlete well-being without interference from lower-resource institutions and conference. All autonomy legislation becomes permissive for the remaining Division I members (NCAA, 2018a, Bylaw 5.3.2.1).

NCAA national office

The NCAA employs more than 350 people at its headquarters in Indianapolis, Indiana. It is important to note the NCAA is its member institutions, as previously discussed. The national office exists to serve the membership and is organised into ten administrative groups, namely executive team, executive affairs, governance, membership services, championships, enforcement, finance and information services, marketing and public affairs. While media and fans often expect the NCAA to solve all of the issues in college athletics, the national office does not have independent rule-making authority over the membership. Similarly, the president of the NCAA, while influential, is not the equivalent of a professional sport commissioner with almost unlimited power.

The role of athletic conferences

As college athletic teams began to proliferate, it was natural for institutions of similar size, academic philosophy, admissions requirements and financial resources to unite and establish uniform playing rules and schedules for their students. Conferences were originally formed around a single sport, with students creating the Intercollegiate Football Association in 1876. Over time, conferences became independent organisations with constitutions and bylaws defining their purpose and mission and their members' responsibilities. The first multisport college athletics conference was the Michigan Intercollegiate Athletic Conference, founded on 24 March 1888 and still operating as a NCAA Division III athletic conference. The Intercollegiate Conference of Faculty Representatives was formed on 11 January 1895, as the first faculty-controlled athletics conference. This organisation is also still operating today as the Big Ten, one of the Autonomy 5 conferences (Smith, 2011).

Athletics conferences have an important role in the governance of college athletics in the United States. The NCAA defines a conference as a group of colleges and/or universities that conducts competition among its members and determines a conference champion in one or more sports (NCAA, 2018a). NCAA recognised member conferences as having the same privileges as institutional members. Conference champions in NCAA-sponsored sports may participate as automatic qualifiers for post-season tournaments in many sports. The NCAA also streamlines some of its administrative load by working through the conference offices.

The organisation of a conference can vary tremendously. Some smaller NCAA Division III conferences operate as voluntary cooperatives in which athletics administrators from member programs carry out leadership and administrative tasks on an assigned or rotating basis. At the other end of the spectrum, most NCAA Division I FBS conferences employ a conference commissioner and a large staff of administrators to provide a wide range of services and generate additional revenue for conference members. While the largest conferences still facilitate scheduling and sponsor conference championships, they have also expanded to handle officiating bureaus, legislative services and rules compliance, education and interpretation.

Conferences also actively promote themselves and their championships through marketing, public relations, media relations and athletics communication. Conference games and championships are broadcast through a variety of television, radio and digital communication platforms that are either produced or procured by the conference. Some conferences own their own television networks. Additional revenues are generated through the sale of conference-licensed merchandise and apparel, through either online stores or physical storefronts – for example, the Atlantic Coast Conference (ACC) stores and restaurants in malls and airports.

In addition, conferences provide leadership, governance and professional development opportunities for athletics administrators and student-athletes of member institutions. Various parties – including presidents, athletics directors, senior women administrators, faculty athletics representatives, coaches, athletics trainers, sports information and athletics communication directors and other athletics administrators or personnel – meet regularly to discuss possible or proposed legislation, issues and concerns related to scheduling and conference championships and various hot topics in intercollegiate athletics. These meetings promote the exchange of ideas and best practices, determine conference policy and provide networking opportunities.

Conference governance is generally determined through member representation, and the conference commissioner and administrators execute the wishes of the membership. However, as the face of the conference, the commissioner generally also possesses a strong voice in discussions about conference policy and may represent conference members in NCAA governance matters. The voice of athletes is represented at the conference level through the conference-sponsored Student-Athlete Advisory Council, through which athletes share ideas, discuss issues and vote whether to support proposed legislation. Conferences may also support students by providing postgraduate scholarships or internship opportunities.

Institutional control

Although the governance and regulation of intercollegiate athletics may appear to be a top-down endeavour, the voluntary nature of membership and enforcement necessitates compliance from the bottom up. The NCAA philosophy of institutional control provides autonomy for the institution to make its own decisions and control its own destiny in choosing what sports to offer, allocating resources and determining the appropriate balance between academics and athletics. However, because intercollegiate sport cannot exist without rules, institutional autonomy is somewhat problematic in the context of athletics competition. From a governance perspective, sport organisations must balance the need of every institution to chart its own course with the need for all competitors to follow the same rules and achieve a standard of fairness on the playing field. Institutional control involves the ability of the college or university to operate the athletics department in a way that abides by the spirit and the letter of the governing rules (NCAA, 2018a, Bylaw 6).

As evidenced by the NCAA governance structure, the organisation operates under a philosophy of presidential control, which extends to the institutional member. The president of the academic institution is the ultimate authority in institutional control of the intercollegiate athletics program. While athletics is only one department within the educational institution, it may generate more attention than most other university departments combined. It is the responsibility of the president to retain a holistic view of the institution's mission and determine what role the athletics department plays in achieving that mission. In theory, the president occupies the best position from which to establish the culture and set the rules and limits for the athletics program. In reality, because the president is responsible for the entire academic institution, he or she may not be particularly interested in devoting much time to the athletics department nor be sufficiently educated about relevant issues to make informed athletics policy decisions.

The athletics director (AD) bears ultimate responsibility for everything that goes on in the athletics program. As the leader of the athletics department, the AD establishes the program's internal compliance culture and serves as the face of the program. An athletics director's job description can vary widely, depending on the type of institution. At smaller institutions with fewer athletics administrators, the AD is tasked with specific duties and general supervisory responsibility, whereas the AD of a larger program assumes a general supervisory role. The AD usually holds approval authority over all athletics department policies and procedures and represents the institution at the conference and national levels. Additionally, institutions are required to designate a Senior Woman Administrator (SWA) who is to be involved in the management of the athletics department (NCAA, 2018a, Bylaw 4.02.4). While there is no specific position description for the SWA designation, this female administrator is not limited to working with women's athletics.

Faculty retain a role in institutional, conference and NCAA governance. The rationale for faculty governance hinges on the educational foundation of intercollegiate athletics and on overarching faculty concern for the students for whom the enterprise exists. However, the role and authority of faculty members on their individual campuses vary depending on institutional structures. A study of faculty governance across thirty-two institutions in three major athletics conferences analysed formal governing documents detailing the role and authority of faculty governing bodies. The study reported minimal faculty participation and authority; participatory faculty committees assumed responsibility for the quality of athletics programs and operation at only two schools (Minor & Perry, 2010). Though few athletics programs appear to operate with a formal faculty advisory committee, many athletic departments do voluntarily include faculty members on a variety of athletic department committees to help bridge the gap between athletics and the academy. Examples include student-athlete academic support advisory committees, Title IX committees and committees related to student-athlete admissions.

The NCAA requires faculty to have a formal role in athletics governance through the role of the Faculty Athletics Representative (FAR) (NCAA, 2018a Bylaw 4.02.2). The FAR is a faculty member or administrator with faculty rank who does not hold a position in the athletics department. The FAR formally represents the view of the faculty in advising the institution's president on athletics-related issues and plays a key communication role on campus by informing the faculty about athletics issues, policies and procedures. Other duties of the FAR vary depending on the academic institution, but most FARs are involved in academic oversight of the athletics program and in ensuring the welfare of student-athletes. The role requires substantial knowledge of university, conference and NCAA rules because the FAR represents the university on various conference and NCAA committees and may serve as the institution's voting delegate if the president is unavailable.

Legally, student-athletes are third-party beneficiaries of the contractual relationship between the institution and its affiliated athletics conference and of the institution's membership in the NCAA. The NCAA requires each institution to establish a Student-Athlete Advisory Committee (SAAC) to provide student-athletes with a voice in the management of the athletics program (NCAA, 2018a, Bylaw 6.1.4). The institutional role of SAAC is not defined, but SAAC members are often leaders on their teams and in service on their campus and in the community.

Conclusion

Governance challenges in intercollegiate athletics and the need for future research

As college sport in the US has evolved from independently operated intercollegiate competitions in a few sports to a multi-billion-dollar industry with high-stakes financial incentives and refined legislative processes, there has been an ever-present tension between the often-conflicting value systems of a student-centric educational enterprise and the competitive entertainment industry. At the institutional level, philosophical tension between the sanctity of the academy as a forum for intellectual exploration and the commercial enticements and financial demands necessary for programs to maintain competitive parity in Division I has facilitated unprincipled behaviour based on a win-at-all costs mentality (Byers, 1996; Desrochers, 2013; Oriard, 2001; Smith, 2011). The actions and policies of the NCAA and its member institutions have been questioned in a burgeoning body of litigation and literature condemning the industry of college sport for its excessive spending; manipulation, exploitation and mistreatment of athletes; and unprincipled methods that have undermined undergraduate education and university operations (Benford, 2007; Sack & Staurowsky, 1998; Sperber, 2000). Calls for reform have been well chronicled (Byers, 1996; Desrochers, 2013; Oriard, 2001; Smith 2011; Thelin, 1996), but actual reform has largely been driven by legal and societal pressure. Each era of reform has been reactive rather than proactive, and temporary, incremental solutions have been enacted to address symptoms of deeper problems. As noted in this chapter, several researchers have chronicled the history of NCAA governance (Smith, 2000; Smith, 2011; Thelin, 1996), but investigation of the impact of the changes in the governance structure and the outcomes for the organisation, its membership and student-athlete beneficiaries, is needed. These broad research topics are explored below.

Institutional control

The NCAA is often blamed generally for the failures of its members, while its members are the ones creating the rules. Many of the scandals plaguing intercollegiate athletics (academic fraud, coach abuse, bribery and fraud) are the result of individual choices to ignore rules and institutional choices to ignore bad behaviour. The difficulty with this governance structure is that every leadership group effectually feels powerless. Institutional athletic directors report to university presidents. University presidents, largely uneducated in the governance structure of intercollegiate athletics, rely on their athletics directors, compliance personnel and conference colleagues to guide them as they navigate athletics-related issues. Conference commissioners report to university presidents, yet they organise and lead conference meetings and processes to designate representatives at the NCAA level. This organisational structure creates a culture filled with leaders who feel powerless to effect significant change (Frey, 1987; Weight, Weight & Schneider, 2013) and perpetuate the passivity relative to "the system" wherein actors simply follow the rules and equate "rule-following" with right or ethical behaviour (Sagas & Wigley, 2014).

Research is needed to examine whether the NCAA's issues are organisational, institutional or inherent in every voluntary membership organisation (Washington, Forman, Suddaby & Ventresca, 2005). Previous research has examined value-based decision-making in college athletics at the institutional level (Cooper, Weight & Pierce, 2014). Authors concluded a leader–value continuum exists within athletic department administrative practices. On the most efficient and transformational side resides administrators who fully embrace values of holistic development through sport and integrate these values into the fabric of the department and decision-making processes. In the middle of the continuum reside administrators who believe the values to be important, and aspire to have the organisation embrace them, but have not built systematic culturalisation of the values. Finally, at the inefficient and ethically questionable end of the continuum, reside administrators who embrace a hypocritical-value approach. Administrators claim values are important, but defy the values they proclaim in culture and decision-making (Cooper et al., 2014). Researchers could utilise this framework to examine the NCAA and its leadership. Related studies could include the impact of member self-interest on organisational governance and how the governance of intercollegiate athletics in the US differs from the governance of other voluntary organizations (Washington et al., 2005).

Organisational values and organisational structure

The core values of the NCAA have been a source of continual debate, revisions and subtle edits as the governance structure has evolved through the various iterations of student-led, faculty-led and administration led – both athletics and/or presidential – leadership. An examination of these changes and the motivators for change could shed light on the forces pushing and pulling the governance of this organisation. "The Collegiate Model", a surrogate term for "amateurism" is an interesting modern example of this process as explored by Southall and Staurowsky (2013). The transition from democratic governance (one-institution, one-vote) to Divisional governance (DI, DII, DIII) to weighted representative governance (in the overall governance and in Division I) would also be an interesting lens through which to view the organisational values and culture. The NCAA is a complex organisation of almost 1,200 academic institutions from all 50 states serving over 460,000 student-athletes. It would be interesting to research how changes in the governance structure have impacted various groups of member–institutions such as the Autonomy 5 conferences, DI FBS, DI FCS, DI, DII and DIII. Is it possible for an organisation with such a diverse membership to effectively represent the interests of all members, and can such a governance organisation control members' constant efforts to gain competitive advantage?

Throughout the history of college athletics, entities external to the governance of the organisation have offered their opinions on reforms to improve intercollegiate athletics (Knight Commission on Intercollegiate Athletics, 2010; Savage, 1929). At the 2019 NCAA Convention,

the membership boldly voted to add five independent representatives outside of higher education to its Board of Governors (Bauer-Wolf, 2019). The extraordinary change to the governance
structure is expected to "enhance the association by injecting our governance processes with
new perspectives, greater diversity of experience and increased levels of objectivity" (Bauer-Wolf,
2019, p. 4). Similarly, the NCAA has modified its enforcement process to include independent
investigators to avoid conflicts of interest for complex cases involving potential violations of core
values (Independent Investigators and Decision Makers, 2018). Further research is needed to
investigate the impact of external constituencies on the governance of college athletics, how the
reports and recommendations of external constituencies have impacted the governance of the
NCAA and whether outside organisations are better equipped to develop policy than members.

The NCAA is the holistic product of member institutions who make, bend, amend and break
the rules while governing intercollegiate athletics. A shared interest brings unique institutions
together to facilitate education, community experiences and institutional branding through
athletics. These institutions simultaneously compete with one another for wins, which, at the
highest level, can be worth millions of dollars. The self-interest of the individual schools or
divisions of schools can influence the types of rules that govern fair play. There is a large body
of research outlining issues within intercollegiate athletics; but there is also a tremendous void
in the literature addressing the impact of governance decisions, and a lack of research to aid in
providing solutions to the issues ailing the industry. As the NCAA has evolved, a patchwork
approach towards governance has been implemented resulting in a 450-page rule book full of
short-term fixes, logical-at-the-time solutions and regulations that can be counter to the core
values of the organisation. Independent research, as outlined above, is necessary to inform the
membership as regulations, enforcement practices and governance structures continue to evolve.

References

247 Sports. (2019). Just So You Know – NCAA Mission Statement/Core Values. Retrieved 13 October
2019, from https://247sports.com/college/louisville/Board/103990/Contents/Just-so-you-know-
NCAA-mission-statementcore-values-71943907/

Bauer-Wolf, J. (2019, January 22). NCAA adds five independent governing board members. Retrieved
from https://www.insidehighered.com

Benford, R. (2007). The College sports reform movement; Reframing the "edutainment" industry. *The
Sociological Quarterly*, 48(1), 1–28.

Byers, W. (1996). *Unsportsmanlike conduct: Exploiting college athletes*. Ann Arbor, MI: University of Michigan
Press.

Carpenter, L. J. (1993). Letters home: My life with Title IX. In G. L. Cohen (Ed.), *Women in sport: Issues and
controversies* (pp. 133–155), Newberry Park, CA. Sage Publishing.

Cooper, C. G., Weight, E. A., & Pierce, D. (2014). The leader-value continuum: NCAA Division I core
values and transformational leadership. *The International Journal of Sport Management*, 15, 1–21.

Desrochers, D. (2013). *Academic spending versus athletic spending: Who wins?* Washington, DC: American
Institutes for Research.

Division I Governance. (n.d.). Retrieved 10 January 2019, from http://www.ncaa.org/governance?divi
sion=d1

Frey, J. H. (1987). Institutional control of athletics: An analysis of the role played by presidents, faculty,
trustees, alumni, and the NCAA. *Journal of Sport and Social Issues*, 11(12), 49–59.

Independent Investigators and Decision Makers. (2018). Retrieved 10 January 2019, from http://www
.ncaa.org/about/independent-investigators-and-decision-makers

Knight Commission on Intercollegiate Athletics. (2010). *Restoring the balance: Dollars, values, and the future of
college sport*. Retrieved 10 January 2019, from http://www.knightcommission.org

Lewis, G. (1970). The beginning of organized collegiate sport. *American Quarterly*, 22, 222–229.

Minor, J. T., & Perry, L. (2010). Faculty involvement in athletic decision making: A review of three athletic
major conferences. Retrieved 10 January 2019, from farawebsite.org

Murphy, C. (2019). Madness Inc. Retrieved 10 January 2019, from https://www.murphy.senate.gov/downl
oad/madness-inc

National Collegiate Athletic Association (NCAA). (2009). *NCAA Division I Manual (2008–2009)*. Indianapolis, IN: Author.

National Collegiate Athletic Association (NCAA). (2018a). *NCAA Division I Manual (2018–2019)*. Indianapolis, IN: Author.

National Collegiate Athletic Association (NCAA). (2018b). *NCAA Division II Manual (2018–2019)*. Indianapolis, IN: Author.

National Collegiate Athletic Association (NCAA). (2018c). *NCAA Division III Manual (2018–2019)*. Indianapolis, IN: Author.

Oriard, M. (2001). *King football: Sport & spectacle in the golden age of radio & newsreels, movies & magazines, the weekly & daily presses*. Chapel Hill, NC: The University of North Carolina Press.

Sack, A. L., & Staurowsky, E. J. (1998). *College athletes for hire: The evolution and legacy of the NCAA's amateur myth*. Westport, CT: Praeger Publishers.

Sagas, M., & Wigley, B. J. (2014). Gray area ethical leadership in the NCAA: The ethics of doing the wrong things right. *Journal of Intercollegiate Sport, 7*(1), 40–57.

Savage, H. J. (1929). *American college athletics*. New York: The Carnegie Foundation for the Advancement of Teaching. Retrieved 10 January 2019, from http://archive.carnegiefoundation.org/pdfs/elibrary/Ame rican_College_Athletics.pdf

Smith, R. A. (2011). *Pay for play: A history of big-time college athletic reform*. Urbana, Chicago, and Springfield, Illinois: University of Illinois Press.

Smith, R. K. (2000). A brief history of the National Collegiate Athletic Association's role in regulating college athletics. *Marquette Sports Law Review, 11*(1), 9–22.

Southall, R. M., & Staurowsky, E. J. (2013). Cheering on the collegiate model: Creating, disseminating, and imbedding the NCAA's redefinition of amateurism. *Journal of Sport and Social Issues, 37*, 403–429.

Sperber, M. A. (2000). *Beer and circus: How big-time college sports is crippling undergraduate education*. New York: Henry Holt and Co.

Thelin, J. (1996). *Games colleges play: Scandal and reform in intercollegiate athletics*. Baltimore, MD: Johns Hopkins University Press.

Washington, M., Forman, P. J., Suddaby, R., & Ventresca, M. (2005, June). The governance of US collegiate athletics. In *Qualitative organizational research volume 1: Best papers from the Davis conference on qualitative research* (p. 113). Greenwich, CT: IAP.

Weight, E., Weight, M., & Schneider, R. (2013). Confronting the arms race: Conference commissioner perspectives on spending within intercollegiate athletics. *The International Journal of Sport Management, 14*(4), 1–21.

Wilson, J. R. (2005). *The history of the National Association of Intercollegiate Athletics: Competition, tradition, character*. Monterey, CA: Coaches Choice Books.

15

Sport event governance models

Becca Leopkey and Milena M. Parent

Introduction

The increasing prevalence and importance of events on the global calendar has led to the development of a burgeoning literature on event studies. An event is a term that can be used to describe a variety of different occurrences; however, it is most commonly associated with the notion of something that happens (Getz, 2007). In the context of this paper, the focus is on "planned events", more specifically, events that include the purposeful organisation of sporting competitions.

There is considerable ambiguity in defining sports events. Many terms including large-scale (cf. Leopkey & Parent, 2009; Parent, 2005), hallmark (cf. Hall, 1992; Whitson & Macintosh, 1993) and mega (cf. Getz, 1989; Horne & Manzenreiter, 2006) sports events, are utilised to characterise varying levels of sport competitions by both academics and practitioners. For example, hallmark events have been described as events that occur regularly in a particular location (Getz, 2007), while others (Hall, 1992; Ritchie, 1984) maintain hallmark events are one-off in nature and are hosted to help draw interest to a local tourism market. Either way, a hallmark sport event can garner legacies for the local region that generally last longer than the event itself and can play a pivotal role in the development of tourism marketing strategies (cf. Ritchie, 1984; Ritchie & Smith, 1991). In addition, hosting the event often relies on public support in the form of tax dollars or savings and has a multifaceted (e.g., cultural, social, economic and infrastructural) impact on the area. Arguably, the defining feature of a hallmark sport event is its relevance to the host community. Todd, Lease and Ensor (2017) emphasised the importance of a hallmark event's impact on the international recognition of the host destination by stating the event and the host city/region "become tangibly and symbolically embedded as permanent institutions within their community or culture" (p. 495).

A mega-sport event, on the other hand, can be described as a massive hallmark event due to the sizeable planning and preparation for the event, as well as cost, infrastructure development, media coverage, international relevance and mass popular appeal (Hall, 1989, 1992; Horne & Manzenreiter, 2006; Roche, 2000). By way of contrast, a large or major sport event may receive less recognition, but it will still attract over 1000 spectators/participants and thus can still result in significant impacts on the host (Emery, 2001). Examples of large/major sports events include the Asian Games, the Pan and Parapan American Games, the World Masters' Games, the Commonwealth

Games and the Youth Olympic Games. In fact, many of these events, especially those for whom athletes' villages and/or internal Games transportation are not provided, can garner greater positive impacts (e.g., economic) for the host region than the larger/mega sports events.

Hosting any of these sports events is a complex project requiring an extensive collective effort on the part of various individuals, groups and organisations (stakeholders) if the event is to be successful. Coordinating these stakeholders is one part of event governance. As such, understanding sport event governance means understanding the structures, processes, constellation of stakeholders and institutional dimensions of the given sport event (cf. Parent, 2016a). In keeping with the theme of this handbook, the purpose of this chapter is therefore to explore ownership models used in the governance of sports events. To do so, an overview of event governance research is provided, followed by event ownership models and event stakeholders. The chapter also examines a contemporary issue in event governance research, namely, sport event legacy governance. The chapter concludes with a critical analysis of existing research, future governance challenges and research opportunities.

Event governance

In a scoping review of the sport governance literature, Dowling, Leopkey and Smith (2018) identified sports events as one of seven main research contexts in the broader sport governance field. They found the majority of the sport event governance research investigated large and mega sports events, with a strong focus on the Olympic Movement. Moreover, event-related research questions adopted a systematic governance perspective (i.e., an area of focus that looks at the key shifts in the way sport organisations are organised and controlled), while paying relatively little attention to political (i.e., a focus on how government bodies steer the behaviour of organisations) and organisational (i.e., a focus on normative and ethically informed behaviours) forms of governance.

Early research on event governance focused on exploring the roles of government, state or parastatal agencies and policy networks; however, the work was limited and descriptive in nature (e.g., Getz & Andersson, 2008; Weed, 2003). Other research exists on the governance of some of the key stakeholders involved in sport event hosting, particularly related to the Olympic Movement. Geereart, Alm and Groll (2014), Geeraert, Mrkonjic and Chappelet (2015) and Chappelet and Kübler-Mabbott (2008), for example, focused on the International Olympic Committee and other international sport governing bodies. Geeraert et al. (2014) argued international sport governing bodies continued to utilise flawed governance practices, which included a lack of accountability arrangements, little transparency with regards to the distribution of monies to association members, a board leadership that reflected a Eurocentric dominance and a severe lack of female representation. Geeraert et al. (2015) confirmed the notion that international sport governing bodies' autonomy, or ability, to self-govern was evolving into a more networked form of governance, where different stakeholders exerted power at different times and in varying contexts. In supporting this notion, the authors identified four different types of autonomy (political, legal, financial and pyramidal), as well as the threats and counterstrategies (e.g., a move to a steering role in the network) used by the sport governing bodies to combat their loss of control (Geeraert et al., 2015). In addition, Chappelet and Kübler-Mabbott (2008) argued there were five governance levels within the Olympic Movement:

1) Management: IOC administration itself and its effective/efficient day-to-day operations;
2) Corporate governance: IOC Session and Executive Board (i.e., the IOC's decision-making structure and control);

3) Governance management: IOC members and IOC commissions "are capable and worthy of fulfilling their role" (p. 176);

4) Harmonisation: Mechanisms for decision challenges and mechanism coordination with those other relevant organisations; and

5) Meta-governance: Respecting fundamental principles related to universal moral and human rights, as stated in international constitutional texts/treaties.

Event governance principles

Based on the analysis of these different levels as well as key Olympic stakeholders, Chappelet and Kübler-Mabbott (2008) suggested five governance principles for the Olympic Movement, namely 1) transparency; 2) democracy; 3) accountability to stakeholders; 4) autonomy from government and corporate backers; and (5) social responsibility (i.e., ensuring Olympic stakeholder activities serve the society). In turn, Parent (2016a) suggested the Canadian Olympic governance model included appropriate leadership, organising committee structural flexibility, a country-wide planned/coordinated stakeholder engagement mechanism, knowledge-seeking activities and a willingness or desire to innovate behind the scenes (management-wise).

Notwithstanding the above works by Chappelet and Kübler-Mabbott (2008) and Parent (2016a) on Olympic Movement governance principles, more recent studies have begun to understand and address broader event governance issues, irrespective of the specific event. Whitford, Phi and Dredge (2014) presented a set of indicators that can help evaluate event governance effectiveness. The principles used to create the set of event governance indicators included relevance, reliability, completeness, clarity, timeliness, verifiability and diversity.

Parent (2016b) addressed different event stakeholder views on the democratic governance process. Results revealed that the accountability, transparency and stakeholder participation principles should be separated into internal and external aspects in order to better understand the governance of sport events. In turn, Geeraert (2017) attempted to theorise the governance of sport mega-events by relying on insights from the principle–agent perspective (cf. Geeraert & Drieskens, 2015). Notably, Geeraert (2017) pointed to how problems such as conflicts of interest and information asymmetries between principals and agents affected the event governance network. To help overcome these issues, the use of control mechanisms including screening processes, contract design, compensation schemes and institutional checks to help moderate stakeholder behaviour within the system were proposed.

Event governance process

Broadly speaking, sports events go through similar phases or modes in their lifecycle, each one having particular goals, issues and stakeholder networks (see Figure 15.1; Parent, 2008; Parent & Smith-Swan, 2013):

- **Bid**: A bid committee is constituted, which will contest for the right to host a particular edition of a sport event at the national and international levels. This (usually) independently incorporated organisation normally hopes to win the right to host the event. However, there are different types of bids; some bids are put together just to garner visibility and/or media attention (i.e., alibi bid) or as a preparation for a future bid (i.e., warm-up bid) (Chappelet, 2005). Notwithstanding, the typical process is to have an idea (origin of the idea), conduct a feasibility study, obtain local political and business support and then go through the formal bidding process as determined by the event rights owner (e.g., Panam

Figure 15.1 Generic sport event stakeholder map.

Sports for the Pan and Parapan American Games and Commonwealth Games Federation for the Commonwealth Games). If there are national and international-level competitions, there will be differences in the stakeholder network relationships (Hautbois, Parent & Séguin, 2012). Finally, it is in this phase (or even before) that potential legacies are conceptualised (Leopkey & Parent, 2017).

- **Transition**: A "successful" sport event governance process will see a six-to-eight-month pre-planned transition phase, where the winning bid committee dissolves and the organising committee is created/incorporated following a particular event governance model (see next section). The transition should be detailed in an agreement signed by the key event partners during the bid process, outlining the legal form and constitution of the future organising committee. For example, the key partners (i.e., the bid committee, host governments, Canadian Olympic and Paralympic committees and Four Host First Nations) of the future Vancouver 2010 Olympic and Paralympic Winter Games signed a multi-party agreement in 2003 during the bid phase (Parent, Rouillard & Leopkey, 2011). The organising committee's first task, one which ends the transition phase, is choosing the organising committee leader.

- **Planning**: In this phase, the organising committee leader creates the organisational structure and develops (with key workforce and stakeholders) the business plan, operational plan and divisional plans or work packages. This phase lasts about half the organising committee's life.

- **Implementation, operationalisation or execution**: Once the conceptual plans are created, they are operationalised or "venuised", meaning they are integrated for each venue of the event, thereby creating specific venue plans. Whereas the planning phase was rather siloed or vertical in nature and termed the "headquarter-centred organising committee", the implementation phase is cross-cutting or horizontal and termed "venue-centred", as integration and coordination between event functions/divisions is key (Parent & Séguin, 2010). After this, the organising committee often breaks itself up into mini-organising committees or venue teams and executes the event itself.

- **Wrap-up**: This phase starts the moment the closing ceremonies are completed. While most workforce members will leave, a core group will remain with the tasks of decommissioning the venues and turning them into their post-event formats, debriefing, writing the final reports, pursuing any legal issues noted during the event (e.g., ambush marketing problems) and transferring legacy responsibilities to previously identified stakeholders (see below). Once these tasks are completed, the organising committee dissolves. During this phase, the organising committee is, once again, headquarter-centred, but it is undertaking performative routines (i.e., those noted above), unlike the ostensive routines undertaken during the planning phase (Parent & Séguin, 2010).

Event governance structure: The organising committee

The central actor, which coordinates the network of stakeholders in a sport event, is usually the organising committee (Parent, 2015). As the event grows larger and becomes more complex, additional workforce and stakeholders are required to play a role in the event governance network (see the section below on event stakeholders).

Event owners (see below) have different options in terms of the organising committee's legal constitution (Getz, 2005). In much of the Western World, large-scale, major and mega events are legally incorporated as a not-for-profit, association, or foundation organisations, such as the organising committees of the London 2012 Olympic and Paralympic Games, the Glasgow 2014 Commonwealth Games, the Toronto 2015 Pan and Parapan American Games and the Gold Coast 2018 Commonwealth Games. However, two other legal constitution options are possible: 1) A public or para-public organisation, essentially an arm of one host government, as was the case with the Beijing 2008 Olympic Games and with the organising committees of the Jeux de la Francophonie when hosted in developing nations, or 2) as a private/for-profit organisation, as is the case with the annual Montreal (Canada) Formula One race and the Red Bull Cliff-Diving World Series.

The legal constitution of an event organising committee is one way to describe its structure. Another way is by the kind of organisation it is. Getz (2005) argued organising committees can be independent organisations created by the key event partners, as is the case with the not-for-profit option noted above. But, "organising committees" can also be found within another organisation, such as an event department within a public or private organisation; in this case the event owner (the public or private organisation) takes the lead in organising the event, including key partners and other stakeholders if and when necessary. The third option is to create a strategic alliance between two key partners and, together, these partners organise the event. In this latter case, however, the strategic alliance "organising committee" must follow strategic alliance best practices (cf. Child & Faulkner, 1998; Faulkner, 1995; Kanter, 2002; Parent, Séguin, Gagné Côté, Leblond & Laperle, 2009).

One key distinction worth noting in terms of organising committees and event governance is the distinction between the role of the board (if present) and the rest of the organising committee (the workforce, especially paid staff and volunteers). The board has a broader strategic or governance role. It is often where the local politics and urban regimes come into play. Sociologists often use the term "organising committee" but they often mean the actors and actions associated with the board. In contrast, the workforce is concerned with the day-to-day operations and event preparations/readiness. Politics can be found at this level, but they are organisational politics, not urban regime-related politics. Management researchers and practitioners usually focus on this level of the organising committee. Still many people (e.g., critical researchers, the media and the general public) sometimes confuse the two. For more information, see Parent (2015).

Although event ownership models are described in the next section, it is worthwhile to explain the structure of the organising committee. Certain events have a single organising committee, which may or may not break up into venue teams come event time, if it is for a multi-sport versus a single-sport event, respectively. In contrast, other events may have a main organising committee and local organising committees (LOCs) if the event takes place in multiple locations, such as for the Fédération Internationale de Football Association (FIFA) World Cup. LOC functions remain largely the same, in that they are operationally-focused in a particular venue and/or location.

Event ownership models

Many events, especially unplanned, spontaneous events, cannot be owned (i.e., belong to a specific individual or organisation). Sport event ownership can also be obscure, as there are many volunteer-driven, informal events occurring on a regular basis. Take, for instance, a pickup baseball game or a local youth soccer jamboree that may occur at the end of a regular season. However, as Getz, MacDonald and Parent (2015) suggested,

> The rights to the name of an event and to produce a planned event within a governed structure can be owned, along with the rights to broadcast it, and to associate with the event as suppliers, sponsors, licensees, cities and destinations. (p. 92)

The International Olympic Committee (IOC), for example, claims ownership of the Olympic (Winter) Games. The official rights to broadcast and sponsor them, as well as use the popular properties associated with the event, such as the Olympic Rings, legally belong to the organisation (internationally) and its subsidiaries, the national Olympic Committees (nationally). Getz et al. (2015) identified four main types of sport event owners:

- Public: Events owned by varying levels of government and their affiliated agencies (e.g., The Vendée Globe, a sailing race organised by the French Department de la Vendée (Getz et al., 2015);
- Private or for-profit: Event businesses that own their particular events and run them for profit (e.g., the X Games is hosted, produced and broadcast by ESPN (cf. X Games, n.d.);
- Not-for-profit organisations: Organisations inspired to serve the community, usually at a loss or to break even. They may also donate profits to charities (e.g., Canada Games is a

national-level, multi-sport event held in the country every two years, which is supported by the Canada Games Council and varying levels of government) (Bodin, 2018); and

- Sport governing bodies (e.g., Ontario Soccer, Biathlon Canada and the International Skating Union, which host regional, national and international championships in their respective sports).

In contrast, Emery (2001) alluded to three levels of event ownership, namely the international level, when sport events are owned by the international sport federations and other international sport organisations (e.g., IOC); the national level, when national federations or equivalents hold sport competitions; and the local level, when the event is operated by a local sport entity or LOC. Given the varying levels and types of sport events, there is a need to differentiate between the varied event governance systems that exist.

Getz et al. (2015) highlighted a number of issues that impact sport event ownership. These concerns revolve around questions, such as who owns the rights to bid on events, and, should a bid contender be successful, who has the privilege to form the local organising committee. In addition, event ownership could change hands. For example, an international sport governing body might completely transfer the rights of the event to an organising committee, as in the case of the Olympic Games, or the sport governing body may retain the majority of the control of the event and rely on the contacts and network of LOCs, as in the case of Union of European Football Association (UEFA) and the European Championships (EURO).

In reality, there is no one basic sport event ownership model. Event ownership models vary and there is no one best approach for all event-related organisations. Moreover, ownership models will be impacted by the nature, size and type of event. International sport organisations, such as the International Olympic Committee and FIFA, delegate the hosting of the sports events to LOCs (Geeraert, 2017). The size and scale of these large and mega sports events require additional support from varying levels of local government to help coordinate the event. As such, it is the combination of the host governments and the LOC that largely determine the success of the event. Geeraert (2017) noted that "Ideally, these agents act in the ISO's [International Sport Organisation] best interests, yet conflicting interests and information asymmetries give rise to agency problems" (p. 27). Andersson and Getz (2009) observed that, as events evolve in size, they become more reliant on stakeholders, such as government and local businesses, for resources (e.g., financial and logistical support), and this, in turn, can result in a loss of independence for event managers and the organising committee.

In sum, event ownership is usually made up of a complex set of relationships between a variety of event stakeholders. There can be significant differences between the event owner's goals (e.g., to make a profit) and the event stakeholders' goals (e.g., to provide community entertainment), which can lead to the failure of events in terms of hosting costs, conflicts and leadership (cf. Parent & Séguin, 2007). As such, the next section elaborates on these event stakeholder issues.

Event stakeholders

Geeraert (2017) suggested the governance of sports events can be conceptualised as a complex network of stakeholders, each with different tasks and responsibilities. Girginov (2012) stated this governance network is responsible for "guid[ing] and steer[ing] collective actors towards a consensus amongst various parties concerned" (p. 543). The management of these stakeholder relationships is critical for the successful planning and implementation of sport events. However, this process is compounded by the complexity of the event planning process, which includes multi-sectoral and multi-level decision-making in both the public and private domains (Parent, Rouillard & Naraine, 2017). In turn, there is a need to include a multitude of stakeholders in order to ensure sustained support and resources throughout the event planning and hosting process (Getz et al., 2007; Parent & Smith-Swan, 2013; Reid, 2011). To better understand this complex system, the stakeholders that influence the decisions made surrounding the governance of sport events is now discussed (see also Figure 15.1).

While the event organising committee often lies at the centre of the event governance system, there has been an effort to identify the sport event stakeholders involved in the sport event planning and implementation process (e.g., Getz, 2009; Reid & Arcodia, 2002). Getz et al. (2007), for example, looked at differentiating these individuals and groups between internal (i.e., those directly involved with the event) and external event stakeholders (e.g., regulators, facilitators, co-producers, etc.). Specific to large-scale sport events, Parent (2008) and later Parent and Smith-Swan (2013) identified eight sport event stakeholder groupings: Host governments, international delegations, sport organisations, media, community, sponsors, organising committee and other stakeholders (e.g., NGOs, consultants) (see Figure 15.1).

Hanstad, Parent and Kristiansen (2013) compared stakeholders across the hosting of the Olympic Winter Games and the Winter Youth Olympic Games. They noted differences between four major stakeholder groupings: Core host, international, sponsors and media and parents, etc. More specifically, Parent, Kristiansen, Skille and Hanstad (2015) explored key stakeholders within the Youth Olympic Games (YOG) context. The International Olympic Committee, media (press and broadcast) and the athletes' parents emerged as central stakeholders. These results support the notion that, while event stakeholder maps may be similar between events, differences in terms of stakeholder dominance or salience will exist as a result of varying goals of the sport events (e.g., participants vs. media vs. spectators).

Other stakeholders can also have a significant impact on the organisation of a sport event. For example, due to the massive amount of dollars given by sponsors and broadcasters to the Olympic Games, organisations like NBC (the United States Olympic broadcaster) has been able to influence specific aspects of the Games, including the scheduling of some marquee events (e.g., swimming finals in Beijing 2008 and Tokyo 2020 and figure skating in Pyeongchang 2018 and Beijing 2022), thereby forcing athletes to adjust to these times (Battaglio, 2017). Moreover, Leopkey and Parent (2017) identified three broad groupings of governance stakeholders (albeit specific to event legacy), namely constant actors (i.e., those that will likely be involved in all editions of the Games – International Olympic Committee and Organising Committee for the Olympic Games); emergent actors (i.e., those that are relatively new to the Games environment but will likely become constant actors in the future – International Paralympic Committee); and context-specific actors (i.e., organisations and groups that play a role in the context-specific network but will not translate to future editions of the event – Green Peace in Sydney 2000, Four Host First Nations in Vancouver 2010).

Satisfying and retaining relationships with stakeholders which the event affects or has the potential to affect is important. Reid (2011) noted that "identifying event stakeholders, monitoring satisfaction levels with their involvement and ensuring improvements to stakeholder relationships can be implemented prior to their withdrawal from involvement" (p. 22). Moreover, it is important to engage the more active stakeholders throughout the entire event management process to ensure that groups such as the community and sponsors are satisfied with and will support the event now and in the future (Ponsford & Williams, 2010). In order to accomplish this, organisers must be able to identify all stakeholders related to their event as this will help them balance the competing needs, tensions and expectations.

Table 15.1 Issues specific to each external event stakeholder group

Issues	Host governments	Community	Sponsors	Sport organisations	Media	Delegations
Financial	X	X	X	X	X	X
Infrastructure	X	X				
Interdependence					X	X
Legacy	X	X		X	X	
Operations				X	X	X
Participation	X	X	X	X		X
Politics	X			X		
Relationships		X	X		X	
Sport		X		X	X	X
Visibility	X	X	X	X	X	

Adapted from Parent (2008) and updated.

A central question that can be asked when dealing with event stakeholders is about their prioritisation. Mitchel, Agle and Wood's (1997) power, legitimacy and urgency framework has been a popular method used to determine stakeholder salience by contending that the more of these attributes a stakeholder possesses, the more important the stakeholder is in terms of managerial attention. Utilising this framework, Parent and Deephouse (2007) found most event stakeholders were perceived to be definitive (i.e., possessing all three attributes) at some point in the event management process; however, their findings also revealed that stakeholder attributes shift throughout the event's lifecycle. Key stakeholder relationships identified in this particular research that focused on the *Jeux de la Francophonie* and the Pan American Games were the various levels of government (e.g., local, provincial and federal), the sport event's owners and their representatives and the local community. Finally, it is important to note that, depending on an individual's role in the organising committee, they will have a different conception of the event's stakeholder map and who is more important (Parent & Deephouse, 2007).

Each event stakeholder will have different goals, needs and wants, including financial, human resources, infrastructure, interdependence, legacy, media, operations, organising, participation, politics, relationships, sport and visibility (Parent, 2008). Table 15.1 notes the issues that are specific to each stakeholder outside the organising committee (i.e., other than the workforce).

Finally, knowledge management has been acknowledged as a crucial function for organisations (Parent, MacDonald & Goulet, 2014). In the event field, especially one-off sport events, the knowledge management process has gained traction given the usually temporal nature of event organising committees. This is because the knowledge-sharing between stakeholders can help reduce risks at the event. In acknowledging this issue, Parent, MacDonald and Goulet (2014) suggested a generic knowledge and transfer management process for sport event stakeholder networks. These steps included knowledge needs identification, knowledge adoption, internal knowledge transfer, knowledge application and knowledge tailoring.

Sport event legacy governance

An area of interest that has progressed in the literature over the last decade is the governance of sport event legacy. Event legacy is generally understood to be what is left behind from the hosting of a sport event that lasts longer than the event itself and can include planned/

unplanned, positive/negative and tangible/intangible impacts (Preuss, 2007). The production of event legacy has become a central focus by event organisers due to the increased scrutiny and accountability on the social, environmental and economic impacts left following the hosting of an event. In fact, Leopkey and Parent (2012) argued event legacy has become institutionalised within the Olympic Movement as a way to help justify the spending of exorbitant sums of money on hosting. Additionally, they suggested the evolution from reactive to proactive strategies by the organising committee and other related event stakeholders requires a governance system to help manage and produce the event legacies. While they showed how the concept of legacy had become consolidated within the Olympic Movement, they argued legacy governance had not become fully institutionalised which may actually allow for localised governance arrangements to flourish.

The concept of sustainability seems to be the newest buzzword being used in the event management realm (e.g., Hall, 2012; Sotiriadou & Hill, 2015). In general, sustainability can refer to the maintenance of the event's legacies over the long-term (Liu, 2018). For example, the 2010 Vancouver Olympic and Paralympic Games had a focus on hosting a sustainable Games for the region (International Olympic Committee, 2010). While the more modern view of sustainability has progressed beyond its "green" roots and environmental focus to include social and economic opportunities, the concepts are often used interchangeably, which can cause confusion for both academics and practitioners. However, it should be clarified that many activities, such as event legacy planning and proper event governance mechanisms, are critical to ensuring sustainable legacies (i.e., long-term sport event legacies) (Leopkey & Parent, 2017; Liu, 2018).

In an effort to illustrate the governance system used to produce event legacies associated with the hosting of an edition of the Olympic Games, Leopkey and Parent (2017) explored the network of actors and the mechanisms responsible for steering collective action towards the event's legacy goals and objectives. Their findings revealed four distinct event legacy governance phases, which start prior to the official bidding for the event and last beyond the conclusion of the event. The legacy governance process (phases) included legacy conceptualisation, legacy planning and implementation, legacy transfer and transformation and post-Games legacy governance. In the same research paper, governance controls impacting the operations of the governance system are also highlighted, including both actors (i.e., individuals and organisations) and mechanisms (i.e., formal and informal rules and policies) that influence the governance system.

Leopkey and Parent (2015a) explored and compared the modes of network governance utilised during the Vancouver 2010 Olympic Winter Games. The authors detailed how the sophistication and formalisation of several contractual documents, policies and agreements played a role in the changing nature of the legacy governance network in this particular setting. In doing so, they proposed a new hybrid form of network governance (cf. Provan & Kenis, 2008), where both a lead organisation and a network administration organisation (NAO) can govern side by side or where more than one NAO can exist together within a network. Leopkey and Parent (2015b) further investigated stakeholder perspectives regarding the governance of event legacy at the Olympic Games. Findings revealed event stakeholders saw proper governance practices including accountability, stakeholder participation, performance and transparency as paramount for the provision of event legacy, which are in line with stakeholder's perceptions of the overall democratic governance of sports events (Parent, 2016b). Moreover, the event stakeholders regularly connected these "good governance" practices to the successful delivery of the event.

Finally, both Christie and Gibb (2015) and Sharp and Finkel (2018) explored the governance of event legacy at the 2014 Commonwealth Games in Glasgow, Scotland. Christie and Gibb (2015) focused on the lessons learned from the collaborative working practices used by the event to generate sustainable legacies. In doing so, they highlighted six important dimensions to facilitate collaborative network governance, namely combining resources and developing joint agendas, strong leadership, involving the community, mutual learning, accountability and trust. Sharp and Finkel (2018) emphasised the need for legacy planning to include the creation of legacy governance structures to ensure the ability to meet overall goals and objectives.

Conclusions and future directions

In sum, this chapter suggests that an increased focus on the governance of sport organisations has led to more research that has focused specifically on events within the sporting context. However, as Dowling et al. (2018) pointed out, only 27 of the 243 articles that formed the basis for their scoping review of the sport domain were clearly linked to the sport event context and, as such, there is still much to learn.

The governance of sports events can be visualised as a complex network of stakeholders. As the organisation of a sport event involves many diverse stakeholders working both individually and collectively in governance networks, the engagement and interactions of relevant sport event stakeholders must be better understood by managers in order to meet hosting goals and objectives and to ensure success. The ability to comprehend these roles and relationships can equip event managers and others within the LOC with tools to enable more effective governance of events. This will become increasingly important as the structure and locations of popular major events continue to evolve. For example, as the International Olympic Committee [Olympic (Winter) Games and the (Winter) Youth Olympic Games] and FIFA (World Cup, Women's World Cup, U-20 events, etc.) continue to move into new territories (e.g., China, Qatar, Senegal, etc.), it will be important to understand the potential changes to these networks given the unique cultural and political systems in these countries. Additionally, the format of these events has the potential to change, as evidenced by the increase in joint bids (i.e., bids made by multiple countries) for these events (e.g., the united bid between Canada/USA/Mexico for the 2026 World Cup and the proposed South Korea/North Korea bid for the 2032 Olympic Games), which will also impact the complexity and nature of the event governance networks.

There also remains a need to explore the event governance system including its characteristics, information flows, communication channels and stakeholder salience and power both at the mega and large-scale event levels. While it has been noted that much of the existing research has focused on the Olympic Movement, there is a necessity to expand our investigations to all levels of sport events and types of event owners (cf. Emery, 2001; Getz et al., 2015) to private for profit, not-for-profit and pubic events at the international, national and local level. For example, there is little knowledge about the FIFA World Cup (beyond the event owner itself) in terms how the event is governed. Moreover, there is limited research on the specific stakeholders beyond the event organising committees, event owners and government bodies. Parent's (2008) and Parent and Smith-Swan's (2013) identification of other event-related stakeholders, such as sponsors, media and the community, provides a starting point for this inquiry.

It has also been argued that sport management scholars in general should adopt a broader definition of sport governance (cf., Henry & Lee, 2004; Dowling et al., 2018; Parent & Hoye, 2018). Given the lack of event governance-related research from the organisational and political governance perspectives, it would be helpful to ask additional research questions in these areas in order to better understand the relationships between the different parts of the governance system. For example, normative and ethically informed standards of managerial behaviour should be assessed in the sport event context. This could include understanding the norms and values associated with the management of major sports events or exploring sport event board dynamics (e.g., developing strategic capability or dealing with board conflict). Another area of research that could be developed centres on political governance or how governing bodies or governments "steer" the behaviour of event organisations and organising committees.

Finally, given that event organisations and organising committees deal with a multitude of issues (e.g., image, political, risk management, operational, financial) (cf. Parent, 2008) on a regular basis during the lifecycle of event, additional efforts should be made to explore how organising committees and stakeholders deal with these concerns.

References

Andersson, T., & Getz, D. (2009). Tourism as a mixed industry: Differences between private, public and not-for-profit festivals. *Tourism Management, 30*, 847–856.

Battaglio, S. (2017). *NBC's 2018 Olympics coverage will air live in all time zones.* Retrieved 3 December 2018, from https://www.latimes.com/business/hollywood/la-fi-ct-olympic-live-coverage-20170328-story.html

Bodin, K. (2018). *The role of the Canada Games in Canadian sport: Canadian celebration and political tool.* Retrieved 29 November 2018, from https://ir.lib.uwo.ca/etd/5449

Chappelet, J.-L. (Ed.). (2005). *From initial idea to success: A guide to bidding for sports events for politicians and administrators.* Lausanne: IDHEAP.

Chappelet, J.-L., & Kübler-Mabbott, B. (2008). *The International Olympic Committee and the Olympic system: The governance of world sport.* Oxon, UK: Routledge.

Child, J., & Faulkner, D. (1998). *Strategies of cooperation: Managing alliances, networks, and joint ventures.* New York: Oxford University Press.

Christie, L., & Gibb, K. (2015). A collaborative approach to event-led regeneration: The governance of legacy from the 2014 Commonwealth Games. *Local Economy, 30*, 871–887.

Dowling, M., Leopkey, B., & Smith, L. (2018). Governance in sport: A scoping review. *Journal of Sport Management, 32*, 438–451.

Emery, P. (2001). Bidding to host a major sports event. In C. Gratton & I. Henry (Eds.), *Sport in the city: The role of sport in economic and social regeneration* (pp. 90–108). London: Routledge.

Faulkner, D. O. (1995). *International strategic alliances: Cooperating to compete.* Maidenhead: McGraw-Hill.

Geeraert, A. (2017). Theorizing the governance of sport mega-events a principal-agent perspective. In S. Frawley (Ed.), *Managing sport mega-events* (pp. 24–36). New York: Routledge.

Geeraert, A., Alm, J., & Groll, M. (2014). Good governance in international sport organizations: An analysis of the 35 Olympic sport governing bodies. *International Journal of Sport Policy and Politics, 6*, 281–306.

Geeraert, A., & Drieskens, E. (2015). Theorizing the EU and sport: The principal-agent model and beyond. *Sport & EU Review, 7*(1), 6–22.

Geeraert, A., Mrkonjic, M., & Chappelet, J.-L. (2015). A rationalist perspective on the autonomy of international sport governing bodies: Towards a pragmatic autonomy in the steering of sports. *International Journal of Sport Policy and Politics, 7*, 473–488.

Getz, D. (1989). Special events: Defining the product. *Tourism Management, 10*(2), 125–137.

Getz, D. (2005). *Event management & event tourism* (2nd ed.). Elmsford, NY: Cognizant Communication Corp.

Getz, D. (2007). *Event studies: Theory, research, and policy for planned events.* Burlington, MA: Elsevier.

Getz, D. (2009). Policy for sustainable and responsible festivals and events: Institutionalization of a new paradigm. *Journal of Policy Research in Tourism, Leisure and Events, 1*(1), 61–78.

Getz, D., & Andersson, T. (2008). Sustainable festivals: On becoming an institution. *Event Management, 12*(1), 1–17.

Getz, D., Anderson, T., & Larson, M. (2007). Festival stakeholder roles: Concepts and case studies. *Event Management, 10*(2/3), 103–122.

Getz, D., MacDonald, D., & Parent, M. M. (2015). The sport event owners' perspective. In M. M. Parent & J.-L. Chappelet (Eds.), *The routledge handbook of sports event management* (pp. 91–108). London: Routledge.

Girginov, B. (2012). Governance of London 2012 Olympic Games legacy. *International Review for the Sociology of Sport, 47*, 543–558.

Hall, C. M. (1989). The definition and analysis of hallmark tourist events. *Geojournal, 19*, 263–268.

Hall, C. M. (1992). *Hallmark tourist events: Impacts, management and planning.* London: Belhaven Press.

Hall, C. M. (2012). Sustainable mega-events: Beyond the myth of balanced approaches to mega-event sustainability. *Event Management, 16*(2), 119–131.

Hanstad, D.V., Parent, M. M., & Kristiansen, E. (2013). The Youth Olympic Games: The best of the Olympics or a poor copy? *European Sport Management Quarterly*, *13*, 315–338.

Hautbois, C., Parent, M. M., & Séguin, B. (2012). How to win a bid for major sporting events? A stakeholder analysis of the 2018 Olympic Winter Games French bid. *Sport Management Review*, *15*, 263–275.

Henry, I., & Lee, P. C. (2004). Governance and ethics in sport. In S. Chadwick & J. Beech (Eds.), *The business of sport management* (pp. 25–41). Harlow, UK: Pearson Education.

Horne, J., & Manzenreiter, W. (2006). An introduction to the sociology of sports mega-events. *The Sociological Review*, *54*(s2), 1–24.

International Olympic Committee. (2010). *VANOC releases final sustainability report*. Retrieved 29 November 2018, from https://www.olympic.org/news/vanoc-releases-final-sustainability-report

Kanter, R. M. (2002). Collaborative advantages: The art of alliances. *Harvard Business Review* , *72*(4), pp. 97–128.

Leopkey, B., & Parent, M. M. (2009). Risk management issues in large-scale sporting events: A stakeholder perspective. *European Sport Management Quarterly*, *9*, 187–208.

Leopkey, B., & Parent, M. M. (2012). The (neo) institutionalization of legacy and its sustainable governance within the Olympic movement. *European Sport Management Quarterly*, *12*, 437–455.

Leopkey, B., & Parent, M. M. (2015a). Vancouver 2010 Olympic Winter Games: Modes of legacy network governance. In D. Ruta & R. Holt (Eds.), *The Routledge handbook of sport and legacy: Meeting the challenge of major sport events.* (pp. 82–96). New York: Routledge.

Leopkey, B., & Parent, M. M. (2015b). Stakeholder perspectives regarding the governance of legacy at the Olympic Games. *Annals of Leisure Research*, *18*, 528–548.

Leopkey, B., & Parent, M. M. (2017). The governance of Olympic legacy: Process, actors and mechanisms. *Leisure Studies*, *36*, 438–451.

Liu, Y.-D. (2018). Legacy planning and event sustainability: Helsinki as the 2012 World Design Capital. *Sustainability*, *10*, 2453–2466.

Mitchel, R. K., Agle, B. R., & Wood, D. J. (1997). Toward a theory of stakeholder identification and salience: Defining the principle of who and what really counts. *Academy of Management Review*, *22*, 853–886.

Parent, M. M. (2005). *Large-scale sporting events: Organizing committees and stakeholders* (PhD doctoral thesis) University of Alberta, Edmonton, Alberta, Canada.

Parent, M. M. (2008). Evolution and issue patterns for major sporting event organizing committees and their stakeholders. *Journal of Sport Management*, *22*, 135–164.

Parent, M. M. (2015). The organizing committee's perspective. In M. M. Parent & J.-L. Chappelet (Eds.), *The Routledge handbook of sports event management* (pp. 43–64). London: Routledge.

Parent, M. M. (2016a). The governance of the Olympic Games in Canada. *Sport in Society*, *19*, 796–816.

Parent, M. M. (2016b). Stakeholder perceptions on the democratic governance of major sports events. *Sport Management Review*, *19*, 402–416.

Parent, M. M., & Deephouse, D. L. (2007). A case study of stakeholder identification and prioritization by managers. *Journal of Business Ethics*, *75*, 1–23.

Parent, M. M., & Hoye, R. (2018). The impact of governance principles on sport organisations' governance practices and performance: A systematic review. *Cogent Social Sciences*, *4*(1), 1–24.

Parent, M. M., Kristiansen, E., Skille, E. A., & Hanstad, D.V. (2015). The sustainabilty of the Youth Olympic Games: Stakeholder networks and institutional perspectives. *International Review for the Sociology of Sport*, *50*(3), 326–348.

Parent, M. M., MacDonald, D., & Goulet, G. (2014). The theory and practice of knowledge management and transfer: The case of the Olympic Games. *Sport Management Review*, *17*, 205–218.

Parent, M. M., Rouillard, C., & Leopkey, B. (2011). Issues and strategies pertaining to the Canadian governments' coordination efforts in relation to the 2010 Olympic Games. *European Sport Management Quarterly*, *11*, 337–369.

Parent, M. M., Rouillard, C., & Naraine, M. L. (2017). Network governance of a multi-level, multi-sectoral sport event: Differences in coordinating ties and actors. *Sport Management Review*, *20*, 497–509.

Parent, M. M., & Séguin, B. (2007). Factors that led to the drowning of a world championship organzing committee: A stakeholder approach. *European Sport Management Quarterly*, *7*, 187–212.

Parent, M. M., & Séguin, B. (2010, July). *Change as routine? Understanding organizational change in Canadian major sporting events.* Paper presented at the International Federation of Scholarly Associations of Management, Paris, France.

Parent, M. M., Séguin, B., Gagné Côté, D., Leblond, O., & Laperle, K. (2009). *Un modèle pour des alliances stratégiques dans le cadre de la gestion d'événements sportifs au Canada*. [A strategic alliance model for managing sports events in Canada]. In B. Séguin (Ed.), *Proceedings of the tourism and sport management division of the 2009 administrative sciences association of Canada conference* (pp. 1–18). Niagara Falls, Ontario, Canada.

Parent, M. M., & Smith-Swan, S. (2013). *Managing major sports events: Theory and practice*. London: Routledge.

Ponsford, I. F., & Williams, P. W. (2010). Crafting a social license to operate: A case study of Vancouver 2010's Cypress Olympic Venue. *Event Management, 14*(1), 17–36.

Preuss, H. (2007). The Conceptualization and measurement of mega sport event legacies. *Journal of Sport and Tourism, 12*(3/4), 207–227.

Provan, K. G., & Kenis, P. (2008). Modes of network governance: Structure, management and effectiveness. *Journal of Public Administration Research and Theory, 18*, 229–252.

Reid, S. (2011). Event stakeholder management: Developing sustainable rural event practices. *International Journal of Event and Festival Management, 2*(1), 20–36.

Reid, S., & Arcrodia, C. (2002). Stakeholder theory to event management contexts, in E. Arola, J. Karkkainen, & M.-L. Siitari (Eds.), *Tourism and Well-Being, The 2nd tourism industry and education symposium* (pp. 342–352), Jyvaskyla Polytechnic, Jyvaskyla.

Ritchie, J. R. B. (1984). Assessing the impact of hallmark events: Conceptual and research issues. *Journal of Travel Research, 23*(1), 2–11.

Ritchie, J. R. B., & Smith, B. H. (1991). The impact of a mega-event on host region awareness: A longitudinal study. *Journal of Travel Research, 30*(1), 3–10.

Roche, M. R. (2000). *Mega-events and modernity: Olympics and expos in the growth of global culture*. London: Routledge.

Sharp, B., & Finkel, R. (2018). Governing major event legacy: Case of the Glasgow 2014 Commonwealth Games. *Event Management, 22*, 903–915.

Sotiriadou, P., & Hill, B. (2015). Raising environmental responsibility and sustainability for sport events: A systematic review. *International Journal of Event Management, 10*(1), 1–11.

Todd, L., Leask, A., & Ensor, J. (2017). Understanding primary stakeholders' multiple roles in hallmark event tourism management. *Tourism Management, 59*, 494–509.

Weed, M. (2003). Why the two won't tango! Explaining the lack of integrated policies for sport and tourism in the UK. *Journal of Sport Management, 17*, 258–283.

Whitford, M., Phi, G., & Dredge, D. (2014). Principles to practice: Indicators for measuring event governance performance. *Event Management, 18*, 387–403.

Whitson, D., & Macintosh, D. (1993). Becoming a world class city: Hallmark events and sport franchises in the growth strategies of Western Canadian cities. *Sociology of Sport Journal, 10*, 221–240.

X Games. (n.d.). *History of X Games*. Retrieved 29 November 2018, from https://www.xgamesmediakit.com

Part IV

Board roles in the governance process

16

Role of the board and directors

Board structure and composition

Josh McLeod

Introduction

Debate around the role of the board of directors is a common feature of the corporate governance literature (Van den Berghe & Baelden, 2005). In the sport governance literature, however, the concept has received far less attention. Similarly, while the structure and composition of boards has been a cornerstone of mainstream governance research for two decades (Mcintyre, Murphy & Mitchell, 2007), it has been neglected by researchers interested in the governance of sport specifically. Thus, there remain significant gaps in our understanding of "what boards do" in sport organisations and how those boards are best structured. The aim of this chapter is to contribute to that research gap by bringing together existing studies in those two areas, assessing current levels of knowledge and identifying avenues for future research.

Before the roles of sport boards are discussed, it is pertinent to provide background on the concept on a general level. Thus, the structure of this chapter is as follows. A brief overview of the generic board roles literature and the related theories is provided first, before existing knowledge of board roles in sport is analysed. This is followed by another short introduction to the generic governance literature on board structure and composition. This issue is then explored in depth in relation to sport boards specifically. Recommendations for future research are provided after the sections on board roles and board structure and composition.

Board roles: A general overview

Central to the task of developing governance research and practice is the need to define the role of the board (Ferkins, Shilbury & Mcdonald, 2005). Without clarity over what boards do, or, rather, what boards are *supposed* to do, it is not possible to assess with accuracy their effectiveness and contribution to organisations (Huse, 2005). The mainstream governance literature indicates that, generally, there are four main roles that boards perform: (1) the control role; (2) the strategic role; (3) the resource provision role; and (4) the advice and counsel role (Madhani, 2017). Definitions of each role are outlined in Table 16.1. It should be noted that there is divergence in the literature regarding the precise definition of each of the four main

Table 16.1 Definitions of board roles

Board role	Definition
Control role	The control role "refers directly to the responsibility of directors to monitor managers on behalf of shareholders". For example, monitoring budgets and operational decisions (Hillman & Dalziel, 2003, p. 384).
Strategic role	The strategic role concerns the board's role in formulating, approving, monitoring, reviewing and implementing an organisation's strategy[a] (Brauer & Schmidt, 2008).
Resource provision role	The resource provision role refers to the responsibility of the board to provide the organisation with access to resources, e.g. human, physical and social capital (Nicholson & Newton, 2010).
Advice and counsel role	The advice and counsel role involves advising the CEO and top managers on various issues such as operational decision-making (Zahra & Pearce, 1989).

[a] There is a notable lack of consensus in the literature regarding the precise nature of the strategic role. Two schools of thought exist. On one hand, there are those that perceive the board to have a "passive" role that is limited to approving and reviewing strategy. On the other, there are those that perceive the board to have an "active" strategic role that involves formulating, reviewing and implementing an organisation's strategy (Nicholson & Newton, 2010).

board roles, however, the definitions offered in Table 16.1 are some of those most commonly adopted. The following section discusses the dominant theories used in the literature to study and explain the role of boards.

Board role theories

A frequent criticism of board role research is that existing governance theories are inadequate in explaining and predicting "what boards do". The dominant theories include the agency, stewardship and resource-dependency perspectives (Hung, 1998; Jonsson, 2013). Although those theories are useful in explaining why a board performs individual roles, they do not encapsulate the heterogeneity of the board's overall function (Van Den Heuvel, Van Gils & Voordeckers, 2006). Table 16.2 outlines the key governance theories, describes their premise for governance and identifies the implications for board roles.

Given the inability of existing theories to explain the entirety of what boards do, many researchers have called for a multi-theoretical approach when studying board roles (Roberts, McNulty & Stiles, 2005; Viganò, Zattoni, Hoskisson & Huse, 2011). This call has been somewhat answered by researchers. For example, Hillman and Dalziel (2003) proposed a model of board function and performance that is underpinned by the integration of agency theory and resource-dependency theory. The authors show how, by applying those theories in concert, a more holistic understanding of the role of boards and their performance can be achieved. Further, the authors note that adopting this integrative approach will be beneficial for researchers and practitioners who have previously relied too heavily on the agency perspective. Despite this effort, much work still needs to be done in order to develop a robust theoretical foundation for board role research.

Although the four generic board roles outlined in Table 16.1 provide a useful overview of the typical functions of boards, existing empirical research shows that board roles are often context specific. That is, the roles performed by individual boards can vary depending on organisational and sectoral circumstances. Indeed, industry factors, organisational size, ownership structure and the organisational lifecycle have all been shown to influence the function of boards (Aguilera,

Table 16.2 Board role theories

Theory	Premise for governance	Implications for board role
Agency theory	Agency theory asserts that managers are motivated by self-interest and that their interests are often different to the owners' interests (Eisenhardt, 1989).	To control and monitor the actions of the CEO
Stewardship theory	Stewardship theory posits that senior management, as stewards of an organisation, are motivated by achievement and recognition. Their interests are said to align with the owners' interests (Donaldson & Davis, 1991).	To partner with the CEO in the interests of the organisation
Resource-dependency theory	Resource-dependency theory asserts that resources are key to organisational success and, therefore, access to and control over resources is a basis of power (Pfeffer & Salancik, 1978).	To provide access to resources
Institutional theory	The central tenet of institutional theory is that the institutional environment can strongly influence the development of organisations and their governance structures (Hoye & Cuskelly, 2007).	To conform to external expectations
Stakeholder theory	Stakeholders have divergent interests and organisational success is dependent on the ability to balance and satisfy those stakeholders (Hung, 1998).	To incorporate stakeholder perspectives into the governing role and to balance stakeholder needs
Managerial hegemony theory	It is inevitable and preferable that managers control organisations and dominate the strategic process (Hung, 1998).	To act as a support mechanism for managers

2005; Gabrielsson & Huse, 2002). As such, it is widely acknowledged that the role of the board is a complex phenomenon that cannot be easily generalised across different settings. The next section reviews the studies that have been conducted on board roles in the sport context.

Board roles in sport

Research on the roles of boards in sport organisations is scarce. Inglis (1997) conducted the first key study in this area, identifying four main roles of boards in amateur sport organisations. These included: (1) setting and monitoring the mission of the organisation; (2) undertaking planning activities such as developing financial policy and setting long-range plans; (3) appointing and monitoring the activities of the CEO; and (4) managing community relations through activities such as fundraising and advocacy. The early work of Inglis (1997) highlighted some key differences between the roles of amateur sport boards and the corporate entities that the majority of mainstream board role research has focused on. Namely, they appeared to have a more prominent operational function that requires, for example, board members to engage in activities related to community development. Indeed, further research by Inglis, Alexander and Weaver (1999) indicated that there are similarities between the role of amateur sport boards and community nonprofit boards in terms of their enhanced operational responsibility.

245

With the advent of the 21st century, however, there has been a marked increase in the professionalisation and modernisation of sport organisations globally. This is manifested, largely, by an increase in paid staff and bureaucratic structures (Shilbury & Ferkins, 2011). Research on Oceanic sport organisations shows that professionalisation has a meaningful impact on the role of sport boards. Specifically, the process has been found to induce a transition from community organisation-style governance, which involves operational activities, to a more corporate-style of governance, which is predominantly non-executive and focuses on strategy and monitoring management (Ferkins et al., 2005; Shilbury, 2001). This is supported by Tacon and Walters (2016), who find that financial oversight and strategy are now considered to be the key roles for boards of national governing bodies (NGB) in the modernised setting of UK sport. Operational functions such as fundraising and community engagement, on the other hand, were no longer viewed as important for UK NGB boards. The impact of professionalisation on sport board roles provides further support to the notion that board roles are highly dependent on contextual factors – a point well documented in the corporate literature (Aguilera, 2005).

The changing nature of sport board roles – induced by professionalisation – has been suggested to lead to tensions between the volunteer directors previously responsible for operational activities and the new paid executives who are acquiring that responsibility (Shilbury, 2001). Other studies have supported this assertion – citing a reluctance of volunteer directors to cede decision-making authority to paid executives due to the challenge it presents to the traditional community- and volunteer-based culture of sport organisations (Amis & Slack, 1996). Shilbury (2001) commented that this reluctance was a significant impediment to the professionalisation process and raised questions over the role of boards in modern sport organisations.

Research conducted in the Taiwanese sport context indicates that boards perform similar roles to those outlined in the seminal work of Inglis (1997), namely that of managing the organisation's vision and purpose; human resource and fundraising; and engaging with stakeholders (Yeh, Taylor & Hoye, 2009). The importance of context in understanding board roles is again clear when drawing together the existing literature. For instance, while Shilbury (2001) and Tacon and Walters (2016) show that the professionalisation of sport in their countries (Australia and the UK respectively) is leading boards to perform roles aligned with the corporate sector, the less modernised setting of Taiwanese sport still requires boards to carry out operational roles such as fundraising (Yeh et al., 2009). Moreover, later research by Yeh, Hoye and Taylor (2011) finds that the importance of particular board roles for Taiwanese sport organisations varies depending on their strategic orientation – further emphasising the context specificity of board roles.

In addition to studies that diagnose "what sport boards do", an alternative stream of research has explored the impact of sport board roles on organisational outcomes. For example, research shows that ambiguity concerning what board members of sport organisations are expected to do is negatively associated with job satisfaction and commitment (Sakires, Doherty & Misener, 2009) and role performance (Doherty & Hoye, 2011).

There has been some focus on the strategic role of the board from sport governance researchers. For instance, studies have indicated that the board's strategic function tends to be a weakness in sport organisations (Ferkins et al., 2005), and that the performance of sport boards can be enhanced by increasing their involvement in the strategic process (Ferkins, Shilbury & Mcdonald, 2009). Other studies highlight how performance of the strategic role can be improved by creating and maintaining collaborative partnerships with key internal stakeholders, particularly within federated governance structures (Ferkins & Shilbury, 2010). More recent research has shown how the strategic capability of sport boards can be enhanced through collaboration on strategy development, collaboration on the integration of strategy and board processes, and the existence of board operational knowledge (Ferkins & Shilbury, 2012, 2015).

Future research on sport board roles

The previous section demonstrated that existing research focused on the role of the board in sport organisations is limited. Still, the paucity of studies conducted in this area have made some important observations. In particular, researchers have identified a link between the profession-alisation of sport organisations and the evolution of their boards' roles. This evolution involves a shift from an operational function to a predominantly non-executive function, thus mirror-ing the corporate sector. In addition, the importance of contextual factors (whether they be geographic, sectoral or organisational) in shaping board roles, has, in line with the corporate governance literature, been demonstrated in the sport governance space. Much work remains, however, so that a deeper understanding of the work of sport boards can be established. This section identifies some key areas for future research.

As previously discussed in this chapter, it has long been established that contextual factors have a significant impact on board roles. However, this has predominantly been shown in rela-tion to corporate board roles, and thus the impact of contextual factors on the role of sport boards specifically remains largely unknown. Thus, future studies could make a meaningful con-tribution to the field by exploring differences in board roles between commercial and nonprofit sport organisations, small and large sport organisations and sport organisations in different coun-tries (Ferkins et al., 2005; Yeh & Taylor, 2008). In addition, researchers can build on the literature that focuses on the professionalisation of sport by exploring the impact of other factors, such as access to funding, on the specification of sport board roles. Such research will help to establish a greater understanding of the nuances of different sport organisations and, subsequently, what roles are most appropriate for their boards.

In the corporate governance literature, researchers have analysed the role of individual direc-tors on boards. Such research has predominantly focused on their responsibility to contribute to board effectiveness by maintaining and demonstrating particular skills, attitudes and behaviours (Huse, Hoskisson, Zattoni & Viganò, 2011; Petrovic, 2008; Roberts et al., 2005). Nevertheless, such investigations are scarce in the sport governance setting. Future research is therefore encouraged to examine the role of individual directors in sport organisations and the char-acteristics required to excel in those positions. This direction of study seems especially salient when considering the idiosyncrasies of sport. For example, sport organisations often experience significant media and public scrutiny (Ferkins et al., 2005), which can add pressure to those in governance positions. It is important, therefore, to identify the characteristics needed to cope with such roles successfully. This point was partially addressed by McLeod (2018) in a study on "fan representatives" on Scottish football club boards, where business experience and a strong personality where considered integral to the role due to the intense fan pressure.

Another issue that remains a pertinent topic for future research is the roles of paid staff and volunteer directors in sport organisations that have, or are, transitioning to a professionalised structure. Although previous studies have pointed to tensions between those groups (Shilbury, 2001), follow-up studies could assist practitioners by exploring how the professionalisation pro-cess is best managed, and how the roles of paid staff and volunteer directors are best divided.

Finally, there remains a shortfall of qualitative research on the roles of sport boards. This mir-rors the broader governance literature, which is similarly dominated by survey-based studies. This problem, faced by both fields of governance research, is symptomatic of the difficulties faced by researchers in gaining access to boards of directors. Nonetheless, it is important for sport governance researchers to overcome this barrier if a deeper understanding of sport board roles is to be established, and the diversity and complexity of sport governance is to be fully captured (Ferkins et al., 2005).

Board structure and composition

Although under-researched in the sport context, board structure and composition has been at the forefront of corporate governance research for three decades (Minichilli, Zattoni & Zona, 2009). In order to provide context to the discussion of board structure and composition in sport organisations, this chapter first provides an overview of the issues from the corporate perspective.

Within the corporate literature, a number of structural factors have received significant scholarly attention. These include:

1. Board independence, which refers to the extent to which there are a majority of non-executive directors on the board of an organisation who also have no previous affiliation with the organisation or any individuals within it (Mcintyre et al., 2007);
2. CEO duality, which refers to the situation in which the two most influential positions within a company, the CEO and chairperson, are held by the same person (Krause & Semadeni, 2013);
3. Board size, which refers to the total head count of directors on an organisation's board (Lawal, 2012);
4. Board diversity, which refers to the range of people on a board in relation to criteria such as gender, ethnicity, age, educational background and skills (Adams, de Haan, Terjesen & van Ees, 2015).

Empirical research on board structure and composition has predominantly focused on the relationship between the aforementioned structural factors and organisational outcomes. Such outcomes include organisational and board performance, with financial performance often being used as a proxy (Minichilli et al., 2009). In general, studies exploring the relationship between these variables have delivered inconsistent results. For instance, while a number of studies indicate that board independence enhances organisational and board performance (e.g., Jackling & Johl, 2009), various others find that there is a negative or no relationship (e.g., Dulewicz & Herbert, 2004). The empirical literature on CEO duality is similar, with contrasting studies showing CEO duality to have both a positive (Boyd, 1995) and negative (Baliga, Moyer & Rao, 1996) effect on organisations.

Linck, Netter and Yang (2009) suggest that the literature on board size is more consistent than on board independence or CEO duality. According to the authors, research generally shows that smaller boards (between 6 and 12 people) enhance board cohesion and organisational performance thereafter. Despite this, a number of studies show that larger boards are more effective in particular circumstances – for example, when directors are not remunerated, a higher number of directors can facilitate a greater division of workload (Cornforth, 2012). Finally, research on board diversity has also delivered inconsistent results. Contrasting studies on gender diversity, for instance, indicate that this variable has a positive relationship (Dezsö & Ross, 2012), no relationship (Chapple & Humphrey, 2014), or a negative relationship (Adams & Ferreira, 2008) with board performance.

The inconsistency of previous research has led to a consensus in the mainstream governance literature that it is too simplistic to focus solely on board structures when assessing board performance (Finkelstein & Mooney, 2003; Sherwin, 2003). In contrast, researchers now point towards board structures as one piece of a broader system of internal and external factors that predicts board performance (Van den Berghe & Levrau, 2004). Consequently, the tendency for governance researchers to focus heavily on board structure appears excessive. This has been acknowledged in the literature, and has, throughout the 2000s, precipitated a growing emphasis by researchers to investigate the impact that social and behavioural factors have on the success of boards (Petri & Soublin, 2010; Zona & Zattoni, 2007). Nevertheless, although board structures are not viewed as the primary antecedent of board performance, they are still considered to be pertinent by researchers and practitioners. This is reflected in various regulatory governance codes around the world. For example, the UK Corporate Governance Code instructs companies to maintain specific structural configurations, as does the Sarbanes–Oxley Act 2002 for corporate boards in the USA, and the Australian Securities Exchange Corporate Governance Council for boards in Australia. Now that the context of board structure and composition research has been set, this issue will be examined in relation to sport organisations specifically (Humphries & Whelan, 2017).

Board structure and composition in sport

The structure and composition of sport boards has received little attention from researchers. Unlike the corporate literature, no studies have explored the relationship between structural characteristics of sport boards and outcomes such as board performance. The few studies that have been carried out in this setting have focused on identifying the extent to which sport organisations conform to generally accepted principles of good governance. These are now reviewed.

In Geeraert, Alm and Groll's (2014) study on structural issues within 35 Olympic sport governing bodies (SGBs), results indicate that SGBs are not implementing many of the governance structures that are widely considered to represent good practice. For instance, none of the SGBs had an independent ethics committee, there was a shortfall of transparency arrangements, there was a lack of diversity and, finally, a notable absence of term limits for board positions. The authors concluded with a call for improved governance in sport. A similar study by Ingram and O'Boyle (2018) assessed the state of sport governance in Australia. Findings highlighted shortfalls in numerous National Sport Organisations (NSOs) with regard to board independence and evaluation. In addition, Taylor and O'Sullivan (2009), after interviewing 22 senior administrators of UK NGBs, found that those organisations would benefit by moving further towards the corporate model of governance, which encourages board independence, smaller boards and separating the CEO and chairperson roles.

Less recently, Hamil, Holt, Michie, Oughton and Shailer (2004) and Michie and Oughton (2005) analysed the corporate governance practices of English football clubs. Both studies identified significant deficiencies in the structure and composition of football club boards, particularly with regard to board independence, inadequate risk assessment processes and a lack of audit committees. As such, the authors concluded that English football clubs were some way short of the governance standards set by listed companies. A more recent survey carried out by Moore Stephens and the Birkbeck Sports Business Centre (2018) finds that, although improvements have been made to the structure and composition of boards in UK sport, a number of issues remain. For instance, only 4 percent of board members surveyed were from an ethnic minority background and 41 percent of boards do not exercise adequate succession planning.

Although limited in volume, the literature on board structure and composition in sport organisations has a consistent narrative that highlights deficiencies in governance standards, particularly in comparison to the corporate sector. Further research is required, however, so deeper understandings can be generated around the structure of sport boards. More specific directions for future study are outlined in the next section.

Future research in sport board structure and composition

A key area for future research identified by sport governance researchers is the relationship between the structural characteristics of sport boards and organisational outcomes (Ferkins et al., 2005; Taylor & O'Sullivan, 2009; Yeh & Taylor, 2008). As discussed earlier, such studies have been commonplace in the corporate literature and, consequently, have played an important role in shaping best practice guidelines. Carrying out similar research in the sport setting could provide those tasked with the governance of sport organisations with invaluable and tailored information on how to operate most effectively. Specifically, research that explores the impact of board independence, the presence of subcommittees, board size and term limits on sport board performance could yield fruitful results (Hoye & Doherty, 2011).

Another related avenue for future study involves investigating the differences between sport organisations in terms of what kinds of board structures and compositions enhance effectiveness. Similar to board roles, the most appropriate structural configuration for a sport board is likely to be dependent on a wide range of sectoral and organisational factors. As such, these differences need to be explored in more detail so the nature and effectiveness of board structure and composition in sport organisations can be fully understood.

Finally, for future research, sport governance scholars should consider how the more advanced corporate governance literature has moved beyond research that focuses narrowly on board structure. Instead, corporate researchers are increasingly adopting a holistic approach to understanding board effectiveness that takes into account social, behavioural and cultural factors (Petri & Soublin, 2010; Zona & Zattoni, 2007). Thus, it may be prudent for researchers interested in sport governance to learn lessons from the corporate literature by focusing on board structures as one aspect of a holistic model of board functioning, rather than as a single dependent variable.

Conclusion

This chapter has reviewed the current state of knowledge with regard to board roles and board structure and composition in the sport setting and has drawn comparisons with the corporate sector. For board roles, it was established that the professionalisation of sport organisations around the world has had a meaningful impact on their configuration. Professionalisation has caused sport board roles to transition from a function that involves operational responsibilities and resembles community organisation governance, to a function that is predominantly non-executive and mirrors the corporate model of board roles. Future research is encouraged to explore this transition in new sport contexts. For board structure and composition, this chapter has highlighted how a limited body of literature shows sport organisations to be falling short of the standards set in the corporate sector with regard to key issues such as board independence and diversity. Given the paucity of studies focusing on the structure of sport boards in general, future research is encouraged in this area, particularly with regard to how board structures influence the effectiveness of sport boards.

References

Adams, R. B., de Haan, J., Terjesen, S., & van Ees, H. (2015). Board diversity: Moving the field forward. *Corporate Governance: An International Review, 23*(2), 77–82.

Adams, R. B., & Ferreira, D. (2008). Do directors perform for pay?. *Journal of Accounting and Economics, 46,* 154–171.

Aguilera, R. V. (2005). Corporate governance and director accountability: An institutional comparative perspective. *British Journal of Management, 16*(s1), 39–53.

Amis, J., & Slack, T. (1996). The size-structure relationship in voluntary sport organizations. *Journal of Sport Management, 10*, 76–86.

Baliga, B. R., Moyer, R. C., & Rao, R. S. (1996). CEO duality and firm performance: What's the fuss? *Strategic Management Journal, 17*(1), 41–53.

Birkbeck Sport Business Centre & Moore Stephens. (2018). *The state of sports governance: Are you leading or lagging?* Retrieved 17 July 2018, from http://www.sportbusinesscentre.com/news/the-state-of-sports-governance-board-report-with-moore-stephens/

Boyd, B. K. (1995). CEO duality and firm performance: A contingency model. *Strategic Management Journal, 16*, 301–312.

Brauer, M., & Schmidt, S. L. (2008). Defining the strategic role of boards and measuring boards' effectiveness in strategy implementation. *Corporate Governance: The International Journal of Business in Society, 8*, 649–660.

Chapple, L., & Humphrey, J. E. (2014). Does board gender diversity have a financial impact? Evidence using stock portfolio performance. *Journal of Business Ethics, 122*, 709–723.

Cornforth, C. (2012). Nonprofit governance research: Limitations of the focus on boards and suggestions for new directions. *Nonprofit and Voluntary Sector Quarterly, 41*, 1116–1135.

Dezsö, C. L., & Ross, D. G. (2012). Does female representation in top management improve firm performance? A panel data investigation. *Strategic Management Journal, 33*, 1072–1089.

Doherty, A., & Hoye, R. (2011). Role ambiguity and volunteer board member performance in nonprofit sport organizations. *Nonprofit Management & Leadership, 22*(4), 107–128.

Donaldson, L., & Davis, J. H. (1991). Stewardship theory or agency theory: CEO governance and shareholder returns. *Australian Journal of Management, 16*, 49–66.

Dulewicz, V., & Herbert, P. (2004). Does the composition and practice of boards of directors bear any relationship to the performance of their companies? *Corporate Governance: An International Review, 12*, 263–280.

Eisenhardt, K. M. (1989). Agency theory: An assessment and review. *Academy of Management Review, 14*, 57–74.

Ferkins, L., & Shilbury, D. (2010). Developing board strategic capability in sport organisations: The national-regional governing relationship. *Sport Management Review, 13*, 235–254.

Ferkins, L., & Shilbury, D. (2012). Good boards are strategic: What does that mean for sport governance? *Journal of Sport Management, 26*, 67–80.

Ferkins, L., & Shilbury, D. (2015). Board strategic balance: An emerging sport governance theory. *Sport Management Review, 18*, 489–500.

Ferkins, L., Shilbury, D., & Mcdonald, G. (2005). The role of the board in building strategic capability: Towards an integrated model of sport governance research. *Sport Management Review, 8*, 195–225.

Ferkins, L., Shilbury, D., & Mcdonald, G. (2009). Board involvement in strategy: Advancing the governance of sport organizations. *Journal of Sport Management, 23*, 245–277.

Finkelstein, S., & Mooney, A. C. (2003). Not the usual suspects: How to use board process to make boards better. *Academy of Management Perspectives, 17*, 101–113.

Gabrielsson, J., & Huse, M. (2002). The venture capitalist and board of directors in SMEs. *Venture Capital, 4*, 125–146.

Geeraert, A., Alm, J., & Groll, M. (2014). Good governance in international sport organizations: An analysis of the 35 Olympic sport governing bodies. *International Journal of Sport Policy and Politics, 6*, 281–306.

Hamil, S., Holt, M., Michie, J., Oughton, C., & Shailer, L. (2004). The corporate governance of professional football clubs. *Corporate Governance, 4*(2), 44–51.

Hillman, A. J., & Dalziel, T. (2003). Boards of directors and firm-performance: Integrating agency and resource dependence perspectives. *Academy of Management Review, 28*, 383–396.

Hoye, R., & Cuskelly, G. (2007). *Sport governance.* London: Routledge.

Hoye, R., & Doherty, A. (2011). Nonprofit sport board performance: A review and directions for future research. *Journal of Sport Management, 25*, 272–286.

Humphries, S. A., & Whelan, C. (2017). National culture and corporate governance codes. *Corporate Governance: The International Journal of Business in Society, 17*(1), 152–163.

Hung, H. (1998). A typology of the theories of the roles of governing boards. *Corporate Governance: An International Review, 6*(2), 101–111.

Huse, M. (2005). Accountability and creating accountability: A framework for exploring behavioural perspectives of corporate governance. *British Journal of Management, 16*(s1), 65–79.

Huse, M., Hoskisson, R., Zattoni, A., & Viganò, R. (2011). New perspectives on board research: Changing the research agenda. *Journal of Management and Governance, 15*(1), 5–28.

Inglis, S. (1997). Roles of the board in amateur sport organizations. *Journal of Sport Management, 11*, 160–176.

Ingram, K., & O'Boyle, I. (2018). Sport governance in Australia: Questions of board structure and performance. *World Leisure Journal, 60*, 156–172.

Inglis, S., Alexander, T., & Weaver, L. (1999). Roles and responsibilities of community nonprofit boards. *Nonprofit Management & Leadership, 10*, 153–167.

Jackling, B., & Johl, S. (2009). Board structure and firm performance: Evidence from India's top companies. *Corporate Governance: An International Review, 17*, 492–509.

Jonsson, E. I. (2013). One role is not big enough: A multi-theoretical study of board roles in SMEs. *International Journal of Business Governance and Ethics, 8*(1), 50.

Krause, R., & Semadeni, M. (2013). Apprentice, departure, and demotion: An examination of the three types of CEO-board chair separation. *Academy of Management Journal, 56*, 805–826.

Lawal, B. (2012). Board dynamics and corporate performance: Review of literature, and empirical challenges. *International Journal of Economics and Finance, 4*(1), 22–35.

Linck, J. S., Netter, J. M., & Yang, T. (2009). The effects and unintended consequences of the Sarbanes-Oxley Act on the supply and demand for directors. *Review of Financial Studies, 22*, 3287–3328.

Madhani, P. M. (2017). Diverse roles of corporate board: A review of various corporate governance theories. *The IUP Journal of Corporate Governance, 16*, 1–20.

Mcintyre, M. L., Murphy, S. A., & Mitchell, P. (2007). The top team: Examining board composition and firm performance. *Corporate Governance: The International Journal of Business in Society, 7*, 547–561.

McLeod, J. (2018). A qualitative inquiry into supporter representation on Scottish football club boards. *Soccer and Society, 19*, 889–902.

Michie, J., & Oughton, C. (2005). The corporate governance of professional football clubs in England. *Corporate Governance, 13*, 517–531.

Minichilli, A., Zattoni, A., & Zona, F. (2009). Making boards effective: An empirical examination of board task performance. *British Journal of Management, 20*(1), 55–74.

Nicholson, G., & Newton, C. (2010). The role of the board of directors: Perceptions of managerial elites. *Journal of Management and Organization, 16*, 201–218.

Petri, T., & Soublin, R. (2010). Turbulent times require a greater focus on board effectiveness. *Strategic HR Review, 9*(4), 20–27.

Petrovic, J. (2008). Unlocking the role of a board director: A review of the literature. *Management Decision, 46*, 1373–1392.

Pfeffer, J., & Salancik, G. (1978). *The external control of organisations: A resource dependence approach.* New York: Harper & Row Publishers.

Roberts, J., McNulty, T., & Stiles, P. (2005). Beyond agency conceptions of the work of the non-executive director: Creating accountability in the boardroom. *British Journal of Management, 16*(s1), 5–26.

Sakires, J., Doherty, A., & Misener, K. (2009). Role ambiguity in voluntary sport organizations. *Journal of Sport Management, 23*, 615–643.

Sherwin, L. (2003). Building an effective board. *Bank Accounting & Finance, 16*(5), 22–29.

Shilbury, D. (2001). Examining board member roles, functions and influence: A study of Victorian sporting organisations. *International Journal of Sport Management, 2*, 253–281.

Shilbury, D., & Ferkins, L. (2011). Professionalisation, sport governance and strategic capability. *Managing Leisure, 16*, 108–127.

Tacon, R., & Walters, G. (2016). Modernisation and governance in UK national governing bodies of sport: How modernisation influences the way board members perceive and enact their roles. *International Journal of Sport Policy, 8*, 363–381.

Taylor, M., & O'Sullivan, N. (2009). How should national governing bodies of sport be governed in the UK? An exploratory study of board structure. *Corporate Governance: An International Review, 17*, 681–693.

Van den Berghe, L., & Baelden, T. (2005). The monitoring role of the board: One approach does not fit all. *Corporate Governance: An International Review, 13*, 680–690.

Van den Berghe, L., & Levrau, A. (2004). Evaluating board of directors: What constitutes a good corporate board? *Corporate Governance: An International Review, 12*, 461–478.

Van Den Heuvel, J., Van Gils, A., & Voordeckers, W. (2006). Board roles in small and medium-sized family businesses: Performance and importance. *Corporate Governance, 14*, 467–485.

Viganò, R., Zattoni, A., Hoskisson, R. E., & Huse, M. (2011). New perspectives on board research. *Journal of Management & Governance, 15*(1), 1–4.

Yeh, C. M., Hoye, R., & Taylor, T. (2011). Board roles and strategic orientation among Taiwanese nonprofit sport organisations. *Managing Leisure, 16*, 287–301.

Yeh, C. M., & Taylor, T. (2008). Issues of governance in sport organisations: A question of board size, structure and roles. *World Leisure Journal*, *50*(1), 33–45.

Yeh, C. M., Taylor, T., & Hoye, R. (2009). Board roles in organisations with a dual board system: Empirical evidence from Taiwanese nonprofit sport organisations. *Sport Management Review*, *12*, 91–100.

Zahra, S., & Pearce, J. (1989). Boards of directors and corporate financial performance: A review and integrative model. *Journal of Management*, *15*, 291–334.

Zona, F., & Zattoni, A. (2007). Beyond the black box of demography: Board processes and task effectiveness within Italian firms. *Corporate Governance: An International Review*, *15*, 852–864

17

Professionalisation of sport governance

Volunteer director motivations

Alison Doherty

The preceding chapter provides insight to the particular roles and responsibilities of volunteer board members – or "governance volunteers" (Inglis & Cleave, 2006, p. 84) – and the changes in them with the increasing professionalisation of sport organisations and the boards that govern them. It is important, then, to consider individual motivations to serve as a director and be part of a board in this evolving context. Motivation explains the decision to pursue and continue with a voluntary board position (Walton, Clerkin, Christensen, Paarlberg, Nesbit & Tschirhart, 2017). Motives, or incentives (Widmer, 1985), relate to individual needs, and motivation is the internal drive to satisfy those needs. Motivation is believed to be critical to performance, as the strength of one's drive to satisfy a need can predict or explain behaviour (Taylor, Doherty & McGraw, 2015). Therefore, it is of interest to know what motivates directors to serve and perform their role, and what are the determinants and outcomes of that drive.

In their multidimensional model of nonprofit sport board performance, Hoye and Doherty (2011) highlight the impact of individual factors, including board member motivation, on the structure (e.g., board and committee composition, diversity) and processes (e.g., group dynamics, decision-making) of the board, with further implications for board performance and ultimately organisational performance. This is undoubtedly connected to being able to ensure a match between an individual's motives for joining and staying and their assigned role (Inglis & Cleave, 2006). However, Jaskyte and Holland (2015) highlight the contemporary issue of "board member disengagement" and suggest it may be due to a poor understanding of directors' "motivation to serve, their interests, needs ... and passions" (pp. 164–165). Further, statistics indicate that citizens are increasingly less likely to volunteer (e.g., Statistics Canada, 2015), and those who are involved are more likely to serve as "peripheral" or "short-term" versus core or career volunteers synonymous with board members (Cuskelly, Hoye & Auld, 2006). Thus, it is critical to effective governance to understand what impels governance volunteers to become involved and remain with an organisation, as boards increasingly vie for capable directors (Agovino, 2013). This chapter synthesises research to date on board member motivation and considers directions for future investigation.

In 2005, Ferkins, Shilbury and McDonald reported that "board motivation" was one of four dominant themes in the limited but growing body of sport governance research to that point.

However, this theme appeared to comprise very few studies focused on board members' reasons for being involved and needs they expected to be met (Inglis, 1994; Searle, 1989). Drawing from board governance literature in the corporate and nonprofit sectors, and the sport subsector specifically, Hoye and Doherty (2011) maintained the hypothetical importance of this element to board functioning and performance, yet they noted that "we [still] have little understanding of what difference [this makes] to the performance of the board" (p. 281). Thus, although "there have clearly been substantial efforts made in measuring and investigating correlates of board performance" (Hoye & Doherty, 2011, p. 272), this does not appear to include a focus on board member attributes in general, and motivation specifically. Of particular importance, it is likely that research has not kept pace with organisational and board changes, and so knowledge to date based on empirical discovery may not reflect the reality of the professionalisation of sport organisations and their boards. This seems to be the case as there continues to be limited attention paid to governance volunteer motivation in the past decade, particularly in the sport context. Cornforth (2012) suggests that too much attention has been given to governance volunteer characteristics – age, gender, socioeconomic background, and so on – with too little consideration of socio-psychological factors that may be particularly relevant to board functioning. Nonetheless, an overview of the research to date is provided here as an indication of current knowledge and a foundation for future research. The focus is specifically on governance volunteer motivation, and not volunteer motivation in general – a common mis-step – as motivation beyond a "core" motive of altruism (Doherty, 2005) may be expected to vary by volunteer type (Doherty, 2005; Prouteau & Tabaries, 2010; Walton et al., 2017). Further, Walton et al. noted as recently as 2017 that we know quite a lot about general volunteering while "the conditions associated with serving on boards remain under-researched" (p. 116).

Published research – from the early work of Widmer (1985), and then Searle's (1989) examination of the sport and recreation board context, up to the findings of Walton et al. (2017) in the general nonprofit board setting – is reviewed here. Research on sport and non-sport governance volunteers is examined, drawing from a reasonably sufficient body of work, in order that some themes may be identified. A multidimensional approach has been used consistently to study governance volunteer motivation, tapping into a range of variables. However, the few studies use a variety of models and measures that render a reasonable synthesis of the findings very challenging. Thus, for the purpose of presentation and further discussion, governance volunteer motives are classified here as generally externally focused (e.g., to help others, support a cause, i.e., altruistic, ideological) and internally focused (e.g., personal gain, i.e., individual, rational, egoistic). While this counters, perhaps, the multidimensional approaches taken by most scholars of governance volunteer motivation, it is a useful basis for understanding the primary motives, and the strength of those, from which we can move to the consideration of more nuanced insights. Indeed, Miller-Stevens, Ward and Neill (2014) acknowledged that distinguishing more nuanced motives within such broad classifications can be difficult, and so the focus here is on the broader categories.

Taking the research to date together, the consistently strongest or most important motivation of governance volunteers appears to be externally focused. It is characterised by a need or desire to "make a difference in the quality of life in my community" (Taysir, Pazarcik & Taysir, 2013, p. 177) or "[do] good for society" in general (Chareonwongsak, 2017, p. 10; also Farris, McKinley, Ayres, Peters & Brady, 2009; Inglis & Cleave, 2006; Ward & McKillop, 2011; Widmer, 1985). Additionally or alternatively, externally focused motivation is to benefit a specific cause through "protect[ing] the interests of one's circle" (Prouteau & Tabaries, 2010, p. 154) because of a "deep loyalty … belief in its specific values" (Taylor, Chait & Holland, 1991, p. 216; also Farris et al., 2009; Inglis, 1994; Inglis & Cleave, 2006; Miller-Stevens et al., 2014; Ward & McKillop,

2011; Widmer, 1985). For the most part, scholars report that governance volunteers are secondarily motivated by internally directed incentives such as "a feeling of accomplishment" (Chareonwongsak, 2017, p. 10), "expansion of networks" (Miller-Stevens et al., 2014, p. 169) and "personal renewal" (Taylor et al., 1991, p. 216). Taysir et al. (2013) concluded that "governance volunteers first look for opportunities to create value for a group or for a whole society and they also expect to receive some social, psychological and material gains" (p. 183). Notably, the limited sport research only distinguishes governance volunteer motives as, for example, addressing "*sport* needs" and "learn[ing] more about *my sport*" (Inglis, 1994) (italics added for emphasis).

A few studies provide further insight with respect to the broad categories of motivation of governance volunteers. In a qualitative study using roundtable discussion with volunteer directors of nonprofit boards, Miller-Stevens et al. (2014) uncovered board members' particular motives for joining their board and notably different motives for continuing on in their role. Specifically, passion for a cause and tackling it together were reportedly most important to joining a board, followed by satisfying an employer's expectation to serve and the personal opportunity for networking. In contrast, board members indicated feeling a sense of purpose, being appreciated and gaining experience as the most important reasons for continuing. This appears to represent a shift over time from an initial combination of externally and internally directed motives to internally directed reasons for remaining with one's board. Further, that initial motivation was directed at a particular cause versus doing good generally; a focus that related research suggests may distinguish board and general volunteers and explain volunteers' move to a governance role.

For example, Prouteau and Tabaries (2010) found that leader and non-leader volunteers in a large sample of French nonprofit associations differed in their primary motives, with leader or governance volunteers more likely to be engaged to support a specific cause and protect the interests of those involved (also Ward & McKillop, 2011). General volunteers reported broader externally directed reasons for engaging with their association. Walton et al. (2017) found no difference between general or programme volunteers and board members with regard to the motivation to "mak[e] a difference in society" (p. 124) in general, however they did not measure more specific cause-related motives, which may have distinguished these types of volunteers. That more focused yet still externally directed motives may be an important distinguishing characteristic of volunteer board members, at least at the outset, would seem consistent with the greater responsibility those volunteers take for the direction and sustainability of the organisations they serve.

A few studies reported variations among cohorts of governance volunteers that provide additional insight to their motivation. Taysir et al. (2013) found that younger board members (less than 35 years) had stronger internally directed motives for developing relationships and learning than their older counterparts. Ward and McKillop (2011) reported similar findings for board volunteers less than 40 years of age. Inglis (1994) reported gender differences such that growth and developing relationships were significantly more important motives for women than men board members (Ward and McKillop also found social interaction to be more important for women). It is possible those gender differences were linked with age, based on their parallels with Taysir et al.'s findings, although Inglis did not consider that variable. Taysir et al. (2013) also examined whether governance volunteer position (president, board member) and organisational mission (culture/recreation, health, social services, environment and so on) explained any variation in motives and found no effect. However, from her data Widmer (1985) reported a typology of governing boards based on the incentives or motives that they primarily serve: "Bureaucratic boards" are those that appear to meet the needs of governance volunteers with employment-related incentives such as the expectation of one's employer to serve and the development of work-based skills; "activist boards" are those that satisfy primarily ideological – and specifically cause-based – incentives to make a difference; and "volunteer boards" meet governance volunteers' primary needs for both social connections and personal development. Widmer provided further insight to the focus of these boards as primarily working with other organisations (bureaucratic), focused on a specific political, social or economic cause (activist) and addressing civic issues (volunteer).

This review of the albeit limited research on board member motives – which is particularly inadequate in the sport organisation setting – nonetheless indicates there are dual broad motives for board members' engagement, with some evidence of further variation by at least individual factors. Notably, it seems likely that governance volunteers become involved for one reason or set of reasons and stay for another based on their lived experience with the board. This shift may happen over time spent with a board, but it may also happen with board changes, such as would be realised with increasing professionalisation. This knowledge has important implications for board member recruitment and retention, which should thus focus on opportunities for the realisation of different needs in order to bring, and keep, valued volunteers on board.

Turning to outcomes, two studies considered whether better board or organisation performance is associated with particular sources of governance volunteer motivation. Chareonwongsak (2017) noted that research has mostly examined motivation to become and serve as a board member but not the relationship between this motivation and performance. Taylor et al. (1991) examined whether board member motives distinguish effective and ineffective boards, finding that volunteers in the two circumstances did not differ in general. However, further analysis revealed that members of effective boards were more likely to indicate the specific cause as their reason for being involved, rather than general externally directed motives. In a more sophisticated study, Chareonwongsak (2017) examined the impact of governance volunteer motivation on performance, with the presumption that the type and degree of directors' motivation will impact their work and the work of the board (cf. Hoye & Doherty, 2011). He found that financial performance and internal management quality of the cooperative organisations that were the focus of the study were significantly and most strongly predicted by board members' drive for accomplishment, receiving honours and awards and being well known in the community because of their involvement; in other words, internally directed motives. Importantly, framed by expectancy theory, that study considered the strength of motivation to serve the board as a function of the value of various incentives and the likelihood of realising those through board engagement. Thus, the study extended the focus to date on *what* motivates board members to join and continue, to the consideration of *how* they are motivated (and ultimately what difference that makes to the organisation). Chareonwongsak was further able to determine that such factors as board function (meaningful decision-making) and composition (informed members) significantly affected the governance volunteers' degree of motivation to serve. While Hoye and Doherty (2011) theorise that the individual factor of board member motivation may be expected to impact board processes, Chareonwongsak's findings indicate that there can be a reciprocal effect of board processes on motivation. This may be an important consideration in the context of increasing board professionalisation, which may, in fact, influence board members' motivations to serve and perform.

While the limited research to date provides some general insights – and perhaps hints at important variations – more questions than answers remain. This chapter turns now to a discussion of directions for future research that can help explain motives, and motivation, in the context of sport boards as they continue to evolve.

Future research

A discussion of direction for the continued investigation of sport governance volunteer motivation should consider suitable theoretical framework(s) for capturing motives, and the determinants and outcomes of those motives. "Good" theoretical models frame description, explanation and prediction of phenomena (Doherty, 2012) – including motivation and behaviour – that may assist with the effective recruitment, retention and performance of board members. Relevant models should be used to explore the nuanced board member motives within broad categories of externally and internally directed drivers, and any relationships between them and meaningful determinants and outcomes. As sport governance volunteer research has likely not kept pace with contemporary organisational and board changes, it is important to consider the context of professionalisation with any examination of board member behaviour. The degree of formalisation, specialisation and expertise, accountability, efficiency and so on, may be expected to shape, and be shaped by, board member motivation.

Board member motivation research to date has relied on general needs theory (Inglis, 1994; Inglis & Cleave, 2006; Searle, 1989), and related incentives-based theory (Taylor et al., 1991; Widmer, 1985) and public servant motivation theory (Miller-Stevens et al., 2014; Walton et al., 2017), as well as social exchange theory (Inglis, 1994; Searle, 1989) and expectancy theory (Chareonwongsak, 2017). These theories explain that behaviour is impelled by the drive to satisfy needs, receive rewards, or fulfil desired benefits, including the desire to serve the greater public good, and by the expectation that such behaviour will engender those valued rewards, respectively. Social exchange and expectancy theories of motivation have the potential to go beyond describing *what* motivates board members to the consideration of *how* they are motivated. The recommendations for future research provided here are delimited to a discussion of how such theories can meaningfully advance our understanding of board member motivation.

The further application of social exchange theory may have particular merit as it allows for the examination of both perceived costs and benefits as determinants of motivation to engage as a volunteer board member. Social exchange theory presumes that individuals are motivated to be involved if they believe the potential benefits of doing so outweigh the costs (Blau, 1994; Thibault & Kelley, 1959). Thus, the motivation or drive to satisfy important needs in a given context is weighed against the perceived costs of doing so. Olson (1965) touted the value of this perspective in the context of collective action. Yet, the work of Searle (1989) and then Inglis (1994) in the sport board context, as well as research by Widmer (1985), Taylor et al. (1991) and Farris et al. (2009), measured the fulfilment or satisfaction of the benefits of volunteering and did not consider the weight of potential costs to board members. Capturing both perceived benefits and costs for governance volunteers, and the relative weight of those, allows a more comprehensive and meaningful modelling of board member motivation by capturing factors that drive and constrain board engagement (cf. Doherty & Patil, 2019; Walton et al., 2017). This may be of particular interest in the context of increasing sport organisation and board professionalisation where different motives and distinct costs of volunteering may come to light.

The theory of planned behaviour is another model that may be used to generate a richer understanding of governance volunteer motivation. This theory contends that motivation to engage in a particular behaviour is a function of one's own positive attitude towards that behaviour in concert with the perceived expectations of others to be involved (Ajzen, 1985). While it does not account for costs or constraints to behaviour, it does consider the strength of one's attitude and the strength of obligation to satisfy others. Obligation to serve – to satisfy an employer, family values or important others – has been identified as a motive for governance volunteers (Miller-Stevens et al., 2014; Ward & McKillop, 2011; Widmer, 1985), and the theory of planned behaviour includes that for a richer explanation of behaviour. The model has been used in the context of sport event volunteering (Bang & Lee, 2014; Lee, Won & Bang, 2014) but does not appear to have been adopted for the study of volunteers in the sport board context.

Expectancy theory (Vroom, 1964) was reportedly valuable for Chareonwongsak's (2017) study of cooperative board volunteer directors. It is unquestionably a complex model to apply as it considers individuals' cognitive processes of determining whether to exert effort in a particular direction. However, the interaction of the perceived ability to carry out one's role, the expectation that certain benefits (or costs) will be realised as a result and the relative value of those benefits to the individual is a powerful model for explaining and predicting board member motivation. Can I do this? If I do this what will happen? Do I value that? Expectancy theory may be particularly useful for examining the motivation of prospective and continuing sport governance volunteers in the context of contemporary boards. It captures volunteers' perceptions about whether they can meet board and organisation expectations, and their motivations to do so based on the anticipation that sufficient intrinsic and extrinsic incentives will be realised as a result.

Framed by any of these theories, it is important to continue to consider whether there is variation in sport governance volunteers' motives, rather than assuming all board members are driven by the same needs. The research reviewed here indicates some variation in governance volunteer motives by age (Taysir et al., 2013) and gender (Inglis, 1994). These factors may be examined further in the contemporary sport board context, along with the consideration of other individual variables that may be particularly relevant to volunteer motives (cf. Wilson, 2012) and board composition in general (e.g., background experience, tenure; Hoye & Doherty, 2011). For example, Inglis (1994) suggests that the primary motives of board members in her study of provincial sport organisations is a reflection of having "come up through the ranks" (p. 182) from the local to provincial level, and the insight and expectations they bring with them. Variation in board member motives associated with particular individual characteristics may provide insight into the importance and impact of board composition for performance.

Given that governance volunteer motives may differ by volunteer type (Prouteau & Tabaries, 2010), there is merit in examining whether there is variation by board roles (e.g., president versus executive board members, versus members at large). Although Taysir et al. (2013) found no differences in the nonprofit context in general, this may not be the case for sport board members' motivations to serve in different board roles, and in the context of increasing professionalisation that may have different implications for different roles. Again, particular nuances within the broad categories of externally and internally directed motives should be considered. An exploratory approach specific to sport governing boards, such as taken by Miller-Stevens et al. (2014), may be useful to uncover any variations in motives. Miller-Stevens et al.'s work is also useful in highlighting a general shift from externally to internally directed motives over time, and this should be examined in the sport board context as well. A more sophisticated inquiry would involve a longitudinal investigation of motives (and constraints) at the outset of board engagement and then at one year and beyond. Such a research design could take into account any critical time points of the board, such as significant shifts in professionalisation (see Thibault, Slack & Hinings, 1991). It may also facilitate consideration of the alignment (or misalignment and potential challenge) of volunteers' externally directed altruistic and ideological motives versus internally directed individual and egoistic motives in the context of more professional sport organisations and boards.

In addition to possible variations in motives for different roles and lengths of time on the board, there may be board- and organisation-level differences that are important to understand for the recruitment, retention and performance of governance volunteers. While Taysir et al.

(2013) found no differences in motives for board members working towards different organisation missions, Widmer (1985) concluded that boards could be classified by the incentives they primarily serve and gave some indication that these are aligned with different missions or mandates. Given the "special features of sport" (Smith & Stewart, 2010, p. 1), with its potential for drama, "intense emotional experiences" and, in some cases, interpersonal connection with elite and celebrity athletes, there may be merit in examining whether the focus or mandate of the board and organisation is associated with particular governance volunteer motives for being involved. Relatedly, and of particular interest to this book, is the possible association between motives and the extent of professionalisation. Do individuals have particular motives for (or constraints to) being involved with a more (or less) sophisticated board?

This leads to the consideration of the outcomes or impacts of board member motivation. Chareonwongsak (2017) found that internally directed board member motives were significantly associated with organisation performance in the cooperative organisation context, highlighting new insight into this direct relationship with objective measures of effectiveness; namely, financial performance and national cooperative quality management ranking. He explains that, perhaps surprisingly, the individual drive for accomplishment, recognition and any public awards that are linked to those, are the most meaningful predictors of organisational outcomes, rather than any sense of altruism. That internally directed drive may be more consistent with board work that is characterised by the complexity of efficiency, accountability, expertise and serving a broader and more demanding group of stakeholders than is the reality for more professional organisations and boards. Does this relationship between internally directed motives and performance hold in the sport board context as well? What impact do sport governance volunteer motives have for board performance?

There is still great opportunity and need for a better understanding of volunteer board member motives and motivation to serve, and the determinants and implications of that for sport board and organisational performance. This chapter provides a review of existing knowledge that only serves to highlight the limited understanding and direction for continued research. Sport is governed by people – and typically volunteers – who shape and serve within given environments and structures. While these are critical considerations for effective governance, it is to the organisation's detriment if it fails to ensure a rich understanding of the motivations of its invaluable governance volunteers to serve.

References

Agovino, T. (2013). So many nonprofits, so few good board members. *Crain's New York*. Retrieved 10 February 2019, from www.crainsnewyork.com/article/20130618/nonprofits/130619867

Ajzen, I. (1985). From intentions to actions: A theory of planned behavior. In J. Kuhl & J. Beckmann (Eds.), *Springer series in social psychology* (pp. 11–38). Berlin: Springer.

Bang, H., & Lee, C. S. (2014). The roles of large-scale sporting event volunteer motivations in predicting behavioural intention within the theory of planned behavior. *International Journal of Hospitality and Event Management, 1*, 111–134.

Blau, P. (1994). *Structural contexts of opportunities*. Chicago, IL: University of Chicago Press.

Chareonwongsak, K. (2017). Enhancing board motivation for competitive performance of Thailand's co-operatives. *Journal of Co-operative Organization and Management, 5*, 1–13.

Cornforth, C. (2012). Nonprofit governance research: Limitations of the focus on boards and suggestions for new directions. *Nonprofit and Voluntary Sector Quarterly, 41*, 1116–1135.

Cuskelly, G., Hoye, R., & Auld, C. (2006). *Working with volunteers in sport: Theory and practice*. London: Routledge.

Doherty, A. (2005). *A profile of community sport volunteers*. Toronto: Parks and Recreation Ontario.

Doherty, A. (2012). Investing in sport management: The value of good theory. *Sport Management Review, 16*, 5–11.

Doherty, A., & Patil, S. (2019). Reflections on major sport event volunteer legacy research. *Journal of Policy Research in Tourism, Leisure and Events, 11*, s34–s42.

Farris, E., McKinley, S., Ayres, J., Peters, J., & Brady, C. (2009). County-level extension leadership: Understanding volunteer board member motivation. *Journal of Extension, 47*, 1–5.

Ferkins, L., Shilbury, D., & McDonald, G. (2005). The role of the board in building strategic capability: Towards an integrated model of sport governance research. *Sport Management Review, 8*, 195–225.

Hoye, R., & Doherty, A. (2011). Nonprofit sport board performance: A review and directions for future research. *Journal of Sport Management, 25*, 272–285.

Inglis, S. (1994). Exploring volunteer board member and executive director needs: Importance and fulfillment. *Journal of Applied Recreation Research, 19*, 171–189.

Inglis, S., & Cleave, S. (2006). A scale to assess board member motivations in nonprofit organizations. *Nonprofit Management and Leadership, 17*, 83–101.

Jaskyte, K., & Holland, T. (2015). Nonprofit boards: Challenges and opportunities. *Human Service Organizations: Management, Leadership, and Governance, 39*, 163–166.

Lee, Y-J., Won, D., & Bang, H. (2014). Why do event volunteers return? Theory of planned behavior. *International Review of Public and Nonprofit Marketing, 11*, 229–241.

Miller-Stevens, K., Ward, K. D., & Neill, K. A. (2014). Public service motivation theory in a nonprofit context: An explanatory study of nonprofit board member motivations. *Journal of Nonprofit Education and Leadership, 4*, 162–178.

Olson, M. (1965). *The logic of collective action* (2nd ed.). Cambridge, MA: Harvard University Press.

Prouteau, L., & Tabaries, M. (2010). The unpaid leaders of French voluntary associations. *Annals of Public and Cooperative Economics, 81*, 131–166.

Searle, M. S. (1989). Measuring recreation board members' needs. *Recreation Research Review, 14*, 41–50.

Smith, A. C.T., & Stewart, B. (2010). The special features of sport: A critical revisit. *Sport Management Review, 13*, 1–13.

Statistics Canada. (2015). General Social Survey: Giving, volunteering and participating, 2013. Retrieved 11 February 2019, from https://www150.statcan.gc.ca/n1/daily-quotidien/150130/dq150130b-eng.htm

Taylor, B. E., Chait, R. P., & Holland, T. P. (1991). Trustee motivation and board effectiveness. *Nonprofit and Voluntary Sector Quarterly, 20*, 207–224.

Taylor, T., Doherty, A., & McGraw, P. (2015). *Managing people in sport organizations: A strategic human resource management perspective* (2nd ed.). London: Routledge.

Taysir, E. A., Pazarcik, Y., & Taysir, N. K. (2013). What motivates nonprofit organizations' top managers to volunteer? *Journal of Transnational Management, 18*, 164–187.

Thibault, J. W., & Kelley, H. H. (1959). *The social psychology of groups*. New York: Wiley.

Thibault, L., Slack, T., & Hinings, B. (1991). Professionalism, structures and systems: The impact of professional staff on voluntary sport organizations. *International Review for the Sociology of Sport, 26*, 83–98.

Vroom, V. H. (1964). *Work and motivation*. New York: Wiley.

Walton, M. A., Clerkin, R. M., Christensen, R. K., Paarlberg, L. E., Nesbit, R., & Tschirhart, M. (2017). Means, motive and opportunity: Exploring board volunteering. *Personnel Review, 46*, 115–135.

Ward, A. M., & McKillop, D. G. (2011). An examination of volunteer motivation in credit unions: Informing volunteer resource management. *Annals of Public and Cooperative Economics, 82*, 253–275.

Widmer, C. (1985). Why board members participate. *Nonprofit and Voluntary Sector Quarterly, 14*, 8–23.

Wilson, J. (2012). Volunteerism research: A review essay. *Nonprofit and Voluntary Sector Quarterly, 41*, 176–212.

18

The interconnected roles of the chair

Géraldine Zeimers and David Shilbury

Introduction

The role of the Chair in the governance function of nonprofit sport organisations has received relatively limited attention by sport management scholars. Comparatively, there has been significant empirical research examining the role of the Chair in the corporate and nonprofit governance literature (Harrison, Murray & Conforth, 2012; Wertheimer, 2007). In the for-profit sector, the Chair is seen "as being relatively less powerful and more ceremonial and symbolic than the CEO position" (Harrison, Torres & Kukalis, 1988, p. 214). In the nonprofit sector, Otto (2003) noted the role of the nonprofit board chair is often not as well defined, leading to ambiguity and even conflicting expectations about the relationships between the Chair, other board members, management and stakeholders. The existing literature on nonprofit board chairs largely concentrates on the outcomes associated with the position (Wertheimer, 2007). For example, what makes for an effective Chair–CEO relationship (Hilland, 2006; Kakabadse, Kakabadse & Barratt, 2006; Ieconvich & Bar-Mor, 2007), the impact of the Chair's leadership on the performance of the CEO, board and organisation (Harrison & Murray, 2012) and the factors influencing the perceptions of Chair leadership effectiveness (Harrison, Murray & Cornforth, 2012).

In the sport governance domain, few scholars have directly explored the role of the Chair although its influential role has often been cited as an important finding (Adriaanse, 2016; Ferkins & Shilbury, 2015; Ferkins, Shilbury & O'Boyle, 2018; Hoye, 2003, 2004; Inglis, 1997). Despite this, the role of the Chair continues to receive global attention largely due to their centrality in chairing/leading board meetings or as a spokesperson for the board and organisation (Balduck, Lucidarme, Marlier & Willem, 2015). Issues such as collective leadership, shared leadership and collaborative governance have been examined in the sport governance literature, but, as yet, the role of the Chair has not been fully explored (Ferkins & Shilbury, 2015; Ferkins et al., 2018). Investigating the leadership contribution of board chairs is important to better understand the extent and nature of the Chair's role as a leader and influence on board strategic functioning (Harrison & Murray, 2012).

This lack of research is particularly surprising given the sport industry's distinctiveness, exemplified by features of intangibility, volunteerism and passion (Taylor & McGraw, 2006). Further, understanding the role of the Chair is needed given that the majority of research on nonprofit governance has been conducted on nonprofit organisations (NPOs) that are not membership-based (Hoye & Cuskelly, 2003). Consequently, much of what is known about the board Chair role in NPOs does not consider membership representation on volunteer boards. Hoye (2002) defined "a board chair as the individual leader of the board who is elected, appointed, invited, or selected to chair meetings of the board and lead the board in fulfilling its duties" (p. 9). The term "Chair" is used generically to identify the person responsible for leading the board and organisation, and, in many cases, this will be the elected president. The purpose of this chapter is to identify, examine and describe the key roles of a sport board Chair, and the interconnectedness of these roles in the context of providing governance leadership.

Based on the review of literature and data collected from four sport board Chairs, Figure 18.1 has been developed to illustrate the main roles of the Chair. Figure 18.1 displays five key themes around which this chapter will be organised. In each theme, the associated sub-themes shown in Figure 18.1 will be used to examine in depth the role of the Chair of a sport board. The non-profit governance scholarship on the role of a Chair showed three sets of interrelationships in which board Chairs may execute their leadership role: (a) board chair–board member relationships; (b) board chair–CEO relationship; and (c) board chair–stakeholder relationships. As shown in Figure 18.1, these three interrelationships are complemented by the need for collaborative governance relationships, particularly salient within a federated sport governance system and professional sport leagues where cooperation between member associations or clubs is critical to a unified vision and strategy for the sport.

After the literature review, four interviews were conducted with current or former Chairs of nonprofit national sport organisations (NSOs) from Australia and Belgium. Table 18.1 provides a summary of the background of each current or former Chair interviewed. It shows a range of experiences from a Chair who has held multiple roles as a Chair in medium to large sports to a Chair of a relatively small sport in terms of staff numbers. Data collection took place in November and December 2018 and the interviews were conducted in French and in English. Traditional coding techniques were used by the first author and discussed in detail with the second author to reach agreement on the key themes and their alignment with the literature.

This chapter is therefore structured around these five themes. The first theme considers the individual Chair board leadership role. Second, the Chair and CEO theme capture the relationship/role of the Chair with the CEO from a shared leadership perspective. The third theme highlights the role of the Chair in managing the group dynamics associated with board members and fostering the notion of collective board leadership and direction setting. The fourth role refers to the Chair and his or her influence and need to work with member associations (regional entities) or club Chairs with a view to establishing a collaborative approach to governance. Finally, the role of the Chair in relation to external partners is examined. External partners may include government and political leaders, sponsors and broadcasters, international/regional federations and in-sport associations (though external to the NSO), such as players', coaches' and referees' associations.

Central to Figure 18.1 is the circle in the middle showing the board leadership role of the Chair and the interconnected nature of the role as the circle passes through each quadrant identifying the four remaining themes. The flow from one quadrant to another is important when examining Figure 18.1. Despite its circular form, Figure 18.1 depicts the extending interconnected roles from the individual Chair by adding other "actors" in each of the subsequent quadrants. The arrow between the CEO quadrant and the board members quadrant illustrates the shared leadership role between the CEO, Chair and board, and the collective leadership role that the board should fulfil.

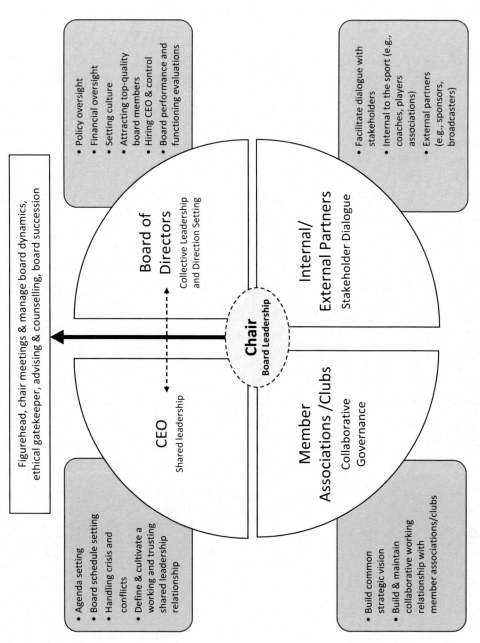

Figure 18.1 Interconnected roles of a sport board chair.

Figurehead, chair meetings & manage board dynamics, ethical gatekeeper, advising & counselling, board succession

Chair
Board Leadership

Board of Directors
Collective Leadership and Direction Setting

CEO
Shared leadership

Member Associations /Clubs
Collaborative Governance

Internal/ External Partners
Stakeholder Dialogue

- Policy oversight
- Financial oversight
- Setting culture
- Attracting top-quality board members
- Hiring CEO & control
- Board performance and functioning evaluations

- Facilitate dialogue with stakeholders
- Internal to the sport (e.g., coaches, players associations)
- External partners (e.g., sponsors, broadcasters)

- Agenda setting
- Board schedule setting
- Handling crisis and conflicts
- Define & cultivate a working and trusting shared leadership relationship

- Build common strategic vision
- Build & maintain collaborative working relationship with member associations/clubs

Table 18.1 Chair backgrounds

Country	Australia (Chair 1)	Australia (Chair 2)	Belgium (Chair 3)	Belgium (Chair 4)
Name of the organisation	Netball Australia	Cycling Australia, Basketball Australia, National Basketball League	Association Royale Belge de Hockey	Fédération Belge de Rugby
Size (paid staff)	46	Various	17	1
Size (participants)	509,000	Various	47,000	12,000
Position	Chair of the board	Past chair	Chair of the board	Chair of the board
Chair appointment date	2017	Chair Cycling Australia 2014–2017, Executive Chairman Basketball Australia, 1993–1997, Chair National Basketball League 1987–1997	2006	2017
Gender	Female	Male	Male	Male
Experience working area	Business manager with operational and strategic experience across a number of industries, own business and recruiter.	CEO of national and international sport organisations, lawyer, company director and lecturer	Private banker	Business manager, self-employed worker
Education	Law degree	Law degree	Finance and economics degree	
Level of education	Master's degree and MBA	Master's degree	Master's degree	Upper secondary
Other relevant functions	Director since 2012	Member of various national and international boards	Member of the executive committee of the Belgian Olympic Committee; Member of the board of directors of international sport federation; Former captain of the national team	Chair of sport club

The Chair: Board leadership

In his work on board leadership and behaviour, Wertheimer (2007) highlighted the need for additional research to focus on Chair leadership. In this context, he wrote: "as the senior volunteer leader of the organisation, the board Chair is responsible for leading the board in the oversight and support responsibilities that are critical to good governance" (p. 7). Scholars have regularly reported on the strategic leadership role of the Chair within the board of directors (Ferkins & Shilbury, 2015; Hoye, 2002, 2003, 2004). As Hoye (2002) described, the role of the Chair is to empower the board's strategic function by seeking agreement (with management) on a vision and strategy defined collectively by the board of directors. Five roles, or sub-themes were identified in this theme of board leadership.

First, the *figurehead role* refers to the responsibility of the Chair to serve as an ambassador and a spokesperson for the organisation. Describing this "public-face" role, a Chair explained:

> Because of the function, I am the figurehead. But what matters is the project, not the people. So, if someone worked on the project more than I, and knows it very well, he or she will be the contact point for the press. Sometimes this role is shared with other board members or with the CEO when the Chair is not the best representative. (Chair 4)

This figurehead role can be divided into a formal and a communication role – for example, a formal figurehead role at an annual general meeting, at organisational programmes or at community events, and a communication figurehead role that contributes to the organisation's annual report, website, newsletter and other communication pieces (Wertheimer, 2007). This role also implies a liaison role that involves cultivating relationships with individual donors, funders and other community stakeholders to increase the visibility and the legitimacy of the organisation (Harrison et al., 2013; Iecovich, 2004; Wertheimer, 2007).

Second, *chairing meetings and managing board dynamics* refers to the responsibility of the Chair to preside over all meetings of the board, executive committee (sometimes shared with subcommittees with dedicated Chairs) and other meetings or events as necessary (Harrison & Murray, 2012; Hoye, 2002; Wertheimer, 2007). Chairing meetings involves organising and structuring the agenda as well as allocating and determining time for each item to ensure efficient use of time to deal with both strategic and routine agenda items. This implies that "the chairperson should be the best prepared person at the meeting. They should know everything that is in the papers" (Chair 2). According to Hoye (2002), a good Chair is needed to aid consensus decision-making. Aiding or facilitating are good words as they imply the need for the Chair to remain neutral or distant enough to avoid defending a particular outcome. As explained by one Chair; "It is not the role of the Chair to have views on everything. It is the Chair's role that everybody else does … It is not conclusive to give your view" (Chair 1).

Another aspect of this role consistently stated by each of the four board Chairs was the need to ensure that every board member has the opportunity to contribute to meaningful dialogue at board meetings (Herman & Heimovics, 1990; Hoye, 2002; Wertheimer, 2007). One Chair noted:

> The Chair needs to try to ensure that everyone is contributing to the meeting and that we are making good decisions, in good spirit. That is an important role of the Chair, to get everyone involved and give the feeling that we are working for a common purpose. (Chair 2)

This illustrates how efficient and satisfying meetings can be by engaging board members and engendering a commitment of board members to the organisation through their full contribution to meetings. Ongoing dialogue and trust within the board is essential for healthy board dynamics. Managing group dynamics on a sport board can be more important, and at times difficult, "because the passion [associated with sport] can create more intense discussions" (Chair 2) and therefore the management of this "passion" is fundamental to a properly functioning board (Brown & Guo, 2010). Consequently, to facilitate board dynamics, the Chair is responsible for handling tensions within the board and this includes handling difficult directors.

Third, the *ethical gatekeeper role* refers to the responsibility to promote ethical and legal compliance to ensure good governance (Wertheimer, 2007). This role involves intervening when unethical behaviour is displayed, showing transparency, handling personal conflict, declaring and managing conflicts of interest and any other internal ethical crisis within the board of directors. As the leader of the board, the Chair is the contact for directors on board issues to ensure "communication with you" rather than "around you" (Wertheimer, 2007). This role is fundamental to ensure the integrity of the board; and it is distinct from the role shared by the Chair and CEO when handling external ethical crises that have a broader scope (Wertheimer, 2007). When managing a crisis within a sport setting, a Chair should be cautious because in sport "Media attention is higher" (Chair 2) and this may have some impact on the decisions made by sport boards and how it is handled.

Fourth, the *advising and counselling role* refers to helping board members to become organised and efficient (Harrison et al., 2013). This also includes mentoring the CEO on key strategic and operational decision-making (Brown & Guo, 2010; Ferkins, 2007). The fifth and last role is the need to *initiate succession planning* on both board and Chair appointments.

Chair and CEO: Shared leadership

As Wertheimer (2007) contends, "the board-chair's relationship with the chief executive is by far the most important relationships he or she will have. It is crucial to forge a working partnership that begins even before you officially become chair" (p. 15). The nonprofit literature has focused on analysing the relationship between the Chair and the CEO, power distribution and its impact on board and organisational performance. In the sport literature, to better understand the board–executive relationship, Hoye and Cuskelly (2007) claimed "The heart of the issue for sport organizations … seems to be clarifying the respective roles of the board and staff in all strategic activities" (p. 117). Similarly, Ferkins and Shilbury (2015) highlighted the need to further examine board shared leadership by clarifying the role of the chairperson. In this quadrant, four sub-themes have been identified.

First, the *agenda setting role* refers to the collaboration between the CEO and the Chair when setting the agenda for board meetings (Ferkins, Shilbury & McDonald, 2009; Ferkins & Shilbury, 2015; Harrison & Murray, 2012; Hoye, 2002; Inglis & Weaver, 2000; Wertheimer, 2007). This is especially relevant when endeavouring to ensure a strategic focus for the board. Ferkins et al. (2009) empirically established that the board's strategic role was enhanced by the integration of strategy into board processes, using the board agenda. When discussing guidelines for identifying key agenda items, all four Chairs recommended that the agenda should endeavour to "place strategic issues up front to have most time during the meeting (not only ticking compliance matters)" (Chair 1).

Second, *board schedule setting* consists of establishing an agreed-upon schedule of board and subcommittee meetings. Often this is jointly undertaken on advice from the CEO, company secretary or equivalent. This involves prioritising items and issues, who should be represented (e.g., invited speakers from management, from regional entities, experts, etc.) and how the issues should be presented (Inglis & Weaver, 2000; Wertheimer, 2007).

Third, the *handling crisis and conflict role* relates to the Chair and CEO working together during a major governance crisis. Contrary to internal crises, one Chair suggested that:

> When there is a situation where your reputation, the reputation of the sport is at risk and this is a consequence of a board decision or if it is both, depending on the circumstances, that is the time where the board should step forward. You need to decide if you want to respond publicly or if you want to sit back. (Chair 1)

Fourth, *define and cultivate a working and trusting shared leadership relationship*. Scholars have pointed to the bridging role of the Chair in the board–CEO shared leadership dynamic (Ferkins, Shilbury & McDonald, 2005, 2009; Ferkins & Shilbury, 2015). They highlighted the balance that exists between the voluntary members of a board and senior management team of a sport organisation and how this balance has increasingly favoured paid executives in decision-making as part of the professionalisation process that has occurred in many sport organisations (Shilbury, 2001). According to Ferkins et al. (2009), more active involvement in strategy by the board advanced the board's ability to perform its strategic function and more importantly oversee and monitor the agreed strategic direction. The shared leadership dynamic is recognition of whether a board is board-led, CEO-led or can find a balance in an environment where directors are typically volunteers and the CEO is often more qualified than the directors. The power dynamic inherent in this role is a result of the professionalisation of the sport sector over the last 30 years. The following citation captures to some extent the complex dynamics associated with shared leadership between the Chair, board and CEO.

> Keeping it strategic and trusting management to actually do the management work. Give them scope but also the opportunity to get up in front of the board so that the board develops trust in management and can see that they are competent and capable. I see them all the time and think they are amazing but if there is a gap, the board will not be as quick to support management. (Chair 1)

Chair and board members: Collective board leadership and enhancing board strategic functioning

In the trend towards integrating strategy into board processes, there is a growing consensus that the Chair has a specific role and impact on the strategic functioning of the board (Ferkins et al., 2005, 2009; Harrison & Murray, 2012). In NSOs, boards should shape rather than merely ratify or "rubber stamp" the strategic direction of the organisation (Ferkins & Shilbury, 2012; Ferkins et al., 2005; Shilbury, Ferkins & Smythe, 2013). Direction setting consists of formulating and approving the vision, mission and strategy for the organisation (Harrison et al., 2013). This includes determining a road map, clarifying the board's role in the direction-setting function with management, setting priorities, strategy and a vision from which paid staff and programme volunteers can deliver programmes and services (Ferkins et al., 2009; Harrison, Murray & Cornforth, 2013; Hoye, 2004; Hoye & Cuskelly, 2003; Inglis, 1997; Inglis & Weaver, 2000). For greater ownership of the strategic governance process, the Chair is expected to play a stronger lead role, "utilising the CEO as an advisor rather than as the leader" (Ferkins, 2007, p. 234). When discussing their strategic role, one Chair observed the need to "take a holistic view and make sure that your board is there, that your management is there, that the subcommittees are binding to the whole picture, not driving the business" (Chair 1).

In seeking to examine the responsibilities of the Chair in relation to the strategic role of other board members, six roles were identified. First, the *policy oversight role* consists of providing guidance for senior management to operationalise the broader strategy into annual practices. This consists of offering guidelines and expertise, monitoring and reviewing operational decisions. Although this issue was not specifically raised by the Chairs interviewed, this role appeared in the literature (Brown & Guo, 2010).

Second, the *financial oversight* role refers to the control function of the board (Brown & Guo, 2010). Setting financial policy and monitoring budget is an important area that the Chair should lead, and individual board members are expected to help ensure the board fulfils its obligations for oversight and monitoring. Third, *setting the culture* of the board and of the organisation. One Chair reported: "Culture has to be set from the top, within the board it is critical. We have a working relationship at stake within our board we are trying to get that right" (Chair 1). Culture can be developed further into a board charter or a code of conduct. The same Chair also insisted on the need to ensure cultural sense checking (oversight) during and after board meeting.

Fourth, *attracting top-quality board members* is also a role highlighted in the literature (Ferkins & Shilbury, 2015) and should be focused on the need to find a balance between industry and sport expertise, functional expertise (e.g., marketing, legal, digital) and strategic thinking. Fifth, is *hiring the CEO and a control role*. This role denotes the importance of monitoring and evaluating the performance of the CEO. Control can be performed through formal annual evaluation or informal discussion (Harrison et al., 2013). Consistent with board strategic function, CEO hiring should reflect the strategic needs of a sport organisation and a match of CEO to strategic direction (Brown & Guo, 2010; Ferkins & Shilbury, 2012). Lastly, the Chair is responsible for initiating, in consultation with directors, an *annual evaluation of board performance and functioning*. Together, these six roles are important for the board to demonstrate collective leadership and to enhance strategic capability.

Chair and member associations/clubs: Collaborative governance

Given the nature of the federated nonprofit sport context, ensuring a positive collaborative working relationship with member associations (MAs)/clubs is a key role of the Chair. The need for the board to consider its MAs/clubs and to engage in a collaborative governing process to achieve the sport's broader strategic outcomes is well established in the sport governance literature (Ferkins & Shilbury, 2010; Shilbury & Ferkins, 2015; Shilbury, O'Boyle & Ferkins, 2016). Ferkins and Shilbury (2010) emphasised the need for a power-sharing approach between MAs (state and regional)/clubs in order for the board of the national body or central commission in a professional sports league to develop its strategic capability. Although not fully explored within the existing literature (O'Boyle & Shilbury, 2016), there are indications that the Chair has responsibilities in encouraging, facilitating and building trust with the MAs/clubs. Three essential roles are mentioned by the Chairs.

First, *build a common and strategic vision for the sport*. This refers to the need to define the role and responsibilities of all MAs to avoid ambiguity and to provide direction around a common vision. Dialogue with MAs is therefore paramount in building a common vision and reducing potential points of tension, as one chaired observed.

> Tensions in the federated model are all about defining roles and responsibilities and who gets to make the final call. It is not unusual. We try to remove ambiguity. Ambiguity will remain as long as you are beholden to regional members. (Chair 1)

Second, *building and maintaining strong collaborative working relationships with regional entities* was a key priority according to each of the four Chairs interviewed. Building a culture of trust (O'Boyle & Shilbury, 2016) and common purpose is fundamental.

> What is very important is understanding the common language around what good consultation looks like, and what is good communication. So, we are all clear, we don't have different expectations, this is what it is going to look like, it is fine if there is no consensus. Clarity takes time and effort. This is the way we do this, this is how they get the information, create a robust system that survives the people. (Chair 1)

As explained by one Chair, this relationship-building is essential in a federated structure because:

> We need to unite with the leagues [i.e., regional entities], the clubs, we do this for the superior interest of Belgium rugby, not for us, clubs need to find their way, it must be the general interest. So, we must be collaborative. We have presented the strategic plan to the other leagues and our clubs at the general assembly as well as the annual report. They must be in line with the project because we want them to be our ambassador to encourage their own members. (Chair 4)

To improve the relationships, Chairs described using different means of communication and touch points. This includes annual meetings that involve MA/club CEOs, the chair travelling (with the CEO) to meet with MA/club boards and discuss strategy and take the time to listen to regional issues, and, in some instances, office-sharing with MAs in the same geographic region. For instance, both Belgian NSOs have decided to share offices with their two regional partners.

Another mechanism used to maintain the relationship was the creation of strategic groups between the CEO and Chair of the MA and NSO.

> These meetings are on all the issues in the hands of the CEOs, for which they need our reflection and our support, and our decision if needed. And what is more strategic remains at the level of the board of the league or federation depending on the topic. (Chair 3)

The Chair also set up dedicated sessions to build the relationship and break down barriers by bringing the respective boards together (not only president and CEO).

> Because it is important for the directors to get to know the whole NSO board. This is really important. If you only meet the president, the problem is that he becomes filled with information (and the filter). When you get them all together, a lot of the unknowns get revealed and people start to understand each other. (Chair 1)

The integration of regional entities into the governing role refers to the need for the board to consider its regional entities as member-owners and to engage in collaborative governance to achieve efficient organisational performance (Ferkins & Shilbury, 2015). Usually, it is the Chair who needs to initiate and action communication with MA/club chairs, and ultimately the boards of MAs.

Chair and stakeholder dialogue

Each of the chairs reported fulfilling a key role in relation to both internal and external stakeholders and partners of the organisation. First, the Chair should *facilitate dialogue and make connections* with internal and external stakeholders, such as sport stakeholders (player, coach, fans, referee associations, national Olympic committee, other national sport federations and international sport federations) and external stakeholders (broadcasters, sponsors, government, public administrations, community partners). This role is highly political and denotes the advocacy, ambassador and public relations role expected of a Chair (an extension of the figurehead role). Interestingly, Chair 1, depending on strategic importance, did not consider that it was the role of the Chair to have contacts with sponsors for instance. In this instance, it is a good example of the delineation of roles between the Chair and CEO. This Chair observed:

> Be available not to everyone but really to the people that are important to the business: the CEO, the seven or eight directors, the eight MA presidents and our key external people. Not the external commercial partners – it is the job of the CEO. Only the in-house people that help you make decision and deliver successes. (Chair 1)

Synthesising the role of the Chair in sport governance

This summary of the current research examining the role of the Chair in sport boards has shown a limited number of studies specifically in relation to this topic. This chapter has shown, however, that in the nonprofit literature such studies are more apparent. When adding the data collected from the four board Chairs to the available literature, it is clear that the Chair is a boundary spanner who should be sensitive to the contextual demands of a respective sport organisation, a figurehead, and should provide a platform for director participation, respect role delineation both on the board and in relation to management, and should be capable of managing complex boardroom dynamics.

In Figure 18.1, the key roles attributed to the Chair are organised around five themes. These distinctions are by no means definitive, and naturally there exists overlap between themes, given different sport contexts. Figure 18.1 therefore shows the overlap of the role of the Chair across the four quadrants. Some roles also feature in studies that might be more strongly associated with the board or with the CEO. Kakabadse, Kakabadse and Barratt (2006) noted "the contribution of the chairman substantially differs from one company to the other, according to variance of context, principally company performance, and the nature of critical decisions required" (p. 141). It is important to acknowledge that the roles described in this chapter stem from a review of the nonprofit and sport governance literature and what four particular Chairs reported they do and how they grapple with each of the themes. Each sport organisation is different, given its strategic capacity, size, age and its stage of professionalisation and it is reasonable to expect some variations in the roles and their relative importance from sport organisation to sport organisation.

This chapter reveals that there is much agreement about the key roles of the Chair generally, including preparing meeting agendas, chairing meetings and ensuring that the board functions well (Harrison & Murray, 2012). However, besides the Chair's leadership during meetings, all four Chairs agreed that they must work across all of the key themes at varying stages in organisational life. After analysing the interviews, two distinctive features of sport governance emerged in relation to the role of the Chair: passion and culture and also federated sport structures. In addition, other less sport-specific areas were also identified as worth further investigation in the future.

Passion and culture

Sport passion and culture are major distinctive features of sport governance compared to the nonprofit and corporate sector. One Chair expressed this as follows: "we are only here

271

for pleasure. It is not us [federation] and you [single], it is us [rugby]. There is only one us [gesture of unity]" (Chair 4). Similarly, another Chair went a step further and explained:

> They [the directors] have netball running in their blood since they were eight. So, for a lot of women it has been a key thing in their life that is giving them a space to compete, to be regarded, to excel. They might get it in their job. Many people don't. There is so much passion invested in it. That makes it tricky. More complex because you deal with personal emotions, personal psyches, volunteerism, grass-roots situations. It is personal. Personal engagement is a strength and danger. (Chair 1).

This quotation points to the difficult role of the Chair to keep highly passionate board members on track strategically and to encourage objective independent and evidence-based decision-making and not fall into the trap of becoming too operational and focused on the playing of the sport.

Each of the Chairs raised two additional negative aspects of sport organisations managed by sport enthusiasts with a passion for the sport. For one Chair, his lack of background and culture in the sport (i.e., a subculture specific to the sport) impeded effective conduct as a Chair, despite excellent experience as a Chair. For another Chair, the negative counterbalance of passion resides in an uncommitted volunteer workforce. The Chair explained:

> The dynamic is different because we are not in a business logic. As a non-profit, we cannot have similar expectations for everyone about his/her performance as a volunteer. Sometimes it is frustrating because there are members of the board who are happy because they are sitting here, but they do not participate a lot. (Chair 3).

The role of sport Chairs is therefore challenging as they endeavour to manage and harness passion and associated culture in a positive way. So far, this area is new and scarcely explored in the sport governance literature. Future research is needed to understand the implications of passion and culture on the governing processes of the board and the implications for sport board Chairs. For instance, the interviews raised questions regarding the legitimacy of being a Chair for individuals without a specific sport background and passion for the particular sport compared to individuals with more traditional corporate and governance skills. As strong emotions are often present in the sports workplace, further investigation is recommended to understand how a passionate association with a sport might positively or negatively influence and impact sport governance behaviour as a Chair and the associated decision-making.

Sport federated structure: Federal model of governance

In Australia, Belgium, Canada, the UK and some European nations, NSOs are often organised under a federal model of governance, where decision-making and the power structure is generally divided between a national governing body and state or regional associations. Scholars have reported inherent challenges within such sport governing systems, where multiple legal entities within one code may work against each other in the governance of the sporting code (O'Boyle & Shilbury, 2016; Shilbury et al., 2013). Shilbury and Ferkins (2015) suggested that collaborative governance has significant relevance for a federally organised sport system and could facilitate trust, transparency and cooperation between entities comprising these networks (Ferkins & Shilbury, 2010; O'Boyle & Shilbury, 2016; Shilbury & Ferkins, 2015). Sport governance scholars have acknowledged the need to recognise multi-level governance structures and how responsibilities are shared between governance actors at different levels. While previous studies have essentially examined collaborative governance between regional and national entities in the sport industry, results shown in this chapter suggest future research is needed on the role of the Chair in collaborative governance between NSOs and MAs and in professional sport leagues. More specifically, research that investigates how a Chair facilitates this collaborative approach and how much time and energy may be required would make a useful contribution to our understanding of the role of a Chair.

Chair leadership skills and Chair diversity

A small but growing number of scholars have focused their attention on what has become known as the leadership skills and behaviours and understanding of where leadership emerges in the interactions and constructions of people in groups or organisations (Harrison et al., 2012; Wertheimer, 2007). As this chapter has focused on the roles performed by a Chair, further research may be relevant when considering leadership skills and competencies associated with being an effective board Chair.

As the current chapter draws on the perspectives of only a limited number of board Chairs, additional research is needed with larger samples to obtain a deeper understanding of board leadership roles that focus on gender and diversity and the differences in styles and role fulfilment. Adriaanse (2016) and Inglis (1997) have called for further research to examine gender diversity in particular. For instance, Inglis (1997) found barriers to the advancement of women to the position of volunteer president. Therefore, the state of women's representation in sport board leadership roles should be further examined to understand the impact of gender diversity on board processes and individual interactions.

This chapter has examined the specific roles and responsibilities of the Chair in sport governance. It has identified five themes and a series of interconnected roles fulfilled by a Chair of a sport board. This chapter has also emphasised the importance of passion and sport federated structures as a unique aspect of sport governance requiring further investigation on how they impact sport board leadership and behaviour. This multi-faceted perspective of the sport board Chair reveals the need to better understand the dynamics between the wider sport governance system and sport governance leadership.

Acknowledgement

The authors would like to thank the four sport board chairs: Malcolm Speed, Paolina Hunt, Marc Coudron and Salvatore Zandonà for their time and expertise in sharing their collective experiences when chairing sport boards. Their collective expertise has helped shape this chapter.

References

Adriaanse, J. (2016). Gender diversity in the governance of sport associations: The Sydney Scoreboard Global Index of Participation. *Journal of Business Ethics, 137*, 149–160.

Balduck, A. L., Lucidarme, S., Marlier, M., & Willem, A. (2015). Organizational capacity and organizational ambition in nonprofit and voluntary sports clubs. *VOLUNTAS: International Journal of Voluntary and Nonprofit Organizations, 26*, 2023–2043.

Brown, W. A., & Guo, C. (2010). Exploring the key roles for nonprofit boards. *Nonprofit and Voluntary Sector Quarterly, 39*, 536–546.

Ferkins, L. (2007). *Sport governance: Developing strategic capability in national sport organisations* (PhD Thesis). Deakin University, Melbourne, Victoria.

Ferkins, L., & Shilbury, D. (2010). Developing board strategic capability in sport organisations: The national–regional governing relationship. *Sport Management Review, 13*, 235–254.

Ferkins, L., & Shilbury, D. (2012). Good boards are strategic: What does that mean for sport governance? *Journal of Sport Management, 26*, 67–80.

Ferkins, L., & Shilbury, D. (2015). Board strategic balance: An emerging sport governance theory. *Sport Management Review, 18*, 489–500.

Ferkins, L., Shilbury, D., & McDonald, G. (2005). The role of the board in building strategic capability: Towards an integrated model of sport governance research. *Sport Management Review, 8*, 195–225.

Ferkins, L., Shilbury, D., & McDonald, G. (2009). Board involvement in strategy: Advancing the governance of sport organizations. *Journal of Sport Management, 23*, 245–277.

Ferkins, L., Shilbury, D., & O'Boyle, I. (2018). Leadership in governance: Exploring collective board leadership in sport governance systems. *Sport Management Review, 21*, 221–231.

Harrison, Y. D., & Murray, V. (2012). Perspectives on the leadership of chairs of nonprofit organization boards of directors a grounded theory mixed-method study. *Nonprofit Management & Leadership, 22*, 4, 411–437.

Harrison, Y. D., Murray, V., & Cornforth, C. (2012). The role and impact of chairs of nonprofit boards. In. C. Cornforth & W. A. Brown (Eds.), *Nonprofit governance innovative perspectives and approaches* (pp. 71–83). New York: Routledge.

Harrison, Y. D., Murray, V., & Cornforth, C. (2013). Perceptions of board chair leadership effectiveness in nonprofit and voluntary sector organizations. *Voluntas. International Journal of Voluntary and Nonprofit Organizations, 24*, 688–712.

Harrison, R. J., Torres, D. L., & Kukalis, S. (1988). The changing of the guard: Turnover and structural change in the top-management positions. *Administrative Science Quarterly, 33*, 211–232.

Herman, R. D., & Heimovics, R. D. (1990). The effective nonprofit executive: Leader of the board. *Nonprofit Management and Leadership, 1*(2), 167–180.

Hilland, M. (2006). Effective board-chair executive director relationships: Not about roles. *The Nonprofit Quarterly, 13*, 49–50.

Hoye, R. (2002). *Board performance of Australian voluntary sport organisations* (PhD Thesis). Griffith University, Gold Coast, Queensland.

Hoye, R. (2003). Who's leading, who's following? Leader-member exchange theory and voluntary sport boards. *Annals of Leisure Research, 6*, 103–113.

Hoye, R. (2004). Leader-member exchanges and board performance of voluntary sport organizations. *Nonprofit Management & Leadership, 15*, 55–70.

Hoye, R., & Cuskelly, G. (2003). Board power and performance within voluntary sport organisations. *European Sport Management Quarterly, 3*, 103–119.

Hoye, R., & Cuskelly, G. (2007). *Sport governance.* New York: Routledge.

Iecovich, E. (2004). Responsibilities and roles of boards in nonprofit organizations: The Israeli case. *Nonprofit Management and Leadership, 15*(1), 5–24.

Iecovich, E., & Bar-Mor, H. (2007). Relationships between chairpersons and CEOs in nonprofit organizations. *Administration in Social Work, 31*(4), 21–40.

Inglis, S. (1997). Roles of the board in amateur sport organizations. *Journal of Sport Management, 11*, 160–176.

Inglis, S., & Weaver, L. (2000). Designing agendas to reflect board roles and responsibilities: Results of a study. *Nonprofit Management and Leadership, 11*, 65–77.

Kakabadse, A., Kakabadse, N. K., & Barratt, R. (2006). Chairman and chief executive officer (CEO): That sacred and secret relationship. *Journal of Management Development, 25*, 134–150.

O'Boyle, I., & Shilbury, D. (2016). Exploring issues of trust in collaborative sport governance. *Journal of Sport Management, 30*, 52–69.

Otto, S. (2003). Not so very different: A comparison of the roles of chairs of governing bodies and managers in different sectors. In C. Cornforth (Ed.), *The governance of public and nonprofit organizations: What do boards do?* London: Routledge.

Shilbury, D. (2001). Examining board member roles, functions and influence: A study of Victorian sporting organizations. *International Journal of Sport Management, 2*, 253–281.

Shilbury, D., & Ferkins, L. (2015). Exploring the utility of collaborative governance in a national sport organization. *Journal of Sport Management, 29*, 380–397.

Shilbury, D., Ferkins, L., & Smythe, L. (2013). Sport governance encounters: Insights from lived experiences. *Sport Management Review, 16*, 349–363.

Shilbury, D., O'Boyle, I., & Ferkins, L. (2016). A research agenda for collaborative sport governance. *Sport Management Review, 19*, 479–491.

Taylor, T., & McGraw, P. (2006). Exploring human resource management practices in nonprofit sport organisations. *Sport Management Review, 9*, 229–251.

Wertheimer, M. R. (2007). *The board chair handbook* (2nd ed.). Washington, DC: Boardsource.

19

Intragroup board dynamics

Geoff Schoenberg

Introduction

A board of directors is a group of individuals who make joint decisions and act together to govern the organisation. As with any group, how directors interact with one another and with the group can affect the work of the group. This chapter uses the term group dynamics – defined as "a shared characteristic of a group that results from group interaction and cannot be structurally regulated, enforced, or implemented" (Schoenberg, Cuskelly & Auld, 2016, p. 2) – to describe these interactions. The very nature of governance makes group dynamics an important consideration as boards are expected to deliberate and debate prior to reaching a decision and acting with one voice (Brown, 2013; Nicholson, Newton & McGregor-Lowndes, 2012). The expectation of and the need for interaction between directors means group dynamics are a fundamental part of how boards enact their responsibility to govern.

The centrality of group dynamics in the board decision-making processes was highlighted in the introduction to this handbook. In this introductory chapter, Shilbury and Ferkins noted that the second sport governance article published in the three major sport management journals was about a form of group dynamics and the majority of the contributions in one of the four quadrants of governance was related to group dynamics. In reviewing Shilbury and Ferkins' approach to classifying papers, group dynamics were an early focus of governance research with topics such as power patterns (Hoye & Cuskelly, 2003a), cohesion (Doherty & Carron, 2003) and norms (Doherty, Patterson & Van Bussel, 2004) making early contributions to the sport governance literature. The early research interest on group dynamics in sport governance differs from early governance research in for-profit contexts. Behavioural approaches in corporate governance only gained prominence in the 2000s (Hillman, Nicholson & Shropshire, 2008) after the early focus on structural elements such as chair–CEO duality (Rechner & Dalton, 1991) and board size (Chaganti, Mahajan & Sharma, 1985).

Research on group dynamics in governance requires a reconsideration of the common theoretical approaches to studying governance. A theory is a "statement of constructs and their relationships to one another that explain how, when, why, and under what conditions phenomena take place" (Cunningham, 2013, p. 1). While theory has played a significant role in governance research, the most commonly used theories are not designed for understanding the inner interactions of the board. Agency theory and resource dependence theory have, for example, been ubiquitous in their contributions to developing an understanding of governance (Daily, Dalton & Cannella, 2003; Miller-Millesen, 2003). Yet, these theories hold significant limitations when considering group dynamics. Both theories tend to treat the board as a singular entity, rather than as a group of individuals, tasked with a specific purpose. This view means the theories' explanatory power for insight into internal behaviours is lacking (Zona, Gomez-Mejia & Withers, 2018). In agency theory, the board (as a principal) is expected to ensure the CEO (the agent) works in the interest of the owners of the organisation (Fama & Jensen, 1983). According to resource dependence theory, the board reduces uncertainty within the organisation through the provision of resources (Hillman, Withers & Collins, 2009). Both these theories tend to ignore the "embedded structural, political, cognitive, and cultural contexts" of a board (Golden-Biddle & Rao, 1997, p. 594).

The "friction of social structure and politics" (Davis, 2005, p. 149) is a real concern in boards and the rational economic approach dictated by agency theory and resource dependence theory does not suitably account for the impact of social relationships on effective governance (Daily et al., 2003). Thus, in understanding group dynamics and governance, theoretical approaches should allow for the social elements and internal dynamics of a board. This requires a shift from economic theories to theories examining the interactions of individuals and groups such as sociology and social psychology. While governance has drawn on institutional theory, there remain many other theories that could provide insight. Examples include social identity theory (Hogg & Reid, 2006), role theory (Turner, 2006) and identity theory (Stryker & Burke, 2000). A detailed review of these theories is outside the scope of this chapter. However, as a general principle, theories within the paradigms of social psychology and sociology provide explanations for behaviours and group dynamics based on the relationships between individuals and groups (Stets & Burke, 2000). These perspectives may provide insight into governance in a way not captured by economic-focused theories.

There has been adequate research into group dynamics through sociological and social psychological perspectives (e.g., Brown, 1978; Stryker & Burke, 2000; Tajfel, Billig, Bundy & Flament, 1971). With well-developed theories and empirical evidence regarding group dynamics, it is worth considering whether these theories are only useful as explanatory tools in a sport context or whether research in sport governance can contribute to theoretical advancements. Why should there be any difference in how group dynamics manifest in a board than in a family, a work group or sport team? While each of the following characteristics are not unique to boards, the combination suggests a setting that contains core differences in which theory should be tested and advanced.

First, boards have a clearly defined membership (Kiel & Nicholson, 2003). There can be little doubt as to whether an individual is a director of an organisation or not. While some social psychological theories, such as self-categorisation theory, argue individuals can self-identify with groups, the nature of governance means individuals either are or are not board members. Identifying as a board member, or not identifying as a board member, makes no difference as to whether one actually is a board member, in the same way that someone may identify as a football fan. Second, all board members have equal votes and therefore, equal structural power in decision-making (with the exception of organisations where the chair gets a deciding vote; a structure that is rare in sport) (Bainbridge, 2002). Third, directors are expected to engage in debate regarding topics, but once a decision is made directors are expected to espouse support for the board's decision regardless of individual beliefs, in contrast to groups – such as families – where internal differences can also be public (Nicholson et al., 2012). Fourth, directors join and leave a board through a formal mechanism (i.e., election or appointment). These mechanisms are described within constitutions or regulations and occur at prescribed times. Therefore, direc-tors often have different tenures within a board, which may lead to differences in knowledge of group norms. Finally, and perhaps most importantly, boards are critical groups by the nature of their role in governing bodies and of great importance to many people – both within sport and outside of it. Even if one was to argue that a board is just like any other group – although the above points indicate otherwise – the nature of the powerful position of boards make them important to understand.

This chapter contains two main sections. The first section reviews the literature on the rela-tionship between group dynamics and sport governance. The second section draws on this analysis to outline a research agenda to further understanding in the field.

Review of group dynamics

The definition of group dynamics acts as an umbrella term that captures a range of specific types of group dynamics. There are several different constructs (e.g., conflict, cohesion, etc.), each of which can be referred to as one type of group dynamic. Recognising the breadth of terminology used, Schoenberg et al. (2016) conducted a systematic review to bring some clarity to the field. Their review highlighted five different types of group dynamics related to board or organisational performance in the nonprofit sector, while noting other dynamics exist such as trust, social capital and shared vision. While not necessarily an exhaustive list, given the focus on relationships with performance, their framework provides an appropriate structure to better understand group dynamics. Four of these dynamics were cohesion, climate, conflict and power patterns. The fifth dynamic, the CEO–board relationship, has been redefined for this chapter as shared leadership. While some of the papers in the systematic review included sport organisa-tions, many did not (Schoenberg et al., 2016).

In specifically considering the sport governance context, there have been two types of studies related to group dynamics. Some studies make group dynamics the focal construct of interest. While not an exhaustive list, examples of the types of group dynamics studied include conflict (Hamm-Kerwin & Doherty, 2010; Van Bussel & Doherty, 2015), cohesion (Doherty & Carron, 2003), power patterns (Hoye & Cuskelly, 2003a), and shared leadership (Hoye & Cuskelly, 2003b). These studies tend to examine the relationship between a specific type of group dynamic and board performance with an exception being the influence of a group dynamic (i.e., norms) on individual behaviours (Doherty et al., 2004).

More commonly, group dynamics are not the focal construct of a sport governance study but emerge as a secondary factor or are used to help explain a relationship. For example, the research agenda of Ferkins and Shilbury between 2005 and 2015 investigated the strategic capability of boards. While this work did not specifically focus on group dynamics, issues of trust, shared leadership and power patterns were frequently cited in their work as critical to the develop-ment of a strategic board (Ferkins & Shilbury, 2012, 2015; Ferkins, Shilbury & McDonald, 2005, 2009; Shilbury & Ferkins, 2011). While these examples were focused on a board performance element, other research drew on group dynamics to explain other issues such as gender balance (Adriaanse, 2016; Adriaanse & Schofield, 2014; Adriaanse & Schofield, 2013) or the perceived roles of the board (Shilbury, 2001).

Ultimately, while these studies can be linked together under the umbrella of group dynamics, the focus on different types of group dynamics reveals a disjointed field. That is, while research exists, there is little consideration of group dynamics in the context of sport governance. Yet, there are some common themes within the findings of these different studies, which shed insight into the role of group dynamics in sport governance.

At the crux of governance in many sport organisations is the balance of leadership between a full-time CEO/executive director/general manager[1] and the part-time board. This shared leadership is the most commonly noted group dynamic in sport governance. Some of the earliest governance work focused on shared leadership (Hoye, 2004, 2006; Hoye & Cuskelly, 2003b) and the theme has evolved and continued into recent studies (Ferkins, Shilbury & O'Boyle, 2018). Shared leadership relates to the balance between a board's legal responsibility for an organisation and a CEO's operational responsibilities for an organisation. Each relies on the other to fulfil their obligations. The CEO relies on the board to provide strategic guidance and advice while the board relies on the CEO for information to create strategy and oversee the organisation. The dynamics of this interdependent relationship are important for its success. Boards need to have a level of trust in the information provided by the CEO (Ferkins & Shilbury, 2012) but also must be willing to scrutinise their work and reports in a way that would suggest less than complete trust (Hoye, 2006).

While shared leadership focuses on the board–CEO relationship, power patterns describe how power is distributed in a board – lending insight into how the board operates. Those with power can influence what is discussed in meetings, how decisions are made and what information is shared. Work by Murray, Bradshaw and Wolpin (1992) identified five types of power patterns: CEO-dominated, chair-dominated, power-sharing, powerless and fragmented, which were subsequently used as a framework by Hoye and Cuskelly (2003a). Within sport, Hoye and Cuskelly (2003a) found that powerless, fragmented and chair-dominated boards tended to be associated with lower board performance.

This problem associated with fragmented boards can, perhaps, be seen in the research related to conflict. Conflict in sport governance is nuanced, as there are different forms of conflict, each of which can influence governance in different ways. There was some evidence that a low level of task conflict (i.e., debate about what should be done) was beneficial for effective governance while process conflict (i.e., how things are done) and relationship conflict (i.e., conflict between people) were not beneficial for governance (Kerwin, Doherty & Harman, 2011; Papadimitriou, 1999). There is likely to be some overlap between fragmented boards and boards experiencing process and relationship conflict. In their work on cohesion, Doherty and Carron (2003) noted the relationships between board members as important. Their findings, echoed by Ferkins and Shilbury (2012), suggested that board members do develop shared social connections and these social dynamics can help the board to perform better. In summary, the research suggests that group dynamics do play a role in effective sport governance, yet there are opportunities to build a stronger research focus on the subject rather than the relatively separate studies conducted thus far.

Research agenda

To this point, research on group dynamics has predominantly focused on investigating how one type of dynamic (e.g., conflict) impacts governance. A systematic analysis of these independent studies argued that there was enough evidence to include group dynamics as a core element of governance models (Schoenberg et al., 2016). While it is important to consider and study these types of relationship (i.e., the influence of one type of group dynamic on performance), an uncoordinated approach to these studies is likely to lead to a disparate body of research emerging with a potentially endless list of types of group dynamics based on different contingencies. These variants may indeed be subtly different from each other and provide slightly different insight into boardrooms, but they are unlikely to provide meaningful and practical insight into governance practices.

Perhaps the best way to avoid this risk is to develop a typology of group dynamics in sport governance. Rather than considering individual types of group dynamics, the conceptualisation and categorisation of group dynamics using macro-level considerations can form a foundation for this emerging field. Thus, a development of a theoretically and conceptually sound typology of group dynamics is a critical next step in the group dynamics literature. Examples of potential elements of a typology of governance group dynamics could include, but is not limited to, continuums such as:

a) Sociological versus social psychological grounding
b) Interactions with individual directors versus interactions with the board as a whole
c) Maintaining versus changing group norms
d) Direct versus mediated effects on board/organisational performance
e) Task focused dynamics versus social focused dynamics
f) Direct interaction (e.g., conflict) versus underlying characteristic (e.g., trust).

A typology or "map" based on theoretically derived characteristics and categorisations of group dynamics in governance would provide multiple benefits. First, it would provide a shared language for examining group dynamics in sport governance. A shared language would help resolve the issues identified by Schoenberg et al. (2016) in the use of different terms to describe similar concepts while also allowing for easier contrast and comparison within the field. Second, a typology would help identify the state of the field. A typology has the potential to provide a framework for understanding what has been studied and where gaps exist as well as mapping how different concepts and studies relate to each other. Third, a typology would create an underpinning framework for "gluing" the field together and creating guidelines and boundaries regarding the study of the role of group dynamics in sport governance. This typology should be a priority for researchers interested in group dynamics in sport governance as it can help organise the existing research and show a platform for further research.

Furthermore, much of the research on group dynamics in sport governance has not explicitly expressed theoretical perspectives in the research (e.g., Hoye & Cuskelly, 2003b; Kerwin, Doherty & Harmon, 2011). Acknowledgement of the theoretical lens is critical to advancing scholarship in this field, given the existing knowledge regarding formation and maintenance of group dynamics in other contexts and the important differences between different theories (Hogg, Terry & White, 1995). The explicit statement of theory will ensure research in sport governance is not simply duplicating existing research from sociological or social psychological domains. Additionally, research on group dynamics in sport governance can only make a significant and original contribution if the research either advances existing theory or if there is a reason to suspect established processes would differ in a sport or governance setting. That is, given the existing research on group dynamics, the key for researchers in sport governance is to explicitly argue, on the basis of sound theory, why the sport governance setting is different from group dynamics in other settings. These differences form the basis for developing conceptual arguments and conducting empirical work that will both inform sport governance research but also make contributions into broader theoretical work.

While subtle, there is a difference between studying the role of group dynamics in sport governance and studying group dynamics in a sport governance context. This forthcoming research agenda focuses on the former, as the latter is merely using governance as a context rather than the topic of interest. Primarily, this focus means understanding how group dynamics affect governance – the primary topic of this handbook – rather than understanding group dynamics.

"Affecting governance" is a broad term and is not intended as a purely performance metric. Thus, it is important to understand how group dynamics can interact with other concepts of governance, such as strategic capability, structures, composition, inter-organisational relationships and networks, oversight and legitimacy, among other governance issues (many of which are discussed in this handbook). Thus, building on the important and overarching theoretical and conceptual work advocated above, the following presents three research questions that require addressing to advance an understanding of group dynamics in sport governance.

RQ1: How do different group dynamics relate with each other and what sort of mediating or moderating effects accompany interactions?

It is well established, both conceptually and empirically, that group dynamics play an important role in governance – particularly related to performance aspects such as board effectiveness. This has been established both through individual studies relating specific group dynamics to performance (Hoye, 2004; Kerwin et al., 2011) and through a systematic review on the topic (Schoenberg et al., 2016). But, as noted earlier, there are many different group dynamics and there is little understanding on how these dynamics interact with each other, especially considering the multidimensional nature of different dynamics. For example, what are the relationships between conflict and cohesion? To address this question, one must consider the types of cohesion and the types of conflict. It may be that groups with strong task cohesion are unlikely to have task conflict, but perhaps will engage more in process conflict (i.e., we agree on what to do, but not on how to do it). What about groups with strong social cohesion? Perhaps this cohesion means they are less likely to engage in relationship conflict, but also perhaps it means the strength of their relationship allows for conflict regarding tasks and processes? These are just some of the potential relationships between two types of group dynamics, let alone considering the relationships with other group dynamics.

Potentially more important than understanding the relationships between different group dynamics is the effect these relationships can have on governance more broadly. How do different group dynamics interact to affect board and organisational performance? Are some group dynamics effective mediators of others? Are there moderating effects on performance between different group dynamics? In addition to developing a better understanding of governance, understanding the relationships between group dynamics could improve the practical implications of this research stream. While it is evident that boards should consider their various group dynamics, understanding the relationships between group dynamics would allow for more impactful recommendations.

RQ2: What are the "non-performance" or indirect effects of group dynamics?

Another research opportunity aligns with the growing interest in systemic governance. As governance becomes more than ensuring an efficient and effective organisation – as noted with concerns related to organisational legitimacy based on governance (Geeraert, 2015) – there are possibilities that group dynamics within the board could have a broader impact outside board performance. Organisations suspected of having poor group dynamics may find the repercussions extend beyond board effects and vice versa. Examples include a reduced pool of interested board and staff/executive/management members (particularly among independent board members), difficulty entering the organisation into new or longer-term contracts or less acceptance of board decisions.

RQ3: How do group dynamics develop within and influence whole-of-sport governing systems?

A critical element of the federated sport system is the relationships between the different governing bodies (e.g., between national and state bodies or between state bodies). These relationships are increasingly important given the shift towards collaborative governance and collective leadership (Ferkins et al., 2018; Shilbury & Ferkins, 2015). Yet, while there is a formal structural relationship between organisations in the federated model, relationships will be based on the people acting on behalf of those organisations (i.e., directors and CEOs). Thus, it is important to consider group dynamics within the broader group of people governing a sport and not just an organisation. For example, board members of national sport federations often have ties, formally or informally, to state sport organisations (O'Boyle & Hassan, 2016). How do these ties influence the group dynamics within the national level, but, more interestingly, in collaboration and coordination efforts between the national body and state bodies? What are the impacts on both within-board group dynamics and between-board group dynamics on a sport and its governance system?

As a final agenda item, while the primary interest of this research agenda is increasing the understanding of group dynamics in sport governance, there are opportunities to use this research context to advance theory. Given the number of different theoretical approaches – alluded to earlier in this chapter – outlining a detailed research agenda on this topic is beyond the scope of this chapter. However, given the unique characteristics of sport governance and the critical role of group dynamics in this sector, it is worth researchers considering how theories (e.g., social identity theory or institutional theory) can be developed and advanced rather than simply tested within this context.

Conclusion

While group dynamics have been an important stream within sport governance research, further work is needed to bring together the disparate work into a connected and unified body of research. Existing research on the topic has demonstrated the roles specific types of group dynamics can play in influencing organisational governance (particularly board performance). The next steps for understanding group dynamics in sport governance require researchers to identify their theoretical lens more explicitly, develop a typology to link together existing research and include a perspective beyond straightforward predictive relationships between group dynamics and performance.

Note

1 Different sport organisations use different terms to indicate the most senior employee in an organisation who reports directly to the board. For the sake of simplicity, the term CEO is used in this chapter.

References

Adriaanse, J. (2016). Gender diversity in the governance of sport associations: The Sydney Scoreboard Global Index of Participation. *Journal of Business Ethics, 137*, 149–160.
Adriaanse, J., & Schofield, T. (2014). The impact of gender quotas on gender equality in sport governance. *Journal of Sport Management, 28*, 485–497.
Adriaanse, J. A., & Schofield, T. (2013). Analysing gender dynamics in sport governance: A new regimes-based approach. *Sport Management Review, 16*, 498–513.

Bainbridge, S. M. (2002). Why a board? Group decision making in corporate governance. *Vanderbilt Law Review, 55*, 1–55.

Brown, R. J. (1978). Divided we fall: An analysis of relations between sections of a factory workforce. In H. Tajfel (Ed.), *Differentiation between social groups: Studies in the social psychology of intergroup relations* (pp. 395–429). Oxford: Academic Press.

Brown, W. A. (2013). Antecedents to board member engagement in deliberation and decision-making. In C. Cornforth & W. A. Brown (Eds.), *Nonprofit governance: Innovative perspectives and approaches* (pp. 100–116). Abingdon: Routledge.

Chaganti, R. S., Mahajan, V., & Sharma, S. (1985). Corporate board size, composition and corporate failures in retailing industry. *Journal of Management Studies, 22*, 400–417.

Cunningham, G. B. (2013). Theory and theory development in sport management. *Sport Management Review, 16*, 1–4.

Daily, C. M., Dalton, D. R., & Cannella, A. A. (2003). Corporate governance: Decades of dialogue and data. *Academy of Management Review, 28*, 371–382.

Davis, G. F. (2005). New directions in corporate governance. *Annual Review of Sociology, 31*, 143–162.

Doherty, A., & Carron, A. (2003). Cohesion in volunteer sport executive committees. *Journal of Sport Management, 17*, 116–141.

Doherty, A., Patterson, M., & Van Bussel, M. (2004). What do we expect? An examination of perceived committee norms in non-profit sport organisations. *Sport Management Review, 7*, 109–132.

Fama, E. F., & Jensen, M. C. (1983). Separation of ownership and control. *Journal of Law and Economics, 26*, 301–325.

Ferkins, L., & Shilbury, D. (2012). Good boards are strategic: What does that mean for sport governance? *Journal of Sport Management, 26*, 67–80.

Ferkins, L., & Shilbury, D. (2015). The stakeholder dilemma in sport governance: Toward the notion of "stakeowner". *Journal of Sport Management, 29*, 93–108.

Ferkins, L., Shilbury, D., & McDonald, G. (2005). The role of the board in building strategic capability: Towards an integrated model of sport governance research. *Sport Management Review, 8*, 195–225.

Ferkins, L., Shilbury, D., & McDonald, G. (2009). Board involvement in strategy: Advancing the governance of sport organizations. *Journal of Sport Management, 23*, 245–277.

Ferkins, L., Shilbury, D., & O'Boyle, I. (2018). Leadership in governance: Exploring collective board leadership in sport governance systems. *Sport Management Review, 21*, 221–231.

Geeraert, A. (2015). *Sport governance observer 2015: The legitimacy crisis in international sport governance.* Copenhagen: Play the Game / Danish Institute for Sports Studies.

Golden-Biddle, K., & Rao, H. (1997). Breaches in the boardroom: Organizational identity and conflicts of commitment in a nonprofit organization. *Organization Science, 8*, 593–611.

Hamm-Kerwin, S., & Doherty, A. (2010). Intragroup conflict in nonprofit sport boards. *Journal of Sport Management, 24*, 245–271.

Hillman, A. J., Nicholson, G., & Shropshire, C. (2008). Directors' multiple identities, identification, and board monitoring and resource provision. *Organization Science, 19*, 441–456.

Hillman, A. J., Withers, M. C., & Collins, B. J. (2009). Resource dependence theory: A review. *Journal of Management, 35*, 1404–1427.

Hogg, M. A., & Reid, S. A. (2006). Social identity, self-categorization, and the communication of group norms. *Communication Theory, 16*, 7–30.

Hogg, M. A., Terry, D. J., & White, K. M. (1995). A tale of two theories: A critical comparison of identity theory with social identity theory. *Social Psychology Quarterly, 58*, 255–269.

Hoye, R. (2004). Leader-member exchanges and board performance of voluntary sport organizations. *Nonprofit Management & Leadership, 15*, 55–70.

Hoye, R. (2006). Leadership within Australian voluntary sport organization boards. *Nonprofit Management & Leadership, 16*, 297–313.

Hoye, R., & Cuskelly, G. (2003a). Board power and performance within voluntary sport organisations. *European Sport Management Quarterly, 3*, 103–119.

Hoye, R., & Cuskelly, G. (2003b). Board–executive relationships within voluntary sport organisations. *Sport Management Review, 6*, 53–73.

Kerwin, S., Doherty, A., & Harman, A. (2011). "It's not conflict, it's differences of opinion": An in-depth examination of conflict in nonprofit boards. *Small Group Research, 42*, 562–594.

Kiel, G., & Nicholson, G. (2003). *Boards that work: A new guide for directors.* Sydney: McGraw-Hill.

Miller-Millesen, J. L. (2003). Understanding the behavior of nonprofit boards of directors: A theory-based approach. *Nonprofit and Voluntary Sector Quarterly, 32*, 521–547.

Murray, V., Bradshaw, P., & Wolpin, J. (1992). Power in and around nonprofit boards: A neglected dimension of governance. *Nonprofit Management & Leadership, 3*, 165–182.

Nicholson, G., Newton, C., & McGregor-Lowndes, M. (2012). The nonprofit board as a team: Pilot results and initial insights. *Nonprofit Management & Leadership, 22*, 461–481.

O'Boyle, I., & Hassan, D. (2016). Board composition in federated structures: A case study of the Gaelic Athletic Association. *World Leisure Journal, 58*, 109–123.

Papadimitriou, D. (1999). Voluntary boards of directors in Greek sport governing bodies. *European Journal for Sport Management, 6*, 78–103.

Rechner, P. L., & Dalton, D. R. (1991). CEO duality and organizational performance: A longitudinal analysis. *Strategic Management Journal, 12*, 155–160.

Schoenberg, G., Cuskelly, G., & Auld, C. (2016). The role of intragroup dynamics in nonprofit governance models: A systematic quantitative literature review. *Managing Sport and Leisure, 21*, 1–22.

Shilbury, D. (2001). Examining board member roles, functions and influence: A study of Victorian sporting organizations. *International Journal of Sport Management, 2*, 253–281.

Shilbury, D., & Ferkins, L. (2011). Professionalisation, sport governance and strategic capability. *Managing Leisure, 16*, 108–127.

Shilbury, D., & Ferkins, L. (2015). Exploring the utility of collaborative governance in a national sport organization. *Journal of Sport Management, 29*, 380–397.

Stets, J. E., & Burke, P. J. (2000). Identity theory and social identity theory. *Social Psychology Quarterly, 63*, 224–237.

Stryker, S., & Burke, P. J. (2000). The past, present, and future of an identity theory. *Social Psychology Quarterly, 63*, 284–297.

Tajfel, H., Billig, M. G., Bundy, R. P., & Flament, C. (1971). Social categorization and intergroup behaviour. *European Journal of Social Psychology, 1*, 149–178.

Turner, R. (2006). Role theory. In J. Turner (Ed.), *Handbook of sociological theory* (pp. 233–254). New York: Springer Science+Business Media.

Van Bussel, M., & Doherty, A. (2015). An examination of the conflict process in nonprofit community sport boards. *European Sport Management Quarterly, 15*, 176–194.

Zona, F., Gomez-Mejia, L. R., & Withers, M. C. (2018). Board interlocks and firm performance: Toward a combined agency–resource dependence perspective. *Journal of Management, 44*, 589–618.

20

Strategy and the strategic function of sport boards

Lesley Ferkins

Introduction

The focus of this chapter is on the board's role in strategy, situated within the context of sport governance. The framing chosen for this chapter follows two questions, which have been derived from an examination of the literature in three specific contexts: for-profit governance, nonprofit governance and sport governance. The first context represents an early scholarly emphasis (some five decades ago), largely from the for-profit governance literature, on the board's compliance and monitoring role, including holding the CEO to account (Stiles, 2001). Supported by agency theory many scholars focused on understanding this aspect of board function, potentially at the expense of exploring its strategic role (Kerr & Werther, 2008). In moving beyond a focus on monitoring and compliance, the question as to "*why should boards be involved in strategy*" was tackled by corporate (for-profit) governance scholars beginning in the 1970s (Pugliese, Bezemer, Zattoni, Huse, Van den Bosch & Volberda, 2009). This focus has directed scholarly efforts of nonprofit and sport governance researchers to explore the board's role in strategy over the past 15 years (Brown & Iverson, 2004; Ferkins, Shilbury & McDonald, 2005).

The second question, "*how do sport boards engage in strategy*", represents the body of work across all three contexts (for-profit, nonprofit and sport governance) that has explored the board's strategic role (McNulty, Pettigrew, Jobome & Morris, 2011). This research theme, developed over the past two decades, has driven a more expansive engagement with theory, and helped to establish the argument for a multi-theoretical approach to the study of governance (detailed in Chapter 2). Of note is the establishment of stewardship theory as a key governance theory to augment agency theory (Donaldson & Davis, 1991). Stewardship theory is considered particularly relevant for nonprofit organisations (including nonprofit sport) and has helped explain and guide the board's strategic role as stewards of the organisation who need to work in partnership with the CEO in strategy design and implementation (Siciliano, 2008). Sport governance researchers have joined this conversation in contributing to the governance literature, also promoting shared leadership and a multi-theoretical approach (Ferkins et al., 2005).

The chapter therefore begins with a discussion of early arguments for the board's role in strategy, teasing out aspects relevant for contemporary sport governance and the ongoing debate regarding tensions between the board's compliance and monitoring role and board involvement in strategy. The next section deals with *how* sport boards are involved in strategy and represents a more recent wave of scholarly efforts. It teases out power dynamics and role definition between the board and CEO in relation to strategy, as well as perspectives on narrow and expansive views of strategy versus strategic function. The conclusion points towards future research directions and urges scholars to continue a focus on this key element of sport governance.

Themes from scholarly endeavours on board strategy

Why should boards be involved in strategy? Establishing the need for board involvement

An appreciation for the evolutionary steps of strategy in organisational governance brings helpful context to the early (and ongoing) debate about the need for board involvement in strategy. As Pugliese et al. (2009) found in a valuable review of literature, the first scholarly articles on the board's role was published in 1972. Clendenin (1972), who presented data from 33 major publicly held US corporations, argued that many boards were too passive, only fulfilling "the requirements of the law, having turned over their authority to executive management" (p. 60). In considering where boards were failing, he found that "most boards do not deal in depth with fundamental matters of long-term direction …" (p. 64) and that they need to take this role more seriously. In the same issue of the *California Management Review*, Heller (1972) asserted that "The board of directors has existed as a legal entity for about five centuries – long enough to be taken for granted as an essential element in industrial organization" (p. 24). He argued that, while the board's usefulness varied considerably from one company to another, "In some situations the board of directors is so ineffective that it is virtually a legal anachronism" (p. 24). Alongside Clendenin's (1972) study, Heller's (1972) article entitled "Legalistic anachronism or vital force" appeared to set the tone for a series of scholarly investigations that evidenced the need for greater board strategic involvement (see Mace, 1976; Machin & Wilson, 1979; Vance, 1979).

The parallel scholarly conversation within the context of sport organisations occurred in the 1990s/early 2000s, beginning with a series of articles by Inglis (1994, 1997a, 1997b) and colleagues (Inglis & Weaver, 2000; Inglis, Alexander & Weaver, 1999). These studies probed the board's role in nonprofit sport organisations arguing for a need to better understand the balance of roles between "policy volunteers" and paid executive directors. This interest reflected a transition from purely voluntary entities (particularly national governing bodies) to the establishment of paid positions for many nonprofit sport organisations (Chelladurai, 1987; Inglis, 1997a). In a seminal study of nonprofit sport organisations, Inglis et al. (1999) established empirical support for sport board involvement in strategic activities. Such activities were determined as setting the mission and vision, an external focus, policy development and planning, as well as evaluating the executive director. This foundation study contributed to an early scoping and defining of the board's strategic role as well as highlighting an imperative for such involvement within the context of sport organisations.

While the practice of governing sport is two centuries old (since the establishment of sport bodies), a focused approach to understanding the board's role in strategy is a recent endeavour. As exemplified above, this was in large part driven by an interest in better understanding the dynamic between paid staff and voluntary board directors (Auld, 1997; Auld & Godbey, 1998). Hinings and Slack (1987) predicted that the professionalisation of voluntary sport organisations would result in them being directed by paid professionals, with volunteers adopting roles in support of professional staff. Some 20 years later, Ferkins, Shilbury and McDonald (2009) found evidence of this in their study of board involvement in strategy within national sport organisations. Ferkins et al. (2009) framed this in terms of the "tail wagging the dog", that is, the board being too passive and the paid CEO dominating strategic impetus and the board agenda with regard to strategy. Shilbury (2001), who examined board roles in state sport organisations, pointed out that increasing CEO influence may not necessarily be a negative outcome and that the CEOs sought board involvement in strategy. He found that "the executive directors were seeking shared control and leadership specifically through their preference for greater influence by the board in the strategic planning process" (p. 275). Later, Hoye and Cuskelly (2007) speculated that at "the heart of the issue for sport organizations seems to be clarifying the respective roles of the board and staff in all strategic activities" (p. 117).

In the nonprofit (non-sport) setting, a similar transition towards professionalisation was occurring with scholars also reporting the latent power of the board (Bradshaw, Murray & Wolpin, 1992; Herman & Heimovics, 1993, 1994; Herman & Renz, 1998, 2000; Herman, Renz & Heimovics 1997). Heimovics and Herman (1990), studied 51 CEOs and presidents representing human service and performing arts organisations. Their results demonstrated that "both chief executives and board presidents believe in the 'psychological centrality' of the chief executive in a hierarchy of responsibility for organizational outcomes" (p. 59). An important focus of this body of work was the drive to understand organisation effectiveness and the board's role within this.

The notion that the board's contribution to strategy is a central component of the board's role, which, in turn, contributes to board and organisation effectiveness, was a link made by several scholars with a focus on the nonprofit context (Brown & Iverson, 2004; Inglis, Alexander & Weaver, 1999; Inglis & Weaver, 2000; Siciliano, 1997). In summary, as Siciliano (1997) observed, "since the 1980s, scholars have encouraged boards of directors in both the for-profit and non-profit sectors to play an active role in strategic management" (p. 152). The insights drawn from this work have provided clear impetus for sport management scholars to also focus on the board's role in strategy led initially by Inglis (1994) and colleagues (see above). So, how has this urging, probing and evidencing of the need for board involvement in strategy played out over the ensuing 30 years?

How do sport boards engage in strategy?

Is there a difference between the board's role in *strategy* and the board's *strategic* role? Thus far, this chapter has referred to these terms as being synonymous. While the need for board involvement in strategy or strategic activities is being established (the discussion so far), this distinction is potentially inconsequential. However, in considering *how* boards engage, this distinction is worth teasing out. To begin with, the considerable body of literature in strategic management strongly indicates that at the apex of the organisation, strategy must be, by its nature, long term and consequential (Wheelen & Hunger, 2010). However, it is useful to consider whether all board strategic activity is about strategy. An early study in sport by Inglis et al. (1999), discussed above, found that while board strategic activities certainly included traditional elements of strategy, such as mission and vision, an external focus, policy development and planning, it also involved evaluating the executive director and many other roles. Later, Ferkins and Shilbury (2015a) emphasised the complexity of the sport governance phenomenon and the need to take a holistic view of the board's strategic role, rather than focussing on one aspect of board function such as strategy.

In a stocktake of scholarly efforts related to board strategic function for sport organisations, Ferkins et al. (2005) pointed out that "There is considerable consensus in the literature regarding an understanding of what is meant by 'strategic'. There is less agreement as to where the strategic role of the board stops and the strategic role of management begins" (p. 215). Discerning the respective roles and responsibilities of the board versus top management is a key question for governance practice and scholarship (Boesso, Cerbioni, Menini & Parbonetti, 2017). In the context of strategy, Stiles (2001) offered that a commonly held perspective was based on distinguishing between formulation and evaluation. From his empirical work, he noted that the board's involvement in formulation varied from "working with management to develop strategic direction to merely ratifying management proposals" (p. 269).

An important influence in this debate (which is ongoing, see Bordean, Borza & Maier, 2011; Boesso et al., 2017; Hendry, Kiel & Nicholson, 2010), was the seminal work of Fama and Jensen (1983). Well known for their thesis on the separation of ownership and control, they distinguished between the tasks of initiating and implementing strategic decisions (referred to as decision management) and ratifying and monitoring strategic actions (referred to as decision control). For Fama and Jensen, decision management was the role of the CEO/top management and decision control was the board's purview. As Pugliese et al. (2009) pointed out, this view has influenced the debate ever since. They explained that "By relying on a clear distinction of responsibilities between boards and management, scholars have viewed the potential contributions of boards to strategy as fairly limited because of their distance from day-to-day operations, the presence of information asymmetries, and the need to remain independent" (p. 293).

Nonetheless, other scholars from nonprofit and for-profit settings who have pursued *how* boards engage in strategy have concluded the need for an expansive view of the board's strategic role. Parker (2007), for example, undertook an in-depth study of two professional (nonprofit) associations to better understand boardroom strategising. He found that the board's strategic role was most potent when the board engaged in strategic discussion and that the role of formal strategic plans was not a major focal point. He concluded that a decoupling occurred between formal planning processes (which largely played a legitimising and ceremonial role) and ad hoc strategic discussions that took place around the boardroom table. These findings encouraged a view of the board's role in strategy to extend beyond planning functions.

In exploring the relationship between organisation and board performance in nonprofits, Brown (2005) also evidenced the need to seek "clarification and differentiation of strategic planning processes as distinct from strategic direction and follow-through" (p. 334). In the for-profit context, the work of Nadler (2004) has been a helpful influence for sport governance researchers (Ferkins & Shilbury, 2015a). In exploring the board's role in strategy development, Nadler (2004) separated formalised strategic planning processes from other elements of strategic engagement. He identified four elements of board strategic activity as: strategic thinking (environmental analysis and discussion); strategic decision-making (involving core directional decisions); strategic planning (a formalised plan and set of budgets); and strategic execution (implementation, monitoring and corrective action). He also offers an explicit differentiation of tasks and roles between the board and CEO in relation to strategy development. This has practical relevance for sport boards and CEOs as they seek to navigate their respective roles in strategy development (Ferkins et al., 2009). Table 20.1 is an adaptation of Nadler's (2004) role differentiation across the four elements of strategic activity and is produced here to offer a practical guide for sport governance practitioners and scholars.

In also seeking to tease out greater understanding of how boards do strategy, Hendry et al. (2010) identified two ways boards engage in strategy. Referred to as strategising practices, the two distinct but complementary approaches involved procedural strategising and interactive strategising. "Procedural Strategising relies on formal administrative activities or events such as strategic plans, planning committees, planning cycles, trend analyses, budgets, forecasts, quarterly reviews and performance targets to influence the development and execution of strategy

Table 20.1 Role differentiation in strategy development for sport boards

Strategic activity	Role of the board	Role of CEO/management
Strategic thinking: Sourcing, analysing and discussing the sport's internal and external environmental issues including societal trends	• Be active in strategic thinking processes • Bring outside perspective and wisdom • Challenge CEO/management thinking • Collaborative with the CEO/management	• Coordinate the process of strategic thinking • Provide relevant and meaningful information/synthesis of information • Participate with the board in discussions • Summarise and synthesise the outcomes of board/CEO strategic discussions
Strategic decision-making: Making the fundamental set of decisions about the sport's strategic design (purpose, values and vision)	• Collaborate with CEO/management in decision-making • Provide ultimate review and approval of major decisions (e.g., resource allocation, initiatives, portfolio changes)	• Collaborate with board in decision-making • Develop proposals for the board for critical directional decisions and major resource allocation • Engage with the board in its review of major decisions
Strategic planning: Translating critical strategic decisions into strategy statements, priorities, objectives and resource allocation actions for implementation	• Review core strategic plan written by CEO/management • Consider potential risks and consequences of written plans • Comment/make suggestions on the presentation of written plans • Formally approve plans	• Develop/write plans, working with staff and operating management • Ensure plans are consistent with strategic thinking and decisions made with the board • Present plans to the board for review
Strategy execution: Undertake initiatives and actions consistent with strategic planning. Revise and adjust over time to account for environmental changes and unanticipated outcomes	• Review process and progress of implementation of key initiatives as per established milestones and objectives • Engage in review and revisions as needed	• Ensure resources and leadership for execution are in place • Monitor progress of execution • Adjust execution or plans as an outcome of board agreement

Source: (Adapted from Nadler, 2004).

in organisations" (p. 36). By contrast, interactive strategising is a more informal and relational approach to strategic activity involving interaction with senior staff and between the board members. "A key characteristic of Interactive Strategising is that it relies on ongoing social exchanges in which individuals or groups communicate, persuade and negotiate; continuously building shared frameworks of meaning about strategy in order to influence each other's behaviour" (p. 37). Of relevance for the current discussion is the conclusion that the nature and extent of board involvement in strategy (whether procedural or interactive) is a matter of board choice and design (Hendry et al., 2010). Equally, informal strategic discussion is as much a part of the board's role as formal strategy development processes. Conceivably, the more board behaviour is understood in relation to strategic function, the more opportunity there will be for conscious choice and contribution by sport boards to this element of their role.

Bailey and Peck's (2013) empirical work also involved understanding styles of strategic decision-making. They analysed eight boards of publicly traded US companies involving in-depth interviews to determine influences on quality strategic decision-making. Key influences included balance in the power relationships between the CEO and the board, shared mental models and chair leadership skill. Such influences are highly relevant for sport boards with power relationships already explored by sport governance scholars, albeit not specifically in relation to the board's strategic role (Auld, 1997; Auld & Godbey, 1998; Hoye & Cuskelly, 2003a, 2003b; Inglis, 1994, 1997b; Kikulis, 2000; Searle, 1989; Shilbury, 2001). These studies seek to address the balance of influence and power between the executive director and voluntary board, referred to as "shared leadership" (Hoye & Cuskelly, 2003a; Hoye, 2006; Inglis, 1997a). Shared leadership between the board and CEO has also emerged as a facilitator for building board strategic capability in sport boards (Ferkins et al., 2009; Ferkins & Shilbury, 2012; Shilbury & Ferkins, 2011).

An earlier series of studies in the for-profit context by Pettigrew (1992) and colleague (McNulty & Pettigrew, 1996, 1999; Pettigrew & McNulty, 1995, 1998) also sought to better understand board power and influence. These studies proved highly relevant for sport governance scholars who sought to probe how boards engage in strategy and strategic activities (Ferkins & Shilbury, 2012, 2015a). A key finding from a study of 108 company directors by McNulty and Pettigrew (1999) revealed that boards "influence processes of strategic choice, change and control by shaping both the ideas that form the content of company strategy and the methodologies and processes by which ideas evolve" (p. 47). Their work also highlighted the informal contribution to strategic discussion by boards. In applying these findings to the context of sport boards, Ferkins and Shilbury (2015a) concluded that "the strategic contribution of the board traverses multiple aspects of the generic governance roles of performance and conformance" (p. 491).

Further consolidating a wide view of board involvement in strategy within the context of sport, Ferkins and Shilbury (2015a) advanced a theory of board strategic capability. They approached board strategic capability as "a dynamic and all-encompassing concept that is enhanced by creating equilibrium in roles and functions that include the design, enactment and monitoring of strategic imperatives" (p. 298). They proposed six dimensions as part of the concept beginning with the contribution of "volunteer part-time board members, or 'will and skill'; board operational knowledge; board integrating regional entities into the governing role; board maintaining the monitoring and control function; board co-leading strategy development; and board co-leading integration of strategy into board processes" (p. 298). In their article, they emphasised the relationships between the six dimensions promoting the idea of board strategic balance. The potential value (and limitation) of this work is in its context-specific focus, which spotlights national sport governing bodies.

Conclusion and looking forward

Conceivably, at the apex of the organisation where boards operate, the distinction between strategy and strategic function is blurred with many scholars arguing for an expansive approach with regard to how the board involves itself in strategy (Bailey & Peck, 2013; Boesso et al., 2017; Nadler, 2004; Parker, 2007). This expansive view certainly moves beyond the board only playing a role in ratifying and monitoring strategy (i.e., strategic plans). The "strategic wheel" has turned a full circle since Clendenin (1972), who argued nearly 50 years ago that boards were too passive and that many had "turned over their authority to executive management" (p. 60). As Heller (1972) stated, "In some situations the board of directors is so ineffective that it is virtually a legal anachronism" (p. 24). As evidenced by the discussion above, 50 years of scholarly efforts across for-profit and nonprofit contexts has helped to drive the work of sport management scholars in first establishing the need for board involvement in strategy and then, more latterly, understanding *how* the board might undertake this role.

As expected from early predictions (Inglis, 1994), these efforts have encouraged sport boards to become an active partner, alongside the CEO and senior management, in the breadth of strategic activities that influence sport organisation performance (Ferkins & Shilbury, 2015a). This line of inquiry targets board members' strategic contribution in order to realise the full potential of those offering their time (largely voluntarily). The ultimate outcome of these efforts is so that sport organisations, many of which are key social institutions, may prosper in societies around the globe.

Future research directions

While there is now a strong cohort of scholars in sport management who have turned their attention to the study of sport governance, there are still few who have specifically focused on the board's strategic role. As professed by Slack (1996) nearly 25 years ago, "despite the centrality of strategy to the operations of all organizations within the sport industry and the links strategy has to other organizational phenomena, there have been very few studies of this topic in our field" (p. 101). Some scholars have taken up this call within the broader sport management discipline (Amis, 2003; Sack & Nadim, 2002; Couvelaere & Richelieu, 2005; Shilbury, 2012; Warner, Chalip & Woolf, 2008) but few have turned their attention to the board's role where significant influence for sport system performance undoubtedly resides.

While a specific focus on how sport boards engage in strategy reveals very few contemporary studies, as illustrated in Chapter 1, there is a growing body of work that has explored other key board functions, namely, integrating regional entities (O'Bolye & Shilbury, 2016) and managing stakeholders (Garcia & Welford, 2015) in the governance process. If an expansive view of the board's strategic role is taken as the large canvas for understanding strategy, then insights from these studies will have bearing on future work (see Table 1.1). This work has begun with a series of more recent studies and an emerging line of inquiry that moves beyond a board level focus to considering governance as part of a system of organisations (Ferkins & Shilbury, 2010, 2012). Referred to as the difference between organisation governance and systemic governance (Henry & Lee, 2004) and explained in other chapters within this handbook, the board's role in strategy is impacted by a view of governance that incorporates multiple organisations (Cornforth, 2012). It is therefore advocated that as scholars pursue such topics, they might also investigate a relationship with the board's strategic role across a sport network, such as in a federated structure.

To supplement the dearth of strategy-based scholarship, sport governance researchers have drawn from the more mature field of corporate governance (for-profit), where the imperative for board involvement in strategy has now been established. The next step – *how* boards engage – is still underdeveloped across all contexts. Bordean et al. (2011) captured this common sentiment in stating that "In academic corporate governance research, it is widely agreed that boards should contribute to corporate strategy. Despite reasonable consensus on the board's responsibility for strategy, how boards should fulfil this responsibility has remained unclear" (p. 986). Moreover, there has also been a regular appeal from the for-profit setting for deeper insights into what has become known as the "black box" of board function. This is because of a need to reveal more about the inner workings of boards than what instruments such as surveys and snapshots in time can offer (Bailey & Peck, 2013; Finkelstein, Hambrick & Cannella, 2009; Leblanc & Schwartz, 2007; Vigano, Zattoni, Hoskisson & Huse, 2011). Thus, understanding board processes over time and using in-depth qualitative methods is also advocated (Pye & Pettigrew, 2005).

This chapter has canvassed the *why* and *how* in relation to the board's strategic role. A final question, and beyond the present scope of this chapter, is *who* should be involved in strategy? This question directs efforts towards board composition and structure as well as stakeholder engagement and collaborative governance (Shilbury, Ferkins & Smythe, 2013). The imperative to engage stakeholders and co-design strategy with "stakeowners" has begun to be explored (Ferkins & Shilbury, 2015b; Shilbury & Ferkins, 2015) but is a topic worthy of more attention. As presented in another chapter, gender and diversity in sport governance is also a growing imperative for sport board composition (Sotiriadou & de Haan, 2019). As this body of work evolves, there is a growing evidence base that points towards the contribution women make to board strategic discussion (Nielsen & Huse, 2010; Pletzer, Nikolova, Kedzior & Voelpel, 2015).

More work focused on how women engage in strategy inside the boardroom will potentially yield rich insights for sport governance strategy research. So too will consideration of greater diversity of thought, experiences and backgrounds (e.g., different ethnic and cultural experiences) and the contribution that a more diverse board can make to sport organisation strategy. Scholarship on board strategic work in sport is in its infancy. The curious dynamics of sport systems, which traverse public, nonprofit and commercial arrangements, often coalescing together, offer many unanswered questions in relation to the board's strategic function. More sport management scholars are needed in the role of developing knowledge for this critical aspect of sport governance.

References

Amis, J. (2003). "Good things come to those who wait": Strategic management of image and reputation at Guinness. *European Sport Management Quarterly, 3,* 189–214.

Auld, C. J. (1997). Professionalisation of Australian sport administration: The effects on organisational decision-making. *European Journal for Sport Management, 4,* 17–39.

Auld, C. J., & Godbey, G. (1998). Influence in Canadian national sport organizations: Perceptions of professionals and volunteers. *Journal of Sport Management, 12,* 20–38.

Bailey, B., & Peck, S. (2013). Boardroom strategic decision-making style: Understanding the antecedents. *Corporate Governance: An International Review. 21,* 131–146.

Boesso, G., Cerbioni, F., Menini, A., & Parbonetti, A. (2017). The role of the board in shaping foundations' strategy: An empirical study. *Journal of Management & Governance, 27,* 375–397.

Bordean, O., Borza, A., & Maier, V. (2011). The involvement of boards in strategy implementation. *Review of International Comparative Management, 12,* 986–992.

Bradshaw, P., Murray, V., & Wolpin, J. (1992). Do nonprofit boards make a difference? An exploration of the relationships among board structure, process, and effectiveness. *Nonprofit and Voluntary Sector Quarterly, 21,* 227–249.

Brown, W. (2005). Exploring the association between board and organizational performance in nonprofit organizations. *Nonprofit Management & Leadership, 5,* 317–339.

Brown, W. A., & Iverson, J. O. (2004). Exploring strategy and board structure in nonprofit organizations. *Nonprofit and Voluntary Sector Quarterly, 33,* 377–400.

Chelladurai, P. (1987). The design of sport governing bodies: A Parsonian perspective. In T. Slack & C. R. Hinings (Eds.), *The organization and administration of sport* (pp. 37–57). London, ON: Sports Dynamics Publishers.

Clendenin, W. D. (1972). Company presidents look at the board of directors. *California Management Review, 14*(3), 60–66.

Cornforth, C. (2012). Nonprofit governance research: Limitations of the focus on boards and suggestions for new directions. *Nonprofit and Voluntary Sector Quarterly, 41,* 1116–1135.

Couvelaere, A., & Richelieu, V. (2005). Brand strategy in professional sports: The case of French soccer teams. *European Sport Management Quarterly, 5*, 23–46.

Donaldson, L., & Davis, J. H. (1991). Stewardship theory or agency theory: CEO governance and shareholder returns. *Australian Journal of Management, 16*, 49–64.

Fama, E. F., & Jensen, M. C. (1983). Separation of ownership and control. *Journal of Law and Economics, 26*, 307–325.

Ferkins, L., & Shilbury, D. (2010). Developing board strategic capability in sport organisations: The national–regional governing relationship. *Sport Management Review, 13*, 235–254.

Ferkins, L., & Shilbury, D. (2012). Good boards are strategic: What does that mean for sport governance? *Journal of Sport Management, 26*, 67–80.

Ferkins, L. & Shilbury, D. (2015a). Board strategic balance: An emerging sport governance theory. *Sport Management Review, 18*, 489–500.

Ferkins, L., & Shilbury, D. (2015b). The stakeholder dilemma in sport governance: Toward the notion of "stakeowner". *Journal of Sport Management, 29*, 93–108.

Ferkins, L., Shilbury, D., & McDonald, G. (2005). The role of the board in building strategic capability: Towards an integrated model of sport governance research. *Sport Management Review, 8*, 195–225.

Ferkins, L., Shilbury, D., & McDonald, G. (2009). Board involvement in strategy: Advancing the governance of sport organizations. *Journal of Sport Management, 23*, 245–277.

Finkelstein, S., Hambrick, D. C., & Cannella, A. A., Jr. (2009). *Strategic leadership: Theory and research on executives, top management teams, and boards.* New York: Oxford University Press.

Garcia, B., & Welford, J. (2015). Supporters and football governance, from customers to stakeholders: A literature review and agenda for research. *Sport Management Review, 18*, 517–528.

Heimovics, R. D., & Herman, R. D. (1990). Responsibility for critical events in nonprofit organizations. *Nonprofit and Voluntary Sector Quarterly, 19*, 59–72.

Heller, M. F. (1972). The board of directors: Legalistic anachronism or vital force. *California Management Review, 14*(3), 24–30.

Hendry, K., Kiel, G., & Nicholson, G. (2010). How boards strategise: A strategy as practice view. *Long Range Planning, 43*, 33–56.

Henry, I., & Lee, P. C. (2004). Governance and ethics in sport. In J. Beech & S. Chadwick (Eds.), *The business of sport management* (pp. 25–41). Essex: Pearson Education.

Herman, R. D., & Heimovics, R. D. (1993, October). *The social construction of nonprofit organizational effectiveness: An interim research report.* Paper presented at the annual meeting of the Association for Research on Nonprofit Organizations and Voluntary Action, Toronto Ontario, Canada.

Herman, R. D., & Heimovics, R. D. (1994). A cross-national study of a method for researching nonprofit organizational effectiveness. *Voluntas, 7*, 86–100.

Herman, R. D., & Renz, D. O. (1998). Nonprofit organizational effectiveness: Contrasts between especially effective and less effective organizations. *Nonprofit Management & Leadership, 9*, 23–38.

Herman, R. D., & Renz, D. O. (2000). Board practices of especially effective and less effective local nonprofit organizations. *American Review of Public Administration, 30*, 146–160.

Herman, R. D., Renz, D. O., & Heimovics, R. D. (1997). Board practices and board effectiveness in local nonprofit organizations. *Nonprofit Management & Leadership, 7*, 373–385.

Hinings, R., & Slack, T. (1987). The dynamics of quadrennial plan implementation in national sport organizations. In T. Slack & R. Hinings (Eds.), *The organization and administration of sport* (pp. 127–151). London, ON: Sports Dynamics Publishers.

Hoye, R. (2006). Leadership within voluntary sport organization boards. *Nonprofit Management and Leadership, 16*, 297–313.

Hoye, R., & Cuskelly, G. (2003a). Board-executive relationships within voluntary sport organisations. *Sport Management Review, 6*, 53–73.

Hoye, R., & Cuskelly, G. (2003b). Board power and performance within voluntary sport organisations. *European Sport Management Quarterly, 3*, 103–119.

Hoye, R., & Cuskelly, G. (2007). *Sport governance.* Sydney: Elsevier.

Inglis, S. (1994). Exploring volunteer board member and executive director needs: Importance and fulfillment. *Journal of Applied Recreation Research, 19*, 171–189.

Inglis, S. (1997a). Shared leadership in the governance of amateur sport. *AVANTE Journal, 3*, 14–33.

Inglis, S. (1997b). Roles of the board in amateur sport organizations. *Journal of Sport Management, 1*, 160–176.

Inglis, S., Alexander, T., & Weaver, L. (1999). Roles and responsibilities of community nonprofit boards. *Nonprofit Management and Leaderships, 10*, 153–167.

Inglis, S., & Weaver, L. (2000). Designing agendas to reflect board roles and responsibilities: Results of a study. *Nonprofit Management and Leadership, 11*, 65–77.

Kerr, J., & Werther, W. (2008). The next frontier in corporate governance: Engaging the board in strategy. *Organizational Dynamics, 37*, 112–124.

Kikulis, L. (2000). Continuity and change in governance and decision making in national sport organizations: Institutional explanations. *Journal of Sport Management, 14*, 293–320.

Leblanc, R., & Schwartz, M. S. (2007). The black box of board process: Gaining access to a difficult subject. *Corporate Governance: An International Review, 15*, 843–851.

Mace, M. (1976, September–October). Attracting new directors. *Harvard Business Review, 54*(5), 46–51.

Machin, J. L., & Wilson, L. S. (1979). Closing the gap between planning and control. *Long Range Planning, 12*, 16–33.

McNulty, T., & Pettigrew, A. (1996). Contribution, power and influence of part-time board members. *Corporate Governance, 4*, 160–179.

McNulty, T., & Pettigrew, A. (1999). Strategists on the board. *Organization Studies, 20*, 47–74.

McNulty, T., & Pettigrew, A., Jobome, G., & Morris, C. (2011). The role, power and influence of company chairs. *Journal of Management & Governance, 15*, 91–121.

Nadler, D. (2004). What's the board's role in strategy development? Engaging the board in corporate strategy. *Strategy & Leadership, 32*, 25–33.

Nielsen, S., & Huse, M. (2010). The contribution of women on boards of directors: Going beyond the surface. *Corporate Governance: An International Review, 18*, 136–148.

O'Boyle, I., & Shilbury, D. (2016). Exploring issues of trust in collaborative sport governance. *Journal of Sport Management, 30*, 52–69.

Parker, L. (2007). Boardroom strategizing in professional associations: Processual and institutional perspectives. *Journal of Management Studies, 44*, 1455–1480.

Pettigrew, A. (1992). On studying managerial elites. *Strategic Management Journal, 13*, 163–182.

Pettigrew, A., & McNulty, T. (1995). Power and influence in and around the boardroom. *Human Relations, 48*, 845–873.

Pettigrew, A., & McNulty, T. (1998). Sources and uses of power in the boardroom. *European Journal of Work and Organizational Psychology, 7*, 197–214.

Pletzer, J. L., Nikolova, R., Kedzior, K. K., & Voelpel, S. C. (2015). Does gender matter? Female representation on corporate boards and firm financial performance - A meta-analysis. *PLOS ONE, 10*(6), e0130005. doi:10.1371/journal.pone.0130005

Pugliese, A., Bezemer, P., Zattoni, A., Huse, M., Van den Bosch, F., & Volberda, H. (2009). Boards of directors' contribution to strategy: A literature review and research agenda. *Corporate Governance: An International Review, 17*, 292–306.

Pye, A., & Pettigrew, A. (2005). Studying board context, process and dynamics: Some challenges for the future. *British Journal of Management, 16*, 27–38.

Sack, A. L., & Nadim, A. (2002). Strategic choice in a turbulent environment: A case study of Starter Corporation. *Journal of Sport Management, 16*, 36–53.

Searle, M. (1989). Testing the reciprocity norm in a recreation management setting. *Leisure Sciences, 2*, 353–365.

Shilbury, D. (2001). Examining board member roles, functions and influence: A study of Victorian sporting organisations. *International Journal of Sport Management, 2*, 253–281.

Shilbury, D. (2012). Competition: The heart and soul of sport management. *Journal of Sport Management, 26*, 1–10.

Shilbury, D., & Ferkins, L. (2011). Professionalisation, sport governance and strategic capability. *Managing Leisure, 16*, 108–127.

Shilbury, D. & Ferkins, L. (2015). Exploring the utility of collaborative governance in a national sport organization. *Journal of Sport Management, 29*, 380–397.

Shilbury, D., Ferkins, L., & Smythe, L. (2013). Sport governance encounters: Insights from lived experiences. *Sport Management Review, 16*, 349–363.

Siciliano, J. I. (1997). The relationship between formal planning and performance. *Nonprofit Management and Leadership, 7*, 387–404.

Siciliano, J. (2008). A comparison of CEO and director perceptions of board involvement in strategy. *Nonprofit and Voluntary Sector Quarterly, 37*, 152–162.

Slack, T. (1996). From the locker room to the board room: Changing the domain of sport management. *Journal of Sport Management, 10*, 97–105.

Sotiriadou, P., & de Haan, D. (2019). Women and leadership: Advancing gender equity policies in sport leadership through sport governance. *International Journal of Sport Policy and Politics.* Advance online publication. doi:10.1080/19406940.2019.1577902

Stiles, P. (2001). The impact of the board on strategy: An empirical examination. *Journal of Management Studies, 38,* 627–651.

Vance, J. O. (1979). The care and feeding of the board of directors. *California Management Review, 21*(1) 93–96.

Vigano, R., Zattoni, A., Hoskisson, R. E., & Huse, M. (2011). New perspectives on board research: Changing the research agenda. *Journal of Management and Governance, 15,* 5–28.

Warner, S., Chalip, L., & Woolf, J. (2008). Fan development strategy: The Austin Wranglers' game plan. *Sport Management Review, 11,* 309–330.

Wheelen, D., & Hunger, J. (2010). *Strategic management and business policy* (12th ed.). Upper Saddle River, NJ: Pearson/Prentice Hall.

21

Integrating regional entities
Unitary and collaborative governance

Trevor Meiklejohn and Ian O'Boyle

Introduction

This chapter explores the nature of the federal model of sport governance with a particular emphasis on investigating intra-sport cohesion between regional and national bodies charged with governing a sport. The federal model of governance refers to the division of powers within a nation where a number of separate and legally autonomous bodies comprise a network of distinct bodies collectively contributing to the governance of that nation. It is a system that has been in place in countries such as Australia and New Zealand and was first introduced under British colonisation. Sport governance in these countries has evolved as something of a mirror image of the political systems in place with little change in these structures, in some instances, for decades.

The chapter begins with a brief depiction of federal sport networks and how they operate, followed by a broader discussion around systemic and network governance, which has direct relevance to these federal systems. The importance of whole-of-sport cohesion is then discussed, highlighting the "compete and collaborate" dynamic that exists in many networks and looking at how sport may overcome this potentially inhibiting factor to increase cohesion. A comprehensive section is then devoted to a discussion on collaborative governance and its potential to facilitate increased collaboration within federally based networks without the requirement for structural change within these systems. Collaborative governance is an arrangement based on behaviours and actions rather than structure and design and therefore may have significant relevance when attempting to increase cohesion, cooperation, and collaboration between regional entities and national bodies.

The final section of the chapter explores the unitary model of sport governance as a potentially viable alternative to the federal model. This chapter relies on the work of O'Boyle and Shilbury (2017) as one of the few studies to examine the unitary model and its perceived efficiencies, weaknesses and benefits in comparison to the federal model. Given the relative infancy of both collaborative and unitary governance research within the sport context, the chapter concludes by exploring future research directions within these domains.

Federal sport networks

A central tenet of a not-for-profit sport system is the systemic or federated nature of the governance structures (Shilbury, Ferkins & Smythe, 2013). Therefore, when attempting to define and frame sport governance within this context, a wider view is required. More specifically, a view that recognises that individual sport organisations, despite being legally autonomous, do not operate in a vacuum. Rather, they are part of a network of organisations and consequently governance roles and processes should reflect this. As an example, the sport of netball in Australia consists of a national governing body (NGB) or national sport organisation (NSO) known as Netball Australia, eight state or regional sport organisations (RSOs) and a network of clubs linked to each state (Netball Australia, 2018). Netball in New Zealand's NSO is Netball New Zealand and the regional structure involves five geographically designated "zones" (Netball NZ, 2018). In these federal networks, there is a series of vertical inter-organisational linkages that exist between the governing bodies and their respective states/zones, and in turn the states/zones with their clubs. Further, there are horizontal connections between clubs within each state/zone and also between states/zones at the national level (Ferkins, Jogula & Meiklejohn, 2013). The foundation of these links is the competition between organisations via organised leagues and matches that Shilbury (2012) aptly described as the "heart and soul of sport management". This is reinforced by the government agency for sport in New Zealand, Sport New Zealand, when discussing the federations via its "nine steps to affective governance". This document high-lighted that clubs provide the opportunities for participation, regions run competitions and sub-elite activity, and the national body oversees high performance, national competitions and links to international bodies and subsequent international competitions (Sport New Zealand, 2018).

Linking systemic and network governance to sport governance

The federated nature of sport systems has a significant impact on the governance of each organi-sation in the network and indeed the governance of the entire sport (Ferkins & Shilbury, 2010; Hoye & Cuskelly, 2007; Taylor & O'Sullivan, 2009; Soares, Correia & Rosado, 2010). Therefore, it is not only the governance "of" organisations that is important, but also the governance "between" organisations and this is the essence of systemic governance. With the above netball example in mind, both the boards of Netball Australia and Netball New Zealand are "charged with not only leading its own organisation, but also mindfully governing a network that is atten-tive to the whole of the sport" (Ferkins, Shilbury & O'Boyle, 2018. p. 222).

Shilbury et al. (2013) captured this when building on Rosenau's (1995) definition of sport governance by stating that systemic sport governance can be defined as "a network of organi-sations which seek to allocate resources, and exercise control and co-ordination" (p. 350). It is here, through the term coordination, that there is a collective aspect to this type of govern-ance. Indeed, there is synergy with the definition of network governance provided by Provan and Kenis (2008) as "use of institutions and structures of authority and collaboration to allo-cate resources and to coordinate and control action across the network as a whole" (p. 231). Stone, Crosby and Bryson (2010) also captured this theme by suggesting that governance is about "making collective decisions about important issues, including the purpose of collec-tive actions, strategies for achieving purpose and oversight and accountability mechanisms" (p. 310). Similarly, Powell, White, Koput and Owen-Smith (2005) described network structure as a framework for "illuminating the structure of collective action" (p. 1133).

The cooperative themes embedded in the above network governance conceptualisations are relevant for nonprofit sports in countries such as Australia, New Zealand, Canada, the UK, and a number of other European countries where the federal model is the predominant sport organisational form. Here, the decision-making and power dynamics are shared across the sport network between the NSO, regional or state organisations and clubs, and subsequently all enti-ties must work together to foster the development of their sport from grass-roots community through to high performance (Ferkins et al., 2018). This was argued by Provan (1983) in his seminal research on federations by emphasising that all affiliated members of a federation should act in the best interests of the network as a whole.

The drive for whole-of-sport cohesion

In practice, a "whole-of-sport approach" and collaborative values are promoted heavily by national sport organisations and lead government agencies for sport. Sport New Zealand (2018) as part of its governance quality standard for sport and recreation highlights the importance of "whole-of-sport plans" and stated that "federations are based on the principles of cooperation, collaboration and the sum of the parts being greater than the whole" (p. 34). The equivalent agency for sport in Australia, Sport Australia (formerly Australian Sports Commission) (2015) via its *Mandatory Sports Governance Principles* emphasised that sports with a federated structure, must demonstrate federation-wide cohesion and adhere to the wider strategic direction set by the NGB/NSO to maximise the interests of the sport. As an example, the national governing body for the sport of cricket in Australia, Cricket Australia, has the vision to be "Australia's favourite sport" and is underpinned by three strategic pillars focussing on delivering excellence for fans, participants and volunteers, and achieving excellence at the elite playing level (Cricket Australia, 2017). As part of this vision, Cricket Australia appears highly aware of the need to work with its six member associations and wider stakeholders to achieve its strategic goals. This is acknowledged by stating in its strategic plan that "we all act collectively in the best interests of the game we love and serve" and "working as a unified sport, we co-design national plans and enable localised delivery of those plans to cricket communities across each state" (Cricket Australia, 2017, p. 3). Finally, the values of being "stronger together" and "go further … collaborate" (p. 16) are highlighted in the plan under the heading of "How We Play".

The discussion thus far leads to a most interesting and unique characteristic pertaining to sport federations and that is the simultaneous and contrasting cooperation and competition dynamic (Shilbury, 1993). Regardless of the level of competition, teams representing clubs, regions/states, franchises or countries exist as both individual entities and as a collection of teams (Dickson, Arnold & Chalip, 2005). Here, the collection of teams often competes as part of a league or tournament and teams may also compete for commercial revenues, funding, media attention, participants and fan engagement. This competition is complemented by ongoing cooperative behaviours such as agreeing to rules such as salary caps (Fort & Quirk, 1995) and numerous conditions relating but not limited to on-field rules, season length, player behaviour, facility requirements and joint marketing initiatives (Stewart, Nicholson & Dickson, 2005). Again, using the Cricket Australia example, this unique and contrasting dynamic is explicitly presented in the strategic plan stating "On the field, we compete in domestic competitions that inspire fans and develop Australian players of the future. Off the field, we collaborate in all areas where it is beneficial to leverage the scale of cricket nationally" (Cricket Australia, 2017, p. 3).

The challenge of achieving sport-wide cohesion

Unfortunately, evidence indicates that, despite the well-intended rhetoric, sport-wide cohesion is not easy to achieve in many sport federations and, at times, the reality is quite the opposite. As far back as 1983, Provan asserted that relationships in federations might become antagonistic. As an example, Meiklejohn, Dickson and Ferkins (2016) studied a unique period in New Zealand rugby during the infancy of professionalism. Here, the regional rugby unions were confronted with new commercial pressures and a newly established professional rugby structure that saw the 26 rugby unions allocated to one of five Super Rugby franchise regions. As part of this structure, five of the larger provincial unions were contracted by New Zealand Rugby to each manage one of the five Super Rugby franchises. They were known as "base unions" as they managed a Super Rugby franchise and the team would be based in that particular province. For example, The Blues franchise consisted of three provincial rugby unions (Auckland, North Harbour and Northland) and Auckland Rugby was the designated "base union" for this franchise as the team was based in Auckland. On its own, this new structure automatically created fragmentation, however what ensued was the formation of a number of cliques underpinned by status rather than region. In the first instance, the five base unions developed unique commercial arrangements between them that did not include the non-base unions.

Similarly, a number of non-base unions (nine to be exact), generally discontented with the above commercial arrangements established by the base unions and the perceived benefits the base unions were able to leverage from their new-found status, also formed their own clique that served as platform for commercial development, resource sharing and to influence the national governing body (Rugby New Zealand). Further, Meiklejohn (2010) observed that the Super Rugby franchises, despite seemingly offering its provincial union members an ideal stage for enhanced collaboration, demonstrated low levels of cooperation and trust, underpinned by a general dissatisfaction by the non-base unions with the relatively newly implemented system to govern in the newly established professional rugby environment.

Collaborative governance as a potential solution to enhancing cohesion

The focus of this chapter now transitions from the key issues inhibiting a cohesive sport system in a federal model to the approaches and alternative structures that provide solutions to achieving greater stakeholder integration and cooperation. The first of which is collaborative governance, which Shilbury and Ferkins (2015) contended has utility within the sport governance arena. Before exploring detailed definitions and relevant conceptualisations of collaborative governance, on the surface, the overarching goals of collaborative governance indicate its relevance within sport federations. In particular, Emerson, Nabatchi and Balogh (2012) emphasised that collaborative governance has the potential to transform a complex situation or issue into a more manageable situation or solution. A prime example of this is the challenging shift in sport from amateurism to professionalism as highlighted above.

This is reinforced by Innes and Booher (1999) who emphasised that collaborative governance seeks to alter a current issue or condition that is deemed undesirable or in need of change. They specifically stated that one of the "most important consequences of collaborative governance may be to change the direction of a complex, uncertain evolving situation, and help move a community towards higher levels of social and environmental importance" (p. 413). With the New Zealand Super Rugby franchise example in mind, Ansell and Gash (2008) emphasised that collaborative governance is not a "winner(s) take all" arrangement, rather it seeks to transform adversarial stakeholder relationships into more cooperative ones.

In very simple terms, Ansell and Gash (2008) assert that collaborative governance brings multiple stakeholders together to engage in consensus-oriented decision-making. As a mode of governance, it has developed as an alternative to multiple agenda-driven interest groups and has become more salient as environments have become more complex and knowledge and expertise has become more specialised, therefore increasing the need for collaboration. Ansell and Gash (2008) specifically defined collaborative governance as:

> A governing arrangement where one or more public agencies directly engage non-state stakeholders in collective decision-making process that is formal, consensus-oriented, and deliberative and that aims to make or implement public policy or manage public programs or assets. (p. 544)

Emerson et al. (2012) highlight that collaborative governance draws from diverse areas of research and practice in public administration and provide a slightly broader definition:

> The processes and structures of public policy decision making and management that engage people constructively across the boundaries of public agencies, levels of government, and/ or the public, private and civic spheres in order to carry out a public purpose that could not otherwise be accomplished. (p. 2)

With reference to the above definition, Shilbury et al. (2016) noted that the delivery of sport for enhanced community outcomes aligns well with delivering a public purpose across a number of connected not-for-profit sport organisations, often supported by government policy and funding. They further emphasised that there is a need for NSOs to drive and facilitate the sharing of information, resources and capabilities among member associations in the same collaborative manner the government agencies are required to do in their respective operational environments. Regardless of the context, collaborative governance is an intentional and formal strategy and thus is inherently linked to the behaviours and actions of those charged to govern (Ansell & Gash, 2008).

Entering into a formal collaborative governance arrangement in a federal network is not something achieved without all parties investing both time and resources. The willingness for mutual adjustment and to attempt to overcome prehistories of conflict or previous failed attempts at collaboration must be addressed. One of the key topics that regularly surfaces in the literature in relation to the "starting conditions" (Ansell & Gash, 2008) and incentives to form a collaborative governance regime (CGR) is the extent to which collaboration and therefore existing collaborative relationships are already in place in a network.

O'Boyle and Shilbury (2016), as noted previously, showed how trust was an essential ingredient and, in some cases, a necessary precondition for the formation of a CGR. The authors showed how high levels of distrust in the governing relationship between national and state bodies could not only inhibit the potential for a formal collaborative governing arrangement to be established but also, in some instances, could lead to a complete breakdown in communication between governing entities. In the networks where distrust was high, prehistories of antagonism and conflict were present, and with minimal effort to overcome these issues being undertaken, it was unlikely that a formal CGR could be adopted.

Further, where the levels of trust were highest within networks, informal collaborative governance behaviours, such as shared understanding, facilitative leadership and openness to explore mutual gains, were already in existence. Trust in these networks was manifested through regular face-to-face dialogue, intentionally seeking intermediate outcomes or "small wins" to create momentum that could act as a platform for larger initiatives, and high levels of transparency across the federal networks, particularly in terms of the decision-making process. O'Boyle and Shilbury's (2016) research clearly showed that distrust was an inhibiting factor in the formation of such a regime.

Shilbury et al. (2016) adapted Emerson et al.'s (2012) work to discuss how current conditions shape and influence collaboration in networks, and they argued that four main "drivers" were crucial, including organisational leadership, consequential incentives, interdependence and uncertainty. Taking a broad view of collaborative sport governance, Shilbury et al. (2016) theorised the potential drivers, collaborative dynamics, actions and contexts within which a sport-based CGR may unfold. The authors grouped together a number of research questions into various themes: "Power and Structure", "People: Leadership and Motivation" and "Decision-Making". Some of these questions directly address the barriers or enablers to developing a CGR in a federal, nonprofit sport system and the authors argued that the exploration of these issues was essential to increase understanding of how CGRs may operate and to build strong foundations for collaborative sport governance theory. Real-life examples of collaborative governance in practice are not well documented and, given the potential rewards of such an approach, it would be encouraging to see more federal-based networks move to adopt such a regime.

The unitary model as an alternative to the federal model

Although the federal model continues to be the prominent model of sport governance within a significant number of nations (particularly those whose political system reflects it), given the complexities of governing in such model, many sports are exploring potentially suitable alternatives. One such alternative that has come to fruition in a small number of sports is known as the unitary model of sport governance. Given the recent emergence of this model in the sporting domain, little is known about the specific benefits and challenges when compared against the federal model (Confederation of Australian Motor Sport (CAMS), 2015).

Essentially, a unitary governance model requires that the board of an NSO holds the balance of power within a sport in relation to decision-making, policy, allocation of resources, direction setting and, ultimately, how the sport manages participation and high-performance issues throughout all regional affiliates (O'Boyle & Shilbury, 2016). Previously existing autonomous regional boards are replaced with either an advisory board or, in some cases, may be dissolved completely. This presents challenges in itself, as it also requires that boards within each region surrender their power and decision-making legitimacy, coupled with the difficult task of attempting to govern an entire sport across potentially expansive landmasses. Nonetheless, the notion and perceived idealism of the unitary model continue to be mooted across the sport industry, which can be assumed to be a direct result of the complexities and challenges that often arise within the federal model, as noted above (CAMS, 2015; Equestrian Australia, 2015; Sport Australia, 2015; TRI, 2015). The increased ability to market a sport to a national sponsor, given that all participants would be members of a single governing body, is also a potentially powerful force underpinning the unitary system.

In keeping with federal models of sport governance mirroring political structures, the versions of unitary models in sport to date ultimately mirror those within political science. Within this domain, the description of what a unitary system of government actually constitutes can become blurred as individual differences often exist between various nations. However, in general, a unitary governance system in relation to political science refers to a central (national) government holding the majority of power and control over all regions in a nation, with only minimal powers being devolved to regions or "states" that comprise the geographical make-up of a nation (Gerring, Thacker & Moreno, 2007).

Interestingly, the dominant political trend of our time is to move away from the idea of "unitarism" and the seeking of increased decentralisation from national to subnational levels in many political systems throughout the world (Gerring et al., 2007). It should also be observed, however, that federalism remains intact in many nations long associated with this structure, such as the United States, Germany, India and Australia. There is no evidence of any democratic nation (to date) moving from a constitutional status of federalism to one that more closely embodies the characteristics of unitary governance (Gerring et al., 2007).

There remains a conspicuous absence of studies in the field of sport governance that afford attention to the issue of unitary models of governance in both nonprofit and for-profit sporting contexts (O'Boyle & Shilbury, 2017). Work such as that of Puig, Martínez and García (2010), and Niemann, García and Grant (2011) have explored issues such as sports policy and the transformation of European football respectively, however, they do not specifically explore key issues of sport governance practice and behaviours in the unitary model.

When soliciting governance reviews of their sports, a small number of Australian NSOs have employed professional consultants to explore issues related to the potential adoption of a unitary model in their networks. These include the Confederation of Australian Motor Sport, Equestrian Australia, Touch Football Australia, Triathlon Australia and Yachting Australia. Golf Australia and most of its state member associations (MAs) have recently adopted the move to a one-management model, which in effect has relieved the MAs of its staff. Staff from five (of the seven) of the MAs are now employed by Golf Australia. The Golf Australia experience shows how difficult it is to implement the full unitary model, as member associations are reluctant to let go, in full, their constitutional power. The prospect of a unitary model was debated as a strategic option, but the obstacles proved too great to implement in its entirety.

O'Boyle and Shilbury's (2017) work is one of the few examples of a direct exploration of the unitary model in comparison to its well-established predecessor, the federal model. In their work, they were able to highlight the challenges of adopting the unitary model, noting particularly the significant barrier of regional entities surrendering power and authority (and assets) in favour of a national and centralised governing structure. This issue would appear to remain a key inhibitor for the increased adoption of unitary models within sport governance networks in Australia and elsewhere.

Summary and future research

The federal model of sport governance continues to remain steadfastly in place in the majority of sporting networks within countries such as Australia, New Zealand, Canada and parts of Europe. This chapter highlighted the now well-documented challenges and barriers to cohesion that can result as a consequence of governing under such a model and has provided a detailed overview of both collaborative and unitary governance approaches to overcome such challenges. In light of the predominant consensus that exists in the research to date that improved whole-of-sport cohesion is both necessary and important for sports codes, the path is now set for ongoing research in this space. This consensus for more collaborative sports networks is also shared by the peak governing bodies, such as those highlighted in this chapter, further reinforcing this avenue of inquiry as salient and important.

The opportunity exists for scholars to explore in greater depth the key elements highlighted thus far, not only to increase understanding, but also to better determine the capacity of sport organisations to both implement and sustain collaborative governance arrangements in the long term. In short, despite early indications that the federal model is well suited to a collaborative governance regime, there are both challenges and barriers for its successful implementation. A deeper deconstruction of these challenges and barriers is needed if scholars are to make a significant contribution to theory development and practice in this space. Acknowledging this,

Shilbury et al. (2016) developed a research agenda to guide inquiry moving forward involving three aforementioned themes in this chapter. Within the theme of "People: Leadership and Motivation", they emphasised that leadership is a vital factor in the initiation and maintenance of a collaborative governance regime. Given this, further work focussing on the role of board leadership is necessary to drive the cultural shift in sport federations from autonomy, self-interest and a combative nature to a more united, collaborative culture.

Within the theme of "Power and Structure", a deeper understanding is required of the power dynamics that exist between smaller and larger legally independent member associations, and how this may influence collaboration. Also, better understanding the existing cooperative arrangements that may exist within a federation as a result of league/federation-wide special initiatives, projects or events that can serve to bring stakeholders together and potentially test the motivation and capacity to cooperate as a precursor to more formal collaborative governance arrangements. The final theme or area of future exploration is "Decision-Making". Here scholars are encouraged to explore how decisions are made within federations as ultimately, if decisions are made independently without the input of all members, a collaborative governance regime will be a challenging proposition. Related areas of trust, shared values and the extent to which the NSO and member associations have a whole-of-sport vision and mission are also important lines of inquiry. In conclusion, Shilbury et al. (2016) stated that regardless of the area being explored, guiding questions should ask: "How the impact attributable to collaborative governance can be determined and assessed, and how the return-on-investment (time and people) to NSOs and MAs in those federal networks which are successful in implementing such a regime can be determined?" (p. 490).

References

Ansell, C., & Gash, A. (2008). Collaborative governance in theory and practice. *Journal of Public Administration Research and Theory, 18*, 543–571.

Confederation of Australian Motorsport. (2015). *Structure*. Retrieved 25 August 2015, from https://www.cams.com.au/about/structure

Cricket Australia. (2017). Australian cricket strategy 2017–2022. Retrieved 10 October 2018, from https://read.e-brochures.com.au/cricketaustralia/2017-strategy-booklet/#page/0

Dickson, G., Arnold, T., & Chalip, L. (2005). League expansion and interorganisational power. *Sport Management Review, 8*, 145–165.

Emerson, K., Nabatchi, T., & Balogh, S. (2012). An integrative framework for collaborative governance. *Journal of Public Administration Research and Theory, 22*(1), 1–29.

Equestrian Australia. (2015). Governance review. Retrieved 25 August 2015, from http://www.equestrian.org.au/sites/default/files/Equestrian%20Governance%20Review:May%202015.pdf

Ferkins, L., Jogula, U., & Meiklejohn, T. (2013). New Zealand. In I. O'Boyle & T. Bradbury (Eds.), *Sport governance: International case studies* (pp. 243–259). Oxon, UK and New York: Routledge.

Ferkins, L., & Shilbury, D. (2010). Developing board strategic capability in sport organisations: The national–regional governing relationship. *Sport Management Review, 13*, 235–254.

Ferkins, L., Shilbury, D., & O'Boyle, I. (2018). Leadership in governance: Exploring collective board leadership in sport governance systems. *Sport Management Review, 21*, 221–231.

Fort, R., & Quirk, J. (1995). Cross-subsidization, incentives, and outcomes in professional team sports leagues. *Journal of Economic literature, 33*, 1265–1299.

Gerring, J., Thacker, S., & Moreno, C. (2007). *Are federal systems better than unitary systems?* Boston, MA: Boston University.

Hoye, R., & Cuskelly, G. (2007). *Sport governance*. Oxford, UK: Elsevier.

Innes, J. E., & Booher, D. E. (1999). Consensus building and complex adaptive systems: A framework for evaluating collaborative planning. *Journal of the American Planning Association, 65*, 412–423.

Meiklejohn, T. W. (2010). *The formation, processes and impacts of interorganisational cliques: A study of New Zealand provincial rugby* (Masters dissertation). Auckland: Auckland University of Technology.

Meiklejohn, T., Dickson, G., & Ferkins, L. (2016). The formation of interorganisational cliques in New Zealand rugby. *Sport Management Review, 19*, 266–278.

Netball Australia. (2018). State member organisations. Retrieved 22 October 2018, from https://netball .com.au/about-netball-australia/member-organisations/

Netball New Zealand. (2018). Choose your zone. Retrieved 22 October 2018, from http://www.netballnz. co.nz/

Niemann, A., García, B., & Grant, W. (Eds.). (2011). *The transformation of European football: Towards the Europeanisation of the national game.* Manchester: Manchester University Press.

O'Boyle, I., & Shilbury, D. (2016). Exploring issues of trust in collaborative sport governance. *Journal of Sport Management, 30*, 52–69.

O'Boyle, I., & Shilbury, D. (2017). Comparing federal versus unitary models of sport governance: A case study investigation. *Managing Sport and Leisure, 21*, 353–374.

Powell, W. W., White, D. R., Koput, K. W., & Owen-Smith, J. (2005). Network dynamics and field evolution: The growth of interorganisational collaboration in the life sciences. *Journal of Sociology, 110*, 1132–205.

Provan, K. G. (1983). The federation as an interorganizational linkage network. *Academy of Management Review, 8*(1), 79–89.

Provan, K. G., & Kenis, P. (2008). Modes of network governance: Structure, management, and effectiveness. *Journal of Public Administration Research and Theory, 18*, 229–252.

Puig, N., Martinez, J., & García, B. (2010). Sports policy in Spain. *International Journal of Sport Policy, 3*, 381–390.

Rosenau, J. N. (1995). Governance in the twenty-first century. *Global Governance, 1*(1), 13–43.

Shilbury, D. (1993). Determining the problem of order in the Australian Football League. *Journal of Sport Management, 7*, 122–131.

Shilbury, D. (2012). Competition: The heart and soul of sport management. *Journal of Sport Management, 26*, 1–10.

Shilbury, D., & Ferkins, L. (2015). Exploring the utility of collaborative governance in a national sport organization. *Journal of Sport Management, 29*, 380–397.

Shilbury, D., Ferkins, L., & Smythe, L. (2013). Sport governance encounters: Insights from lived experiences. *Sport Management Review, 16*, 349–363.

Shilbury, D., O'Boyle, I., & Ferkins, L. (2016). Towards a research agenda in collaborative sport governance. *Sport Management Review, 19*, 479–491.

Soares, J., Correia, A., & Rosado, A. (2010). Political factors in the decision-making process in voluntary sports associations. *European Sport Management Quarterly, 10*, 5–29.

Sport Australia. (2015). *Mandatory sport governance principles.* Retrieved 2 October 2018, from https://ww w.sportaus.gov.au/governance/mandatory_sports_governance_principles

Sport New Zealand. (2018). Nine steps to effective governance. Retrieved 2 October 2018, from https://sp ortnz.org.nz/assets/Uploads/attachments/managing-sport/strong-organisations/Nine-Steps-to-Effec tive-Governance-Building-High-Performing-Organisations.pdf

Stewart, B., Nicholson, M., & Dickson, G. (2005). The Australian Football League's recent progress: A study in cartel conduct and monopoly power. *Sport Management Review, 8*, 95–117.

Stone, M. M., Crosby, B. C., & Bryson, J. M. (2010). Governing public–nonprofit collaborations: Understanding their complexity and the implications for research. *Voluntary Sector Review, 1*, 309–334.

Taylor, M., & O'Sullivan, N. (2009). How should national governing bodies of sport be governed in the UK? An exploratory study of board structure. *Corporate Governance: An International Review, 17*, 681–693.

Triathlon Victoria (TRI). (2015). Special General Meeting: 6th October 2013. Retrieved 25 August 2015, from http://www.triathlon.org.au/Assets/Triathlon+Australia+Digital+Assets/VIC/PDFs/Explan atory+Memorandum.pdf

22

Managing stakeholders

Michael L. Naraine and Milena M. Parent

Introduction

Governing sport organisations in the current global climate is fraught with many challenges, including the need to manage a complex and diverse set of stakeholders. Whether voluntarily or reluctantly embraced, organisations are linked with other organisations, institutions, clients and publics (Carroll, 1999; Mainardes, Alves & Raposo, 2011). Their association with a focal organisation, whether through financial, legal, material or intellectual means (Knoke & Yang, 2008), creates relevance for these actors, each of whom bear intrinsic value to the focal organisation (Phillips, 2003).

For example, Churchill Downs Incorporated, owners of the famed Churchill Downs racetrack that organises the perennial Kentucky Derby racehorse event, cannot be concerned solely with the dyadic relationship between themselves and consumers/spectators. The organisation should consider the needs and attitudes of horse owners, trainers and jockeys; without them, there is no race. Beyond these obvious stakeholder groups, corporate partners, such as Coca-Cola and Chrysler agreeing to multi-million-dollar deals, could want a greater opportunity to voice their concerns about the direction of the event, and organisers may have to collaborate with NBC, the television rights holder, to determine the schedule of events. There is also the influence borne by local government vis-à-vis traffic and safety management, and activist groups such as People for the Ethical Treatment of Animals (PETA) who protest against the use of animals for sport and entertainment, which could affect the event. Indeed, this one case of the Kentucky Derby emphasises that sport organisations do not operate in isolation; rather, there are multiple stakeholders with their own agendas and interests involved in the discourse.

But what constitutes a stakeholder? Freeman (1984) suggested stakeholders are all the organisations, groups and individuals who affect or are affected by the actions of a focal organisation. The ambiguity in this definition produces a rather wide view of an organisation's stakeholder environment; essentially anyone could be a stakeholder. As such, researchers started narrowing the definition. In the 1990s, management researchers mostly thought stakeholders included employees, shareholders, suppliers and consumers – actors with a direct business-oriented relationship with the firm (i.e., a for-profit organisation; Clarkson, 1995).

The more modern view of stakeholder classification argues moral obligations, power and contributions to the focal organisation's wealth-creating capacities are necessary for a constituent to be called a stakeholder of the organisation. Phillips (2003) argued "stakeholders are those groups from whom the organization has voluntarily accepted benefits and to whom there arises a moral obligation … stakeholder status may also be derived from the power to affect the organization and its normative stakeholders" (p. 135). In turn, Post, Preston and Sachs (2002) argued "stakeholders in a corporation are the individuals and constituencies that contribute, either voluntarily or involuntarily, to its wealth-creating capacity and activities, and that are therefore its potential beneficiaries and/or risk bearers" (p. 19).

Alongside this conceptual sophistication has been a substantial rise in stakeholder-related research (Laplume, Sonpar & Litz, 2008). The stakeholder approach has also become popular for governance-related research in the management and public management fields (Clarke, 2004), as using a stakeholder approach means recognising the reciprocal interdependencies between the focal firm and its stakeholders, which form the specific stakeholder network of that focal organisation (cf. Post et al., 2002), a network that must ultimately be governed. This is also the case with sport management, for example for major sport event organising committees needing to coordinate their stakeholder network in order to prepare and host the sport event – organising committees cannot do it alone.

Despite this advance, sport governance research has generally focused on boards, organisational structure (e.g., federated models), and strategic management, including works advanced by Ferkins and Shilbury (2010, 2015a, 2015b), Hoye and Doherty (2011), and Shilbury, O'Boyle and Ferkins (2016). This general line of inquiry, while needed, has a limited view of sport governance due to its internal perspective. This view has the potential to overlook stakeholders situated outside the organisation's borders. Though many of these groups have traditionally remained dormant or silent in sport organisation governance, technological advancements in communication, such as social media, have given stakeholders a voice and a means to engage with other stakeholders to advance a collective interest (Parent, Naraine & Hoye, 2018). Moreover, the evolution of sport has produced new lines of inquiry, such as eSports (Cunningham, Fairley, Ferkins, Kerwin, Lock, Shaw & Wicker, 2018), which have in turn introduced new actors and relationships into the sector. While stakeholders are not tasked with governing (with the exception of federated governance models), they can influence organisational governance as well as influencing decision-making towards favourable decisions on issues or positions of concern to those groups. This sentiment highlights the need to examine collaboration and coordination between these groups (e.g., Naraine, Schenk & Parent, 2016), particularly in light of these new trends and operational realities (Parent et al., 2018). As such, there remains a need to shift the sport governance lens towards a stakeholder management perspective to extend our comprehension of sport governance in the contemporary landscape (Parent, Rouillard & Naraine, 2017).

The purpose of this chapter is therefore to examine stakeholder management as it relates to the sport governance discourse. Stakeholder management is critical to temper expectations and obtain support for organisational directives. However, this relationship is not unidirectional. As noted above, stakeholders can advance their own agendas and interests onto the sport organisation. Thus, it is important to expand our understanding of stakeholders in the sport governance context. To do so, we begin by identifying the types of stakeholders that occupy a position within a sport organisation's network, including their salience, and the overall process of stakeholder management. Next, emergent trends are discussed, including enduring and temporary stakeholder management, as well as the emerging saliency of social media. The chapter concludes with a brief summary, a critical view of the trends and gaps present in the stakeholder management literature, and opportunities for future directions.

The stakeholder management process

The stakeholder management process has four basic questions (cf. Friedman, Parent & Mason, 2004): (1) Who surrounds the organisation? (2) What do they want? (3) Who is more important? And (4) What does the organisation need to do to ensure the most important stakeholders are satisfied? We briefly review each step below.

Who surrounds the organisation?

Sport managers need to consider a number of key stakeholders, both internal and external to the organisation, such as (see also Figure 22.1; cf. Parent & Deephouse, 2007):

- Internal stakeholders: The paid staff/employees and/or volunteers involved in the organisation;
- External stakeholders:
  - The athletes and their entourage (e.g., coaches, nutritionists, psychologists, agents and delegation staff);
  - Customers/clients;
  - Sponsors (local/regional, national and/or international);
  - The governments under whose jurisdiction(s) the sport organisations fall;
  - The media (print/press, radio, internet/digital media, broadcast/television);
  - Other sport organisations (e.g., local, regional, national, continental and/or international sport federations and clubs, leagues and event rights owners);

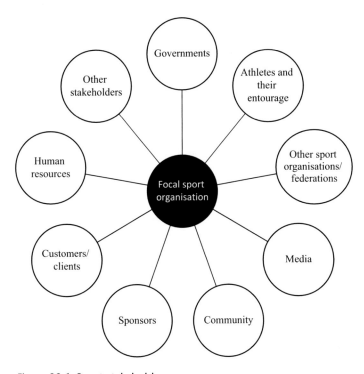

Figure 22.1 Sport stakeholder map.

- The community (e.g., residents, community groups, schools, activists and local businesses); and
- Other stakeholders: other individuals, groups and organisations that have a direct or indirect connection to the organisation (Starik, 1994), have a stake in the organisation, affect its wealth-creating capacity and/or other relevant attribute.

What do they want?

It is not enough to know who surrounds the focal organisation. A sport manager must also understand what each stakeholder (group) wants. Stakeholder interests can be defined by the type of stake or claim the stakeholder has on the organisation (Freeman, 1984); this stake can be benefit-related or cost-related and be associated to money, time or another resource (Freeman, 1984; Clarkson, 1995; Phillips, 1999). For example, employees give their time in exchange for monetary benefit, whereas volunteers give their time in exchange for some other benefit (e.g., new skills, networks, make friends or for leisure; Parent & Smith-Swan, 2013). In turn, event sponsors give cash or in-kind donations in return for the right to be associated with the event and its activities and for potential return-on-investments, while spectators (i.e., the community) give money in return for access to the event and for the experience of seeing their favourite team or event live. Overall, stakeholders can have the following types of interests (Parent, 2008; Reichart, 2003):

- Material: the gain or loss of tangible benefits;
- Affiliative: the need to belong and the need for human relationships;
- Informational: knowledge-based benefits;
- Political: political power as well as the distribution of influence;
- Symbolic: benefits associated with a symbol (e.g., image, identity and reputation).

It is important to note, however, that it cannot be assumed all stakeholders within a given stakeholder group have the exact same interests; this is called stakeholder heterogeneity (Parent, 2008; Parent & Deephouse, 2007; Putler & Wolfe, 1999). For example, Parent (2008) found that for a major sport event, while all three host government levels (i.e., municipal, provincial/state and federal) had financial and visibility concerns, the municipal government also concerned itself with participation and legacy, while the provincial/state government had political and legacy concerns, and the federal government had political and participation concerns.

Who is more important?

So with varying stakeholder interests and usually limited organisational resources, the next step is to determine who is more important. Although stakeholder theorists argued "the interests of all (legitimate) stakeholders have intrinsic value, and no set of interests is assumed to dominate the others" (Jones & Wicks, 1999, p. 207), some stakeholders are more salient (important) than others. This is typically associated with the type of stake and/or degree of impact of the stakeholder on the focal organisation. There are numerous ways to determine stakeholder salience, such as Carroll's (1996) generic and specific stakeholders, Post et al.'s (2002) resource-based, industry structure-based and sociopolitical arena-based stakeholders, Sirgy's (2002) internal, external and distal stakeholders, and Phillips' (2003) normative and derivative stakeholders. We outline two popular approaches as well as an emerging approach.

Clarkson's (1995) primary and secondary stakeholders. Primary stakeholders are those individuals, groups and organisations without "whose continuing participation the corporation cannot survive" (p. 106). If the primary stakeholder becomes dissatisfied, the organisation would be significantly damaged. If the primary stakeholder leaves or breaks the partnership, the organisation may not survive. For instance, customers are a primary stakeholder group for any apparel company like Puma, Adidas or Nike. In turn, secondary stakeholders are those individuals, groups and organisations that can influence or affect, or can be influenced or are affected by, the organisation's actions. But they are not engaged in direct transactions with the focal organisation and they are not critical to the focal organisation's survival. For apparel companies, activist groups would likely be considered as a secondary stakeholder group.

Mitchell, Agle and Wood's (1997) power-legitimacy-urgency typology. Here, power can be *coercive* (the use of force or threat), *utilitarian* (the use of material resources or financial incentives) and/or *normative* (the use of symbolic influences) (Etzioni, 1964). In terms of legitimacy, a stakeholder's action or claim will be seen as legitimate if it is perceived as appropriate, socially acceptable and expected (Mitchell et al., 1997; Agle, Mitchell & Sonnenfeld, 1999). For example, an official event sponsor will be seen as having a more legitimate claim on the organising committee than a local company that is only tangentially associated with an event. Legitimacy depends on the established standards of the network within which the focal organisation and stakeholders operate, which means legitimacy can result in an organisation actually becoming a stakeholder for the focal organisation even if it doesn't want to recognise that stakeholder (cf. Carroll, 1993; Scott & Lane, 2000). For example, the organising committee may wish to ignore local indigenous group's claims, but if they are seen as legitimate by others in the event network, they de facto become stakeholders, whether the organising committee likes it or not. Finally, if a stakeholder's claims are seen as time sensitive and/or highly important from the stakeholder's point of view, then the stakeholder has urgency. Mitchell et al. (1997) argued that the more of these three attributes a stakeholder possesses, the more salient they are. Parent and Deephouse (2007) added that having different types of each attribute increases a stakeholder's salience. Of course, any stakeholder can be critical at any point in time for any particular issue; also, stakeholder salience will depend on the manager's individual cognitive abilities and perceptions, as well as their position in the organisation (Parent & Deephouse, 2007).

Stakeowners. Another way to view stakeholders is regarding the extent to which legitimate stakeholders have rights and responsibilities towards the focal organisation; it is a reciprocal perspective, as opposed to the one-way focal organisation-to-stakeholder perspective. This *stakeowner* view focuses attention on the prominent, legitimate stakeholders, those from whom the focal organisation expects something in return (see Fassin, 2009, 2012). These can be the sport organisation's fans, members or sponsors, to name a few. The stakeowner approach is a revisiting of Clarkson's (1995) primary stakeholders. In the case of a national sport organisation (NSO), a stakeowner could be the provincial/state associations that are the members of the NSO and have voting power to elect the NSO's board members. Fifty percent of Canadian NSOs have seats on their boards for key stakeowners; this shows the decision-making power and responsibilities these stakeholders can have within the context of governance-based boards (cf. Parent et al., 2018, 2019). For Fassin (2009, 2012), the secondary stakeholders would be termed *stakewatchers* (e.g., the media, activists and athlete unions) and *stakekeepers* (e.g., regulatory bodies). In the NSO example, broadcasters could be stakewatchers while the federal government would be a stakekeeper. What is important, however, is to ensure these stakeowners understand their responsibilities towards the focal organisation (cf. Ferkins & Shilbury, 2015b).

What to do to ensure the most important stakeholders are satisfied?

Once the more important stakeholders are identified and their needs known, the sport manager must compare these needs and expectations with what the organisation can offer. At a minimum, the organisation must satisfice (satisfy + suffice) its primary stakeholders or stakeowners in order to survive. Depending on the type of interest, need or expectation, this may mean, for example, adjusting policies or procedures so desired outcomes are reached, conducting a press conference to increase the visibility of an organisation's partners (e.g., sponsors), or hiring individuals to act as liaisons with the stakeholder group and provide information to the stakeholder. As such, what has been discussed above is a means to manage the stakeholder network surrounding a focal organisation. It allows the sport organisation to govern not only inside their own organisation but across its sport (Ferkins & Shilbury, 2015b).

Stakeholder management trends

Emanating from the preceding section are emergent trends. The focus here is on pressing, relevant issues to managing stakeholders. Specifically, the differences between enduring (e.g., national sport organisation) and temporary (e.g., event organisers) sport organisation stakeholder management are discussed, as well as the saliency of new stakeholders, specifically athlete entourages and social media users.

Enduring and temporary organisations

As the sport industry matures and the number of permanent, enduring sport organisations rises, so, too, has the number of sport events. Events seem "the *it* thing to do" for organisations today to gain visibility, fundraise, thank partners or simply to showcase one or more sports and their athletes. Parent and Chappelet (2015) discussed the typology of sport events, detailing the existence and dichotomy of for-profit/nonprofit and mono-sport/multi-sport schemes around the world and, in doing so, the complexity that exists in managing stakeholders for enduring and temporary organisations. Here, two examples of sport organisations and their stakeholders are presented from data collected a posteriori.

Examining a typical enduring sport organisation, such as Canada Snowboard, the NSO for snowboard sports in Canada, there are many unsurprising stakeholders (see Figure 22.2). Certainly, the organisation would be expected to deal with the federal government given they are a national sport entity, but the inclusion of staff, volunteers, athletes and its international federation, the *Fédération Internationale de Ski* or FIS, would be expected, as these stakeholders are essential to the organisation's survival from a financial, human and legal resource perspective. Concurrently, sponsors, media and community groups are also important stakeholders for an enduring sport organisation. In this specific instance, Canada Snowboard is linked with Under Armour and Burton, key apparel and equipment sponsors of the organisation's athletes, traditional media outlets like TSN on television and Globe and Mail in print, and even First Nations communities who might be negatively impacted by snowboard events and facilities on their land.

The quantity of stakeholders in this example highlights the potential variance of wants and needs that can impact strategic and operational decisions by the sport organisation. For instance, Canada Snowboard cannot simply disregard the position of snow resorts because it is focused on an upcoming world championship event; this stakeholder is vital to grass-roots snowboard development and providing opportunities for snowboard athletes to train. The organisation

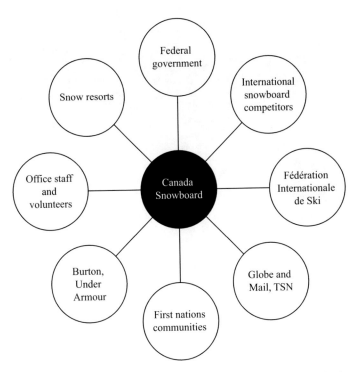

Figure 22.2 Example of stakeholders for enduring sport organisation: Canada Snowboard.

would also have to be mindful of the position of international snowboard athletes and organisations for, without their participation, domestic events could suffer from a lack of high calibre participation. Indeed, enduring sport organisations must consider these stakeholders and their interests because they bear intrinsic value (Donaldson & Preston, 1995); considering the interests of stakeholders deemed legitimate is mutually beneficial (cf. the primary stakeholder and stakeowner concepts). Enduring organisations are unable to forecast when a stakeholder might be more relevant to their interests, hence the need to consider multiple touchpoints with stakeholders, cementing a long-term view of stakeholder management. At the board level specifically, there are primary stakeholders or "stakeowners" with which board members/directors may concern themselves. For instance, liaising with government officials and major media outlets is not outside the realm of jurisdiction for directors, particularly given the visibility and profile of senior directors, and the network and connections they bear. As boards move towards being governance boards, they focus on long-term strategic planning and governance issues, whereas the staff focus on more operational issues (Parent et al., 2019); hence, the types of stakeholders/stakeowners each group will interact with will differ (cf. Parent & Deephouse, 2007).

Conversely, temporary sport organisations may not have as many touchpoints and may opt to concentrate on a core group of stakeholders. The 2018 Melbourne eSports Open (MEO), a regional eSports competition held in Victoria, Australia, emphasises this sentiment (see Figure 22.3). Although the organising committee is tied to a range of stakeholders akin to enduring sport organisations, the level of importance that directors have to place on certain groups becomes more apparent. For instance, though the MEO is tied to community stakeholders like Harry's Doughnuts food truck, a local business operating at the event, this stakeholder is far less important to the governance of the event than the local Melbourne government,

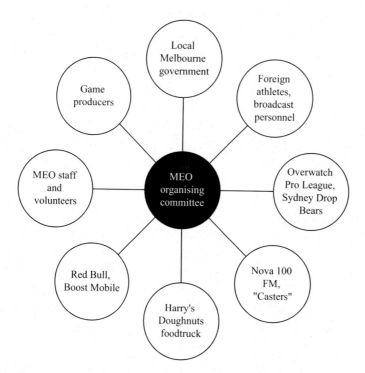

Figure 22.3 Example of stakeholders from a temporal event: The 2018 Melbourne eSports Open.

foreign delegations and game producers who create and own the rights to popular eSports games (e.g., Electronic Arts, Activision). The same can be said for sponsors. Though Red Bull and Boost Mobile are important partners and offer incremental revenue for the event, they are not as vital to the event compared to "casters", popular eSports influencers who live-record themselves at the event as they play an eSports title, and who broadcast to hundreds of thousands, if not millions, around the world. Traditionally, managing and liaising with these primary stakeholder groups would be relegated to executive officers and managers handling the day-to-day operations of the event. However, the current reality of sport governance has led to an increased awareness of these groups, and active involvement in their management. With new environments like eSports, capable directors are able to exercise their social capital to reach out and liaise with directors from stakeowner groups. In effect, the directors of these organisations, who are experts in eSports events and tournament hosting, can serve as front-line ambassadors to balance the influence from stakeowner groups, and bring those discussions to the forefront of board meetings.

At the same time, different types and scales of events will change the relative importance of a given stakeholder group. It cannot be assumed that an important stakeholder group for one event has the same degree of saliency for another event. For example, at the Olympic (Winter) Games, sponsors are critical – they bring in significant financial and material resources to put on the Games – whereas athletes' parents are essentially relegated to the status of spectator despite their years of support of their athlete. In contrast, Parent, Kristiansen, Skille and Hanstad (2015) found parents to be one of three central stakeholder groups for the (Winter) Youth Olympic

Games, this time with sponsors relegated to secondary stakeholder status. This variance seems to be less noticeable in enduring sport organisations, or rather, stakeholder maps seem to be converging (Parent et al., 2018), though this remains to be confirmed in future studies. Nevertheless, this highlights the importance of knowing who your critical stakeholders are – not assuming they are the same as other similar organisations – as these stakeholders have an impact on the organisation's success.

Athlete entourages and social media users

Another key trend in stakeholder management is the emergence of two salient stakeholder groups, notably athlete entourages and social media users. As we saw above, the athlete entourage stakeholder refers to those directly associated with and supporting an athlete, including their parents, family and close friends, as well as personal coaches, lawyers/agents, sport psychologists, personal trainers, nutritionists and other health professionals. These individuals form an entourage that can travel with the athlete from event to event, offering social, mental and emotional support as they compete (Kristiansen, Roberts & Lemyre, 2015). Traditionally, this amalgamation of support remained in the background, siphoned away from the spotlight, emphasising the relationship between the sport organisation and the athlete. However, the current reality of stakeholder management is that this group is active and vocal in athlete affairs and, given their influence, organisations have had to give more credence to the group (Naraine et al., 2016). The International Olympic Committee is one of those organisations recognising the importance of managing this group, establishing an athletes' entourage commission to facilitate the relationship with athlete supporters (The International Olympic Committee, 2018).

Part of the explanation as to why this group has become more vocal in recent years has been the emergence of social media communication. Social media empowers stakeholders to air their grievances to a mass audience without filtering or dilution (Naraine & Parent, 2017). It simultaneously provides a direct link between stakeholders, allowing groups to communicate with one another while circumventing the focal sport organisation (see Figure 22.4). What exacerbates this trend from a stakeholder management perspective is that major social media platforms like Facebook, Instagram and Twitter have millions of monthly active users, including athletes, sponsors and sport organisations, seeking to interact and engage with one another (Naraine & Parent, 2016). Furthermore, because social media is open and available to any and all stakeholders, there is an increased risk of narrative manipulation and false information, which can affect how others perceive the focal sport organisation and cause support to dwindle.

Concurrently, directors have become more conscious of social media. Although social media has previously been viewed as an operational, marketing or communication tool within sport organisations (Naraine & Parent, 2017), traditional boards have begun to consider social media (and digital more broadly) as a matter of strategy. At this level, social media is considered as a strategic tool for outward-facing communication, but also as a damage control mechanism for image repair. However, considering social media at the board level is not simply another line item. Social media has multiple layers, including an ability to generate revenue (through sponsor activation) and to provide more data from athletes, fans, officials and other stakeholders active in the online space. It is important for board members/directors to consider the strategic value of social media for their organisation given these new realities (Parent et al., 2018), but this also requires a recognition of the ambiguity that remains in the space and, as yet, there is not enough shared knowledge about social media and its use in governing sport organisations (Naraine & Parent, 2017).

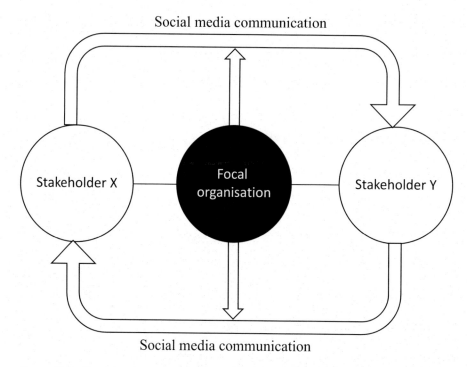

Figure 22.4 Circumventing communication with the focal organisation through social media.

Conclusions and future directions

This chapter has made the case for the importance of stakeholders in the sport world, and therefore of the need to include a stakeholder perspective within sport governance. Sport governance has traditionally focused on board management and managing member associations. However, with new shifts in the sport landscape, board members and directors are becoming more actively involved in liaising with stakeowner/stakeholder groups and applying their strategic vision to these trends (e.g., social media). As noted above, organisations cannot undertake all their actions and activities alone; they need stakeholders. These stakeholders must therefore be considered in the ongoing governance of a particular sport. What is important to remember, however, is the distinction to make between the stakeholders involved in operational aspects of the organisation versus those involved in the strategic/governance aspects.

To help with this task, this chapter provides an overview of the stakeholder concept as well as the four steps to stakeholder management: identifying the stakeholders, understanding their needs, determining their salience, and determining what the organisation needs to do to satisfice the more important stakeholders. Moreover, two additional trends have been identified: the emergence of the athlete's entourage and social media stakeholders. For boards and directors, this chapter expands the gaze of governance towards these new trends affecting sport organisations and, as a result, governance practice. As stakeowners gain greater visibility and access to the sport organisation through new means (e.g., social media) and new sport forms (e.g., eSports), there are increased opportunities to engage with these stakeholders to steer the organisation. Thus, it is critical that boards and directors harness their stakeholder management capacity to alleviate the pressures already existing within the organisation and become more strategic in the use of social media (Parent et al., 2018).

Although we understand the stakeholder management process, researchers still appear "stuck" on defining the stakeholders, labelling them and classifying them. To wit, the stakeowner concept, while drawing attention to the reciprocity of the organisation–stakeholder relationship, remains a new version of the primary stakeholder label, and it remains on a dyadic level of analysis. Given the complex (stakeholder) environment sport managers now face, this chapter has argued that it is time researchers move beyond the dyadic and focus their attention on governing the *network* of stakeholders, realising the interdependencies and interrelationships within a sport's stakeholder network and between stakeholder networks. Now more than ever, stakeholders are able to influence the focal organisation and its governance; it therefore becomes critical to better understand this influence and its governance impact. Does the influence go both ways? What aspects of governance do these stakeholders influence? What is the impact of this governance influence on organisational performance?

On this point, the convergence of the stakeholder network requires further examination. Parent and colleagues (2018) noted this convergence at the Canadian NSO level. Does this convergence hold for other levels? For other countries? For other types of organisations (e.g., for-profit and public)? As well, if there is convergence, how or when is this convergence occurring? Is it only occurring when a regulatory body forces sport organisations to follow a new policy or regulations (e.g., a new law) or is it occurring due to similar uses of communication practices or board co-optation, for instance?

In addition, it is important to explore how the dynamics between the stakeholders are changing/have changed due to the emergence of digital and social media in order to understand whether existing stakeholder management strategies and approaches should remain appropriate or require modifications. For example, Savage, Nix, Whitehead and Blair (1991) prescribed generic strategies (collaboration, involvement, defend, monitor) while Shepard, Betz and O'Connell (1997) described four strategies used by proactive organisations to deal with stakeholder activism and social embeddedness: cooperation, participation, negotiation and direct anticipation. The question remains: are these still appropriate in today's digital era and what are the implications for boards of major sport organisations and events?

References

Agle, B. R., Mitchell, R. K., & Sonnenfeld, J. A. (1999). Who matters to CEOs? An investigation of stakeholder attributes and salience, corporate performance, and CEO values. *Academy of Management Journal, 42*, 507–525.

Carroll, A. B. (1996). *Business and society: Ethics and stakeholder management* (3rd ed.). Cincinnati, OH: South-Western College Publishing.

Carroll, A. B. (1999). Corporate social responsibility: Evolution of a definitional construct. *Business & Society, 38*, 268–295.

Carroll, G. R. (1993). A sociological view on why firms differ. *Strategic Management Journal, 14*, 237–249.

Clarke, T. (Ed.). (2004). *Theories of corporate governance: The philosophical foundations of corporate governance*. New York, NY: Routledge.

Clarkson, M. E. (1995). A stakeholder framework for analysing and evaluating corporate social performance. *Academy of Management Review, 20*, 92–117.

Cunningham, G. B., Fairley, S., Ferkins, L., Kerwin, S., Lock, D., Shaw, S., & Wicker, P. (2018). eSport: Construct specifications and implications for sport management. *Sport Management Review, 21*, 1–6.

Donaldson, T., & Preston, L. E. (1995). The stakeholder theory of the corporation: Concepts, evidence, and implications. *The Academy of Management Review, 20*, 65–91.

Etzioni, A. (1964). *Modern organizations*. Englewood Cliffs, NJ: Prentice Hall.

Fassin, Y. (2009). The stakeholder model refined. *Journal of Business Ethics, 84*, 113–135.

Fassin, Y. (2012). Stakeholder management, reciprocity and stakeholder responsibility. *Journal of Business Ethics, 109*(1), 83–96.

Ferkins, L., & Shilbury, D. (2010). Developing board strategic capability in sport organisations: The national-regional governing relationship. *Sport Management Review, 13*, 235–254.

Ferkins, L., & Shilbury, D. (2015a). Board strategic balance: An emerging sport governance theory. *Sport Management Review, 18*, 489–500.

Ferkins, L., & Shilbury, D. (2015b). The stakeholder dilemma in sport governance: Toward the notion of "stakeowner". *Journal of Sport Management, 29*, 93–108.

Freeman, R. E. (1984). *Strategic management: A stakeholder approach*. Boston, MA: Pitman.

Friedman, M. T., Parent, M. M., & Mason, D. S. (2004). Building a framework for issues management in sport through stakeholder theory. *European Sport Management Quarterly, 4*, 170–190.

Hoye, R., & Doherty, A. (2011). Nonprofit sport board performance: A review and directions for future research. *Journal of Sport Management, 25*, 272–285.

Jones, T. M., & Wicks, A. C. (1999). Convergent stakeholder theory. *Academy of Management Review, 24*, 206–221.

Knoke, D., & Yang, S. (2008). *Social network analysis* (2nd ed.). Thousand Oaks, CA: SAGE.

Kristiansen, E., Roberts, G. C., & Lemyre, P-N. (2015). The sport parents' and athlete entourage's perspectives. In M. M. Parent & J-P. Chappelet (Eds.), *Routledge handbook of sports event management* (pp. 183–202). Oxon, UK: Routledge.

Laplume, A. O., Sonpar, K., & Litz, R. A. (2008). Stakeholder theory: Reviewing a theory that moves us. *Journal of Management, 34*, 1152–1189.

Mainardes, E. W., Alves, H., & Raposo, M. (2011). Stakeholder theory: Issues to resolve. *Management Decision, 49*, 226–252.

Mitchell, R. K., Agle, B. R., & Wood, D. J. (1997). Toward a theory of stakeholder identification and salience: Defining the principle of who and what really counts. *Academy of Management Review, 22*, 853–886.

Naraine, M. L., & Parent, M. M. (2016). Illuminating centralized users in the social media ego network of two national sport organizations. *Journal of Sport Management, 30*, 689–701.

Naraine, M. L., & Parent, M. M. (2017). This is how we do it: A qualitative approach to national sport organizations' social-media implementation. *International Journal of Sport Communication, 10*, 196–217.

Naraine, M. L., Schenk, J., & Parent, M. M. (2016). Coordination in international and domestic events. Examining stakeholder network governance. *Journal of Sport Management, 30*, 521–437.

Parent, M. M. (2008). Evolution and issue patterns for major-sport-event organizing committees and their stakeholders. *Journal of Sport Management, 22*, 135–164.

Parent, M. M., & Chappelet, J-P. (Eds.). (2015). *Routledge handbook of sports event management*. Oxon, UK: Routledge.

Parent, M. M., & Deephouse, D. L. (2007). A case study of stakeholder identification and prioritization by managers. *Journal of Business Ethics, 75*(1), 1–23.

Parent, M. M., Kristiansen, E., Skille, E. Å., & Hanstad, D.V. (2015). The sustainability of the Youth Olympic Games: Stakeholder networks and institutional perspectives. *International Review for the Sociology of Sport, 50*, 326–348.

Parent, M. M., Naraine, M. L., & Hoye, R. (2018). A new era for governance structures and processes in Canadian national sport organizations. *Journal of Sport Management, 32*, 555–566.

Parent, M. M., Rouillard, C., & Naraine, M. L. (2017). Network governance of a multi-level, multi-sectoral sport event: Differences in coordinating ties and actors. *Sport Management Review, 20*, 497–509.

Parent, M. M., & Smith-Swan, S. (2013). *Managing major sports events: Theory and practice*. Oxon, UK: Routledge.

Parent, M. M., Taks, M., Naraine, M. L., Hoye, R., Séguin, B., & Thompson, A. (2019). Canadian national sport organizations' governance landscape study: Survey results. Retrieved 25 September 2018, from https://www.researchgate.net/publication/331983098_Canadian_National_Sport_Organizations'_Governance_Landscape_Study_-_Survey_Results

Phillips, R. (1999). On stakeholder delimitation. *Business and Society, 38*, 32–34.

Phillips, R. (2003). *Stakeholder theory and organisational ethics*. San Francisco, CA: Berrett-Koehler Publishers.

Post, J. E., Preston, L. E., & Sachs, S. (2002). *Redefining the corporation: Stakeholder management and organizational wealth*. Stanford, CA: Stanford University Press.

Putler, D. S., & Wolfe, R. A. (1999). Perceptions of intercollegiate athletic programs: Priorities and tradeoffs. *Sociology of Sport Journal, 16*, 301–325.

Reichart, J. (2003). A theoretical exploration of expectational gaps in the corporate issue construct. *Corporate Reputation Review, 6*(1), 58–69.

Savage, G. T., Nix, T. W., Whitehead, C. J., & Blair, J. D. (1991). Strategies for assessing and managing organizational stakeholders. *Academy of Management Executive, 5*, 61–75.

Scott, S. G., & Lane, V. R. (2000). A stakeholder approach to organizational identity. *Academy of Management Review, 25*(1), 43–62.

Shepard, J. M., Betz, M., & O'Connell, L. (1997). The proactive corporation: Its nature and causes. *Journal of Business Ethics, 16*, 1001–1010.

Shilbury, D., O'Boyle, I., & Ferkins, L. (2016). Towards a research agenda in collaborative sport governance. *Sport Management Review, 19*, 479–491.

Sirgy, M. J. (2002). Measuring corporate performance by building on the stakeholders model of business ethics. *Journal of Business Ethics, 35*, 143–162.

Starik, M. (1994). The Toronto Conference: Reflections on stakeholder theory: Essay by Mark Starik. *Business and Society, 33*, 89–95.

The International Olympic Committee. (2018). Athletes' entourage commission. Retrieved 25 September 2018, from https://www.olympic.org/athletes-entourage-commission

23

Sport board performance

A contribution to the integrated board performance model

Tracy Molloy, Lesley Ferkins and Geoff Dickson

Introduction

An effective board is a critical determinant of a sport organisation's performance, at grass roots, on the podium, on the balance sheet and in securing stakeholder confidence. This is the message communicated by government sport agencies to their national sport organisations (NSOs) in a range of "good governance" documents (e.g., Australian Institute of Sport (AIS), 2015; Australian Sports Commission (ASC), 2012; Sport Canada, 2011; Sport England & UK Sport, n.d.; Sport New Zealand (Sport NZ), n.d.(b), 2015). In academic circles, many authors support these industry assertions however there has been limited scholarly focus on verifying the relevant sport board performance factors, associated with sport industry guidelines, and their contributions to sport board and organisational performance (Hoye & Doherty, 2011; Parent & Hoye, 2018). This chapter therefore concentrates on board performance in overviewing the environmental and internal factors considered influential in the successful performance of a sport board. A review and critique of the Hoye and Doherty (2011) integrated board performance model (IBP) provides the basis for this overview, which is then expanded to capture contemporary work and to advance this model.

This chapter is organised in the following manner. First, a summary of the IBP model and the for-profit and nonprofit models on which it draws are provided. This gives both a vehicle for exploring the relevant concepts and a platform from which to critique the IBP model. Next, the critique identifies grounds for a conceptual advancement, expanding the IBP model to include a distinct director selection factor and a board intragroup dynamics factor. In Chapter 24, the expanded integrated board performance model (EIBP) model then provides the framework through which to identify a significant gap in sport research related to director selection factors and associated board processes of director development and evaluation.

Board performance

In any examination of board performance, it is necessary to determine the board roles against which to assess such performance. Board roles have been described in various ways but generally fall within the objectives of providing oversight (compliance-related functions and tasks), foresight (performance-related functions and tasks) and insight (higher-level critical/ethical thinking) on behalf of an organisation (Ferkins & Kilmister, 2012; Nahkies, 2009). For the purposes of the IBP model, board performance is "defined as how well the board fulfils its role in relation to setting and monitoring the mission, planning and policy development, appointing and monitoring the CEO, and managing external relationships" (Hoye & Doherty, 2011, p. 276). This definition provides the basis for the "integration" of three nonprofit board performance models and three for-profit models (the foundation models). The nonprofit foundation models are those developed by Cornforth (2001), Miller-Millesen (2003) and Brown (2005). The for-profit foundation models are those developed by Zahra and Pearce (1989), Nicholson and Kiel (2004a, 2004b), and, Murphy and McIntyre (2007). Following is the aforementioned summary of, first, these foundation models and then the IBP model.

A summary of the foundation and integrated board performance (IBP) models

In the earliest nonprofit foundation model, Cornforth (2001) examined postal surveys from 737 charity boards in England and Wales and proposed an input (board structure and processes)/ output (performance of board functions) model. Examples of these input, structure, process and output factors, and their allocation under the IBP model and subsequent EIBP model, are provided in Table 23.1. Ultimately, the Cornforth (2001) study suggests that:

> Board inputs and three process variables are important in explaining board effectiveness, namely; board members have the time, skills and experience to do the job; clear board roles and responsibilities; the board and management share a common vision of how to achieve their goals; and the board and management periodically review how they work together.
>
> *(p. 217)*

The chief weakness of the model is found in its simplicity (Hoye & Doherty, 2011). Cornforth himself, whilst taking some assurance from the similarity of his findings to the Bradshaw, Murray and Wolpin (1992) study, acknowledged the likelihood of other causal variables and possible explanations.

The Miller-Millesen (2003) study offered a theory-based typology of board behaviour using three theoretical perspectives: agency, resource dependence and institutional theory. For example, in the director recruitment context, agency theory (where the board monitors and controls management on behalf of the owners/members) suggests that directors are likely recruited to better manage such power dynamics. Resource dependence theory explains the recruitment of directors with links to the external resources required for organisational survival/success. Institutional theory (where the board secures legitimacy by conforming to institutional pressures – mimetic, normative and/or coercive) might explain board diversity not as ideologically motivated but as a response to these external pressures. Ultimately, the theory-based typology "identifies the conceptual links between two environmental factors, three organizational factors and board behaviours" (p. 523) with these environmental and organisational factors also influencing composition. This suggests a link between director recruitment practices and board performance of its functions. The relevant factors are summarised in Table 23.1. See also the Miller-Millesen (2003) tables for useful summaries of "normative board roles and responsibilities" (p. 523) and the "theoretical origins of best practice literature" (p. 529).

Table 23.1 Allocation of integrated board performance (IBP) factors

Model authors	Model summary	Factors (as allocated from the foundation models' factors by Hoye & Doherty, 2011, to their IBP model factors, then reallocated as proposed by the authors of this chapter, with reallocation noted by the strike out for deletions and italics for new/shifted allocations)						Board performance (of its role/ responsibilities/ activities/ functions/ outputs)
		Environmental	Individual	Organisational	Board factor (structure)	Board factor (process)	Board factor (dynamics/behaviours)	
IBP Model								
Hoye and Doherty (2011)		Institutional pressures, interorganisational relationships, etc.	Age, education, motivation, competencies, etc.	Size, professionalisation, age/lifecycle, etc.	Subcommittees, composition, etc.	Meetings, ~~group dynamics~~, decision-making, etc.	*Group dynamics, decision-making (e.g., groupthink), etc.*	Roles: Set/monitor mission, plan/ develop policy, appoint/ monitor CEO, manage external relationships.
Nonprofit foundation models								
Cornforth (2001)	Inputs engage with the board structures and processes to translate into outputs or board performance of its functions.		Inputs: Right mix of director skills and experience, appropriate time committed (now commonly described as the "skill and will" inputs)		Board structures: Size, meetings (frequency, attendance rates), subcommittees, written job descriptions, induction/ training, etc.	Board processes: 14 items spread under 6 main headings: Common vision, clear roles and responsibilities, regular board management reviews, ~~board management communication, conflict management~~ and meeting practices (notices, agenda, etc.).	*Communication, conflict management,*	Outputs: 17 tasks under the 5 function headings of: Strategy and policy-making, stewardship, supervising and supporting management, board maintenance (e.g., recruitment), and external relations and accountability.

Study	Key proposition	*Resource/funding pressures* / *Institutional/regulatory pressures*	*Composition: Demographic characteristics*	*Composition: Board size*	*Director recruitment practices* (*Note: Proposed reallocation to a new EIBP factor: Director selection factors*)	Board behaviours / competencies
Miller-Millesen (2003)	Environmental and/or organisational factors likely influence board behaviour, both directly, and through their impact on board composition, thus suggesting a link between director recruitment strategies and board behaviour.		Age (lifecycle), organisational stability, professionalisation, constitutional requirements relating to board composition and recruitment practices			Board behaviours in the context of performance of its functions (x 3): Monitoring (e.g., evaluate CEO, strategy), boundary spanning (e.g., raise money, enhance image) and conforming (e.g., legal compliance, implement mandates).
Brown (2005)	Six board competency dimensions contribute to board and organisational performance with the strategic and interpersonal dimensions being the most significant.	Political (e.g., community connections)	Contextual (e.g., organisational history, mission)	Strategic (e.g., long-term planning), analytic (e.g., effective decision-making, processes), educational (e.g., role descriptions, orientation processes), ~~interpersonal (e.g., group relations)~~	*Interpersonal (e.g., group relations, collegiality, cohesion, etc.)*	Board competencies (x 6): Contextual, political, strategic, analytic, educational and interpersonal, with organisational performance measured by financial performance indicators and perceptions of organisational performance.

(Continued)

Table 23.1 Continued

Model authors	Model summary	Factors (as allocated from the foundation models' factors by Hoye & Doherty, 2011, to their IBP model factors, then reallocated as proposed by the authors of this chapter, with reallocation noted by the strike out for deletions and italics for new/shifted allocations)						Board performance (of its role/ responsibilities/ activities/ functions/ outputs)
		Environmental	Individual	Organisational	Board factor (structure)	Board factor (process)	Board factor (dynamics/behaviours)	
For-profit foundation models								
Zahra and Pearce (1989)	Internal and external contingencies influence 4 board attributes, their relationships with board, performance of its roles and organisational performance (the temporal relationship between the attributes is indicated by the ordered numbering in this table, with interactive relationships contemplated).	External contingencies, e.g., industry type, legal requirements	*Board attribute (2a): Characteristics (director background), e.g., age, education, values, experience*	Internal contingencies, e.g., ownership type, size, life cycle, CEO style, corporate resource situation	Board attribute (1): Composition, e.g., size, insider vs. outsider directors, minorities Board attribute (3): Structure, e.g., number, types, membership of committees, unitary vs. dual board leadership	Board attribute (4): Process, e.g., meeting frequency and length, formality, CEO–board interface, level of consensus, self-evaluation ~~Board attribute (2b): Characteristics (board personality), e.g., style, independence from management influence~~	*Board attribute (2b): Characteristics (board personality), e.g., style, independence from management influence*	Roles: Service, strategy and control, with organisational performance measured by corporate financial performance.

| Nicholson and Kiel (2004b) | Inputs (through the application of board intellectual capital (BIC), in the context of the performance of board roles, as impacted by internal/external environmental context factors), are transformed into the outputs of board (individual/team) effectiveness and organisational effectiveness. | External environment (context), e.g., socioeconomic trends, competitive environment *Inputs, e.g., relevant legislation* | BIC (individual, human), e.g., director knowledge, skills, experience BIC (individual, cultural), e.g., director morals/motivations BIC (individual, social), e.g., extra/inter-organisational relationships | Inputs, e.g., organisation type, constitution, history/culture/values, resource allocation strategy *Internal environment (context), e.g., fit between the board and the organisation's culture/people/systems.* | BIC (team, structural), e.g., routines re: Agenda, minutes, etc., policies ~~and culture including board values/norms~~ ~~BIC (team, social), e.g., intra-board, board management goodwill, and extra-corporate relationships~~ | BIC (team, structural), *e.g., culture including board values/norms* BIC (team, social), *e.g., intra-board, board management goodwill, and extra-corporate relationships* *"Board dynamics are the 'sparks' that fly from … the 'flints' of intellectual capital" (p. 452)* | Board (individual/team) effectiveness in relation to the functions of: Control/monitor, advice/counsel, and access to resources, with organisational performance noted as usually measured by accounting/market-based indicators in the for-profit sector and fulfilment of members' mandate, in the nonprofit sector. Note: The Nicholson and Kiel (2004a) model also includes strategy as a distinct board function. *(Continued)* |

Table 23.1 Continued

Model authors	Model summary	Factors (as allocated from the foundation models' factors by Hoye & Doherty, 2011, to their IBP model factors, then reallocated as proposed by the authors of this chapter, with reallocation noted by the strike out for deletions and italics for new/shifted allocations)						Board performance (of its role/responsibilities/activities/functions/outputs)
		Environmental	Individual	Organisational	Board factor (structure)	Board factor (process)	Board factor (dynamics/behaviours)	
Murphy and McIntyre (2007)	Board characteristics influence board functionality, both independently influence board performance, with internal and external contextual variables moderating the relationships between board characteristics and performance, characteristics and functionality and functionality and performance, with board performance influencing organisational performance	Moderating variables: External, e.g., operating environment, competitive pressure, globalisation	Board characteristics, e.g., director tenure, age, race, gender, skills, expertise, experience, values *Board functionality, e.g., director commitment*	Moderating variables: Internal, e.g., organisation size, lifecycle stage, product lifecycle	Board characteristics, e.g., size, inside vs. outside directors	Board characteristics, e.g., meeting frequency, agenda processes Board functionality, e.g., ~~director commitment,~~ ~~group social capital,~~ trust, role clarity, ~~team satisfaction~~	*Board characteristics, e.g., team personality elevation vs. team personality deviation* *Board functionality, e.g., reflexive, adaptable, flexible, group social capital, trust, mutual respect, team satisfaction*	Activities expected of a well-functioning board: Environmental scanning, monitoring, strategic advice, feedback/guidance to CEO, external resourcing: Financing, e.g., financing, networks, knowledge, and succession planning, with a variety of financial indicators referenced as the traditional organisational performance measure.

Brown (2005) also included a theoretical component within his framework. In a study involving data (surveys and financial data) from 202 American nonprofit organisations (mainly in human service, health care and public benefit sectors), Brown tested his board performance model. The model proposed relationships between three major governance theories, six board performance dimensions and organisational effectiveness. The nonprofit governance theories are agency, resource dependence and group decision-making theories. The six board performance dimensions are those developed by Chait, Holland and Taylor (1991): contextual, political, strategic, analytic, educational and interpersonal. Organisational performance is measured through financial performance indicators and perceptions of organisational performance (Brown, 2005). Examples of the performance dimensions and their allocation under the IBP model are provided in Table 23.1. In conclusion, Brown found support for all three theories and described positive associations between five of the board performance dimensions (excluding education) and organisational performance. The strongest support lies in the strategic board contributions to financial performance, with such contributions also accounting for executive perceptions of organisational performance. Interestingly, the interpersonal dimensions are also linked with financial performance (net financial surplus) and account for both executive and board member perceptions of organisational performance (Brown, 2005). Again, there is acknowledgement that the factors under examination, in this case the six board dimensions, are likely incomplete. Of the three nonprofit board studies, only the Brown model "explicitly explored the link between board and organizational performance" (Hoye & Doherty, 2011, p. 275).

In the earliest of the for-profit foundation models, Zahra and Pearce (1989) synthesised the empirical studies on board contributions to corporate financial performance. Studies relating to board composition, board/director characteristics and board structure and process are summarised along with their effects on organisational financial performance. Zahra and Pearce utilised four corporate governance theories, legal (with a board focus on legal responsibilities), class hegemony (board preservation of capitalist elite power structures), resource dependence and agency theories, to explain these contributions. Each theory drives the production of a distinct board performance model, with relevant factors, whilst similar, varying accordingly in terms of some content and prioritisation. The synthesis of these four perspectives results in an integrated model of board attributes and roles. Zahra and Pearce proposed a model in which "internal and external contingencies determine the mix of the board attributes and, in turn, a board's performance of its three roles and, ultimately, on company performance" (1989, p. 306). These contingencies and attributes are summarised in Table 23.1. The board roles considered critical to organisational (financial) performance are service, strategy and control. Importantly, Hoye and Doherty (2011) note that subsequent studies support their preferred board roles of monitoring and controlling, setting strategy, providing advice and counsel and facilitating access to resources.

The intellectual capital approach of Nicholson and Kiel (2004a) provided "a model of board effectiveness that uses the construct of board intellectual capital to integrate the predominant theories of corporate governance" (p. 5). The authors assert that board intellectual capital is a product of three sub-domains: human (director knowledge, skills and abilities), structural (process, procedures, routines and practices) and social (intra-board, board management and extra-organisational relationships) capital. This intellectual capital approach is then linked with their Corporate Governance Charter model (Kiel & Nicholson, 2003) to assist scholars and practitioners alike in their understanding and application of quality board performance. In Nicholson and Kiel (2004b), an expanded input–output model of board intellectual capital is proposed. The authors described the board as "a system that transforms inputs into outputs – a process that is facilitated by its intellectual capital and is contingent on the roles required of it" (p. 454), with such roles influenced by internal and external environmental factors. A summary of the inputs, intellectual capital (with board dynamics represented as an expanded product of both individual and team intellectual capital) and the context of roles and internal/external influential factors is provided in Table 23.1. The final governance outputs being board effectiveness (a combination of team and individual effectiveness) and organisational performance.

Murphy and McIntyre (2007) based their approach on the view that a board of directors (BoD) is a team, with similar characteristics to many other types of team. Accordingly, this conceptual piece involved a synthesis of relevant governance and organisational behaviour literature, in particular, team and group dynamics. The resultant model of board performance asserts that:

> Both BoD characteristics and functionality may each independently influence performance, and BoD characteristics may also influence functionality (indirectly influencing performance). ... [They] also contend that contextual factors from within and outside the organization will moderate the relationships between BoD characteristics and performance, BoD characteristics and functionality, and BoD functionality and performance.
>
> *(p. 212)*

Examples of the model's BoD characteristics, BoD functionality and internal and external moderating variables are provided in Table 23.1. A board that is well composed and high functioning is more likely to effectively perform its expected activities of environmental scanning, monitoring, advice, strategy, access to resources and succession planning. However, Murphy and McIntyre (2007) do caution that BoD effectiveness is only one of the inputs in organisational performance.

In integrating the aforementioned foundation models, Hoye and Doherty (2011) proposed a model that "acknowledges that environmental, individual and organizational factors directly impact board factors (structure and process), which directly impacts board performance, and ultimately organizational performance" (p. 276). They note that board-level factors "mediate the influence of environmental, individual and organisational factors on board performance" (p. 276) and that both environmental and organisational factors influence the performance of the board in a direct way. In their model they make explicit the relationship between board and organisational performance. This integration is achieved by the allocation of the elements and relationships of the aforementioned foundation models to the IBP model elements of environmental, organisational, individual and board-level factors.

The Cornforth (2001) input (will and skill) (board structure and processes)/output (performance of functions) are readily transposed. Likewise, for Miller-Millesen's (2003) environmental and organisational factors. The Chait et al. (1991) six dimensions utilised in the Brown (2005) model require a little more analysis with the political dimension allocated to environmental factors, the contextual dimension to organisational factors and the strategic, analytic, educational and interpersonal dimensions to board factors (processes). In terms of the Zahra and Pearce (1989) approach, the internal organisational factors and the external environmental factors are readily transposed. Their four board attributes are assigned as follows: directors' characteristics to individual factors, board composition and structure to board factors (structure) and board process to board factor (process). The Nicholson and Kiel (2004a, 2004b) approach also includes the readily transferrable external and internal factors. However, their board attributes of human, structural and social capital are not, by nomenclature, as obvious. The human capital of knowledge, skills and experience is allocated to individual factors. The structural capital, of board structures, processes and routines is allocated to the relevant board factor, structure or process.

Hoye and Doherty (2011) allocated social capital, revolving around relationships between board members, the staff and stakeholders to the board factor (process). Here, questions arise as to whether concepts attached to social capital (Nicholson & Kiel, 2004b) and Chait et al.'s (1991, as cited in Brown, 2005) interpersonal dimension, would be more appropriately allocated to the individual factors or a new board factor regarding board dynamics/behaviours? Similarly, with the Murphy and McIntyre (2007) framework, the internal and external environmental factors and the board composition (board structure) factors are readily transposed. However, again, questions arise relating to the allocation of some of the board functionality features, such as trust and group social capital, to the board factor regarding process. From the six foundation models, some of the variables clearly sit within the board process factor, such as induction, meeting practices and board evaluations, but others, such as the aforementioned trust, cohesion and relationships, may warrant a separate category? Also noteworthy is the omission of a distinct director recruitment factor as posited in the Miller-Millesen (2003) model.

To summarise, Hoye and Doherty (2011) have, in synthesising a range of theories and factors drawn from both the for-profit and nonprofit sectors, achieved their aim of "developing a model of board performance that is both conceptually clear and able to be operationalized for research" (p. 276). This chapter's overview of the foundation models provides a useful and timely reminder of some of the key concepts attached to board performance. A summary that, for the sport governance student, serves as an introduction to these key concepts. For the scholar, it may prompt reflection on alternate, previously overlooked, avenues of investigation. It also provides the platform from which to explore the questions raised above relating to board factor (process) and the omission of a director recruitment factor. What follows is an exploration of these questions resulting in suggested additions to the IBP model.

A critique of and contribution to the IBP model

The suggested contributions to the IBP model are the express inclusion of the Hoye and Doherty (2011) preferred board roles under board performance, the division of the board factors (processes) into two separate board factors and the addition of a new director selection factor. These contributions are depicted in Figure 23.1 with the new content highlighted in italics and the proposed modifications of director selection factors and board factor (intragroup dynamics), and potential relationships, denoted by the broken lines.

Justification for these contributions is drawn from the preceding overview of the IBP foundation models supported by associated literature from both academia and industry. The inclusion of board roles under board performance requires little explanation other than to assert the benefits for the sake of consistency, clarity and completion. The Hoye and Doherty (2011) preferred roles are included by way of example noting that each board performance study will need to ascertain the relevant functions against which the particular board is to be assessed. Substantive justification is however provided, first, for the separation of board factor (processes) into board factor (processes) and board factor (intragroup dynamics) and, second, for the addition of the director selection factors.

IBP model contribution: Board processes (intragroup dynamics). The recent focus on the concepts of group fit (Elms, Nicholson & Pugliese, 2015) and intragroup dynamics (Schoenberg, Cuskelly & Auld, 2016), together with a review of the foundation board performance models, supports the division of the IBP model board factor (processes) into the separate board factor (processes) and board factor (intragroup dynamics). Starting with the IBP model, an intuitive distinction is made between the board factors (processes) examples of "meetings, group dynamics, [and] decision making" (Hoye & Doherty, 2011, p. 277). Board process features, such as meeting frequency, annual calendar-driven agenda and role clarity are different in nature to group dynamics. Even the example of decision-making can be divided into decision-making processes (e.g., majority or consensus decision-making) and decision-making styles or behaviours (e.g., groupthink).

This intuitive differentiation leads to a closer examination of the foundation models in terms of identified board processes and board group behaviours. The features that more closely align with board processes include clear roles, regular reviews, meeting practices (Cornforth, 2001), meeting frequency and length (Zahra & Pearce, 1989) and agenda/calendar-driven processes (Nicholson & Kiel, 2004a). The features that align with group behaviours include communication, conflict management, decision-making (Cornforth, 2001), interpersonal behaviours (Brown, 2005), board personality (Zahra & Pearce, 1989), meeting dynamics (Nicholson & Kiel, 2004a), goodwill, trust, culture (Nicholson & Kiel, 2004b), team personality elevation, team personality diversity and intragroup trust (Murphy & McIntyre, 2007). The Brown (2005) use of group decision-making theory and Murphy and McIntyre's (2007) focus on team/group dynamics literature add weight to the proposed recognition of board factors (intragroup dynamics) as a distinct factor. Again, intuitively, it appears that such board processes could influence board behaviour and that board behaviour could similarly influence board processes. Represented in Figure 23.1, this new factor is contained within the relevant broken line box and the proposed relationships by the broken line double arrow.

Turning to associated academic literature, Elms et al. (2015) and Schoenberg et al. (2016) both espouse the importance of group dynamics. Elms et al. (2015) proposed that group fit is as important as role fit in determining the criteria for director selection. It is "group fit" that enables the fulfilment of a director's "role fit" contribution to the board. Schoenberg et al. (2016),

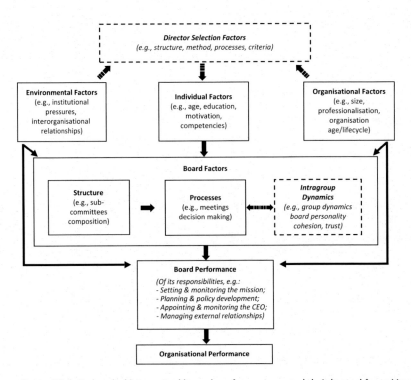

Figure 23.1 Expanded integrated board performance model. Adapted from Hoye, R. & Doherty, A. (2011). Non-profit sport board performance: A review and directions for future research. *Journal of Sport Management, 25,* 272–285.

in a systematic quantitative literature review focussing on intragroup dynamics, confirm positive relationships between factors such as the board–CEO relationship, cohesion, boardroom climate and performance. A review of industry "good governance" codes/guides (AIS, 2015; ASC, 2012; Australian Securities Exchange Corporate Governance Council, 2014; Financial Reporting Council, 2014; New Zealand's Exchange, 2017; Securities Commission, 2004; Sport and Recreation Alliance, 2015; Sport Canada, 2011; Sport England & UK Sport, n.d.; Sport NZ, n.d.(a), n.d.(b)) reveals that all reference the concept of ethics and/or integrity. Such principles can be attributed to individual director factors or the board (process) factor but they can equally be attributed to the collective behaviour of a group or board. Whilst some attention is paid in the industry guides to board culture (Financial Reporting Council, 2014; Sport Canada, 2011; Sport England & UK Sport, n.d.; Sport NZ, n.d. (a)) and climate (Sport Canada, 2011), few overtly address the "group fit" element in their recommendations regarding director selection criteria.

Perhaps, in light of the observation that "huge corporate scandals such as Enron have happened although they 'were supervised by an all-star board [adhering to the formal system], with qualifications far beyond what any regulator would impose'" (Hansell, 2003, p. 15, as cited by Maharaj, 2009, p. 108), the issue of board culture/intragroup behaviour merits closer attention by industry and academics alike? In summary, support is drawn from Schoenberg et al. (2016) who proposed that "intragroup dynamics such as cohesion and power patterns do not reflect processes and, conceptually, would fit better as a third factor" (p. 16) in the Hoye and Doherty (2011) IBP model. Accordingly, such terminology is adopted to describe this separate "behaviour"-related board factor (intragroup dynamics).

IBP model contribution: Director selection factors. The primary logic driving the proposed addition of director selection factors to the IBP model is that director selection is, in a temporal sense, the first step. In order to enjoy the performance-enhancing benefit of directors with the appropriate backgrounds and skill sets (individual factors) to compose a board with appropriate diversity (board factor, structure) that will constructively engage (board factor, intragroup dynamics) with relevant practices and policies (board factor, process), such directors must first be identified and recruited. Of the foundation models, the Miller-Millesen (2003) typology expressly situated director recruitment practices central to the board performance formula: recruitment practices and composition being both directly impacted by environmental and organisational factors and having a direct link with board behaviour. Other foundation models acknowledged the importance of director selection (Cornforth, 2001; Murphy & McIntyre, 2007; Nicholson & Kiel, 2004a, 2004b; Zahra & Pearce, 1989) in the development of their board performance models. The Hoye and Doherty (2011) IBP model situated both board composition and the existence of nomination committees, along with audit, risk and remuneration committees, as part of the board factor (structure). However, director selection factors, the realm of the nomination committee, are more elemental than, for example, the control and compliance focus of an audit or risk committee, and, as such, merit separate recognition, distinct from board factor (structure) and/or board factor (processes).

In associated literature, Clune, Hermanson, Tompkins and Ye (2014) endorsed the elemental nature of director selection factors describing the nomination committee as the "foundational committee as it builds the other board committees and the overall board" (p. 783). Brown (2007) found support for the "contention that board development practices lead to stronger board members, and stronger board members are a significant predictor of board performance" (p. 312). In particular, out of board recruitment, orientation and evaluation practices, the "strongest pathway was between recruitment practices and perceptions of board member competency" (p. 311). In a review of industry "good governance" codes/guides, both the nonprofit and for-profit sectors stress the importance of director selection processes and outcomes (AIS, 2015; ASC, 2012; ASX Corporate Governance Council, 2014; Financial Reporting Council, 2014; NZX, 2017; Securities Commission, 2004; Sport and Recreation Alliance, 2015; Sport Canada, 2011; Sport England & UK Sport, n.d.; Sport NZ, n.d. (a), n.d. (b)). Director selection factors extracted from these sources can be organised under four headings: structure (e.g., constitutional constraints such as director tenure and rotation), method (e.g., delegation, election, co-option and/or appointment), process (e.g., use of a nomination committee, board skills matrices, public advertising, interviews, etc.) and criteria (related to role fit and/or group fit objectives). These are included as examples in the associated broken line box in Figure 23.1. However, in the absence of empirical data no attempt is made to infer relationships between these factors, making it a matter for future investigation and empirical testing.

IBP model contribution: Summary. In summary, the proposed additions of director selection and board intragroup dynamics factors to the "good governance" equation are justified through the review and critique of the IBP model (Hoye & Doherty, 2011), including a reanalysis of the foundation models, and is supported also with reference to associated literature. The EIBP model outlines seven factors (environmental, organisational, director selection, individual, board structure/process/intragroup dynamics) and their purported relationships with overall board and organisational performance. Overlaying this model are the theoretical explanations promoted in the foundation models: agency (Brown, 2005; Miller-Millesen, Zahra & Pearce, 1989); resource dependence (Brown, 2005; Miller-Millesen, 2003; Zahra & Pearce, 1989); institutional (Miller-Millesen, 2003); legal (Zahra & Pearce, 1989); class hegemony (Zahra & Pearce, 1989); and group decision-making theory together with the concepts represented in the team/group dynamics literature (Brown, 2005; Murphy & McIntyre, 2007).

Conclusion

As identified earlier in this chapter, the challenge for sport governance scholars remains to "more clearly define … how improved governance may be objectively measured" (Parent & Hoye, 2018, p. 22). The elusive nature of board performance assessment and verification of causal relationships, between factors and with overall organisational performance, is recognised in the aforementioned foundation models. The complexities associated with such measurements are replicated in the sport sector. For nonprofit sport, commonly delivered through federated member-benefit structures and organisations, indicators other than financial carry significant weight and are notoriously difficult to measure. For example, how to measure a board's contribution to an NSO's constitutional objectives of both sport participation/development and elite sport performance (Ingram & O'Boyle, 2018) or the extent to which a sport board satisfies the stakeowner mandate under which it operates (Ferkins & Shilbury, 2015b)?

In the delivery of professional sport competitions and team franchises, with their coopetition [simultaneous need for both cooperation and competition] dimension, unusual challenges also arise. Despite such challenges, or perhaps, because of them, it is crucial that we heed the calls for coordinated, yet context-specific, empirical verification of the actual impact of board performance factors, and associated good governance principles, on both board and organisational performance (Hoye & Doherty, 2011; Parent & Hoye, 2018). The EIBP model, with contributions developed in this chapter, is offered as a framework to assist academics in this regard. It may also foster beneficial awareness, for policy-makers and practitioners alike, of the complexities at play in their pursuit of good governance.

Finally, whilst the rallying cries for sport-specific performance measurements are mounting, the theoretical developments associated with sport governance and board performance cannot be neglected. To the more traditional theories utilised in the foundation models, can be added those emerging in the sport governance literature such as board strategic balance (Ferkins & Shilbury, 2015a) and collaborative governance theories (Shilbury, O'Boyle & Ferkins, 2016). Indeed, in conjunction with the opportunity identified by Ferkins and Shilbury (2016) for indigenous sport governance theory development is the opportunity for indigenous sport board/organisational performance measurements. Perhaps, given the evolving maturity of sport governance scholarship the time is right for both.

References

ASX Corporate Governance Council. (2014). *Corporate governance principles and recommendations* (3rd ed.). Retrieved 13 May 2016, from https://www.asx.com.au/documents/asx-compliance/cgc-principl es-and-recommendations-3rd-edn.pdf

Australian Institute of Sport. (2015). *Mandatory sports governance principles*. Canberra, Australia: Author.

Australian Sports Commission. (2012). *Sports governance principles*. Canberra, Australia: Author.

Bradshaw, P., Murray, V., & Wolpin, J. (1992). Do nonprofit boards make a difference? An exploration of the relationships among board structure, process, and effectiveness. *Nonprofit & Voluntary Sector Quarterly, 21*, 227–249.

Brown, W. A. (2005). Exploring the association between board and organizational performance in nonprofit organizations. *Nonprofit Management & Leadership, 15*, 317–339.

Brown, W. A. (2007). Board development practices and competent board members: Implications for performance. *Nonprofit Management & Leadership, 17*, 301–317.

Chait, R., Holland, T. P., & Taylor, B. E. (1991). *The effective board of trustees*. New York, NY: MacMillan.

Clune, R., Hermanson, D., Tompkins, J., & Ye, Z. (2014). The nominating committee process: A qualitative examination of board independence and formalization. *Contemporary Accounting Research, 31*, 748–786.

Cornforth, C. (2001). What makes boards effective? An examination of the relationships between board inputs, structures, processes and effectiveness in non-profit organisations. *Corporate Governance: An International Review, 9*, 217–227.

Elms, N., Nicholson, G., & Pugliese, A. (2015). The importance of group-fit in new director selection. *Management Decision, 53*, 1312–1328.

Ferkins, L., & Kilmister, T. (2012). Sport governance. In S. Leberman, C. Collins & L. Trenberth (Eds.), *Sport business management in New Zealand and Australia* (3rd ed., pp. 137–159). Melbourne, Australia: Cengage Learning Australia Pty Ltd.

Ferkins, L., & Shilbury, D. (2015a). Board strategic balance: An emerging sport governance theory. *Sport Management Review, 18*, 489–500.

Ferkins, L., & Shilbury, D. (2015b). The stakeholder dilemma in sport governance: Toward the notion of 'stakeowner'. *Journal of Sport Management, 29*, 93–108.

Ferkins, L., & Shilbury, D. (2016). Developing a theory of board strategic balance. In G. Cunningham, J. Fink & A. Doherty (Eds.), *Routledge handbook of theory in sport management* (pp. 114–131). New York, NY: Routledge.

Financial Reporting Council. (2014). *The UK corporate governance code*. Retrieved 20 March 2016, from https://www.frc.org.uk/getattachment/59a5171d-4163-4fb2-9e9d-daefcd7153b5/UK-Corporat e-Governance-Code-2014.pdf

Hansell, C. (2003). *What directors need to know: Corporate governance*. Toronto, Canada: Thomson Carswell.

Hoye, R., & Doherty, A. (2011). Nonprofit sport board performance: A review and directions for future research. *Journal of Sport Management, 25*, 272–285.

Ingram, K., & O'Boyle, I. (2018). Sport governance in Australia: Questions of board structure and performance. *World Leisure Journal, 60*, 156–172.

Kiel, G. C., & Nicholson, G. J. (2003). *Boards that work. A new guide for directors*. Sydney, Australia: McGraw Hill.

Maharaj, R. (2009). Corporate governance decision-making model: How to nominate skilled board members, by addressing the formal and informal systems. *International Journal of Disclosure & Governance, 6*, 106–126.

Miller-Millesen, J. L. (2003). Understanding the behavior of nonprofit boards of directors: A theory-based approach. *Nonprofit and Voluntary Sector Quarterly, 32*, 521–547.

Murphy, S. A., & McIntyre, M. L. (2007). Board of director performance: A group dynamics perspective. *Corporate Governance: The International Journal of Business in Society*, 7, 209–224.

Nahkies, G. (2009). The fully 'sighted' board. *Philanthropy News*, 3(5), 12.

Nicholson, G. J., & Kiel, G. C. (2004a). Breakthrough board performance: How to harness your board's intellectual capital. *Corporate Governance: The International Journal of Business in Society*, 4, 5–23.

Nicholson, G. J., & Kiel, G. C. (2004b). A framework for diagnosing board effectiveness. *Corporate Governance: An International Review*, 12, 442–460.

NZX. (2017). *NZX corporate governance code 2017*. Retrieved 26 November 2018, from https://s3-ap-s outheast-2.amazonaws.com/nzx-prod-c84t3un4/comfy/cms/files/files/000/002/818/original/Corp orate_Governance_Code_2017.pdf

Parent, M. M., & Hoye, R. (2018). The impact of governance principles on sport organisations' governance practices and performance: A systematic review. *Cogent Social Sciences*, 4, 1–24.

Schoenberg, G., Cuskelly, G., & Auld, C. (2016). The role of intragroup dynamics in nonprofit governance models: A systematic quantitative literature review. *Managing Sport and Leisure*, 21, 1–22.

Securities Commission. (2004). *Corporate governance in New Zealand: Principles and guidelines. A handbook for directors, executives and advisers*. Wellington, New Zealand: Author.

Shilbury, D., O'Boyle, I., & Ferkins, L. (2016). Towards a research agenda in collaborative sport governance. *Sport Management Review*, 19, 479–491.

Sport and Recreation Alliance. (2015). *The voluntary code of good governance*. Retrieved 13 May 2016, from http://sramedia.s3.amazonaws.com/media/documents/Voluntary%20Code%20of%20Good%20 Governance%20-%20V3.pdf

Sport Canada. (2011). *Pursing effective governance in Canada's national sport community*. Retrieved 13 May 2016, from http://sportlaw.ca/wa-content/.../FINALGoverancePrinciples.EN.doc

Sport England, & UK Sport. (n.d.). *A code for sports governance*. Retrieved 24 January 2019, from https://ww w.uksport.gov.uk/resources/governance-code

Sport New Zealand. (n.d.a). *Governance framework: For the New Zealand sport and recreation sector*. Retrieved 13 May 2016, from https://www.sportnz.org.nz/assets/Uploads/attachments/managing-sport/strong -organisations/Governance-Document-2-7-Links.pdf

Sport New Zealand. (n.d.-b). *Nine steps to effective governance: Building high performance organisations* (3rd ed.). Retrieved 13 May 2016, from https://sportnz.org.nz/assets/Uploads/attachments/managing-sport/ strong-organisations/Nine-Steps-to-Effective-Governance-Building-High-Performing-Organisations. pdf

Sport New Zealand. (2015). *Governance benchmarking review 2014*. Retrieved 13 May 2016, from https:// www.sportnz.org.nz/assets/Uploads/attachments/managing-sport/strong-organisations/Governance -Benchmarking-Summary-May-2014.pdf

Zahra, S. A., & Pearce, J. A. (1989). Boards of directors and corporate financial performance: A review and integrative model. *Journal of Management*, 15, 291–334.

24

Director selection, development and evaluation

Tracy Molloy, Geoff Dickson and Lesley Ferkins

Introduction

The power of human potential to contribute to quality sport governance is the theme of this chapter. In particular, there is a focus on the recruitment and development of directors with the requisite skills, experiences, attributes and perspectives to contribute to a highly functioning board. Whilst embracing the possibilities of emerging systemic governance theories (as highlighted in Chapter 2), this chapter serves to caution against neglect of the individual and the interactions between individual board members. The premise of this chapter rests on the assertion that for the "board to be greater than the sum of its people", there is a need to first find the right people and then maximise their individual (human and social) and combined (intra/inter-board relationships) potential. A holistic approach is promoted whereby evaluation is integral, informing both director selection and development.

This chapter draws from the Expanded Integrated Board Performance (EIBP) model (Hoye & Doherty, 2011; see Chapter 23) as a way to position the foci of sport board performance research published since 2009, as it relates to selection, development and evaluation. This synthesis incorporates the scoping and systematic literature reviews of Dowling, Leopkey and Smith (2018) and Parent and Hoye (2018) respectively, together with the "mapping" of sport governance articles undertaken in Chapter 1 of this handbook. In the absence of any substantial research focusing on director selection within nonprofit sport organisations, this review then draws upon the wider nonprofit and for-profit literature related to director selection, director development and evaluation processes and use of nomination committees. Nomination committees (NCs) are recognised as a means of advancing selection, development and evaluation processes and outcomes. To conclude, the issue of how to measure director and board performance is discussed.

Director selection, development and evaluation research in sport: An overview

In the mapping of sport governance articles in the three major sport management journals undertaken in Chapter 1, 33 of the 49 articles were published post-2008. Of these, only one was categorised under a director selection theme. However, closer examination reveals that while the context was director selection, the focus was on gendered self-descriptions in French national sport organisation (NSO) election profiles (Ferrand, Henry & Ferrand, 2010). Similarly, for the board processes of director development and evaluation, two articles were themed as "evaluation/performance" and two as "monitoring and compliance", but only one, Sherry & Shilbury (2009), addressed the actual practices under examination in this chapter (finding director selection processes and director education influential in reducing conflict-of-interest risks).

In the Dowling et al. (2018) scoping review, 243 sport governance articles were identified, of which 74 articles were classified as relating to organisational (as opposed to systemic or political) governance. In their analysis of reoccurring themes, sub-themes, topics and contexts there were no overt references to director selection, or the board processes/practices of director development or evaluation. The Parent and Hoye (2018) systematic review focussed on the impact of governance principles on sport organisations' governance practices and performance. A wide-ranging search of the academic and grey literature revealed 2,155 records, which were narrowed down to 19 that met their search criteria. Of these 19 records, 12 were journal articles published post-2008. Over half of these 12 article summaries did reference board structure issues such as size, tenure, duality, independence and quotas but only one (Bradbury & O'Boyle, 2015) evidenced a strong director selection methods/process theme in the findings. None of the journal article summaries focussed on director development or evaluation practices. However, the Birkbeck Sport Business Centre report (Walters, Trenberth & Tacon, 2010) summary does record the importance of board induction, training and evaluation.

To summarise, the above reviews suggest that minimal attention has been paid to the actual board practices of director development and/or evaluation. In terms of director selection, while appearing as a context for, or in the periphery of, some of these studies, there is a near-complete absence of this factor at the centre of sport governance research. Positioned in the EIBP model as influencing, through director competencies, board composition, processes and intragroup dynamics, director selection is thus considered fundamental to board performance. The focus of the next section is therefore on director selection, followed by a discussion on board practices for director development and evaluation. An examination of NCs is then offered as a potential vehicle for improving such processes and outcomes.

Director selection

In this section, for-profit, nonprofit and grey literature are used to describe key concepts related to director selection. The focus then turns to relevant sport governance literature.

Key concepts

Director selection has been described as the "formal process by which individuals are identified, screened, nominated and elected (or appointed) to corporate boards" (Withers, Hillman & Cannella, 2012, p. 245). In the nonprofit sport sector, director selection processes reflect interorganisational network structures. The most common network structure for NSOs is the federated network (Dickson, Arnold & Chalip, 2005). In this structure, the voting members of the NSO are the regional sport entities and the voting members of the regional sport entities are the clubs. Historically, the board structure followed a delegate model of director selection (Shilbury, 1993). In this model, the NSO directors were often nominated delegates of the regional sport entities. Alternatively, various interest groups, whether based on membership class, sporting code, geographical region or otherwise, elected delegates to the national board (more likely a management committee than a true governing board) to represent their interests as in a democratic (Cornforth, 2004) governance model. With the twin pressures of commercialisation and professionalisation, the independent and hybrid models (described in more detail later in this section) became more prevalent. In these models, directors can be selected by election, appointment and/or co-option, and the appointment of additional board members is by the existing directors.

Government sport agencies have advocated these more recent approaches in their prescriptive sport governance guidelines (Australian Sports Commission, 2012; Sport England & UK Sport, n.d.; Sport New Zealand, n.d. (c)), reflecting the importance of director selection and associated development and evaluation practices. Table 24.1 provides a summary of relevant Sport New Zealand (Sport NZ) guidelines.

As is evident from Table 24.1, director selection "key concepts" can be categorised under four factors: structure (e.g., independent board), method (e.g., appointment), process (e.g., use of an NC) and criteria (e.g., skills, experience, attributes, perspectives). The recommendation for director/board evaluation to inform director selection and development affirms their real-world connectedness.

From a theoretical perspective, Withers et al. (2012), provide a multidisciplinary examination of the corporate director selection literature. The main discussion focussed on the supply (i.e., characteristics of potential directors) and demand (i.e., characteristics of the appointing firm) features from both the "rational economic" and "social embeddedness" perspectives. First, the rational perspective assumes that directors are selected to best meet the governance and resource needs of the organisation as explained by agency and resource dependency theory. Second, the social embeddedness perspective recognises the board as a complex social system with inherent social biases and inconsistencies whereby those in control of the selection will likely perpetuate the current board norms. Withers et al. (2012) make the case for integrating these theoretical approaches to reflect the integration in the actual process of director selection. In responding to this argument, Elms, Nicholson and Pugliese (2015) interviewed 10 individuals in relation to 24 selection processes across a mix of 20 corporate, public and nonprofit organisations. Interestingly, some director selection processes were labelled as "rigorous and formal" whilst others were considered "ad hoc, informal and at times heavily influenced by a single decision maker" (p. 1320). They caution against an overemphasis on "role fit" and stress the need for balance, as "role fit reflects the board's economic needs and group fit acknowledges the board's social needs. It is only by having an appropriate group fit that the equally necessary role fit of a director can be harnessed" (p. 1324).

Sport organisations

Director selection for nonprofit sport organisations is equally important and arguably more challenging than in the corporate/commercial domain. Like other nonprofits, nonprofit sport organisations' performance objectives go beyond the financial to the social and/or sporting objectives for which they are established. Unlike many other nonprofits, sport organisations are often member-owned (benefit) organisations (O'Boyle & Shilbury, 2016), providing sport services to their members, with some directors likely to also be customers of these services (Hoye & Cuskelly, 2004). Additionally, sport organisations face integrity issues of increasing complexity with high expectations not just from their members, but also from the media and the community (Sherry & Shilbury, 2009). For many NSOs, the professionalisation of their management/governance systems is linked to their reliance on government funding (Ferkins & Shilbury, 2010;

Table 24.1 Summary of key director selection, development and evaluation guidelines (Sport NZ)

Director selection
* General:
- Board responsible for director succession planning, ensuring ongoing mix of appropriate board skills (9 Steps, BC); and
- Open, systematic and deliberate recruitment process (GF, 9 Steps).

* Structure:
- Specified tenure and rotation of directors (GF); and
- Appropriate ratio of independent directors – defined as those with "no formal connection with the sport for a fixed prior period" (9 Steps, p. 55).

* Methods:
- Election and/or appointment process; (9 Steps, BC);
- Depends on unique needs of each organisation (9 Steps); and
- Recommended mix of elected and appointed directors (GF).

* Processes:
- Establish appointments panel – with terms of reference (GF), including independent governance specialists (9 Steps, GF) and board members (9 Steps);
- Appointment panel interviews candidates, appointing directors and recommending "best fit" candidates for election (9 Steps);
- Develop board skills/needs matrix (9 Steps, GF);
- Develop director recruitment profiles (9 Steps); and
- Possible use of advertising/professional search agency (9 Steps).

* Criteria:
- Skills (e.g., strategic thinking, financial literacy, interpersonal skills);
- Attributes (e.g., integrity, independence, emotional intelligence);
- Experience (e.g., professional, sport, life);
- Perspectives (e.g., gender, ethnic, age diversity);
- Operational knowledge; and
- Broader conceptual abilities (9 Steps).

Director development
* Induction:
- Role clarity – achieved via role descriptions and letters of appointment/commitment (9 Steps, GF);
- Review relevant documents (e.g., constitution, charter, policies, annual report, recent meeting papers) (9 Steps, BC);
- Meetings with chair (governance) and CEO (operational) (9 Steps, BC);
- Use of board mentors where appropriate (9 Steps).

* Education:
- Development policy and plan (GF);
- Individual professional development activities encouraged (BC); and
- Board development workshops (9 Steps).

(*Continued*)

Board/director evaluation

* General:

- Documented commitment to governance evaluations (GF);
- Governance evaluations inform succession planning, board/director development (9 Steps, BC) and provides accountability to stakeholders (9 Steps);
- Governance evaluations to include chair, director and senior management perceptions (GF); and
- Board performance report provided to key stakeholders (GF).

* Process/criteria:

- Board performance reviewed every 2 years (BC);
- Director performance reviewed annually (BC);
- Criteria based on relevant policies and other board agreed criteria (BC);
- Interviews (9 Steps) and self-/peer-assessment surveys (9 Steps, BC) optional;
- Ideally conducted by an independent and external facilitator (9 Steps);
- Report/recommendations provided to board (BC).

* Costs:

- Annual "Cost of Governance" budget – to include board/director development and assessment costs (BC).

---

* Source abbreviations
9 Steps = Nine Steps to Effective Governance: Building High Performing Organisations (Sport NZ, n.d. (c)).
BC = Board Charter –Sport NZ template – updated 10 October 2018 (BoardWorks International Ltd, 2018).
GF = Governance Framework (Sport NZ, n.d. (b)).

Hoye & Cuskelly, 2004). All of this takes place in an environment where "a non-executive director is typically a volunteer" (Sherry & Shilbury, 2009, p. 48).

In this dynamic governance environment, director selection processes in nonprofit sport organisations are also evolving. One early study described the top three director selection criteria as "interest" in the organisation, ability to commit the "time" and sharing "common views" with the existing board members (Inglis, 1997). A more recent study hints at greater sophistication: "extensive experience at the grassroots … is no longer regarded as sufficient preparation for work at higher levels of sporting structures" (Ferrand, Henry & Ferrand, 2010, p. 547). Whilst sport experience may no longer be a sufficient qualification, for member-benefit organisations, the director selection process will likely remain connected to the issues of membership ownership, control and representation.

The importance of membership "voice" is reflected in the Hoye and Cuskelly (2004) study comparing the director selection, induction and evaluation practices of seven state sporting organisations in Australia to a list of recommended board practices. The recommended board practices included five director selection items (i.e., ability to co-opt external directors, use of board profile, nominee interviews, use of nomination or board development committee and written selection criteria), two orientation items (i.e., board manual and orientation process) and four evaluation items (i.e., individual director evaluations, feedback to individual directors, board self-evaluations and collective board self-evaluations). All four of the "effective" boards used at least one of these practices whereas the three "ineffective" boards used none. Director selection issues centred on the efficacy concerns attached to directors elected by the members (i.e., popularity versus ability, conflict of interest versus sport knowledge) and the recognised value of appointed external directors. In summary, Hoye and Cuskelly (2004) concluded that effective boards "utilised more recommended board processes to *select*, orientate and evaluate board members" (p. 77, emphasis added). More recent studies, involving director selection and associated developments, are now explored under four director selection factor headings of board structure, selection method, processes and criteria.

Board structure and selection methods

A repeated debate in the board structure literature concerns the merits of three models of board structure – delegate, independent and hybrid (O'Boyle & Hassan, 2016). Some authors advocate for the 100 percent independent model (Bradbury & O'Boyle, 2015) and others for a hybrid approach, at least during a transition phase (Ferkins & Shilbury, 2010). There is also acknowledgement that the delegate model "may remain … suitable … in less commercial and professionalized sporting environments" (O'Boyle & Hassan, 2016, p. 110). Table 24.2 summarises the key themes of this debate.

The themes shown in Table 24.2 suggest the need to disentangle the concepts of structure and selection methods. As previously described, the traditional delegate board structure was based on representation (with director selection occurring via nomination and/or election by various constituencies). The independent board is described as 100 percent appointed with the hybrid board comprising both elected delegates and appointed independents. However, in the modern environment, most sport boards will have a duty to promote the best interests of the organisation as a whole (i.e., be "independent" in behaviour). A director can act "independently" regardless of whether they are elected (by/from within the membership), co-opted (by the existing board) or appointed. Hence, by this analysis, there are two sport board structures: the delegate/representative (competitive democracy) model and the independent (whole-of-sport) model. It is the selection method that can then be more accurately described as "hybrid" with either structure utilising a range of director selection methods (to best secure the desired outcomes). Reflecting a view that behaviour/mind-set is the critical component of independence, the Australian Sports Commission requires "all directors to be independent, regardless of whether elected or appointed" (Australian Institute of Sport, 2015, p. 5). Jurisdictional restrictions may also impact selection methods such as the Canadian "non-profit" legislative requirement that only members elect directors (Parent, Naraine & Hoye, 2018) with those elected directors having limited co-option powers (Canada Not-for-profit Corporations Act, 2009, s. 128(8)).

There are other structural factors related to director selection. These include the number of directors, tenure and diversity quotas (reflecting gender, race, etc.). See Parent and Hoye (2018) for a summary of recent scholarly perspectives. In addition to these structural composition and selection methods dictated in the constitution, a sport organisation must consider the process of director selection.

Process

In 2013, New Zealand Cricket (NZC) transitioned to an independent (100 percent appointed) model described as "leading the nonprofit sporting world in governance practices" (Bradbury & O'Boyle, 2015, p. 352), In particular, the key elements of the NZC director selection process include:

- Skills matrix to assess key organisational challenges and requisite director skill sets. The matrix is re-evaluated each year in consultation with the six major association members;

Table 24.2 Themes: Board structure and selection methods

Themes	Delegate (representative)	Independent
Legitimacy and logic	Upholds democratic legitimacy and/or traditions (Enjolras & Waldahl, 2010; O'Boyle & Shilbury, 2016; Shilbury, 1993; Tacon & Walters, 2016)	Professional/commercial logic prevailing over the traditional volunteer/democratic logic (Ingram & O'Boyle, 2018; Tacon & Walters, 2016)
Affiliate interests vs. network interests	Adversarial approach to governance (Bradbury & O'Boyle, 2015) reflecting the competitive/representative type of democracy (Enjolras & Waldahl, 2010). Promotes parochialism, politics and "affiliation" interests over broader interests of the sport/network (Bradbury & O'Boyle, 2015; Enjolras & Waldahl, 2010; Ingram & O'Boyle, 2018; O'Boyle & Hassan, 2016; Shilbury, 1993; Taylor & O'Sullivan, 2009). Increases conflict-of-interest risk (Bradbury & O'Boyle, 2015; Ingram & O'Boyle, 2018; Sherry & Shilbury, 2009).	Promotes best interests of the sport/network (Bradbury & O'Boyle, 2015; O'Boyle & Hassan, 2016). Reduces conflict-of-interest risk (Bradbury & O'Boyle, 2015; Ferkins & Shilbury, 2010; Hoye & Cuskelly, 2004; Sherry & Shilbury, 2009).
Member ownership/control/mandate vs. member alienation	Preserves/protects membership voice (Ferkins & Shilbury, 2010; Tacon & Walters, 2016). Members are the most important stakeholder for a nonprofit sporting network (Bradbury & O'Boyle, 2015).	May lack member/owner mandate (Ferkins & Shilbury, 2010). Risks disconnection/alienation of members (Bradbury & O'Boyle, 2015; Ferkins & Shilbury, 2010; Hoye & Cuskelly, 2004; O'Boyle & Hassan, 2016; Taylor & O'Sullivan, 2009).
Knowledge/skills/expertise	Selections often based on popularity rather than skills/attributes (Sherry & Shilbury, 2009). Operational knowledge can aid strategic decision-making (O'Boyle & Hassan, 2016).	Selections based on business expertise/skill sets (Hoye & Cuskelly, 2004; O'Boyle & Hassan, 2016; O'Boyle & Shilbury, 2016; Taylor & O'Sullivan, 2009). Appropriate mix of sport/business experience, merit-based appointments (Bradbury & O'Boyle, 2015). May lack practical level understanding of the sport (Ferkins & Shilbury, 2010). Intended independent director quality vs. democracy "trade off" not guaranteed (O'Boyle & Hassan, 2016).
Board conversations	Emphasis on sport-specific topics (Ingram & O'Boyle, 2018).	Emphasis on strategic and financial issues (Ingram & O'Boyle, 2018).

(Continued)

Table 24.2 Continued

Themes	Delegate (representative)	Independent
Candidate pool	Candidate pool limited in terms of size, skills and/or expertise (Hoye & Cuskelly, 2004; Sherry & Shilbury, 2009).	Expanded candidate pool with increased skills and expertise (Hoye & Cuskelly, 2004; Taylor & O'Sullivan, 2009). AGM "election" filters may be a disincentive for independent candidates (Bradbury & O'Boyle, 2015).
Planned vs. unplanned	Uncertainty whether election outcomes will match current governance needs (Bradbury & O'Boyle, 2015; Hoye & Cuskelly, 2004).	Independent appointments more likely to align with current governance needs (O'Boyle & Hassan, 2016), performance challenges (Bradbury & O'Boyle, 2015) and experience/skill set needs (Hoye & Cuskelly, 2004).

Themes	Hybrid
Balance	Balances sport knowledge (Ingram & O'Boyle, 2018), representative voices and commercial skills-based mix (Hoye & Cuskelly, 2004; Ferkins & Shilbury, 2010; Taylor & O'Sullivan, 2009).
	Supports power-sharing (Ferkins & Shilbury, 2010; O'Boyle & Shilbury, 2016) and the promotion of collaboration over competition (Ingram & O'Boyle, 2018).
	Requires elected representatives to take a "whole-of-sport" approach (Bradbury & O'Boyle, 2015) and appointed independents to minimise "disharmony" risks (Ingram & O'Boyle, 2018).
Ratio	Participant debate divided between preferring a 50/50 balance vs. a majority of delegate representatives (O'Boyle & Hassan, 2016).
	Members want a majority of directors to be elected (Ingram & O'Boyle, 2018).
	Even as a minority, independent directors are still able to influence decision-making (Taylor & O'Sullivan, 2009).
Transition	Fully appointed board to a hybrid board (Tacon & Walters, 2016, citing Ferkins & Shilbury, 2010).
	Fully elected board to a hybrid board (Tacon & Walters, 2016, citing Ferkins & Shilbury, 2015).

- Nationwide "open" campaign to attract quality director candidates;
- Short-listed candidates are interviewed by a nomination committee;
- Nomination committee makes merit-based appointments;
- Nomination committee is comprised of the NZC president, chairpersons of three of the six major associations (rotating with the other three each alternate year), and a Sport NZ representative.

The NZC model is an example of evolving director selection processes. The members have sacrificed the right to "elect" their directors but their "voice" is still heard. They play an active role in determining the board skills matrix. The members also retain ultimate control because they constitute the majority of the nomination committee.

A range of similar (Ingram & O'Boyle, 2018) and more traditional (Enjolras & Waldahl, 2010; Sherry & Shilbury, 2009) director selection processes are described by other authors. However, the NZC example is the only known reported study where the negotiation of the skills matrix goes beyond the board and senior management to the member associations. In the O'Boyle and Hassan (2016) study on board composition of the Gaelic Athletics Association, one participant noted, regarding the democracy "trade-off" debate, "if we move to a mixed model we need to ensure that the external candidate is of an extremely high standing" (p. 119). How then to identify candidates, both internal and external, of the requisite quality? A key step, addressed below, is the development of appropriate director selection criteria.

Selection criteria

A distinction is drawn between structural criteria that pertains to all director selection processes within an organisation and the context-specific criteria that is developed for each director selection process. Structural criteria would normally be prescribed in the organisation's constitution (e.g., quotas, number of appointed/elected directors). Context-specific criteria are developed to address the organisation's strategic needs (as influenced by relevant environmental and organisational factors).

Two types of context-specific criteria are proposed. Allocating the Sport NZ (n.d. (c)) criteria to the Elms et al. (2015) concepts are "role fit" (skills and experience) and "group fit" (attributes and perspectives) criteria. Role fit is driven by the desire to "ensure that appropriate knowledge and expertise is present within the board in order to deliver on strategic imperatives" (Bradbury & O'Boyle, 2015, p. 357). In doing so, there is the need to balance business acumen with sport-specific knowledge. The shift towards independent (appointed/hybrid) boards created an emphasis on business skills and experience. However, it is not only the internal legitimacy issues (relating to membership and democracy) that merit inclusion of sport-specific skills and experience but also the contention that "operational detail may be a necessary element of strategic decision making" (Ferkins & Shilbury, 2010, p. 238). Regardless of the relevant experience, consider an executive's observation that it is "better to have board members who [can] think in broad strategic terms for the sport rather than have a board full of skill-based appointments" (Hoye & Cuskelly, 2004, p. 92).

Second, there is a need to balance these "role fit" criteria with the equally important "group fit" criteria (Elms et al., 2015). Group fit is necessary to effectively harness the potential role fit contributions of a director. There is a need for personal attributes that are compatible with the group, yet with sufficient diversity of thought and perspective (e.g., gender, culture, age, etc.) to minimise the risk of groupthink. Balduck, Rossem and Buelens (2010) affirm the importance of personal attributes such as emotional intelligence. After their study of 23 sport boards across 12 different sports, they concluded that "possessing cognitive competencies such as technical abilities, strategic skills or financial skills is not enough to be an outstanding performing board member. Emotional intelligence and social intelligence competencies are important pillars in perceptions of competencies" (p. 228). Such "group fit" director selection criteria contribute to intragroup dynamics that enable the directors to engage in constructive scepticism whilst maintaining cohesion and a healthy board climate (Schoenberg, Cuskelly & Auld, 2016).

This need to balance group fit and role fit criteria is reflected in the prescriptive material of government sport agencies. For example, see Table 24.3 for a board needs matrix (adapted from Sport NZ, n.d. (a)), which enables a board to weight relevant areas and assess the skills/attribute needs of the board as a whole. Although the absence of the important "diversity perspectives" from this matrix is noted.

Table 24.3 Board needs matrix

Desired characteristics	Weighting (optional)	Self	Name 2	...	Unweighted total	Total
Attributes						
Ethical, open, honest, trustworthy, high levels of integrity	x 2					
Independence and inquisitiveness	x 1.5					
Ability to establish quality relationships						
Ability to work as a team player	x 2					
Preparedness to work hard and commit time and effort to do the job	x 1.5					
Has an outcomes focus						
Strong stewardship orientation/consumer focus						
Skills						
Ability to think strategically	x 2					
Analytical, critical reasoning and problem-solving skills						
Strong financial literacy and analytical ability	x 1.5					
Oral communication skills	x 1.5					
Ability to understand and relate to stakeholders						
Experience						
Corporate governance experience						
Understanding of and experience in the sport	x 1.5					
Community/stakeholder influence and connections						
Broad business experience	x 1.5					
Meeting performance						
Well prepared for meetings						
Adds value to board dialogue	x 2					
Able to focus at the governance level of issues						

(Continued)

Table 24.3 Continued

Desired characteristics	Weighting(optional)	Self	Name 2	…	Unweighted total	Total
Able to disagree without being disagreeable						Total
Scale	5	4	3		2	1
Competence (see Sport NZ, n.d. (a) for full-scale description & matrix use suggestions)	Exceptional competence	Fully competent	Mostly competent		Basic competence	Minimal/no competence

Adapted from Sport NZ (n.d. (a)): Board needs matrix.

To close this section is an endorsement for future attention to the practice, as much as the policies, of director selection. It is as true today as it ever was that it is important to examine "how the selection process really operates" (O'Neal & Thomas, 1995, p. 82).

Director development and evaluation: Board processes

Director selection is not the only variable contributing to board performance. Other important factors include those falling within the EIBP model of board process factors: induction (Brown, 2007; Grassi, Giorgino, Raimondo & Romani, 2016), training (Gazley & Nicholson-Crotty, 2018) (considered under director development) and evaluation (Gazley & Nicholson-Crotty, 2018). Director induction has been described as "a structured process of introduction of directors into the boardroom and into the context of the company, with the aim to give fundamental information to play their role actively in the shortest possible time" (Grassi et al., 2016). Ongoing training and development are then necessary to keep directors abreast of relevant organisational and environmental factors (Grassi et al., 2016). Evaluation closes the loop and informs the next iteration of succession planning, recruitment, induction and director development.

Many of the previously mentioned nonprofit sport studies assert the benefits of the board practices of induction, education and evaluation, but few position these board practices at the centre of their research. Regarding induction, only one of the seven boards in the Hoye and Cuskelly (2004) study used orientation practices. This absence was attributed by one participant to "a lack of resources rather than will" (p. 92). The authors observed that directors who "have not been adequately oriented to an organisation, may find it difficult to contribute optimally to the board and thereby impact negatively on board performance" (p. 95). Regarding director development generally, the associated benefit of overcoming role ambiguity is well supported (Hoye & Cuskelly, 2004; Ingram & O'Boyle, 2018; Sherry & Shilbury, 2009). Sherry and Shilbury (2009) noted the sport organisation "has a responsibility to ensure that directors are educated in the responsibilities and requirements of their role" (p. 58). Failure to do so potentially limits the board's ability to perform effectively (Hoye & Cuskelly, 2004).

In terms of board evaluation practices, the Hoye and Cuskelly (2004) study revealed that the three "ineffective" boards did not use any form of evaluation. Of the "effective" boards, one used a board self-evaluation process and one used three of the recommended evaluation practices. In the Brunzell and Söderman (2012) study of top Nordic football clubs, 34 (52 percent) of clubs reported annual board evaluations, albeit mainly through informal discussions led by the chair. More recently, the assessment methods of the five NSOs in the Ingram and O'Boyle (2018) study ranged from "no formal appraisal; self-assessment; peer assessment; an internal Nomination Committee being responsible for the process ... [to] an external consultant interviewing board members" (p. 166). In line with the earlier Hoye and Cuskelly (2004) study, the NSO with no assessment process attributed this to "other priorities" rather than a lack of perceived value. Further barriers to evaluation included process/criteria issues (i.e., how, by whom and against what criteria?) and the negative impact that evaluation might have on director recruitment and retention for unpaid directors recruited in a non-competitive environment (Hoye & Cuskelly, 2004). Given the potential for board evaluation practices to positively impact perceptions of board performance, including activities related to business plans, strategy, objectives and budget (Brunzell & Söderman, 2012), further scholarly attention to this board practice is warranted. Questions for further examination include: do boards evaluate themselves, against what criteria, is there a benefit to doing so, and, how is such evaluation being performed?

The use of the NC to inform director selection (Brunzell & Söderman, 2012) and director evaluation (Ingram & O'Boyle, 2018) is an emerging phenomenon of significant potential for nonprofit sport organisations. Whilst at face value, the NC may appear to fit within a director selection discussion, the NC also has the potential to enhance and integrate other important board responsibilities. In light of this potential, before turning to the topic of board evaluation instruments, the corporate NC literature is introduced together with implications for the sport sector.

Nomination committees

The NC has been described, in the for-profit sector, as the "primary institutional mechanism designed to strengthen director selection processes" (Kaczmarek, Kimino & Pye, 2012, p. 474). NC functions include: the implementation of a robust process (Carson, 2002; Kaczmarek et al., 2012), the design of director candidate profiles (Kaczmarek et al., 2012; Kallamu, 2016), the recommendation of director candidates for ratification by the board and/or shareholders (Kaczmarek et al., 2012; Kallamu, 2016), individual director performance assessment (Kallamu, 2016), ongoing succession planning and, critically, board evaluation (Carson, 2002; Kaczmarek & Nyuur, 2016). As with director selection generally, it is the actual practice/behaviours of those engaged with the NC processes that determine their effectiveness (Walther & Morner, 2014; Walther, Morner & Calabrò, 2017). Ultimately, NCs should contribute to organisational performance by building a well-composed and value-creating board of directors (Kaczmarek & Nyuur, 2016). Despite this NC centrality to good governance, scholarly interest in the sport governance domain is nascent.

Nonprofit and sport organisations

As early as 1991, NCs were recognised in the nonprofit domain as "the key to leading an effective recruitment practice" (Brown, 2002, p. 45, citing Joyaux, 1991). Similar to the for-profit literature, a wide range of functions are referenced including the identification of board needs, recruitment, induction, role allocation, development and evaluation (Brown, 2002; Renz, 2004). The use of NCs is linked to improved perceptions of both board effectiveness (Herman, Renz & Heimovics, 1997) and board member competence (Brown, 2007).

In the sport sector, Hoye and Cuskelly (2004) determined that effective boards had more effective director selection processes than ineffective boards but that "neither group of boards used a nominating or board development committee ..." (p. 90). Six years later, Enjolras and Waldahl (2010) noted that NCs are "common within voluntary organizations, trade unions and political parties in Norway" (p. 228) and speculated on the possible role of NCs in reducing oligarchs within the Norwegian Olympic and Paralympic Committee and Confederation of Sports. NC functions in nonprofit sport include succession planning, director recruitment, candidate assessment, recommendation, appointment and director/board evaluation (Bradbury & O'Boyle, 2015; Brunzell & Söderman, 2012; Enjolras & Waldahl, 2010; Ferkins & Shilbury, 2010; Ingram & O'Boyle, 2018). In particular, Brunzell and Söderman (2012) revealed that of 44 Nordic football clubs with NCs, 37 (84 percent) reported their board evaluation results to their NC. These studies, in Australia, Norway, Denmark, Finland, Iceland, Sweden and New Zealand, whilst not focussing on NCs, signal their emergence as an important governance tool for sport organisations. However, unlike the corporate sector, little is actually known about the NC, its benefits, attributes, behaviours and/or performance, within the modern nonprofit sport environment.

The NC potential to maximise the benefits, in a holistic way, associated not only with director selection but also with director development and evaluation practices, merits urgent attention. As does the need to measure NC performance, and director and board performance generally. Accordingly, the chapter now provides a brief overview of director and board evaluation instruments (as opposed to the existence/impact of board evaluation practices) available to assist with such performance assessments.

Evaluation instruments: Individual (director) and collective (board and nomination committee)

For the purposes of this section, the term board evaluation encompasses the evaluation of the board, board subcommittees and its directors. Expanding on the work of Minichilli, Gabrielsson and Huse (2007), the for-profit literature emphasises the importance of designing context-specific strategies for such evaluations (Nordberg & Booth, 2019; Rasmussen, 2015; Roy, 2008). This requires thoughtful consideration to the following questions: why, what criteria, how, by whom, of whom, for whom and to what use will the results be applied?

Within this literature, the assessment of "behavioural dynamics" as well as the more traditional for-profit financial indicators is promoted (Nordberg & Booth, 2019; Rasmussen, 2015). Importantly, the "value creating" board will avoid the trap of evaluation for compliance purposes alone and maximise the associated performance enhancement opportunities (Nordberg & Booth, 2019; Rasmussen, 2015; Roy, 2008).

As identified earlier in this chapter, sport boards do engage in performance evaluation (Brunzell & Söderman, 2012; Ingram & O'Boyle, 2018) with this board process positively impacting perceptions of board effectiveness (Brunzell & Söderman, 2012). Despite this potential, Ingram and O'Boyle (2018) observed the "minimal scholarly attention" (p. 159) directed to this area. Board evaluation instruments referenced by sport governance academics include the Self-Assessment for Non-profit Governing Boards Scale (SANGBS) (Slesinger, 1991), the Board Self-Assessment Questionnaire (BSAQ) (Jackson & Holland, 1998) and the Governance Self-Assessment Checklist (GSAC) (Gill, Flynn & Reissing, 2005). Hoye and Cuskelly (2007) identified a stream of research in the early 2000s "adapting the SANGBS for the context of nonprofit sport organizations" (p. 154). More recent studies have departed from the SANGBS approach and developed their own scales to explore season-ticket holder perceptions of board performance (McDonald & Sherry, 2010), chair perceptions of board performance (Brunzell & Söderman, 2012; Tacon & Walters, 2016) and a "glocalised" measure of sport board performance (Ghadami & Henry, 2015).

The literature relating to nonprofit sport director and board committee evaluation is even more sparse. In terms of director evaluation, leading sport management researchers assert reliance on the work of Preston and Brown (2004) (Doherty & Hoye, 2011; Hoye, 2007). To measure individual director performance, Preston and Brown (2004) utilised three strategies: executive assessment (via the "Executive Perceived Participation" scale), peer assessment (via the "Board Member Value" scale) and self-assessment (via the "Self-Reported Involvement" scale). In the nonprofit sport studies on "commitment, involvement and board member performance" (Hoye, 2007) and "role ambiguity and board member performance" (Doherty & Hoye, 2011), directors rate their own performance according to five items (i.e., adequacy of role fulfilment, the quality, meaningfulness and strength of their contributions, plus their contribution "strength" compared to others). Akin to some board evaluation tools, there is little emphasis on the important personality traits/behaviours that contribute to effective intragroup dynamics. Unfortunately, in relation to governance committees, in particular NCs, there are no known sport studies using evaluation instruments to assess their effectiveness.

Government sport agencies may be leading the field in terms of the utilisation of evaluation instruments. Subsequent to their increased investment in quality NSO governance is an increased emphasis on evaluation. For example, in 2017, Sport NZ released a revised Online Governance Evaluation System (OGES) (Sport NZ, n.d. (d)). The OGES aligns with the Sport NZ Governance Framework (GF) and Governance Mark (GM) accreditation system (Sport NZ, n.d. (b)). It involves five modules: whole-of-board (i.e., skills, behaviour, processes and outputs), chair (i.e., leadership, personal qualities and relationships with management and stakeholders), individual directors (i.e., role, contribution and behaviour), management (evaluation of the board) and nine essential questions for the board (i.e., a discussion framework for the board to consider critical governance areas) (Sport NZ, 2017).

The online tool has the capacity to generate multi-year "whole-of-board" report comparisons as well as re-evaluation questions and development plans based on low-scoring areas (Sport NZ, 2017). The reference to "behaviours" at both the collective and individual levels is reassuring. However, one concern is the omission of the membership/stakeholder perspective from the OGES. In addition, from a review of publicly available website information, as at 2018, there is no evidence of similar evaluation of governance committees (e.g., NCs).

A key benefit of the Sport NZ OGES appears to be its potential to capture the "power of integration" (Roy, 2008), of board/director evaluation, director selection and development (induction and education) strategies. Sport governance scholars, policy-makers and practitioners alike are therefore encouraged to progress such integration to maximise the associated board and organisational performance objectives. In addition, for sport governance scholars, empirical validation of the reliability of industry instruments such as the OGES would be a timely and meaningful contribution.

Conclusions: Implications for industry and future research

There is no "one size fits all" for nonprofit sport governance. This is reflected in the shift from "best practice" to "good practice" recommendations in the prescriptive literature. The challenge for sport sector practitioners is to identify the particular context-specific drivers and strategically designed fit-for-purpose director selection, development (induction/education) and evaluation practices accordingly. The challenge for scholars is to help practitioners understand why this is needed, and to identify (in a resource-poor environment), where and how best to allocate their governance resources (Parent & Hoye, 2018).

Director selection, development and evaluation is fertile ground for future research for at least two reasons. First, there is a dearth of empirical studies in these fields, particularly for nonprofit sport. Second, the evidence to date supports the contribution of improved director selection, development and evaluation to board performance. Of particular importance for director selection is the behavioural component and the interactions between CEO, chair, board, NC (Kaczmarek & Nyuur, 2016; Walther, Morner & Calabrò, 2017) and, arguably for nonprofit sport, the organisation's voting members. In the case of director development and evaluation, concepts from human resource and volunteer management studies of nonprofit sport organisations may be useful complements (Taylor & McGraw, 2006; Wicker, 2017). Attention is directed to the NC as a means of advancing/integrating these board practices so that director selection and development can be both informed by, and inform, evaluation, in an ongoing succession planning cycle.

Finally, the need to evolve the empirical measurement of board (including director and NC) effectiveness is pressing. Such measures need to address the challenges of assessing "group fit" type criteria such as attributes/behaviour and intragroup dynamics. Collaboration between scholars, policy-makers and practitioners may assist in identifying, developing and validating sport-/context-specific evaluation instruments, such as the Sport NZ OGES. Closer analysis of the interconnected nature of director selection, development and evaluation (inherent in the OGES) perhaps paves the way for significant scholarly contributions to sport board, and hence, organisational performance.

References

Australian Institute of Sport. (2015). *Mandatory sports governance principles*. Canberra, Australia: Author.

Australian Sports Commission. (2012). *Sports governance principles*. Canberra, Australia: Author.

Balduck, A.-L., Van Rossem, A., & Buelens, M. (2010). Identifying competencies of volunteer board members of community sports clubs. *Nonprofit and Voluntary Sector Quarterly, 39*, 213–235.

BoardWorks International Ltd. (2018). *Board charter and governance policies*. Retrieved 11 February 2019, from https://sportnz.org.nz/managing-sport/search-for-a-resource/guides/nine-steps-to-effective -governance-building-high-performing-organisations

Bradbury, T., & O'Boyle, I. (2015). Batting above average: Governance at New Zealand Cricket. *Corporate Ownership & Control, 12*, 352–363.

Brown, W. A. (2002). Racial diversity and performance of nonprofit boards of directors. *The Journal of Applied Management and Entrepreneurship, 7*, 43–57.

Brown, W. A. (2007). Board development practices and competent board members: Implications for performance. *Nonprofit Management & Leadership, 17*, 301–317.

Brunzell, T., & Söderman, S. (2012). Board evaluation in the top Nordic football clubs. *Sport, Business and Management: An International Journal, 2*, 210–224.

Canada Not-for-profit Corporations Act, S.C. 2009, c. 23 (2009).

Carson, E. (2002). Factors associated with the development of board sub-committees. *Corporate Governance: An International Review, 10*, 4–18.

Cornforth, C. (2004). The governance of cooperatives and mutual associations: A paradox perspective. *Annals of Public and Cooperative Economics, 75*, 11–32.

Dickson, G., Arnold, T., & Chalip, L. (2005). League expansion and interorganisational power. *Sport Management Review, 8*, 145–165.

Doherty, A., & Hoye, R. (2011). Role ambiguity and volunteer board member performance in nonprofit sport organizations. *Nonprofit Management & Leadership, 22*, 107–128.

Dowling, M., Leopkey, B., & Smith, L. (2018). Governance in sport: A scoping review. *Journal of Sport Management, 32*, 438–451.

Elms, N., Nicholson, G., & Pugliese, A. (2015). The importance of group-fit in new director selection. *Management Decision, 53*, 1312–1328.

Enjolras, B., & Waldahl, R. H. (2010). Democratic governance and oligarchy in voluntary sport organizations: The case of the Norwegian Olympic Committee and Confederation of Sports. *European Sport Management Quarterly, 10*, 215–239.

Ferkins, L., & Shilbury, D. (2010). Developing board strategic capability in sport organisations: The national-regional governing relationship. *Journal of Sport Management Review, 13*, 235–254.

Ferkins, L., & Shilbury, D. (2015). Board strategic balance: An emerging sport governance theory. *SMR, 18*, 489–500.

Ferrand, C., Henry, I., & Ferrand, A. (2010). Gendered identities in self-descriptions of electoral candidates in a French national sport federation. *European Sport Management Quarterly, 10*, 531–552.

Gazley, B., & Nicholson-Crotty, J. (2018). What drives good governance? A structural equation model of nonprofit board performance. *Nonprofit and Voluntary Sector Quarterly, 47*, 262–285.

Ghadami, M., & Henry, I. (2015). Developing culturally specific tools for the evaluation of good governance in diverse national contexts: A case study of the National Olympic Committee of the Islamic Republic of Iran. *The International Journal of the History of Sport, 32*, 986–1000.

Gill, M., Flynn, R. J., & Reissing, E. (2005). The Governance Self-Assessment Checklist: An instrument for assessing board effectiveness. *Nonprofit Management & Leadership, 15*, 271–294.

Grassi, L., Giorgino, M., Raimondo, S., & Romani, G. (2016). The induction of board directors: A case study perspective. *Corporate Ownership & Control, 13*, 207–223.

Herman, R. D., Renz, D. O., & Heimovics, R. D. (1997). Board practices and board effectiveness in local nonprofit organizations. *Nonprofit Management & Leadership, 7*, 373–385.

Hoye, R. (2007). Commitment, involvement and performance of voluntary sport organization board members. *European Sport Management Quarterly*, 7, 109–121.

Hoye, R., & Cuskelly, G. (2004). Board member selection, orientation and evaluation: Implications for board performance in member-benefit voluntary sport organisations. *Third Sector Review*, 10, 77–100.

Hoye, R., & Cuskelly, G. (2007). *Sport governance*. Oxford, UK: Elsevier.

Hoye, R., & Doherty, A. (2011). Nonprofit sport board performance: A review and directions for future research. *Journal of Sport Management*, 25, 272–285.

Ingram, K., & O'Boyle, I. (2018). Sport governance in Australia: Questions of board structure and performance. *World Leisure Journal*, 60, 156–172.

Inglis, S. (1997). Shared leadership in the governance of amateur sport: Perceptions of executive directors and volunteer board members. *Avante*, 3, 14–33.

Jackson, D. K., & Holland, T. P. (1998). Measuring the effectiveness of nonprofit boards. *Nonprofit and Voluntary Sector Quarterly*, 27, 159–182.

Joyaux, S., (1991). The nominating committee: Effective tool for improving the board. *Fund Raising Management*, 21, 38–42.

Kaczmarek, S., Kimino, S., & Pye, A. (2012). Antecedents of board composition: The role of nomination committees. *Corporate Governance: An International Review*, 20, 474–489.

Kaczmarek, S., & Nyuur, R. (2016). Review of the literature on board committees: Taking stock and looking ahead. *International Journal of Business Governance and Ethics*, 11, 89–115.

Kallamu, B. S. (2016). Nomination committee attributes and firm performance: Evidence from finance companies in Malaysia. *Journal of Economic and Social Thought*, 3, 150–165.

McDonald, H., & Sherry, E. (2010). Evaluating sport club board performance: A customer perspective. *Journal of Sport Management*, 24, 524–543.

Minichilli, A., Gabrielsson, J., & Huse, M. (2007). Board evaluations: Making a fit between the purpose and the system. *Corporate Governance: An International Review*, 15, 609–622.

Nordberg, D., & Booth, R. (2019). Evaluating the effectiveness of corporate boards. *Corporate Governance: The International Journal of Business in Society*, 19, 372–387.

O'Boyle, I., & Hassan, D. (2016). Board composition in federated structures: A case study of the Gaelic Athletic Association. *World Leisure Journal*, 58, 109–123.

O'Boyle, I., & Shilbury, D. (2016). Comparing federal and unitary models of sport governance: A case study investigation. *Managing Sport and Leisure*, 21, 353–374.

O'Neal, D., & Thomas, H. (1995). Director networks/director selection: The board's strategic role. *European Management Journal*, 13, 79–90.

Parent, M. M., & Hoye, R. (2018). The impact of governance principles on sport organisations' governance practices and performance: A systematic review. *Cogent Social Sciences*, 4, 1–24.

Parent, M. M., Naraine, M. L., & Hoye, R. (2018). A new era for governance structures and processes in Canadian national sport organizations. *Journal of Sport Management*, 32, 555–566.

Preston, J. B., & Brown, W. A. (2004). Commitment and performance of nonprofit board members. *Nonprofit Management & Leadership*, 15, 221–238.

Rasmussen, J. (2015). Do board evaluations measure board effectiveness? *International Studies of Management & Organization*, 45(1), 80–98.

Renz, D. O. (2004). *An overview of nonprofit governance*. Midwest Center for Nonprofit Leadership at UMKC. Retrieved 18 February 2019, from http://energycollection.us/Board-Of-Directors/Governance/Ove rview-Nonprofit-governance.pdf

Roy, M.-J. (2008). Building board expertise through key supporting processes. *Measuring Business Excellence*, 12, 38–49.

Schoenberg, G., Cuskelly, G., & Auld, C. (2016). The role of intragroup dynamics in nonprofit governance models: A systematic quantitative literature review. *Managing Sport and Leisure*, 21, 1–22.

Sherry, E., & Shilbury, D. (2009). Board directors and conflict of interest: A study of a sport league. *European Sport Management Quarterly*, 9, 47–62.

Shilbury, D. (1993). Determining the problem of order in the Australian football league. *Journal of Sport Management*, 7, 122–131.

Slesinger, L. H. (1991). *Self-assessment for nonprofit governing boards*. Washington, DC: National Centre for Nonprofit Boards.

Sport England, & UK Sport. (n.d.) *A code for sports governance*. Retrieved 24 January 2019, from https://www.uksport.gov.uk/resources/governance-code

Sport New Zealand. (n.d. a). *Board needs matrix*. Retrieved 11 February 2019, from https://sportnz.org.nz/managing-sport/search-for-a-resource/guides/nine-steps-to-effective-governance-building-high-performing-organisations

Sport New Zealand. (n.d. b). *Governance in the New Zealand sport and recreation sector*. Retrieved 11 February 2019, from https://sportnz.org.nz/assets/Uploads/SportNZ-GovernanceDocument.pdf

Sport New Zealand. (n.d. c). *Nine steps to effective governance: Building high performance organisations* (3rd ed.). Retrieved 13 May 2016, from https://sportnz.org.nz/assets/Uploads/attachments/managing-sport/strong-organisations/Nine-Steps-to-Effective-Governance-Building-High-Performing-Organisations.pdf

Sport New Zealand. (n.d. d). *Welcome to the governance evaluation system*. Retrieved 26 February 2019, from https://snz.directorevaluation.com/home

Sport New Zealand. (2017). Sport New Zealand governance evaluation system user guide. An online approach to board assessment and development. Retrieved 26 February 2019, from https://snz.directorevaluation.com/guides/participant_guide.pdf

Tacon, R., & Walters, G. (2016). Modernisation and governance in UK national governing bodies of sport: How modernisation influences the way board members perceive and enact their roles. *International Journal of Sport Policy and Politics, 8*, 363–381.

Taylor, T., & McGraw, P. (2006). Exploring human resource management practices in nonprofit sport organisations. *Sport Management Review, 9*, 229–251.

Taylor, M., & O'Sullivan, N. (2009). How should national governing bodies of sport be governed in the UK? An exploratory study of board structure. *Corporate Governance: An International Review, 17*, 681–693.

Walters, G., Trenberth, L., & Tacon, R. (2010). *Good governance in sport: A survey of UK national governing bodies of sport*. London, UK: Birkbeck Sport Business Centre.

Walther, A., & Morner, M. (2014). Opening the black box of nomination committees: A case study of non-executive director selections in German supervisory boards. *International Journal of Business Governance & Ethics, 9*, 136–154.

Walther, A., Morner, M., & Calabrò, A. (2017). The role of behaviorally integrated nominating committees in non-executive director selection processes. *European Management Journal, 35*, 351–361.

Wicker, P. (2017). Volunteerism and volunteer management in sport. *Sport Management Review, 20*, 325–337.

Withers, M., Hillman, A., & Cannella, A. (2012). A multidisciplinary review of the director selection literature. *Journal of Management, 38*, 243–277.

Part V

Future sport governance challenges

25

Leadership in governance

The potential of collective board leadership

Ian O'Boyle

Introduction

There has been a growing appreciation for the importance of effective leadership within sport governance. As the industry continues to evolve, it requires the need for effective leadership at many levels but especially at the upper echelons of governance. Although leadership and management in general have long been associated with each other, leadership and governance have seldomly been explored simultaneously. Soucie (1994) suggested that leadership pervades all the managerial activities of the sport administrator. This is clearly based on everyday practical examples within the sport industry where leaders are required to plan, organise, control, delegate and empower others to achieve organisational objectives as effectively and efficiently as possible. But little has been known about the inner workings of sport boards, thus potentially giving rise to this lack of exploration of the leadership issue within these settings. Given the repeated high-profile examples of "poor" leadership in the sport governance environment reported via the media (e.g., Fédération Internationale de Football Association (FIFA), International Olympic Committee (IOC), National Collegiate Athletic Association, etc.), it is even more surprising that this stream of research has not received more attention.

It is unquestionable that the notion of leadership in any environment is most often complex and can contain many different layers, definitions and practices. The sport context is no different. For example, in nations where a federal model of governance exists, directors of an organisation are not only expected to lead a singular entity but also have an explicit, or at the very least, an implicit responsibility to enact leadership across a network of associated organisations (Ferkins, Shilbury & O'Boyle, 2018). This has been described in a variety of ways and under various frameworks, such as facilitative leadership, collaborative leadership, shared or distributed leadership and, most recently, collective leadership. The purpose of this chapter is to chronicle the rise in attention that leadership in the sport governance setting is receiving, relying on an exploration of previous work in the field combined with real-life examples of leadership in the sport governance environment. The chapter will also detail some potential avenues for future research to explore how this could help both scholars and practitioners increase understanding of this complex and multi-faceted concept.

Ian O'Boyle

Siloed concepts: Leadership and governance research

Both leadership and governance research are well-established fields of inquiry. Leadership research permeates many academic disciplines in one form or another, and governance research, although not as ubiquitous, has attracted scholarly interest from various perspectives including research centred on the corporate, nonprofit, and public administration contexts. Organisational governance typically includes boards, chairpersons and CEOs as those who would often be described as the leaders of an organisation. Governance exists at the apex of the organisation where a natural connection to leadership can be rightly assumed. What is therefore interesting is the realisation that a dearth of research exists that focusses on the intersection of leadership and governance, with a relatively small number of studies (given the breadth and scope of leadership research) affording specific attention to this area (Erakovic & Jackson, 2012). For isolated instances of focussed leadership in governance work, see examples from Davies (2006), Holloway and van Rhyn (2005) and Pye (2002).

Historically within governance systems, and certainly within the sport governance domain, there exists an issue of cultural ambiguity over the exact role of those charged to govern in organisations (Doherty & Hoye, 2011). This issue relates to those structural, policy-based, procedural tasks noted previously (the orthodox components of governance) versus the more intangible yet equally important areas such as reputational image, establishing of vision, developing relationships and networks and delivery of mission. It is in the latter area that leadership skills, qualities, characteristics and traits in the traditional sense of leadership (i.e., leader-centric approach) as well as leadership as a social construct (i.e., relational, collective achievement) can come to the fore. The latter intangible elements of leadership are potentially more fitting for a modern board of directors, evolving from a results-oriented focus to viewing governance as a multidimensional practice combining elements of traditional governance roles and leadership (Chait, Ryan & Taylor, 2005; Huse, 2007).

As an amalgamation of governance and leadership research (in the general sense) currently does not exist as a legitimate stream of inquiry, it is not surprising that the same can be said for leadership and *sport* governance. Nevertheless, like the general context, a handful of scholars have ventured directly into this area with areas of facilitative and, more recently, collective leadership coming to the fore. The next section of this chapter explores the concept of facilitative leadership before taking a more acute view of the emerging notion of collective leadership and its potential positive impact on the sport governance environment.

Facilitative leadership in sport governance

Although collective leadership in sport governance appears to be where the dial currently sits in terms of exploring this complex issue, there have been several other concepts that have led researchers to this destination with facilitative leadership being one of those. Facilitative leadership as a concept has been synonymous with collaborative governance, which has received significant attention in the sport governance domain of late (O'Boyle & Shilbury, 2016; Shilbury & Ferkins, 2015; Shilbury, O'Boyle & Ferkins, 2017). Sporting bodies within a network may have a history of strong collaboration and individuals may have built relationships with their counterparts in other organisations that have allowed for the sharing of ideas or mutual benefits for each organisation. Likewise, organisations within a particular network may have a deep history of antagonism and conflict that may act as a barrier to a collaborative approach to leadership within their sport. "Unassisted" negotiations are often possible within sport if there have indeed been positive interactions between entities previously, but to ensure that all parties within a network

354

are engaging in a collaborative spirit, many authors have argued that facilitative leadership is crucial (Ansell & Gash, 2008; Reilly, 2001; Susskind & Cruikshank, 1987).

Leadership at the sport governance level is clearly an important mechanism for setting policy and rules, building trust, facilitating face-to-face and other dialogue, and exploring mutually beneficial gains. Even if these are small in nature, they may contribute to momentum building and increase the level of trust within inter-board relationships. Effective leadership can empower affiliated organisations to create collaborations that lead to outcomes at a higher level than could have been achieved if these entities continued to work without interaction with other organisations in their network (Vangen & Huxham, 2003). Lasker and Weiss (2003) suggested that the facilitative leader(s) should have ability to: promote broad and active participation; ensure broad-based influence and control; facilitate productive group dynamics; and extend the scope of the process.

Facilitative leadership also relies on the willingness of other leaders within the network to engage in the process, both formally and informally, which may lead to more successful collaborations (Bradford, 1998; Lasker & Weiss, 2003). One of the major benefits of implementing a facilitative leadership approach within sport governance is that "weaker" stakeholders such as those at the bottom of the pyramid structure (clubs/grass-roots sports) become more involved in the decision-making process. Empowering and representing these stakeholders is seen as an integral component of the facilitative leadership process (Ozawa, 1993). It is important to note, however, that although collaborative governance and facilitative leadership have been explored in federal sporting networks, much of this work has focussed on collaboration between national and state bodies and has generally not accounted for the community level of the sporting pyramid as referenced above.

Ansell and Gash (2008) argued that within a facilitative leadership approach, the traditional balance of power that exists within a network becomes less critical and mediation procedures help to ensure all stakeholders enter the process on an equal footing. They add that "this style of facilitative leadership also helps stakeholders to explore possibilities for mutual gain" (p. 555). This view is further supported by work undertaken by Lasker and Weiss (2003) who also suggest that facilitative leaders must give meaningful voice to all participants and encourage participants to listen to each other. The facilitative leader should stimulate creativity by taking on board the diverse views of all stakeholders within the sporting network and synthesising those views so new directions and ideas can be established and acted upon.

As noted above, a prior history of conflict, which can often exist within sporting networks, may severely limit the state of collaboration and interplay between governing boards within a network. Likewise, if parties feel there is little incentive to participate in a collaborative process, or that the balance of power is unjust, leadership then becomes an all-important mechanism for bringing these parties together and attempting to build trust and cooperation between affiliated entities. The qualities and characteristics required of boards and CEOs to enact facilitative leadership will often depend on the levels of conflict, distrust and antagonism that currently exist within the network. When incentives to participate are seen to be lacking, or lines of communication have completely broken down, the board or CEO will often be required to intervene in order "to keep stakeholders at the table or empower weaker actors" (Ansell & Gash, 2008, p. 555). Shilbury, Ferkins and Smythe (2013) argued that deft skill is required to coordinate wholly or partially autonomous organisations on behalf of interests to which they both contribute. They suggest that "leadership, and the skill-sets of the personnel involved therefore, are also important factors" (p. 13). Henry and Lee (2004) also highlighted the importance of the skills-set of individuals in leadership positions within sport management. They argued that leaders should not simply have skills in planning and directing but should also have the ability to negotiate effectively and be willing to undergo mutual adjustment for the benefit of the sport as a whole and, ideally, for the benefit of all parties in the network.

These varying functions of the facilitative leader(s) can unquestionably create tensions within the network, particularly if they are required to intervene to empower underrepresented stakeholders, which others may view as favouritism. If there is a significant prehistory of conflict within the network, Ansell and Gash (2008) suggest that the only viable alternative may be to obtain an external mediator to replace the board or CEO as the facilitative leader(s) within the collaborative process. This of course is far from an ideal situation as external parties or individuals may struggle to gain acceptance and exert influence over the actions of affiliated bodies in the absence of any real leverage or preconceived levels of trust. In order for both external mediators or the current board or CEO to gain the trust of the network they must remain impartial to any self-interested views of affiliated parties and be seen to act in a transparent manner upholding the integrity of the collaborative/facilitative leadership process while clearly working towards whole-of-sport outcomes.

Trust and distrust

Central to the issue of leadership in sport governance, regardless of which frame is being explored (e.g., facilitative, collaborative, shared, distributed, collective), is the issue of trust and distrust. Within the networked model that many sport organisations find themselves operating in, trust within and between organisations can be a crucial factor in determining the level and ability for successful leadership within that network (O'Boyle & Shilbury, 2016). If trust therefore is an integral ingredient for success, the facilitative leader must ensure that strategies are in place to build trust within the network, particularly if there has been a prehistory of conflict where distrust may exist between parties limiting the capabilities for collaboration. This may prove extremely difficult for the board or CEO who are attempting to build trust within the network, as parties may have had negative experiences with organisations in the past and may enter new collaborative arrangements with scepticism due to these past experiences. Ring (1997) suggested that even if trust is non-existent within a network, it may emerge from formal or informal processes of "transacting". However, the same can be said of distrust, and long histories of distrust within the network will present major challenges for the "would-be" facilitative leader.

It is more than likely that in some networks distrust will be a major obstacle in attempting to undertake collaborative arrangements through a facilitative leadership approach (Weech-Maldonado & Merrill, 2000). The facilitative leader may have to undertake specific trust-building initiatives within the network, such as intentionally seeking intermediate outcomes (small wins) that help to build momentum and act as a platform for greater collaboration in the future. Ansell and Gash (2008) suggest "the building of trust can be a time-consuming process that requires a long-term commitment to achieving collaborative outcomes" (p. 559). An additional feature that has been acknowledged as helping to build trust between parties is the extent of face-to-face dialogue that is undertaken within the network. Within some networks, face-to-face dialogue may take place on a regular basis whereas, in contrast, in countries such as Australia with a large geographical size, face-to-face contact may only take place within the network at an annual general meeting. Developments in technology such as video conferencing have allowed organisations in such situations to have increased face-to-face dialogue and may be an adequate substitute for in-person correspondences.

Face-to-face dialogue allows for the breaking down of stereotypes or preconceived notions about individuals or entities within a network (Bentrup, 2001). Warner (2006) argued that face-to-face dialogue is the core component for trust-building, creating shared understanding and ensuring parties are committed to the collaborative process. The facilitative leader must exploit all opportunities for face-to-face dialogue within the network and encourage parties to correspond as often as possible through this medium. Of course, it is important to also note that face-to-face dialogue in some instances may in fact reinforce negative stereotypes and increase antagonism and distrust within the network. In this case, the facilitative leader will need to intervene to examine ways in which the relationship can be repaired. Regardless of this possible situation, effective collaboration based on high levels of trust is unlikely without significant face-to-face dialogue between parties within the network (Ansell & Gash, 2008).

The keys to being a facilitative leader

Facilitative leadership at the governance level within federated networks such as sporting environments, requires the leader to actively engage key stakeholders in the network so talents and contributions can be maximised. There are abundant instances of the need for individuals with facilitation skills within the sporting setting, most notably at the governance level, where the majority of these relationships are enacted. With increased pressure from funding bodies to ensure that affiliated sport organisations are working towards common goals (Australian Sport Commission, 2015), the need for board members and CEOs to possess the traits of a facilitative leader is becoming even more important. Furthermore, the increase in professionalism and the expertise of individuals working across all levels of sport should be brought to the fore of the decision-making process, which the facilitative leader can help to achieve. Based on Cufaude's (2014) synopsis of facilitative leadership, there are several key traits that are important to becoming an effective facilitative leader that appear relevant the sport governance environment:

Make connections with issues across the sport

The sport industry is a fast-paced environment where information regarding financial, operational and strategic issues can change rapidly across various areas of the industry. The ability to make connections between all these pieces of information is crucial for the facilitative leader to attempt to join pieces of the puzzle together and ensure accurate up-to-date information is received by key stakeholders. It is the facilitative leader's responsibility to listen to the concerns of a group of stakeholders and make connections with the concerns of other stakeholders within the network. An effective facilitative leader at the governance level must periodically ask the question: "How do the concerns of these stakeholders fit in with the concerns of others within the network?"

Providing direction

It is important that the facilitative leader(s) provides direction for the sport or the issues at hand while still actively engaging stakeholders in the collaborative process. It often requires deft skill to balance the need for providing direction while simultaneously ensuring stakeholders "own" the process, as in the absence of ownership true commitment to the process may not be sustainable. The facilitative leader(s) must be concerned with guiding the collaborative process through asking the right questions at the appropriate times, as opposed to a more traditional directive style that may lead to adversarial encounters (Shilbury et al., 2013).

Balancing the agenda and the collaborative process

The facilitative leader(s) is required to ensure that an appropriate collaborative process comple-ments the content of matters discussed by parties in the network. Ensuring that the collaborative process is undertaken correctly provides the greatest opportunity for additional collaborative processes to be accepted in the future and helps to establish the all-important issue of trust within the network. Pre-empting the collaborative process by establishing agreements of how interaction will take place between parties in the network allows the facilitative leader(s) to evaluate the process itself irrespective of the outcomes that are achieved. Ignoring the group process and solely focussing on the outcomes or decisions that have been made runs the risk of alienating individuals or groups within the network who may feel that their contributions have not been appropriately acknowledged and considered.

Bringing the core issues to the fore (the elephant in the room)

The facilitative leader(s) is required to tease out the underlying obstacles to effective collabora-tion within the network. There may be personality clashes, a prehistory of conflict or antagonism, or personal and professional issues that are preventing the network from collaborating effectively. Individuals may be reluctant to discuss these issues or attempt to avoid them. However, if these issues are truly preventing the network from achieving outcomes, it is the role of the facilitative leader(s) to use either subtle or forceful questioning to bring these issues to the fore so they can be addressed and the network can move forward. When the network can freely raise concerns and issues without fear of retaliation, openness, honesty and trust can be increased.

Facilitating sustainable collaboration

Facilitative leadership is not simply about achieving immediate outcomes or once-off collabora-tions within the network. The true value in employing a facilitative leadership approach lies in the establishment of the collaborative process itself where future collaborations may continue within the network based on the momentum, trust and goodwill that has been forged through initial outcomes and collaboration. This long-term focus ensures that the facilitative leader(s) does not assume all responsibility for future collaborations. After the initial collaborative process where strong facilitative leadership is clearly required, the ideal situation is that the facilitative leader simply oversees future processes as opposed to becoming directly engaged with additional collaboration in the network.

Commitment by the facilitative leader

Finally, the facilitative leader(s) must ensure that they themselves are fully committed to enact-ing this style of leadership and must be authentic in their relations with others in the network (Takos, Murray & O'Boyle, 2018). Enacting this style of leadership with some parties and not with others serves little benefit to the collaborative process and the leader(s) may be judged to be insincere or even manipulative. Facilitative leadership requires thoughtful planning and execution to ensure its success. Leaders who spontaneously alter the way in which they interact and engage with stakeholders in the network must be sensitive to how parties may react and speculate on true intentions. Openness and honesty about the alteration of leadership style may relieve some of the concerns of the parties in the network. A staggered change to a more facilitative leadership style may prove to be more palatable for the network as parties get used to more involvement in the decision-making process and become comfortable with increased collaboration.

The potential for collective leadership

The above discussion and articulation of the concept of facilitative leadership leads to the notion of collective leadership and its potential to positively impact the sport governance environment. Collective leadership has only recently received a small amount of attention regarding sport governance but has begun to be explored in depth in other non-sport contexts over the past decade.

One of the main proponents of this concept, Cullen and Yammarino (2014), highlighted the need for additional research to focus on collective engagement in leadership by multiple individuals through both formal and informal relationships, which reflects the increasingly complex workplaces and non-work situations leaders may face. As collective leadership is ultimately an informal and non-traditional leadership process, understanding the connection between formal and informal leadership structures is important to increase an understanding of how a board can engage in collective leadership (Cullen-Lester & Yammarino, 2016). While the concept of collective leadership is gaining favour with an increasing number of scholars (Chrobot-Mason, Gerbasi & Cullen-Lester, 2016; Friedrich, Griffith & Mumford, 2016; Friedrich, Vessey, Schuelke, Ruark & Mumford, 2009; Manz & Sims, 1991; Yukl, 2009), limited research sheds light on how to develop and enhance collective leadership capacity, although efforts are being made to move away from the traditional view of leadership and associated theories (Cullen, Palus, Chrobot-Mason & Appaneal, 2012).

The traditional notion of leadership often encompasses some form of hierarchical component, frequently reflecting a leader-centric, individual level phenomenon (Friedrich et al., 2009; Pearce & Manz, 2005). As research surrounding the topic of leadership has evolved, we have begun to understand the limitations of this traditional view of leadership for varied settings including sport organisations (Kihl, Leberman, & Schull, 2010). Yukl (2009) suggested that leadership should not only be viewed as a person but as a role, and that leadership itself could be explained as a process. Similarly, Grint (2005) proposed that leadership has been viewed in four very different ways: leadership as person, leadership as results, leadership as position and leadership as process. While all perspectives potentially have implications for the notion of collective leadership, it is perhaps leadership as process (where multiple contributions are possible) that has the most obvious symmetry with collective board leadership.

This view of leadership is arguably more in line with how leadership plays out in many practical settings including the federal sport governance model where leadership is often a complex and dynamic process potentially involving multiple stakeholders, where roles are shared across a group dynamic and leadership is generated through multiple interactions (Dansereau & Yammarino, 1998; Day, Gronn, & Salas, 2004; Friedrich et al., 2009). In this way leadership is seen as a phenomenon, and the focus of research is on the multiple interactions rather than the characteristics or behaviours of the "person in charge" (Jackson & Parry, 2011).

Conceptualising leadership as a collaborative, social, relational experience, where leadership is viewed as a collective achievement not something that belongs to an individual (Cullen-Lester & Yammarino, 2016; Kihl et al., 2010; Ospina & Foldy, 2009), is an important theoretical transition for governance research. In the context of leadership in sport governance, such a conceptualisation draws attention to the board's ability to share information, collaborate among themselves, and arrive at consensus-driven decisions (Ansell & Gash, 2008; Friedrich et al., 2009).

It is also important to note that collective leadership cannot be seen as a static concept. As a board attempts to enact increased collaboration in a sporting network, multiple challenges will inevitably arise requiring various skills and expertise to ensure they are overcome. Uhl-Bien, Marion and McKelvey (2007) alluded to this general concept in their leader complexity theory, in which an adaptive leadership capacity can emerge through the interaction and exchange between individuals with different information. In essence, this capacity is dynamic and can be dictated by the situation at any given time (Friedrich et al., 2009).

Given the need for sharing information and collaboration with member association boards across a network, consensus decision-making processes at the board mean that board dynamics and cohesion are clearly important to the concept of collective leadership. Board dynamics and cohesion appear to be one of the few areas related to collective leadership that have previously been explored in the sport governance literature (Doherty & Carron, 2003; Schoenberg, Cuskelly & Auld, 2016; Soares, Correia, & Rosado, 2010). As board members of a national sport organisation (NSO) are all seen as equal, as noted previously, a formal designated notion of leadership is absent when conceptualising collective board leadership. This, in and of itself, may be a challenge for board members in the sporting context, given the hierarchical culture within the industry, particularly from an on-field perspective, where many board members may have developed their leadership capacities (O'Boyle, Murray & Cummins, 2015).

In fact, certain team processes may be preconditions for collective leadership to emerge and be successful (Friedrich et al., 2009). For example, if sharing of information does not occur as a result of limited interaction between boards and board members, the prospect of enacting collective board leadership is slim (Uhl-Bien et al., 2007). It is within situations such as these that it is possible to see how collective board leadership acts as a stimulant for wider collaborative behaviours across the network, as it is likely similar issues would resonate in the broader context across the network. In other words, a culture of collaboration and collective thinking and action is essential to drive behaviour throughout the network at a board-to-board level.

Can collective leadership be applied to sport governance?

As noted previously, there is little work that has specifically explored the relationship between collective board leadership and governance systems within the sport organisation context (Ferkins et al., 2018). Further, as explored earlier in the chapter, facilitative leadership is needed to harness pre-existing relationships and processes and to culturally shape future board leadership roles. Thus, understanding the required skills and behaviours for voluntary directors working within a network of sport organisations and further theorising about potential leadership roles is paramount when considering the potential impact of collective board leadership in sport governance systems.

What is currently unknown in the sport governance space is how exactly collective leadership can be *enacted* and what *impact* collective leadership might have on governance systems. The need to systemise and sustain a collective leadership approach in a federal network may be a daunting challenge for NSO board members. This is largely due to the voluntary nature of governance positions and the potential for high levels of both director and executive turnover. Studies related to voluntary boards have provided insight into the correlates of volunteer board performance in the nonprofit sporting context (Doherty & Carron, 2003; Doherty & Hoye, 2011; Hoye, 2004, 2006; Hoye & Auld, 2001; Hoye & Cuskelly, 2003, 2004; Schoenberg et al., 2016), yet investigations of board relationships and dynamics specifically within a federal model have not been well documented.

Attempts to systemise collective leadership behaviours may go some way to transitioning an NSO and its member associations from traditional hierarchical thinking, in a governance sense, to achieving a more consensus-based and sustainable-networked approach to governance. However, the interpersonal and informal nature of collective leadership, as noted previously (Cullen & Yammarino, 2014), raises questions about how to ensure directors possess those required skills and behaviours. Moreover, how do NSOs identify and recognise these skills and behaviours and ultimately influence the appointment of directors with the requisite skills? These volunteer decision-makers come from different backgrounds and have varying understandings and abilities to enact collective leadership for the purposes of facilitating a more collaborative approach to governance.

Ferkins et al. (2018) argued that enacting collective board leadership by the NSO is critical when seeking to implement smooth collaborative functions for all arms of governance in a sport network. How this form of leadership is operationalised in nonprofit boards within a federated structure is largely unknown but, intuitively, unity of action in the quest for whole-of-sport outcomes is contingent on the NSO board acting in unison to provide direction for both task and process outcomes. By implication, task (e.g., strategic direction, mission, vision) and process outcomes (e.g., communications, trust) implemented across the network and performed by the NSO board constitute collective board leadership, but the relative importance of each to collective leadership is not well documented. Such a collaborative approach alongside collective leadership will likely be time-intensive, as noted by Huxham and Vangen (2000), given consultation and engagement with all boards in a network, with time being a potentially limited resource for volunteer directors. In this context, investigating the impact of time on implementing collective leadership is also an important area for future research. If implementing collective leadership for the purpose of collaborative behaviours is time-intensive, it is also important to understand what exactly the efficiency gains over time are if a network is to adopt such an approach to governance.

Ultimately, the voluntary nature of these positions and the need for skills-based directors with an understanding of collective leadership raise questions about the delegate system of board composition that is synonymous with the federal governance model (Hoye & Cuskelly, 2007; O'Boyle & Bradbury, 2013). This representative system sees delegates elected to represent the interests of their own state or regional affiliations and not necessarily those of the entire sport network (Shilbury et al., 2013) and, arguably, little consideration is given to the leadership capabilities of these individuals from a whole-of-sport, collective perspective. In the nonprofit context in general, Kearns (1995) suggested that board members should possess specific talents that add value to the board and possess a clear understanding of their role and selflessness, both of which would appear to be useful for embedding a culture of collective leadership. Current nonprofit sport governance models within a federal system may not necessarily facilitate this situation, hence the need for collective leadership skills and behaviours in this context. Where boards are composed of a mix of delegates and independently appointed directors, future research could investigate the extent to which the appointment of independent directors impacts collective leadership throughout a sport network. This focus is interesting, because it is in this space that national governing bodies can directly choose the skill sets required to complement board composition.

The move to incorporate more independent directors within such boards has enabled greater inclusion of individuals with specific skills relevant to the increasingly diverse challenges boards face, including those related to effective leadership. However, it is still assumed that many NSO boards do not consider leadership capabilities and styles of potential board members when co-opting or appointing independent directors in order to foster collective leadership and cross-network collaboration (O'Boyle & Shilbury, 2016). Moreover, the issue of term lengths on boards can act as a barrier to collective leadership if prehistories of conflict are present and cannot be overcome via constitutional turnover (Ansell & Gash, 2008; O'Boyle & Shilbury, 2016).

In amalgamating work in the sport governance domain and other fields related to collaborative governance and leadership, several salient themes come to light. For a federal sporting network, sustainability of a collaborative approach to governance is grounded in the ability of these systems to produce "organic leaders"; those with an overriding interest in promoting collaboration who come from within the network itself (Ansell & Gash, 2008; Shilbury & Ferkins, 2015). From empirical work conducted in the field it is known that this leadership must be vested in the board members of the NSO as a collective unit, as they have the influence to potentially systemise collaborative behaviours and provide some prospect of long-term sustainability (O'Boyle & Shilbury, 2016; Shilbury & Ferkins, 2015). As noted previously in the chapter it is also known there are specific skills and behaviours required of facilitative/collaborative leaders in a federal network that are largely based on an ability to communicate and negotiate effectively, along with a willingness for mutual adjustment (Henry & Lee, 2004; O'Boyle & Shilbury, 2016). These skills and behaviours are required internally within the board to enact collective leadership to facilitate the adoption of more consensus-seeking forms of governance such as collaborative governance.

What is currently not known in relation to collective board leadership as a precondition for a collaborative approach to sport governance are the various roles that the board must fulfil, which has been highlighted as a fundamental starting point (Contractor, DeChurch, Carson, Carter & Keegan, 2012; Friedrich et al., 2009). To understand and bring to light these varying roles, it is necessary to take a more acute view of the collective leadership variable when pursuing a collaborative approach to sport governance. Exploring the roles that make up the notion of collective board leadership is important as the identification and articulation of these roles may help the cogs of a collaborative approach to governance turn more easily. Thus, the basis of an important stream of future research is formed with the potential to identify these roles and the conditions under which they might be more effective.

Summary

This chapter explored the emerging context of contemporary leadership practice in sport governance systems. The old view of leadership as a leader-centric concept has clearly been replaced with more complex and relevant notions of describing leadership. The need for leaders in sporting networks such as those operating in a federal model to be more facilitative and far less authoritarian has now been well established but there remains much to uncover about how this new relational view of leadership in sport governance can be fully adopted and implemented.

One of the focus areas for research in this domain currently revolves around the notion of collective board leadership. Collective board leadership may present itself in different ways depending on the situational context of the network (Friedrich et al., 2009; Uhl-Bien et al., 2007). Tasks such as building trust, improving transparency and facilitating face-to-face dialogue may all require different techniques and skills from leaders, all of which reinforce the need for multiple leaders but nonetheless require a contingency approach to explain collective leadership within the sport governance context. As Ansell and Gash (2012) described, "a contingency approach assumes that there is no single 'best way' to exercise leadership … but that different tasks, goals, and contexts will place distinctive kinds of demands on leaders" (p. 3). Examining the variety of these conditions that shape collective board leadership behaviour is critical, as is the potential for different sports themselves to shape these conditions.

References

Ansell, C., & Gash, A. (2008). Collaborative governance in theory and practice. *Journal of Public Administration Research and Theory, 18*, 543–571.

Ansell, C., & Gash, A. (2012). Stewards, mediators, and catalysts: Toward a model of collaborative leadership. *The Innovation Journal: The Public Sector Innovation Journal, 17*(1), 1–21.

Australian Sports Commission (ASC). (2015). *Mandatory sports governance principles*. Author: Canberra.

Bentrup, G. (2001). Evaluation of a collaborative model: A case study of analysis of watershed planning in the Intermountain West. *Environmental Management, 27*, 739–748.

Bradford, N. (1998). Prospects for associative governance: Lessons from Ontario, Canada. *Politics & Society, 26*, 539–573.

Chait, R. P., Ryan, W. P., & Taylor, B. E. (2005). *Governance as leadership: Reframing the work of nonprofit boards*. Hoboken, NJ: John Wiley and Sons.

Chrobot-Mason, D., Gerbasi, A., Cullen-Lester, K. L. (2016). Predicting leadership relationships: The importance of collective identity. *The Leadership Quarterly, 27*, 298–311.

Contractor, N. S., DeChurch, L. A., Carson, J., Carter, D. R., & Keegan, B. (2012). The topology of collective leadership. *The Leadership Quarterly, 23*, 994–1011.

Cufaude, J. (2014). Facilitative leadership: Maximising the contributions of others. *The Systems Thinker, 15*(10), 2–5.

Cullen, K. L., Palus, C. J., Chrobot-Mason, D., & Appaneal, C. (2012). Getting to "we": Collective leadership development. *Industrial and Organizational Psychology: Perspectives on Science and Practice, 5*, 428–432.

Cullen, K., & Yammarino, F. J. (2014). Special Issue on collective and network approaches to leadership. *The Leadership Quarterly, 25*, 180–181.

Cullen-Lester, K., & Yammarino, F. (2016). Collective and network approaches to leadership: Special Issue introduction. *The Leadership Quarterly, 27*, 173–180.

Dansereau, F., & Yammarino, F. (1998). *Leadership: The multiple-level approaches*. (Volume B). Stamford, CT: JAI Press.

Davies, A. (2006). *Best practice in corporate governance: Building reputation and sustainable success*. Aldershot, UK: Gower.

Day, D. V., Gronn, P., & Salas, E. (2004). Leadership capacity in teams. *The Leadership Quarterly, 15*, 857–880.

Doherty, A., & Carron, A. (2003). Cohesion in volunteer sport executive committees. *Journal of Sport Management, 17*, 116–141.

Doherty, A., & Hoye, R. (2011). Role ambiguity and volunteer board member performance in nonprofit sport organizations. *Nonprofit Management and Leadership, 22*, 107–128.

Erakovic, L., & Jackson, B. (2012). Promoting leadership in governance and governance in leadership: Towards a supportive research agenda. In A. Davila, M. Elvira, J. Ramirez & L. Zapata-Cantu (Eds.), *Understanding organizations in complex, emergent and uncertain environments* (pp. 68–83). Basingstoke, UK: Palgrave Macmillan.

Ferkins, L., Shilbury, D., & O'Boyle, I. (2018). Leadership in governance: Exploring collective board leadership in sport governance systems. *Sport Management Review, 21*, 221–231.

Friedrich, T. L., Griffith, J. A., & Mumford, M. D. (2016). Collective leadership behaviors: Evaluating the leader, team network, and problem situation characteristics that influence their use. *The Leadership Quarterly, 27*, 312–333.

Friedrich, T. L., Vessey, W. B., Schuelke, M. J., Ruark, G. A., & Mumford, M. (2009). A framework for understanding collective leadership: The selective utilization of leader and team expertise within networks. *The Leadership Quarterly, 20*, 933–958.

Grint, K. (2005). Problems, problems, problems: The social construction of 'leadership'. *Human Relations, 58*, 1467–1494.

Henry, I., & Lee, P. C. (2004). Governance and ethics in sport. In J. Beech & S. Chadwick (Eds.), *The business of sport management* (pp. 25–41). Essex: Pearson Education.

Holloway, D. A., & van Rhyn, D. (2005). Effective corporate governance reform and organisational pluralism: Reframing culture, leadership and followership. Corporate Governance: Does Any Size Fit? *Advances in Public Interest Accounting, 11*, 303–328.

Hoye, R. (2004). Leader-member exchanges and board performance of voluntary sport organizations. *Nonprofit Management and Leadership, 15*, 55–70.

Hoye, R. (2006). Leadership within Australian voluntary sport organization boards. *Nonprofit Management and Leadership, 16*, 297–313.

Hoye, R., & Auld, C. (2001). Measuring board performance in nonprofit voluntary sport organisations. *Australian Journal on Volunteering, 6,* 108–116.

Hoye, R., & Cuskelly, C. (2003). Board power and performance in voluntary sport organizations. *European Sport Management Quarterly, 3,* 103–119.

Hoye, R., & Cuskelly, G. (2004). Board member selection, orientation and evaluation: Implications for board performance in member-benefit voluntary sport organisations. *Third Sector Review, 10,* 77–100.

Hoye, R., & Cuskelly, G. (2007). *Sport governance.* Oxford: Elsevier Butterworth-Heinemann.

Huse, M. (2007). *Boards, governance and value creation: The human side of corporate governance.* Cambridge, MA: Cambridge University Press.

Huxham, C., & Vangen, S. (2000). Leadership in the shaping and implementation of collaboration agendas: How things happen in a (not quite) joined-up world. *Academy of Management Journal, 43,* 1159–1175.

Jackson, B., & Parry, K. (2011). *A very short, fairly interesting and reasonably cheap book about studying leadership* (2nd ed.). London, UK: Sage Publications.

Kearns, K. P. (1995). Effective nonprofit board members as seen by executives and board chairs. *Nonprofit Management and Leadership, 5,* 337–358.

Kihl, L. A., Leberman, S., & Schull, V. (2010). Stakeholder constructions of leadership in intercollegiate athletics. *European Sport Management Quarterly, 10,* 241–275.

Lasker, R. D., &. Weiss, E. S. (2003). Broadening participation in community problem-solving: A multidisciplinary model to support collaborative practice and research. *Journal of Urban Health: Bulletin of the New York Academy of Medicine, 80,* 14–60.

Manz, C. C., & Sims, H. P. (1991). Super leadership: Beyond the myth of heroic leadership. *Organizational Dynamics, 19*(4), 18–35.

O'Boyle, I., & Bradbury, T. (Eds.). (2013). *Sport governance: International case studies.* London, UK: Routledge.

O'Boyle, I., Murray, D., & Cummins, P. (Eds.). (2015). *Leadership in sport.* Oxon, UK: Taylor & Francis.

O'Boyle, I., & Shilbury, D. (2016). Exploring issues of trust in collaborative sport governance. *Journal of Sport Management, 30,* 52–69.

Ospina, S., & Foldy, E. (2009). A critical review of race and ethnicity in the leadership literature: Surfacing context, power and the collective dimensions of leadership. *The Leadership Quarterly, 20,* 876–896.

Ozawa, P. (1993). Improving citizen participation in environmental decision making: The use of transformative mediator techniques. *Environment and Planning C: Government and Policy, 11,* 103–117.

Pearce, C., & Manz, C. (2005). The importance of self- and shared leadership in knowledge work. *Organizational Dynamics, 34,* 130–140.

Pye, A. (2002). Corporate directing: Governing, strategising and leading in action. *Corporate Governance: An International Review, 10,* 153–163.

Reilly, T. (2001). Collaboration in action: An uncertain process. *Administration in Social Work, 25*(1), 53–73.

Ring, P. S. (1997). Transacting in the state of union: A case study of exchange governed by convergent interests. *Journal of Management Studies, 34*(1), 1–25.

Schoenberg, G., Cuskelly, G., & Auld, C. (2016). The role of intergroup dynamics in non-profit governance models: A systematic quantitative literature review. *Managing Sport and Leisure, 21,* 1–22.

Shilbury, D., & Ferkins, L. (2015). Exploring the utility of collaborative governance in a National Sport Organization. *Journal of Sport Management, 29,* 380–397.

Shilbury, D., Ferkins, L., & Smythe, L. (2013). Sport governance encounters: Insights from lived experiences. *Sport Management Review, 16,* 349–363.

Shilbury, D., O'Boyle, I., & Ferkins, L. (2017). A research agenda for collaborative sport governance. *Sport Management Review, 19,* 479–491.

Soares, J., Correia, A., & Rosado, A. (2010). Political factors in the decision making process in the voluntary sports associations. *European Sport Management Quarterly, 10,* 5–29.

Soucie, D. (1994). Effective managerial leadership in sport organization. *Journal of Sport Management, 4,* 211–223.

Susskind, L., & Cruikshank, J. (1987). *Breaking the impasse: Consensual approaches to resolving public disputes.* New York: Basic Books.

Takos, N., Murray, D., & O'Boyle, I. (2018). Authentic leadership in nonprofit sport organization boards. *Journal of Sport Management, 32,* 109–122.

Uhl-Bien, M., Marion, R., & McKelvey, B. (2007). Complexity leadership theory: Shifting leadership from the industrial age to the knowledge era. *The Leadership Quarterly, 18,* 298–318.

Vangen, S., & Huxham, C. (2003). Enacting leadership for collaborative advantage: Dilemmas of ideology and pragmatism in the activities of partnership managers. *British Journal of Management, 14,* 61–76.

Warner, J. F. (2006). More sustainable participation? Multi-stakeholder platforms for integrated catchment management. *Water Resources Development, 22*(1), 15–35.

Weech-Maldonado, R., & Merrill, S. (2000). Building partnerships in the community: Lessons from the Camden healthcare improvement learning cooperative. *Journal of Healthcare Management, 45*(3), 189–205.

Yukl, G. (2009). *Leadership in organizations.* Upper Saddle River, NJ: Prentice Hall.

26

Gender and diversity in sport governance

Popi Sotiriadou and Adele Pavlidis

Introduction

This chapter draws on information from two separate studies on women in the governance of sport to discuss the nuances and challenges in the area of gender and diversity in sport. Using this information, this chapter projects future areas of importance in sport governance and particular challenges for women in sport leadership roles (e.g., board of directors) as they relate to integrity, social responsibility and collective governance structures.

The movement to gender equality in sport (i.e., equal access or gender-neutral access to social goods, services and resources and opportunities) has gained exponential support worldwide in the last decades (Rubin & Lough, 2015). Efforts to increase women's inclusion in sport have resulted in advancements in participation at grassroots levels via programs and competitions. Advancements are also prevalent in women's representation in the media and other communication platforms, as well as their successes at higher levels of competition such as the Olympic Games and World Championships. However, women's inclusion in decision-making (i.e., holding leadership roles in the governance of key sport organisations) has not reached equivalent milestones. Indicatively, the 2016 International Sports Report Card on Women in Leadership Roles (Lapchick, 2016) showed men chair 33 of the 35 International Federations (IFs) affiliated with the Olympics, and only two women lead IFs. A significantly small number of women (5.7%) are IF presidents or vice-presidents (12.2%), and only 24.4% of the IOC members are women.

The Australian Sports Commission's (ASC, re-branded in 2018 as *Sport Australia*) (2015) Mandatory Sports Governance Principles requires that National Sport Organisation (NSO) boards be represented by at least 40% women directors. Quotas however do not address the near exclusion of women from national and international sport organisation boards. Women's inclusion in decision-making, through their appointment to leadership positions in sport organisations, is, and has been, limited. In light of this challenge, the authors of this chapter conducted two research projects in order to (a) understand the factors that influence gender diversity in the governance of sport and (b) demonstrate the persistent and enduring marginalisation of women from sport governance and hence the urgent need for change.

This chapter offers a brief review of literature on sport governance and gender politics in sport. Then, the chapter presents an overview of the methods used to collect data for the two studies, followed by reporting key findings and their ramifications in the governance of sport. Based on the findings and a subsequent summary discussion, the chapter draws conclusions on the future challenges for women in sport governance and ways these might be mitigated to further enable collective governance in sport organisations.

Governing bodies and gender politics in sport

Worldwide, understanding the underrepresentation of women in sport governance has been, and remains, a stream of research for sport management scholars and for policy makers concerned with the broader participation of women in sport (Welty Peachey, Zhou, Damon & Burton, 2015). Governance is critical to any sport organisation since it is concerned with issues of policy and sets the strategic direction of the organisation (Ferkins & Shilbury, 2012). Therefore, the board can influence attitudes towards gender through its own composition and actions. In the general organisational literature there has been great strides in the ways gender and governance are conceptualised (e.g., Acker, 2006, 2012; Britton & Logan, 2008). The sport governance literature has also contributed towards this rethinking (e.g., Cunningham, 2009; Geeraert, Alm & Groll, 2014; Leberman & Burton, 2017; Ryan & Dickson, 2018; Shaw & Slack, 2002; Sibson, 2010). Yet, as a sociocultural site of movement and bodies (for sport is primarily concerned with moving bodies), these insights can be extended further.

As Knoppers, Hovden and Elling (2018, p. 4) noted, governance "should also be seen as political process". "Sport" is often considered outside of the realm of government – as a voluntary, civic pursuit – yet of course this is often, if not always, not the case. First, sport is tightly woven into a range of lucrative and important markets including gambling and sport media (broadcasting and advertising) (e.g., Smart, 2007). Second, and more importantly, "power", as Foucault (1972) observed, is always present. Power and politics are not the preserve of government, but are instead part of even our most intimate relationships, and is certainly part of sport in all its myriad of forms (including formal, informal, structured and unstructured) (e.g., Houlihan, 2002). This means that sport governance, including who is, and how they are, appointed to the board, the rules and regulations that regulate and shape decision-making and the activities being governed are all inherently political (Claringbould & Knoppers, 2007). Sport governance is hence never "neutral" and decisions that are made reverberate into other fields with a range of known and unknown effects.

If sport governance is political, then the question of gender diversity in this context is also political. Using Hargreaves (1990) phrasing, "gender" is on the "sports agenda" for sport governance. Therefore, it is important to unpack what we mean by "gender" and acknowledge the various and sometimes vastly different approaches to gender inclusion. As Hovden, Elling and Knoppers (2018) write, it is "important to examine who is in the position to shape determinations about which equality norms are applied in the development of politics that aim to remove gender inequalities and bring about social change" (p. 192). As they go on to note "…the definition of the problem influences the selection and implementation of gender political strategies" (p. 192). There are numerous ways to conceptualise women's inclusion/exclusion in sport governance. These include a) liberal feminism, where the goal has been to provide equal access and rights, usually in law, b) radical feminism, concerned with critiquing and dismantling patriarchy (systems of male dominance and power) (Scraton & Flintoff, 2002) and (c) post-structural feminism, focusing on the notion of "phallocentrism", which "denotes male control of language, symbols, definitions, discourses, sexuality, theory and logocentric thinking" (Wearing, 1998, p. 39). Although not exclusive – as there are many other types of feminist theories – these three have been central to understanding women's long exclusion and marginalisation in sport governance. In the following section, we outline the two case studies that form that basis of this chapter's discussion, demonstrating the diverse ways gender inclusion has been conceptualised in practice and theory.

Methods and case studies

This chapter reports findings from two studies. The first case study reports on findings from a study that was funded by the IOC and was led by the first author in this chapter with two colleagues residing in the Netherlands to investigate the role that men can play in working towards gender equity in sport governance. That study (Sotiriadou, de Haan & Knoppers, 2017b) used a qualitative approach to investigate gender balance across the boards from various sport organisations; and it focused on triathlon and rowing in Australia and the Netherlands, two countries that have announced their support for and engagement with gender balance in governance. The full report is available online at the Olympic Studies Centre library.

The study drew information from organisational documents and semi-structured interviews with 22 men and 12 women from organisations involved in sport governance at the national or international level. These organisations included two NOCs, the two international sport federations (IFs) and their national level counterparts (i.e., four national sport federations [NFs], two from each country). Besides convenience on location and access to data, the Netherlands and Australia were selected because these countries are committed to gender-balanced boards (critical mass of a minimum of 30%). This commitment is also consistent with worldwide trends that indicate that these countries rank between 10th and 15th in women in corporate board seats suggesting a relatively similar commitment to gender equality in other sectors (Catalyst, 2017). The two sports included in this study (i.e., triathlon and rowing) were also chosen carefully, as they have a strong organisational commitment to gender equality, as shown by consistently working towards gender balance on and off the field, their boards attain a gender-balanced representation, and they employ campaigns targeting the appointment of women to sport boards.

The second case study focuses on an Australian example, the Australian Football League (AFL) and the development of the Australian Football League Women's (AFLW) competition. The second author of this chapter was awarded funding to research the rise of women's participation in contact sport and related management and governance issues. Central to these projects was an emphasis on innovative theories, taking a new lens to the enduring problem of women's marginalisation in sport more broadly. Relevant to this chapter were the in-depth interviews conducted with administrators involved in a range of AFL governance bodies, including community boards, state organisations and the national office (n = 16). Analysis of public documents, including annual reports, media articles, books and policies also supported this case study. The interviews were focused on asking participants to reflect on issues of leadership related to the first season of AFLW. This included questions about governance, women as players, women as leaders and the efficacy of the decision-making processes in relation to women in the sport.

Case 1: Women in leadership roles in sport governance

Sotiriadou et al. (2017b) discussed a paradox related to gender supply versus demand in sport leadership and governance. They suggested that, on one hand, knowledge on gendering, heroic masculinity, social and other barriers offer a good understanding of why there is an underrepresentation of women in sport organisations (low demand). However, evidence suggests that there are many females (supply) that can take on various leadership roles in boards of directors (BoDs) including marketing, finance and law (Pletzer, Nikolova, Kedzior & Voelpel, 2015). Hence, as Burton (2015) alluded to, it is likely that there are certain contextual, sport-system related, cultural, social and psychological factors that potentially act as barriers to gender equity (i.e., macro, meso and micro level research/factors).

The macro level in this case is the sport sector where masculinity is institutionalised and the gendered structure of sport is an operating principle. Therefore, in their investigation, Sotiriadou et al. (2017b) examined "What do BoDs *think* and *do* about gender and sport governance?" The meso level is an analysis within sport organisations (policies and procedures in place). Specifically, in their research, Sotiriadou, de Haan and Knoppers (2017a) explored the question: "What evidence is there of stereotypes, discrimination and gendered organisational cultures?" Last, the micro level is individual experiences, practices and interactions. The question at the micro level was: "What do individuals perceive to be the roles of males/females on implementing or bringing about changes on gender leadership?" What follows is a discussion of the key findings at the macro, meso and micro levels, respectively.

The results at the macro level show that the BoDs "thinking" is that they see a lot of "room for improvement" and a "need for a lot more" that needs to be done to improve gender equity and shift the existing gendered culture in the boardroom. What many participants thought was that "the board should reflect what's going on in society. It cannot be that only men are in charge…. That may have happened because that [male dominance] is also part of the world of sports" (Sotiriadou et al., 2017b, p. 20). That thinking however was not aligned with the "doing", because when it came down to strategies and actions that the BoDs had in place to ensure more women take up leadership roles in the governance of sport organisations, these led predominantly to a sense of equality and represented short-term solutions. For example, efforts to bring about a balanced gender ratio on BoDs and enforcing a quota of 30 percent representation of women in boards reflect gender equality strategies.

Another strategy to balancing BoDs was the creation of women's groups/commissions within federations. Both of these approaches have limited results (Women in Sport, 2015), as merely including more women on sport boards and in leadership positions does not change the gender constructs (Knoppers & Anthonissen, 2001). This is because gender equality may change the gender ratio but does not explicitly encourage men to collaborate with women or to be involved in changing male-dominated governance cultures and producing gender equity (Knoppers, 2016). Gender equality is equal treatment of women and men in laws and policies with equal access to resources and services, whereas gender equity reflects fairness in the distribution of opportunities, responsibilities and benefits available to men and women and the strategies used to achieve gender equality (United Nations Population Fund [UNFPA], 2017). Therefore, a focus on gender equity requires an exploration of what men and women think and do and the practices they engage to bring about changes (Martin, 2003). Consequently, to enable equity in sport leadership, it is important that the thinking and doing of BoDs is more aligned.

The results at the meso level report on gender stereotypes and board culture/interactions. The participants drew on several stereotypes to describe behavioural- and skill-related differences between male and female directors and leaders. When highlighting differences in perceived confidence between men and women in a meeting environment, one of the participants explained: "Even if they have no clue what they are doing, men say 'yes, I can'. And women think, 'I've never done that, so I don't think that I can do that'". Another participant pointed out that "Many men like to demonstrate that they are smarter or more strategic, that is an ego thing. I think females bring sensitivity to discussions and ego comes out of it" (Sotiriadou et al., 2017b). Overall, males were quoted as being "ambitious" and "opinionated", with "strong egos" and "confidence" and "very good at lobbying", "politicking" and "networking" and "competitive". Some participants attributed these male traits to the nature of sport being gendered and one female participant claimed that sport governance "does tend to attract those who have operated at a very high level within their sports. It is quite often a sort of high ego environment…in my experience men have a little more tendency to be like this". Women, on the other hand, were portrayed as "emotional", "insulated" and "lacking confidence".

As Knoppers (2016) explained, the prevalence of these stereotypes means that even when sport organisations strive for gender equality by focusing on reducing the male to female ratio, they continue to (re)produce social relations based on gender. Males were seen as "dominant", "assertive" and "results-oriented" directors, whereas women combine leadership with "sensitivity", "passion" and "realism". In the context of this finding, it was not surprising when data supported the notion that women "help dominant males maintain their status quo" precisely because they are not a threat. A quotation from a director at the triathlon federation illustrating this point was as follows: "I think the previous president was so dominant that he probably didn't surround himself with alpha males. That he surrounded himself with good quality people that weren't after his position. Three of those happen to be women". These findings suggest that stereotypes on women's availability and traits could result in situations where women are less likely to be considered for certain positions (e.g., the top job) that are perceived to require masculine attributes and behaviours. However, upon reflection, there is no evidence in the leadership literature suggesting that sensitivity, passion and realism are weaknesses in leaders (Sotiriadou & de Haan, 2019). Therefore, at the meso level, what participants perceived as gender differences are leadership traits that could potentially allow for skill complementarity in BoDs. Therefore, women add value and their leadership traits may offer a competitive advantage to gender-balanced boards.

The results at the micro level revealed several nuances related to the role of individuals within BoDs in advancing gender equity in sport leadership. The findings revealed that both males and females in leadership positions play a key role in gender diversity when they actively support other women in taking up leadership roles or mentor and promote their interests. Previous research has indicated how males can act as change agents (Claringbould & Knoppers, 2008) and this study shows how women too, when they hold positions of power, can support gender equity practices. In particular, strategies include "active approaching" and "selecting and recruiting" of women on boards, as well as adopting a "whole of sport approach" where equity is evident in all aspects of the sport (e.g., sport participation, coaching, competitions and prize money). In comparison to female champions of change, the results show that males can play a significant role in "advocacy" for women's inclusion and for women to be heard on gender equity issues. It is quite likely that this active and pro-active positioning of male equity champions has the potential to enable sport boards to reach high levels of female representation on the board. Because of their dominant and powerful position, male leaders, more so than their female counterparts, can have more influence when acting as equity champions for gender equity in sport. Champions of change have the ability to influence or even undo stereotypes and promote a gender-friendly culture where women on boards say it "doesn't feel forced, it feels like something that's natural and the people who are there are the best people for the job".

Case 2: AFL, women and governance

> …we're sitting in this board room and there's all these kinds of chairmen of the AFL around the wall, like it was really blokey. (Kelly)

AFL is a code of football, indigenous to Australia, and the most popular football code in Australia. According to the Australian Bureau of Statistics (ABS) (2012), the AFL is the most popular spectator sport in Australia. It is also the most lucrative. The AFL reported AUD$650.6 million in revenue in their 2017 annual report (AFL, 2017) compared to AUD$313,005 million by Cricket Australia (2017) and AUD$354 million by the National Rugby League (NRL) (2017). AFL is popular Australia-wide, but predominately in Victoria, Western Australia and Queensland. "Footy", as AFL is commonly referred to in Australia, has been historically a game for men and boys. This is despite girls and women making up a growing proportion of AFL fans (Toffoletti, 2017) with a long history of women competing (Wedgwood, 2005).

The game itself is a contact sport. Nikki Wedgwood (2005) has called it "a local variant of the rugby family of football games". The ball is kicked in the air and play moves forward, with teams of 18 pitched against each other on a large grass field. Girls and women have played, but their participation has been hampered, and, in some instances, they have been actively excluded. The AFL presented the launch of AFLW as unique and ground-breaking, but as sports historian Hess (2017) writes:

> However the AFL presents the AFLW, women's football is not a "revolution" that starts with the first whistle on Friday [3 February 2017]. Nor did it begin with the advent of the modern women's leagues in the 1980s. It began in 1915, when 36 pioneering young women in modest and cumbersome outfits took to the field and showed that women belonged there, too. (n.p.)

Considering this history, it was not until the 2000s that the numbers of girls and women wanting to compete in AFL grew. There had been some opportunities for youth girls under 12 to play, but they were unsupported from 12 onwards due to a ban on mixed-gender competitions (and there being no girl competitions). This ban was overturned in 2003 when three teenage girls (Helen Taylor, Emily Stanyer and Penny CullaReid) challenged the Victorian Civil and Administrative Tribunal arguing it was contrary to the Equal Opportunity Act 1995 (Victoria State Government, 2010). This legal win pushed AFL Victoria to provide competitions for girls in the 2000s, while the senior women continued, in the Victorian case[1] to be organised and governed by the majority-women board of the Victorian Women's Football League. As one participant went on to explain,

> once that (the youth girl's competition) was happening then we (AFL Victoria) started looking at the senior women's space and that was the Victorian Women's Football League. So, we worked closely with them to look at well, what is the future of the Victorian Women's Football League, what's the best governance and management structure. They were an independent organisation that crossed over all regions. So, it wasn't consistent with the model we'd put in place for the youth girls (Gerry).

The reasons given for the AFL Victoria intervention into VWFL's board and overall structure were that, first, there needed to be an alignment between the youth girls pathways and the plans for the national women's competition; and second, as stated by a participant, "to provide greater service to the clubs from a governance and management point of view" (Gerry). He went on to explain:

> We restructured the Victorian Women's Football League where we transitioned the governance and management into AFL Victoria so that we could then restructure how it was

managed with a view to then transitioning those competitions into community leagues as well. So (we) sort of replicated the model of what we did with the youth girls.

In short, AFL Victoria, with the support of many women from the VWFL, "wound up" the entire governance structure of the VWFL. This was a highly emotionally charged and sensitive issue, as women who had volunteered and committed to the VWFL for many years were losing all decision-making power.

This was an important event in understanding gender and governance in women's AFL. Where previously women held the majority of decision-making power through the board of the VWFL, through this event and the dismantling of the board of the VWFL – a board of women, (with the exception of one man) – men now had control. Hence, the predominately all-male board of AFL Victoria decided that it was "in the best interests" of women for them to be subsumed/incorporated into the governance and hence political power of AFL Vic. AFL Victoria sent in employees to dismantle the board of the VWFA and bring the women's competition "into the fold" so to speak – to bring women's football into the governance realm of the AFL, creating new pathways and ultimately leading to the development and launch of AFLW – a national, televised and "professionalised" women's competition. These pathways were previously unsupported by the AFL, and women had operated independently of AFL Victoria prior to this.

The governance of sport is complex, where there are, as Pavlidis and Fullagar (2014) noted, "multiple focus points – for example, community/elite, profitable/voluntary, spectators/players" (p. 40). These multiple focus points are sometimes in tension, yet it is often forgotten that central to sport governance are decisions about athletes/players. These athletes are "mobile, diverse, corporeal bodies" (p. 40). Women's corporeal bodies are often positioned as less rational, undisciplined and vulnerable, whereas men's corporeal bodies are often assumed to behave in rational and controlled ways (Grosz, 1994; Pavlidis & Fullagar, 2014). This assumption spills over to governance where, in this case of the AFL, women are assumed to be less able to fulfil leadership roles. As Pippos (2017) noted, the AFL has an "unofficial policy of one woman (in leadership) at a time" (p. 208).

The VWFL was a space where women took up most of the roles in sport, including governance. Whereas in the AFL and AFL Victoria it was, and remains to a large extent, men who are in positions of power and authority to govern. The answer is, of course, not simple. In line with Ashcraft (2001) we argue that there is a need to discard the notion that "the only way to manage competing goals is to subordinate one to the other" (p. 1317).

It is on the record that it was a woman, the AFL's first woman commissioner, Sam Mostyn, who began conversations about a national women's AFL competition (Pippos, 2017). This was supported by the league's second woman commissioner, Linda Dessau, and the pair persisted in the boardroom until change began to happen. It is worth noting at this point that Sam Mostyn was appointed in 2005 as the first women only because they had *created a position on the Commission especially for a woman* (Wilson, 2012). They were not alone in their efforts, of course, as there were a number of key – woman – employees who were on the ground working hard to support women's football to grow and nurture talent and mentor the next generation of leaders, including women such as Jan Cooper. There was, and continues to be, a push for the inclusion of women and girls in AFL at all levels (girls, youth, women) and in a range of spaces (boards, fields, stadiums, change rooms). Yet, despite this push, women continue to be marginalised in decision-making processes, which potentially has a direct influence on the opportunities for women and girls to make their mark in AFL more broadly.

Women have enjoyed playing Australian football for over 100 years (Lenkić & Hess, 2016). They have played in their own competitions, organised and governed by (mostly) women.

Despite this history of involvement, AFL has been, in all intents and purposes, considered a "man's game", and women have been excluded. As one research participant stated, "I went back and looked at the 2005 AFL report and there's nothing even in there about female participation. And then it talks about women being volunteers and helping in canteens and raising money for uniforms – even in 2005". Moira Gatens (1997), in her hugely influential article, "Corporeal representation in/and the body politic", draws our attention to the way the modern body politic "uses the human body as its model or metaphor" (p. 80). This "human body" is a masculine image of unity and independence from women and nature, "the infantile wish for independence from the maternal body" (p. 82). Gatens goes on to argue that women are "made part of the corporation not by pact, nor by covenant, but by incorporation" (p. 82). One woman interviewed, articulated this experience of not being represented in the (masculine) model of AFL governance:

> …you have the advantage of being in the heart of footy, you know how it works, you don't ever have to think outside the box. You're in a position of control, you're a man, you belong in the space, you can operate as a man would in that space, you don't have to question how you work, it just works for you, really restricts the skills you develop in terms of thinking about how things could work differently. Whereas if you've been excluded from those positions of power and that way of operating you have to think much more creatively, you have to have a much more flexible world view and thinking to make what you're excluded from and what isn't necessarily how you work, work for you.

This form of feminist theory has yet to be considered in the context of sport governance research - indeed to speak of these things is certainly an anomaly in the field – yet we do speak of "bodies" all the time. Governing bodies, national sport bodies, state sport bodies. These "bodies" also regulate other bodies, directing who and what and where a body can move and play (Woodward, 2016).

These bodies have been, overwhelmingly, male. Anderson's (2009) review article in *Sport Management Review* takes a detailed look at the persistent masculine cultures in sport organisations and presents a comprehensive review of the literature. His insights as to the ongoing promotion and recruitment of men in leadership positions and sport governance resonates with Gatens' (1997) arguments regarding the masculine body politic. He noted:

> In order for men to be successful in sport, they must spend most of their youth and young adulthood dedicated to their athletic endeavours. Accordingly, they predicate their social and personal identities as that of an athlete. This then means that when they fail to make their athletic dreams, they desire to be associated with sport in an ancillary fashion. In this aspect, *it is failed athletes who self-segregate into sporting-related occupations, like sport management.* (Anderson, 2009, p. 10, emphasis added)

Anderson (2009) described how managers hire men who have sporting experience, hence preventing those without this experience from entering many professions related to sport. This also, he argued, "influences the system to forego a more rigorous manner for judging the abilities of a job candidate" (Anderson, 2009, p. 10).

There is a view that the "best person for the job" is someone with experience in the sport. Anderson (2009) explained that "Gatekeepers (ex-sportsmen) are likely to consider that their former sporting histories have well prepared them for their current occupation; accordingly, they would seek similar qualities in people they hire – appointing clones to reproduce the masculinized nature of their sport" (p. 11). In this case study one participant commented on the promotion practices of the AFL board, reflecting on the recent appointment of the new CEO of one of the teams, stating:

> I mean, classic to me was the Gold Coast Suns CEO. It was never put out there. It was just whoever is on the…the president just went straight to somebody that he wanted and never considering that it could be a female to add a different perspective to everything. Then up the line it goes, okay, well, the next person in line is yet another male, so we will elevate him to football ops and no advertising of the role, nothing like that. No going broader into the organisation to say, Sue, would you like to be general manager of football ops? (Sue)

Whether at an international level, or a small sport club, governing bodies in sport are granted power (through terms of reference, constitutions and so forth) to regulate the practice, representation and organisation of sport. In much sport governance literature little reflection is given to the taken-for-grantedness of these "bodies" and how women – previously refused admission completely – might be included. This refusal or reluctance to interrogate the model of governance currently in place is often predicated on an assumption of functionality – "it works". Yet, those people saying "it works" are those that are included in governance. These people are, in the huge majority, men.

> The first home game that the Western Bulldogs had was against Fremantle, an interstate team. Not one senior management or board member from Fremantle attended Fremantle's first AFLW game ever. Then at the function for Western Bulldogs, every keynote speaker was a male. (Lisa)

The lack of support for the AFLW by the BoDs and the lack of foresight, in terms of gender diversity at major functions, were major faux pas that visibly demonstrate the ways men in decision-making positions in AFL have been failing to support women. This failure is in the spotlight, and the need for diversity in AFL governance clear. As the participant noted,

> It definitely has to be that the influences and decision-making groups within our industry change because, whilst everything going into the talent programs is changing at a rate of knots to improve player welfare, improve the talent pathway, that's great and needed to happen as well, but what has to be front and centre is making all of those changes quite sustainable, because the decision-making groups such as the board, senior management, are all across diversity. It reflects our community, so we have to have a variety of ages. We have to have a variety of genders. (Sue)

Yet, despite the clarity of voices calling for diversity, there remains a persistent cultural norm that is difficult to shift without concerted effort. Many of the women interviewed had been involved in Australian Rules football for 20 years or more – as players, administrators and board members, as well as parents of players and volunteers. Yet their experience, and the experience of many women in sport, is sidelined as irrelevant because they haven't been involved in the "men's game" (read as "the main game").

> I've been involved with it (my local club) for 20 years and I hate the f… stupid blokes who run it. I'm sorry. It breaks my heart that something I love so much with these kids that I could be really good at, always feels like a battle. It's really, really sad and it's just because they

won't even talk to you about how things could be done differently or how you can make this place….They just go, the answer always is "oh we've tried that before. Oh, that doesn't work. Oh, we know what we're doing and it's just so dumb". (Peita)

There is a struggle to account for women's historical, cultural and social marginalisation in terms of power to govern, and the situation is becoming more complex. As an organisation, the AFL have had a number of parallel processes 1) the development of AFLW, 2) the inclusion of women in AFL (the men's game) governance and 3) women in community and grassroots Australian football. These processes overlap and interlink, and together they provide an informative demonstration of the ways bodies – governing bodies and corporeal bodies – are gendered masculine and in need of change at all levels.

Discussion: Shifting cultures, processes and stereotypes

Wood (2013) argued that the underrepresentation of women in leadership positions in the governance of sport prevents sport organisations from making better use of their available talent and improving decision-making. Studies over time reiterated the need for women to have greater involvement in decision-making (e.g., Adriaanse & Claringbould, 2016; Toohey, Taylor & Vescio, 1999). The results from the exploratory study that Sotiriadou et al. (2017b) conducted showed that women and men might have different leadership styles and attributes that complement each other. This skill complementarity means that the inclusion of women in leadership positions is not just a matter of fairness; gender diversity can increase this skill complementarity and subsequently improve decision-making and organisational efficiencies (Hartarska & Nadolnyak, 2012). A study conducted by the Commonwealth Secretariat (2013) on the connection between gender, skills and leadership styles revealed differences in the behaviours of women and men and found that these differences influence and shape decisions on boards. However, it is unclear how these differences influence board performance and how the gender-related capabilities (skill-sets) of male and female directors complement each other in the governance setting. The Commonwealth Secretariat report stressed that a nation's competitiveness depends significantly on how it utilises its female talent and suggested that if women (who comprise half of the population) are not represented in a nation's decision-making processes, then that country's economic potential is inhibited. However, little is known about the ways skill complementarity in a gender-balanced sport governance setting can increase socioeconomic value.

Directors are collectively able to influence board attitudes to gender equality (i.e., equal access to social goods, services, resources and opportunities) and equity (i.e., fairness of treatment by gender needs) (Knoppers, 2016) throughout a sport organisation. However, men's perceptions (or thinking) about women's skills are not always positive (Sotiriadou et al., 2017b), particularly if they perceive women's attributes (e.g., empathy and asking questions) as a burden to decision-making rather than enabling skill complementarity. Therefore, as this chapter has demonstrated and other authors have reiterated in their work (e.g., Knoppers, 2016), understanding existing attitudes, stereotypes and organisational culture is necessary to enable sustainable changes in sport governance.

There is an increasing expectation in society that women be included in governance. Yet, despite this expectation, and, as Case Study 2 serves to demonstrate, sport has been very slow to change. This resistance can be understood through the persistent and enduring coupling of sport and masculinity (Anderson, 2009), where sport is considered to be the preserve of men, with women participating for "fun" and usually preferring non-competitive endeavours (see Pavlidis & Fullagar, 2014 for a more nuanced account of these ideas). If "sport" is for men, then including women in the governance of sport does not "make sense". This is despite consistent and oftentimes passionate efforts of women to gain entree to sport, be included in all aspects and levels of sport and contribute their skills and capabilities in decision-making, governance and law.

Making space (literal and figurative) for women in sport governance is about more than the discursive; it is about more than a written policy, target, or even quotas; it also about financial and social benefits, it is about political and cultural change at the molecular level. Scholars, such as Hovden et al. (2018) and Fullagar (2017), have begun to note this, but on a broader level, theory and approaches to gender and sport governance have predominantly focused on either individual strategies (e.g., mentoring for women) or structural changes (policies and procedures). As demonstrated in Case Study 2, despite the AFL providing resources to launch the AFLW, the status quo – privileging men over women and failing to shift the organisational culture – persisted. In this chapter, we use a range of theoretical approaches that specifically look at the "gendering of governance" (Hovden et al., 2018, p. 214) to demonstrate the ways future challenges in sport governance might be addressed.

Anderson (2009) concluded his review by arguing for a completely new approach to thinking about gender diversity in sport, moving away from liberal feminist perspectives (see also de Haan & Dumbell, 2019) and towards structural and material change. He argued, "gender-equality in sport is not enough; we need to instead experiment with the gender-integration of both sporting programs and their management" (Anderson, 2009, p. 11). In the case of the AFL, this could be an exciting and potentially successful experiment, as the co-existing men's and women's teams learn to work *together* for their shared club, rather than in competition. A shift in discourse from gender equality to gender equity is necessary if we are to *undo gender* in sport leadership roles. This can be achieved by converging thinking into explicit strategies that enable active recruitment, support, advocacy and mentoring of women.

Unconscious bias remains an inconvenient truth in sport organisations, even the ones that are set up to cater for gender equity (Sotiriadou & de Haan, 2019). There appears to be so much more *doing* that is needed before change in the context and culture where governance takes place is pervasive enough to lift the burden of stereotypes, empower women to join and stay engaged as leaders and act as advocates for other women to follow suit. Therefore, in answering a rhetorical question – whether gender can be undone in sport governance – the most powerful message in this chapter is the need to harness the role of *equity champions of change* (both by conducting further research with a focus on the micro level and in terms of practical recommendations) to advance positive changes in gender equity in sport leadership.

Conclusion

Modern sport management practice and governance points towards examining sport business with an integrity focus. Integrity is a fundamental pillar of all good sport administration (ASC, 2015), as it ensures sport organisations and programs meet social obligations, reduce social disadvantage and eliminate barriers to participation. The social responsivity that sport organisations carry is becoming increasingly important. In August 2018, the Federal sports minister Bridget McKenzie released the findings of an integrity review of Australian sport, which recommended comprehensive governance changes (Gowthorp, 2018). This legislative and policy framework recommended the establishment of a national integrity commission signposting the need to strengthen public confidence in the Australian government, address corruption and misconduct in sport and show stronger respect to men and women's human rights. To protect the integrity of sport and the decisions made from BoDs for sport, two of the ASC's fundamental principles for good governance dictate the need for (a) balanced board composition, roles and powers and (b) ethical and responsible decision-making (ASC, 2015).

Governance structures have a significant impact on the performance of sporting organisations, and the lack or low representation of women in decision-making is seen as a sign of poor governance (ASC, 2015). Social responsibility offers a platform where accountability for gender-inclusive leadership becomes a requirement. Organisations at various levels within the sporting sphere have increasingly focused their social responsibility efforts on creating opportunities for women and girls. For example, campaigns like "Girls make your move" and organisations like "Women Sport Australia" show a devotion to providing women and girls with access to opportunities to play sport and advance women in sport. This capacity-building is important. However, if women remain out of the boardroom and outside the realm of leadership roles then the decision-making is compromised.

Prior Catalyst research (Carter, Joy & Wagner, 2007) has established that companies with the highest representation of women leaders financially outperform companies with the lowest. Further to this, data that is more recent suggests that gender-inclusive leadership and corporate social responsibility are also linked and that both companies and society win when leaders are gender-diverse (Soares, Marquis & Lee, 2011). Hence, the gains are far more than economic, they are social too. A key area of social responsibility is concerned with initiatives and changes on ethical business practices including gender-inclusive leadership and governance. Social responsibility and gender-diverse leadership are highly correlated with one positively influencing the other. Sport organisations with both women and men leaders in the boardroom and at the executive table are bound to achieve sustainable wins for both sport and society.

In conclusion, increased gender leadership in the governance of sport organisations is necessary if gender equality is to be addressed by all the main actors in emerging new systems of societal governance. In their discussion on collective leadership, Ferkins, Shilbury and O'Boyle (2018) challenge our thinking and pose the question "How can boards enable and enact collective leadership?" They argued that "the need for unity of purpose brings into question the skills and behaviours of the board as a collective in relation to their ability to enact collective leadership" (p. 229). In that sense, skill complementarity presents the potential to strengthen efforts towards enabling collective leadership. This chapter concludes that gender-balanced leadership and an equal representation of women in the governance of sport may offer an enabler to collective leadership advancements in the world of sport. To this end, future research is needed in this area to not only attend to the numbers of women on boards, but to explore why this seemingly more diverse voice is needed – taking an intersectional approach focused on race, class, sexuality, ethnicity, (dis)ability, indigeneity – and what keeps these diverse bodies out of board rooms. More importantly, future research is needed to explore what sport governance researchers can do to support boards to include more diverse bodies for collective leadership.

Note

1 Each state and territory had a different governance structure for women's football. However, it is outside of the scope of this chapter to provide a historical account of all states.

References

Acker, J. (2006). Inequality regimes: Gender, class, and race in organizations. *Gender & Society*, *20*, 441–464.
Acker, S. (2012). Chairing and caring: Gendered dimensions of leadership in academe. *Gender and Education*, *24*, 411–428.

Adriaanse, J. A., & Claringbould, I. (2016). Gender equality in sport leadership: From the Brighton Declaration to the Sydney Scoreboard. *International Review for the Sociology of Sport*, *51*, 547–566.

Anderson, E. D. (2009). The maintenance of masculinity among the stakeholders of sport. *Sport Management Review*, *12*, 3–14.

Ashcraft, K. L. (2001). Organized dissonance: Feminist bureaucracy as hybrid form. *Academy of Management Journal*, *44*, 1301–1322.

Australian Bureau of Statistics (ABS). (2012). *Sports and physical recreation: A statistical overview, Australia, adult attendance*. Cat. *41560*. Retrieved 31 October 2018, from http://www.abs.gov.au/ausstats/abs@.nsf/Latestproducts/5B4A9042741FA657CA257AD9000E283D?opendocument

Australia Football League (AFL). (2017). *Australian Football League annual report*. Retrieved 31 October 2018, from https://indd.adobe.com/view/3dab2f7a-5539-4c78-a88e-76d91cea5788

Australian Sports Commission (ASC). (2015). *Mandatory sports governance principles*. Canberra: Author.

Britton, D. M., & Logan, L. (2008). Gendered organizations: Progress and prospects. *Sociology Compass*, *2*(1), 107–121.

Burton, L. J. (2015). Underrepresentation of women in sport leadership: A review of research. *Sport Management Review*, *18*, 155–165.

Carter, N., Joy, L., & Wagner, H. M. (2007). The bottom line: Corporate performance and women's representation on boards (2004–2008). *The Catalyst*. Retrieved 31 October 2018, from https://www.catalyst.org/system/files/The_Bottom_Line_Corporate_Performance_and_Womens_Representation_on_Boards.pdf

Catalyst. (2017). *Quick take: Statistical overview of women in the workplace*. New York: Author.

Claringbould, I., & Knoppers, A. (2007). Finding a 'normal' woman: Selection processes for board membership. *Sex Roles*, *56*, 495–507.

Claringbould, I., & Knoppers, A. (2008). Doing and undoing gender in sport governance. *Sex Roles*, *58*, 81–92.

Commonwealth Secretariat. (2013). *Gender differences in leadership styles and the impact within corporate boards*. Retrieved 12 July 2018, from http://www.cpahq.org/cpahq/cpadocs/Genderdiffe.pdf

Cricket Australia. (2017). *Financial report for the financial year ended June 30, 2017*. Retrieved 31 October 2018, from https://www.cricketaustralia.com.au/about/annual-report/annual-report-16-17

Cunningham, G. B. (2009). Understanding the diversity-related change process: A field study. *Journal of Sport Management*, *23*, 407–428.

de Haan, D., & Dumbell, L. (2019). From the battlefield to the boardroom: The place of gender in sex-integrated sport. In N. Lough & A. N. Geurin (Eds.), *Handbook of the business of women's sport* (pp. 134–150). London: Routledge.

Ferkins, L., & Shilbury, D. (2012). Good boards are strategic: What does that mean for sport governance? *Journal of Sport Management*, *26*, 67–80.

Ferkins, L., Shilbury, D., & O'Boyle, I. (2018). Leadership in governance: Exploring collective board leadership in sport governance systems. *Sport Management Review*, *21*, 221–231.

Foucault, M. (1972). *Power/knowledge. Selected interviews and other writings. 1972–1977*. New York: Pantheon Books.

Fullagar, S. (2017). Post-qualitative inquiry and the new materialist turn: Implications for sport, health and physical culture research. *Qualitative Research in Sport, Exercise and Health*, *9*, 247–257.

Gatens, M. (1997). Corporeal representation in/and the body politic. In K. Conboy, N. Medina, & S. Stanbury (Eds.), *Writing on the body: Female embodiment and feminist theory. Columbia University Press* (pp. 80–89). New York: Columbia University Press

Geeraert, A., Alm, J., & Groll, M. (2014). Good governance in international sport organizations: An analysis of the 35 Olympic sport governing bodies. *International Journal of Sport Policy and Politics*, *6*, 281–306.

Gowthorp, L. (2018). *The National Sport Plan has ambitious ideas, but not enough specifics*. The Conversation. Retrieved 31 October 2018, from http://theconversation.com/the-national-sport-plan-has-ambitious-ideas-but-not-enough-specifics-100817

Grosz, E. (1994). *Volatile bodies*. Bloomington: Indiana University Press.

Hargreaves, J. A. (1990). Gender on the sports agenda. *International Review for the Sociology of Sport*, *25*, 287–307.

Hartarska, V., & Nadolnyak, D. (2012). Board size and diversity as governance mechanisms in community development loan funds in the USA. *Applied Economics*, *44*, 4313–4329.

Hess, R. (2017). Growth of women's football has been a 100-year revolution – it didn't happen overnight. *The Conversation* (Politics & Society). Retrieved 31 October 2018, from https://theconversation.com/growth-of-womens-football-has-been-a-100-year-revolution-it-didnt-happen-overnight-71989

Houlihan, B. (2002). *Sport, policy and politics: A comparative analysis.* London: Routledge.

Hovden, J., Elling, A., & Knoppers, A. (2018). Meta-analysis. In A. Elling, J. Hovden & A. Knoppers (Eds.), *Gender diversity in European sport governance* (pp. 179–191). London: Routledge.

Knoppers, A. (2016). Sociology of sport: The Netherlands. In K. Young (Ed.), *Sociology of sport: A global subdiscipline in Review* (pp. 245–263) (Research in the Sociology of Sport, Volume 9), Bingley, UK: Emerald Group Publishing Limited.

Knoppers, A., & Anthonissen, A. (2001). Meanings given to performance in Dutch sport organizations: Gender and racial subtexts. *Sociology of Sport Journal, 18,* 302–316.

Knoppers, A., Hovden, J., & Elling, A. (2018). Introduction. In A. Elling, J. Hovden & A. Knoppers, A. (Eds.), *Gender diversity in European sport governance* (pp. 3–10). London: Routledge.

Lapchick, R. (2016). *Gender report card: 2016 International sports report card on women in leadership roles.* The Institute for Diversity and Ethics in Sport, University of Central Florida, USA. Retrieved 25 October 2018, from www. tidesport. org/women-sleadershipin-international-sports. html

Leberman, S., & Burton, L. J. (2017). Why this book? Framing the conversation about women in sport leadership. In L. J. Burton & S. Leberman (Eds.), *Women in sport leadership: Research and practice for change* (pp. 1–15). London, UK: Routledge.

Lenkić, B., & Hess, R. (2016). *Play on! The hidden history of women's Australian rules football.* Melbourne: Echo Publishing.

Martin, P. Y. (2003). "Said and done" versus "saying and doing" gendering practices, practicing gender at work. *Gender & Society, 17,* 342–366.

NRL. (2017). *Before/beyond, annual report.* Retrieved 31 October 2018, from https://www.nrl.com/siteassets/documents/nrl-annual-report-2017.pdf

Pavlidis, A., & Fullagar, S. (2014). *Sport, gender and power: The rise of roller derby.* London: Routledge.

Pippos, A. (2017). *Breaking the mould.* Melbourne: Affirm Press.

Pletzer, J. L., Nikolova, R., Kedzior, K. K., & Voelpel, S. C. (2015). Does gender matter? Female representation on corporate boards and firm financial performance - A meta-analysis. *PLOS ONE, 10*(6), e0130005. doi:10.1371/journal.pone.0130005

Rubin, L. M., & Lough, N. L. (2015). Perspectives of Title IX pioneers: Equity, equality and need. *Journal of Intercollegiate Sport, 8,* 109–130.

Ryan, I., & Dickson, G. (2018). The invisible norm: An exploration of the intersections of sport, gender and leadership. *Leadership, 14,* 329–346.

Scraton, S., & Flintoff, A. (2002). Sport feminism: The contribution of feminist thought to our understandings of gender and sport. In S. Scraton & A. Flintoff (Eds.), *Gender and sport: A reader* (pp. 30–46). London: Routledge.

Shaw, S., & Slack, T. (2002). 'It's been like that for donkey's years': The construction of gender relations and the cultures of sports organizations. *Sport in Society, 5,* 86–106.

Sibson, R. (2010). "I was banging my head against a brick wall": Exclusionary power and the gendering of sport organizations. *Journal of Sport Management, 24,* 379–399.

Smart, B. (2007). Not playing around: Global capitalism, modern sport and consumer culture. *Global Networks, 7,* 113–134.

Soares, R., Marquis, C., & Lee, M. (2011). Gender and corporate social responsibility: It's a Matter of sustainability. *The Catalyst.* Retrieved 31 October 2018, from https://www.catalyst.org/system/files/gender_and_corporate_social_responsibility.pdf

Sotiriadou, P., & de Haan, D. (2019). Women and leadership: Advancing gender equity policies in sport leadership through sport governance. *International Journal of Sport Policy and Politics, 11,* 365–383.

Sotiriadou, P., de Haan, D., & Knoppers, A. (2017a, May 31–June 4). Rocking the boat? Changing the underrepresentation of women in sport governance. NASSM Conference Orlando Florida. Retrieved 25 October 2018, from https://www.nassm.org/files/conf_abstracts/2017-032.pdf

Sotiriadou, P., de Haan, D., & Knoppers, A. (2017b). *Understanding and redefining the role of men in achieving gender equality and equity in sport leadership/governance.* Research report to the IOC, Advanced research award programme 206/17. Lausanne, Switzerland: The Olympic Studies Centre. Retrieved 25 October 2018, from https://library.olympic.org/Default/doc/SYRACUSE/171304/understanding-and-redefining-the-role-of-men-in-achieving-gender-equity-in-sport-leadership-popi-so

Toohey, K. M., Taylor, T. L., & Vescio, J. A. (1999). An exploration of sports participation by girls from non-English speaking backgrounds. *ACHPER Australia Healthy Lifestyles Journal, 46*(2–3), 14–19.

Toffoletti, K. (2017). *Women sport fans: Identification, participation, representation*. London: Routledge.

United Nations Population Fund (UNPF). (2017). Gender equality and equity: A summary review of UNESCO's accomplishments since the Fourth World Conference on Women (Beijing 1995). Retrieved 31 October 2018, from http://unesdoc.unesco.org/images/0012/001211/121145e.pdf

Victoria State Government. (2010). Victorian Legislation and Parliamentary Documents. Version No. 059 Equal Opportunity Act 1995 No. 42 of 1995.

Wearing, B. (1998). *Leisure and feminist theory*. Thousand Oaks, CA: Sage.

Wedgwood, N. (2005). Doin' it for themselves! A case study of the development of a women's Australian Rules Football Competition. *The International Journal of the History of Sport, 22*, 396–414.

Welty Peachey, J. W., Zhou, Y., Damon, Z. J., & Burton, L. J. (2015). Forty years of leadership research in sport management: A review, synthesis, and conceptual framework. *Journal of Sport Management, 29*, 570–587.

Wilson, C. (2012). Meet the AFL commissioners. *The Age*. Retrieved 31 October, from https://www.theage.com.au/sport/afl/meet-the-afl-commissioners-20121019-27xau.html

Women in Sport. (2015). *Trophy women? 2015: No more board games*. Retrieved 31 October 2018, from https://www.womeninsport.org/wp-content/uploads/2015/11/FINAL_report_Trophy-Women_November-2015.pdf?938151

Wood, R. (2013). *Building a business case for gender diversity*. Melbourne VIC: Centre for Ethical Leadership. University of Melbourne.

Woodward, K. (2016). *Embodied sporting practices: Regulating and regulatory bodies*. London: Springer.

27

The social responsibilities of sport governing bodies and the role of sport governance

Jonathan Robertson, Rochelle Eime and Hans Westerbeek

Introduction

Social responsibility is defined as the "responsibility of an organisation for the impacts of its decisions and activities on society" (International Standards Organisation, 2010, p. 3). For an organisation to behave in a socially responsible manner, it must meet minimal behavioural standards expected by society by not causing harm to the organisation's stakeholders and rectifying any harm caused once it is identified (Campbell, 2007). National sport organisations (NSOs) have been defined as overseeing the "administration, financing and strategic development of their sport at the national level" (Kennelly & Toohey, 2014, p. 408). They rely on a "mixture of paid professional staff and volunteers…[and] exist to serve their membership and advance their sport in their place of operation" (Naraine & Parent, 2016, p. 142) and "develop their sport from the grassroots to an elite level…operate under government funding and are regarded as not-for-profit organisations" (Abeza & O'Reilly, 2014, p. 104). Given the centrality of the decision-making power of NSOs within federated sport systems and the subsequent influence of non-executive directors overseeing NSOs, it is important to understand the influence of sport governance practices on the social impact of NSOs and the broader federated sport system.

Over the past decade, NSOs have come under increasing public scrutiny for a range of social issues related to participation at the community and elite levels. Some of these issues are occupational health and safety (e.g., concussion); regulating gender norms and ideologies (e.g., intersex and transgender athletes); the protection of minors (e.g., coaching accreditation and police background checks) and corruption (e.g., match fixing). Such social issues are magnified given the substantial public interest in sport, public subsidy (e.g., state funding) and legislative assistance (e.g., antitrust laws, tax exemptions) that NSOs are afforded by society based on the assumption that management of a sport is in society's best interests. Viewed from this perspective, NSOs, like any organisation, have certain responsibilities to the society in which they operate; however, the exact nature of what that is has not been investigated or defined.

The board of directors of an NSO oversees, and is ultimately responsible for, the performance and impact of the organisation. Sport governance enacted by a board of directors, therefore, can be considered the ability "to steer an organisation and to make decisions that are consequential, strategic and impactful, usually on the behalf of others" (Shilbury, Ferkins & Smythe, 2013, p. 349).

The board of directors is often a collective of individuals who volunteer their time and are responsible for providing foresight, oversight and insight to management (Robertson, Walzel & Shilbury, 2019). Material breaches of social expectations of responsible behaviour may be considered a failure of effective governance *oversight*. As Carroll (1979) noted, "as the times change, so does emphasis on the range of social issues business must address" (p. 501); consequently, *foresight* is an important governance function to mitigate risks associated with changing social mores. Finally, *insight* is the "intangible director skill required to balance a raft of competing priorities and to synthesize large amounts of information" (Robertson, Walzel & Shilbury, 2019, p. 121), and this is required to choose between competing alternatives and the extent to which an NSO chooses to proactively engage in socially responsible activities.

Socially responsible governance requires the board of directors to consider the scope of social issues and the extent to which the NSO can and should take responsibility to deliver on those issues. Counterintuitively, this may require an NSO to narrow the scope to those issues that materially impact the organisation for which they are responsible. In other words, to do less better. This approach builds on Campbell's (2007) conception of social responsibility that requires organisations to "not knowingly do anything that could harm their stakeholders…and rectify it whenever the harm is discovered and brought to their attention" (p. 951). The role of governance in the first instance can be thought of as akin to mitigating implicit risks that are often considered to be obvious when stated plainly. This may be because behaviours have been institutionalised within a given setting and go unquestioned, or there are assumptions of good behaviour in lieu of appropriate checks and balances. Sport is replete with such breaches (e.g., corruption, concussion, child abuse, doping for but a few examples). Consequently, it is the role of the board to set the organisational appetite for socially responsible behaviours and risk mitigation.

So where does this leave NSOs and directors regarding their social contract with society? Like all contracts, a contract delimits the scope of available options and specifies the responsibilities of both parties. In this case, society is generally considered responsible for funding, patronising and participating in sport. In return, NSOs are traditionally responsible for the governance and management of the sport delivery system. However, a singular focus on the delivery of sport increasingly seems a limiting remit for NSOs. Considerations for ethics, the environment, inclusion, safety and integrity are prevalent amongst an array of competing demands from NSO stakeholders. In many post-industrial western economies, funding requirements are increasingly reflective of changing social expectations.

Sport Australia (formerly the Australian Sport Commission) provides an illustrative example. In 2018, *Sport Australia* released a plan entitled *Sport 2030*, outlining four strategic priorities for the coming decade in the areas of physical activity, sporting success, integrity and economic impact of sport (Sport Australia, 2018). A stronger focus on social outcomes of sport, as evidenced by inclusion of integrity and physical activity, relative to the traditional pillars of elite performance and community-level participation signals a strategic shift or, more accurately, an expansion of the social remit of sport within federal sport policy. The broader strategic tasks set by the central funding body in return for NSOs to continue being a recipient of government funding means that the scope of their responsibilities to society must increase to meet these changing social and governmental expectations.

The corporate sector faced similar challenges to their ongoing legitimacy in the 1960s and 1970s. Davis (1973) neatly summed up this position in his now infamous *iron law of responsibility* stating that "in the long run, those who do not use power in a manner that society considers responsible will tend to lose it" (p. 314). On the back of significant professionalisation and commercialisation over the past four decades, sport and the organisations that govern it, are starting to face similar societal pressures as corporations in the 1970s. Hence, if NSOs continue to want to be seen as legitimate social actors and retain the power to govern sport, they will have to extend their governance structures and operate transparently in a way that society deems appropriate. Nearly four decades after the legitimate behaviour of corporations was called into question (Carroll, 1979), it appears similar pressures are beginning to be applied to NSOs (Pope, Bromley, Lin & Meyer, 2018). This chapter therefore draws on the results of a study that aimed to determine the responsibilities of NSOs regarding the impact of their decisions and activities on society and also to understand the influence of sport governance structures on social responsibility at the institutional level.

Method

This research surveyed a range of academic and industry experts using the Delphi method. The purpose of this method is to generate expert consensus from a wide range of viewpoints on a particular topic (Martino, 1983). The Delphi method has been used to better understand a wide range of issues including: Health promotion in community sport organisations (Kelly et al., 2013); environmental responsibility in sport facilities (Mallen, Adams, Stevens & Thompson, 2010) and the future of the sport management field (Costa, 2005). This study included 56 experts from 12 countries, including 33 senior academics (professor, associate professor) and 23 senior managers/directors of NSOs. The expert panel represented 32 universities and 14 different sports (Table 27.1).

The expert panel were asked to review social responsibility items in three iterative surveys that were distributed over the course of three months. The survey items were developed from the *Global Reporting Initiative 3.1 - International Sustainability Reporting Standards* (Global Reporting Initiative, 2011), the International Standards Organisation (ISO) *ISO 26000 Guidance on Social Responsibility* (International Standards Organisation, 2010) and an extensive review of the social responsibility in sport literature. The social responsibility items were mapped into seven dimensions, namely product responsibility, governance, economic, human rights, labour practices, community development and the environment.

Table 27.1 Expert panel

	Academic (n = 33)	Industry (n = 23)
Gender	13 female, 20 male	5 female, 18 male
Position	24 full professors, nine associate professors	18 executive managers, 5 middle managers
Organisation	United States (13); Canada (9); United Kingdom (4); Australia (2); Germany (1); Greece (1); Netherlands (1); New Zealand (1); Norway (1)	Australia (5); New Zealand (5); United Kingdom (3); South Africa (3); Canada (2); USA (2); Finland (1); Netherlands (1); Singapore (1)
Broad topic areas/ sports governed	Race, gender, economics, organisational studies, marketing, ethnicity, management, physical activity, policy, volunteerism, sociology, community development, diversity, governance, inequality, culture, sponsorship	Basketball, handball, hockey, netball, rugby league, rugby union, softball, soccer, squash, swimming, table tennis, tennis, volleyball, water polo

The Delphi method consisted of three sequential survey rounds (Robertson, 2016). The first and second round aimed to generate consensus among the expert group, whilst the third round aimed to discriminate between the most important social responsibility issues that had reached consensus. Each survey round had both Likert scaled and open-ended questions and asked experts to rank social responsibility items on a five-point Likert scale of importance (from very low to very high importance) (see Table 27.2). Eight additional items were identified as important in the first round and subsequently included for ranking in the second round. Additionally, those items on which no consensus was reached were redistributed to the panel to be reconsidered. The third round aimed to discriminate between the highest social responsibility priorities for an NSO identified in the previous two rounds. Panel members were asked to identify their five highest social responsibility priorities for an NSO. Based on this data each social responsibility item was ranked from the highest perceived social responsibility priority for the organisation to the lowest.

Determining the scope of social responsibility: What do Boards of Directors need to consider?

The scope of an NSO's social responsibility was conceptualised at two levels. First is the organisational level, which considers the direct social impacts of the decisions made by the board of directors and senior management on the organisation and its staff. This discussion proceeds by considering the *relative* importance of seven social responsibility areas that directors need to consider, namely product responsibility, governance, economic, human rights, labour practices, community development and the environment. Second is the institutional level responsibilities, which account for the indirect social impacts that decisions made within NSOs have as they reverberate throughout the sport system they govern. This section discusses the broader social impacts that NSOs can have via (de)regulating types of pro- and anti-social behaviours and normalising shared understandings of what is and is not acceptable within a given sport (see Figure 27.1).

Organisational level responsibility and the Board of Directors

Five of the seven areas of organisational responsibility were considered central to the social responsibility considerations of the NSO (product responsibility, governance, economic, human rights, labour practices). These issues are generally related to the fulfillment of the core sport product in a safe and inclusive manner. In contrast to the majority of social responsibility literature, community programs and environmental activities were considered discretionary and of lower importance *relative to core operational functions*. Table 27.2 shows those social responsibilities considered most important for an NSO to fulfil.

Responsibility for the sport product. This was included as an item on the basis that it is oftentimes overlooked in social responsibility research that may seek to include a range of activities into the perceived social responsibility of an organisation. The highest priority for an NSO was to maximise participation in the sport they govern. The expert panel identified that maximising participation in the sport by "promoting sport as widely and actively as possible" (Participant 1, Sport Management Professor, United Kingdom) was a central function of responsible NSO practice. Part of the social responsibility discourse for NSO boards should be to make the implicit explicit. For the board of directors, this may mean consistently monitoring programs that seem intuitively obvious when explicitly stated, such as participation growth and retention over the lifespan. NSOs are constitutionally bound to proliferate their sport within a

Table 27.2 List of social responsibilities perceived as most important to an NSO

Perceived organisational priority	Weighted R3 mean	Round 2 (n)	Social responsibility item	Social responsibility dimension
1	6.54	49	Maximise participation in the sport	Product responsibility
2	6.08	49	Ensure the appropriate organisational governance frameworks are in place to effectively identify and manage the organisation's social objectives	Governance
3	5.68	49	Ensure financial viability	Economic
4	5.57	48	Create an accessible and inclusive sport setting	Human rights
5	5.23	49	Safeguard individuals from potential harm by assuring people in positions of trust have gone through relevant background checks and possess appropriate training	Labour practices
6	5.2	47	Develop equality and diversity resources to implement within the sport	Human rights
7	5.09	49	Complying with relevant equity and anti-discrimination legislation	Human rights
8	4.96	48	Ensure fiscal responsibility to owners/ members	Economic
9	4.92	49	Publicly stating social goals and performance indicators	Governance
10	4.87	49	Actively promote anti-corruption practices that support the 'uncertainty of outcome' within a sporting contest and/or the organisation's integrity	Product responsibility
11	4.81	49	Raise awareness of social issues within the organisation's sphere of influence	Governance
12	4.78	48	Develop and implement injury prevention strategies for players and officials	Labour practices
13	4.74	49	Ensure disability inclusion and equity standards	Human rights
14	4.7	49	Ensure gender inclusion and equity standards	Human rights
15	4.67	49	Ensuring up to date occupational health and safety standards and procedures	Labour practices
16	4.67	48	Setting social equality policies and procedures	Governance

(Continued)

Table 27.2 Continued

Perceived organisational priority	Weighted R3 mean	Round 2 (n)	Social responsibility item	Social responsibility dimension
17	4.65	47	Ensure the organisation is an equal opportunity employer	Human rights
18	4.51	49	Guarantee data protection and privacy	Labour practices
19	4.44	49	Provide personal development and training opportunities for staff and members	Labour practices
20	4.42	48	Maximise the use of the organisation's sports facilities	Community development
21	4.36	48	Actively abide by anti-competitive behaviour regulation to ensure fair competition within the organisation's market(s)	Product responsibility
22	4.19	49	Provide equitable access to disadvantaged groups through subsidies, access times, locations, etc.	Community development
23	4.14	48	Maximise volunteer participation	Labour practices
24	3.94	49	Abide by principles of environmental responsibility and sustainability	Environment
25	3.94	49	Prioritise on-field sporting success within the organisation	Product responsibility
26	3.92	49	Maximise health promotion opportunities for staff, volunteers and community	Community development
27	3.88	49	Actively identifying the organisational resource capacity for socially responsible programs	Governance
28	3.76	49	Provide community education opportunities	Community development
29	3.71	49	Contribute to increasing social capital and community cohesion through community involvement	Community development
30	3.71	48	Implement socially responsible procurement practices within the supply chain	Product responsibility
31	3.37	49	Overtly express the freedom to associate and collectively bargain	Labour practices
32	3.33	48	Maximise local investment, suppliers and employment	Community development
33	2.96	48	Contribute surplus resources to social benefit organisations that are not business-related	Community development

Figure 27.1 Organisational and institutional levels of social responsibility influenced by the board of directors.

given geography – it is their *raison d'etre*. Consequently, if an NSO was to do nothing else but safely delivering sport to its community in a sustainable manner, then it is meeting the objective function for its existence. Pragmatically, this provides guidance regarding the manner in which a board of directors can develop a socially responsible culture within an NSO by narrowing the scope of their perceived responsibility around the few actions that lead to the fulfilment of the primary purpose of the organisation, the provision of the sport product.

The safeguarding of uncertainty of outcome, is key to having a competitive sport (contest) product and central to the notion of "fairness" (Paul, Wachsman & Weinback, 2011), as such, dealing with corruption and the extent to which anti-competitive behaviour is allowed within sport were seen as another central aspect of managing the sport product. A central consideration for the board of directors of an NSO is, therefore, the extent to which they develop and implement mechanisms of competitive balance, such as hard vs soft salary cap, draft rules and concessions and a variety of decisions that may affect the notion of fairness (e.g., such as where finals are played). The effect of corruption and corruption allegations in the management of sport threatens its moral and financial integrity. The International Federation of Association Football (FIFA) for example, has lost several of its major sponsors, in part, due to recent corruption allegations, including Sony, Emirates and Johnson & Johnson. Corruption allegations at the organisational level raise questions about the (lack of) ability of such organisations to regulate corruption within their sport system. The development of transparent and accountable organisational practices and applicable legislation to address competitive balance and anti-corruption in sport is therefore considered a key component of a national sport organisation's responsibility to society.

Governance. Understandably effective governance was perceived to be a key area of responsibility for the NSO and its board of directors. The results indicated that areas such as governance frameworks, equality and diversity resources, publicly stating social goals, raising awareness of social issues and setting social equality policies and procedures were important social issues for an NSO to consider as part of its organisational governance. In principle, the board of directors oversees the responsible management of an NSO via governance practices and policies that compel management to operate within a given scope. The ISO 26000 stated that "organisational governance is the most crucial factor in enabling an organisation to take responsibility for the impacts of its decisions and activities and to integrate social responsibility throughout the organisation and its relationships" (International Standards Organisation, 2010, pp. 21–22). The capacity for delivering organisational responsibility is predicated on the capability of the board and management to develop and deliver on such actions.

At the organisational level, the board of directors sets the appetite for social responsibility practice within the NSO. Within this domain, participants had a number of suggestions regarding how a board of directors could implement socially responsible governance practices including "developing a programme of awareness raising" (Participant 16, Sport Management Professor, UK); "provide educational programmes for staff, players, participants" (Participant 20, CEO, New Zealand NSO) and "review the governance structure, management decisions, policies and procedures to ensure they include social objectives" (Participant 7, Sport Management Professor, Canada). These actions align with what Robertson, Walzel and Shilbury (2019) identify as an integrative approach in which "social responsibility is the responsibility of the whole organization that starts with the board of directors" (p. 127). In this case, the board of directors is manifestly responsible for setting the cultural parameters of (ir)responsible organisational behaviours (foresight), the type and nature of social issues to pursue (insight) and ongoing adherence to meeting organisational objectives in a socially responsible way (oversight).

Economic responsibilities. Results indicated that within the economic dimension, the items of financial viability (third highest) and fiscal responsibility to members (eighth highest) remained important elements of the organisational responsibility of an NSO. Ensuring financial viability and fiscal responsibility to members aligns with the concept of social performance (Carroll, 1979). Within NSOs sound financial management, overseen by the board of directors, facilitates the ongoing attainment of the organisation's objectives. Participants identified standard financial management and accounting practices be implemented as part of the board of directors due diligence and fiduciary responsibilities as directors of the organisation including "long-term budgets and forecasting" (Participant 21, CEO, New Zealand NSO); "annual published financial targets and accounts and policies that support modest expenditure by Board and staff" (Participant 20, CEO, New Zealand CEO); and "establish revenue-generating systems, make sure expenditures do not exceed revenues" (Participant 12, Sport Management Professor, United States). Whilst such measures are intuitively obvious, sound financial management is far from universal in sport governance. In the German context, Wicker and Breuer (2014) investigated the financial condition of 1080 sport governing bodies. They found that only 72.4% of German governing bodies could break even in 2011, and revenue diversification was higher in NSOs than other industrial sectors. Furthermore, the researchers found that strategic actions such as revenue diversification, hosting major events and cost optimisation may improve the financial position of an NSO (Wicker & Breuer, 2014). Improving the financial position is congruent with the social responsibility literature that suggests "all other responsibilities are predicated upon economic responsibilities, because without it the others become moot considerations" (Carroll, 2012, p. 8). Like all organisations, pragmatic financial management by the NSOs management, overseen by the board of directors, is required to produce and allocate appropriate resources to facilitate the achievement of the organisation's objectives and social responsibilities.

Human rights. NSOs are also becoming increasingly responsible for protecting the human rights of individuals within their sport. All six indicators were perceived as highly important for an NSO to address including creating an inclusive environment, complying with anti-discrimination legislation, ensuring inclusion and equity on the basis of ability and ensuring equal opportunity employment both within the NSO itself and within the broader sport institution. Within this domain, NSOs are required to create an accessible and inclusive environment that is non-discriminatory towards diverse social groups. For example, NSOs establish how breaches of human rights are arbitrated rather than deferring to a human rights commission; produce gender, transgender and intersex definitions that establish the parameters for gender inclusivity; fund or support the upgrading of facilities to be accessible to persons with disabilities; and, oftentimes, create inclusion programs and policies to be implemented throughout the sport system. The implementation of inclusion strategies and the presence of inclusion statements could be seen as a measure of the degree to which an NSO can/will act in a socially responsible manner. Conceptually, the board of directors could consider a tool, such as the "inclusion spectrum", that integrates people with a disability into sport participation on a continuum from full and modified forms of integration to parallel, adapted and discrete forms of the sporting activity (Misener & Darcy, 2014).

Labour practices. At the organisational level, the responsibility of NSOs to assure equitable labour practices was similar to other organisations. Participants identified the need to "appoint or contract a [health and safety] professional" (Participant 47, CEO, New Zealand NSO) and to "proactively exceed the minimum requirements and stand for this" (Participant 48, Senior Manager, Australian NSO), to be able to work within a safe working environment. In that regard, an NSO has a responsibility to hire and manage paid staff and volunteers under similar labour and human resource management systems as profit-orientated organisations. However, in Australian state sport governing bodies, paid staff were identified as operating under more formal human resource management systems than volunteers and, in general, state sporting bodies "deployed human resource management in a relatively unsophisticated way" (Taylor & McGraw, 2006, p. 247). Striking a balance between internal (organisational) and external (institutional) human resource and labour management systems, in combination with (in)directly working with a dual paid and voluntary labour force, presents unique responsibility challenges for an NSO. NSOs therefore possess dual responsibilities internally to effectively manage both paid staff and volunteers; and, externally to ensure appropriate policies are developed for organisations that fall under its governance to do the same.

Community development. The expert panel was divided over the importance of the community development dimension. Maximising and providing equitable access to sporting facilities were considered of moderate importance but five of the lowest eight priorities came from the community development dimension including, volunteer participation, philanthropy and promoting health and educating and investing in local communities. The participants perceived the community involvement of the NSO as relatively indirect. Unlike existing perceptions of philanthropic activities in the community (e.g., professional staff volunteering in communities), the community benefit delivered by NSOs is implicit in the everyday delivery of sport to participants. Philanthropy in the form of "contributing surplus resources to social benefit organisations that are not business-related" was the lowest priority identified by participants. This is a major difference from existing literature. Philanthropy is not considered important in the way experts construct social responsibility for NSOs. The responsibilities of an NSO should focus on matters such as human rights, governance, labour practices and fair operating practices in an economically responsible way before dealing with non-core business activities, such as overt community development.

Environment. The level of importance for an NSO to abide by principles of environmental responsibility and sustainability was different compared to literature on social responsibility in sport. Respondents identified it as moderately important, whereas, in the literature, environment and sustainability feature highly on the list of corporate social responsibilities. Whilst it is understood that social responsibilities may be achieved simultaneously, the results indicate that participants perceived it to be a lower priority than many operational and ethical considerations. Furthermore, lower normative pressures associated with a lower public profile of NSOs in comparison to elite sport teams and large multinational corporations may place less pressure on these organisations to demonstrate their environmental responsibility. There is further scope for investigating environmental responsibility in national sport organisations. Critically, our research has demonstrated that environmental responsibility may be less of a priority for organisations when competing interests are considered.

Institutional level responsibilities of an NSO

In this section it is argued that NSOs also have responsibilities that extend beyond the organisational boundaries of the NSO itself. The level of responsibility of an NSO may be influenced by the impact that NSO-specific policies have on society. In this sense, it is conceptualised that NSOs possess responsibilities that extend more broadly into and across the federated sport system (e.g., concussion policies). For the purpose of clarity, here we identify the federated sport system of a given sport (e.g., tennis), within a given geography (e.g., Australia) as an organisational field consisting of "those organisations that, in the aggregate, constitute a recognised area of institutional life: Key suppliers, resource and product consumers, regulatory agencies and other organisations that produce similar services or products" (DiMaggio & Powell, 1983, p. 148). To this end, it is conceptualised that regulative actions of an NSO implicitly and explicitly influence member associations operating within the organisational field. As these responsibilities exist at the institutional level of analysis, as opposed to the organisational or individual level of analysis, these responsibilities are referred to as "institutional responsibilities" of NSOs to the broader sport environment and are classified into two categories, namely regulative and normative responsibilities.

Regulative responsibilities

According to Scott (1995), the regulative function of institutions refers to "rule-setting, monitoring and sanctioning activities…regulative processes involved the capacity to establish rules, inspect or review others' conformity to them and as necessary, manipulate sanctions – rewards and punishments – in an attempt to influence future behaviour" (p. 35). Combining this with this chapter's working definition of social responsibility as "responsibility of an organisation for the impacts of its decisions and activities on society and the environment" (International Standards Organisation, 2010, p. 3), regulative responsibilities of NSOs therefore constitute the responsibility of an NSO for the impacts of the rules, conformity and sanctions it imposes on the broader sport system that it governs.

This dimension relates directly to coercive institutional pressures NSOs can apply to organisations it governs to collaboratively maintain and enhance integrity within the sport. Typically, regulative pressures come from outside the organisation such as from government or regulatory agencies (Scott, 1995). Conversely, in this case, a regulatory agency (i.e., the NSO) *is* the object of study and the way in which NSOs regulate, or choose not to regulate, areas of social behaviour become part of the concept of responsibility. In other words, it would be socially and morally irresponsible for an NSO not to act when corruption behaviour is detected in a team that operates under the regulation of an NSO. As one participant described, "without integrity, nothing will work effectively…institutionalised procedures are crucial" (Participant 5, Sport Sociology Professor, United States).

Relative to state legislation, regulative responsibilities for NSOs may impede or enable the extent to which actions are socially accepted within the institution of sport. Rule 46 in the National Hockey League rulebook regulates "fighting", the punishments for which are significantly less than in the workplace in which an individual would be arrested and charged with a legal misdemeanour, such as assault (NHL, 2015). Regulative responsibilities in this domain impede what is socially accepted in society and could be detrimental to the health of sport participants (e.g., concussion). Violence is more socially accepted on the ice hockey rink than on the street. Conversely, regulative responsibilities may enable prosocial behaviours to a higher degree than can be legislated by the state. Recognising the underrepresentation of females in positions of decision-making power (i.e., NSO board representation) *Sport Australia* regulated that NSO boards were required to demonstrate 40 percent female board member representation in order to receive funding. These actions enabled prosocial actions to be taken towards gender equity in the Australian sport system at a time that similar actions were not yet institutionalised via state legislation. The examples of fighting and gender equity demonstrate that the regulative responsibility of NSOs is a relative concept, on the one hand regulation in the form of rules and sanctions can impede the promotion of responsible behaviour, whilst simultaneously, in alternative social domains, prosocial behaviours can be enhanced via regulation created in NSOs.

Future research may investigate a number of premises that base the social responsibility of an NSO not only on an audit of the internal actions, but on an audit of the rules/policies it enacts and the associated sanctions. Does the NSO regulate regarding concussion, anti-discrimination, equitable access, fighting/violence? What are the impacts of these policies on society? What responsibility does an NSO have for negating or promoting such social issues within its domain? A logical extension of such lines of enquiry may be to investigate how effectively such policies are implemented at the local club level where policy implementation and scarcity of resources collide (Donaldson, Leggett & Finch, 2012).

Normative responsibilities

According to Scott (1995), the normative pillar of institutions refers to normative systems that "define goals or objectives (e.g., winning the game or making a profit) but also designate the appropriate ways to pursue them (e.g., conceptions of fair business practices)" (p. 37). For NSOs, normative systems consist of values that are underpinned by norms to achieve these values. NSOs are charged with the responsibility to manage sport based on principles/values such as uncertainty of outcome (e.g., sport is an equal playing field). The pursuit of uncertainty of sporting outcomes normalises further regulative responsibilities that are contrary to those that are socially acceptable outside the institution of sport, such as restricting player movements (trade), randomising the assignment of human resources (draft) and capping the available financial resources (salary cap). Consequently, normative responsibilities are generally deeply embedded within the fabric of the institution and are based on goals and objectives that NSOs set.

From a responsibility perspective, NSOs set the terms of reference, beyond explicit regulation, for what is accepted and not accepted behaviour within the sport institution that they govern. For example, whilst shaking an opponent's hand following a game is not regulated by an NSO, the organisation sets the normative conditions for such an action to become an unwritten rule (i.e., a socially expected norm of good sportsmanship and fair play). Although an NSO does not have sanctioning power if a player does not adhere to this norm, it is likely to be informally sanctioned by individuals within a team structure. At the national level, it is suggested

391

NSOs are responsible for the systematic construction of normative expectations that can be deeply embedded within sport. For example, whilst conformity to eliminating discriminatory behaviours is both legislated and regulated against in the form of rules and sanctions, proactive behaviours to produce inclusive environments, advocate on behalf of social causes and engage in the community are not. Ultimately, normative responsibilities complement regulative responsibilities to outline the means by which NSOs can achieve their desired goals.

NSOs most often pursue dual goals, elite sporting success and maximising mass participation. By further outlining appropriate means to achieve these goals (e.g., junior "taster" programs, inclusive positioning, high-performance centres), NSOs set normative expectations within the institution they govern. The central normative responsibility identified by an NSO was the maximisation of participation. Future research could focus on what are the longitudinal implications of shifting sport goals between elite sport success and mass participation. For example, if the funding for NSOs is justified on the basis that it is a public good, but the majority of funding accrues to the development of a few elite athletes, at the expense of the many whom consume amateur sport, is this a responsible way to spend taxpayer money? Framed differently, if the premise that sport is beneficial to population health, via normalising physical activity in the form of community sport, does it not hold that diverting funding away from this domain to an elite few is institutionally irresponsible for those in positions of decision-making power?

Discussion and conclusion

Socially irresponsible behaviour, or breaches in communities' expectations of what are the social responsibilities of sport organisations, have significantly compromised NSOs around the world. Simultaneously, such breaches have had considerable negative impacts on the health, wellbeing and careers of individual athletes. Concussion, long overlooked by the NFL and other contact sports has cost the sport over US$1 billion and arguably affected the long-term health of many of its players (Belson, 2014). Inaction and a lack of oversight in USA Gymnastics created an environment in which Larry Nassar was accused by more than 265 gymnasts for various forms of abuse and molestation, creating untold pain for those involved. In England, the Rugby Football Union dealt with 141 cases of misconduct involving adults and children in 2015–2016. The athletics world and other sporting codes, such as Australian Football, have had to challenge an ideological view of gender as a binary construct to accommodate athletes that fall outside binary conceptions of gender (i.e., intersex or transgender). Last, but not least, the Russian Federation has been plagued by cases of state-sponsored doping in various sporting domains. Not understanding or, worse, avoiding one's social responsibilities, is of consequence, because it impacts on the individuals involved in the sport and can potentially impair the reputation, finances and culture of an NSO.

This chapter offers two main directions for future research. The first positions this research within the broader shift towards organisational responsibilities that apply across sector boundaries (i.e., to nonprofits, government, etc.) and are not delimited to a corporate organisational form (Pope et al., 2018). Whilst substantial research on "corporate" social responsibility has occurred, research into the role non-executive directors can have in influencing social responsibility practices is currently lacking. Utilising integrative frameworks of socially responsible behaviour may go some way to challenge institutionalised norms and values at the intersection of sport governance and social issues. Explicit critique and empirical research of sports institutionalised, normative practices, coupled with pragmatic managerial tools, such as integrative social responsibility reporting, can have substantive implications within the sport industry. For example, explicitly applying a critical lens to the implied notion of "sport for good", may further enlighten the causes of a number of systemic failures in sport systems around child safety, concussion, corruption and health. Pragmatically, such knowledge could then be utilised by non-executive directors to set the parameters for socially responsible behaviours, processes and policies to be enacted by management.

The second future research direction offered by this chapter addresses the level of analysis of social responsibility research. Traditionally, social responsibility has been conceptualised at the organisational level of analysis (e.g., a corporation possesses a specific set of responsibilities). A specific contribution offered from this research is the conceptual expansion of social responsibility from the organisational level of analysis to the institutional level of analysis. Non-executive directors, via their collective oversight of the central regulator of a given sport system, set the normative and regulative parameters of socially responsible behaviour. For example, the introduction of a concussion policy is unlikely to influence the direct employees of a national sport organisation in their place of employment (e.g., the finance manager is unlikely to suffer concussion from producing the annual report). However, the presence, or lack thereof, of a concussion policy throughout the sport system, from elite leagues down to modified youth sport, reverberate well beyond organisational boundaries and have substantive impacts on society (e.g., the avoidance of hundreds of thousands of concussive incidents). Of consequence to social responsibility research, this chapter suggests that the combination of centralised decision-making by non-executive directors, in combination with the systemic, exponential impact from these decisions places an emphasis on the need for future research to investigate social responsibility at an institutional level of analysis.

This research investigated social responsibilities obligations for NSOs and what is the influence of the governance of sport on their social responsibilities within the broader organisational field. Key findings from the research presented in this chapter indicated that NSOs are perceived to have a wide range of social responsibilities that include the appropriate management of the sport product (e.g., fair operation and participation within the game) as well as a range of economic, human rights, labour practices and governance responsibilities. Areas of environmental and community development were deemed lower priorities. A focus on well-governed, financially stable, inclusive and accessible sport participation opportunities contradicts much of the literature on social responsibility, which is framed around overt community actions such as philanthropy, community education and environmental activities as core to their social responsibilities. While these may be a part of the construction of social responsibility for some highly commercial organisations and leagues (e.g., major US sport leagues), for NSOs, the findings indicate social responsibilities are more implicitly linked to the core business. It is the implicit avoidance of harm (i.e., the health and safety of participants, anti-corruption and anti-discrimination policies and policing), rather than the explicit promotion of some loosely defined social good (i.e., community development) that defines the responsibility of an NSO.

In practice, NSOs receive significant public funding, hold regulative and normative power and directly influence society. With an increasing number of breaches in responsible behaviour, particularly in high-profile sport organisations, it is likely that the ongoing legitimacy of NSOs right to govern will continue to be called into question. It is recommended that directors audit and report on their organisational and institutional level responsibilities to better understand the social impact of their decisions both internally, and externally, to the NSO.

References

Abeza, G., & O'Reilly, N. (2014). Social media platforms' use in building stakeholder relationships. *Journal of Applied Sport Management, 6*(3), 103–126.

Belson, K. (2014, July 10). Altered N.F.L. settlement wins judge's approval. *The New York Times*. Retrieved from http://www.nytimes.com/2014/07/08/sports/football/judge-approves-preliminary-nfl-settlement. html

Campbell, J. L. (2007). Why would corporations behave in socially responsible ways? An institutional theory of corporate social responsibility. *Academy of Management Review, 32*, 946–967.

Carroll, A. B. (1979). A Three-dimensional conceptual model of corporate performance. *Academy of Management Review, 4*, 497–505.

Carroll, A. B. (2012). *A corporate social responsibility journey: Looking back, looking forward.* Paper presented at the 5th International Conference on CSR, Humboldt University, Berlin, Germany.

Costa, C. A. (2005). The status and future of sport management: A Delphi Study. *Journal of Sport Management, 19*, 117–142.

Davis, K. (1973). The case for and against business assumption of social responsibilities. *Academy of Management Journal, 16*, 312–322.

DiMaggio, P. J., & Powell, W. W. (1983). The iron cage revisited: Institutional isomorphism and collective rationality in organizational fields. *American Sociological Review, 48*(2), 147–160.

Donaldson, A., Leggett, S., & Finch, C. F. (2012). Sport policy development and implementation in context: Researching and understanding the perceptions of community end-users. *International Review for the Sociology of Sport, 47*, 743–760.

Global Reporting Initiative. (2011). *Sustainability reporting guidelines version 3.1.* Amsterdam, The Netherlands: Author.

International Standards Organisation. (2010). *ISO 26000 - Guidance on social responsibility.* Geneva, Switzerland: Author

Kennelly, M., & Toohey, K. (2014). Strategic alliances in sport tourism: National sport organisations and sport tour operators. *Sport Management Review, 17*, 407–418.

Kelly, B., King, L., Bauman, A. E., Baur, L. A., Macniven, R., Chapman, K., & Smith, B. J. (2013). Identifying important and feasible policies and actions for health at community sports clubs: A consensus-generating approach. *Journal of Science and Medicine in Sport, 17*(1), 61–66.

Mallen, C., Adams, L., Stevens, J., & Thompson, L. (2010). Environmental sustainability in sport facility management: A Delphi Study. *European Sport Management Quarterly, 10*, 367–389.

Martino, J. P. (1983). *Technological forecasting for decision-making* (2nd ed.). New York: Elsevier.

Misener, L., & Darcy, S. (2014). Managing disability sport: From athletes with disabilities to inclusive organisational perspectives. *Sport Management Review, 17*, 1–7.

Naraine, M., & Parent, M. (2016). "Birds of a feather": An institutional approach to Canadian national sport organizations' social-media Use. *International Journal of Sport Communication, 9*(2), 140–162.

NHL. (2015, July 15). *National hockey league official rules 2014–2015.* Retrieved from http://www.nhl.com/nhl/en/v3/ext/rules/2014-2015-rulebook.pdf

Paul, R., Wachsman, Y., & Weinbach, A. (2011). The role of uncertainty of outcome and scoring in the determination of fan satisfaction in the NFL. *Journal of Sports Economics, 12*, 213–221.

Pope, S., Bromley, P., Lim, A., & Meyer, J. (2018). The pyramid of nonprofit responsibility: The institutionalization of organizational responsibility across sectors. *Voluntas, 29*, 1300–1314.

Robertson, J. (2016). *Exploring the social responsibility of sport organisations* (Doctor of Philosophy). Victoria University, Melbourne.

Robertson, J., Walzel, S., & Shilbury, D. (2019). Intersections of governance and social responsibility in sport. In C. Anagnosopoulos & M. Winand, (Eds.), *Research handbook on sport governance* (pp. 118–132), Cheltenham Gloucestershire: Edward Elgar Publishing.

Scott, W. R. (1995). *Institutions and organizations.* Thousand Oaks, CA: Sage.

Shilbury, D., Ferkins, L., & Smythe, L. (2013). Sport governance encounters: Insights from lived experiences. *Sport Management Review, 16*, 349–363.

Sport Australia. (2018). *Sport 2030: Participation, performance, integrity, industry.* Canberra: Department of Health. Commonwealth of Australia.

Taylor, T., & McGraw, P. (2006). Exploring human resource management practices in nonprofit sport prganisations. *Sport Management Review, 9*, 229–251.

Wicker, P., & Breuer, C. (2014). Examining the financial condition of sport governing bodies: The effects of revenue diversification and organizational success factors. *Voluntas: International Journal of Voluntary & Nonprofit Organizations, 25*, 929–948.

28

Sport integrity systems

A proposed framework

Lisa A. Kihl

In our industry, nothing is more important than integrity. If we are to earn and retain the trust of the public, then our sport must not only be clean and fair, but also must be seen to be clean and fair. It is what sets us apart from illegal gambling operators. Going forward we need to strengthen education of all participants and work across borders with partners, sharing information and intelligence to combat our common foe and uphold the trust in our racing product.

—Kim Nag Soon, Chairman and Chief Executive Officer
Korea Racing Authority (*Asian Racing Federation, 2019*)

Importance of integrity in sport governing bodies

Integrity breaches are a consistent feature in national sport governing bodies. Both high profile and less notable cases involving corruption, such as those involving Russian state sponsored doping (McLaren, 2016), illegal gambling operators in horsing racing, or abusive behaviours reported by the Vermont high school hockey team members who participated in hazing (Farrey, 2018), illustrate that sporting integrity is a concern for local sport establishments as well as high performance sporting federations. Sport integrity violations encompass both non-corrupt and corrupt behaviours. For example, the United States Gymnastics Association and the United States Olympic Committee were both criticised for their fundamentally flawed processes to address sexual assault of athletes along with an organisational culture that valued reputations and winning over the safety of athletes. A recent Independent Review of Integrity in Tennis noted that, "tennis faces a serious integrity problem" (Lewis, Wilkinson & Henzelin, 2018, p. 2) as the sport lends itself to manipulation for betting purposes. Given the regularity and, in some cases, systematic nature of integrity violations across the sporting industry, critics have voiced their lack of confidence in the ability of sport governing bodies (SGB) to uphold standards of integrity. Constant occurrences of integrity violation across the sport industry and at all levels (e.g., community sport, intercollegiate athletics and professional sport have led to declarations, similar to Kim Nag Soon's of the importance of integrity in sport and the call to change the perception of sport competitions to one of fairness and cleanliness. This would require reform by means of an integrity system in order to restore the public's trust in sport. Sport governing boards play an important role in preventing integrity violations and institutionalising a sport integrity system.

Critics have called on SGBs to adopt various mechanisms to address integrity concerns in sport, such as the need for integrity management, honest competitions and outcomes, good governance, cultural change and national and international legislation. As a result, sport integrity has become a priority for many SGBs as well as national governments and/or international agencies to address specific forms (e.g., fraud and bribery) and types (e.g., match fixing, doping and event and/or sponsorship bribery) of corruption. Various integrity systems or governance frameworks to enhance the integrity of sport have been implemented though not necessarily by SGBs. For example, *The Sport Integrity Global Alliance (SIGA)* (2018) developed "Universal standards on sports betting integrity" to assist sport organisations in providing "a coordinated, holistic universal framework to protect the integrity of sport" (p. 1). The Australian government (2012) instituted the "National Integrity of Sport Unit" (NISU), which is responsible for "national oversight, monitoring and coordination of efforts to protect the integrity of sport" and preventing various forms and types of corruption (para. 1). International, national and state sport governing bodies (e.g., International Association of Athletics Federations, England Cricket Board, New South Wales Badminton) have also implemented integrity (or anti-corruption) units to assist in maintaining corrupt free sport, free from match fixing and doping. The Australia "Integrity in Sport" unit works in partnership with various government agencies to provide resources for national, state and local organisations to help build their "capacity and capability to provide safe, ethical and inclusive sporting environments" (Sport Australia, 2019, para. 1).

UK Sport has adopted a code of sport governance that involves realising five broad gold governance principles for sport organisations seeking government funding (UK Sport, 2019). Some national governing bodies (NGB's) have implemented specific integrity policies (e.g., SafeSport)[1] to prevent certain kinds of integrity breeches rather than an overarching system to enhance integrity more broadly. Such frameworks operate alongside existing institutions and policies such as government agencies, courts of arbitration, auditing bodies, education programs and codes of conduct. Arguably, all of these institutions and structures constitute a sport integrity system.

Pope (1996) argued, "the long-term success of integrity and anti-corruption depends on holistic rather than piecemeal reform" (p. 5). Sport Australia, UK Sport and the NISU seem to approach the protection of sport integrity in a broad manner that includes coordination, monitoring and national oversight. However, in many respects SGBs are in the nascent stages of conceptualising and developing an overarching effective sport integrity system for national governing bodies. Many research opportunities exist for determining methods to evaluate the effectiveness of an integrity system.

One of the aims of this chapter is to start a conversation on what such a sport integrity system would look like. In particular, the purpose of this chapter is to broaden an understanding of concepts of integrity in sport and to present a framework to conceptualise a sport integrity system. Public administration, legal and governance scholars have discussed, mapped and evaluated various national integrity systems (e.g., Head, Brown & Connors, 2008; Huberts, 2014; Six & Lawton, 2013). The proposed framework in this chapter draws from this scholarship and acknowledges the complexity in creating an integrity system that works. Despite this challenge, a sport integrity system is important for the integrity of SGBs and sport competitions to maintain the public's trust in sport. The next section discusses the meaning of integrity in sport as well as a range of violations that are considered integrity breaches. An understanding of a sport integrity system is presented followed by an overview of a proposed framework.

Integrity in sport: More than anti-corruption mechanisms

The terms "integrity in sport" or "sport integrity" are used ubiquitously throughout the sport industry. To conceptualise these two terms, a number of different perspectives are used that seem to vary based on context. In the broader literature there are several approaches used to conceptualise integrity. These approaches can be organised into two main perspectives. First, integrity as wholeness or consistency with values and behaviours over time (Huberts, 2014). Brown, Griffith University Key Centre for Ethics, Law, Justice and Governance & Transparency International, (2005) suggested 'integrity' is conceptually opposite to 'corruption', which "means decay, deterioration or perversion from an original or 'whole' state; in physical terms, corruption is 'the destruction or spoiling of anything, especially by *disintegration* …' (p. 9). In the context of understanding integrity in sport, this notion of integrity as the antithesis of corruption (e.g., doping, match fixing and hosts rights bribery) is dominant. Furthermore, integrity is perceived as a principle of good governance rather than a quality of sport and/or sport system. For example, Chappelet and Mrkonjic's (2013) *Better indicators for better governance in international sport* and the European Commission's (2019) pledge to good sport governance both list integrity as a principle to adhere to in seeking good sport governance. This chapter argues that sport governance is an internal element of an overarching sport integrity system. An integrity system is much broader and involves both internal and external mechanisms that seek integrity of an SGB.

In the second perspective, integrity reflects a moral perspective that emphasises right and wrong (i.e., a moral component) (Six, Bakker & Huberts, 2007). Integrity focuses on morals, norms and values that help determine right or wrong in different contexts (e.g., the administration of sport competitions, sport governance and sporting organisations. For example, sport integrity is conceived as individuals (i.e., sport stakeholders) upholding a range of moral values (e.g., honesty, sportspersonship, respect and trustworthiness) in fulfilling their sport organisational roles (professional responsibility) as well as within wider society (personal responsibility). In the specific context of sport, sport integrity has also been referred to as providing an inclusive, safe and fair environment. For example, Vanden Auweele (2015) defined integrity as "the reapplication of values and norms in sport practice such as wellness and well-being, fair play, solidarity and health that are generally promoted and considered positive" (p. 18). While sport philosophers have conceptualised sport integrity as a virtue upholding the ethos of the game (e.g., Archer, 2016; Zakhem & Mascio, 2018)

The meaning of sport integrity also incorporates both perspectives (i.e., wholeness and moral) where integrity relates to ensuring honest competitions and outcomes as well as management practices. For example, the Australian Sport Integrity Unit defined sport integrity as a "manifestation of the ethics and values which promote community confidence in sports" that is demonstrated by honest sport performances and administrative conduct (Australian Government, 2018, para. 1). The sport industry has yet to critically discuss and agree on a definition of integrity and has yet to clearly articulate and accept a common set of standards and practices (Gardiner, Parry & Robinson, 2017). Despite the absence of an agreed-upon understanding of the term, it seems apparent that integrity in sport represents a range of moral values and norms that sport stakeholders and organisations should uphold in different contexts such as sporting and administrative behaviors, decision-making and governance systems.

Based on these understandings of integrity in sport, it is clear that integrity is a multifaceted term that takes on different meanings depending on the level of the organisation and context. Integrity in sport involves both behavioural violations and integrity risks carried out by individuals, organisations and/or systems. Adapting from Molina (2016, 2018), sport integrity violations are actions taken by sport stakeholders that can undermine an SGB's integrity at various levels of governance. As noted previously, violations may involve illegal behaviours, but can also include conduct that is inconsistent with both an SGB and its respective member organisation's purposes and values. Integrity risks are comprised of conditions and behaviours within a sport system that increase its vulnerability to integrity violations.

Integrity in sport therefore has two connotations. First, competition encroachments where sport stakeholders fail to adhere to standards of competition (to the ethos of the sport itself) and to ensure that competition outcomes are the result of skill (and not manipulation). Second, integrity in sport concerns sporting administration carried out through various systems that both the public and sport stakeholders trust and by individuals who accept and maintain professional responsibility in the effective and efficient governing of sport. It is important to acknowledge and distinguish between individual and organisational forms of integrity (cf. Bauman, 2013; Erhard & Jensen, 2014) that occur within a system of sport governance. Integrity exists within individuals and organisations and understandings of integrity overlap and are intertwined with each context and through interrelated systems in the contexts of governing, delivering sport and competing in sport. From an individual/stakeholder perspective, integrity can mean representing a range of values (e.g., being incorruptible) or acting in accordance with laws and codes of exemplary moral behaviour and professional responsibility (Huberts, 2014). Organisational integrity is generally understood as a "condition in which an organisation functions in a manner that is consistent with the purposes and values for which it was created" (Molina, 2016, p. 6). Understanding the term "sport integrity system" and what features make it effective in preventing integrity violations and minimising integrity risks will greatly depend on how an SGB defines "integrity." Critical to establishing an SGB's understanding of integrity is engaging in initial stakeholder dialogue at individual and organisational levels that will assist with "owning authorship" (Gardiner et al., 2017, p. 10). Ongoing dialogue should also occur to discuss new meanings of integrity as novel events occur that could extend the original meaning of the term.

Types of sport integrity violations and risks

Integrity in sport is a widely used term in society. In developing a sport integrity system, it is important to identify potential integrity risks in a system as well as the types of violations that an integrity system is seeking to prevent. A starting point is to create a typology based on a framework founded on the morals, values and norms an SGB seeks to represent. Integrity in an SGB means sport stakeholders are acting in accordance with relevant morals, values and rules established by the SGB as well as with systems that function effectively to mitigate integrity risks.

A typology of sport integrity violations and risks is presented in Table 28.1. The typology is based on cases of violations and risks reported in the literature and media. Sport integrity violations in an SGB represent a wide range of illicit behaviours. Integrity violations in a sport integrity system concern actions in governance processes and sporting competitions that violate relevant moral values, norms and rules. Violations may involve bribery (e.g., match fixing, doping, money laundering and host rights bribery), fraud (e.g., salary cap breeches, election rigging, doping and embezzlement), conflict of interest (e.g., accepting gifts), favouritism (e.g., nepotism), misuse and manipulation of information (e.g., concealing information), indecent/illegal treatment of sport stakeholders (e.g., child trafficking and sexual harassment), waste and abuse of organisational resources (e.g., luxury travel and accommodations) and misconduct in private time (e.g., domestic violence). Several legal activities are considered integrity violations. Examples include off-the-field behaviours, such as conflict of interest, improper use of authority,

Table 28.1 Typology of sport integrity violations and risks

Integrity violations	Types
Bribery: Actively offering a bribe (e.g., gift or other inducement) or passively receiving a bribe.	Host rights to secure events Match and spot-fixing (betting and non-betting) Recruiting athletes Tanking
Fraud: "Involves some form of trickery, swindle or deceit" that can involve "a manipulation or distortion of information, facts and expertise" (Andvig & Fjeldstad, 2001, p. 9).	Academic fraud Doping Competing with ineligible athletes Embezzlement Election rigging Illegal transfers Illegal/irregular gambling Match-fixing Money laundering Nobbling Ring ins Salary cap breeches
Conflict of interest: An actual or perceived personal interest that comes into conflict with the interest of another party (Boatright, 1992, p. 189).	Accepting gifts Influence peddling Kickbacks Self-dealing
Favouritism: Misuse of authority or position to favour family (nepotism), friends (cronyism), or party (patronage).	Nepotism, cronyism, patronage
Misuse and manipulation of information: The intended or unintended abuse of (access to) information.	Breaching confidentiality of information, concealing information, and match-fixing
Indecent/illegal treatment of colleagues, athletes, other sport stakeholders and citizens: Unacceptable treatment that may include discrimination (based on gender, race, or sexual orientation), intimidation, harassment, and also slavery and other improper behaviours.	Child trafficking, child labour, over-aggressive adults (e.g., trainers, coaches, and parents) who place exaggerated pressure on young athletes for their own egocentric reasons; bullying, hazing, sexual harassment, third-party player contracts, and gossiping
Waste and abuse of organisational resources: Failure to comply with organisational standards and/or improper performance or incorrect/dysfunctional internal behaviour.	Luxury travel and accommodations; excessive equipment purchases and number of coaching staff
Misconduct in private time: Conduct during private time that harms trust in the organisation.	Driving while under the influence, domestic violence, tax evasion, solicitation of prostitutes
Integrity risks	
Poor governance practices: A lack of accountability, transparency, democracy and responsibility.	Failure to thoroughly investigate, failure to sanction integrity violations, lack of financial reporting, failure to hold elections, inadequate stakeholder representation

Source: Adapted from Lasthuizen, Huberts and Heres (2011, p. 389) and Masters (2015).

excessive team and administrative budgets (e.g., travel, accommodations, equipment and number of paid staff), subtle forms of favouritism and patronage; or on-field behaviours, such as doping, tanking, or faking injuries.

Integrity risks are generally created through poor governance practices. The typology illustrates that integrity violations and risks occur in different SGB contexts (e.g., on-field and off-field behaviours) within stakeholder roles and behaviours (e.g., administrators, athletes, coaching staffs, parents, medical staff and sponsors) and internal (e.g., codes of conduct, disciplinary rules and regulations, working and playing rules and professional ethics) and external (e.g., national laws, rules, regulations, media and society) organisational systems.

The typology is not meant to be exhaustive but aims to illustrate the range of integrity violations and risks that can occur at the club, regional, state and national levels of sport governance. These risks warrant an integrity system that can assist an SGB in developing a coherent and consistent approach to creating and maintaining sport integrity.

Sport integrity system: A framework

Based on the concept of integrity in sport presented above, an integrity sport system consists of individuals, institutions, policies, practices and agencies that contribute to safeguarding the integrity of an SGB (Head et al., 2008; Huberts & Six, 2012). A sport integrity system is responsible for monitoring, preventing and tackling integrity violations and minimising integrity risks. The central focus of an integrity system is outlining the elements and conditions necessary for preventing integrity violations and minimising integrity risks in governance and sports competitions. This requires an integrity system to first assist with the effective coordination of value-based policies and practices, institutions and agencies to ensure high-integrity performance and second, to "ensure that power is exercised in a manner that is true to the values, purposes and duties for which that power is entrusted to, or held by, institutions" (Brown, Griffith University Key Centre for Ethics, Law, Justice and Governance & Transparency International, 2005, p. i) and sport organisational stakeholders. An SGB's integrity system includes both internal organisational and ethical management practices (e.g., anti-doping or match fixing education, governance practices, codes of ethics and rules compliance) as well as external integrity guardians of an SGB's administration (e.g., national sport integrity units, INTERPOL-like agencies, media and legislation). The components that comprise an SGB's integrity system (e.g., actors, policies, practices) and their respective relationships should ideally act coherently to ensure integrity risk containment including the appropriate exercise of power throughout a federated sport system. In such a system, SGBs collaboratively support and coordinate with state/provincial and territorial/regional sport governing bodies who in turn coordinate with local clubs to adopt and implement specific measures, policies and practices considered important to ensuring integrity within their respective levels of governance.

Components of a sport integrity system

The basic components of a sport integrity system framework outline the elements and conditions considered important for the integrity of an SGB. A sport integrity system is multidimensional and elements comprising the system can vary significantly depending on the sport governing body, the level in which the elements operate, the location (e.g., urban or rural) and the political and economic environment. The elements of the system include sport actors, internal organisational components and external components that perform different but interrelated functions.

Actors

Several actors have the responsibility to serve as generators and guardians of integrity in an SGB. It is important that an SGB determine which internal and external actors are concerned about sport integrity. These actors might include SGB sport stakeholders who are internal to the organisation at the club, regional, state and national levels (e.g., governing board members, administrators, staff, parents, coaches and athletes) as well as external actors (e.g., local government, watchdog groups, media and community members). Including both internal and external actors in a sport integrity system assumes the need for external accountability, which has not been traditionally accepted by SGBs. However, given that an integrity system includes individuals, institutions and agencies that contribute to safeguarding integrity, external actors are required.

In order for an SGB to develop an agreed-upon understanding of sport integrity and what violations and risks are associated with a sport integrity system, all relevant actors must be included in the discussion. Each actor brings to the discussion their own moral code that is comprised of personal values, attitudes, beliefs and ethical sensitivities, which influences their perception of integrity. Obviously, not all actor's moral codes coincide with one another and many actor's moral codes contradict an organisation's mission and values. Nonetheless, no matter the level of governance actors participate in, or the external role they fulfil, they contribute to generating the meaning and/or understanding of integrity. Furthermore, these actors should identify whose integrity within the SGB needs to be managed, that is, which individuals the sport integrity system is directed at in limiting risks and deterring violations. Sport governing boards, administrators, coaches and athletes are perhaps the central actors the integrity system is seeking to manage, but other individuals, such as medical staff, parents and sponsors, should also be identified as actors whose integrity needs to be managed.

Internal environment

The internal environment includes organisational characteristics and ethical management practices that require working in harmony within a sport integrity system.

Organisational elements. The central aim of an integrity system is to guide organisational decision-making and practices towards ethical behaviour and avoiding corrupt behaviours and system failures. In order to accomplish an effective integrity system, an SGB should develop a moral framework that serves as its foundation that guides and underpins policies, practices and decision-making from national to club levels. It is important that an SGB's structure and culture are reflective of a moral framework that fosters and maintains integrity throughout the organisation. Ideally, the moral framework should strengthen organisational decision-making towards high integrity.

Organisational elements can be categorised into two components: 1) Organisational structure and 2) the organisational culture. Organisational elements are comprised of formal and informal systems, processes and interactions (Cohen, 1993; Schein, 2010) that contribute to the creation, implementation and coordination of a sport integrity system. Components of an organisational structure include governance structure, leadership, policies, reward systems, socialisation mechanisms and decision processes (Schein, 2010). Organisational culture is comprised of behavioural norms, morals, myths, rituals, symbols, stories and language. The moral framework is expressed through these various informal and formal organisational elements that shape and reflect the type and extent of integrity standards that stakeholders expect to be upheld.

The moral framework of an SGB governance structure is first articulated through its mission statement that describes the organisation's purpose and emphasises "values, positive behaviours and guiding principles within the framework of the corporation's announced belief system and ideology" (Swales & Rogers, 1995, p. 227). A mission statement, therefore, represents an SGB's conceptualisation of integrity and serves as its charter for achieving integrity. Increased commercialisation and professionalisation and other influences and/or pressures can steer governing boards' decision-making and values from their core mission. Both organisational leadership and governing boards therefore are responsible for communicating the mission and integrity standards through their decision-making and actions. An SGB should aim to maintain the relevance and salience of its mission, vision and integrity charter throughout the levels of governance (i.e., club, regional and state). It is important that formal policies and practices (e.g., incentive systems, performance and evaluation processes and job and/or role processes) are used to emphasise an SGB's ethical behavioural expectations and goals and objectives (both economic and non-economic goals). In many high-performance contexts, SGB levels of funding and bonuses awarded by the state are tied to regular season winning, playoff winning and/or medal placing, whereas at the local and regional levels, where bonuses and funding are generally not applicable, unethical behaviour has been ignored and/or forgiven due the status of the stakeholder (coach, athlete and board director). Cohen (1993) argued "when performance goals are excessively demanding, the message conveyed to employees is that any means available may be used to achieve these goals, regardless of the legitimacy of these means" (p. 347).

The socialisation processes of each level of sport governance emphasises the organisational values that are rewarded and celebrated on a daily basis. Hence, sport stakeholders learn which ethical behaviours are valued and which integrity violations are accepted and over time these violations become normalised. For example, athletes have rationalised doping practices because it was part of the culture to compete at an elite level. Engelberg, Moston and Skinner (2015) argued that the culture of doping has normalised using performance-enhancing substances because "everyone was doing it" and the practice was reinforced by a "silent pressure" from peers, coaches and health professionals. This elite performance culture emphasised "winning and doing what it takes to win" and the financial investments of the sport made "it almost 'necessary' for doping to continue" (p. 274). This example of a doping culture illustrates the need for an integrity system that creates and maintains consistency between organisational mission and values and priorities.

The various dimensions of sport governance (e.g., structures, regulations, democratic processes, competent governing board, equity, responsibility, accountability and transparency) are also critical in preventing integrity violations. For example, instituting and carrying out good governance principles and practices including accountability, transparency and democracy guide decision-making to ensure fairness, fiscal responsibility and equal distribution of power/authority. In practice, these principles equate to: Term limits for elected and appointed board members and executives; legitimate athlete representation at all levels of governance; public release of budgets and meeting minutes; fair and open competition and disclosure of information related to event bidding and other business relationships; and fair procedures for alleged abuses.

The 2018 sexual molestation case involving Larry Nassar, the USA Gymnastics and Michigan State University sports medicine specialist who was found guilty and sentenced for sexually molesting over 350 girls and women over approximately two decades (Connor & Fitzpatrick, 2018), is a good example of integrity risks and violations that occur when organisations fail to implement effective accountability and transparency policies and practices. Governance practices for suitably investigating alleged child molestation were inadequate as former female athletes stated that USA Gymnastics and Michigan State University ignored complaints of Nassar's abuse made as early as 1997. Both institutions' organisational cultures contributed to the ongoing abuse by valuing reputations, the sport and winning over the safety of athletes. Athletes worked within a culture of fear, intimidation and humiliation. Athletes that reported Nassar's abuse to adults (i.e., parents, coaches, athletic trainers and others [doctors]) were chastised and told they misunderstood his treatment and that they didn't know the difference between medical treatment and sexual abuse. Coaches, trainers and administrators defended Nassar and instructed the athletes to trust him because he was a world-renowned doctor that treated elite athletes, and they were therefore not to question his methods of treatment.

Nassar's abuse appeared to be part of a broader national governing sport problem as the United States Olympic Committee (USOC) and over 45 national governing bodies for individual sports were aware of allegations of sexual abuse by numerous coaches and officials since the early 1980s but did little to investigate or develop policies and practices that would protect athletes (Harrison & Wolf, 2018). Recently, the USOC has made several attempts to appoint suitable ethical leadership as well as instate a safe sport policy that appears to be implemented throughout local, regional and national sport organisations. It is too early to determine the effectiveness of the safe sport policy strategy in achieving integrity. Nonetheless, governance processes should assist with the coordination and control mechanisms of an effective integrity system to ensure that diverse efforts of organisational stakeholders, state bodies, associations, clubs and their respective units work together to reach their goals in an ethical manner. Strong ethical leadership, strong governing boards, governance practices, ethical codes and compliance practices must all work in unison to create a consistent message about integrity expectations throughout an SGB. This consistency in message, policies and practices strengthens the organisations' moral framework and leads to normalising integrity as stakeholders and wider society internalise integrity as valued and expected.

Ethical management. The internal environment also includes organisational ethics strategies comprised of compliance- and values-based programs that outline the integrity standards that sport stakeholders should accept and uphold. Both governing boards and top management are responsible for aligning ethical management mechanisms through appropriate governance structures, processes and procedures. A high-performance integrity ethical management system will focus on potential integrity violations and moral awareness (organisational values).

Compliance-based ethics programs use codes of ethics and regulatory structures that outline permissible behaviours for sport organisational stakeholders. Compliance programs act as a control system that stresses strict compliance to a system of rules and regulations. Procedures are instituted, monitoring systems are implemented to detect violations, and regulator actors are given investigative and sanctioning powers. Such programs use coercive techniques that help individuals focus on conforming to organisational rules and regulations. Compliance ethics programs (e.g., NCAA compliance education and training programs relative to match fixing, anti-doping, sexual harassment and child safety) typically provide training that includes rules education and training related to competition rules, sportspersonship and responsible behaviours as well as threats of punishment for noncompliance with the rules. The NCAA's rules compliance system is one of the extreme examples of a compliance-based rules program.

An effective integrity system also requires a values-based approach to ethical behaviour that works in unison with a compliance program. Compliance systems tend to encourage sports stakeholders to use a rulebook understanding of integrity where they apply ethical reason to the level of the rules (Kihl, 2006). Verhezen (2010) argued that a compliance-based framework assumes "that adherence to the rules, codes and regulations will suffice to guide ethical behaviour" (p. 194) and avoid illegal or unethical behaviour. Informal ethics approaches encourage sport stakeholders to think about their ethical role within the organisation and how their actions coincide with ethical expectations from both wider society and the organisation itself. A values-approach promotes ethical dialogue that enhances moral awareness and moral decision-making while aiming to promote responsible behaviours and practices. High-performing integrity systems balance both compliance- and values-based approaches that enhance resource-capacity building capabilities of board member management, paid staff and volunteers. Compliance-based programs might include monitoring, education, training, investigative processes, adjudication and sanctioning mechanisms. Values-based programs could also entail moral awareness and decision-making training, whistle-blower protections (e.g., World Anti-Doping Agency [WADA] whistle-blower program), ethics reporting hotlines and mobile device apps (e.g., Stop Matchfixing app, CCES Report Doping App). Incorporating both kinds of programs can deepen individuals' understandings and valuing of ethics which, in turn, induces trust and close collaboration across organisations and sport stakeholders.

External environment

External guardians. External guardians function as external checks and balances. Checks and balances are the mechanisms for guardianship and accountability that ensure that local, regional and national sport governing boards operate within legal and social boundaries. The continued occurrence of integrity breaches has highlighted SGBs' inability to self-regulate and hold themselves accountable. Sport governing boards and administrators conceivably hold too much autonomy from the external and social environment, which in many instances has led to failures in managing integrity risks and holding perpetrators and systems accountable. SGBs inability to self-regulate thus warrants external guardians as a key component within a sport integrity system. External guardians consist of an independent regulatory environment and the social environment that serves as a network of actors with formal and/or informal oversight responsibilities. External guardians, in essence, are a collective or network of outside agencies that are mutually supportive and assist in integrity coordination with the SGB and its internal organisations (i.e., club, state and national).

Regulatory environment refers to the laws, regulations and external regulatory oversight agencies that serve to work in coordination with a sport integrity system. Standard regulatory watchdogs include law enforcement, state and national legislation, government regulations and so forth. Despite the fact that many countries have adopted fraud and bribery legislation, many of these laws have substantial loopholes where the legislation does not pertain to sport match fixing, illegal betting or doping. It is important that SGBs work with their respective government judicial authorities to enact specific legislation prohibiting and sanctioning such sport corrupt behaviours. The regulatory environment includes specific sport and non-sport regulatory oversight bodies including anti-corruption and safe sport agencies. For example, international anti-corruption agencies include WADA, INTERPOL and government agencies such as the Australian National Integrity in Sport Unit who can aid SGBs in combating corruption in sport. Safe sport agencies such as the US Center for SafeSport aim to end different forms of abuse in sport. Integrity-specific watchdog groups have also emerged including organisations such as the Sport Integrity Global Alliance and the Sport Integrity Unit, which focus on promoting integrity by providing various governance resources and leadership.

The social environment refers to media and community members serving in their respective roles as guardians of sport integrity. In a sport integrity system, the main role of the media and the community is exposing sport integrity risks and violations by informing governing bodies at the local, regional, state and national levels of any problems in the delivery of sport and its governance. Community members can serve in a variety of capacities within sport organisations (e.g., governing board members, volunteers, coaches). In these roles, they can serve as active participants in ensuring transparency and accountability of sporting organisations by raising concerns, placing pressure on organisations to change, as well as working to develop solutions by reforming policies and procedures. For example, sport activist Jaimie Fuller and sports compression manufacturer SKINS formed a pressure group and through different campaigns (e.g., #ChooseTheRightTrack and #RainbowLaces) raised awareness and concerns about corruption and gender equality in sport.

By accessing public information, the media, in particular, play a critical role in seeking accountability by exposing to the public important integrity risks and violations in sport organisations. In particular, the media's reporting on corrupt practices, such as illegal gambling on sport, match fixing, state doping systems and poor governance practices (e.g., the USOC failure to address numerous cases of sexual harassment by coaches and/or support staff) has assisted in exposing both systematic integrity risks and violations that have undermined the public's trust in sport. Exposing these cases to the public places pressure on SGBs and their partners to investigate integrity breeches. Furthermore, the media's accountability role can assist with ensuring that perpetrators are sanctioned and that SGBs change their systems to prevent integrity risks. For example, the media's reporting of United States Anti-Doping Associations' investigation of Lance Armstrong and the Larry Nassar sexual assault cases illustrates the important roles they played in exposing critical violations and breakdowns in SBG governance. Important reforms have and are in the process of being implemented to prevent further instances of doping and address sexual assault of athletes.

External guardians function in a mutually accountable role rather than a horizontally accountable role. Mutual accountability requires each actor to be accountable to each other and watch and advise one another in managing integrity in legislative bodies, government agencies, public oversight agencies and both national and international sport governing bodies. It is important that a balance exists between external and internal regulations. Too much emphasis on external regulations can lead to an SGB integrity system relying too much on external oversight (e.g., law enforcement, government regulators, media). As a result, stakeholders are less likely to accept the importance of adopting and adhering to organisational values and compliance-based initiatives.

Effective functioning of components

Ideally, an integrity system should influence organisational stakeholders to act with integrity and at a minimum avoid violations (e.g., conflicts of interest, harassment, bribery). An integrity system should also create functional systems and practices that properly contain integrity risks (e.g., match fixing, doping, lack of checks and balances). An effective system should limit integrity breaches, contain sufficient capacity (e.g., resources, financial support, individuals) and involve coherent institutional cooperation (functional system interactions). SGBs should work to ensure that, within the system, each level of sport governance contains the necessary human and financial resources to realise their integrity goals. Many local sport clubs currently lack the resources to address match fixing and therefore national governing boards will need to assist with providing suitable resources to prevent this type of corruption. In addition, government and legal agencies need to ensure that laws are enacted that criminalise match fixing to ensure that offenders can be suitably sanctioned. Integrity institutions will need to work collaboratively to achieve high levels of support and coordination to ensure the system functions effectively at each level of sport governance. The extent of the system to effectively promote and realise integrity in competitions, in the governing of sport and in the public's trust in sport is a measure of integrity success.

SGBs generally have some form of integrity system in place; however, for many SGBs, it is not recognised as such and there may not be a clear communication strategy and/or coordination of the system from clubs to regional leagues to state associations up to the national level. For example, both Badminton Canada and USA Badminton display on their websites their organisational missions, operational policies and practices, competition rules, governance principles, codes of ethics, athlete safety policies and governance by laws. Badminton Canada also contains a partner's page with links to various provincial associations, while USA Badminton provides information on membership and competitions. Whilst both SGBs appear to have robust integrity systems in place, it is unclear how they communicate and infuse integrity from the club level up to the SGB. In conducting a general scan this appears to be the case for many US and Canadian NGBs.

Recognising the potential differences in the structures of SGBs and their sport integrity systems, the number and nature of institutions, policies, practices, stakeholders and agencies that make up the system is not prescribed. The nature (e.g., sport, funding, size, actors, location and so forth) of the SGB will influence which components are the best fit for an effective sport integrity system. An SGB will naturally use existing external and internal components in addition to other elements that can enhance the effectiveness of an integrity system. Noteworthy, there is no one size fits all that leads to creating an effective sport integrity system. Rather, an SGB could quite possibly select a number of different configurations to achieve high integrity. The SGB and its respective governing boards and stakeholders will need to determine the appropriate configuration of policy, practices and agencies that best suit their mission and context. Additionally, since sport occurs in a dynamic context the integrity system configuration will require adaptation over time. As new integrity risks emerge and integrity breaches occur, the system will require some adjustments to address such situations.

Conclusion

The issue of integrity in sport is under a global spotlight. Society's lack of trust in sport competitions along with systematic integrity violations have led integrity scholars and agencies to generate integrity standards towards enhancing the governance of sport and to ensure competitions are played honestly. Whilst there have been attempts to instil integrity in sport through good governance practices, this chapter aimed to propose a sport integrity system. Creating such a system is an arduous task and there is no suggesting that this is an easy framework to create in achieving integrity in sport. It is acknowledged that each country and SGB is unique in how they might approach constructing an internal (organisational structure and culture) and an external (regulatory environment) environment. However, similarities in a sport integrity system do exist and elements are transferrable. A sport integrity system is comprised of several elements. Those discussed in this chapter include actors, internal components (organisational elements and ethical management) and external components (regulatory and social environments). The effective functioning of components within a sport integrity system requires coordination, capacity building and ongoing evaluation of the effectiveness of the system as a whole as well as its individual components. Individual SGBs will need to determine how a sport integrity system is initiated and managed as well as decide the criteria for assessing high-performing integrity systems. Providing sufficient capacity support to various levels of a governing body that lacks sufficient resources is important, because gaps in the system could undermine the reform.

Lastly, SGBs will need to develop performance targets and monitoring systems to evaluate progress towards reduced integrity risks and violations. Carrying out such performance appraisals can help build public trust by demonstrating that SGB leaders are serious about integrity, and that sport is both clean and fair and sport is also *perceived* as being clean and fair.

The proposed sport integrity system provides opportunities for a research agenda that aims at developing and assessing the effectiveness of a sport integrity system. The proposed integrity system in this chapter is prescriptive in nature and thus future research could empirically examine what comprises an effective sport integrity system and why? To carry out this objective, exploratory research is necessary to determine the various elements of a sport integrity system, as well as the criteria with which to evaluate its performance. Possible research questions that could be posed to address this aim might include the following: What elements of the system are included at the local, regional/state and national levels? How do the various environments and actors interact with one another to ensure a harmonious integrity system? What is the nature of the interrelationships within and between environments and actors? Last, what is the most appropriate means for assessing the effectiveness of a system in limiting integrity breaches? As Hubert and Six (2012) noted, "there may be several configurations that lead to high integrity, rather than just one best way" (p. 169). Thus, it is important to develop and test theory on the components that comprise an integrity system and the relationships between them.

An important secondary research agenda involves conducting comparative analysis across national sport integrity systems and over time (longitudinal comparisons). Comparative analysis would allow for determining what structures, mechanisms, elements and evaluative criteria broadly apply to developing a sport integrity system and which components and measures are better suited to specific SGBs. The data collected about both the components of the integrity system and the performance of different SGBs integrity systems can be used to highlight deficiencies in capacity and coordination. In addition, comparative data could assist in determining a range of "different configurations of policies, practices and institutions that can lead to the same outcome of high integrity performance and high integrity risk containment" (Six & Lawton, 2013, p. 654). Last, longitudinal comparisons and evaluations can assist with generating new knowledge and detect changes of systems that enhance integrity. The research agendas suggested are not exhaustive but provide a road map to initiate and enhance our understanding of sport integrity systems.

Note

1 https://safesport.org/

References

Andvig, J. C., & O. Fjeldstad, O. (2001). *Corruption: A review of contemporary research report.* Oslo, Norway: Michelsen Institute for Development Studies and Human Rights.

Archer, A. (2016). On sporting integrity. *Sport, Ethics and Philosophy, 10*, 117–131.

Asian Racing Federation. (2019). *Sports and racing integrity under the microscope at 37th Asian Racing Conference.* Retrieved 30 October 2018, from http://www.asianracing.org/article.aspx?articleid=283

Australian Government. (2018). *National integrity of sport unit.* Department of Health. Retrieved 2 December 2018, from http://www.health.gov.au/internet/main/publishing.nsf/Content/national-integrity-of-sport-unit

Bauman, D. C. (2013). Leadership and the three faces of integrity. *The Leadership Quarterly, 24*, 414–426.

Boatright, J. (1992). Conflict of interest: An agency analysis. In N. Bowie & R. Freedman (Eds.), *Ethics and agency theory: Introduction* (pp. 187–203). New York: Oxford University Press.

Brown, A. J., Griffith University Key Centre for Ethics, Law, Justice and Governance, Transparency International. (2005). *Chaos or coherence?: Strengths, opportunities and challenges for Australia's integrity systems, national integrity systems assessment (NISA)*. Blackburn South, Victoria: Transparency International.

Chappelet, J.-L., & Mrkonjic, M. (2013). Existing governance principles in sport: A review of published literature. In J. Alm (Ed.), *Action for good governance in international sports organisations final report* (pp. 222–239). Copenhagen: Play the Game/Danish Institute for Sports Studies.

Cohen, D. V. (1993). Creating and maintaining ethical work climates: Anomie in the workplace and implications for managing change. *Business Ethics Quarterly, 3*, 343–358.

Connor, T., & Fitzpatrick, S. (2018, January 28). Gymnastics scandal: 8 times Larry Nassar could have been stopped. *NBCNews.com*. Retrieved 30 October 2018, from https://www.nbcnews.com/news/us-new s/gymnastics-scandal-8-times-larry-nassar-could-have-been-stopped-n841091

Engelberg, T., Moston, S., & Skinner, J. (2015). The final frontier of anti-doping: A study of athletes who have committed doping violations. *Sport Management Review, 18*, 268–279.

European Commission. (2019). *A pledge to implement good governance in European sport*. Retrieved 30 October 2018, from https://ec.europa.eu/sport/policy/organisation-of-sport/pledge_en

Erhard, W., & Jensen, M. C. (2014, April). *Putting integrity into finance: A purely positive approach (No. w19986)* (ECGI Working Paper Series in Finance Working Paper No. 4/17)Brussels, Belgium.

Farrey, T. (2018, June 3). *Athlete abusing athletes*. Retrieved from https://www.espn.com/otl/hazing/mon day.html

Gardiner, S., Parry, J., & Robinson, S. (2017). Integrity and the corruption debate in sport: Where is the integrity? *European Sport Management Quarterly, 17*, 6–23.

Harrison, K., &. Wolf, A. L. (2018, April 5). Larry Nassar wasn't the only abuser in Olympic sports. Opinions. *Washington Post*. Retrieved from https://www.washingtonpost.com/opinions/larry-nassar-wasnt-t he-only-abuser-in-olympic-sports/2018/04/05/1bfdf994-3809-11e8-8fd2-49fe3c675a89_story.htm l?utm_term=.faa905004e98

Head, B. W., Brown, A. J., & Connors, C. (Eds.). (2008). *Promoting integrity: Evaluating and improving public institutions*. Burlington, VT: Farnham Ashgate.

Huberts, L. W. J. C. (2014). *The integrity of governance. What it is, what we know, what is done, and where to go*. Basingstoke, UK: Palgrave Macmillan.

Huberts, L. W., & Six, F. E. (2012). Local integrity systems: Toward a framework for comparative analysis and assessment. *Public Integrity, 14*(2), 151–172.

Kihl, L. A. (2006). What's morality got to do with it? An examination of compliance officers' approaches to rule interpretations. *Journal of College & Character Special Issue- Sport Ethics, 7*, 1–8.

Lasthuizen, K., Huberts, L., & Heres, L. (2011). How to measure integrity violations. *Public Management Review, 13*, 383–408.

Lewis, A., Wilkinson, B., & Henzelin, M. (2018, December 19). Independent review of integrity in tennis: Final report. Retrieved from http://www.tennisintegrityunit.com/storage/app/media/Independent% 20Reviews/Final%20Report_191218.pdf

Masters, A. (2015). Corruption in sport: From the playing field to the field of policy. *Policy and Society, 34*(2), 111–123.

McLaren, R. (2016). *WADA investigation of Sochi allegations. An independent investigation*. Montréal: World Anti-Doping Agency.

Molina, A. D. (2016). *Ten recommendations for managing organizational integrity risks*. Washington, DC: IBM Center for the Business of Government. Retrieved 30 October 2018, from http://www.businessofgove rnment.org/sites/default/files/Ten%20Recommendations%20for%20Managing%20Organizationa l%20Integrity%20Risks.pdf

Molina, A. D. (2018). A systems approach to managing organizational integrity risks: Lessons from the 2014 veteran's affairs waitlist scandal. *The American Review of Public Administration, 48*, 872–888.

Pope, J. (1996). (Ed.). *The TI source book*. Berlin: Transparency International.

Schein, E. H. (2010). *Organizational culture and leadership* (4th ed.). San Francisco, CA: John Wiley & Sons.

Six, F. E., De Bakker, F. G., & Huberts, L. W. (2007). Judging a corporate leader's integrity: An illustrated three-component model. *European Management Journal, 25*(3), 185–194.

Six, F., & Lawton, A. (2013). Towards a theory of integrity systems: A configurational approach. *International Review of Administrative Sciences, 79*, 639–658.

Sport Australia. (2019). *Integrity in sport*. Retrieved 2 December 2018, from https://www.sportaus.gov.au/ integrity_in_sport

Sport Integrity Global Alliance. (2018). Universal standards on sports betting integrity. Retrieved 2 December 2018, from http://siga-sport.net/wp-content/uploads/2018/05/SIGA-Universal-Standa rds-on-SBI-General-Assembly-13.09.2016.pdf

Swales, J. M., & Rogers, P. S. (1995). Discourse and the projection of corporate culture: The mission statement. *Discourse & Society*, *6*, 223–242.

UK Sport. (2019). *A code for sports governance*. Retrieved 2 December 2018, from http://www.uksport.g ov.uk/resources/governance-code

Vanden Auweele, Y. V. (2015). Restoring sport's integrity: Beyond ad-hoc solutions in challenging aberrations in sport. In Y. Vanden Auweele, E. Cook & J. Parry (Eds.), *Ethics and governance in sport* (pp. 42–50). London: Routledge.

Verhezen, P. (2010). Giving voice in a culture of silence. From a culture of compliance to a culture of integrity. *Journal of Business Ethics*, *96*(2), 187–206.

Zakhem, A., & Mascio, M. (2018). Sporting integrity, coherence, and being true to the spirit of a game. *Sport, Ethics and Philosophy*, *13*, 227–236.

29

Sport governance
A point in time for reflection

David Shilbury and Lesley Ferkins

The commissioning of a research handbook in any field is a wonderful opportunity for a point-in-time reflection on the progress and status of a field of study. In this case, the commissioning of a research handbook of sport governance by Routledge has provided the opportunity for, at a macro level, a review of scholarship and progress in sport management and at a micro level, a specific focus on sport governance and its growing body of knowledge and as a critical set of processes shaping organisational life. Sport management as a field has progressed at different rates globally, but in nearly all countries, the theme of professionalisation is consistent, as has been the transition from a volunteer workforce to a professional cadre of staff managing and leading sport organisations. In all countries where professionalisation of sport management has been evident, commercialisation has been a driving factor, which ultimately has shaped governance practice in terms of accountability, transparency, timelines of decision-making, setting strategic direction, risk mitigation and, in general, a greater understanding of the role of the board in leading and directing organisations.

Given the role of boards in leading and directing sport organisations (many of which remain voluntary), it is somewhat paradoxical to note that the professionalisation of sport management has largely occurred through the transition from a volunteer to paid workforce and then a qualified workforce. It has only been in relatively recent times that the focus has shifted to professionalising governance practices in sport organisations. The catalyst for this shift has often been the result of major crises confronted by high-profile sport organisations including, for example, FIFA and the IOC. Of course, there have been numerous sport-governing bodies that have dealt with similar crises, and in most instances these crises can be tracked back to governance processes and practices. In general, outdated systems that were rooted in former leisure-oriented and volunteer cultures were in need of updating to keep pace with a professionalising and increasingly commercialised sector. The challenge of such a systems update is to do this in a way that protects and integrates the social mission of sport organisations – many of which remain as nonprofit entities striving to be more professional in their approach.

This handbook has provided a wonderful insight to the progress made in sport governance scholarship, much of which is now evident in practice to varying degrees by professional sports (international, national and regional) organisations the world over. The scholarship contained in this handbook therefore has provided a "point-in-time" audit of the research undertaken to date in sport governance including a detailed list of relevant literature. Significantly, each chapter has mapped and highlighted future research directions for scholars pursuing sport governance studies. Chapters 1 and 2 made clear the relatively limited research published in the field's three major journals and the lack of an overarching theoretical framework guiding sport governance scholarship. Chapter 1, in particular, showed that sport governance scholarship was somewhat limited from 1996 to 2008. Post 2008, there was evidence of an increasing interest in sport governance research, at least as it is reflected in the three main sport management journals.

Of the articles published, the bulk of the studies focused on key board functions (Table 1.4), with an emphasis on integrating regional networks in federated sport models, strategy formulation by directors, managing stakeholders and monitoring and compliance. Eighteen of the 19 articles in this category were published after 2004, highlighting the nascent state of sport governance. Not surprisingly, defining governance roles and responsibilities (Table 1.1) showed the next largest suite of published articles. This analysis reinforced the focus on professionalisation, firstly of volunteers and paid staff, but with an emphasis on how this was affecting volunteer directors as board members. Chapter 1 therefore set the scene for the chapters that followed, highlighting the evolving state of sport governance scholarship.

Chapter 2 examined the theoretical foundations shaping sport governance scholarship. Eight theories drawn from the for-profit and nonprofit literature and applied to sport governance were identified. Typically, the nature of the problem has determined the choice of theory through which to engage with the identified problem. Few indigenous theories were shown to exist specific to sport governance. The emerging theory of board strategic balance shown in Figure 2.1 is an exception, and its design is specific to federated structures where national and state governing body boards must interact for the overall good of a sport.

With an increasing emphasis on sport governance scholarship, future work could focus on theory development to help explain specific phenomena that might exist in sport governance. Some of these phenomena include: The dynamic between an increasingly qualified professional staff and volunteer directors; the board's appreciation of and ability to embrace a social mission for the sport while chasing high-performance aspirations and commercial opportunities; and board practices and processes in a leisure domain often replete with high levels of emotion and familiarity with sport to the extent that "expertise" is assumed by the actors. Indeed, in Chapter 18, Zeimers and Shilbury highlight the role of passion for sport board chairs as an area of future research, as it affects how the chair manages boardroom dynamics, as well as his or her own cultural understandings and background in the sport. Sport governance is a dynamic yet invisible process with results often the subject of intense media scrutiny in ways most other industries and corporations do not confront.

Part 2 of the handbook grapples with the environmental context of sport policy and its influence on sport governance. In other words, as government funding supports sport in many countries, how does government policy shape and influence sport governance? Part 2 draws on an overview of the broad legal environment with Jonson and Thorpe articulating the important role of corporate law on governance and the prevalence of international treaties such as the World Anti-Doping Code as special features of the sport industry. Moreover, the extent to which international governing bodies should be self-regulating or autonomous versus more direct government intervention is raised as an interesting issue. Identifying which governments and which laws would be applied in such a circumstance remain a challenge. As Chapters 4, 5 and 6 demonstrate, there is a clear link between sport organisations at a domestic level and government policy. The focus in these chapters is on how policy shapes sport governance. Articulated sport governance principles were shown to exist in a number of countries highlighting the need for government to "demand" improved governance practices.

The European context provided a unifying approach across numerous countries to assess current governance practice. Results of research undertaken through the National Sports Governance Observer project and detailed in Chapter 4 highlight the increasing importance of understanding and improving sport governance in practice. The role of scholarly research in the process is important. In relation to government policy, Anagnostopoulos, van Eekeren and Solenes, observed in Chapter 4: "In conclusion, given that incidents of poor governance have not gone unnoticed by governments (irrespective of the degree of intervention), national sport federations must gain and/or retain their legitimacy". The right to govern by national sport organisations, or remain legitimate, emerges as a key policy issue in relation to governance practices. Sam and Schoenberg, in Chapter 5, reinforce the need for further research to understand the relationship between government sport policy and governance, and this might, for example, include questions such as: How does policy impact governance of sport organisations? Why do government agencies prescribe particular governance structures and practices over others? What is the effectiveness of government support resources in helping governance? What flows from this work is a broader research question, as to how this range of government policies changes governance behaviours, rather than just providing direction on a checklist of items that constitute good governance. In Chapter 6, Bravo and Haas identify at least two different issues in the governance of sport in Latin America, which will demand the attention of policy makers. For many sports in Brazil and other Latin American countries, the presence and voice of the president remains influential, and NSOs remain president-dependent. An important principle of good governance is that the chair or president is the first among equals on a board of directors, and, to that extent, the overbearing voice of the president is an outdated principle of governance – and one that is likely to attract the interest of government policy in the future. The other issue raised in Chapter 6 is the role of athletes in the governance process. Bravo and Hass stated in Chapter 6 that athletes have "attained a unique status inside the governance of many sport organisations, and it is unknown what role and contribution athletes make to the governance of sport". Logically, from a research perspective, it begs the question: Should they and, if so, in what capacity?

The final two chapters of Part 2 grapple with sport systems and structures used by national sport organisations and the role of non-traditional sport structures in systemic governance. In other words, organisations that support the delivery of sport. In Chapter 7, O'Boyle and Shilbury examine federal forms of governance highlighting the role of the (now outdated) delegate system of governance and the move to appoint independent directors to a board. Although it was noted that the delegate system is no longer "fit for purpose", little research has examined board dynamics and decision-making on boards where there remain elected directors by member associations (although not delegates of the member association) and some independently appointed directors. The chapter also highlights the potential of a unitary model in the governance of national sport organisations. Again, little research has been undertaken on the efficacy of such an approach, in part, because there are few sports willing to adopt this structure. These structural changes directly affect processes on how directors are appointed to boards and how they discharge their responsibilities.

Chapter 8 focused on the governance of non-traditional sport structures including facilities, sport trusts, sport federations and Active Partnerships in the UK and other related entities. From a governance perspective, this chapter is an important contribution and raises questions about the relevance of collaborative governance arrangements between these entities and participating sports, or sport organisations that rely on the use of the facility or related service. Stakeholder theory in relation to governance is also important, as often representatives from stakeholder sports form the governance mechanism for such an entity. Spencer and Phillips illustrate this example through the Melbourne and Olympic Park Trust and how stakeholders are represented and how stakeholder agreements are brokered. From a stakeholder or collaborative governance perspective, there are some interesting and relevant research questions worthy of future examination. Power in these relationships is also as a potential research focus.

Part 3 of the handbook examines ownership structures and governance models in professional sport clubs, international federations, intercollegiate sport and hallmark events. Chapters 9, 10, 11 and 12 provide a unique and rarely written about insight to the various ownership structures of professional sport clubs in a variety of countries. Norm O'Reilly, in Chapter 9, describes four types of club ownership models in the most corporate sport market in the world. In Chapter 10, Gammelsaeter and Walters focus on football club ownership models in Europe, a reflection of the dominant code in that region of the world. Similarly, in Chapter 11, Karg and Ingley examine ownership structures in Australia, New Zealand and South Africa, which typically reflect different sport systems and therefore ownership models when compared to European football clubs and the USA. Finally, Kang, Yoshida and Liu, in Chapter 12, provide an Asian perspective using South Korea, Japan and China to provide a focus on ownership models in professional sport clubs. Although diverse ownership models exist in different areas of the world, little research has been undertaken in relation to ownership models and how they affect governance. A change in ownership structure, either private or member-based, will inevitably affect governance practices. The broad research question of interest here is – What changes (governance practices) when ownership changes? Little research has addressed this question, but each of the four chapters in varying ways addresses this concern in terms of the governance of privately owned professional sport clubs, member-owned clubs or hybrid forms of ownership.

Chapters 13, 14 and 15 outline the research challenges and options for governance in international sport federations, intercollegiate athletics in the USA and governance models used for mega and hallmark events such as the Olympic Games. In Chapter 13, Chappelet, Clausen and Bayle describe international federations as straddling corporate and political governance, thereby highlighting the constraints to enhanced sport governance. The authors point to the need for future research to examine the leadership styles and national networks of the international federations as both can negatively affect the governance of these entities. A key question raised in this chapter is: How can international federations impose governance standards on its national sport federations or push its leaders to improved governance practice? Given the various scandals besetting international federations and the complex web of political activity between regional member associations and the international federations and governments of the world generally, it is not clear whether it is a good idea for these governing bodies to impose their will in relation to governance practice on national member associations. Sport governance at the international federation level is complex and characterised by a myriad of cultures, value systems and political networks that impede the potential for consistent governance practices. This remains a fertile area for further research.

Intercollegiate governance reflects one of the many variances in sport systems throughout the world. Sport in the USA is largely grounded in the educational system, making it somewhat of an outlier in terms of sport systems. This therefore means the university and college system plays a central role as an outlet for sport at elite levels. The burden for the governance of university and college sport is shared between the individual universities and colleges, the NCAA and its conference systems and other intercollegiate agencies that coordinate and govern sport competitions across the university sector. Like professional sport across the world, Osborne and Weight observed, in Chapter 14, that university and college sport in the US has grown to become a multimillion-dollar business for many universities. The authors note an ever-increasing tension between the often-conflicting value-systems of a student-centric educational enterprise and the competitive entertainment industry, in which television broadcasting revenues are increasingly important to many universities. In a classic member-owned, agent arrangement, the NCAA is often blamed for various failures while it is the member universities creating and approving the rules. A delicate balance between governance independence and autonomy and member-owned outcomes is evident in this chapter. Therein lies a plethora of research opportunities to examine these tensions through a governance lens.

Events are central to sport management. They are the instrument through which the sport product is often delivered to the public. Mega and hallmark events usually involve a dense network of government agencies and private providers to deliver the event. The Olympic Games is an example, as is the FIFA World Cup. In Chapter 15, Leopkey and Parent examine the ownership and governance models used in major events. They note that the governance of sport events involves a complex array of stakeholders and therefore engagement and interactions with these stakeholders must be better understood. Often, key stakeholders are members of an organising committee, and this facet of event governance requires further investigation in terms of how stakeholder involvement shapes governance practice. Event governance systems and examination of information flows, communication channels and stakeholder salience and power are also areas of future investigation as noted by Leopkey and Parent.

Part 4 provides a collection of nine chapters overviewing key board roles and processes. This section, in particular, should engage sport governance students and practitioners with the key research themes detailing what is known across the nine themes. In Chapter 16, McLeod assesses board roles and observes that there has been limited research on board roles in sport governance. One of the main outcomes from this synthesis has been the evolution of board roles from a predominantly operational to a non-executive function, where strategy and oversight are more important than actually delivering sport services by directors. This is consistent with the professionalisation literature and the changing role of staff and directors.

Another area, noted by McLeod, in need of further investigation is an examination of the characteristics of sport board directors to excel in this role. McLeod makes the point that sport organisations often confront extreme media and public scrutiny, which adds pressure to those in a governance role. He also contends that board composition, in terms of board size, term limits and use of sub-committees are all areas in need of further investigation to understand optimum composition under varying circumstances. Although board composition and structures have been important areas of research, McLeod notes the need to move beyond research that focuses narrowly on such structures to that which adopts a holistic approach to board effectiveness, through an examination of social, behavioural and cultural factors. This aligns well with extending the value and use of governance principles observed as part of government policy in previous chapters. A focus on behaviours and cultural factors is likely to reveal more insight to good governance practice than the checklist approach provided by governance principles.

This focus could also include a better understanding of individual director motivations to assume a role as a governance volunteer. This is the focus of Chapter 16, in which Doherty examines board member motivation. Framed by a number of generic motivation theories, Doherty observed the need to examine whether volunteer board member motivation is any different to corporate or nonprofit board members. Extending this research theme, Doherty also asks in relation to the special features of sport with its potential for drama, intense emotional experiences and, in some cases, interpersonal connection with elite and celebrity athletes, if there is merit in examining whether the focus or mandate of the board and organisation is associated with particular governance volunteer motives for being involved?

In Chapter 18, the focus shifts to the interconnected roles of the chair, or president, depending on the terminology used by individual sport organisations. Little research has examined the diverse roles of the chair in sport governance. Five themes were identified and include board leadership, shared leadership with the CEO, collective board leadership and enhancing board strategic functioning, collaborative governance with member associations and stakeholder dialogue. A number of sub-themes describing the various roles of the chair supports each theme. Two future research areas emerged in the context of what might be special about chairing a sport board. The first related to the role of passion and culture as potentially distinctive features of sport governance. Based on data collected, it was found by Zeimers and Shilbury in Chapter 18 that the role of "sport Chairs is…challenging as they endeavour to manage and harness passion and associated culture in a positive way". Passion relates to volunteer directors and their enthusiasm to shape direction and culture of their sport and the need to ensure this enthusiasm is well directed. Passion and culture also flowed over into the legitimacy of the chair to oversee the board and organisation. In other words, did the chair have a sufficiently developed cultural background and passion in and for the sport compared to an experienced chair from the corporate sector but without the cultural heritage and passion for the sport? The second special feature of chairing a sport board related to collaborative governance in a federated sport network and the role of the chair in working with the chairs and boards of member associations. Future research in this area would add to the growing body of knowledge in collaborative governance adding insight to the role of the chair in facilitating this approach.

The role of the chair in managing the dynamics of boardroom meetings, illustrated in Chapter 18, is a nice segue to Chapter 19, which examines intragroup dynamics. Schoenberg highlights the importance of understanding group dynamics and the potential impact on board performance. He poses three questions that shape future research. 1) How do different group dynamics relate with each other and what sort of mediating or moderating effects accompany interactions? 2) What are the "non-performance" or indirect effects of group dynamics? 3) How do group dynamics develop within and influence whole-of-sport governing systems? Understanding board dynamics and finding a balance between open robust debate and conflict is critical in shaping the strategic direction boards set for management. Lesley Ferkins, in Chapter 20, addressed the direction-setting function of the board, or the role the board plays in determining strategy. This has become an important focus of research, as it charts a sport board's progress from an operational to a strategic focus. Moreover, Ferkins asks the important question: Is there a difference between the board's role in strategy and the board's strategic role? In essence, the strategic role is more encompassing, shaping an overall approach to all issues – or, in other words, to adopt a strategic perspective. The board's role in shaping strategy is important, but it is just one facet of thinking and acting strategically across all areas of the organisation.

A major challenge for a network of sport organisations in a federated model is how strategy either devolves or evolves between national sport organisations and member associations. Although a national sport organisation may have a board who understand their strategic role, this may not extend to the boards of member associations. Achieving a whole-of-sport approach is a challenge in a federated model. Increasingly, however, it is clear that if boards of all member associations work collaboratively with the national sport organisation and vice versa, governance processes are likely enhanced. This is the focus of Chapter 21. Meiklejohn and O'Boyle explore how regional or member associations are integrated in a federated structure. The key research question to emerge from this chapter is whether the solution to integration and a more consistent whole-of-sport approach is about adopting collaborative governance processes, or is it structural, by implementing a unitary structure which automatically integrates and subsumes all member associations as one national identity with regional branch offices. This is a rich area

415

of future research, which returns the focus to a similar theme observed in relation to professional sport clubs – what changes (in governance) when structures change?

In Chapter 22, Naraine and Parent tackle the task of exploring the management of stakeholders. They observe that boards increasingly have to be more active in liaising with stakeholder groups. This is because many may be influential and generous sponsors or politically aligned with scope to influence government. They also note that stakeholders must be considered because sport organisations rely on them to help conduct the business of the sport organisation. This chapter also points to the digital world and the potential for issues to escalate rapidly via social media. Ultimately, these issues and "viral" effect may influence perceptions of key stakeholders.

The final two chapters of Part 4 tackle sport board performance, director selection, director development and evaluation. In these chapters Molloy, Ferkins and Dickson firstly examine how improved governance can be objectively measured and significantly, the link between governance and organisational performance. Little, if any, research has been undertaken in sport governance to understand how governance affects organisational performance. This is a complex area, yet there is a need to develop a stream of research in this domain. Secondly, the authors examine director selection, development and board evaluation. In relation to director selection or appointment, ownership structures shape how directors are appointed to sport boards. This, the authors observe, may present some limitations to the range and quality of candidates. In addition, the role of the nominations committee in this process is considered, and it is noted that typical corporate processes have been adopted. In the context of nonprofit member-based organisations, this corporate approach to a nominations committee may or may not be appropriate. Consequently, further research is recommended to evaluate not only how a nominations committee should function in this environment but also the value and contribution of board/ board member evaluation processes and the potential of nomination committees to also be involved in board development and evaluation.

Part 5 brings together some future challenges for sport governance. The first of these is an examination of collective board leadership and its implications for understanding good governance. A key point to emerge from Chapter 25 is that leadership theory has a greater role to play in sport governance research. Boards work at the apex of a sport organisation and, in a unique way, need to construct a collective style of leadership through which to direct their sport. Understanding leadership through a socially constructed perspective of leadership is central to O'Boyle's examination of collective board leadership in Chapter 25. By contrast, in an earlier chapter examining sport policy in Latin America, Bravo and Haas observed "presidential" influence as a potential governance weakness. When viewed in the context of collective board leadership and emerging theory in this domain, the strong, dominant and charismatic (authoritarian) voice of the president is not consistent with current thinking in relation to collective behaviour of boards and their leadership styles. This facilitative style of leadership may fit well with collaborative approaches to governance in a federated sport network, or a professional sport league.

Leadership styles arise in many forms. Another future issue of importance is the role of women on boards and the need to obtain gender balance on boards. This may also bring greater diversity in leadership styles. In Chapter 26, Sotiriadou and Pavlidis draw on a concept known as skill complementarity in arguing why gender balance in sport governance matters. A strong female representation on sport boards sends a powerful cultural signal to young girls who see successful women "participating" in sport organisations. In terms of socio-economic value, what is lost to the board, in the range of skills women bring to the board, by not having gender balance? However, little is known about how skill complementarity increases socio-economic value in dollar terms and productivity through gender-balanced boards. Gendered leadership, economics and sport management theories could combine to provide the lens for an interesting body of research in this domain.

Chapter 27 explores the role of the board in establishing a socially responsible approach to organisational life. For example, women's role in sport addressed in the previous chapter highlights an increasing responsibility by sport organisations to promote women's participation at all levels. In this chapter, Robertson, Eime and Westerbeek identify two key areas for future research. The first argues for the expansion of social responsibility from corporate settings to nonprofit organisations including sport organisations. For example, the authors stated in Chapter 27 that "explicitly applying a critical lens to the implied notion of 'sport for good', may further enlighten the causes of a number of systemic failures in sport systems around child safety, concussion, corruption and health". The point is clear. Sport organisations grapple with many and varied social issues, and, ultimately, the board bears the responsibility for setting the tone for a socially responsible organisation. The second area of research to emerge from this chapter is the need to extend the level of analysis from the individual level (i.e., organisations) to institutional, which, in this case, is the sport industry. In other words, a collective view on what constitutes a socially responsive sport organisation may create a more unified understanding of what is socially responsible in the context of changing societal standards over time. How this is achieved is an interesting challenge and presents a meaningful research focus.

Finally, Chapter 28 tackles one of the most challenging areas for sport organisations in an increasingly globalised sport community. Sport integrity has become a key term in defining the range of issues that can compromise the conduct of sporting competitions. Doping and match fixing are two of the most well-known issues sport organisations confront. Off the field, it can also extend to host event bribes in the quest, for example, of the Olympic Games or other major world championships. Increasingly, as Kihl contends in this chapter, integrity has become a principle of good governance. Kihl also notes that the sport industry has yet to agree on a definition of integrity, arguing that it is more than just the high-profile cases of match fixing and corruption, and it represents a range of moral values and norms that sport organisations should uphold. In an effort to promote discussion and definitions of sport integrity, Chapter 28 provides a sport integrity typology, which naturally becomes a tool to be tested, assessed and used to direct research efforts. The issue of sport integrity is clearly one of the most challenging future issues for sport governance.

Conclusion

The purpose of this handbook was to map the sport governance literature as well as provide an authoritative account of the theory and practice of sport governance. It also aimed to provide direction for future research in sport governance. As exhaustive as this handbook has been, it covers many, but not all, topics relevant to governance. For example, risk management and compliance generally are two important areas not covered. Simply, there has been no research specific to sport governance in these two areas, but, nonetheless, they are important. There may well be other areas, or those that will emerge in the future, but, as a point-in-time audit of sport governance research, it is reasonable to claim it is comprehensive if not exhaustive.

This handbook captures the journey sport has been on in its quest for professionalisation. It captures the transition from leisure-oriented volunteer cultures to a field more businesslike in focus, but never so business-focussed that it overlooks the important role of sport as a social institution and as an outlet for volunteers to appreciate the "playful" leisure-oriented nature of sport through participation in all its manifestations. Volunteers have assumed an important role in the handbook, as the majority of non-executive directors of sport organisations are volunteers and "give" of their time freely for the good of the sport. This is both a strength and weakness. A strength because it is a measure of community support for sport and an appreciation for the social contribution sport can make to society. It is a weakness, because volunteers may not always possess the knowledge and understanding of what it means to be a good director and contribute to board decision-making in order to have the desired impact. This includes finding the delicate balance between rational decision-making and passion for the sport. Nonetheless, it is "our" system, and our role as scholars is to make sense of what appears sometimes as a complex array of interactions. Consequently, good scholarship should add value to how sport governance systems, practices and processes improve. We hope that this handbook has provided an important point-in-time for reflection of sport governance research and brought an enhanced understanding of sport governance and the context in which it exists. Finally, we hope that it stimulates further research and theory testing and development in order to influence positively the various sport systems of the world as they continue to evolve.

Index

Page numbers in **bold** denote tables, those in *italic* denote figures.

Made in United States
North Haven, CT
14 August 2024

56022168R00246